Excess of Powers in International Commercial Arbitration

Excess of Powers in International Commercial Arbitration

Compliance with the Arbitral Tribunal's Mandate in a Comparative Perspective

Piotr Wiliński

eleven
international publishing

Published, sold and distributed by Eleven International Publishing
P.O. Box 85576
2508 CG The Hague
The Netherlands
Tel.: +31 70 33 070 33
Fax: +31 70 33 070 30
email: sales@elevenpub.nl
www.elevenpub.com

Sold and distributed in USA and Canada
Independent Publishers Group
814 N. Franklin Street
Chicago, IL 60610, USA
Order Placement: +1 800 888 4741
Fax: +1 312 337 5985
orders@ipgbook.com
www.ipgbook.com

Eleven International Publishing is an imprint of Boom uitgevers Den Haag.

ISBN 978-94-6236-991-7
ISBN 978-94-6094-512-0 (e-book)

Z dedykacją dla Alfreda i Alberta

Foreword

Though many assume otherwise, Albert Einstein won the Nobel Prize in Physics not for developing the Theory of Relativity but, rather, for his work on the Photoelectric Effect. Building on the work of Louis de Broglie, Max Planck, Niels Bohr and others, Einstein confirmed that light has a dual nature. In other words, he postulated that photons – quantums of light – behave as both wave and particle. Nonetheless, the term 'wave-particle duality' is, as a matter of fact, a misnomer: there is but one nature of light; it is divided by human perception alone.

Like the natural sciences, the legal domain is not immune to similar conceptual difficulties, much as they may be artificially construed. In his research on excess of powers, Mr. Wiliński has identified and addressed in a comprehensive manner one such theoretical imprecision that is of particular relevance to the field of international arbitration: the dual – adjudicative and contractual – nature of an arbitral tribunal's mandate. As Mr. Wiliński points out, the term 'arbitral mandate' has long escaped accurate legal definition. This has left open the precise scope of grounds for challenges in the post-award phase, which has found different articulations in different legal systems. It also plays out on the international level in the form of the limited grounds for refusal of the recognition and enforcement of foreign awards envisaged in the New York Convention of 1958. I am delighted that in his comparative analysis Mr. Wiliński has taken up some of my recommendations for amending the New York Convention in the interest of clarity – may it serve as a catalyst for reform.

This brings me to the third – and final – duality: that of scholar and practitioner. As a professional with over three decades of experience in both academia and sitting as an arbitrator, I can undoubtedly assert that it is a false dichotomy. Legal rules require a solid philosophical foundation, yet many practitioners may not be impressed by elaborate theoretical deliberations with little implications for the practical realm. A certain degree of balance is required. Mr. Wiliński has managed to bridge this ostensible divide by creating an impressive piece of scholarship that takes due account of academic discourse without losing sight of the practical dimension. As I myself have attempted – and, hopefully, at times achieved – to strike this balance throughout my work, it is encouraging to see that a young scholar who dared embark on this challenging mission completed it so successfully.

Prof. Albert Jan van den Berg
Brussels, June 2020

Table of Contents

List of Abbreviations **xxiii**

Part I

I Introduction **3**
1 Preliminary remarks 3
1.1 The power to resolve disputes 3
1.2 The role of legal theories on arbitration 4
1.3 The discourse over "the excess of mandate" type of challenge 5
1.4 The concept of the arbitral tribunal's mandate and potential problems in testing its excess 6
1.5 Working definition of the arbitral tribunal's mandate 6
1.6 Two dimensions of the mandate and their competing characteristics 7
1.7 The exceptional character of the post-award procedure 7
1.8 The place of the "excess of mandate" type of challenge within other grounds for review of the arbitral award 8
2 Research question(s) and objectives/problem statement 8
3 Methods and methodology 9
3.1 Methods and legal sources 9
3.2 The functional comparison 11
4 The structure of the research 11

II The UNCITRAL Model Law on International Commercial Arbitration **13**
1 Introduction 13
2 Court standard of review at the post-award stage 15
2.1 The universal "pro-arbitration" approach 15
2.2 The scope of the court's review 16
2.3 Remedies at the court's disposal 20
3 The concept of the arbitral tribunal's mandate under the Model Law 22
3.1 Temporal aspect of the tribunal's adjudicative function 22
3.2 Violation of the scope of the submission to arbitration 23
4 Limits to the arbitral tribunal's "mandate" 24

4.1 Agreement to arbitrate 25
4.2 Parties' (subsequent) submissions 26
4.3 Mandatory rules of law of public policy character 27
4.4 The importance of the consent, the request and the law: the three keyholes test 29
5 The Model Law approach to the "excess of mandate" type of challenge 30
5.1 Differences in the official language versions of the Model Law and the implementation of the Model Law 30
5.2 Textual interpretation of Article 34(2)(a)(iii) of the Model Law 33
5.2.1 The importance of "the submission to arbitration" 33
5.2.2 The difference between "the terms of the submission to arbitration" and "the scope of the submission to arbitration" 35
5.2.3 The meaning of a "dispute" 37
5.2.4 The meaning of "matters" 38
5.2.5 Conclusion of the textual analysis 39
5.3 The interface between grounds for challenge prescribed by the Model Law 39
6 Application of the three keyholes test to selected issues that might fall outside the arbitral tribunal's "mandate" 41
6.1 Decisions on parties' claims 42
6.1.1 Decision on contractual claims 42
6.1.2 Decision on contractual counterclaims 43
6.1.3 Decision on set-off 45
6.1.4 Decision on claims/counterclaims based on torts or pre-contractual liability 49
6.1.5 Decision on new claims/counterclaims and change of claims/counterclaims 51
6.1.6 Decision not covering all claims/counterclaims 53
6.2 Process of application of law by the arbitral tribunal 55
6.2.1 Determining the method of selection of applicable law 55
6.2.2 Decision on applicable law 58
6.2.3 Ascertaining the content of applicable law by the arbitral tribunal 59

6.2.4 Application of mandatory rules of law (of public policy character) by the arbitral tribunal 62
6.2.5 Decision reached *ex aequo et bono* or as *amiable compositeur* 64
6.3 Decisions on remedies 66
6.3.1 Decision on damages 66
6.3.2 Decision on specific performance 69
6.3.3 Decision on contract adaptation and filling of gaps in the contract 69
6.4 Decisions accessory to the parties' main submissions and the merits of the case 72
6.4.1 Decision on interest 72
6.4.2 Decision on costs 74
6.4.3 The procedural decisions of the arbitral tribunal 76
7 Concluding remarks 76

III France and Book IV of the Code of Civil Procedure **79**
1 Introduction 79
2 Dualism of the French arbitration regime: different statutory architecture for domestic and international arbitration 81
2.1 Legal framework for international arbitration 81
2.2 The importance of domestic arbitration law 84
3 Court standard of review during the setting aside 86
3.1 Pro-arbitration approach towards the arbitration award 86
3.2 The scope of the court's review 87
3.3 Remedial powers of the courts 90
4 Delineation of the mandate: the importance of the consent, the request and the law: the three keyholes test 91
4.1 Agreement to arbitrate 91
4.2 Relevance of parties' submissions: reference of a dispute and other requests of the parties 93
4.3 Mandatory rules of law of (French international) public policy and their impact 95
5 The French concept of the arbitral tribunal's mandate and testing its excess at the post-award stage 96
5.1 The functional aspect of the arbitral tribunal's mandate 98
5.2 The contractual framework of the arbitral tribunal's mandate 99

5.3 The time limits for the execution of the arbitral tribunal's mandate 101
5.4 The concept of the mandate (and of its excess) under Article 1520(3) of the CCP 102
5.5 (Contractual) waiver of the right to set an arbitral award aside 104
6 Application of the excess of mandate ground to selected decisions of the arbitral tribunal 105
6.1 Decisions on parties' claims 105
6.1.1 Decision on contractual claims 106
6.1.2 Decision on contractual counterclaims 110
6.1.3 Decision on set-off 113
6.1.4 Decision on claims/counterclaims based on torts or pre-contractual liability 116
6.1.5 Decision on new claims/counterclaims and change of claims/counterclaims 117
6.1.6 Decision not covering all claims/counterclaims 119
6.2 Process of application of law by the arbitral tribunal 121
6.2.1 Decision on the method of determining applicable law 121
6.2.2 Decision on applicable law 123
6.2.3 Ascertaining the content of applicable law by the arbitral tribunal 125
6.2.4 Application of mandatory rules of law by the arbitral tribunal 128
6.2.5 Decision reached as *amiable compositeur* or on equity 132
6.3 Decisions on remedies 136
6.3.1 Decision on damages 137
6.3.2 Decision on specific performance 139
6.3.3 Decision on contract adaptation and filling of gaps in the contract 140
6.4 Decisions accessory to the parties' main submissions and the merits of the case 143
6.4.1 Decision on interest 143
6.4.2 Decision on costs 145
6.4.3 Decision on procedure 147
7 Concluding remarks 152

IV England and the Arbitration Act of 1996 **157**
1 Introduction 157
2 Historical overview of the development of judicial scrutiny over arbitral awards under English arbitration law 161
2.1 Judicial control of arbitral awards before the 1889 Act 162
2.2 Judicial review of arbitral awards before the 1996 Act 165
2.3 The 1996 Act: work in progress 168
3 The three-headed concept for the challenge procedure 169
4 Testing the scope of the substantive jurisdiction: the importance of the contractual framework for the arbitral tribunal's powers 171
4.1 The court standard of review when faced with the challenge 172
4.1.1 The scope of the court's review 172
4.1.2 Remedies at the court's disposal 174
4.2 Limits to the scope of the arbitral tribunal's substantive jurisdiction 177
4.2.1 The agreement to arbitrate and its scope 178
4.2.2 Relevance of parties' submissions 180
4.2.3 Overriding and mandatory rules of public policy 180
5 Substantial injustice and the concept of "serious irregularities" and its relevance for testing the mandate 181
5.1 The court's standard of review as conditioned upon the seriousness of irregularity 181
5.1.1 The scope of the court's review limited to the irregularities listed 182
5.1.2 The two-step test exercised by the courts faced with challenge 183
5.1.3 The high threshold for the irregularity to amount to substantial injustice 185
5.1.4 Remedies at the court's disposal 186
5.2 Selected "irregularities" relevant in the context of the arbitral tribunal going beyond the parties' requests 189
5.2.1 Breach of general duties of the arbitral tribunal 189
5.2.2 Excess of powers 192
5.2.3 Failure to deal with all the issues that were brought before the arbitral tribunal 195
5.2.4 Uncertainty or ambiguity as to the effect of the award 198

6 "Appeal on point of law": a limited safeguard of the system and the arbitral tribunal's discretion to apply the law 198
6.1 The court's standard of review when faced with challenge 199
6.1.1 Review based on factual findings made in the arbitral award 199
6.1.2 Remedies at the court's disposal 200
6.2 Distinctive features of the Section 69 challenge 200
6.2.1 The opt-out character of the system 200
6.2.2 Appeal on point of law not fact 201
6.2.3 Appeal on point of English law only 202
7 The application of a three-headed concept to selected issues that might fall outside the arbitral tribunal's authority 202
7.1 Decisions on parties' claims 203
7.1.1 Decision on contractual claims 203
7.1.2 Decision on contractual counterclaims 206
7.1.3 Decision on set-off 208
7.1.4 Decision on claims/counterclaims based on torts and pre-contractual liability 211
7.1.5 Decision on new claims/counterclaims and change of claims/counterclaims 214
7.1.6 Decision not covering all claims/counterclaims 216
7.2 The process of application of law by the arbitral tribunal 218
7.2.1 Determining the method of selection of applicable law 219
7.2.2 Decision on applicable law 221
7.2.3 Ascertaining the content of the applicable law by the arbitral tribunal 222
7.2.4 Application of mandatory rules of law by the arbitral tribunal 225
7.2.5 Decision based on equity or reached *ex aequo et bono* 228
7.3 Decisions on remedies 230
7.3.1 Decision on damages 231
7.3.2 Decision on specific performance 233
7.3.3 Decision on contract adaptation and filling of gaps in the contract 235
7.4 Decisions accessory to the parties' main submissions and the merits of the case 238
7.4.1 Decision on interest 238

7.4.2 Decision on costs 241
7.4.3 Decision on procedure 242
8 Concluding remarks 244

V The United States and the Federal Arbitration Act of 1925 249
1 Introduction 249
2 The legal context of international commercial arbitration in the United States 251
2.1 The Federal Arbitration Act of 1925 and its supremacy 252
2.2 State laws and their (marginal) significance 253
2.3 The role of the courts and the organization of the judicial system in the United States 255
2.4 The role of the United States Supreme Court in (re)structuring the system of arbitration 257
3 Court standard of review of arbitral awards 258
3.1 Pro-arbitration stand in the context of vacatur 258
3.2 The scope of the court's review 259
3.3 The remedial powers of the courts 261
4 Limits to the arbitral tribunal's powers 263
4.1 Agreement to arbitrate 263
4.2 Parties' (subsequent) submissions 266
4.3 Mandatory rules of public policy character 267
5 The United States standards for excess of arbitral tribunal's powers 268
5.1 The concept of the "excess of powers" 269
5.2 The notion of "imperfect execution of powers upon the subject matter submitted" 273
5.3 The Restatement's take on the post-award challenge architecture 276
6 The impact of non-statutory grounds on the Federal Arbitration Act framework: "manifest disregard of the law" and other concepts 277
6.1 Judicially created non-statutory grounds for vacatur 277
6.1.1 Decision in manifest disregard of the law 277
6.1.2 Violation of public policy 282
6.1.3 Arbitrary, capricious and completely irrational awards: the award that fails to draw its essence from the underlying contract 282
6.2 Attempts to judicially expand the "excess of powers" challenge on the federal level 283

7	Application of the United States standard of excess of powers to selected issues that might fall outside the arbitral tribunal's authority		286
	7.1	Decisions on jurisdictional/threshold issues	286
	7.1.1	Decision on the validity and existence of an agreement to arbitrate	288
	7.1.2	Decision on the scope of an agreement to arbitrate	291
	7.1.3	Decision on arbitrability of claims	294
	7.1.4	Decision on class arbitration	296
	7.2	Decisions on parties' claims	297
	7.2.1	Decision on contractual claims	297
	7.2.2	Decision on contractual counterclaims	299
	7.2.3	Decision on set-off	302
	7.2.4	Decision on claims/counterclaims based on torts and pre-contractual liability	305
	7.2.5	Decision on new claims/counterclaims and change of claims/counterclaims	307
	7.2.6	Decision not covering all claims/counterclaims	308
	7.3	Process of application of law by the arbitral tribunal	310
	7.3.1	Determining the method of selection of applicable law	310
	7.3.2	Decision on applicable law	311
	7.3.3	Ascertaining the content of applicable substantive law by the arbitral tribunal	313
	7.3.4	Application of mandatory rules of law (of public policy character) by the arbitral tribunal	314
	7.3.5	Decision based on equity or reached *ex aequo et bono*	316
	7.4	Decisions on remedies	318
	7.4.1	Decision on damages in general	318
	7.4.2	Decision on punitive damages	320
	7.4.3	Decision on specific performance	323
	7.4.4	Decision on contract adaptation and filling of gaps in the contract	324
	7.5	Decisions accessory to the parties' main submissions and the merits of the case	325
	7.5.1	Decision on interest	326
	7.5.2	Decision on costs	328
	7.5.3	Decisions on procedure	331

8 Concluding remarks 335

VI The New York Convention of 1958 on the Recognition and Enforcement of Foreign Arbitral Awards 337

1 Introduction 337
2 Court standard of review at the enforcement stage 338
2.1 Approach favoring enforcement of arbitral awards 339
2.2 The scope of the court's review 341
2.3 Remedies at the court's disposal 342
3 Limits to the arbitral tribunal's "mandate" at the enforcement stage 343
3.1 Agreement to arbitrate 344
3.2 Parties' (subsequent) submissions 345
3.3 Mandatory rules of public policy character 346
3.4 The relevance of the parties' consent, their requests and the law: the three keyholes test 347
4 The New York Convention approach to the "excess of mandate" type of challenge 348
4.1 Historical overview 348
4.2 Differences in the authentic versions of the text of the New York Convention 351
4.3 Textual interpretation of Article V(1)(c) of the New York Convention 352
4.3.1 The meaning of the "submission to arbitration" 353
4.3.2 The difference between the "terms" and the "scope" of the submission to arbitration 355
4.3.3 The meaning of "a difference" 357
4.3.4 The meaning of "matters" 358
4.4 Competing defenses: the interplay between the grounds for resisting recognition and enforcement under Article V(1) of the Convention 360
5 Application of the "excess of mandate" type of challenge to selected decisions of the arbitral tribunal 363
5.1 Decisions on parties' claims 364
5.1.1 Decision on contractual claims 364
5.1.2 Decision on contractual counterclaims 366
5.1.3 Decisions on set-off 367
5.1.4 Decision on claims/counterclaims based on torts or pre-contractual liability 369

5.1.5 Decision on new claims/counterclaims and change of claims/counterclaims 370
5.1.6 Decisions not covering all claims 371
5.2 Process of application of law by the arbitral tribunal 374
5.2.1 Decision on the method of determining applicable law 374
5.2.2 Decision on applicable law 375
5.2.3 Ascertaining the content of applicable law by the arbitral tribunal 377
5.2.4 Application of mandatory rules of law by the arbitral tribunal 379
5.2.5 Decision reached *ex aequo et bono* or as *amiable compositeur* 381
5.3 Decisions on remedies 384
5.3.1 Decision on damages 384
5.3.2 Decision on specific performance 388
5.3.3 Decision on contract adaptation and filling of gaps 388
5.4 Decisions accessory to the parties' main submissions 389
5.4.1 Decision on interest 390
5.4.2 Decision on costs 391
5.4.3 Decision on procedure 392
6 Conclusions 393

Part II

VIIThe Comparative Law Analysis 399
1 Preliminary remarks 399
1.1 Setting the scene 399
1.2 "If it ain't broke don't fix it" and the legislative timeline 400
1.3 Harmony and divergence: the impact of the Model Law 402
1.4 Apples and oranges: distinctive features of analyzed systems 403
2 Court standard of review of arbitral awards 404
2.1 The pro-arbitration approach of national courts in the context of the challenge 405
2.2 The scope of the court's review 407
2.3 Remedies at the national courts' disposal 409

3 Different standards for the "arbitral tribunal's mandate" and variations of recourse against its excess 411
3.1 Limits to the arbitral tribunal's "mandate" 411
3.1.1 Agreement to arbitrate 412
3.1.2 Parties' (subsequent) submissions 413
3.1.3 Mandatory rules of public policy character 414
3.2 The analysis of different concepts of "mandate", "mission", "powers", "authority" 415
3.2.1 The notion of "mandate" and "mission" 415
3.2.2 The notion of "powers" 416
3.2.3 The notion of "authority" 418
3.3 Different approaches to the "excess of mandate" type of challenge 418
3.4 The place of the "excess of mandate" type of challenge in the post-award architecture of selected systems 420
4 The application of different standards of the "excess of mandate" type of challenge to selected issues that might fall outside the arbitral tribunal's adjudicative authority 423
4.1 Decisions on jurisdiction 423
4.2 Decisions on parties' claims 424
4.2.1 Decision on contractual claims 424
4.2.2 Decision on contractual counterclaims 426
4.2.3 Decision on set-off 427
4.2.4 Decision on claims/counterclaims based on torts and pre-contractual liability 429
4.2.5 Decision on new claims/counterclaims and change of claims/counterclaims 430
4.2.6 Decision not covering all claims/counterclaims 432
4.3 Process of application of law by the arbitral tribunal 434
4.3.1 Determining the method of selection of applicable law 434
4.3.2 Decision on applicable law 435
4.3.3 Ascertaining the content of applicable substantive law by the arbitral tribunal 436
4.3.4 Application of mandatory rules of law (of public policy character) by the arbitral tribunal 437
4.3.5 Decision based on equity or reached *ex aequo et bono* 439

4.4 Decisions on remedies 440
4.4.1 Decision on damages 440
4.4.2 Decision on specific performance 442
4.4.3 Decision on contract adaptation and filling of gaps in the contract 442
4.5 Decisions accessory to the parties' main submissions and merits of the case 443
4.5.1 Decision on interest 444
4.5.2 Decision on costs 445
4.5.3 Decisions on procedure 448
5 Comparative assessment 451
5.1 Leading similarities and differences 451
5.2 Explaining the similarities 455
5.2.1 The harmonizing effect of the New York Convention and the UNCITRAL's undertakings 456
5.2.2 The importance of party autonomy in structuring the adjudicative mandate 457
5.2.3 The tribunal's autonomy: the significance of the arbitral tribunal's managerial toolbox 458
5.3 Explaining the differences 459
5.3.1 The ongoing competition between the leading arbitral centers 459
5.3.2 Historical development and legal heritage 460

VIII Conclusions and recommendations **463**
1 Conclusions 463
1.1 Preliminary observations 463
1.2 Pro-arbitration standard eliminating the possibility of review on the merits 463
1.3 Two dimensions of the "tribunal's mandate" and limits that might be exceeded 464
1.4 The use of the "mandate" in statutory frameworks in the analyzed legal systems 466
1.5 Possible difficulties in selecting appropriate grounds to challenge awards on the basis of "excess of the tribunal's mandate" 466
1.6 Availability of the "excess of mandate" type of challenge against the tribunal's decisions on claims 467

1.7 Availability of the "excess of mandate" type of challenge to the process of application of law 468
1.8 Availability of the "excess of mandate" type of challenge to tribunal's decisions on remedies 469
1.9 Availability of the "excess of mandate" type of challenge to tribunal's decisions accessory to the parties' main submissions 470
1.10 Application of the "excess of mandate" type of challenge to the tribunal's procedural decisions 470
1.11 Looking at the concept of the tribunal's mandate through lenses of the post-award challenge against its excess 472
1.12 Potential changes in the shape of the arbitral tribunal's mandate 472
2 Recommendations 473
2.1 Recommendations for parties 473
2.1.1 Shaping the mandate 473
2.1.2 Exclusion agreements 474
2.1.3 Inclusion of the appeal mechanism 476
2.2 Recommendations for arbitrators and judges 476
2.2.1 Active participation of the tribunal in structuring the mandate 476
2.2.2 Following "no review on the merits" approach by judges 477
2.3 Recommendations for legislators/the UNCITRAL 477
2.3.1 Abolishing the reference to the tribunal's mandate at the post-award stage 478
2.3.2 The Swiss model 478
2.3.3 The "van den Berg formula" 479
2.3.4 The UNCITRAL Recommendation regarding the interpretation of its instruments 482
3 Directions for further research 483
4 Concluding observations 484

Annexes **485**

List of cases **489**

References **507**

List of Abbreviations

AA	Arbitration Act
AAA	American Arbitration Association
AAA Rules	Commercial Arbitration Rules of American Arbitration Association
ALI	American Law Institute
BJC	The Belgian Judicial Code
CCP	Code of Civil Procedure
CEPANI	The Belgian Centre for Arbitration and Mediation
cf	*confer*
CFA	Comité Français de l'Arbitrage
DAC	The Departmental Advisory Committee
DCCP	The Dutch Code of Civil Procedure
DIS	The German Arbitration Institute
DIS Rules	Arbitration Rules of the German Arbitration Institute
e.g.	*exempli gratia*
EAA	The English Arbitration Act
FAA	The Federal Arbitration Act
FCCP	The French Code of Civil Procedure
GCCP	The German Code of Civil Procedure
Geneva Convention	The Geneva Convention on the Execution of Foreign Arbitral Awards
HKIAC	Hong Kong International Arbitration Centre
i.a.	*inter alia*
i.e.	*id est*
ICC	The International Chamber of Commerce
ICC Rules	Rules of Arbitration of the International Chamber of Commerce
ICCA	International Council for Commercial Arbitration
ICCA Guide	The ICCA Guide to Interpretation of the New York Convention
ICDR	International Centre for Dispute Resolution
ICDR Rules	Arbitration Rules of International Centre for Dispute Resolution
ILA	International Law Association

ILA Committee	International Law Association International Commercial Arbitration Committee
LCIA	London Court of International Arbitration
LCIA Rules	Arbitration Rules of London Court of International Arbitration
LMAA	London Maritime Arbitration Association
LMAA Rules	Terms of Arbitration of London Maritime Arbitration Association
Miami Draft	The Hypothetical Convention on the International Enforcement of Arbitration Agreements and Awards
ML or the Model Law	The UNCITRAL Model Law on International Commercial Arbitration
NYC or the Convention	The New York Convention on Recognition and Enforcement of Foreign Arbitral Awards
Restatement or (draft) Restatement	The Restatement on International Commercial Arbitration
SIAA	The Singapore International Arbitration Act
SIAC	The Singapore International Arbitration Centre
SIAC Rules	Arbitration Rules of the Singapore International Arbitration Centre
UNCITRAL Digest	The UNCITRAL Digest of Case Law on the Model Law on International Commercial Arbitration
UNCITRAL or the Commission	United Nations Commission on International Trade Law
UNCITRAL Rules	Arbitration Rules of the United Nations Commission on International Trade Law

Part I

"The highest proof of virtue is to possess boundless power without abusing it."
Lord Thomas Babington Macaulay

I Introduction

1 Preliminary remarks

1.1 The power to resolve disputes

The power to settle disputes between parties is exceptional. Historically reserved for gods or kings,[1] in modern democracies it remains an exclusive domain of a judiciary in accordance with Montesquieu's model for the separation of powers. It means, in turn, that it constitutes the reflection of sovereignty. It is truly remarkable that arbitral tribunals can be granted such a vast authority. However, as Justice Kagan once quoted: "*in this world, with great power there must also come – great responsibility.*"[2]

Without a doubt, the power to resolve a dispute constitutes a great responsibility. It therefore comes with an obligation not to exceed the authority. If such a power is abused, parties will have a legitimate reason to challenge the decision. In a traditional court system, it is evidenced with a review of court judgments by the courts of higher instance (appeal mechanism). Importantly, the scrutiny of the reviewing court may also involve the lower court's findings on the facts and on the law.

In arbitration, however, the system operates differently. It is based on a limited court intervention in the arbitral process and the tribunal's findings. In principle, the post-award court review is narrow and allowed only in a listed number of cases. This is why it may be tempting for the parties to apply the grounds for recourse ever so broadly.

The ground directly relevant to the tribunal's dispute resolution power is the "excess of mandate" type of challenge. In principle, every legal system will guarantee a post-award recourse against an alleged "excess of mandate" even though they often do not define what the "mandate" itself entails. This, in turn, attracts a broad interpretation made by the aggrieved parties and may frustrate the fundamental value of arbitration – the finality of the arbitral award.

It is therefore essential to determine how the national courts review arbitral awards on the basis of "excess of mandate" and consequently in what instances they accept the argument that the tribunal acted in violation of its mandate. This study aims at recognizing the similarities and differences of the "excess of mandate" type of challenges in selected

1 Clay, *L'arbitre* (2001) pp.33-35.

2 Albeit in a different context. See *Kimble v. Marvel Entm't, LLC*, 135 S. Ct. 2401, 2415, 192 L. Ed. 2d 463 (2015).

legal systems (namely the UNCITRAL Model Law,[3] France, England, the U.S. and the New York Convention[4]).It is expected that looking through the eyes of what selected legal systems (and their national courts) consider to be an "*excess*" of the elusive "mandate" and identifying the common features of the "excess of mandate" type of challenge in reviewed jurisdictions may contribute to a better understanding of the concept of the arbitral tribunal's mandate itself. Accordingly, this research's objective is to add a building block to a definition of the tribunal's mandate.

1.2 The role of legal theories on arbitration

Historically there have been some attempts to produce legal theory explaining the concept of arbitration.[5] The practical significance of these developments, however, has been rather limited.[6] A brief introduction of competing theoretical frameworks will be helpful in the context of the "excess of mandate" debate, because the same characteristics of arbitration are being balanced during the assessment when the tribunal exceeds its "mandate".

Sanders observed that:

> [o]n the one hand, arbitration must be based on an agreement to arbitrate. This could lead to underlining the contractual nature of arbitration. On the other hand, the jurisdictional nature could be stressed because arbitral proceedings lead to an award, binding upon the parties and enforceable in the same way as a final court judgement.[7]

One may therefore easily deduct that those two features of arbitration stand out clearly: the first one is a contractual basis for arbitration to go forward, and the second one is the adjudicative function with which the tribunal is entrusted. These elements provide, in turn, the basis for the two competing theories of arbitration: the contractual and the jurisdictional theory. There is also a third theory, the mixed one that focuses on the arbitration's hybrid nature, namely it underlines that both aspects of arbitration are

---

3 The UNCITRAL Model Law on International Commercial Arbitration (1985) (hereafter "UNCITRAL Model Law" or "ML").

4 The Convention on the Recognition and Enforcement of Foreign Arbitral Awards (1958) (hereafter "New York Convention" or "NYC").

5 See Born, *International Commercial Arbitration* (2014) p.214 and the literature therein.

6 Sanders, *Arbitration* (1996) p.5 ("*Dealing with arbitration theories, in my opinion, therefore is a fascinating exercise, but for the solution of practical problems, these theories are hardly of any assistance to a legislator*"), and Born, *International Commercial Arbitration* (2014) p.214 ("*Although the practical implications of this debate are often unclear there is little academic agreement on these various theories.*").

7 Sanders, *Arbitration* (1996) p.5.

important.[8] As elegantly put by Motulsky: "*[t]here is always, in arbitration, an intrusion/interference of the contractual component in the judicial function, which makes its difficulty and appeal.*"[9] In evaluating whether the tribunal exceeded its mandate, the same two elements – the contractual nature and the adjudicative function – are at stake. Since, as explained above, no precise definition of mandate is available, the outstanding question is which of these aspects of the mandate is being tested for its excess or, in the alternative, what is the relation of these two aspects whenever the mandate is being tested.

1.3 The discourse over "the excess of mandate" type of challenge

The legal discourse on the concept of "mandate" is rather limited and it usually refers to the contractual paradigm of the mandate.[10] When a reference is made to the "excess of mandate", authors usually do refer to the same grounds for recourse although they might not have (exactly) the same meaning[11] or the analysis focuses on one jurisdiction only.[12]

One should note that there are only three commonly known examples where the legislator allowed for a challenge of an award on the basis of the "excess of mandate", namely France, the Netherlands and Sweden.[13] In each system, it seems to be recognized that this ground can be overly capacious. Recent studies of the French system[14] confirmed, however, that the French courts are in favor of a restrictive interpretation. Similarly, the Dutch legislator in a newly introduced legislative reform qualified the use of this ground upon the seriousness of a violation.[15] Most recently, Swedish legislator followed this

8 For further reading, see Born, *International Commercial Arbitration* (2014) pp.215-216.

9 Motulsky (2010) p.289 ("*Il y a toujours, dans l'arbitrage, une immixtion, qui fait sa difficulté et son attrait, de la composante contractuelle dans la fonction juridictionnelle.*"). An alternative translation of the same text would read as follows "*in arbitration, there is always an intrusion of the contractual component in the judicial function, which makes its [arbitration] difficulty and attractiveness.*"

10 See, *e.g.*, Schöldstrom (1998). As such it falls outside of the scope of this research. For further reading, see also Poudret & Besson (2007) pp.367-376.

11 Thus, referring for example to Art. 1520(3) of the French Code of Civil Procedure (hereafter "FCCP") and Art. V(1)(c) of the NYC.

12 See Giraud (2017).

13 See Art. 1520(3) of the FCCP, Art. 1065(1)(c) of the Dutch Code of Civil Procedure (hereafter "DCCP"), Section 34(3) of the Swedish Arbitration Act (hereafter "SAA"). For the translations used see accordingly, http://www.iaiparis.com/pdf/FRENCH_LAW_ON_INTERNATIONAL_ARBITRATION.pdf [last accessed 23 April 2018], http://www.nai-nl.org/downloads/Text%20Dutch%20Code%20Civil%20Procedure.pdf [last accessed 23 April 2018] https://sccinstitute.com/media/408924/the-swedish-arbitration-act_1march2019_eng.pdf [last accessed 23 April 2019].

14 See Giraud (2017).

15 Art. 1065(4) of the DCCP.

approach, limiting the scope of the "excess of mandate" challenge to those instances that affect the outcome of the case.[16]

In other jurisdictions, one may observe two models that can be qualified as the "excess of mandate" type of challenge. In the first model, most likely stemming from the English arbitration system, the recourse against the arbitral award can be made when a party alleges that the tribunal "exceeded its powers". This argument is available, for example, in England, the U.S. amongst others.[17] The second model has been universally introduced by the New York Convention and allows for a recourse when "*the award deals with a difference not contemplated by or not falling within the terms of the submission to arbitration or it contains decisions on matters beyond the scope of the submission to arbitration [...]*".[18] In the similar shape, it has been offered in the Model Law and implemented as a national legislation by a number of jurisdictions (even though the way countries implement the Model Law does differ).[19] It is necessary to reflect further if those three models do refer to the same concept or in what instances they do differ.

1.4 *The concept of the arbitral tribunal's mandate and potential problems in testing its excess*

As suggested above, there is no legal definition of the "arbitral tribunal's mandate". Yet it is a central element in the functioning of arbitration itself and essential to evaluate the scope of the "excess of mandate" type of challenge. Therefore, it is necessary to introduce a working definition for the concept (section 1.5), followed by a brief reflection on the relevant aspects of the mandate (section 1.6). Finally, one should stress the importance of the exceptional character of the post-award review (section 1.7) and the place of the "excess of mandate" type of challenge among other grounds for recourse (section 1.8).

1.5 *Working definition of the arbitral tribunal's mandate*

For the purpose of the study at hand it is suggested that the arbitral tribunal's mandate is a relationship between arbitrators and parties where arbitrators accept to finally and

16 See https://sccinstitute.com/media/408924/the-swedish-arbitration-act_1march2019_eng.pdf [last accessed 23 April 2019]; also http://kluwerarbitrationblog.com/2015/10/17/time-to-upgrade-review-of-the-swedish-arbitration-act/ [last accessed 23 April 2018] and http://arbitrationblog.kluwerarbitration.com.eur.idm.oclc.org/2018/04/09/the-swedish-government-revives-efforts-to-modernise-the-arbitration-act/ [last accessed 23 April 2018].

17 See Section 68(2)(b) of the English Arbitration Act (hereafter "EAA"), Section 10(a)(4) of the Federal Arbitration Act (hereafter "FAA").

18 See Art. V(1)(c) of the NYC.

19 See Chapter II.

effectively resolve the dispute(s) between the parties. At the same time, they (arbitrators) accept restrictions, rights and obligations imposed on them by the parties' agreement to arbitrate, the parties' submissions and the mandatory provisions of applicable law. The tribunal's mandate entails what it can and cannot do within the limits imposed to fulfill its *adjudicatory function*, thus resolving the dispute between the parties. Consequently, the mandate gives autonomy to the tribunal in fulfilling its adjudicative function which creates a layer of inherent powers necessary to complete its prescribed role.

1.6 *Two dimensions of the mandate and their competing characteristics*

There is no doubt that the adjudicative function of the tribunal remains a central concept defining the mandate of the arbitral tribunal. At the same time, however, it is necessary to recognize that the tribunal has an authority to adjudicate only because the parties themselves commission it.

These two concepts become essential when the scope of the mandate is being assessed. As highlighted above,[20] both concepts address a different aspect of the tribunal's mandate, and both are vital in evaluating which of the tribunal's undertakings can be found to be *beyond* the tribunal's mandate. At the same time, one should note that, potentially, they may also compete. On the one hand, party autonomy is of paramount importance in international arbitration. On the other hand, the tribunal should have its own autonomy to properly fulfill its adjudicative function. Whenever two dimensions of the mandate compete, it might be necessary to evaluate which notion should be given priority. Consequently, it raises a problem for the tribunals that wish to ensure the enforceability of their decisions.

1.7 *The exceptional character of the post-award procedure*

As suggested above, the setting-aside procedure is an extraordinary means of recourse against the award.[21] Therefore, it should never be equated with the review of the merits of the case. Nevertheless, since the "excess of mandate" type of challenge inevitably relates to the tribunal's performance of its judicial function, the question is how far it can be used by the parties displeased with the tribunal's conclusions. As long as the mandate itself is not defined, the "excess of mandate" type of challenge may serve as a capacious vehicle for challenges of different types of tribunal's decisions.

20 See section 1.2.

21 The exceptional character of the recourse equally applies to the enforcement procedure pursuant to the New York Convention.

1.8 *The place of the "excess of mandate" type of challenge within other grounds for review of the arbitral award*

One should note that not only is the "excess of mandate" type of challenge potentially broad, it is also problematic because it competes with other grounds for review. It may happen, when the same factual circumstances give rise to different challenges at the post-award stage. In principle, there are two layers of tensions: firstly, it might be occasionally difficult to distinguish whether the tribunal exceeded its "mandate" or "jurisdiction"; secondly, it might be equally troublesome in assessing what ground should be raised in the case of the tribunal's procedural wrongdoing. In other words, one should reflect if the "excess of mandate" type of challenge or rather due process violation should be a basis for an allegedly excessive tribunal's undertaking. Further, it raises the question regarding what the added value is for the (elusive) "excess of mandate" type of challenge in the post-award review system if the potential violation of the tribunal's authority can be addressed under other grounds.

2 Research question(s) and objectives/problem statement

The previous section was devoted to highlighting in which areas the application of the "excess of mandate" type of challenge gives rise to potential obstacles. It has led to the formulation of the following central research question:

> How is the tribunal's "mandate" being reviewed under the selected systems and does this test constitute an essential element of the post-award review architecture?

This question, in turn, triggers a number of subquestions:

1. What is the court standard of review when faced with an "excess of mandate" type of challenge? What are the court's remedies to mitigate the potential "excess of mandate"?
2. What are the limits to the "tribunal's mandate" that can be exceeded, and do they differ depending on the system?
3. What concepts are being used in the different systems to address the "excess of mandate" type of challenge?
4. How does the "excess of mandate" type of challenge fit as an element of the post-award review mechanism of selected legal systems?

and finally

5. What are the issues that might fall outside the scope of the tribunal's mandate?

6. How does the principle of party autonomy and the tribunal's autonomy compete in the context of the "excess of mandate" type of challenge? What dimension of the mandate is being challenged under the "excess of mandate" type of challenge?

This research focuses on the concept of the tribunal's "mandate" from the perspective of the post-award review of its alleged violation. It is expected that the study will provide the actors active in international arbitration (*i.e.* judges, arbitrators, parties) with a better understanding of what might be considered as a tribunal's mandate and what its dimensions are.

The objective of this research is to fill *lacunae* in international arbitration scholarship and to contribute to the important debate regarding the tribunal's "mandate" and its autonomy, by analyzing in what instances challenge against its excess is allowed. Additionally, the research addresses how the "excess of mandate" type of challenge may potentially evolve should it remain available as a ground for recourse. Importantly, the study is limited to the analysis of the "excess" of the "tribunal's mandate". Therefore, it does not focus on the legal nature of the "mandate" itself. Instead, it concentrates on the post-award review of its excess. At the same time, however, it is distinguished from the issues of the "excess of the tribunal's jurisdiction" and that of due process, which fall outside of the scope of a detailed analysis.

3 Methods and methodology

3.1 *Methods and legal sources*

The research at hand constitutes a classical legal research. It means that it was conducted with the use of the traditional legal research method. Consequently, the statutory text and case law are of primary importance. Whenever possible the *travaux préparatoires* are also consulted.[22] Finally, scholarly writings and commentaries provide a useful insight in understanding and conceptualizing the scope of the post-award review against the alleged "excess of mandate".

This study is of a comparative character. Therefore, the analysis focuses on different "excess of mandate" type challenges as introduced in three national legal regimes (*i.e.* France, England, and the U.S.) and two international legal systems (*i.e.* the Model Law and the New York Convention).

22 Namely in the case of England, the Model Law, and the New York Convention.

In principle, however, the analysis does not follow the classical comparative law divide between common law and civil law systems, because it is not as useful as in other areas of law. Instead, arguably, a line should be drawn between the Model Law jurisdictions (that includes both civil and common law countries *i.a.* Canada, Germany, Poland, Singapore etc.) and jurisdictions which do not follow the Model Law structure (*i.a.* France, England, the U.S., the Netherlands, Switzerland, Sweden, etc.). One may observe that the states which do not follow the Model Law scheme are the major arbitration centers with established arbitration practice.[23] The rationale for *not* following the Model Law might be explained with the goal of preserving their competitive edge, providing for a unique set of tools sought by the users of international arbitration. Selected representatives of these countries (*i.e.* France, England and the U.S.) constitute a sample for the comparison at hand.

The comparison has to be made at two levels. At the first level, the comparison between different mechanisms to challenge the alleged excess needs to be carried out at the national level. It means that, one should examine the Model Law, which, as explained, constitutes the framework that national legislators (from both civil and common law countries) may rely upon while drafting their arbitration acts. The Model Law approach, in turn, needs to be contrasted with the rules applicable to the setting-aside procedure in France,[24] England[25] and the U.S.[26] These four legal systems may be evaluated at the same level.[27]

The second level, which is the enforcement stage, requires an analysis of the application of the New York Convention. Mostly, national courts, while interpreting the Convention, do so in a uniform and consistent manner.[28] In principle, they also resist the temptation of transplanting the national concepts to the international level. It does not change the fact, however, that the challenging parties often keep insisting on relying on those alluring (national) notions. Therefore, the vertical comparison might also be relevant.

---

23 De Ly, *Paradigmatic Changes – Uniformity, Diversity, Due Process and Good Administration of Justice: The Next Thirty Years* (2016) p.23 ("*Notwithstanding the major breakthrough brought by the Model Law, the picture remains one of divergence in the western world with major arbitration centres in London, Paris, New York, Zurich or Geneva having arbitration laws based on different traditions, assumptions, approaches and rules.*").

24 See Chapter III.

25 See Chapter IV.

26 See Chapter V.

27 A horizontal comparison.

28 See Chapter VI.

3.2 The functional comparison

Since the concepts introduced in the systems slightly differ, it is only reasonable to undertake a functional comparison. As suggested elsewhere,[29] the selected legal systems are each an example of one of the three models of the "excess of mandate" type of challenge.

According to the first model, the award may be challenged if the "*tribunal's ruling without complying with the mandate conferred upon it.*"[30] This model operates in France. The second model is employed in the English and the U.S. arbitration regimes. In these systems, in principle, the recourse is available when the tribunal "*exceed[s] its powers*".[31] The last model is introduced by the New York Convention and the Model Law.[32] It allows for the challenge of a tribunal deciding on "differences not contemplated by or not falling within the terms of the submission to arbitration" and on "matters beyond the scope of the submission to arbitration". All in all, the study aims at highlighting similarities and differences between these three models for the review of the tribunal's mandate and assesses what dimension of the mandate proves to be relevant for the review.

4 The structure of the research

As explained above, the research is conducted on a comparative basis. Therefore, in Part I of the research, each of the reviewed legal systems is analyzed independently. In turn, in Part II, the comparative assessment and general conclusions will be offered.

Additionally, it should be noted that each substantive chapter has a similar structure which is also two-fold. It means that the first sections of the chapter are dedicated to more general (procedural) elements related to the challenge against the award at the post-award stage (such as court standard of review of the award and remedies available to the parties), whereas the subsequent sections aim to identify (i) the limits to the arbitral tribunal's mandate and (ii) how the "excess of mandate" type of challenge applies to different decisions taken by the tribunal throughout the arbitral process.

The latter part of the studies indicated above (*i.e.* application of the "excess of mandate" type of challenge to selected tribunal's decisions) is essential for the study at hand, because it has been dedicated to the application of the "excess of mandate" type of challenge to selected issues that arguably may fall outside the scope of the arbitral tribunal's powers.

29 See section 1.3.

30 See Art. 1520(3) of the FCCP.

31 See Section 68(2)(b) of the EAA and Section 10(a)(4) of the FAA. The exact wording slightly differs. It will be discussed in detail in the next chapters.

32 See Art. 34(2)(a)(iv) of the ML and Art. V(1)(c) of the NYC.

The selection of the issues that may fall outside the scope of the tribunal's mandate has been divided thematically into four parts: the first is devoted to the arbitral tribunal's decisions on parties' claims (including *i.a.* contractual claims, set-off claims and tort claims); the second explains the process of application of law by the arbitral tribunal (starting from the application of the relevant choice of law rules through decision on the applicable law and finishing with ascertaining the content of the applicable law by the arbitral tribunal); the third part focuses on the excess of the arbitral tribunal's powers when awarding different types of remedies (such as damages, punitive damages, specific performance, contract adaptation and filling the gaps); the fourth and final part is contributed to the arbitral tribunals' decisions on interest and costs which are decisions accessory to the parties' main submissions. Decisions on the procedure are also taken into account.

Chapters II and VI deal with the important international instruments, namely the Model Law and the New York Convention. Both include a similar, rather descriptive provision that requires a burdensome interpretation. It is therefore necessary to closely examine it and explain its scope of application.

Chapters III, IV and V introduce national reports on (subsequently) France, England and Wales and the U.S. Notably, the French regime is the only system that in its setting-aside mechanism makes a reference to the tribunal's mandate. Yet, the English and the U.S. references to the "excess of powers" also require further analysis.

Part II (Chapters VII to VIII) reflects the comparative assessment of all the reviewed systems (Chapter VII) and general conclusions of the research (Chapter VIII). The comparative chapter mirrors the structure of the chapters introduced in Part I (Chapters II to VI), therefore it first deals with more general elements of the post-award challenge and subsequently reflects on the application of the "excess of mandate" type of challenge to the different tribunal's decisions.

II The UNCITRAL Model Law on International Commercial Arbitration

1 Introduction

Undoubtedly the UNCITRAL Model Law on International Commercial Arbitration (1985) ("Model Law" or "ML") is a milestone in the history of international arbitration. As observed by Born: "*[the Model Law] is the single most important legislative instrument in the field of international commercial arbitration. It has been adopted in a substantial (and growing) number of jurisdictions and served as a model for legislation and judicial decisions in many others.*"[1] The question at hand is, however, whether (and if so how) the drafters of this legal instrument defined the challenge for the alleged "excess of the tribunal's mandate".

Although the Model Law itself *does* refer to the mandate of the arbitral tribunal, it does so in a different context than with a reference to the post-award recourse. For the purpose of the setting-aside provision, the system operates with the concept that can be broadly summarized as a violation of the scope of the submission to arbitration. Consequently, in this chapter the analysis will primarily focus on Article 34(2)(a)(iii) of the Model Law. According to this provision, the court may test whether an arbitral award deals with a dispute not contemplated by or not falling within the terms of the submission to arbitration, or contains decisions on matters beyond the scope of the submission to arbitration. If, in turn, the court finds that any of the objections above are justified, it may set aside the arbitral award.

At the outset it is necessary to briefly outline the underlying principles of the courts' review at the post-award stage. In principle, one should discuss the "pro-arbitration" stand of the courts, the scope of their scrutiny regarding the award and the remedial tools they have at their disposal when faced with challenge.

In turn, the limits to the "arbitral tribunal's mandate" will be explained. Put differently, when faced with the "excess of mandate" type of challenge, the reviewing court will have to look at three important elements structuring the tribunal's authority to adjudicate: (i) what is the scope of the parties' consent to arbitration, (ii) whether the party or parties requested the arbitral tribunal to decide a particular dispute or a matter, and finally (iii) whether the applicable law allows a particular decision of the arbitral tribunal to be made (thus whether the decision accords with the public policy rules of the country of the seat). Those reflections will lead to the introduction of the "three keyholes test" which the

1 Born, *International Commercial Arbitration* (2014) p.134.

court should undertake when determining whether the arbitral tribunal "exceeded its mandate" or not.

Furthermore, in order to explain the Model Law's approach to the "excess of the arbitral tribunal's mandate", it is important to closely analyze the language that is being used in Article 34(2)(a)(iii) of the Model Law. It is so, because the text of the provision is rather descriptive and repetitive. Pursuant to this article an award may be set aside when "*the award deals with a dispute not contemplated by or not falling within the terms of the submission to arbitration, or contains decisions on matters beyond the scope of the submission to arbitration [...].*" Consequently, it raises some interpretative difficulties which should be tackled. In particular, the meaning of "the submission to arbitration" and the difference between "the terms of the submission to arbitration" and "the scope of the submission to arbitration" need to be determined. For a better understanding, the *travaux préparatoires* of the original Model Law from 1985 and its amended 2006 version will be studied. Following the textual study, it is also necessary to reflect on the place of the "excess of mandate" type of challenge within the framework of the post-award review system.

The final – and the most important – part of this chapter will focus on the application of the "three keyholes test" to the particular situations. The analysis will be based on case law and hypothetical cases which together should make up for the comprehensive catalogue of instances when the mandate can be potentially exceeded. The first type of tribunal decisions that needs to be tested targets the parties' claims. It other words, one should consider if torts, counterclaims, cross-claims and the like will fall within the scope of the arbitral tribunal's mandate in the Model Law jurisdictions. Secondly, it is necessary to examine if the process of application of law by an arbitral tribunal (including *i.a.* determination of the applicable law and the application of mandatory rules of law) can be reviewed under the "excess of mandate" type of challenge. Similar considerations relate to the tribunal's power to decide *ex aequo et bono*. Thirdly, the tribunal's remedial power will be analyzed. Final reflections relate to the tribunal's decisions that are of an accessory character to the main claims, namely decisions on interest, costs and even the procedural decision of the arbitral tribunal. These should also be tested for their availability against the "excess of mandate" type of challenge. In the Model Law structure the same type of ground is included not only as a basis for setting aside (see Article 34(2)(a)(iii)) but also as a basis to refuse recognition and enforcement of the arbitral award (see Article 36(1)(a)(iii)). Both grounds differ only in the timing when they can be invoked. Thus, the only difference is that Article 34(2)(a)(iii) of the Model Law can be used as an offensive tool against the arbitral award (in the setting-aside proceedings), whereas Article 36(1)(a)(iii) of the Model Law is a defensive mechanism protecting the losing party at the enforcement stage of the arbitral award. Arguably, however, the instances where these grounds can be successfully invoked remain the same. For this reason, although the focus in this chapter is on the setting-aside mechanism, the sources (especially the case law) dealing with Article 36(1)(a)(iii) of the Model Law will also be used.

2 Court standard of review at the post-award stage

The initial inquiry should commence with a brief analysis of the court's approach to the post-award challenge in the Model Law jurisdictions. Three aspects of the review need to be highlighted: the "pro-arbitration" attitude of the courts (section 2.1), the deferential standard of the judicial scrutiny (section 2.2) and the availability of the remedial tools given to the courts (section 2.3).

2.1 *The universal "pro-arbitration" approach*

What can be considered as a hallmark of the Model Law is its pro-arbitration philosophy. Essentially it means that national courts should endorse the parties' choice to arbitrate their disputes and refrain from intervening in the process. Additionally, they should recognize the exceptional character of the setting-aside proceedings and the limited nature of their control over the award.

According to the UNCITRAL analytical commentary on the draft text of the Model Law, the Article 34 recourse is designed to be an exclusive means of recourse available against the award, available only shortly after it is rendered and only for a limited (exhaustive) number or reasons.[2] This philosophy has been adhered to by the countries adopting the Model Law. For example, in Germany, it has been recognized that Article 1059 of the German Code of Civil Procedure ("GCCP") "*has a limiting function*" eliminating the possibility of the review on the merits and allowing the review on the closed list of internationally recognized grounds instead.[3] Similarly in Belgium, "*the procedure for setting aside is the exclusive recourse by which a party may challenge an arbitral award before a State court.*"[4] Also in Singapore "*[i]t is to be emphasized that the ability to challenge the award is limited to jurisdictional, procedural and public policy issue[s] [...]*".[5]

---

2 A/CN.9/264 pp.71-72.

3 See Kröll & Kraft, *Recourse against the Award, § 1059 – Application for Setting Aside* (2015) p.386. See also Kreindler et al., *Commercial Arbitration in Germany* (2016) p.335.

4 Verbruggen, *Commentary on Part VI of the Belgian Judicial Code*, Chapter VII: Article 1717 (2016) p.461.

5 Merkin & Hjalmarsson, *Singapore Arbitration Legislation Annotated* (2009) p.116.

National courts in the Model Law jurisdictions follow the pro-arbitration principle. Consequently, they affirmed the exhaustive character of grounds for setting aside.[6] The same goes for the presumptive finality of the award,[7] and the minimal and restrictive character of the judicial intervention at the setting-aside stage.[8]

2.2 *The scope of the court's review*

As already hinted above, the fundamental idea of the Model Law is to limit the scope of intervention of the courts in the arbitration itself. It has, in turn, consequences for the attitude the courts should exercise when faced with the "excess of mandate" type of challenge. These consequences, explained in details below, are two-fold: (i) the courts are not allowed to review the merits of the case and, arguably and (ii) they should only allow the most grievous instances of the alleged "excess of mandate".

The first aspect is rather clear.[9] Already at the drafting stage of the Model Law, it has been observed that "*[t]here was very wide support for the view that an award rendered in international commercial arbitration should not be subject to court review on its merits.*"[10]

6 *CRW Joint Operation v. PT Perusahaan Gas Negara (Persero) TBK* [2011] SGCA 33, [2011] 4 SLR 305 at [25] ("*The court's power to set aside an arbitral award is limited to setting aside based on the grounds provided under Art 34 of the Model Law and s 24 of the IAA.[...].*").

7 See, *e.g.*, *Bayview Irrigation District #11 v. United Mexican States*, 2008 CanLII 22120 (ON SC), par. 63, http://canlii.ca/t/1wwtf#par63 [last accessed on 27 April 2018] ("*While the decisions of international arbitral tribunals are not immune from challenge, any challenge advanced is confronted with the "powerful presumption" that the tribunal acted within its authority. An arbitral decision is not invalid because it wrongly decided a point of fact or law. [Corporacion Transnacional, at p. 192]. The grounds cited by the Applicants under Article 18 and Article 34(2)(a)(ii), 34(2)(a)(iii) and 34(2)(b)(ii) of the Model Law must therefore be construed narrowly and the Applicants must satisfy a high threshold to succeed in having the Award set aside.*").

8 See, *e.g.*, *CRW Joint Operation v. PT Perusahaan Gas Negara (Persero) TBK [2011] SGCA 33, [2011] 4 SLR 305 at [25] ("As declared by this court in Soh Beng Tee & Co Pte Ltd v. Fairmount Development Pte Ltd [2007] 3 SLR(R) 86 ("Soh Beng Tee") at [59], the current legal framework prescribes that the courts should not without good reason interfere in the arbitral process. This policy of minimal curial intervention by respecting finality in the arbitral process acknowledges the primacy which ought to be given to the dispute resolution mechanism that the parties have expressly chosen."). Quintette Coal Ltd. v. Nippon Steel Corporation,* 1991 CanLII 5708 (BC CA), par. 32, http://canlii.ca/t/231lq#par32, [last accessed on 27 April 2018] ("*It is meet therefore, as a matter of policy, to adopt a standard which seeks to preserve the autonomy of the forum selected by the parties and to minimize judicial intervention when reviewing international commercial arbitral awards in British Columbia. That is the standard to be followed in this case.*").

9 See, *e.g.*, Lew et al., *Comparative International Commercial Arbitration* (2003) pp.673-674 ("*The grounds listed in Article 34 Model Law unequivocally suggest that judicial review in the context of an application to challenge an award can only be based on natural justice and legality grounds. There can be no review on the merits.*"). See also Roth (2009) p.1116: ("*The selection of the grounds in both sub-paragraphs avoids court review 'on the merits'*"), UNCITRAL, *Digest of Case Law on the Model Law on International Commercial Arbitration* (2012) pp.140-141.

10 A/CN.9/216 paras 107-108.

This vision of the system has been consequently adopted by the Model Law countries.[11] For example, in Germany, "*[t]he exhaustive character of s 1059 para 2 ZPO distinguishes setting aside application from appeals as it in particular excludes the incorrect decision of the dispute as a ground for setting aside (no révision au fond).*"[12] The same standard is also recognized *i.a.* in Belgium[13] and in Singapore.[14] The Model Law case law repeatedly confirms that the courts may not reevaluate the merits of the dispute during the setting-aside stage.[15]

The second characteristic of the standard for the review requires perhaps a bit more explanation. Although the leading guideline for the setting-aside court is the principle of "no review on the merits", "*[t]he content of the award may [...] be relevant in connection with an alleged excess of authority [that is the "excess of mandate" type of challenge].*"[16] It is so because the review of the "mandate" is closely intertwined with the merits of the case. Consequently, it has been observed that

> [w]hile it is uncontroversial that a reviewing court must not re-examine the merits of an arbitral award when it determines whether a tribunal has exceeded its powers, there is currently no uniform approach regarding the degree of deference that courts are willing to accord to the arbitral tribunal's interpretation of its competence, as set out in the Parties' submissions or the arbitration agreement.[17]

---

11 Notably, Roth reported that "*Tunisia empowers the court which sets aside the award to decide on the merits, if necessary and upon the application of all parties.*" See Roth (2009) p.1110.

12 Kreindler et al., *Commercial Arbitration in Germany* (2016) p.335, see also Kröll & Kraft, *Recourse against the Award, § 1059 – Application for Setting* Aside (2015) p.397.

13 Verbruggen, *Commentary on Part VI of the Belgian Judicial Code*, Chapter VII: Article 1717, 2016, p.461 ("*The court will not review the merits of the case but only examine the criticism made by claimant against the award in light of the limited grounds for setting aside.*").

14 Merkin & Hjalmarsson, *Singapore Arbitration Legislation Annotated* (2009) p.116 ("*It is to be emphasized that the ability to challenge an award is limited to jurisdictional, procedural and public policy issues: there is no basis for a challenge based on error of law, and there is a need to ensure that challenges are genuinely made on the permitted grounds rather than amounting to disguised attempts to attack awards on their merits.*").

15 See, *i.a.*, *ABC Co. v. XYZ Ltd.*, High Court, Singapore, 8 May 2003], [2003] 3 SLR 546: ("*The Court also noted that an application under article 34 MAL is not a process designed for purposes of seeking review of a pre-existing judicial decision by way of appeal [...] A setting aside application is not a process whereby facts which have been already established in the arbitration are being reassessed.*"), *Quintette Coal Ltd. v. Nippon Steel Corporation*, 1991 CanLII 5708 (BC CA), par. 32, http://canlii.ca/t/231lq#par32, [last accessed 14 August 2020] ("*It is meet therefore, as a matter of policy, to adopt a standard which seeks to preserve the autonomy of the forum selected by the parties and to minimize judicial intervention when reviewing international commercial arbitral awards in British Columbia. That is the standard to be followed in this case.*"); *Nearctic Nickel Mines Inc. c. Canadian Royalties Inc.*, 2012 QCCA 385 (CanLII), http://canlii.ca/t/fqcwz, [last accessed 14 August 2020]; see also UNCITRAL, *Digest of Case Law on the Model Law on International Commercial Arbitration* (2012) p.134.

16 Kröll & Kraft, *Recourse against the Award, § 1059 – Application for Setting Aside* (2015) p.397.

17 Pulkowski (2010) p.127.

There are two explanations for the difficulties with the scope of the review and, arguably, both relate to the way the Model Law is adopted. The first reason relates to the very nature of the "excess of mandate" type of challenge. The second one is associated with the (discretionary or not) power of the court to set aside the arbitral award.

As to the first reason, one may observe, that in some jurisdictions the ground introduced in Article 34(2)(a)(iii) of the Model Law is perceived as a jurisdictional ground relating directly to the scope of the parties' consent. If this is the case, the courts may reasonably expect that they are allowed to have a closer look at the tribunal's findings, because the allegations that the tribunal's conclusions fall outside the scope of the underlying arbitration consensus requires careful judicial control in order to safeguard legitimacy of the system. The opposite view is that the "excess of mandate" type of challenge "simply" concerns the assessment of the tribunal's decision in the light of the parties' submissions, but without any objections to the existence or scope of the original consent to arbitrate (thus to the original jurisdiction of the tribunal).[18]

The second reason relates to the opening sentence of Article 34(2) of the Model Law, which reads that "*an arbitral award may be set aside by the court [...].*" This wording raised the question whether a setting-aside court is obliged (forced) to set aside the award whenever satisfied that the challenge is justified or, rather, the court has a discretion to save the award (notwithstanding the existence of some deficiencies in the award itself). Unfortunately, there is no uniformity in the interpretation.

If one looks at the *travaux préparatoires* of the Model Law, one will observe that it was taken under consideration by the working group to replace the permissive 'may' with the peremptory "shall' "*for the sake of certainty and predictability.*"[19] In the end, however, the "may be refused" wording has been reinstated.[20] The rationale for keeping "may" can be described as follows: it was designed as a sifting mechanism that would allow the court to accept only serious and material challenges. Holtzman and Neuhaus explained that: "*[a]s noted by the Commission Report, a non-material error can give rise to grounds for setting aside the award, but, as noted during the debates, a setting-aside court has discretion not to*

18 For further reading see also section 3.2 and section 5.

19 A/CN/233 para 140.

20 Holtzmann & Neuhaus (1989) p.1058, with reference to A/CN.9/245 paras 139, 141: ("*at its next meeting the Working Group rejected this change, and reinstated the 'may be refused' wording. Its Report offers no explanation, but it may be inferred that, in addition to the general desire to align article 36 with the New York Convention, it was thought preferable to provide a general power of "flexibility" with respect to granting or refusing recognition or enforcement.*").

set aside the award when such grounds are present."[21] Importantly, also other official translations of UNCITRAL Model Law use permissive language.[22]

That being said, one should note, however, that the understanding of the (allegedly) discretionary power may differ among the Model Law jurisdictions. Arguably the application is different in countries of civil and common law tradition.

For example, German commentators have observed that

> [i]n the light of the general approach of German procedural law to discretionary powers of the courts, the 'may be set aside' in §1059 (2) ZPO has to be read as 'shall be set aside'. Whenever a ground for setting aside exists, courts have no discretionary power to refuse the setting aside of the award.[23]

Kröll and Kraft argue, however, that

> [i]n practice, the need for such discretionary powers is limited due to the broad interpretation of the 'effects on the award' requirement and of the grounds for preclusion. As a consequence, in most cases where courts in Model Law countries have made use of their discretion to refuse the setting aside of the award, German courts would already deny the existence of a ground for setting aside or find that a party is precluded from relying on a certain ground.[24]

Conversely, courts from common law countries (that have adopted the Model Law) tend to accept the idea that they have discretionary power (and not the obligation) to set aside the arbitration award. In one case, the Canadian court noted that:

> [...] the seriousness of the defect in the arbitral procedure should be considered when this Court is deciding whether to exercise its discretion to either set aside an award under s. 34 or refuse to enforce an award under s. 36. Like s. 36(1),

---

21 Holtzmann & Neuhaus (1989) p.922. Similarly, Roth (2009) p.1102 ("*[...], as indicated by the word 'may' in the opening sentence of para (2), the court has discretion not to set aside the award*"). For further reading see also A/CN.9/SR.318 para 65.

22 See, for example, the French translation: "*La sentence arbitrale ne peut être annulée par le tribunal visé à l'article 6 que si [...]*" or the Spanish translation "*El laudo arbitral sólo podrá ser anulado por el tribunal indicado en el artículo 6 cuando [...]*". It is an important linguistic argument in favor of discretion considering the analogous discussion that takes place in the context of Art. v. of the New York Convention on Recognition and Enforcement of Foreign Arbitral Awards ("New York Convention" or "NYC"). For further reading see Chapter VI.

23 Kröll & Kraft, *Recourse against the Award, § 1059 – Application for Setting Aside* (2015) p.398.

24 Kröll & Kraft, *Recourse against the Award, § 1059 – Application for Setting Aside* (2015) p.398.

> s. 34(2) is permissive in nature because it states that an arbitral award may be set aside if one of the conditions contained in clauses (a) or (b) is met.[25]

Equally, the New Zealand court observed that "*[a] finding of a breach of the rules of natural justice does not mean that the arbitral award must be set aside. As already noted, the power of the court to set aside an award under art 34 is discretionary and will not be exercised automatically in every case.*"[26]

The aim of this section was to highlight differences that might potentially affect the challenge against the "excess of mandate" type of challenge depending on how the Model Law is adopted. As a general conclusion, one should argue that notwithstanding the details, the courts do follow the same "pro-arbitration" philosophy which encourages them to save the arbitral awards whenever possible; they do so either by accepting discretionary powers to set aside the award or by heightening the standard for the challenge. The effect is, in principle, the same. In any event, it is advocated that on the Model Law level (i) no review of the merits should ever be allowed, (ii) the discretionary power of the courts was intended and (iii) the "excess of mandate" type of challenge should not be classified as a jurisdictional objection.[27]

2.3 *Remedies at the court's disposal*

When faced with a setting-aside challenge, courts have an array of tools that are tailored to protect the arbitral award.[28] As already observed above, the first mechanisms that reinforce the finality of the award are the absence of the merits review and high onus for bringing a successful challenge. Notably, however, the Model Law prescribes two additional tools, namely (i) partial enforcement and (ii) remission that allows the court to protect the healthy part of the arbitral award while setting aside its defective section (if any).

Pursuant to the second part of Article 34(2)(a)(iii) of the Model Law: "*if the decisions on matters submitted to arbitration can be separated from those not so submitted, only that part of the award which contains decisions on matters not submitted to arbitration may be*

---

25 *United Mexican States v. Metalclad Corp.*, 2001 BCSC 664 (CanLII), para 129, http://canlii.ca/t/4xfw#par129 [last accessed 14 August 2020].

26 *Kyburn Investments Limited v. Beca Corporate Holdings Limited* [2015] NZCA 290 para 41, http://www.nzlii.org/nz/cases/NZCA/2015/290.html [last accessed 14 August 2020]. *Brunswick Bowling & Billiards Corporation v. Shanghai Zhonglu Industrial Co. Ltd. and Another* [2009] HKCFI 94 at [29-39], http://www.hklii.hk/eng/hk/cases/hkcfi/2009/94.html [last accessed 14 August 2020].

27 This will be explained further in this chapter. See section 3.2 and section 5.

28 Arguably, the award can be considered as a glare of the parties' bargain to arbitrate their disputes.

set aside."[29] The proviso is quite clear.[30] This mechanism should be considered as another element of the pro-arbitration policy behind the Model Law. It safeguards the finality of the arbitral awards, allowing the part of the decision that is within the scope of submission to survive the challenge against the part that goes beyond the agreed scope. The possibility to sever the arbitral award has been used by courts in Model Law jurisdictions.[31]

The additional power to remit is available under Article 34(4) of the Model Law which reads that

> [t]he court, when asked to set aside an award, may, where appropriate and so requested by a party, suspend the setting aside proceedings for a period of time determined by it in order to give the arbitral tribunal an opportunity to resume the arbitral proceedings or to take such other action as in the arbitral tribunal's opinion will eliminate the grounds for setting aside.

It shows that, in limited circumstances ("*where appropriate*") and upon the request of a party, the court is permitted "*to allow the arbitrators an opportunity to take further steps or decisions, which might render the annulment application unnecessary or inappropriate.*"[32] Importantly, not all Model Law jurisdictions have adopted the remission provision.[33] Some

---

29 The question whether the partial enforcement can be granted in the case of grounds other than Art 34(2)(a)(iii) of the Model Law, falls outside the scope of this study. Usually it is considered as a general rule applicable to all setting-aside grounds. For further reading, see, *e.g.*, UNCITRAL, *Digest of Case Law on the Model Law on International Commercial Arbitration* (2012) p.141, Born, *International Commercial Arbitration* (2014) pp.3180-3181, Kreindler et al., *Commercial Arbitration in Germany* (2016) p.333, Kröll & Kraft, *Recourse against the Award, § 1059 – Application for Setting Aside* (2015) p.418.

30 Kröll & Kraft, *Recourse against the Award, § 1059 – Application for Setting Aside* (2015) p.463 ("*[a]s explicitly stated, the court may only set aside that part of the award which is not covered by the submission to arbitration or beyond the arbitral tribunal's power*").

31 See *United Mexican States v. Metalclad Corp.*, 2001 BCSC 664 (CanLII), http://canlii.ca/t/4xfw, [last accessed 14 August 2020], and as reported in UNCITRAL, *Digest of Case Law on the Model Law on International Commercial Arbitration* (2012) p.154: *Jaral Decoración, S.L v. Peñasco Rodilla, SL*, Madrid Court of Appeal, Spain, 2 February 2007, case No. 94/2007—7/2005; decision on enforcing part of the arbitral award but on the basis of public policy, see also CLOUT case no 687 [*J. J. Agro Industries (P) Ltd. v. Texuna International Ltd.*, Supreme Court of Hong Kong, High Court, 12 August 1992], [1992] 2 HKLR 402]. See also Oberlandesgericht Dresden, 3 Sch 3/12, 26 July 2012 as reported in Kröll & Kraft, *Recourse against the Award, § 1059 – Application for Setting Aside* (2015) p.407, fn.147.

32 Born, *International Commercial Arbitration* (2014) p.3153. See also *AKN and another v. ALC and others and other appeals* [2015] SGCA 63.

33 Born, *International Commercial Arbitration* (2014) p.3153 with a reference to Art. 34 of the Russian Arbitration Act, Art. 34 of the Ukrainian Arbitration Law, Art. 34(4) of the 2011 Costa Rican Arbitration Law, 2011, Arts. 52-54 of the Egyptian Arbitration Law, Art. 78 of the Tunisian Arbitration Code.

have adopted it in a slightly different form[34] and others in *verbatim*.[35] All in all, albeit not often used, it may be a useful tool to remedy the deficiencies of the award.[36]

3 The concept of the arbitral tribunal's mandate under the Model Law

As it has been initially observed in the introduction, the Model Law *does* operate with the concept of the mandate, yet, it is used in a different context than the challenge of the award itself. Therefore, it is necessary to briefly reflect on aspects of the "mandate" in the context of the Model Law. Firstly, the temporal aspect of the tribunal's adjudicative function will be discussed (section 3.1). Secondly, what follows is the introduction of the concept of a violation of the scope of the submission to arbitration (section 3.2).

3.1 Temporal aspect of the tribunal's adjudicative function

If one looks at the text of the Model Law, one will notice that the term "mandate" is repeated seven times and, in all cases, it refers to the temporal characteristic of the tribunal's adjudicative function.[37] Since the countries adopting the Model Law decided to use, in principle, the same language, only the Model Law provisions will be discussed below.[38]

In Article 14(1) of the Model Law the reference to the mandate is used to express the fact that the arbitrator's (adjudicative) function is terminated the moment "*he withdraws from his office or if the parties agree on the termination.*"[39] In Articles 14(2) and 15 of the Model Law it is used to explain the consequences that follow the termination of the mandate. Finally, pursuant to Article 32(3) "*[t]he mandate of the arbitral tribunal terminates with the termination of the arbitral proceedings, subject to the provisions of articles 33 and 34(4).*" This last Article deals, therefore, with the *functus officio* of the arbitral tribunal which is

34 See Art. 1059(4) of the GCCP. In principle, the remission would take place after setting-aside of the award.

35 See the Model Law as adopted in Singapore.

36 For further reading see, *i.a.*, Roth (2009) pp.1108-1109, Binder (2010) p.385 and p.404. UNCITRAL, *Digest of Case Law on the Model Law on International Commercial Arbitration* (2012) p.165, Born, *International Commercial Arbitration* (2014) pp.3153-3154, Kröll & Kraft, *Recourse against the Award, § 1059 – Application for Setting Aside* (2015) pp.393-394, 418, Kreindler et al., *Commercial Arbitration in Germany* (2016) p.352.

37 See Art. 14(1), Art. 14(2), Art. 15 and Art. 32(3) of the ML.

38 See, *e.g.*, (the English translations of) the German Law (Art. 1038(1), Art. 1038(2), Art. 1039 and Art. 1056(3) of the GCCP) or Belgian Law (Art. 1688 §1 and §3, Art. 1689 §1 and Art. 1714 §3 of the Belgian Judicial Code ("BJC")). See also Section 10(6)(b) of the Singaporean International Arbitration Act ("SIAA"). Notably, under Belgian Law, the notion of "mandate" is used along with the notion of "mission" (see Art. 1685 §7 and Art. 1713 §2 of the BJC).

39 Art. 14(1) of the ML.

"[...] the point when the arbitral tribunal has discharged its duty in full and can no longer act."[40]

Notably, Articles 14 and 15 of the Model Law make a reference to the mandate of *an arbitrator*, whereas Article 32 of the Model Law deals with the mandate of *a tribunal*. One may therefore wonder if there is any difference between the mandate of an arbitrator and that of a tribunal. Arguably, however, this difference is of little significance for the research at hand. What those Articles do have in common, however, is a reference to the point in time when the tribunal is no longer able to decide on the dispute of the parties.

Similar conclusions may be drawn when looking at the official French version of the Model Law. The term "*mandat*" is also used seven times and in the same circumstances as in the English version. Interestingly, not only the reference to the tribunal's mandate has been made but also the one to the tribunal's "*mission*" which has been placed instead of the term "function" used in the English version.[41]

All in all, although the concept has been used in the Model Law, it is not employed as a part of the ground for challenge. It is useful to the extent that it shows that the "mandate" is related to the tribunal's adjudicative function.

3.2 *Violation of the scope of the submission to arbitration*

What can be concluded from the previous section is that the concept of the mandate is used in the Model Law and that it does refer to the tribunal's power to resolve the dispute. Notably, however, at the post-award stage, a different mechanism is introduced for testing the tribunal's decision. For the sake of convenience, it should be reiterated that the award can be challenged if "*[it] deals with a dispute not contemplated by or not falling within the terms of the submission to arbitration, or contains decisions on matters beyond the scope of the submission to arbitration [...].*"[42]

One may easily observe that no reference to the "mandate" or its potential "excess" is made. Instead, the challenge is directed at what can be broadly described as a "violation of the scope or terms of the submission to arbitration".[43] At the same time, however, whenever the Article 34(2)(a)(iii) challenge is discussed reference is often made to the "mandate".

40 Fullelove (2016) p.257.

41 Compare Art. 14(1) of the ML in the French version ("*Lorsqu'un arbitre se trouve dans l'impossibilité de droit ou de fait de remplir sa mission [...]*") and the English version ("*If an arbitrator becomes de jure or de facto unable to perform his functions [...]*"). See also fn.38.

42 Art. 34(2)(a)(iii) of the ML.

43 Below it will be also categorized as an "excess of mandate" type of challenge.

This was the case, for example, during the discussion on the early draft of Article 36(1)(a)(iii) of the Model Law. It read that the recognition and enforcement of the award may be refused when "*(c) [t]he award [deals with] [decides on] a dispute of matter [not submitted to arbitration] [outside the scope of the arbitration agreement or not referred to the arbitral tribunal].*"[44] In the explanatory note it was observed that: "*[...] the second alternative attempts to indicate [...] that the question of the arbitrators' exceeding their authority has to be answered by using two standards: the arbitration agreement (in particular an arbitration clause) and the often narrower mandate given to the arbitrators by way of reference, submission of statement of claim.*"[45] Although the debate dealt with the ground at the enforcement stage, it is, arguably, equally applicable to Article 34(2)(a)(iii) of the Model Law.[46]

Similarly, the UNCITRAL Digest reports that "the scope of [the] submission to arbitration" is the same as "the scope of the mandate of the arbitral tribunal".[47] Consequently, these terms have been used interchangeably therein while discussing the "excess of mandate" type of challenge.[48] It is also frequently the case that the Article 34(2)(a)(iii) applicants describe their challenge as one against an "excess of mandate".[49] In conclusion, it seems that the general understanding of the tribunal's "mandate" for the purpose of the Article 34(2)(a)(iii) challenge is that of the parties' submission to arbitration. What it exactly entails will be discussed further in this chapter.[50]

4 Limits to the arbitral tribunal's "mandate"

The power to resolve disputes between parties is exceptional and it is not given without any constraints. Therefore, one should reflect on the traditionally defined limits to this power, namely, the agreement to arbitrate (section 4.1), parties' requests (section 4.2) and public policy rules (section 4.3). Eventually, these three elements will constitute a useful test applicable to the Article 34(2)(a)(iii) challenge (section 4.4).

---

44 See A/CN.9/WG.II/WP.42 p.92.

45 A/CN.9/WG.II/WP.42 p.92.

46 See the explanation above, section 1.

47 UNCITRAL, *Digest of Case Law on the Model Law on International Commercial Arbitration* (2012) p.151.

48 See UNCITRAL, *Digest of Case Law on the Model Law on International Commercial Arbitration* (2012) pp.151-154.

49 See, *e.g.*, *CRW Joint Operation v. PT Perusahaan Gas Negara (Persero) TBK* [2011] SGCA 33, [2011] 4 SLR 305 at [17], *Blanalko Pty Ltd v. Lysaght Building Solutions Pty Ltd* [2017] VSC 97 at [45].

50 See sections 4 and 5 of this chapter.

4.1 Agreement to arbitrate

Any of the arbitral tribunal's powers start with the parties' consent. It means that a valid agreement to arbitrate, which is a medium transmitting the parties' consent, does shape the scope of arbitral tribunals' rights and obligations. At the same time, however, the agreement to arbitrate itself is often broadly drafted and vague in defining the scope of the tribunal's adjudicative function. The reflections introduced below are two-fold. It means that one should (i) highlight its relevance for the "excess of mandate" type of challenge and (ii) identify the most important features of the agreement to arbitrate.

As has been observed in the previous section,[51] the Model Law operates with the notion of "the submission to arbitration" in the context of Article 34(2)(a)(iii) which is in stark contrast with the explicit reference to the "arbitration agreement" under Article 34(2)(a)(i).[52] Yet, the importance of the agreement to arbitrate cannot pass unnoticed, since the parties' consent to arbitrate is expressed through it. Consequently, one should conclude that the agreement to arbitrate is important not only to establish the jurisdiction of the arbitration tribunal, but also its "mandate" which is generally narrower[53] but equally dependent on the underlying parties' consent. The conclusion that the agreement to arbitrate is important for the "excess of mandate" type of challenge can be supported by the French version of the Model Law where the reference to both submission agreement and arbitration clause is made.[54]

What is relevant for the research at hand is that both the arbitration clause (which is the agreement to refer to arbitration future disputes) and the submission agreement (which is the agreement between the parties to have an existing dispute resolved by the arbitral tribunal) can be considered as an agreement to arbitrate. This is explicitly stated in Article 7 of the Model Law.[55] Additionally, since the agreement to arbitrate is the contractual framework of the parties' consent, it needs to be drafted very carefully. It is particularly true if parties intend to narrow the scope of the powers available to the tribunal. Finally, one should also take into account that the choice of a certain set of institutional rules will also impact the shape of the tribunal's adjudicative powers.[56]

---

51 See section 3.2.

52 See also section 5.3.

53 Because it is limited to the dispute submitted to the tribunal by the parties.

54 See the French version of Art. 34(2)(a)(iii) of the ML ("*Que la sentence porte sur un différend non visé dans le compromis ou n'entrant pas dans les prévisions de la clause compromissoire, ou qu'elle contient des décisions qui dépassent les termes du compromis ou de la clause compromissoire, [...].*"). It does not change the fact, however, that even the French version operates with a different terminology for the purpose of Art. 34(2)(a)(iii) and Art. 34(2)(a)(i) of the ML. Compare "*le compromise*" and "*la clause compromissoire*" (Art. 34(2)(a)(iii) of the ML) and "*la convention d'arbitrage*" (Art. 34(2)(a)(i) of the ML).

55 See Art. 7(1) of the ML (option I) and Art. 7 of the ML (option II).

56 Since the agreement to arbitrate is usually broad and addressed mostly to the parties themselves (as to what disputes they may bring to arbitration), it does not provide sufficient explanation as to how the tribunal

4.2 *Parties' (subsequent) submissions*

Article 34(2)(a)(iii) of the Model Law makes a reference to the "scope" and the "terms" to "submission to arbitration". It gives a clear indication that it is not the agreement to arbitrate alone that is relevant for this ground for challenge.[57] Although a more detailed textual analysis as to what "submission to arbitration" entails will be made in the next section,[58] one should preliminarily conclude that the court when faced with the "excess of mandate" type of challenge, apart from reviewing the agreement to arbitrate, should also take into consideration the relief sought by the parties and other examples of the parties' communications.

The parties' subsequent submissions are of utmost importance because they might explicitly or impliedly alter the original scope of the arbitral tribunal's adjudicative function prescribed initially in the agreement to arbitrate. In principle, isolated requests of the party in the arbitration (for example stated in a request for arbitration, memorial, or counter-memorial) will usually define (and limit) the realm where the arbitral tribunal may make use of its adjudicative powers. Occasionally, however, a request may also expand the adjudicative mandate beyond the parties' initial consent expressed in the agreement to arbitrate. It will all depend on the conduct of the other parties in arbitration. Their silence to broadening the scope of the submission might constitute their acceptance.

The courts in the Model Law jurisdictions have confirmed, for example, that Article 34(2)(a)(iii) of the Model Law deals with the matters that have been actually submitted to arbitration[59] and that the scope of the submission is expressed in the request for arbitration.[60] Similarly, the UNCITRAL Digest reports that "*[s]everal courts have stated that, in determining the "terms of the submission" to arbitration and "scope of the submission" in paragraph (2)(a)(iii), the arbitration agreement and other relevant contractual provisions, the notice of request for arbitration, and the pleadings exchanged between the parties are to be taken into account.*"[61]

Additionally, it is necessary to highlight the importance of Terms of Reference as a characteristic feature of some institutional rules.[62] By and large, the Terms of Reference

should exercise its adjudicative function. Consequently, it is the institutional rules that serve as a guidance as to what powers the parties consented to vest in arbitrators.

57 Compare with Art. 34(2)(a)(i) of the ML. See also section 4.1.

58 See section 5.2.

59 *CRW Joint Operation v. PT Perusahaan Gas Negara (Persero) TBK* [2011] SGCA 33, [2011] 4 SLR 305 at [31].

60 *Quintette Coal Ltd. v. Nippon Steel Corporation*, 1991 CanLII 5708 (BC CA), par. 33, http://canlii.ca/t/231lq#par33, [last accessed 14 August 2020].

61 UNCITRAL, *Digest of Case Law on the Model Law on International Commercial Arbitration* (2012) p.151.

62 See, *e.g.*, Art. 23 of the (draft) 2021 ICC Rules, Art. 23 of the 2017 ICC Rules or Art. 22 of the 2013 CEPANI Rules.

become a useful tool to delimit and define the scope of the dispute and consequently the tribunal's adjudicative function. In principle, all parties to arbitration shall participate in drawing up the Terms of Reference, agree on their content and sign them. From the perspective of the tribunal, the Terms of Reference give a clear indication as to the parties' expectations in the process.

Finally, it is concluded that both the agreement to arbitrate and the parties' subsequent submissions are relevant to determine what the "submission to arbitration" entails in the context of Article 34(2)(a)(iii) of the Model Law. That being said, one should know, however, that this ground is not adapted and is not applied the same way in all of the Model Law jurisdictions. It consequently means that the interpretation of "submission to arbitration" may differ.[63]

4.3 *Mandatory rules of law of public policy character*

According to Article 34(2)(b)(ii) of the Model Law an award may be refused if the setting-aside court finds that the award is in conflict with the public policy of the place of the seat of the arbitral tribunal. These rules of public policy, albeit elusive, constitute the most basic elements of any legal regime. As aptly explained by Wolff, "*public policy consists of those rules that regulate crucial issues which affect the basis of public and economic life due to specific political or economical visions or fundamental ideas of justice.*"[64]

In the context of the research at hand, one should note that the public policy rules are also an important element constraining the tribunal's adjudicative function, because the national court when reviewing an alleged excess of the arbitral tribunal's mandate will ultimately condition its analysis not only upon the parties' consent but also upon the conformity of the award with public policy rules. Importantly, it will do so on *ex officio* basis.

Additionally, although it is mostly accepted that the public policy test should have a narrow application,[65] there is no uniformity in the way this provision is interpreted. There are two aspects that need to be carefully reviewed when analyzing the public policy test in the Model Law jurisdiction: first, whether a distinction is made between "national"

63 For example, it has been suggested by Wolff in Kreindler et al., *Commercial Arbitration in Germany* (2016) p.339 that Art. 1059(2)(1)(c) of the GCCP refers to the excess of the arbitration agreement. Similarly under the Polish arbitration regime, the reference is made only to the agreement to arbitrate. Pursuant to Art. 1206(1)(3) of the Polish Code of Civil Procedure ("Polish CCP") the award may be set aside "*if [it] deals with a dispute not contemplated by the agreement to arbitrate or goes beyond the scope of the agreement to arbitrate [...]*" ("*wyrok sądu polubownego dotyczy sporu nieobjętego zapisem na sąd polubowny lub wykracza poza zakres takiego zapisu*").

64 Kreindler et al., *Commercial Arbitration in Germany* (2016) pp.346-347.

65 UNCITRAL, *Digest of Case Law on the Model Law on International Commercial Arbitration* (2012) p.159.

and "international" public policy (and which standard is applied in the setting-aside provision) and, second, whether public policy includes both "procedural" and "substantive" public policy.

The better view is to conclude that the Model Law in itself refers to the concept of international public policy, because of the overarching pro-arbitration philosophy behind the Model Law.[66]

As an illustration, however, one should point out that according to German arbitration law, "*[t]he public policy standard to be applied in s 1059 ZPO is that of so-called national public policy.*"[67]

Belgian law seems to be more nuanced. According to commentators:

> [w]hen Belgian law applies to the arbitration, the award may be annulled for a violation of (Belgian) public policy. In the circumstances, however, where the arbitration takes place in Belgium but the parties have opted to have their dispute governed by a foreign law (i.e., not Belgian law), the reference to substantive Belgian public policy is not adequate. It is generally considered that, in that case, annulment will only be justified if the award is contrary to the principles of substantive international public policy.[68]

In Singapore, a court held that "*the concepts of public policy for setting aside a 'domestic' award under article 34 and for the enforcement of a foreign award are identical. The court saw no need to distinguish between the two regimes as all awards falling within the ambit of the legislation on international arbitration are considered to have an 'international focus'.*"[69] Notably, however, the Singaporean International Arbitration Act extends the catalogue of the *ex officio* grounds. The court will be able to set aside the award if (i) the making of the award was induced or affected by fraud or corruption or (ii) a breach of the rules of natural justice occurred in connection with the making of the award by which the rights of any party have been prejudiced.[70]

The question whether public policy refers to procedural or substantive public policy generally falls outside the scope of this research and again depends on how the Model Law is adopted. In principle, both public policy grounds might be available for violations of

66 See section 2.1.

67 Kreindler et al., *Commercial Arbitration in Germany* (2016) p.347, as opposed to the international public policy standard at the enforcement stage. See also Kröll & Kraft, *Recourse against the Award, § 1059 – Application for Setting Aside* (2015) p.411 ("*Awards can be set aside if their enforcement would be contrary to German public policy*").

68 Verbruggen, *Commentary on Part VI of the Belgian Judicial Code*, Chapter VII: Article 1717, 2016, p.480.

69 UNCITRAL, *Digest of Case Law on the Model Law on International Commercial Arbitration* (2012) p.160.

70 See Section 24(a) and Section 24(b) of the SIAA.

both types of public policy.[71] As an example, violation of the procedural public policy would usually entail non-compliance with the basic principles of procedural fairness, whereas substantive public policy will be violated, *e.g.*, when "*[...] the compliance with the award would constitute a criminal offence, violate price fixing provisions, [...] or contravene [...] antitrust law.*"[72]

All in all, one should conclude that the rules of public policy are relevant in structuring the arbitral tribunal's adjudicative mandate and indirectly affect the review of the "mandate" at the post-award stage.

4.4 *The importance of the consent, the request and the law: the three keyholes test*

The previous three sections were intended to describe the essential limits to the tribunal's adjudicative function. In principle, the shape of the "mandate" depends on the parties, save for the underlying values of each legal system.

Consequently, the three steps test has to be exercised in order to determine whether the tribunal acted within its adjudicative authority: first and foremost the reviewing court has to examine the agreement to arbitrate, *i.e.* whether there was a consent of the parties to arbitrate certain categories of disputes or matters;[73] the next step is to establish whether the parties' requests, thus the parties' (subsequent) submissions, allow one to assume that an arbitral tribunal was truly asked to grant the relief sought.[74] Finally, the court should also take into account the impact of public policy rules which will inevitably affect both the consent and the request of the parties in arbitration in the process of determining the arbitral tribunal's "mandate".[75] It is argued that in cases of the post-award review of the tribunal's "mandate", the award should pass the three keyholes test.[76] It means that the arbitral tribunal's decision should comply with the mandatory rules of law (of public policy character) and fit within the scope of the agreement to arbitrate and the parties' reliefs sought. It is important to mention, however, that the level of deference employed by the court might depend on which step (of the three keyholes test) the national court exercises.

---

71 For general overview of approaches to the public policy challenge, see Hwang & Lai (2005).

72 Kreindler et al., *Commercial Arbitration in Germany* (2016) p.348. See also UNCITRAL, *Digest of Case Law on the Model Law on International Commercial Arbitration* (2012) pp.161-164.

73 For further reading see section 4.1.

74 For further reading see section 4.2.

75 For further reading see section 4.3.

76 The notion of the "two keyholes test" was suggested by David Caron during the International Academy for Arbitration Law in 2013 albeit in different context. Since it is evocative in nature it is also used in the context of the research at hand.

5 The Model Law approach to the "excess of mandate" type of challenge

The "excess of mandate" type of challenge introduced in the Model Law is rather descriptive in nature. For the sake of convenience it should be highlighted that, pursuant to Article 34(2)(a)(iii) of the Model Law, the award may be set aside if

> [it] deals with a dispute not contemplated by or not falling within the terms of the submission to arbitration, or contains decisions on matters beyond the scope of the submission to arbitration, provided that, if the decisions on matters submitted to arbitration can be separated from those not so submitted, only that part of the award which contains decisions on matters not submitted to arbitration may be set aside.

One should note that different authors refer to this provision in a way suggesting its affiliation with an "excess of mandate" type of challenge (*e.g.* "the excess of authority",[77] "the excess of power"[78] or even "*excès de pouvoir*"[79]). At the same time, however, it is necessary to reflect if it is justified or else if by doing so they transpose the concept known from other jurisdictions which does not necessarily fit with an intended scope of Article 34(2)(a)(iii). Consequently, it is necessary to conduct a textual analysis of the discussed provision (section 5.2) and explain its place in the system of the post-award review (section 5.3). Before going further into details, it is useful to highlight the main differences in adopting the Model Law that might potentially influence the difficulty with the application of Article 34(2)(a)(iii) of the Model Law (section 5.1).

5.1 *Differences in the official language versions of the Model Law and the implementation of the Model Law*

Although there are many similarities between the systems that adopt the Model Law, one should be careful in drawing general inferences from the way the system is applied in the Model Law jurisdictions to the general Model Law level. This is particularly true for the post-award review mechanism and the "excess of mandate" type of challenge. Therefore, one should reflect on the different language versions of the Model Law and give examples of the peculiarities of how the review mechanism has been adopted by the Model Law

77 See, *e.g.*, Born, *International Commercial Arbitration* (2014) pp.3287-3309.

78 See, *e.g.*, Blackaby et al. (2015) pp.584-585.

79 See Pulkowski (2010) pp.119-134.

jurisdictions. Some of the observations will also be introduced in the sections that follow, yet it is reasonable to collect them and present them together in an orderly manner.

This study was based on three official language versions of the Model Law as available on the official UNCITRAL website.[80] For the sake of convenience, the relevant fragments of the text of the provisions have been repeated below.

Table 1

	The English version	The French version	The Spanish version
1.	*the award deals with a dispute not contemplated by or not falling within the terms of the submission to arbitration*	*Que la sentence porte sur un différend non visé dans le compromis ou n'entrant pas dans les prévisions de la clause compromissoire*	*que el laudo se refiere a una controversia no prevista en el acuerdo de arbitraje*
2.	*or contains decisions on matters beyond the scope of the submission to arbitration*	*ou qu'elle contient des décisions qui dépassent les termes du compromis ou de la clause compromissoire*	*o contiene decisiones que exceden los términos del acuerdo de arbitraje*

One might observe that all three variations refer to two hypotheses in which the award is susceptible to challenge.[81] The differences are also noticeable, however. Whereas in the most common English variation of the Model Law the reference is made to both "the terms" and "the scope" of the "submission to arbitration" without further explanation on whether there is a difference between those terms, one will notice that the French text, in both hypotheticals, refers explicitly to the submission agreement ("*le compromis*") and to the arbitration clause ("*la clause compromissoire*") making it clear what the "submission to arbitration" actually entails. The Spanish text in both instances refers to arbitration agreement ("*acuerdo de arbitraje*"), notably in the same fashion as it is used in Article 34(2)(a)(i) of the (Spanish version) of the Model Law.[82] Arguably, one might consider these versions to support an argument that Article 34(2)(a)(iii) of the Model Law would be directed at the scope of the tribunal's jurisdiction (and not at the "excess of mandate" type of challenge).

Moreover, although the French and the Spanish texts do refer to the "terms" (Fr. "*termes*" and Spa. "*términos*") in the second hypothesis, they make no use of similar terms in the first hypothesis. Put differently, the first hypothesis explains that the decision

80 The remaining three, the Arabic and the Chinese and the Russian, were not included due to the language capacities of the author.

81 This division has also been presented and explained in section 5.2.2. For further reading, see that section.

82 The Spanish version of Art. 34(2)(a)(i) of the Model Law reads that: "*que una de las partes en el acuerdo de arbitraje a que se refiere el artículo 7 estaba afectada por alguna incapacidad, o que dicho acuerdo no es válido en virtud de la ley a que las partes lo han sometido, o si nada se hubiera indicado a este respecto, en virtud de la ley de este Estado*".

was made on a dispute not included in the "arbitration agreement", whereas the second hypothesis allows for setting aside where the award contains a decision that goes beyond the "terms" of the "arbitration agreement". Arguably, it might be still difficult to distill the difference between an "arbitration agreement" and the "terms" of an "arbitration agreement". Still, by not using the term "matters" (as in the English text "decisions on matters") and avoiding the distinction between "the terms" and "the scope", the language comes across simpler. Therefore the Model Law system may evolve differently when adopted, depending on which language variation it is based on.

The underlying goal of the Model Law is to ensure the pro-arbitration philosophy worldwide. This pursuit for harmonization and uniformity is to be praised. Yet, at the end of the day, everything depends on the countries that adopt the Model Law. This is particularly relevant in the case of Article 34(2)(a)(iii) of the Model Law, because this remedy against the arbitral award is perceived differently in different jurisdictions.[83]

Careful analysis of each legal system allows to observe that sometimes Article 34(2)(a)(iii) of the Model Law is perceived only as the challenge of the scope of the tribunal's jurisdiction. It might depend, however, on the text used in the relevant arbitration statute, which does not necessarily adopt the Model Law in *verbatim*. For example, according to the Polish Code of Civil Procedure, the award may be set aside if "*the award deals with a dispute not contemplated by the agreement to arbitrate or it goes beyond the scope of this agreement [...]*".[84] Therefore, the way the Model Law has been implemented in the Polish legal system, this ground for challenge refers only to the arbitration agreement, thus the basic realm of the tribunal's jurisdiction and not to the mandate. In Singapore, possibly because of the influence of the English legal tradition, this ground is likely to also be qualified as the jurisdictional one.[85]

Another issue that might be relevant for the analysis of the "excess of mandate" type of challenge in the Model Law jurisdictions is whether they have included only the grounds for recourse listed in the Model Law itself or, else, whether they adjusted the Model Law to their national legal system. Two examples come to mind. One is Belgium, where the Model Law has been recently implemented. Yet, it was decided that the concept of "excess of powers" will remain a valid reason to challenge the award.[86] It might give an additional layer of difficulty in determining what ground for challenge is the most suitable for the "excess of mandate" type of challenge. Similarly, in Singapore, the typical Model Law

83 See examples in section 5.3.

84 See Art. 1206(1)(3) of the Polish CCP ("*wyrok sądu polubownego dotyczy sporu nieobjętego zapisem na sąd polubowny lub wykracza poza zakres takiego zapisu [...]*").

85 In the English system, the question regarding "*what matters have been submitted to arbitration in accordance with the arbitration agreement*" is identified in Section 30(1)(c) of the English Arbitration Act as one of the questions of substantive jurisdiction. For further reading see Chapter IV.

86 See Art. 1717(3)(vi) of the BJC.

post-award mechanism has been supplemented by recourse in cases where "the making of the award was induced or affected by fraud or corruption" or when "a breach of natural justice occurred".[87] Although these will be challenges on the level of public policy violations, it might be necessary to remain cautious on how those concepts influence constraints on the "tribunal's mandate".

Although there might be some discrepancies in the system, the Model Law's "excess of mandate" type of challenge is a suitable candidate for the comparison between the French notion of the "tribunal's failure to comply with its mandate" and generally the Anglo-American model of the "excess of powers".

5.2 *Textual interpretation of Article 34(2)(a)(iii) of the Model Law*

The working hypothesis is that the long and descriptive provision does not make the application of Article 34(2)(a)(iii) of the Model Law easy. Because of the ambiguity of some of the terms used, it is therefore necessary to discuss each expression separately. The analysis will begin with the term "submission to arbitration" (section 5.2.1) and continue with the closely related "terms of the submission to arbitration" and the "scope of the submission to arbitration" (section 5.2.2). What follows are reflections on the meaning of a "dispute" (section 5.2.3) and "matters" (section 5.2.4). Finally, the general conclusion arising from the textual analysis will be presented (section 5.2.5).

One should observe that the provision has been designed to correspond to the same provision of the New York Convention and to enhance the uniform application of the UNCITRAL texts. Consequently, the linguistic analysis offered in the context of the New York Convention might have persuasive value, also in the context of the Model Law.[88]

5.2.1 The importance of "the submission to arbitration"

If one considers that, in some cases, the term "submission to arbitration" is directly equated with the mandate of the tribunal,[89] one should conclude that determining the meaning of "the submission to arbitration" constitutes the key to understanding what is covered by the "excess of mandate" type of challenge under the Model Law regime.[90]

The general view is that "the submission to arbitration" is a broad term. Therefore, it should *not* be narrowly understood as a submission agreement *i.e.* the agreement to arbitrate

87 See Section 24(a) and Section 24(b) of the SIAA.

88 For further reading, see Chapter VI.

89 See UNCITRAL, *Digest of Case Law on the Model Law on International Commercial Arbitration* (2012) p.151 ("*The scope of [the] submission to arbitration, also referred to as the scope of the mandate of the arbitral tribunal, is primarily determined by the parties.*").

90 For similar considerations at the enforcement stage, see Chapter VI.

an already existing dispute.[91] Similarly, it should not be limited only to the parties' subsequent submissions with disregard of the agreement to arbitrate.[92] Consequently, one should conclude that both an agreement to arbitrate and the parties' subsequent submissions are relevant for testing the award against the Article 34(2)(a)(iii) matrix.[93]

Such a notion is supported by the draft provision of Article 36(1)(a)(iii) of the Model Law [then Article 37(1)(c)] which reads that recognition and enforcement of the arbitral award may be refused if: "*[t]he award [deals with] [decides on] a dispute or matter [not submitted to arbitration][outside the scope of the arbitration agreement or not referred to the arbitral tribunal; [...].*"[94] Although the provision did not survive in said shape, it shows the intention of the drafters to invoke both the agreement to arbitrate and the parties' references as a source reviewed under this post-award mechanism.[95] According to the explanatory note:

> [w]hile the first alternative may be regarded as sufficient for all practical purposes, the second alternative attempts to indicate more clearly that the question of the arbitrators' exceeding their authority has to be answered by using two standards: the arbitration agreement (in particular arbitration clause) and the often narrower mandate given to the arbitrators by way of reference, submission or statement of claim.[96]

Equally, the UNCITRAL Digest reported that "*[s]everal courts have stated that, in determining the "terms of the submission" to arbitration and "scope of the submission" in paragraph (2)(a)(iii), the arbitration agreement and other relevant contractual provisions, the notice of request for arbitration, and the pleadings exchanged between the parties are to be taken into account.*"[97]

Also scholars seem to favor a broad interpretation of the submission to arbitration. For example, Born argues that the "excess of mandate" type of challenge "*[...] is directed towards cases where a valid arbitration agreement existed, but the matters decided by the tribunal either exceeded the scope of that agreement or the scope of the issues presented to the tribunal by the parties in the arbitration.*"[98] Similarly, Kröll and Kraft when discussing

91 For further reading see section 4.1 and section 4.2.
92 Born, *International Commercial Arbitration* (2014) p.3288.
93 For further reading see section 4.1 and section 4.2.
94 Second Draft A/CN.9/WG.II/WP.42 Art. 37(1)(c); the quotation follows the original wording (this also applies to the square brackets).
95 The only reason why the provision did not survive in the said shape is because it was decided that it should be harmonized with Art. v. of the NYC; see A/CN.9/245 paras 139 and 141.
96 Second Draft A/CN.9/WG.II/WP.42 Article 37(1)(c), note 4.
97 UNCITRAL, *Digest of Case Law on the Model Law on International Commercial Arbitration* (2012) p.151.
98 Born, *International Commercial Arbitration* (2014) p.3288.

the Article of the German Code of Civil Procedure mirroring Article 34(2)(a)(iii) of the Model Law stated that "*[a]n award may be set aside if the arbitral tribunal has exceeded its authority, either because the dispute or parts of it were outside the scope of the arbitration agreement or the arbitral tribunal has acted ultra petita, awarding more or something different than the parties have requested.*"[99]

Not all commentators agree, however. For example, Wolff argues that under German law the ground corresponding to Article 34(2)(a)(iii) of the Model Law is dedicated to dealing with the challenge of the scope of the arbitration clause and the provision mirroring Article 34(2)(a)(iv) of the Model Law or even Article 34(2)(b)(ii) of the Model Law can be used for the setting aside of the *ultra petita* decisions.[100] The better view, however, is to accept *ultra petita* challenges also within the ambit of Article 34(2)(a)(iii) of the Model Law. Arguably, had this ground referred to the agreement to arbitrate alone, it would have so indicated in the same way as the reference to the agreement to arbitrate is made in Article 34(2)(a)(i) of the Model Law.

Although it is concluded that both the agreement to arbitrate and the parties' subsequent submissions should be consulted in case of the "excess of mandate" type of challenge, one should observe that certain interpretative difficulties arise because of the use of two different references in the text of the analyzed provisions, namely (i) "the terms of submission to arbitration" and (ii) "the scope of the submission to arbitration". It requires therefore further analysis which is presented in section 5.2.2 below. At the later stage, some reflections need to also be added with respect to the terms "dispute" and "matters".[101]

5.2.2 The difference between "the terms of the submission to arbitration" and "the scope of the submission to arbitration"

As suggested above, the difficulty with interpreting the "excess of mandate" type of challenge under the Model Law system goes further than problems with interpreting what the "submission to arbitration" entails. This is the case, because Article 34(2)(a)(iii) of the Model Law operates with two distinctive concepts, those of (i) "the terms of submission to arbitration" and (ii) "the scope of the submission to arbitration". Consequently, the use of different wording ("the terms" and "the scope") might suggest that there is a variation between these two expressions.

If it is accepted that both terms constitute distinctive concepts, one would need to recognize the following construction of Article 32(2)(a)(iii) of the Model Law, where the award can be set aside if:

99 Kröll & Kraft, *Recourse against the Award, § 1059 – Application for Setting Aside* (2015) pp.406-607

100 Kreindler et al., *Commercial Arbitration in Germany* (2016) pp.339-340.

101 See section 5.2.3 and section 5.2.4.

Table 2

1.	[it] deals with *a dispute*	not contemplated by or not falling within	*the terms* of the submission to arbitration
2.	[or] contains decisions on *matters*	beyond	*the scope* of the submission to arbitration

It would entail two distinctive categories of challenges to be dealt with under the same ground for recourse. Notably, it also ties the term "dispute" to the notion of "the terms of the submission to arbitration" (see ad. 1 in the table 2) and the term "matters" (or even "decisions on matters") to the concept of "the scope of the submission to arbitration" (see ad. 2 in the table 2). Such an interpretation is to be preferably avoided, because it might make Article 34(2)(a)(iii) applicable to jurisdictional objections (ad. 1) and "mandate"-type objections (ad. 2). These two categories of challenges, however, are distinct and might result in a different scope of the court's judicial control of the award.[102]

The preferred view, therefore, is to treat both terms ("the terms" and "the scope") as synonyms. This way it would be clear that Article 34(2)(a)(iii) of the Model Law is limited to the "excess of mandate" type of challenges.[103] If one looks, for example, at the former version of Article 37(1)(c) of the Model Law, one would read that the arbitral award may be refused if "*[it] [deals with][decides on] a dispute or matter [not submitted to arbitration][outside the scope of the arbitration agreement or not referred to the arbitral tribunal]*".[104] Arguably, it shows that both "dispute" and "matter" do refer to a single (broad) concept of the submission to arbitration. This argument would also be supported by the French text of the Model Law, which in both counts (*i.e.* in the context of "dispute" and "matter") makes a reference to the same notion of a submission to arbitration.[105]

Notably, the UNCITRAL in its Digest also reports that

> [s]everal court[s] have stated that, in determining the "terms of the submission" to arbitration and "scope of the submission" in paragraph (2)(a)(iii) [of Article 34 of the Model Law], the arbitration agreement and other relevant contractual

102 See section 2.2.

103 This would leave the jurisdictional objectives to be fitted under Art. 34(2)(a)(i) of the ML.

104 Second Draft A/CN.9/WG.II/WP.42 Art. 37(1)(c); the quotation follows the original wording (it also applies to the alternatives in square brackets).

105 The French version of Art. 34(2)(a)(iii) of the ML reads: "*Que la sentence porte sur un différend non visé dans le compromis ou n'entrant pas dans les prévisions de la clause compromissoire, ou qu'elle contient des décisions qui dépassent les termes du compromis ou de la clause compromissoire [...].*" One will, therefore, notice that the reference is constantly made to both the submission agreement ("*le compromis*") and the arbitration clause ("*la clause compromissoire*").

provisions, the notice of request for arbitration, and the pleadings exchanged between the parties are to be taken into account.[106]

To conclude, on the Model Law level, treating the "terms of the submission to arbitration" and "the scope of the submission to arbitration" as synonyms will better serve the consistent application of Article 34(2)(a)(iii) of the Model Law and the underlying pro-arbitration philosophy behind of the Model Law.[107] That being said, one should always consult how the Model Law is adopted in the jurisdiction in question to determine the suitable interpretation of the "excess of mandate" type of challenge.

5.2.3 The meaning of a "dispute"

Apart from some difficulties in establishing what the term "submission to arbitration" entails, the two other notions "dispute" and "matters"[108] also require a brief explanation. As to the first concept, the general idea is that the "mandate" may be violated if the award deals with a dispute that is not submitted to arbitrators, which means that it resolves a disagreement between the parties that has neither been envisaged by the agreement to arbitrate nor by the parties' subsequent submissions.

Considering that the Model Law mirrors solutions introduced in the New York Convention,[109] one should observe that the use of the term "dispute" in Article 34(2)(a)(iii) of the Model Law is one of the eminent deviations from the text of Article V(1)(c) of the New York Convention (at least in the English version of the provision) which refers to "difference".[110] Arguably, such a modification should be welcomed, because it offers more coherence with the language used in the modern (model) arbitration clauses.[111]

Occasionally, the (rather jurisdictional) argument is raised that a "dispute" is needed for the tribunal to exercise its adjudicative function.[112] If such an argument is accepted, it

---

106 UNCITRAL, *Digest of Case Law on the Model Law on International Commercial Arbitration* (2012) p.151.

107 See section 2.1.

108 See section 5.2.4.

109 For further reading see Chapter VI.

110 A modification can also be observed in the Spanish texts: in the Spanish text of the NYC the term "*una diferencia*" is used, whereas the Spanish version of the ML operates with the term "*una controversia*". Notably, in the French version of the NYC and of the ML the same term is used ("*un différend*").

111 See, for example, the ICC Model Clause, the LCIA Model Clause, the HKIAC Model Clause, the UNICTRAL Model Clause, the SIAC Model Clause). All of them use the term "disputes" instead of "differences". Interestingly, "dispute" for the purpose of the English Arbitration Act ("EAA") has been defined as including "any difference". See Section 82 of the EAA.

112 See as discussed *e.g.* in Pryles & Waincymer, *Multiple Claims in Arbitration Between the Same Parties* (2009) p.443 ("*Even if the claims bear the necessary connection with the defined legal relationship and therefore prima facie fall within the jurisdiction of the tribunal, it is sometimes contended that the claims cannot be put forward because there is no 'dispute' between the parties. For example if a claim is made for payment of monies due under a contract and it is clear that the respondent has no defence and seeks to raise no defence other than its impecuniosity, is there a 'dispute' which can be referred to arbitration? In our opinion there is*

will have further consequences for the "excess of mandate" type of challenge.[113] The better view, however, is to follow Pryles and Waincymer's argumentation that the dispute will exist if "*the claim has been made and has not been satisfied.*"[114] Additionally, one should note that Article 34(2)(a)(iii) of the Model Law operates with a reference not only to the concept of a "dispute" but also "matters" which suggests that all issues (not only a "dispute" in the narrow sense) brought to the tribunal within the limits of the "submission to arbitration"[115] deserve a tribunal's decision.

5.2.4 The meaning of "matters"

The expression "matters" (or rather "decisions on matters") referred to in the second part of Article 34(2)(a)(iii) of the Model Law, which has been paired up with "the scope of submission to arbitration", complements the first part of the provision since it allows the reviewing court to test not only an arbitral tribunal's decisions on "disputes" but also on "matters".[116]

A decision on matters should be considered as a decision on issues that are not necessarily disputed between the parties, but nonetheless have been brought before the arbitral tribunal for a determination.[117] This might happen, for example, when the parties concluded a long-term gas sales and purchase agreement which gives the parties right to request the arbitral tribunal to review the price of the gas. Additionally, one might also recognize instances when the parties envisage in the arbitration agreement that the arbitral tribunal will have discretion to modify certain terms of the underlying contract. In these cases, it is also plausible that without the existence of a "dispute" between the parties, an arbitral tribunal will be asked to render a decision.

---

a dispute because the claim has been made and has not been satisfied. In any event such esoteric arguments can be avoided by drafting an arbitration clause to include a 'claim' and a 'difference' as well as a 'dispute'. Well drafted clauses allow for all disputes which could conceivably flow from the contract between the parties. Nothing should turn on the distinction between terms such as 'dispute' and 'difference'.").

113 For example, one may try to argue (invoking Art. 34(2)(a)(iii) of the ML) that "a dispute" is an essential element of the "submission to arbitration". Consequently, since there was no dispute, the tribunal is unable to act (on a claim submitted by claimant).

114 Pryles & Waincymer, *Multiple Claims in Arbitration Between the Same Parties* (2009) p.443.

115 No distinction is made between "the terms" and "the scope". See section 5.2.1 and section 5.2.2.

116 The category of "matters" might be particularly useful, if one considers the concept of a "dispute" narrowly. For further reading see fn.112 and section 5.2.3.

117 Distinction between the notion of a "dispute" and "matters" can be illustrated by reference to Art. 1020(1) and Art. 1020(4) of the Dutch Code of Civil Procedure. Whereas the former gives a general definition that "*[t]he parties may agree to submit to arbitration disputes which have arisen or may arise between them out of a defined legal relationship, whether contractual or not*", the latter explains that "*Parties may also agree to submit the following matters to arbitration [...]*". Three distinctive items have been categorized as "matters" in Art. 1020(4) of the Dutch Code of Civil Procedure, namely: "*(a) the determination only of the quality or condition of goods; (b) the determination only of the quantum of damages or monetary debt; (c) the filling of gaps, or modification of, the legal relationship between the parties [to an arbitration agreement]*".

Notably, neither the French nor the Spanish versions of the Model Law make any reference to "matters". Instead, these texts operate only with the notion of the tribunal's "decision" going beyond the terms of the submission to arbitration.[118] Arguably, such a solution leaves less interpretative doubts than the English text, because one does need to tie the term "dispute" with "terms of the submission to arbitration" and the term "(decision on) matters" with the "scope of the submission to arbitration".

All in all, arguably, not only "disputes" but also "matters" might be submitted to the tribunal's determination. Additionally, whenever the question arises whether "matters" have been submitted to arbitration, one should consult both the agreement to arbitrate and the parties' subsequent submissions.[119]

5.2.5 Conclusion of the textual analysis

Following the analysis presented above, one should conclude that when the confines of the submission to arbitration are tested by the court pursuant to Article 34(2)(a)(iii) of the Model Law, the court should, firstly, disregard that two different expressions are being used (i.e. "the terms of the submission to arbitration" and "the scope of the submission to arbitration") and consider that they have the same meaning and, secondly, it should accept that both decisions on disputed (i.e. "a dispute") and "undisputed" (i.e. "matters") issues that fall outside the scope of the submission to arbitration might be successfully challenged in light of Article 34(2)(a)(iii) of the Model Law. All in all, the better view is not to accept jurisdictional challenges under "the excess of mandate" type of challenge to better ensure the consistent application of this ground for challenge.

5.3 *The interface between grounds for challenge prescribed by the Model Law*

The "excess of mandate" type of challenge is an element of the post-award review mechanism. This means that it is closely intertwined with other grounds that could be invoked by the parties in the process of challenging the arbitral award. Consequently, the same factual underpinning might trigger different grounds for recourse. Further, it is likely that the parties intending to challenge the award will substantiate their objections on a number of other competing grounds rather than raise them only on the basis of Article 34(2)(a)(iii) of the Model Law hoping that such an isolated claim will suffice in the context of the "excess of mandate" type of challenge.

118 See the relevant part of the French text of the ML ("*[...] qu'elle contient des décisions qui dépassent les termes du compromis ou de la clause compromissoire [...]*") or of the Spanish text ("*[...] contiene decisiones que exceden los términos del acuerdo de arbitraje [...]*").

119 See also section 5.2.1 and section 5.2.2.

The competition between challenges can be observed in two realms. In the first one, which is closely related to the tribunal's jurisdiction, parties might have difficulties on deciding whether to invoke Article 34(2)(a)(i)[120] or Article 34(2)(iii) of the Model Law. In the second one, the tension exists between "excess of mandate" type of challenge and "procedural" grounds for challenge (namely Article 34(2)(ii)[121] and Article 34(2)(iv)[122] of the Model Law).

In the first dimension, it may occasionally be cumbersome to distinguish whether the challenge stated in Article 34(2)(a)(i) of the Model Law (no valid arbitration agreement, thus no jurisdiction of the arbitral tribunal) or rather the challenge of Article 34(2)(a)(iii) of the Model Law (*i.e.* going beyond the submission to arbitration, hence "exceeding the mandate" of the arbitral tribunal) is an appropriate ground to invoke against the arbitral tribunal's actions. As an example, both grounds were raised when this challenge was brought based on the argument that the award had been made against a non-signatory. In these circumstances, as reported in one of the CLOUT cases, the German court accepted the challenge of the tribunal's jurisdiction based on Article 34(2)(a)(i) of the Model Law.[123] Conversely, in another reported case, the Canadian court seemed to agree that the award affecting a third party goes beyond the scope of submission to arbitration.[124] The better view, however, is to apply Article 34(2)(a)(i) of the Model Law when the mere fact that there was an arbitration agreement is being questioned, while Article 34(2)(a)(iii) should serve strictly as a challenge against the tribunal's decisions on the issues that go beyond the issues that have been submitted. Separating these two issues is important to limit the scope of the courts' review under the "excess of mandate" type of challenge.[125]

The second realm is where the potential tension may exist between the "excess of mandate" type of challenge and violation of due process challenge(s). For example, in

120 Art. 34(2)(a)(i) of the ML states that the award may be set aside if the party furnishes proof that "*a party to the arbitration agreement referred to in article 7 was under some incapacity; or the said agreement is not valid under the law to which the parties have subjected it or, failing any indication thereon, under the law of this State [...]*".

121 Art. 34(2)(a)(ii) of the ML states that the award may be set aside if the party furnishes proof that "*the party making the application was not given proper notice of the appointment of an arbitrator or of the arbitral proceedings or was otherwise unable to present his case*".

122 Art. 34(2)(a)(iv) of the ML states that the award may be set aside if the party furnishes proof that "*the composition of the arbitral tribunal or the arbitral procedure was not in accordance with the agreement of the parties, unless such agreement was in conflict with a provision of this Law from which the parties cannot derogate, or, failing such agreement, was not in accordance with this Law*".

123 See CLOUT case No. 562 [Hanseatisches Oberlandesgericht Hamburg, Germany, 6 Sch 04/01, 8 November 2001].

124 CLOUT case No. 12 [*D. Frampton & Co. Ltd. v. Sylvio Thibeault and Navigation Harvey & Frères Inc.*, Federal Court, Trial Division, Canada, 7 April 1988]. The argument was brought also in Singapore, albeit at the enforcement stage, see *Aloe Vera of America, Inc v. Asianic Food (S) Pte Ltd and Another* [2006] 3 SLR 174; [2006] SGHC 78 at [64-69].

125 See section 2.2.

instances where the tribunal decides *ex aequo et bono* without explicit authorization, it has been successfully argued that the tribunal "exceeded the mandate" (Article 34(2)(a)(iii) of the Model Law)[126] or that the procedure was not in accordance with the parties' agreement (Article 34(2)(a)(iv) of the Model Law).[127] Additionally, it is not clear how to qualify a tribunal's decision on the merits that "surprises" parties with regard to the choice of applicable law, choice of legal theories and the like. On the one hand, one might argue that the tribunal's decision which relies on its independent research and does not follow the parties' views (thus their submissions), goes beyond what was expected from the tribunal. On the other hand, surprise decisions can better be treated as a due process violation (*e.g.* inability to present one's case)[128] or a violation of public policy.[129] The general reflection is that parties need to be cautious with the application of the "excess of mandate" type of challenge in the Model Law framework. It will always depend on the way the Model Law has been adopted under national law. All in all, the same tribunal's wrongdoing might trigger different grounds for challenge and the "excess of mandate" type of challenge might not be immediately available notwithstanding its potentially broad application.

6 Application of the three keyholes test to selected issues that might fall outside the arbitral tribunal's "mandate"

In order to determine whether the three keyholes test serves its purpose, it should be evaluated by applying it to different arbitral tribunal decisions. The division suggested in this section aims to arrange in certain categories all issues (or at least the majority of them) that may be decided by the arbitral tribunal during arbitration. The first group relates to the general concept of the parties' claims brought before the arbitral tribunal in their submissions to arbitration and the tribunal's powers over them (section 6.1). The common feature of the second group of decisions is that they deal with the process of application of law (section 6.2). The third group focuses on reliefs that might be granted by the arbitral tribunal (section 6.3). Finally, the last group comprises decisions of an accessory character

126 Cairo Court of Appeal, Egypt, 8 January 2002, case No. 72/117 as reported in UNCITRAL, *Digest of Case Law on the Model Law on International Commercial Arbitration* (2012) p.153.

127 Oberlandesgericht München, Germany, 34 Sch 10/05, 22 June 2005 as reported in UNCITRAL, *Digest of Case Law on the Model Law on International Commercial Arbitration* (2012) p.157. See also Kreindler et al., *Commercial Arbitration in Germany* (2016) p.345.

128 See Kreindler et al., *Commercial Arbitration in Germany* (2016) p.341. See also *Louis Dreyfus, s.a.s. (SA Louis Dreyfus & Cie) c. Holding Tusculum, b.v.*, 2008 QCCS 5903 (CanLII), http://canlii.ca/t/21v03, [last accessed 14 August 2020].

129 See, for example, Regional Court in Katowice judgment of 23 November 2010, XIII GC 183/10 *(not published)* as referred to in Dziurda & Zielińska (2015) p.327. For further reading see Dziurda & Zielińska (2015) pp.315-329. See also *Louis Dreyfus, s.a.s. (SA Louis Dreyfus & Cie) c. Holding Tusculum, b.v.*, 2008 QCCS 5903 (CanLII), http://canlii.ca/t/21v03 [last accessed 14 August 2020].

to the award, such as decisions on interest or cost (section 6.4). The categories may intertwine with each other.

6.1 *Decisions on parties' claims*

The overarching feature of the subsections presented below is the nature of the claims (thus whether they are contractual or not) and who brought it (whether is it submitted by claimant or respondent). Therefore, the following section will focus on, *i.a.*, the tribunal's decisions on parties' contractual claims (sections 6.1.1 and 6.1.2) and claims based on torts (section 6.1.4). In addition, set-offs (section 6.1.3), potential modifications of claims during the process (section 6.1.5) and decisions not covering all claims (section 6.1.6) will be discussed.

6.1.1 Decision on contractual claims

Under this section, the focus will be directed only on contractual claims brought by the claimant. According to the simplified meaning of Article 34(2)(a)(iii) of the Model Law, the reviewing court should determine if the relief granted in the arbitration award was higher or somewhat different from the relief sought in the parties' submissions.[130] In other words, in the core of said provisions lies the question whether the arbitral tribunal's decision on contractual claims mirrors what the arbitral tribunal has been requested to award.

The first step in the Article 34(2)(a)(iii) test is to review if the tribunal's decision fits well within the limits imposed by the agreement to arbitrate.[131] In general, the (model) agreements to arbitrate are drafted in broad fashion which would entail that most, if not all, potential disputes that may arise between the parties are covered. The contractual claims are certainly suitable to be resolved by the arbitral tribunal. In fact, resolving contractual claims is most likely an underlying reason for the parties to draft an agreement to arbitrate. That is why, arguably, even if the agreement is narrower than usual, the decision on contractual claims will have a high chance of surviving the post-award challenge. Following the "one-stop arbitration" model[132] parties will be presumed, for the reasons of

130 See, for example the wording of the Miami Draft which reads in Art. 5(3)(c) that the award shall be refused recognition if "*the relief granted in the award is more than, or different from, the relief sought in the arbitration*". See also Chapter VI.

131 For further reading, see section 4.1.

132 The term is persuasively used in *Fiona Trust & Holding Corporation & Ors v. Privalov & Ors.* [2007] 1 C.L.C. 144 at [19] ("*One of the reasons given in the cases for a liberal construction of an arbitration clause is the presumption in favour of one-stop arbitration. It is not to be expected that any commercial man would knowingly create a system which required that the court should first decide whether the contract should be rectified or avoided or rescinded (as the case might be) and then, if the contract is held to be valid, required*

procedural efficiency and cost economy, to prefer the system where all disputes are resolved during a single proceedings rather than employing separate settlement mechanisms to different categories of disputes.[133] In turn, should the parties intend to constraint the tribunal's adjudicative powers they should do so in their agreement expressly.

In turn, one should review the claimant's subsequent submissions initiating arbitration (*i.e.* the request for arbitration, the statement of claim and eventually Terms of Reference) as a source for a tribunal's mandate.[134] The arbitral tribunal's decision on contractual claims (which are within the scope of the initial agreement to arbitrate) may be susceptible to the "excess of mandate" type of challenge, if the decision grants a request beyond the one sought by claimant. Importantly, the tribunal's alleged mistakes in the interpretation of claims might survive the challenge, because of the exclusive power given to the tribunal to adjudicate the dispute. Therefore, for example, if the claim is vague and yet granted, it should be enforced if no arguments against the scope of said claim were raised (by the respondent) in the arbitration. Respondent's reaction is also relevant if claimant seeks a relief that goes beyond the original agreement to arbitrate. If respondent fails to contest this relief during arbitration proceedings, it may be considered to impliedly agree to an extension of the original agreement to arbitrate.

Lastly, it is important to determine if the claims can be brought in the arbitral proceedings at all, *i.e.* whether they are arbitrable.[135] Consequently, it means that any decision granting claims that are not arbitrable will exceed the general notion of the arbitral tribunal's mandate by violating public policy.[136]

6.1.2 Decision on contractual counterclaims

By and large, a counterclaim is defined as a claim, "*procedural law mechanism or demand*"[137] brought by respondent which is independent from the claimant's initial claim.

the arbitrator to resolve the issues that have arisen. This is indeed a powerful reason for a liberal construction."). Although this is an English case the argument is equally valid in the Model Law context.

133 See, *e.g.*, Kreindler et al., *Commercial Arbitration in Germany* (2016) p.66.

134 For further reading, see section 4.2.

135 For further reading, see section 4.3.

136 As an illustration *Despetaux v. Éditions Chouette (1987) Inc.*, Quebec Court of Appeal, 18 April 2001, [2001] J.Q. No. 1510; JEL/2001-203 can be mentioned. As reported by Alvarez et al. (2003) p.211: "*The court held that by deciding on the legal status of D and H with respect to the Caillou character, a work protected by the Copyright Act, the arbitrator had acted beyond his jurisdiction because, pursuant to article 2639 of the Quebec Civil Code and 946.5 of the Code of Civil Procedure, questions regarding the status and capacity of persons and other questions of public order could not be submitted to arbitration*"; It is necessary to stress that this decision has been reversed by the Supreme Court of Canada in its ruling; *Desputeaux v. Éditions Chouette (1987) inc.*, [2003] 1 SCR 178, 2003 SCC 17 (CanLII), http://canlii.ca/t/1g2jh, [last accessed 14 August 2020].

137 See Carducci (2013), p.175.

Consequently, it means that as a stand-alone claim it will survive withdrawal or any aspects of invalidity of the primary claim.[138]

Similarly to the issue of (claimant's) claims, the first question regarding counterclaims relates to the parties' consent. Generally, little controversy arises when the contractual counterclaim is based on the same contract as the initial claim. The mere fact that the claim is brought by respondent in response to the primary claim of claimant does not affect that it shall be assessed as an independent relief sought by respondent. Thus, counterclaims should fit within the scope of the "*all claims*" formula. In addition, some additional guidance might be provided in the applicable arbitration rules and for this reason they should be always consulted.[139]

The more difficult issue, however, is to decide on counterclaims that are based on other contracts than the one relevant for the claimant's initial claim. As mentioned by Pryles and Waincymer:

> because a counterclaim remains alive even if the primary claim is withdrawn or invalid, it must be based on its own independent evidence of consent. As always, such consent should be found to emanate from the arbitration agreement itself, either directly or through a lex arbitri that expressly allows for counterclaims. Even then the counterclaim should be linked to the original arbitration agreement.[140]

If, however, the original arbitration agreement is sufficiently broad and allows the resolution of disputes, *e.g.*, *in connection with* the main contract, the counterclaims arising out of a closely connected contract may still survive the post-award challenge. That being said, it is concluded that this is a matter of the tribunal's jurisdiction rather than of the "mandate".[141] Additionally, the parties must be reminded to raise the objections to the arbitral tribunal's jurisdiction on counterclaims in a timely manner to avoid instances

138 Pryles & Waincymer, *Multiple Claims in Arbitration Between the Same Parties* (2009) p.448. Additionally, it may so occur that the arbitral tribunal will grant counterclaims and dismiss claimant's claims. see, *e.g.*, *ABC Co. v. XYZ Ltd.*, High Court, Singapore, 8 May 2003], [2003] 3 SLR 546.

139 See Art. 19(3) of the 1976 UNCITRAL Rules, with the strict requirement for counterclaims and claims for the purpose of a set-off to be based on the same contract as the initial claims. Notably, this requirement has been relaxed in Art. 21(3) of the 2010 UNCITRAL Rules (in the relevant part), which reads that "*[...] the respondent may make a counterclaim or rely on a claim for the purpose of a set-off provided that the arbitral tribunal has jurisdiction over it.*" The modified provision, therefore, does not set the requirement for the claims to arise out of the same contract. See also, *e.g.*, Art. 5(5) of the (draft) 2021 ICC Rules, Art. 5(5) of the 2017 ICC Rules, Art. 5(5) of the 2012 ICC Rules.

140 Pryles & Waincymer, *Multiple Claims in Arbitration Between the Same Parties* (2009) p.448.

141 See section 5.3.

where the tribunal finds that there was an implied agreement of the parties on accepting counterclaims.[142]

Similarly to the previous section, in the process of review of the arbitral tribunal's decision, submissions of the parties *do* matter.[143] It means that an arbitral tribunal needs to address the relief sought by respondent. Consequently, under no circumstances may it decide to grant a relief not requested. If the relief granted goes beyond the relief sought, the award might be successfully exposed to the "excess of mandate" type of challenge.

Again, one should note that the decision on counterclaims will be controlled for its compliance with the public policy of the seat[144] similarly to the decision on claimant's claims.[145] Therefore, the award may be set aside if the counterclaim granted was not arbitrable or violated substantive public policy rules of the seat (*e.g.* violated certain provisions of competition law).

6.1.3 Decision on set-off

The issue of set-off in international commercial arbitration has attracted a notable amount of attention over the years.[146] Yet, it will continue to be a topic of a heated debate. The initial problem with set-offs arise when determining its legal character. Put differently, the question is whether a set-off is a substantive mechanism of extinguishing claims or rather a procedural tool.[147]

142 See, *e.g.*, Art. 21(3) of the 1976 UNCITRAL Rules ("*A plea that the arbitral tribunal does not have jurisdiction shall be raised [...] with respect to a counterclaim, in the reply to the counterclaim*"), Art. 23(2) of the 2010 UNCITRAL Rules ("*A plea that the arbitral tribunal does not have jurisdiction shall be raised [...], with respect to a counterclaim or a claim for the purpose of a set-off, in the reply to the counterclaim or to the claim for the purpose of a set-off.*").

143 It goes without saying that it applies to both claimant's and respondent's submissions. As explained earlier in this section, claimant's submissions (namely its objections) would be relevant when the counterclaims submitted exceed the scope of the initial agreement to arbitrate.

144 See section 4.3.

145 See section 6.1.1.

146 For the major studies see, in particular, Fountoulakis (2011) and Pichonnaz & Gullifer (2014). For articles see also, *i.a.*, Berger, *Set-off in International Economic Arbitration* (1999), Karrer, *Jurisdiction on set-off defences and counterclaims* (2001), Pavić (2006), Schöll (2006), Poudret & Besson (2007) pp.274-280, Mourre, *The Set-off Paradox in International Arbitration* (2008), Fortún (2010), Carducci (2013) and Scherer, *The Award and the Courts, Set-Off in International Arbitration* (2015).

147 This might, in turn, trigger difficult applicable law questions and the scope of the post-award review. For example, if the tribunal grants set-off as a substantive law mechanism based on its interpretation of the applicable law (of country B), to what extent may its conclusion be reviewed by the reviewing court at the seat (which is in country A) following the post-award challenge. See also another illustration offered by Pryles and Waincymer in Pryles & Waincymer, *Multiple Claims in Arbitration Between the Same Parties* (2009) p.441: "*[C]omplexities may arise if a set-off emanates from a different arbitration agreement which in turn could call for a different applicable law. Even where the set-off emanates from the same agreement, if the conflict of approach adopted is to look for the law most closely connected to the individual claim, that may differ between claims and various forms of counterclaims. Some legal systems draw a distinction between*

For the research at hand, set-off will be considered as a substantive law mechanism.[148] As such, set-off is a defensive tool against the initial claim,[149] which will share the fate of the initial claim should the latter be withdrawn, found inadmissible or without merit.[150] In addition, set-off, being closely linked to the initial claim, may not exceed the amount of the initial claim.[151] Finally, set-off, in principle, can be made only against monetary claims.[152]

That being said, one should reflect if the decision on set-offs satisfies the requirements of the "excess of mandate" type of challenge. Three scenarios can be distinguished: (i) the set-off is governed by the same agreement to arbitrate, (ii) in a multi-contract reality, the set-off arises out of a different contract (falling outside the scope of the underlying agreement to arbitrate), and finally (iii) the tribunal grants the set-off *ex officio*. All of these scenarios assume that set-offs are properly objected to (by the opposing party).

The first scenario is rather clear-cut. If the set-off has been brought in a timely manner and is covered by the same agreement to arbitration[153] as the primary claim,[154] there should be no doubts that an arbitral tribunal can decide on the set-off defense without risking its award being set aside under the "excess of mandate" type of challenge.[155] In principle, it

---

counterclaim and set-off and link substantive law of the set-off to the law of the primary claim on the basis that the law of a defence should follow the law of the claim.".

148 This limitation is also related to the fact that there no uniform answer could be given that applies to all jurisdictions that apply the Model Law.

149 Be it as either the initial claim of claimant or the counterclaim of respondent. Carducci in Carducci (2013), p.176 argues, however, that "*[i]t seems that there is no reason to exclude from set-off the case where a respondent invokes the existence of two mutual debts or obligations of the same kind between respondent and claimant even if the claimant's primary claim did not allege the existence of such respondent's debt and rather sought a different remedy, for instance specific performance, delivery of goods or other.*".

150 Counterclaims, on the other hand, may survive any deficiencies of the primary claims as they are considered as independent claims. See section 6.1.2.

151 Berger, *Set-off in International Economic Arbitration* (1999) p.61.

152 Carducci in Carducci (2013), p.175 suggests that "*[s]et-off is obviously important and commonly used between mutual debtors of a monetary obligation or of another obligation, for instance to deliver identical or equivalent goods, allowing set-off to operate.*".

153 Similarly to counterclaims, one should always consult how the issue of set-offs is dealt with in applicable institutional rules. See, *e.g.*, Art. 19(3) of the 1976 UNCITRAL Rules ("*the respondent may make a counter-claim arising out of the same contract or rely on a claim arising out of the same contract for the purpose of a set-off.*"). Compare with Art. 21(3) of the 2010 UNCITRAL Rules ("*[...] the respondent may make a counterclaim or rely on a claim for the purpose of a set-off provided that the arbitral tribunal has jurisdiction over it.*"). Although not immediately relevant in the Model Law context, see, however, the broad formulation of Art. 21(5) of the Swiss Rules ("*The arbitral tribunal shall have jurisdiction to hear a set-off defence even if the relationship out of which the defence is said to arise is not within the scope of the arbitration clause, or falls within the scope of another arbitration agreement or forum-selection clause.*").

154 Arguably, in this case it does not even matter whether the set-off is of substantive or procedural nature.

155 As mentioned in A/CN.9/264 pp.52-53, for the purpose of the set-off defense Art. 23 of the Model Law will apply. It means that set-off should be raised in the Statement of Defense. Additionally, the commentary explained that the set-off claim may be amended at the later stage of the proceedings in accordance with Art. 23(2) of the ML assuming that amendment fits within the scope of the agreement to arbitrate. The

might also cover multi-contract disputes where there is no controversy that the tribunal has jurisdiction to hear claims arising out of different contracts.

The second hypothetical presupposes that the claim for the purpose of set-off arises out of the contract that is not covered by the underlying agreement to arbitrate. Consequently, the set-off cannot even be entertained by the broad wording of the agreement to arbitrate.[156] It triggers, yet again, the question of parties' consent.[157] On the one hand, if the claim for the purpose of set-off goes beyond the initial scope of the agreement to arbitrate, one may question the tribunal's jurisdiction over it.[158] On the other hand, however, the contractual bargain to arbitrate is to resolve the disputes that arise out of the parties' legal relationship. It should, in turn, include also all available defenses.[159] Otherwise, the respondent might have inadequate opportunity to fully present its case. This, in turn, may jeopardize the fate of the award, making it vulnerable to the due process violation claims.[160]

The better view is to allow the tribunal to decide on the admissibility of (substantive law) set-offs without risking the award being set aside at the post-award stage under the Model Law "excess of mandate" type of challenge.[161]

For example, Karrer strongly advocates that:

> the parties must be presumed to prefer the dispute about the set-off defence to be resolved by the arbitral tribunal already in place. After all, the claimant started the arbitration before that arbitral tribunal, and the respondent who is setting off prefers to use the second obligation the other way, as a defence in the existing arbitration, or the respondent would not have raised it there and would have commenced arbitration elsewhere. All this makes good sense to me, and the claimant's insistence that the obligation used as a set-off defence should be brought before a different arbitral tribunal that first must be set up

---

Model Law jurisdictions approach the issue in a similar manner. See, for example, Art. 1046(3) of the GCCP and the commentary of Sachs & Lörcher (2015) p.276 and Kreindler et al., *Commercial Arbitration in Germany* (2016) p.197.

156 Therefore, it will not be allowed even if the agreement to arbitrate includes the "*in connection with*" formula or the like.

157 And, again, one should be reminded that the protest against set-off is necessary to avoid the situation where the tribunal considers that the initial consent has been impliedly broadened.

158 This might involve the Art. 34(2)(a)(i) challenge.

159 At this point the distinction of the legal nature (substantive or procedural) of set-off might be relevant. Additionally, one might argue that set-off is still made "*in connection with*" since it is aimed at distinguishing claims raised by claimant.

160 See Art. 34(2)(a)(ii) of the ML or Art. 34(2)(b)(ii) of the ML.

161 This is not to say that the risk is excluded with regard to other challenges, *e.g.*, of jurisdictional character. As has been discussed elsewhere, certain jurisdictions adopt Art. 34(2)(a)(iii) of the ML as a jurisdictional (scope) objection. In these cases, this ground will be applicable. See also section 5, in particular, section 5.2.1 and section 5.3.

> appears abusive of the legal process. The legal process should bring peace quickly and efficiently and should not be an all-out battle.[162]

Moreover, Berger concludes that

> [...] there is a growing tendency to assume that, as a rule, an international arbitral tribunal has jurisdiction to hear a set-off defence based on a cross-claim that is subject to a different arbitration agreement or jurisdiction clause. This view applies only to those set-offs that have a substantive nature, e.g. the 'Aufrechnung' or 'Verrechnung' under German or Swiss law, the 'compensation légale' under French law and the equitable or 'transaction' set-off under English law. Being a substantive defence which denies the existence of the claim, the set-off has the same quality as any other substantive defence. The tribunal should therefore be authorized to decide on all defences which are raised against the claim ('le juge de l'action est le juge de l'exception'), and consequently also on the merits of the set-off.[163]

This view is not approved by all. Rieder and Kreindler observe, in the context of the German legal regime, that "*[w]here the counterclaims or claims subject to set-off are governed by no or another arbitration agreement, the arbitral tribunal generally lacks jurisdiction [...] The claims introduced by way of set-off need to be disregarded by the arbitral tribunal.*"[164] Even these authors, however, admit that if these claims are (i) undisputed, or (ii) based on a final and binding judgment or award, then they might be entertained by the tribunal.[165] Additionally, the authors acknowledge that "*there is a strong view that set-off with claims resulting from an agreement that is commercially closely connected to the agreement giving rise to the main claims is to be accepted by the tribunal.*"[166]

The last scenario relates to the tribunal invoking set-off *ex officio*. As always, the tribunal is bound by the parties' submissions. It entails that parties should educate the tribunal about all relevant claims and defenses. It means that the tribunal may expose its award to risk if it invokes (and asks for comments) that a certain set-off defense is available to a party. By doing so, it might be considered to effectively plead for the party that did not raise such a defense although it should have had. The situation may slightly differ if the set-off would operate *ipso iure* and if one accepts that arbitrators should know the law.

162 Karrer, *Jurisdiction on set-off defences and counterclaims* (2001) p.177. See also Pichonnaz & Gullifer (2014) p.59. For a useful set of "best practices" in dealing with set-off, see Schöll (2006) pp.131-136.

163 Berger, *Set-off in International Economic Arbitration* (1999) pp.72-73.

164 Kreindler et al., *Commercial Arbitration in Germany* (2016) p.73.

165 Kreindler et al., *Commercial Arbitration in Germany* (2016) p.73.

166 Kreindler et al., *Commercial Arbitration in Germany* (2016) pp.73-74.

Even then, however, it is perhaps more sensible for the well-being of the award for the tribunal to refrain from raising a set-off issue on its own motion. Finally, raising set-off *ex officio* without consulting parties will result in "surprising" them and, in turn, will likely result in a successful post-award challenge.[167]

6.1.4 Decision on claims/counterclaims based on torts or pre-contractual liability

Occasionally, parties invoke the "excess of mandate" type of challenge against the tribunal's decision that grants claims based on torts or pre-contractual liability. The issue once again relates (mostly) to the scope and the wording of the arbitration agreement. Yet it also triggers the question of the possibility for the tribunal to requalify claims. These two issues will be discussed accordingly.

As to the first question, it is largely settled that the parties who use broad (model) arbitration clauses[168] wish to have all disputes (including those of non-contractual nature) resolved before the same forum.[169] The wording of the agreement to arbitrate would be controlling, however.

For example, Rieder and Kreindler concluded that: "*[a]s a rule of thumb, the formula "all disputes arising out of this agreement" is considered not to include pre-contractual claims or at least to pass the burden of proof to the opposing party. By contrast, the broader term "all disputes arising out of or in connection with this agreement" would generally cover pre-contractual claims.*"[170] The same authors also observed that "*[a]n arbitration agreement on disputes arising out of or in connection with a commercial contract [...] typically covers tort claims to the extent tort claims result from the same facts that give rise to breach of contract.*"[171] Similarly, Pryles and Waincymer consider that: "*[...] now it is accepted that such claims [claims based on tort or founded on statute] fall within an arbitration clause*

167 Likely on a different ground than Art. 34(2)(a)(iii) of the ML. Possibly Art. 34(2)(b)(ii) of the ML. See, *e.g.*, in Dziurda & Zielińska (2015) pp.315-329.

168 See, *e.g.*, the UNCITRAL Model Clause ("*Any dispute, controversy or claim arising out of or relating to this contract, or the breach, termination or invalidity thereof, shall be settled by arbitration [...].*"), the SIAC Model Clause ("*Any dispute arising out of or in connection with this contract, including any question regarding its existence, validity or termination, shall be referred to and finally resolved by arbitration [...].*"), the DIS Model Arbitration Agreement ("*All disputes arising in connection with this contract or its validity shall be finally settled in accordance with the Arbitration Rules of the German Institution of Arbitration (DIS) without recourse to the ordinary courts of law.*"), the ICC Standard Clause ("*All disputes arising out of or in connection with the present contract shall be finally settled [...].*").

169 The notion of "one-stop arbitration" as evocatively used by the English judges. See *Fiona Trust & Holding Corporation & Ors v. Privalov & Ors.* [2007] 1 C.L.C. 144 at [19].

170 Kreindler et al., *Commercial Arbitration in Germany* (2016) p.73. See also Lew et al., *Comparative International Commercial Arbitration* (2003) p.151 ("*The ICC model clause for example covers "All disputes arising out of or in connection with the present contract." It is generally recognised that this wording covers all differences and claims arising from a given contractual relationship and even to non-contractual and tortious claims.*").

171 Kreindler et al., *Commercial Arbitration in Germany* (2016) p.73.

provided that they bear a sufficient nexus to the contractual relationship established between the parties."[172]

Importantly, even if the agreement to arbitrate does not include an "in connection with" formula, the tribunal's decisions on claims based on torts might still survive the challenge. As argued by Lew, Mistelis and Kröll:

> [i]n the absence of clear intention to the contrary "it would be illogical to suppose that the parties would have wanted a 'split' jurisdiction." Therefore arbitration agreements without an express limitation should in general be interpreted to cover all claims in connection with a contract, irrespective of whether they are claims in contract, in tort or of statutory nature.[173]

In one case when "[t]he agreements *between the parties [...] both provide that any disputes between them shall be "settled by" or "determined by" arbitration*",[174] the Canadian court was satisfied to conclude that "*[...] the tribunal had power to award damages in tort.*"[175]

As always, the national court reviewing the award in the context of the "excess of mandate" type of challenge should analyze what the parties requested from the tribunal. In any event, it should be argued that both counterclaims and set-off defenses deserve the same standards of interpretation as the primary claims. Therefore, if the wording of the arbitration agreement is broad enough, then claims based on torts can be brought not only as initial claims but also as counterclaims or claims for the purpose of set-off. As suggested by Berger: "*[...] the set-off has to involve a claim concerning a 'dispute which has arisen out of or in connection with the contract' that contains the arbitration agreement. The wording covers not only contractual claims. Thus, from this procedural standpoint, the cross-claim can also be of a tortious nature.*"[176]

Another question may arise in cases where the arbitral tribunal admitted a set-off defense based on pre-contractual liability arising out of a different contract. This hypothetical would require further analysis of the scope of arbitration agreements governing both contracts. If both arbitration agreements are broad (thus covering claims based on torts) and both contracts are closely related, it can be argued that both claims (*i.e.* the initial claim and the set-off defense based on torts arising out of a different contract) may be brought before one arbitral tribunal. It would be a reasonable solution tailored to avoid

172 Pryles & Waincymer, *Multiple Claims in Arbitration Between the Same Parties* (2009) p.441.

173 Lew et al., *Comparative International Commercial Arbitration* (2003) p.153.

174 *Dunhill Personnel System Inc. v. Dunhill Temps Edmonton Ltd.*, 1993 CanLII 7171 (AB QB), par. 6, http://canlii.ca/t/28p21#par6, [last accessed 14 August 2020].

175 *Dunhill Personnel System Inc. v. Dunhill Temps Edmonton Ltd.*, 1993 CanLII 7171 (AB QB), par. 6, http://canlii.ca/t/28p21#par6, [last accessed 14 August 2020].

176 Berger, *Set-off in International Economic Arbitration* (1999) p.65.

parallel proceedings and conflicting judgments.[177] As explained above, however, entertaining set-off claims arising from a different contract might be controversial.

As to the second main question, the tribunal should rather refrain from requalifying the parties' claim. This is particularly the case when it relies on its own legal expertise without asking parties for their opinion. "Surprising" the parties is always a bad idea as it puts the award at risk.[178] Even if the tribunal invites the parties to address its suggestion of requalifying the claim, it should do so cautiously. Otherwise it might put the award at risk for the allegation of the violation of the equal treatment of the parties. This, arguably, will not be a question of the violation of the scope of submission anymore.

6.1.5 Decision on new claims/counterclaims and change of claims/counterclaims

The situation where a party decides to submit an additional claim or to change a relief sought will invariably influence the "arbitral tribunal's mandate". The question herein, however, focuses on the extent to which the tribunal's decision on new or changed claims may be subjected to the subsequent "excess of mandate" type of challenge.

At the outset, one should observe the unique feature of the Model Law. Article 23(2) of the Model Law provides that "*[u]nless otherwise agreed by the parties, either party may amend or supplement his claim or defence during the course of the arbitral proceedings, unless the arbitral tribunal considers it inappropriate to allow such amendment having regard to the delay in making it.*" This rule is an important power for the tribunal to control an arbitral process. Notably, however, this rule has two limitations, namely (i) it can be contracted out by the parties ("*unless otherwise agreed*" *by the parties*") and, arguably, (ii) it can only be used if the modification affects the duration of the proceedings ("*unless the arbitral tribunal considers it inappropriate to allow such amendment having regard to the delay in making it*").[179] Importantly, however, one should always consult the applicable institutional rules, because they do differ in the context of the tribunal's power over the modifications of parties' submissions.[180]

In principle, any modification to the initial submissions should fit within the underlying agreement to arbitrate. Otherwise Article 34(2)(a)(iii) may be triggered similarly to the other types of claims.[181] Notably, Rieder and Kreindler, in the context of the German arbitration regime, observe that:

177 See section 6.1.3.

178 For further reading see, *e.g.*, Tan & Ahmad (2014), Dziurda & Zielińska (2015).

179 Similar conclusions have been offered by Broches who explained that: "*[d]elay in submitting an amendment or supplement would then, along with non-observance of the equality of the parties, be the sole bases for disallowing the amendment or supplement.*" See Broches (1990) p.113.

180 See, *e.g.*, Art. 20 of the 1976 UNCITRAL Rules, Art. 22 of the 2010 UNCITRAL Rules, Rule 20.5 of the 2016 SIAC Rules, Art. 23(4) of the (draft) 2021 ICC Rules, Art. 23(4) of the 2017 ICC Rules, Art. 23(4) of the 2012 ICC Rules. Notably the DIS Rules do not have a similar provision.

181 See other subsections under section 6.1.

> [...] where the opposing party agrees to the amendment, the principle of party autonomy prevails and there is no basis for rejection by the tribunal based on delay. The same applies if the amended part exceeds the arbitration agreement but the other party at least impliedly agrees to this extension of the arbitration agreement.[182]

It shows how important the parties' conduct may be. The parties' conduct, thus their subsequent submissions, will be particularly relevant if they wish to oppose the modification of the claims. If the additional claim goes beyond the relief already sought before the tribunal (but not necessarily beyond the agreement to arbitrate), one should not automatically assume that the tribunal could and should assume jurisdiction over those claims. Instead, it might be indispensable for the parties to initiate separate proceedings. Pryles and Waincymer rightly observe that: "*the fact that the new claims fall within the ambit of the arbitration agreement is not necessarily sufficient. It may be contended that the new claims go beyond the dispute or difference referred to the arbitration already commenced and thereby require the commencement of a new arbitration.*"[183] This is when objections of the adversaries become essential.

It is important to note that the tribunal might not be willing to reject (new or changed) claims if not properly objected to by the parties. As explained above, the tribunal may rely on the power to reject the modifications to avoid potential delays in the process pursuant to Article 23(2) of the Model Law.[184] Yet, at the same time, any (substantial) delays might not be readily obvious. Instead, the risk lies with the tribunal violating the parties' right to present their case. Consequently, the tribunal might refuse to use the powers available to it.[185] As suggested by Rieder and Kreindler: "*[t]he only way for the arbitral tribunal to limit an ever-increasing scope of the case is to exercise its discretion and impose a time limit beyond which, in the absence of a valid excuse, such supplements are no longer admissible, in particular new facts and offers of evidence.*"[186]

All these lead to two conclusions. Firstly, rejecting amendments will not trigger Article 34(2)(a)(iii) of the Model Law, yet it might put the award at risk under a different ground (namely violation of the right to present one's case).[187] Secondly, accepting the new or modified claims will only be susceptible to the "excess of mandate" type of challenge

182 Kreindler et al., *Commercial Arbitration in Germany* (2016) pp.195-196.

183 Pryles & Waincymer, *Multiple Claims in Arbitration Between the Same Parties* (2009) p.470.

184 Or its alternatives as provided by the institutional rules. For examples see fn.180.

185 Especially if the other party does not object to the extension. See also Kreindler et al., *Commercial Arbitration in Germany* (2016) pp.195-196.

186 Kreindler et al., *Commercial Arbitration in Germany* (2016) p.196.

187 Art. 34(2)(a)(ii) of the ML.

in traditional circumstances, therefore only if the (submitted) claims go beyond the agreement to arbitrate or if the tribunal grants a claim that has not been requested.

6.1.6 Decision not covering all claims/counterclaims

If an arbitral tribunal fails to address all claims raised in the arbitration or decides to render an award only on part of the claims, it will render an award *infra petita.* This scenario is by far undesirable, because it leaves some of the issues unresolved between the parties. As such, it goes against the parties' expectations towards the tribunal's adjudicative function.

As pointed out by some authors:

> [t]he significance of the issues that were not dealt with has to be considered in relation to the award as a whole. For example, it is not difficult to envisage a situation in which the issues that were overlooked were of such importance that, if they had been dealt with, the whole balance of the award would have been altered and its effect would have been different. In such circumstances, it seems fair that the aggrieved party should have a right of recourse against the entire award.[188]

Yet, the *infra petita* decisions are not included in the exhaustive list of grounds under Article 34 of the Model Law.[189] This leaves the question whether the *infra petita* decisions can be covered by the "excess of mandate" type of challenge (or any other ground for challenge).

In principle, thus on the level of the Model Law, the answer should be given in the negative. One argument emanates from the drafting process of the Model Law, where *infra petita* decisions were brought to the attention of the Working Group as one of the separate grounds for setting aside,[190] but was eventually dismissed and not included in the final text of the Model Law.[191] Additionally, arguably, recourse against the award is unnecessary, because the Model Law includes a different mechanism, namely an additional award, which is designed to mitigate shortcomings of the *infra petita* decision.

Pursuant to Article 33(3) of the Model Law:

> [u]nless otherwise agreed by the parties, a party, with notice to the other party, may request, within thirty days of receipt of the award, the arbitral tribunal to make an additional award as to claims presented in the arbitral proceedings

188 Blackaby et al. (2015) p.585. See also Born, *International Commercial Arbitration* (2014) p.3294.

189 See also section 2.1.

190 See A/CN.9/WG.II/WP.42, Art. 41, note 27(a).

191 See A/CN.9/233, para 187.

> but omitted from the award. If the arbitral tribunal considers the request to be justified, it shall make the additional award within sixty days.

One may easily observe that this provision can be contracted out by the parties. Notably, according to one interpretation it means that an additional award could not have been designed as the sole way of dealing with an *infra petita* decision.[192] Even though the argument is not without merits, it should not automatically lead to the conclusion that *infra petita* decisions are covered by the (limited) list of grounds under Article 34.[193] It merely gives an opportunity to exclude certain types of recourse against the award if the parties make a conscious decision to do so, with all its consequences. In any event, it may also be adopted differently by the Model Law jurisdictions.[194]

Although, as argued above, the Model Law does not allow recourse against the *infra petita* decisions,[195] one should (again) closely observe how the Model Law was adopted. For example, in Germany[196] or in Belgium[197] *infra petita* will escape the challenge pursuant to Article 34(2)(a)(iii) of the Model Law. In Canada, one court refused to set aside the award on the basis that the tribunal failed to address all questions.[198] In Singapore, however, *infra petita* decisions have been seriously considered as a reason to review the award under Article 34(2)(a)(iii) of the Model Law. In one case, the court held that: "*[...] Art 34(2)(a)(iii) of the Model Law applies where an arbitral tribunal exceeds its authority by deciding matters beyond its ambit of reference or fails to exercise the authority conferred on it by failing to decide the matters submitted to it, which in turn prejudices either or both of the parties to the dispute.*"[199] Similarly, in two different court decisions the court reflected allegedly an *infra petita* award on grounds of breach of natural justice and Article 34(2)(a)(iii) of the

192 Tan & Ahmad (2014) p.416.

193 See section 2.1.

194 See, for example, Art. 1715(3) of the BJC that follows the structure of the Model Law and Art. 1058(1)(3) of the GCCP that does not use the "unless otherwise agreed by the parties" formula.

195 Apart from the request for an additional award under Art. 33(3) of the ML.

196 Kröll & Kraft, *Recourse against the Award, § 1059 – Application for Setting Aside* (2015) p.407 ("*By contrast, awards ruling infra petita cannot, in principle, be set aside pursuant to (c).*"). The authors acknowledge that "*[...] some authors have supported the analogous application of (c) to the incorrect denial of jurisdiction by the arbitral tribunal [...].*" For further reading see Kröll & Kraft, *Recourse against the Award, § 1059 – Application for Setting Aside* (2015) p.407 and p.404.

197 Piers (2016) p.447 ("*It is important to note that 1717, § 3(a)(iii) B.J.C. does no longer provide that an award omitting to decide on one or more issue[s] of the dispute constitutes an annulment ground.*").

198 *United Mexican States v. Metalclad Corp.*, 2001 BCSC 664 (CanLII), paras. 119-132, http://canlii.ca/t/4xfw#par119, [last accessed 14 August 2020]. The argument discussed, however, did not relate to the Model Law *per se*.

199 *CRW Joint Operation v. PT Perusahaan Gas Negara (Persero) TBK* [2011] SGCA 33, [2011] 4 SLR 305 at [33].

Model Law.[200] Although the award in one case had been set aside,[201] the court signaled that a request for an additional award is better suited for dealing with *infra petita* decisions.[202]

In conclusion, one should observe that the "excess of mandate" type of challenge should not be considered a fit for the *infra petita* decisions. Instead, one should consider a request for an additional award. If it fails, one might examine if an *infra petita* decision violated a party's opportunity to present its case or public policy.[203] The difficulty will remain, however, with proving the tribunal's failure to deal with the issue.[204] Therefore a recourse might be successful in truly exceptional circumstances.

6.2 Process of application of law by the arbitral tribunal

The common denominator of the (sub)sections that will follow is the process of determination and application of law in the arbitral process. Therefore the process of selection and decision on applicable law should be explained (sections 6.2.1 and 6.2.2) among the process of application of law including mandatory rules of law (sections 6.2.3 and 6.2.4). Finally, it is necessary to reflect on decisions reached *ex aequo et bono* (section 6.2.5).

6.2.1 Determining the method of selection of applicable law

This section focuses on the first of salient questions on applicable law, namely deciding on the method of the selection of the applicable law. Because of the complexity of this issue, it needs to be narrowly addressed.[205] The study shall be thus limited to the problem as to whether the tribunal's choice of the method to select the applicable law is open for

---

200 *TMM Division Maritima SA de CV v. Pacific Richfield Marine Pte Ltd* [2013] SGHC 186 at [41], *BLB and another v. BLC and others* [2013] SGHC 196 at [94-99].

201 *BLB and another v. BLC and others* [2013] SGHC 196.

202 *BLB and another v. BLC and others* [2013] SGHC 196 at [103] ("*I note, parenthetically, that this would have been the type of case that Art 33(3) of the Model Law would have been intended to provide redress for. Art 33(3) permits parties to request (within a specified time period) the arbitral tribunal to make an additional award as to claims presented in the arbitral proceedings but omitted from the award. It is to be hoped that parties in future cases of a similar nature would first attempt to avail themselves of any available opportunities to seek redress from the tribunal itself, before turning to the courts (assuming of course that this is possible in the circumstances).*").

203 Raising the argument of public policy violation might not be easy however. See Tan & Ahmad (2014) p.419 ("*Further, it is unlikely that a breach of public policy has occurred if an arbitrator fails to rule on an issue or head of claim. Although the phrase 'public policy' does cover fundamental principles of justice in substantive and procedural respects, this requires a high threshold, with instances such as corruption, fraud, and bribery as examples that could constitute breaches of public policy. Setting aside an award infra petita on the ground of a breach of public policy is an unnatural fit.*").

204 Especially if the tribunal concludes its award with the formula "*rejects any and all other claims*" or the like.

205 For further reading, see for example Ferrari & Kröll, *Conflict of Laws in International Commercial Arbitration* (2010).

a challenge under Article 34(2)(a)(iii) of the Model Law.[206] There are three hypothetical scenarios in which each case may unwind, namely (i) the parties designate an applicable law, (ii) the parties designate an applicable method of selection or (iii) the tribunal needs to determine an appropriate method for selecting the applicable law on their own (or by using the opposing submissions of the parties).

An express choice of law clause should be an ideal solution. In consequence, a clear intention of the parties would guide an arbitral tribunal through the process of determining the law applicable to the merits.[207] As explained by Ferrari and Silberman: "*[...] an explicit choice not only clarifies the appropriate choice of legal regime for application by the arbitrators, but also manifests an expression of intention by the parties that should be interpreted as a mandate to the arbitrators in respect of their scope of jurisdiction.*"[208] In other words, it frames the basis on which the arbitral tribunal can decide.[209]

For this reason, Ferrari and Silberman argued further that:

> where parties make an express choice of national law to govern the substance of their dispute and the arbitrators fail to honor that choice – by applying general principles of commercial law or disregarding a choice to apply a particular substantive legal regime – that action should be considered outside the scope of the arbitrators' authority and regarded as an excess of power by the arbitrators.[210]

Although Ferrari and Silberman submit that acting in violation of the express choice of law should be open for the "excess of mandate" type of challenge,[211] Wolff (albeit in

206 The problem of finding applicable law is a difficult one and more recently it has been given an extra layer of complexity due to the fact that different law may apply to the substantive law issues (validity or existence in particular) surrounding the agreement to arbitrate and different law may apply to the substantive law issues arising out of main contract (thus issues at the core of the dispute). This distinction, albeit important, is not relevant for the analysis of this section. Consequently, this division will not be used. At the same time, however, the conclusions would be equally valid in both instances.

207 Or the law applicable to the substantive law issues with regard to the agreement to arbitrate. See fn.206.

208 Ferrari & Silberman (2010) p.120.

209 With all its consequences. An example is *ICC Case No.10625* as reported by Gaillard in Gaillard, *The Role of the Arbitrator in Determining the Applicable Law* (2004) pp.188-189; in this case, an arbitral tribunal respected the parties' choice of Portuguese law, however, it noted that the solution they needed to follow "was in contrast to most continental European law of the civil law type."

210 Ferrari & Silberman (2010) p.120.

211 Ferrari & Silberman (2010) pp.117-118 ("*For present purposes, our main concern is choice of law, and it is the express choice of law clause that suggests an analogy to situations where arbitrators have exceed their mandate or acted beyond the scope of their submission. Why do we think that the express choice of law provision should be treated as a "scope" matter? Why do we say disregard of an "express choice" is different from any other error on choice of law that violates the direction on choice of law given to arbitrators by an arbitration statute or institutional rule – an error which we treat as a mere mistake – like any other error of law made by arbitrators – and not subject to set aside or non-recognition?*").

minority) suggests that: "*application of an incorrect standard including of a national law other than that chosen by the parties or a decision ex aequo et bono without express authorization is considered a violation of procedure.*"[212] In the context of the Model Law, the better view is to subsume such a tribunal's wrongdoing as the flaw in the procedure and challenge it under Article 34(2)(a)(iv) of the Model Law.

When a choice of law clause has not been included in the contract, the parties may jointly (and occasionally do) request an arbitral tribunal to determine the applicable law in accordance with specific conflict of laws rules chosen after a dispute has arisen.[213] If the tribunal follows selected conflict of laws rules, but decides incorrectly, its decision is not open for post-award review.[214]

If the parties did not designate any conflict of laws rules to be applicable, the Model Law includes a fallback mechanism. Pursuant to Article 28(2) of the Model Law "*failing any designation by the parties, the arbitral tribunal shall apply the law determined by the conflict of laws rules which it considers applicable.*" It means that if the parties failed to specify the applicable law or determine the method of selection of the applicable law, the tribunal will be authorized to select the law it deems fit after undertaking a conflict of laws analysis.[215] In addition, it shows that a decision of the arbitral tribunal is released from the duty to follow the conflict of laws rules applied by a national court at the seat of arbitration.[216] At the same time, however, the choice of applicable law needs to be supported by the conflict of laws analysis.[217] Consequently, the tribunal may not designate the law

212 See Kreindler et al., *Commercial Arbitration in Germany* (2016) p.345. See also Jarvin, *Irregularity in the Composition of the Arbitral Tribunal and the Procedure* (2008) p.730 ("*A tribunal's disregard of the parties' instructions pertaining to the governing law does not, as a rule, fall within the scope of procedural irregularity; it is an excess-of-power defence. But not all countries take this approach: in German law the application of a different law from that chosen by the parties has been found to amount to an admissible procedure.*").

213 *ICC Award No.1250 (1964), ICC Award No.2680 (1977)* as reported by Gaillard in Gaillard, *The Role of the Arbitrator in Determining the Applicable Law* (2004) p.200.

214 No review on the merits. See section 2.2.

215 As always, the parties' submissions are of relevance; even if no consensus had been reached as to the applicable conflict of laws rules, the parties' submissions may limit the arbitral tribunal's deliberations to the conflict of laws rules indicated by the parties.

216 *ICC Case No.11264 (2002)*, unpublished, as reported by Gaillard in Gaillard, *The Role of the Arbitrator in Determining the Applicable Law* (2004) p.196 ("*In the absence of a designation of the applicable law of the parties, article 28(2) [of the 1985 UNCITRAL Model Law on International Commercial Arbitration] authorizes the Arbitral Tribunal to apply "the law determined by the conflict of laws rules which it considers applicable." This clearly frees the Arbitral Tribunal from having to follow the choice of law rules which would be applied by a local court.*").

217 See, however, *e.g.* Art. 1051(2) of the GCCP which limits the tribunal's freedom. It reads that "*[f]ailing any designation of the applicable rules of law by the parties, the arbitral tribunal shall apply the law of the State with which the subject-matter of the proceedings is most closely connected.*" See also Schmalz (2015) p.304.

directly without following said analysis.[218] Yet again, such a violation is of (rather) procedural nature and is as such better suited for an Article 34(2)(a)(iv) challenge.[219]

6.2.2 Decision on applicable law

Before the tribunal may decide the case on the basis of the applicable law, it must first select it. It is undisputed that the determination of the applicable law by an arbitral tribunal may have a substantial effect on a subsequent decision on the merits of the dispute. Consequently, it is necessary to reflect if the tribunal's decision on the applicable law may be challenged under the "excess of mandate" type of challenge. This type of tribunal's decision has some common features with the tribunal's decision on the *method* of selecting applicable law.[220] For this reason, the reflections presented above would be equally valid in this case. In any event, one should consider three hypotheticals, where (i) the parties have included a valid choice of law provision in their contract; (ii) the parties, in the absence of choice of law provision, have submitted their pleadings on applicable law to the arbitral tribunal when the dispute arose; and (iii) the parties have not included any choice of law provision nor have they pleaded what law they consider applicable for the arguments they submit.

In principle, and as explained above, an explicit (and undisputed) choice of the parties is controlling for the tribunal. It means that the tribunal's decision that goes against the parties' choice should be susceptible to the post-award recourse. Since no review on the merits is possible, however unintended mistake by the arbitral tribunal is beyond court's control at the setting-aside stage.[221] Therefore, only a *deliberate* disregard of the parties' directives might be considered. As explained above, this is usually considered to fall within the category of "excess of authority",[222] which would suggest that it is reasonable to employ Article 34(2)(a)(iii) of the Model Law.[223] At the same time, an alternative view is to challenge

218 In principle, however, since the tribunal may employ "conflict of laws rules which it considers appropriate", it will, arguably, be able to reach the same conclusions as if given full freedom to determine the applicable law through *voie directe*.

219 See ILA, *ILA Report on Ascertaining the Contents of the Applicable Law in International Commercial Arbitration* (2008) pp.15-16 ("*Since the determination of the contents of the applicable law is by and large a matter of procedure, in the absence of pertinent mandatory rules of the law of the seat, the arbitrators will have to deal with it as with any other procedural matter. According to the almost universally accepted principle, this means that the arbitrators must have regard to the direct or indirect will of the parties, absent which they should follow the rules or approach of their choice.*").

220 See section 6.2.1.

221 See section 2.

222 Ferrari & Silberman (2010) p.120.

223 Lewis in Lewis (2016) p.161 reports that "*[i]n Hong Kong in Brunswick it was submitted that [Article 34(2)(a)(iii) of the Model Law] was engaged because the underlying contract specified Illinois' law and the tribunal decided that PRC law applied. Lam J held that this was a simple decision on the interpretation of the contract by the tribunal and was not within this ground.*" A reference is given of *Brunswick Bowling & Billiards Corp. v. Shanghai Zhonglu Indus. Co., Ltd. & Another*, [2011] 1 HKLRD 707 at [22]. This passing of the

the award that blatantly disregards the choice of law selected by the parties as the procedural violation that triggers Article 34(2)(a)(iv) of the Model Law.[224] Irrespective of the choice made the threshold to successfully challenge the award would be extremely high.

In the second scenario, the parties will submit their views on the applicable law (either in the absence of a contractually agreed choice of governing law or in case its validity is contested). The parties may still reach a consensus as to what law applies or submit contrasting arguments regarding governing law. In case they are unanimous as to what law should apply to their dispute, the same reflections from the first hypothetical would apply. Therefore, the tribunal would have to follow their joint conclusion on the issue. If, however, the parties cannot reach an agreement, it will be in the arbitral tribunal's discretion to follow one of the views presented to it. Arguably, it will also be in the arbitral tribunal's discretion to independently select the legal regime, provided that the tribunal will communicate its intention to the parties and allow them to comment on the selection before any decision is rendered. In this case, the tribunal's conclusion should survive at the post-award stage.

In the third and highly unusual scenario, and in the absence of an explicit choice of law and without the legal framework of the arguments of the parties, the power of the arbitral tribunal to determine the applicable law might be perceived as a state of necessity and will be rooted in Article 28(2) of the Model Law.[225] An arbitral tribunal's decision, in that case, should not be subject to challenge under Article 34(2)(a)(iii) of the Model Law. Importantly, in any event, the tribunal should give the parties the opportunity to comment on its findings. In this case, the decision on applicable law is a better fit for challenge under Article 34(2)(a)(ii), if any.

6.2.3 Ascertaining the content of applicable law by the arbitral tribunal

The dispute resolution function of the arbitral tribunal inevitably requires the tribunal to apply and interpret the law.[226] At the same time, following the underlying principle of the

---

judgment shows the rather unusual circumstances of the case, however. The court held therein that: "*[t]he last point can be disposed of shortly. The extent to which the choice of law clause is applicable to the various disputes was a subject of arguments before the Tribunal. As shown above, the Respondents contended in their closing submissions in the arbitration that the validity of the OIS was to be determined according to PRC law (see para.382 of the closing quoted above). The Tribunal agreed with them. It does not lie in their mouth to contend in the present proceedings that the validity of the OIS should be determined by Illinois law. I therefore hold that there is no merit in the Respondents' reliance on Article 34(2)(a)(iii) in this context. Neither can the Respondents rely on Article 34(2)(a)(iv) which deals with arbitral procedure. The determination on the applicability of the choice of law clause to the validity of the OIS is not a matter of arbitral procedure.*"

224 See Kreindler et al., *Commercial Arbitration in Germany* (2016) p.345.

225 Which still refers to the applicable choice of law rules. No direct application of substantive law is, thus, possible under the Model Law.

226 The process of application of the law has been analyzed in a number of studies. For further reading, see, *i.a.*, (Lew, Applicable Law in International Commercial Arbitration, 1978), Grigera Naón (2001), and ILA,

finality of the arbitral tribunal's conclusions, its legal findings should be immune to any of the post-award recourse. This applies, in principle, also to the "excess of mandate" type of challenge. It means that Article 34(2)(a)(iii) should not become a gateway for review of the merits of the arbitral awards.[227]

Although the tribunal's legal conclusions should escape the court's scrutiny, one should reflect whether the process of reaching these conclusions may generate a post-award challenge under Article 34(2)(a)(iii) of the Model Law. Put differently, it is necessary to observe if the tribunal is limited by the parties' legal pleadings or it may independently reach certain legal conclusions based on its own legal expertise.

In principle, the process of ascertaining law has two aspects: on the one hand, the parties have a burden of educating the tribunal on the contents of the applicable law,[228] on the other hand, arbitrators are often chosen for their legal expertise and as such they should be able to make use of it.[229] Without going further into details,[230] it should be highlighted that it is the parties' responsibility to present legal arguments and inform the arbitral tribunal on the contents of applicable law. Irrespectively, an arbitral tribunal's right to investigate the applicable law on its own motion should be likewise endorsed. It is particularly important if the applicability of the mandatory rules of law is at stake.[231] In this case the tribunal should be able to inspect any implication that mandatory rules may have, even if it had not been raised by the parties.

All in all, one should observe that applying the law is one of the tribunal's duties and is important for fulfilling its mandate.[232] Consequently, it should be possible for the tribunal to raise new legal issues, if considered relevant and subjected to a due process requirement.

As suggested by Dimolitsa:

ILA Report on Ascertaining the Contents of the Applicable Law in International Commercial Arbitration (2008).

227 See section 2.2. Additionally, it is submitted that the process of application of law or rules of law will not fit comfortably in the three keyholes test. It is so because the test prescribed in Art. 34(2)(a)(iii) of the Model Law is limited to the arbitral tribunal's decisions on claims rendered beyond a request sought by the parties. Therefore, one might argue that ascertaining law beyond the parties' expectations can only be challenged on the basis of the third step of the three keyholes test (*i.e.* public policy).

228 For further reading see Kurkela, *'Jura Novit Curia' and the Burden of Education in International Arbitration - A Nordic Perspective* (2003).

229 See, *i.a.*, Kurkela, *'Jura Novit Curia' and the Burden of Education in International Arbitration - A Nordic Perspective* (2003), Kaufmann-Kohler, *"Iura Novit Arbiter" - est-ce bien raisonnable? Réflexions sur le statut du droit de fond devant l'arbitre international* (2004), Lew, *Iura Novit Curia and Due Process* (2011).

230 The issue of an arbitral tribunal ascertaining law is a topic of ongoing debate and as such has been the subject of many detailed studies. Of particular relevance is ILA, *ILA Report on Ascertaining the Contents of the Applicable Law in International Commercial Arbitration* (2008).

231 See also section 6.2.4.

232 See ILA, *ILA Report on Ascertaining the Contents of the Applicable Law in International Commercial Arbitration* (2008) p.19.

> [i]n contrast to the fundamental principles [i.e. right to be heard, equal treatment of the parties and impartiality], the principle of 'ne ultra petita partium' does not enter into play as much when arbitrators introduce ex officio new issues of law. Indeed, introducing new issues of law does not equate with granting non-requested remedies.[233]

In other words, as long as an arbitral tribunal acts in due process, consults the introduction of new legal rules or the requalification of claims with the parties and gives them an opportunity to comment on its actions,[234] the tribunal's decision should survive the "excess of mandate" type of challenge.[235] If the tribunal, however, does not invite the parties to comment on their legal findings and "surprises" them with its legal conclusions,[236] the award will likely to be set aside for violation of one's right to present one's case,[237] which is better suited than the "excess of mandate" type of challenge.[238]

---

233 Dimolitsa, *The equivocal power of the arbitrators to introduce ex officio new issues of law* (2009) p.438; the author qualifies her statement (albeit with reference to the Swiss case) by pointing out that: "*[i]t is not excluded, however, that a party challenges an award for violation of this very principle [i.e. ne ultra petita] in situations where arbitrators have raised new issues or have recharacterized legal relationships; but such challenge should normally fail as long as the arbitrators have ultimately adjudicated not more or other than what was claimed.*".

234 See *e.g. Full Joy Foods Pty Ltd v Australian Dairy Park Pty Ltd* [2020] VSC 672 [118], www.austlii.edu.au/cgi-bin/viewdoc/au/cases/vic/VSC/2020/672.html, [last accessed 3 November 2020] ("*The applicant's submission that it was not incumbent on it to make submissions in response to the arbitrator's invitation can be accepted. There was no obligation for it to do so. And no obligation on the arbitrator to ensure that the applicant made submissions on the point. The issue is whether the applicant had a reasonable opportunity to present its case, not whether it took best advantage of the opportunities afforded to it.*").

235 Landolt (2012) p.192 ("*The predominant tendency in arbitration is to treat as ultra petita only those awards which decide beyond the relief sought by the parties, and not those in which the reasoning goes beyond the parties' submissions, if in fact the result of this is an award within the relief sought by the parties. By consequence, arbitrators need not usually fear interference with their award on the basis of a challenge of ultra petita*") also Born, *International Commercial Arbitration* (2009) p.2608 ("*[...] an arbitral tribunal does not exceed its authority under Article 34(2)(a)(iii) by relying on arguments or authorities not raised by the parties to support their claims.*").

236 See, *i.a.*, Dziurda & Zielińska (2015).

237 *Louis Dreyfus, s.a.s. (SA Louis Dreyfus & Cie) c. Holding Tusculum, b.v.*, 2008 QCCS 5903 (CanLII), paras. 76-103, http://canlii.ca/t/21v03#par76 [last accessed 14 August 2020]. For further reading on competition between the grounds, see section 5.3.

238 *Brunswick Bowling & Billiards Corp. v. Shanghai Zhonglu Indus. Co., Ltd. & Another* [2009] HKCFI 94, available at http://www.hklii.hk/eng/hk/cases/hkcfi/2009/94.html [last accessed 14 August 2020]. Notably, in para 28 of the judgment, the court held that: "*[...] the Tribunal should have canvassed with the parties the particular provision in the PRC law on the topic and [given] them an opportunity to respond before making a decision on the same. The failure of the Tribunal in this regard furnished the Respondents a valid ground of complaint under Article 34(2)(a)(ii). I prefer to rest my decision on this limb instead of Article 34(2)(a)(iii) because I can contemplate cases where an arbitral tribunal may feel obliged in the interest of justice to canvass issues not raised by the parties for the proper determination of the disputes submitted for arbitration. Provided that the parties were given opportunity to present their case on the 'new' issues, the determination of the tribunal would still be within the scope of submission.*".

6.2.4 Application of mandatory rules of law (of public policy character) by the arbitral tribunal

Mandatory rules have an exceptional status in each legal system, since they are its backbone.[239] The mandatory character also entails that parties may not contractually derogate from their application. It is necessary, however, to distinguish two types of mandatory rules.[240] The most important are the rules of public policy character which might be eventually reviewed at the post-award stage. The second category of (non-public policy) mandatory rules might have, arguably, less significance, because parties in international arbitration may effectively exclude their application by their choice of governing law.[241] In the analysis below, the rules of public policy will be predominantly discussed.

For the purpose of this research, it is necessary to reflect if the tribunal that applies mandatory rules of law puts its award at risk under the "excess of mandate" type of challenge. Therefore, following the three keyholes test, one should consider whether an arbitral tribunal's application of mandatory rules of law can violate (i) the agreement (to arbitrate) between the parties, (ii) the parties' requests, or (iii) mandatory rules of public policy character.

Under the first hypothesis one would have to assume that the tribunal went beyond the parties' agreement to arbitrate by applying mandatory rules of law. This is rather unlikely. In principle, it would require the parties to expressly narrow their consent to the effect that the tribunal will not be able to invoke any mandatory rule of law.[242] In fact, such a qualification made in the agreement to arbitrate would make the tribunal's decision compliant with it open for a public policy challenge.[243]

In the alternative, one may also try to argue that the tribunal went beyond the parties' agreement when it decided to apply (likely *ex officio*) mandatory rules of (substantive) law that were not chosen by the parties as the governing law. In these circumstances it is possible

239 For further reading on mandatory and public policy rules, see, *i.a.*, Mayer, *Mandatory rules of law in international arbitration* (1986), Barraclough & Waincymer (2005), ILA, *ILA Report on Ascertaining the Contents of the Applicable Law in International Commercial Arbitration* (2008) Recommendation 13, p.23, Paulsson J., *Thinking Simply about Public Policy* (2011), Radicati di Brozolo (2012).

240 See, *i.a.*, Radicati di Brozolo (2012) p.50.

241 If parties from respectively country A and B decide that law from country C applies to their contract, such a choice will be binding on the arbitrators. It would, in principle, prevent otherwise applicable mandatory rules to apply (unless they are crucial to safeguard public interest, thus unless they are of public policy nature).

242 It will make the arbitrator, as eloquently put by Paulsson in Paulsson J., *Thinking Simply about Public Policy* (2011) p.477, "*the slave of the contract*" disallowing him to apply corrective measures prescribed by the mandatory rules of law.

243 If the tribunal decides on contractual claims which would be found to be illegal, then its award would be most probably successfully challenged on the public policy basis, not to mention the potential liability for aiding and abetting illegal activities. See Radicati di Brozolo (2012) pp.70-71.

that the tribunal considered that the choice of the parties was made to circumvent an application of otherwise applicable mandatory rules of law and decided to address them, shielding the award from a potential public policy challenge. This is where the distinction between public policy and non-public policy rules becomes useful. If the rules applied by the tribunal are of public policy character, they would inevitably override any agreement of the parties. If, however, the mandatory rules invoked by the tribunal are not of a public policy nature, the tribunal might be (effectively) modifying a valid choice of law, which might be open for a challenge, but, arguably, on another ground than the "excess of mandate" type of challenge.[244] As always, it is essential to allow the parties to address the tribunal's findings.[245]

The second hypothesis presupposes that the arbitral tribunal allegedly decided beyond the request sought when it substantiates its findings with the mandatory rules of law *ex officio*.[246] This argument, as well, would not fit under Article 34(2)(a)(iii) of the Model Law.

Furthermore, as observed by Radicati di Brozolo: "*[...] there is an expectation, perhaps even a requirement, that arbitrators apply mandatory rules.*"[247] The author aptly concludes that "*[w]hile it is true that arbitrators are primarily at the service of the parties, it is now recognized that they are not their mere servants and that in some way they are also under a broader duty to see that justice is done.*"[248] Therefore, even if the parties forgot or deliberately omitted to plead for the application of mandatory rules of law, it is still at a tribunal's discretion to investigate whether these (mandatory) rules apply.[249]

According to the report of the International Law Association:

> [i]n disputes implicating rules of public policy or other rules from which the parties may not derogate, arbitrators may be justified in taking measures appropriate to determine the applicability and contents of such rules, including by making independent research, raising with the parties new issues (whether legal or factual), and giving appropriate instructions or ordering appropriate measures insofar as they consider this necessary to abide by those rules or to protect against challenges to the award.[250]

---

244 See Art. 34(2)(a)(iv) of the ML. See also section 6.2.2.

245 See also section 6.2.3.

246 Conversely to the situation discussed in the preceding paragraph, under this scenario it is presumed that the mandatory rules (not raised by the parties) constitute the part of the law chosen by them.

247 Radicati di Brozolo (2012) p.66.

248 Radicati di Brozolo (2012) p.68.

249 See section 6.2.3.

250 ILA, *ILA Report on Ascertaining the Contents of the Applicable Law in International Commercial Arbitration* (2008) Recommendation 13, p.23.

Yet again, the tribunal needs to give the parties the opportunity to present their case.

The third hypothesis raises the question whether the application of (mandatory) rules may violate the rules of public policy. In principle, indeed it might. At the same time, however, one should consider that disregarding public policy rules and not their application will give higher chances of the award being susceptible to the Article 34(2)(b)(ii) challenge.[251] Therefore, the tribunal will better ensure enforceability of the award by investigating potentially applicable public policy rules rather than shying away from them.

All in all, the conformity with mandatory rules of law might play a decisive role in the review process of the arbitral award. Taking into account that the tribunal should be concerned with the fate of the award rendered,[252] application of mandatory rules of law by the arbitral tribunal might be justified if not indispensable. In principle, it should not be, reviewable pursuant to Article 34(2)(a)(iii) of the Model Law.

6.2.5 Decision reached *ex aequo et bono* or as *amiable compositeur*

The power to decide *ex aequo et bono* encompasses the ultimate trust the parties have in arbitrators that they will render a just decision. It is reasonable therefore that it requires explicit authorization. This rule is also prescribed in Article 28(3) of the Model Law. Pursuant to said Article: "*[t]he arbitral tribunal shall decide ex aequo et bono or as amiable compositeur only if the parties have expressly authorized it to do so.*"

Importantly, however, even if this power is given, it might be subjected to certain restrictions imposed by Article 28(4) of the Model Law. This Article gives clear indication that: "*[i]n all cases, the arbitral tribunal shall decide in accordance with the terms of the contract and shall take into account the usages of the trade applicable to the transaction.*" It has been concluded that "*[t]he effect of this provision is largely limited to [...] confirming that agreements of the party and trade usages supersede even those decisions rendered ex aequo et bono*".[253]

Yet, Born submits compelling argument that

251 The tribunal risks more by not applying mandatory rules rather than by applying them (even if not correctly); see *Desputeaux v. Éditions Chouette (1987) inc.*, [2003] 1 SCR 178, 2003 SCC 17 (CanLII), http://canlii.ca/t/1g2jh, [last accessed 14 August 2020] ("*An error in interpreting a mandatory statutory provision would not provide a basis for annulling the award as a violation of public order, unless the outcome of the arbitration was in conflict with the relevant fundamental principles of public order.*"). See also CLOUT case No. 639 as reported in A/CN.9/SER.C/ABSTRACTS/58 (failure to apply legal norms does not amount to violation of the fundamental principles of Russian Law).

252 Craig, *The arbitrator's mission and the application of law in international commercial arbitration* (2010) p.285 ("*Nevertheless, while the grounds for judicial review are narrow, a wise arbitrator will want to make sure that his award correctly addresses any issue subject to review in a way to satisfy any court.*").

253 Schmalz (2015) p.317.

> [t]he better view, adopted by a majority of commentators and other authorities, is that arbitrators may depart from the terms of the parties' contract in fashioning a fair and equitable result, provided that they do not rewrite the structure of the agreement. Of course, arbitrators sitting ex aequo et bono or as amiable compositeur may not ignore applicable mandatory law.[254]

For the research at hand, however, it is important to determine whether the tribunal's decision *ex aequo et bono* is susceptible to the "excess of mandate" type of challenge. In this case it is assumed that the tribunal departs from applying the law without the parties' express authorization.[255]

Although it is clear that the tribunal's decision based on powers it had never possessed should be open for the (successful) post-award challenge,[256] it is uncertain if the "excess

254 Born, *International Commercial Arbitration* (2014) pp.2775-2776. For further reading on mandatory law see section 6.2.4.

255 Occasionally, parties try to argue that the tribunals (effectively) usurp the power *ex aequo et bono* by the way the arbitrators apply the applicable law (usually, in the opinion of the applicants incorrect). For example, in *American International Group and AIG Capital Corporation v. X Company* [2016] HCCT 60/2015 [8], http://legalref.judiciary.hk/lrs/common/search/search_result_detail_frame.jsp?DIS=105848&QS=%2B&TP=JU [last accessed 14 August 2020], it was argued that: "*[...] the Majority had (it is claimed) ignored or consciously disregarded basic principles of New York law concerning the enforceability of liquidated damages clauses, and the inadmissibility of parol[e] evidence to vary or contradict the express terms of a written contract, in order to arrive at what the Majority considered to be the fair or equitable result. This, it was argued, goes beyond mere erroneous application of New York law, but amounts to the Majority impermissibly deciding the dispute ex aequo et bon[o] or as amiable compositeur.*" These types of arguments, however, go dangerously close to the review of the merits which is impermissible (see section 2.2). In the mentioned case, the application to set aside was rejected and the court concluded that: "*[i]f, as the Plaintiffs submit, the Majority had made errors of law in their findings on the enforceability of the liquidated damages clause and in considering parole evidence, they may simply have made these errors because they failed to understand the correct analyses of the binding New York authorities, and this in my judgment is just as equally probable as the Majority having made a conscious and deliberate choice to ignore the binding New York authorities, to come to a contrary conclusion in order to arrive at what the Majority perceived to be the fair result in the Arbitration. The latter inference involves a quantum leap which is not justified by a fair, objective reading of the Award.*" See *American International Group and AIG Capital Corporation v. X Company* [2016] HCCT 60/2015 [26], http://legalref.judiciary.hk/lrs/common/search/search_result_detail_frame.jsp?DIS=105848&QS=%2B&TP=JU [last accessed 14 August 2020] It shows that the burden of proving that the tribunal allegedly decided *ex aequo et bono* while applying the law is rather high.

256 See, *e.g.*, Cairo Court of Appeal, Egypt, 8 January 2002, case No. 72/117 (see UNCITRAL, *Digest of Case Law on the Model Law on International Commercial Arbitration* (2012) p.153). In this case, a court in Egypt set aside an award where the arbitrator decided *ex aequo et bono* and disregarded the parties' choice of law. See also *Louis Dreyfus, s.a.s. (SA Louis Dreyfus & Cie) c. Holding Tusculum, b.v.*, 2008 QCCS 5903 (CanLII), par. 107, http://canlii.ca/t/21v03#par107, [last accessed 14 August 2020], where the court held that: "*[t]he Tribunal erred in determining that it had the power to ...fashion appropriate remedies and ...to find a just solution notwithstanding its dismissal of the parties' respective claims,... irrespective of whether the particular dispute in question or remedy requested fell within the ambit of Section 13 of the Agreement. In so determining, the Tribunal took on the role of amiable compositeur, when it was never asked, mandated, or permitted to do so. It failed to observe the applicable domestic and international arbitration procedure by assuming this role without the requisite of the parties.*".

of mandate" type of challenge in the Model Law context is the best mechanism for doing so. One should always have in mind the whole wording of Article 34(2)(a)(iii) of the Model Law, because it does not only refer to "the award going beyond the scope of the submission to arbitration",[257] but rather it makes a reference to *disputes* not contemplated by or *matters* going beyond the terms (or scope)[258] of the submission to arbitration. Deciding *ex aequo et bono* is the *way* the tribunals decide on disputes or matters which may very well fall within the scope of the submission. Consequently, as argued by Wolff: "*[...] a decision ex aequo et bono without express authorization is considered a violation of procedure.*"[259] As such it would be better suited under Article 34(2)(a)(iv) of the Model Law.[260]

6.3 *Decisions on remedies*

Resolving a dispute between parties inevitably means that the tribunal answers the relief sought by granting (or rejecting) remedies requested by the parties. The study at hand focuses on three basic categories of the remedies that may be potentially sought by the parties. These are: damages (section 6.3.1), specific performance (section 6.3.2) and contract adaptation (section 6.3.3).

6.3.1 Decision on damages

It is undisputed that damages are a traditional and important remedy sought. The types of damages that the parties can seek depend, however, on the applicable law.[261] Nonetheless, in the context of the Model Law, without reference to a single legal system, no unequivocal answer can be given as to the question whether an arbitral tribunal's decision granting damages can be successfully contested as being beyond the scope of submission to arbitration.

In any case, there are several scenarios that need to be highlighted: (i) the arbitral tribunal awarded more damages than claimed, (ii) the arbitral tribunal recharacterized damages sought, and (iii) the arbitral tribunal granted damages that have been specifically excluded by the parties in their agreement or (iv) granted damages that are unknown at the seat of arbitration.

The first scenario is rather clear-cut and thus does not require further elaboration: in the case when the arbitral tribunal grants more than the parties sought, it would clearly

257 This could, arguably, entail also the matters on *how* the tribunal should decide.

258 See section 5.2.2.

259 See, *e.g.*, Kreindler et al., *Commercial Arbitration in Germany* (2016) p.345.

260 See section 5.3.

261 Different legal systems may offer, for example punitive, exemplary or treble damages, liquidated damages, moral damages, consequential damages, statutory damages, or incidental material damages.

render the decision *ultra petita* which would constitute a valid reason to challenge the award on the basis of the second step of the three keyholes test. Therefore, the award will be susceptible to the "excess of mandate" type of challenge.

The second scenario is closely related to the process of ascertaining the content of the applicable law.[262] In principle, whenever the tribunal is convinced that the damages should be granted, but on a somewhat different legal basis than the one presented by the parties, it should always give the parties the right to address its findings.[263]

On the one hand, it has been reported that the domestic award has been set aside in Poland in a case where:

> the claimant demanded a contract should be declared invalid on the grounds of exploitation pursuant to Article 388 §1 KC, and the arbitral tribunal accepted this provision as a valid basis for the claim. Instead, however, of declaring the contract invalid the arbitral tribunal awarded an alternative remedy available under Article 388 §1 KC, namely a modification of the claimant's consideration under the contract.[264]

In addition, the authors have questioned whether

> [...] the annulment of the award could have been avoided if the arbitral tribunal had notified the parties that it was considering applying Article 388 §1 KC in extenso. The answer appears to be negative since an arbitral tribunal's discretional powers are limited by the parties' dispositive right to define their claims (including their scope).[265]

On the other hand, a court in Hong Kong held that the tribunal did not "exceed its mandate" when it issued an award on the basis of loss of revenue and set-off and not on loss of profit as pleaded by the claimant.[266] It further held that

> [t]he issue of quantum is one of the matters submitted to the Tribunal for determination. The Tribunal is not bound by the positions taken by the parties

262 See section 6.2.3.

263 Otherwise it might expose its award to a setting-aside challenge under Art. 34(2)(a)(ii) or Art. 34(2)(b)(ii) of the ML.

264 Dziurda & Zielińska (2015) pp.327-328, with a reference to Regional Court in Katowice judgment of 23 November 2010, XIII GC 183/10 *(not published)*.

265 Dziurda & Zielińska (2015) p.328.

266 *Brunswick Bowling & Billiards Corp. v. Shanghai Zhonglu Indus. Co., Ltd. & Another* [2009] HKCFI 94 at [51], available at http://www.hklii.hk/eng/hk/cases/hkcfi/2009/94.html [last accessed 14 August 2020].

> if it can, on the basis of the evidence canvassed, come to a different conclusion. The Tribunal did not act in excess of its jurisdiction when it made a determination based on loss of revenue and setoff. There is no ground for complaint under Article 34(2)(a)(iii).[267]

All in all, whenever the tribunal recharacterizes the legal basis for the claim for damages, it might be necessary to consult grounds for challenge other than the "excess of mandate" type.

In the third hypothetical, it might be necessary to reflect whether the remedial powers of the tribunal are limited in the agreement to arbitrate itself or elsewhere in the contract. Arguably, if it is included in the agreement to arbitrate, it would be controlling for the tribunal.[268] Conversely, if a similar limitation is included in the main contract (for example by prohibiting the parties to request damages or certain types of damages), it would be within the tribunal's powers to interpret the contract. As such, it should escape the courts scrutiny (no review on the merits).[269]

The last reflections concern granting damages unknown at the seat of arbitration. This would be the case when punitive damages are requested, and the tribunal needs to decide whether they may be granted. As long as an arbitral award granting punitive damages may very well fit within the scope of the parties' submission to arbitration (*i.e.* first two parts of the three keyholes test), the likelihood that the unknown type of damages may violate public policy is rather high. This risk may emerge at both stages of the post-award review, namely at the setting-aside stage at the country of the seat and during the enforcement of the award.[270] At this point, the analysis reflects the public policy of the seat. For example, in Germany, the award granting punitive damages will be found to be against substantive (international) public policy.[271] Arguably, however, following the recent court decision where punitive damages have been granted for breach of contract in Singapore law,[272] it is plausible that the tribunal's decision to the same effect might survive at the setting-aside stage.

In any event, as a concluding reflection, one should consider that:

---

267 *Brunswick Bowling & Billiards Corp. v. Shanghai Zhonglu Indus. Co., Ltd. & Another* [2009] HKCFI 94 at [51], available at http://www.hklii.hk/eng/hk/cases/hkcfi/2009/94.html [last accessed 14 August 2020].

268 If the agreement to arbitrate states (however unlikely) that the tribunal may not grant damages, the question still remains if it is a matter that should be tackled under Art. 34(2)(a)(iii) of the ML or rather the matter of "agreed procedure" to be dealt with under Art. 34(2)(a)(iv) of the ML.

269 See section 2.2.

270 See also Chapter VI.

271 See Kreindler et al., *Commercial Arbitration in Germany* (2016) p.90.

272 *Airtrust (Hong Kong) Ltd v. PH Hydraulics & Engineering Pte Ltd* [2015] SGHC 307, http://www.singaporelaw.sg/sglaw/laws-of-singapore/case-law/free-law/high-court-judgments/18260-airtrust-hong-kong-ltd-v-ph-hydraulics-amp-engineering-pte-ltd [last accessed 14 August 2020].

> [...] it is preferable for arbitral tribunals to treat any award in respect of punitive damages or any other penalties as an entirely separate claim, in order to ensure that the punitive portion of the award is severable in the event of a successful challenge in the courts at the place of enforcement.[273]

6.3.2 Decision on specific performance

Specific performance is yet another remedy available to the parties. Similar to the analysis on damages,[274] no comprehensive answer can be provided in the context of the Model Law as to the instances when granting such remedy will be an option. Contrary to the difficulties that may arise with respect to certain types of damages, an arbitral tribunal's decision on specific performance will not, by and large, be considered outside the arbitral tribunal's "mandate".[275] The only exception, similar to the ones discussed above with regard to tribunal's decisions on damages, that one could envisage is an arbitral tribunal's decision truly rendered *ultra petita* or made against the parties' explicit limitation regarding the tribunal's remedial powers. These would be, in principle, instances where the award may be open for the Article 34(2)(a)(iii) challenge.

6.3.3 Decision on contract adaptation and filling of gaps in the contract

The power of an arbitral tribunal to revise the contract and to fill the gaps therein might be of paramount importance, particularly in the context of complex long-term contracts. In these cases, the parties cannot reasonably be expected to foresee all problems that may occur along the way. Consequently, they might need a fallback mechanism allowing an arbitral tribunal to alter the initial agreement of the parties to maintain their *status quo*.

The exercise of the power to adapt the contract, however, might be controversial at times. It is undisputable that the adjudicative function of the arbitral tribunal entails that it will interpret the underlying contract and give its provisions a meaning. Yet, the power to adapt the contract is occasionally considered to go beyond this classical (adjudicative) function.[276] It is then argued that the contract adaptation exercise involves creative analysis and not only interpretation of the contract. Consequently, it is often required that the parties expressly authorize the tribunal with these powers.[277] In addition, the law of the

---

273 Blackaby et al. (2015) p.519.

274 See section 6.3.1.

275 Blackaby et al. (2015) p.519 ("*The question of whether an arbitral tribunal is empowered to order specific performance is thus rarely an issue in international arbitration. However, the question of whether it is an appropriate remedy, and whether it can be effectively granted in the circumstances of any particular case was not definitely established at the time of writing.*").

276 Bernardini, *Stabilization and adaptation in oil and gas investments* (2008) pp.108-109.

277 Bernardini, *Stabilization and adaptation in oil and gas investments* (2008) p.107.

seat[278] and the law applicable to the merits of the case might also be of relevance when the tribunal needs to determine if it can accept the power to revise the contractual provisions.[279]

When it comes to the Model Law, it does not contain any express provision on powers of the arbitral tribunal to revise the contract and fill the gap in the contract.[280] For this reason, it might be prudent to consult the national legislation adopting the Model Law and find out whether any provision on contract adaptation has been included therein.[281] All in all, however, the Model Law court faced with the "excess of mandate" type of challenge against an arbitral tribunal's decision on the revision of the contract would need to follow the three keyholes test.

On the first level, the court should determine, in absence of authorization by the law of the seat or the law applicable to the merits, whether express consent to adapt the contract has been provided in the parties' agreement.[282] The need for the unequivocal consent of the parties has been suggested during the drafting of the Model Law:

> [...] the decisive factor may be the generally recognized principle that a contract is binding on a party only if he agreed to it. By adapting or supplementing a contract the arbitral tribunal creates new contractual obligations for the parties and, therefore, such contractual obligations can become binding only when the parties have agreed to be bound. The parties may demonstrate their agreement to be bound by expressly conferring such a mandate to the arbitral

278 See *e.g.* Art. 1020(4) of the Dutch Code of Civil Procedure (expressly allowing the parties to delegate the power fill the gaps or modify the legal relationship between the parties to the agreement to arbitrate).

279 For further reading on the importance of *lex arbitrii* and the law applicable to the merits of the case, see, *e.g.*, Berger, *Power of Arbitrators to Fill Gaps and Revise Contracts to Make Sense* (2001) pp.5-11, Bernardini, *Stabilization and adaptation in oil and gas investments* (2008) pp.107-108. Parenthetically, it should be mentioned that arbitral tribunals are rather reluctant in accepting their role to adapt or revise the contract. See, *e.g.*, Hunter & Redfern, *Law and Practice of International Commercial Arbitration* (2004) p.539 ("*[...] arbitral tribunals have proved very reluctant to substitute their own views of a fair allocation of contractual risk for that of the parties at the time the contract was originally concluded*"); Gaillard & Savage, *Fouchard Gaillard Goldman on International Commercial Arbitration* (1999) p.25 ("*[discussing the approach in the absence of a hardship clause] The trend in international arbitral case law is in favor of a fairly narrow, conservative conception of the arbitrator's powers. Arbitrators will generally be reluctant to accept the doctrine of change in circumstances even in long-term, non-speculative contracts. Instead, they will often consider that parties to international contracts are, generally speaking, experienced professionals well able to protect themselves in their agreements from changes in circumstances.*"). See also *Himpurna California Energy Ltd v. PT (Persero) Perusahaan Listruik Negara*, Final Ad Hoc Award of 4 May 1999, XXV Y.B. Comm. Arb. 13 (2000).

280 Although no provision on adaptation and supplementation of contracts has been included in the text of the Model Law, it was discussed. For an informative analysis see A/CN.9/WG.II/WP.41, paras 2-11 and A/CN.9/WG.II/WP.44, paras 1-32.

281 Or in the law applicable to the merits.

282 It can be included either directly in the arbitration clause or in a specific hardship or renegotiation clause contained in the same contract that refers to the arbitration agreement. See Berger, *Power of Arbitrators to Fill Gaps and Revise Contracts to Make Sense* (2001) p.8.

> tribunal. Thus, the usual arbitration clauses may be interpreted as being limited to the mandate to adjudicate legal disputes arising from breach of non-performance of contracts.[283]

On the second level (of the three keyholes test), arguably, the reviewing court needs to be satisfied with the evidence showing that the parties requested the tribunal to revise their contractual provisions. Importantly, even if the arbitration agreement is broad enough to entertain contract revision, the tribunal shall refrain from intervening with the sanctity of the contract if not specifically requested to do so.

On the third level, it has been suggested that "*[t]he contract terms established by a decision on adaptation or supplementation, like any other contract, should not be contrary to mandatory rules of the applicable law.*"[284] It means that the contractual provisions redrafted by the tribunal should comply with the mandatory rules of the applicable law. In addition, it needs to be emphasized that the mere notion of the tribunal intervening with the contract (thus, going outside its adjudicative function) may be set aside based on violation of public policy.

In addition to a traditional, three-step analysis, the final question that needs to be addressed separately is whether an arbitral tribunal vested with power to decide *ex aequo et bono* or act as *amiable compositeur* can modify the contract terms. According to Jarvin "*the terms of the contract may not be modified by the arbitrator acting as amiable compositeur.*"[285]

Conversely, Berger argues that:

> [...] this procedural notion of arbitration is incompatible with the creative character of decisions required in cases of adaptation and gap-filling which involve the evaluation of economic issues and the rewriting of the parties' contract. From this perspective, gap-filling and contract adaptation are not arbitrable, unless the arbitrator is freed from the constraints of substantive law and is authorized by the parties to act as 'amiable compositeur'.[286]

Taking into account the application of Article 28(4) of the Model Law, it is more sensible for the tribunal to refrain from modifying the contract terms under its *ex aequo et bono* mandate.[287]

283 A/CN.9/WG.II/WP.41 para 8.
284 A/CN.9/WG.II/WP.44 para 32.
285 Jarvin, *The sources and limits of the arbitrator's powers* (1996) p.71.
286 Berger, *Power of Arbitrators to Fill Gaps and Revise Contracts to Make Sense* (2001) p.2.
287 See section 6.2.5.

6.4 *Decisions accessory to the parties' main submissions and the merits of the case*

Three types of tribunal's decisions need to be discussed under this section. At first, the analysis will focus on the tribunal's decision on interest (section 6.4.1). It will then be followed by reflections on costs (section 6.4.2) and on procedure (section 6.4.3).

6.4.1 Decision on interest

Due to the fact that an arbitral tribunal's decision on interest may be as important as a decision on an underlying claim in terms of a monetary value, the way how it is tackled by the arbitrators may be of substantial relevance. The court testing the arbitral award of interest against allegations arising out of Article 34(2)(a)(iii) of the Model Law would need to approach it cautiously.

At the outset, one should conclude that no conclusive answer can be given as to the character of the power to award interest (procedural or substantive) in the Model Law jurisdictions. It has been reported that

> [t]he laws that govern the power of a tribunal to award interest also vary. In some jurisdictions, for example Bermuda, Hong Kong, England, and Scotland, the power to award interest is governed by the law of the place of arbitration. In others, for example under German conflict-of-laws rules, the liability to pay interest is a question of substantive law and this is governed by the law of the contract.[288]

Additionally, it is necessary to point out that the Model Law in itself does not include any provision on interest.[289] Yet,

> [a] number of states that have adopted the Model Law have modified the statute, to include an express authorization for the arbitrators to award interest, but typically without specifying any standards governing such awards. The typical formulation in such legislation is '[u]nless otherwise agreed by the parties, the arbitral tribunal may award interest'.[290]

---

288 Blackaby et al. (2015) p.528. In Singapore, the power to award interest would be a matter of procedure as well. See Merkin & Hjalmarsson, *Singapore Arbitration Legislation Annotated* (2009) p.44.

289 It has been discussed by the UNCITRAL, however. See A/CN.9/460 paras 101-106, A/54/17 paras 367-369.

290 Born, *International Commercial Arbitration* (2014) p.3103.

For example, in Singapore, the power of the tribunal to award interest is prescribed by Sections 12(5)(b) and 20 of the SIAA. "*Even in the absence of express statutory authority, there should be no doubt concerning the authority of an arbitral tribunal to award interest.*"[291]

By and large, the broad arbitration clause should (impliedly)[292] encompass interest claims.[293] It stems from the fact that interest claims would be accessory to the underlying claims and as such interest claims will follow the fate of the underlying contractual claims.[294] For this reason, if the reviewing court will not find any qualification within the agreement to arbitrate prohibiting the tribunal to award interest, the challenge on the first level of the three keyholes test will likely fail.

The general considerations of the second step of the three keyholes test will apply in the context of awarding interest. It means that the starting but also the end point of the relief granted is the parties' request. The UNCITRAL Digest reported that "*[a]n award was partially set aside in a case where the arbitral tribunal awarded interests on the sums in arrears without being asked to do so. Thus, only the part of the award relating to the interests claimed was set aside.*"[295] Another award was also set aside in New Zealand when it departed from the parties' submissions on interests and costs.[296] Consequently, interest being awarded by the tribunal on its own initiative might satisfy the reviewing court that the tribunal acted beyond the parties' submissions and to (partially) set aside the award.[297]

It has been observed, however, that

---

291 Born, *International Commercial Arbitration* (2014) p.3103.

292 Notably, the 1976 UNCITRAL Rules, the 2010 UNCITRAL Rules, the (draft) 2021 ICC Rules, the 2017 ICC Rules, the 2012 ICC Rules and the 1998 DIS Rules are silent on the power of the tribunal to award interest. Rule 32.9 of the 2016 SIAC Rules is, therefore, an exception.

293 Born, *International Commercial Arbitration* (2014) p.3104 ("*The parties' arbitration agreement must, of course, encompass interest claims in order for the arbitrators to be able to make a valid award of interest. In virtually all cases, an arbitration agreement applicable to an underlying claim will be interpreted to encompass claims for interest in connection with that claim. The conclusion is almost always (correctly) assumed without discussion.*").

294 If the main claim will be found inadmissible or will fall outside the scope of the arbitration agreement, it will have the same effect as to the accessory interest claims. If the main claim fits within the ambit of the agreement to arbitrate (in the absence of the contrary stipulation), it will also include claims for interest in connection with the main claim. See also Blackaby et al. (2015) p.528 ("*Most institutional rules of arbitration do not contain express provisions for the payment of interest, largely because their draftsmen assumed that an arbitral tribunal has the power to make an award in respect of interest in just the same way as it has the power to make an award in respect of any other claims submitted to it.*").

295 UNCITRAL, *Digest of Case Law on the Model Law on International Commercial Arbitration* (2012) p.154, with a reference to *Jaral Decoración, S.L v. Peñasco Rodilla, SL*, Madrid Court of Appeal, Spain, 2 February 2007, case No. 94/2007—7/2005.

296 See *Parts & Services Limited v. Brooks* [2005] NZHC 293.

297 Pulkowski (2010) p.121. One should note that the judgment mentioned therein is not from a Model Law jurisdiction. It is expected, however, that such a challenge would succeed also before the court in a Model Law country.

> [i]n exercising this discretion [to award interest], the tribunal will typically invite submissions and evidence from the parties on these issues in the same way as it would in respect of any other request for relief. Thus, parties will usually have an opportunity to set out their respective positions on the rate of interest to be applied, the period for which it should be applied, and whether a different rate (for example a statutory legal interest rate) should be applied for the period following the rendering of an award up until payment. In making such submissions, parties would do well to make an award of interest as easy for a tribunal as possible by providing the calculations upon which such an award would be based.[298]

Consequently, the tribunal might be granted a certain degree of discretion regarding the decision on interest. Therefore, arguably, if the decision on interest (i) is consulted with the parties and (ii) does not violate public policy (of the country of the seat), it might survive the challenge even if the issue of interest has been raised by the tribunal on its own initiative.

Finally, it should be expected that the reviewing court will also test an arbitral award regarding interest against its compliance with the legal rules of public policy of that country.[299] Notably, in some jurisdictions (*e.g.* Muslim countries) the general notion of awarding interest might be against public policy.[300]

6.4.2 Decision on costs

The costs incurred in arbitration may represent substantial amounts. Additionally, the method for costs allocation differ greatly between jurisdictions. For these reasons, parties may be tempted to challenge the tribunal's (costs) findings at the post-award stage. At the same time, one should not disregard, however, the value of the decision on costs as an important managerial tool given to the tribunal.

298 Blackaby et al. (2015) pp.529.

299 Which would be in turn either the law of the seat or the law where the possible enforcement will take place. Other legal regimes might be also at stake, for example (i) law governing the arbitration agreement or (ii) the law governing the contract. The focus of the analysis at hand should be narrowed to the question, on how the national courts approach "the excess of mandate" type of challenge. Consequently, the courts during the setting-aside and enforcement proceedings are not competent to review the merits of the award, therefore they will not test the arbitral award against compliance with the public policy of every possible legal system involved (thus for example the law applicable to the arbitration agreement or the law applicable to the contract, unless of course it is their own law).

300 Blackaby et al. (2015) pp.527-528.

As in the case of power of the tribunal over interest,[301] the Model Law does not provide any express provision on awarding costs.[302] "*Nonetheless, there is no question but that the Model Law permits arbitrators to make awards of the costs of the arbitration and legal costs (absent to the contrary agreement).*"[303] The lack of a Model Law provision might, however, be remedied by states adopting the Model Law. By doing so states may design a useful fallback mechanism for the tribunals. This is the case, for example, with Germany that included an express provision that authorizes the tribunal to decide on costs.[304] Additionally, often and even in the absence of a statutory provision, the tribunals will be able to rely on costs provisions in the applicable institutional rules.[305]

"*A claim in respect of the costs incurred by a party in connection with an international arbitration is, in principle, no different from any other claim, except that it usually cannot be quantified until the end of the arbitral proceedings.*"[306] In essence, therefore, the "excess of mandate" type of challenge will become operational in the context of the decision on costs in the traditional three hypotheticals, namely, (i) the agreement of the parties limits the tribunal's authority over costs (or expressly directs how the costs should be allocated),[307] (ii) the costs granted are higher or granted although not requested, and (iii) the costs granted violate the public policy rules. Put differently, the general considerations of the three keyholes test will be correspondingly applicable in the case of costs. Thus, a tribunal's decision on costs must, in principle, respect the parties' agreement to arbitrate,[308] costs must have been sought by a party and a decision on costs may be reviewable on the public policy ground.

This paradigm may change, however, depending on the governing law of the seat and applicable arbitration rules. For example, in the German context, Wolff observes that "*[t]o the extent that the arbitral tribunal has jurisdiction to rule on costs, it will decide sua sponte,*

301 See section 6.4.1.

302 This possibility of including an express provision on the power of the arbitral tribunal to award costs has been considered by the UNCITRAL as potential future work, before the text of the Model Law was amended in 2006; see A/CN.9/460 paras 107-114.

303 Born, *International Commercial Arbitration* (2009) p.2490.

304 See Art. 1057 of the GCCP.

305 See, *e.g.*, Arts. 40-43 of the 2010 UNCITRAL Rules, Art. 38 of the (draft) 2021 ICC Rules, Art. 38 of the 2017 ICC Rules, Art. 37 of the 2012 ICC Rules, Arts. 32-36 of the 2018 DIS Rules, Section 35 of the 1998 DIS Rules, Rule 35-37 of the 2016 SIAC Rules.

306 Blackaby et al. (2015) p.532.

307 *Telestat Canada and Juch-Tech, Inc.*, 2012 ONSC 2785 (CanLII), par. 64, http://canlii.ca/t/fr848#par64, [last accessed 14 August 2020] ("*The arbitrators cannot give what the arbitration clause does not permit or provides for otherwise.*"). See Kreindler et al., *Commercial Arbitration in Germany* (2016) p.297 ("*The arbitral tribunal's discretion is limited by party agreements on a cost allocation standard. [...] However, the price for such foreseeability is the lack of flexibility when it comes to finding a suitable cost allocation for a specific case.*").

308 See fn.306.

ie even if the parties have not requested a cost decision."[309] Additionally, tribunals, while deciding on costs, should be able to take into account the parties' conduct in the proceedings, which means that it should have a power to sanction the parties' delaying tactics and failure to proceed in a cost effective manner.[310] As a consequence, arguably, the tribunal's decision on costs might still survive the "excess of mandate" type of challenge even not aligned with parties' underlying agreement and requests.

6.4.3 The procedural decisions of the arbitral tribunal

The procedural decisions of an arbitral tribunal should not be susceptible to the "excess of mandate" type of challenge. Instead, one should consider invoking Article 34(2)(a)(iv) of the Model Law which in relevant part reads that the award may be set aside if "*the arbitral procedure was not in accordance with the agreement of the parties, unless such agreement was in conflict with a provision of this Law from which the parties cannot derogate, or, failing such agreement, was not in accordance with this Law [...].*"

7 Concluding remarks

The Model Law is a remarkable instrument that makes it possible to harmonize the general perception of international arbitration and to improve its efficiency as a dispute resolution system. Together with the New York Convention, it can be perceived as one of the milestones of the modern architecture of arbitration. In order to provide essential coherence with the enforcement regime prescribed by the New York Convention, the Model Law mirrors legal norms envisaged in the New York Convention. This statement holds true also in the case of the "excess of mandate" type of challenge. On the one hand, this solution (*i.e.* the similarity of provisions in these texts) can be praised for its harmonizing effect; on the other hand, however, the wording of Article 34(2)(a)(iii) of the Model Law can easily be criticized for its unclear wording.

By and large, the Model Law design serves its purpose: it favors arbitration, grounds for refusal are limited, national courts generally refrain from reviewing the merits of the arbitral decisions. Notwithstanding the above, the "excess of mandate" type of challenge calls for an improvement. Such a development has already been proposed by van den Berg

309 See Kreindler et al., *Commercial Arbitration in Germany* (2016) p.295.

310 See, *e.g.*, Art. 38(5) of the (draft) 2021 ICC Rules, Art. 38(5) of the 2017 ICC Rules, Art. 37(5) of the 2012 ICC Rules. Schütze (2013) p.178 ("*[...] [the] arbitral tribunal will take account of the parties' conduct throughout the proceedings, considering in particular whether the party has conducted the arbitration in an expeditious and cost effective manner or whether it has applied delaying tactics [...].*").

in his "Miami Draft" and will be discussed further in the New York Convention chapter.[311] It is argued that a simple change in the language of Article 34(2)(a)(iii) of the Model Law would enhance a clearer and, thus, more uniform application of the recourse mechanism.

Generally, it has been concluded that "the submission to arbitration" should be interpreted broadly in a way that includes not only the arbitration agreement but also the parties' subsequent submissions. Furthermore, in determining the scope of the submission to arbitration, the reviewing court should accept the notion that the parties may have requested the tribunal to decide on the issues that are disputed (*i.e.* disputes) but also on the other questions that are not necessarily disputed by the parties (*i.e.* matters).

A national court in a Model Law jurisdiction, when faced with the challenge on the basis of the "excess of mandate" should only test whether (i) an arbitral tribunal's decision grants either party something more or something different than the parties consented to arbitrate in their submissions to arbitration or whether (ii) an arbitral award goes beyond the parties' request stated in their submissions. These considerations may be supplemented by the courts' reflections on the question whether (iii) the arbitral award violates rules of public policy character. The court's review on these three levels would constitute the proposed three keyholes test.

Accordingly, one should consider that the challenge pursuant to Article 34(2)(a)(iii) of the Model Law is limited to a comparison of the relief sought by the parties and the relief granted by the arbitral tribunal. Therefore, it is argued that in the Model Law the "excess of mandate" type of challenge is exceptionally narrow and can be used only against an award *ultra petita*. Consequently, a challenging party might need to invoke different grounds of Article 34(2)(a) of the Model Law in order to challenge the arbitral award that they perceive to be granted in "excess" of "the tribunal's mandate".[312]

In conclusion, it should be reasonably expected that most arbitral tribunals will not dare to render a decision beyond the parties' request and thus the challenge on the basis of Article 34(2)(a)(iii) of the Model Law will be successful only in exceptional circumstances.

311 Pursuant to proviso 5(3)(c) of the Miami Draft: "*Enforcement of an arbitral award shall be refused if, at the request of the party against whom the award is invoked, that party asserts and proves that [...] the relief granted in the award is more than or different from, the relief sought in the arbitration and such relief cannot be severed from the relief sought and granted.*".

312 For example, the inability to present its case (Art. 34(2)(a)(ii) of the ML) or failure to follow the agreed procedure (Art. 34(2)(a)(iv) of the ML).

III France and Book IV of the Code of Civil Procedure

1 Introduction

"*Paris, the Home of International Arbitration*" is the praise found on one of the websites[1] which aims at attracting users of arbitration to choose Paris as the seat of arbitration and it is just one of many examples that evidences that the French are active (and successful) in promoting the French legal system and Paris as a preferred place for commencing arbitral proceedings.[2] Indeed, France maintains it is the venue that is regularly selected by parties because of the expertise of the French courts in arbitral matters and modern legislation that is supportive of arbitration.

France adopted the new arbitration law with the Decree No. 2011-48 of 13 January 2011 which went into force on 1 May 2011 and was included in Book IV of the Code of Civil Procedure (hereafter "the CCP"). The new arbitration law replaced the previous regime that had been introduced at the beginning of the 1980s. It is said to "update" the previous law by "incorporating rules developed by case law" and by "adopting new provisions".[3] The French arbitration law is divided into two parts: the first (Title I) is applicable to domestic arbitration and the second (Title II) provides rules for the international arbitration proceedings. What is relevant for the research at hand is what type of recourse against the mandate of the arbitral tribunal is recognized under French law for international arbitration.

According to Article 1520(3) of the CCP "*An award may only be set aside where [...] the arbitral tribunal ruled without complying with the mandate conferred upon it [...].*"[4] This provision precisely corresponds to the research question and for this reason it will be a key target for the analysis below.

---

1 See http://www.parisarbitration.com/home/ [last accessed on 28 April 2018].

2 See, *e.g.*, Born, *International Commercial Arbitration* (2014) p.142 ("*France is one of the leading centers for international commercial arbitration in Europe and, indeed, the world.*").

3 Derains & Kiffer, *National Report for France* (2013) Chapter I(1). Notwithstanding these developments, some academic writings and case law pre-dating the enactment of the new law remain relevant and will be taken into account. References made to the preceding act (*i.e.* the 1981 Act) will be qualified as the references to "the Old CCP".

4 ("*Le recours en annulation n'est ouvert que si [...] [l]e tribunal arbitral a statué sans se conformer à la mission qui lui avait été confiée [...].*"). In this chapter, the translations of the French Arbitration Law as provided by Gaillard, Leleu-Knobil and Pellarini will be used. For their translation see http://www.parisarbitration.com/wp-content/uploads/2014/02/French-Law-on-Arbitration.pdf [last accessed on 28 April 2018].

By and large, as long as the concept of an arbitral tribunal's mandate relates mainly to the tribunal's adjudicative role, other types of "non-compliance" (other than the adjudicative one)[5] may very well be successfully invoked when challenging the award. The reason for this may be traced back to the dualistic nature of the tribunal's mandate. On the one hand, as pointed out above, the mandate relates to adjudicating the disputes between parties. At the same time, however, it relies on the parties' consent and is constrained by their contract. This in turn creates two sets of obligations that the tribunal needs to observe.[6] Before elaborating further on this topic, a few brief comments (of more general nature) shall be made.

Firstly, it is necessary to recognize the dualistic nature of the French arbitration regime. In brief, it means that different legal rules applies to domestic arbitrations and different ones to international cases. It is necessary to assess what the impact of this distinction on a challenge procedure is.

Secondly, one should elaborate on the main characteristics of the court's standards of review. It means that one should determine what the grounds are for a recourse to the court and to what extent a court is able to scrutinize an arbitral tribunal's decision, and what types of remedies are at the court's disposal.

Thirdly, after explaining the basic concepts governing the setting-aside procedure, it is necessary to focus in detail on the French approach to the mandate and the possibility to challenge its excess. Additionally, the analysis should include reflections on the limitations that structure the scope of the arbitral tribunal's mandate, namely the agreement to arbitrate, the parties' submissions and underlying principles of international public policy as seen by the French courts.

Finally, different categories of tribunal's decisions will be tested in order to determine if (and if so when) they can be successfully challenged under the French concept of the excess of the arbitral tribunal's mandate. These decisions have been grouped thematically: the first group focuses on the basis of the claim (for example whether the claim or the counterclaim is based on contract or not), the second one deals with the particularities of the process of the tribunal's application of law, the third addresses the tribunal's ability to grant remedies and in the fourth and final part decisions accessory to the parties' main submissions are grouped (*e.g.* decision on costs or interest). The underlying goal is to comprehensively catalogue (most of) the tribunal's decisions that are crucial in fulfilling the tribunal's adjudicative mission. It is envisaged that such a model will make it possible to pinpoint what the crucial factors are that allow the successful application of the excess of mandate ground. The concluding section will aim at summarizing the reflections

5 For example, decisions in violation of the parties' procedural agreement.

6 See also Giraud (2017) p.94.

presented in this chapter. Generally, it should clarify how to apply excess of mandate challenges regarding specific issues that arise in the arbitral process.

2 Dualism of the French arbitration regime: different statutory architecture for domestic and international arbitration

As mentioned above, the French arbitration law accommodates the concept of an autonomous international arbitration regime, which is, to a certain extent, more liberal than the French statutory rules applicable in the domestic setting (section 2.1). Importantly, however, domestic rules are still relevant in the international context (section 2.2).

2.1 Legal framework for international arbitration

The unique status of international arbitration was embedded in the French arbitration system, even before the introduction of the Decree of 1981.[7] The reform of the early 1980s constituted an "*[...] affirmation of the specific nature of international arbitration [which] is one of the most significant features of French law. Following these statutory reforms, the more liberal regime applicable to international arbitration was maintained and reinforced by the French courts.*"[8] This characteristic of the French arbitration law was reconfirmed by the most recent reform of 2011.

An independent statutory framework for international arbitration is, by and large, tailored to offer a maximum amount of flexibility for the users of international arbitration. At this point, however, reflections should be limited only to the details of the international arbitration law relevant for the research at hand. Therefore, it is necessary (i) to determine when arbitration can be qualified as international, (ii) to list the basic features of the international arbitration regime, and (iii) to highlight those that may be relevant with regard to the challenges against the tribunal's mandate at the post-award stage.

As to the first point, the French international arbitration law gives a short and broad definition of international arbitration. Pursuant to Article 1504 of the CCP, "*[a]n arbitration is international when international trade interests are at stake*".[9] From the perspective of this definition it is, therefore, the character of *the transaction* that is relevant in order to

7 Poudret & Besson (2007) p.26.

8 Gaillard & Savage, *Fouchard Gaillard Goldman on International Commercial Arbitration* (1999) p.64. Although this reference was made to the Old CCP, it holds true for the new CCP as well.

9 ("*Est international l'arbitrage qui met en cause des intérêts du commerce international*"). The same definition was available before the 2011 reform. See Art. 1492 of the Old CCP. No changes had been proposed by the Comité Français de l'Arbitrage; see Art. 1490 of the Proposal CFA, *Texte proposé par le Comité Français de l'Arbitrage pour une réform du livre IV NCPC* (2006).

determine whether it is appropriate to apply the French international arbitration law.[10] "*The criterion is purely objective, focusing essentially on the object of the contract which gives rise to the arbitration and not the nationality, domicile or seat of the parties.*"[11]

Consequently, one should note that other connecting factors would be irrelevant *per se*:

> [t]he international character of an arbitration must be determined on the basis of the economic reality of the transaction out of which it arises; in this connection, it suffices that the economic transaction in question gives rise to the transfer of goods, services or funds across borders, irrespective of the nationality of the parties, the law applicable to the contract or to the arbitration, and also of the place of arbitration.[12]

In other words, the nationality of the respective parties,[13] the law applicable to the merits[14] or to the procedure,[15] or even the parties' will to define an arbitration as international[16] might not be important at all and would not automatically trigger the application of the French international arbitration regime.[17] "*The essential criterion lies therefore in a material or immaterial crossborder transfer.*"[18]

The second point aimes at listing the features of the French law on international arbitration which make it an attractive choice for the parties. Arguably, the outstanding elements of the French arbitration regime that deserve to be mentioned are the following:

---

10 See also Carducci, *The Arbitration Reform in France: Domestic and International Arbitration Law* (2012) p.149 ("*Consequently*, the French law regime for international arbitration applies as to a dispute submitted to arbitration concerning a transaction which is not economically limited within the boundaries of a country") with a reference to Cour de Cassation Civ 1ère, 26 January 2011, *INSERM v. Fondation Letten F. Saugstad*, No. 09-10198 ("*L'internationalité de l'arbitrage fait appel à une définition économique selon laquelle il suffit que le litige soumis à l'arbitre porte sur une opération qui ne se dénoue pas économiquement dans un seul Etat.*").

11 Poudret & Besson (2007) p.31. For further reading on the economic criterion, see also *i.a.* de Boisséson (1990) pp.424-427, Robert (1993) pp.226-229, Rouche et al. (2009) pp.29-31.

12 CA Paris, 14 March 1989, *Murgue Seigle v. Coflexip*, Rev. Arb. 1991, p.355. Translation after Rouche et al. (2009) pp.30-31. See also CA Paris, 29 March 2001, *Carthago Films v. Babel Productions*, Rev. Arb. 2001, p.543, and Clay, *Code de l'arbitrage commenté* (2015) pp.169-174.

13 CA Paris, 29 March 2001, *Carthago Films v. Babel Productions*, Rev. Arb. 2001, p.543.

14 CA Paris, 29 March 2001, *Carthago Films v. Babel Productions*, Rev. Arb. 2001, p.543; see also CA Paris, *Sporprom Service B.V. v. Polyfrance Immo*, Rev. Arb. 1984, p.87.

15 CA Paris, 29 March 2001, *Carthago Films v. Babel Productions*, Rev. Arb. 2001, p.543.

16 Cour de Cassation Civ 1ère, 20 November 2013, *Giepac Bourgogne/Saica Pack v. Automation Group*, No. 12-25266.

17 One should also note, however, the argument by the authors in Derains & Kiffer, *National Report for France* (2013) Chapter I(1): "*Although the transaction is decisive and not the parties' nationality or will, Art. 1504 looks at the dispute that is the subject of the arbitration, as this may be determined by other facts and circumstances than the transaction. Thus, a domestic contract may lead to an international arbitration if the dispute implicates international commercial interests. The reverse situation is also possible.*"

18 Poudret & Besson (2007) p.32.

the centralized jurisdiction of the President of the *Tribunal de grande instance* of Paris who has the role of a judge acting in support of the arbitration ("*juge d'appui*")[19] and, importantly, who can act (*i.a.*) "*when one of the parties is exposed to a risk of a denial of justice*",[20] the freedom to opt out from the rules introduced by the French arbitration law (both domestic and international),[21] and the relaxed standards as to the form of the arbitration agreement.[22]

The third and final point deals with the two characteristics of French international law that directly influence the scope of the tribunal's mandate and the challenge against its mandate. The first relates to the tribunal's freedom to select rules applicable to the merits of the dispute (in the absence of the parties' choice). The second concerns the possibility to waive the right to set the award aside in France.[23]

Pursuant to Article 1511 of the CCP, "*[t]he tribunal shall decide the dispute in accordance with the rules of law chosen by the parties or, where no such choice has been made, in accordance with the rules of law it considers appropriate. In either case, the tribunal shall take trade usages into account.*"[24] This provision offers the tribunal an extensive power to *directly* determine the applicable *rules of law*. The consequences are two-fold: the first is that the tribunal is not obliged to conduct any conflict of laws analysis in order to decide what law applies to the dispute. The second is that the tribunal, in the absence of the parties' express or implied choice, may opt for non-national rules of law (such as the UNIDROIT Principles) as applicable to the merits of the case.[25] In any event, the tribunal should also take into consideration trade usages. Since the process of application of law by the arbitral tribunal will be discussed in further detail at a later stage, for now, it suffices to say that France promotes a liberal approach with regard to the process of the application of law.[26]

Pursuant to Article 1522 of the CCP:

19 See Art. 1505 of the CCP. A judge acting in support of arbitration will exercise his/her competence only when parties did not designate any other body or institution to enforce the arbitral bargain. Therefore, if parties had agreed that the arbitral institution will act as an appointing authority, their choice will prevail over the default mechanism including *juge d'appui* involvement. See further Bensaude (2015) pp.1144-1145.

20 See Art. 1505(4) of the CCP. Notably, in cases of a risk of denial of justice (by and large with regard to the constitution of the arbitral panel), the *juge d'appui* may be competent even if there is no connection with France at all. See, *e.g.*, Gaillard, *France Adopts New Law on Arbitration* (2011), Carducci, *The Arbitration Reform in France: Domestic and International Arbitration Law* (2012) p.149, Bensaude (2015) p.1145.

21 See in particular Art. 1506 of the CCP. Also, section 2.2 below and *i.a.* Carducci, *The Arbitration Reform in France: Domestic and International Arbitration Law* (2012) pp.149-150.

22 Art. 1507 of the CCP.

23 See further section 5.5.

24 ("*Le tribunal arbitral tranche le litige conformément aux règles de droit que les parties ont choisies ou, à défaut, conformément à celles qu'il estime appropriées. Il tient compte, dans tous les cas, des usages du commerce.*").

25 See also Carducci, *The Arbitration Reform in France: Domestic and International Arbitration Law* (2012) pp.152-153, and Bensaude (2015) pp.1156-1157.

26 For further reading, see section 6.2.

> by way of a specific agreement the parties may, at any time, expressly waive their right to bring an action to set aside. Where such right has been waived, the parties nonetheless retain their right to appeal an enforcement order on one of the grounds set forth in Article 1520. Such appeal shall be brought within one month following notification of the award bearing the enforcement order. The award bearing the enforcement order shall be notified by service (signification), unless otherwise agreed by the parties.[27]

This provision was introduced by the 2011 reform. What is essential is that when a party decides to waive its right to set aside, it is still able to resist enforcement (if sought in France) by appealing against the enforcement order[28] on the same grounds used for the setting-aside proceedings. As a result of such a successful appeal against the enforcement order, the arbitral award will not be annulled. It will "only" be denied recognition in France, which means that a party successful in arbitration will still be able to enforce it elsewhere.[29]

2.2 *The importance of domestic arbitration law*

Although the initial idea of the Comité Français de l'Arbitrage was to introduce two fully independent sets of rules, one for domestic arbitration and the other one for international arbitration,[30] this concept was eventually replaced by the system whereby some of the domestic arbitration provisions apply to international arbitration unless parties have agreed otherwise. "*Thanks to this extension [of the domestic arbitration regime], fewer provisions are listed in the shorter 'International Arbitration' Title II of the Decree, whose objective is to set out exclusively those provisions truly specific to international arbitration.*"[31] Therefore, although international arbitration is meticulously distinguished from the domestic

27 ("*Par convention spéciale, les parties peuvent à tout moment renoncer expressément au recours en annulation. Dans ce cas, elles peuvent toujours faire appel de l'ordonnance d'exequatur pour l'un des motifs prévus à l'article 1520. L'appel est formé dans le délai d'un mois à compter de la notification de la sentence revêtue de l'exequatur. La notification est faite par voie de signification à moins que les parties en conviennent autrement.*").

28 This is the only instance where the challenge against an enforcement order can be filed. See Art. 1524 of the CCP.

29 Bensaude (2015) p.1175: "*[...] in the case of such a waiver, there will be no possibility for either party to obtain the setting aside (or annulment) of the award at the place where the award was rendered.*"

30 Carducci, *The Arbitration Reform in France: Domestic and International Arbitration Law* (2012) p.129. For the proposal see CFA, *Texte proposé par le Comité Français de l'Arbitrage pour une réform du livre IV NCPC* (2006). For the explanatory note to the proposal see Devolvé (2006). Still, even the proposal made a minor cross reference to the (proposed) Arts. 1483 and 1484 that constitute a part of the domestic arbitration law.

31 Carducci, *The Arbitration Reform in France: Domestic and International Arbitration Law* (2012) pp.149-150.

arbitration system, it does refer to the relevant principles that are set out in the domestic regime.

Pursuant to Article 1506 of the CCP:

> Unless the parties have agreed otherwise, and subject to the provisions of the present Title, the following Articles shall apply to international arbitration:
> (1) 1446, 1447, 1448 (paragraphs 1 and 2) and 1449, regarding the arbitration agreement;
> (2) 1452 through 1458 and 1460 regarding the constitution of the arbitral tribunal and the procedure governing application to the judge acting in support of the arbitration;
> (3) 1462, 1463 (paragraph 2), 1464 (paragraph 3), 1465 through 1470 and 1472 regarding arbitral proceedings;
> (4) 1479, 1481, 1482, 1484 (paragraphs 1 and 2), 1485 (paragraphs 1 and 2) and 1486 regarding arbitral awards;
> (5) 1502 (paragraphs 1 and 2) and 1503 regarding means of recourse other than appeals or actions to set aside.[32]

For the purpose of the research at hand, the application of the last two provisions may be relevant. Article 1502 of the CCP in the first two paragraphs contemplates *recours en révision* which is an exceptional recourse against the arbitral award and "*[i]t is the only possible basis on which to challenge an award on the grounds of fraud.*"[33] Importantly, application should be made to the arbitral tribunal.[34] Additionally, Article 1503 of the CCP further clarifies that "*no opposition may be filed against an arbitral award, nor may the Cour de Cassation be petitioned to quash the award.*"[35] Overall, as long as the international arbitration regime is shaped upon its independent structure, it relies on certain fallback

---

32 ("*A moins que les parties en soient convenues autrement et sous réserve des dispositions du présent titre, s'appliquent à l'arbitrage international les articles: «1° 1446, 1447, 1448 (alinéas 1 et 2) et 1449, relatifs à la convention d'arbitrage; «2° 1452 à 1458 et 1460, relatifs à la constitution du tribunal arbitral et à la procédure applicable devant le juge d'appui; «3° 1462, 1463 (alinéa 2), 1464 (alinéa 3), 1465 à 1470 et 1472 relatifs à l'instance arbitrale; «4° 1479, 1481, 1482, 1484 (alinéas 1 et 2), 1485 (alinéas 1 et 2) et 1486 relatifs à la sentence arbitrale; «5° 1502 (alinéas 1 et 2) et 1503 relatifs aux voies de recours autres que l'appel et le recours en annulation*").

33 Derains & Kiffer, *National Report for France* (2013) Chapter VII(4)b).

34 Art. 1502 (paragraph 2) of the CCP states that "*Application shall be made to the arbitral tribunal.*"

35 ("*La sentence arbitrale n'est pas susceptible d'opposition et de pourvoi en cassation.*"). As explained by the authors of the translation: "*Opposition is a form of a recourse under French law, available when a judgment is rendered by default because a defendant was not properly notified of a hearing. The defendant can then "oppose" the judgement.*" See http://www.parisarbitration.com/wp-content/uploads/2014/02/French-Law-on-Arbitration.pdf [last accessed on 28 April 2018].

mechanisms introduced already in domestic arbitration law. That being said, following the language of Article 1506 of the CCP, parties may always contract out of these rules.

3 COURT STANDARD OF REVIEW DURING THE SETTING ASIDE

At the post-award stage, the French courts are prone to take a pro-arbitration stand on arbitration awards (section 3.1) as is demonstrated by the scope of the review undertaken (section 3.2), as well as the remedies exercised as to the arbitral award (section 3.3).

3.1 Pro-arbitration approach towards the arbitration award

The French arbitration regime constitutes a model design when it comes to pro-arbitration fashion; the "pro-arbitration approach" entails that the legal framework does not allow for much interference in the arbitral process.[36] Most importantly, however, the French courts are willing to enforce the parties' bargain to arbitrate their disputes without getting involved, unless the most basic principles are at stake.

When it comes to testing the arbitral award after it is rendered, the French system of international arbitration prescribes only a short list of the most grievous irregularities that can be invoked by a challenging party.[37] This list is exhaustive[38] and cannot be altered.[39] In other words, parties may not agree to add other grounds to the list or to expand the court's control over the award to the merits of the case.[40] It goes without saying that at the

36 It is also expressed *i.a.* by the so called negative competence-competence. According to this principle, the courts will only test *prima facie* if the parties concluded an agreement to arbitrate, thus they will not interfere and let the tribunal address the question of its own competence in the first place. Importantly, however, this mechanism favoring arbitration is relevant at the outset of the arbitration and during the proceedings instead of at the post-award stage.

37 Pursuant to Art. 1520 of the CCP, the award may be set aside when (i) the tribunal wrongly upheld or declined its jurisdiction, (ii) the tribunal was not properly constituted, (iii) the tribunal ruled without complying with the mandate conferred upon it, (iv) due process was violated, or (v) recognition or enforcement of the award is contrary to international public policy. For the research at hand primarily the third ground is important.

38 See, *e.g.*, Seraglini & Ortscheidt (2013) pp.853-854, Loquin (2015) p.420. See also CA Paris, 10 January 2012, *Société Sharikat al Ikarat Wal Abnieh (SIWA) S.A.L. v. Société Butec S.A.L.*, Rev. Arb. 2012, p.203 which reads that "*the action to set aside in international matters is available only under grounds exhaustively listed in Article 1502 of the Code of Civil Procedure.*" ("*Le recours en annulation d'une sentence arbitrale rendue en matière internationale n'est ouvert que dans les cas limitativement énumérés par l'article 1502 du Code de procédure civile.*").

39 Bensaude (2015) p.1176.

40 Bensaude (2015) p.1176, Seraglini & Ortscheidt (2013) p.854 ("*L'appel, voie de recours ouverte dans l'arbitrage interne […] est exclu à l'encontre d'une sentence rendue en France en matière internationale.*").

same time parties cannot remove any of the grounds for challenge. The only alternative is to opt out of the setting-aside procedure at large.[41]

The pro-arbitration approach is also manifested by the fact that the arbitral award (at the post-award stage) is reviewed at the level of the Court of Appeal[42] and that challenges are only rarely accepted. It is important to note that the same factual underpinning may trigger different challenges.[43] Notably, however, "*if a party fails to specify the grounds for the action or chooses the wrong grounds, the courts may be inclined to re-characterize the basis of the action rather than declaring it inadmissible.*"[44]

3.2 The scope of the court's review

As highlighted above, the scope of the court's review during the setting aside is of a limited nature. It means that this type of recourse will by no means allow the court to review the merits of the case.[45] This principle has been defined by Chantebout in the following way: "*the principle prohibits the judge to consider the merits of arbitral awards referred to him and to refuse exequatur or to set aside the arbitral awards on the grounds that he finds a disagreement [with the tribunal's findings] or that they [the merits] seem incorrect to him.*"[46] At the same time, (i) the French courts have the right to review the arbitral award based on the statutory grounds for setting aside and (ii) this notwithstanding they often give a deference to the arbitral tribunal.

41 See section 5.5. For further reading, see also Scherer, *The fate of parties' agreements on judicial review of awards: a comparative and normative analysis of party-autonomy at the post-award stage* (2016) pp.437-457.

42 Pursuant to Art.1519(1) of the CCP: "*[a]n action to set aside shall be brought before the Court of Appeal of the place where the award was made.*" ("*Le recours en annulation est porté devant la cour d'appel dans le ressort de laquelle la sentence a été rendue.*").

43 The usual difficulty and the risk of confusion exist between the challenge against the excess of mandate and (i) the excess of jurisdiction (Art. 1520(1) of the CCP) and (ii) the violation of due process (Art. 1520(4) of the CCP).

44 Derains & Kiffer, *National Report for France* (2013) Chapter VII(2)(B)(a). See also Seraglini & Ortscheidt (2013) p.881, Loquin (2015) pp.420-421. Clay, *Code de l'arbitrage commenté* (2015) p.208.

45 For example Loquin reflects that "*[t]he principle of no review on the merits of the award has been gradually developed by the courts which deduced that any criticism of the motivation of the award is inadmissible.*" See Loquin (2015) p.413 ("*Le principe de non-révision au fond de la sentence a été progressivement dégagé par la jurisprudence qui en déduit que toute critique de la motivation de la sentence est irrecevable.*"). See also Gaillard & Savage, *Fouchard Gaillard Goldman on International Commercial Arbitration* (1999) p.923, Seraglini & Ortscheidt (2013) pp.880-881, Racine (2016) p.588.

46 Loquin (2015) p.413 with the reference to Chantebout (2007): "*[u]n auteur [Chantebout] a défini ce principe pas son objet: il interdit au juge de tenir compte du bien-fondé des sentences arbitrales qui lui sont déférées et de leur refuser l'exequatur ou de les annuler au motif qu'il éprouve un désaccord ou qu'elles lui paraissent erronées.*".

The level of scrutiny allowed to the courts is rather high. For example, already in 1987, the *Cour de Cassation* in one of its decisions stated that, although the role of the setting-aside court is limited to the examination of the setting-aside grounds enumerated therein,

> there is no restriction upon the power of the court to examine, as a matter of law and in consideration of the circumstances of the case, elements pertinent to the grounds in question [...] in particular, it is for the court to construe the contract in order to determine itself whether the arbitrator ruled in the absence of an arbitration clause.[47]

It therefore means that the setting-aside court will enjoy the power to review all the issues of the case[48] to the extent that it is necessary to assess the challenge of the award itself.

Similarly, in another, more recent case the *Cour de Cassation* held that the

> annulment judge reviews the arbitral tribunal's award on jurisdiction, regardless of whether it is positive or negative, by enquiring into all the legal and factual elements [of the dispute] enabling him to determine the scope of the arbitration agreement and to determine the consequences for the compliance with the mission entrusted to the arbitrators.[49]

The same has been observed by Bensaude:

> [i]n deciding upon the setting aside of an award, or upon the appeal of an enforcement order under art. 1520, the Court of Appeal has the power to examine any evidence and factual or legal submissions that it considers relevant to determine whether the action should succeed on any of the grounds specified

47 (“*Mais attendu que, si la mission de la Cour d'appel, saisie en vertu des articles 1502 et 1504 du nouveau Code de procédure civile, est limitée à l'examen des vices énumérés par ces textes, aucune limitation n'est apportée au pouvoir de cette juridiction de rechercher en droit et en fait tous les éléments concernant les vices en question; qu'en particulier, il lui appartient d'interpréter le contrat pour apprécier elle-même si l'arbitre a statué sans convention d'arbitrage*”); translation after 26 International Legal Materials (1987) pp.1004-1007 slightly different translation offered in *Southern Pacific Properties Ltd. v. Southern Pacific Properties (Middle East) Ltd., The Arab Republic of Egypt*, Cour de Cassation [Supreme Court], Not Indicated, 6 January 1987, Y.B. Comm. Arb. 152, 154 (1988).

48 Poudret & Besson (2007) p.724.

49 Cour de Cassation Civ 1ère, 6 October 2010, *Fondation Albert Abela Family v. Fondation Joseph Abela Family*, Rev. Arb. 2010, p.969 (“*Le juge de l'annulation contrôle la décision du tribunal arbitral sur sa compétence, qu'il se soit déclaré compétent ou incompétent, en recherchant tous les éléments de droit ou de fait permettant d'apprécier la portée de la convention d'arbitrage et d'en déduire les conséquences sur le respect de la mission confiée aux arbitres.*”). Translation after Born in Born, *International Commercial Arbitration* (2014) p.3209 with the modification to the last part of it (“*et d'en déduire les conséquences sur le respect de la mission confiée aux arbitres.*”), which was omitted in the original translation.

> in art. 1520. Moreover, the Court of Appeal has the power to review de novo any issue that may provide a basis for action under art. 1520 regarding jurisdiction [...], the regular constitution of the tribunal, as well as alleged violations of [procedural and substantial public policy].[50]

One can thus conclude that the Court of Appeal in its capacity of setting-aside court is not restricted by the tribunal's conclusions, but rather is able to exercise an independent analysis. "*Having said this, the Court of Appeal tends to give deference to findings of arbitral tribunals, particularly with respect to questions of fact.*"[51]

Respecting the tribunals' findings, however, is a sensible solution, especially when the existence or validity of the arbitration agreement is *not* questioned. In the end, one should always conclude that the parties accepted that it would be the arbitral tribunal and not the court that decides the dispute. It might be particularly important with regard to the review of (i) the scope of the jurisdiction and (ii) the excess of mandate.

In the former instance (which would generally be challenged under Article 1520(1) of the CCP), as pointed out above, there is no objection as to the existence or validity of the agreement to arbitrate and the only concern relates to the *scope* of the jurisdiction. In turn, if the setting-aside court is willing to examine the scope of the jurisdiction of the arbitral tribunal anew (without any consideration to the tribunal's findings on the issue) it may lead to the situation where the same (scope) question is disputed at length before two different *fora*. Such a scenario is undesirable to say the least.

In the latter instance, the reviewing court, in principle, should focus on whether the prayers for relief sought by the parties have been answered in the award. If the reviewing court is vested with the power of independent determination of all circumstances of the case, only a fine line separates it from reevaluating the merits of the case and thus acting as an appellate body. For example, if the challenge is based on the allegation that the tribunal exceeded its mission by requalifying the claim defined in the Terms of Reference,[52] a reviewing court that does not give any deference to the tribunal's analysis may come to different conclusions as to what constitutes a claim. Consequently, and arguably, it may be eager to accept the challenge only because its findings differ from those of the tribunal.

For the above reasons, the power of *de novo* review is well balanced in France by the great deference given to the arbitral awards by setting-aside courts. At all times one should remember that the analysis of the setting-aside courts is strictly limited to the grounds listed and the review of the merits is strictly prohibited.[53]

---

50 Bensaude (2015) p.1178.

51 Bensaude (2015) pp.1178-1179. Cour de Cassation Civ 1ère, 10 October 2012, *Neoelectra Group v. Tecso*, No. 11-20299.

52 For example, on the basis of the subsequent submissions.

53 Born, *International Commercial Arbitration* (2014) pp.3183-3184, Loquin (2015) p.420.

3.3 *Remedial powers of the courts*

Taking into account the pro-arbitration stand of the French international arbitration regime, one can expect that only the most flagrant wrongdoing of the arbitral tribunal will justify the annulment of the award. For this reason, setting-aside courts have been equipped with tools that can be used to limit the consequences of the award being set aside. Therefore, it is necessary to briefly reflect on the availability of measures of (i) partial setting aside, (ii) remission and (iii) sanction for the abuse of the right to challenge the award.

Arguably, one of the most pro-arbitration mechanisms at the courts' disposal is the partial setting aside of the award. It means that the court carefully examines an arbitral award and annuls only the part of the award that meets the requirements of Article 1520 of the CCP. Consequently, the setting-aside court can use this tool when faced with challenges as to the scope of the tribunal's jurisdiction or as to the ambit of the tribunal's mandate. The basis for the partial setting aside of the award can be, albeit implicitly,[54] found in Article 1527(2) of the CCP, which reads that: "*[a] decision denying an appeal or application to set aside an award shall be deemed an enforcement order of the arbitral award or of the parts of the award that were not overturned by the court.*"[55] As aptly explained by Bensaude, "*with respect to international awards rendered in France, art. 1527 provides that if the Court of Appeal rejects an action for setting aside an award in whole or in part, the rejection of the setting aside action constitutes an enforcement order for the corresponding part of the award in France.*"[56]

The power to remit, however used infrequently, might serve as a useful tool to rectify a flawed award. In essence, remission "*permits a court, presented with an annulment application, to allow the arbitrators an opportunity to take further steps or decisions, which might render the annulment application unnecessary or inappropriate.*"[57] Alas, the remission is generally not available as a remedy at the post-award stage of international arbitration proceedings in France.[58] Without going into further details, one should note that, as argued by Derains, "*the only exception is fraud.*"[59] Additionally, it is necessary to stress that application for revision ("*recours en révision*") should be done directly to the tribunal that

54 See Seraglini & Ortscheidt (2013) p.872.

55 ("*Le rejet de l'appel ou du recours en annulation confère l'exequatur à la sentence arbitrale ou à celles de ses dispositions qui ne sont pas atteintes par la censure de la cour.*").

56 Bensaude (2015) p.1186. See also CA Paris, 18 September 2012, *S.A. Buildinvest et autres v. M. Guy Roy*, Rev. Arb. 2012, p.867 where the court concluded that nothing in the Code of Civil Procedure prevents an action for a partial annulment ("*Aucune disposition du Code de procédure civile ne fait obstacle à l'exercice d'une action en annulation partielle d'une sentence arbitrale.*").

57 Born, *International Commercial Arbitration* (2014) p.3152.

58 Seraglini & Ortscheidt (2013) pp.872-873.

59 Derains & Kiffer, *National Report for France* (2013) Chapter VII(2)(B)(b) with the reference to Cour de Cassation Civ 1ere, 25 May 1992, *Société Fougerolle v. Société Procorance*, Rev. Arb. 1993, p.91.

rendered the award[60] or to the newly constituted one, if the former cannot reconvene.[61] Finally, French courts take a strong position against the abusive use of the right to set aside.[62] As reported by Bensaude: "*[i]n recent years, the Paris Court of Appeal increasingly sanctions parties who frivolously seek to block enforcement or recognition of international awards under art. 1520 [...], or file claims under this provision that are found to be clearly inadmissible and filed for the sake of generating adverse publicity [...]*."[63] All things considered, both the partial setting aside and sanctions for the abuse of right seem to be sufficient and work effectively for achieving the pro-arbitration philosophy of arbitration regime in France.

4 DELINEATION OF THE MANDATE: THE IMPORTANCE OF THE CONSENT, THE REQUEST AND THE LAW: THE THREE KEYHOLES TEST

Having established that the arbitral tribunal's mandate for the purpose of Article 1520(3) of the CCP is *the function* of resolving the dispute within the limits imposed by the parties,[64] one should conclude that the mandate of the arbitral tribunal is unequivocally set by the parties' consent. Therefore, it is necessary to identify sources evidencing that consent, namely an agreement to arbitrate (section 4.1) and the parties' submissions (section 4.2). In addition, the possible implications of legal rules should also be analyzed (section 4.3).

4.1 Agreement to arbitrate

An agreement to arbitrate is the ultimate source of the parties' consent and inevitably the starting point for any arbitral process. It also constitutes one of the cornerstones of the tribunal's mandate.[65] Therefore, when deciding the case, the tribunal should closely follow

---

60 See Art. 1502(2) of the CCP.

61 Bensaude (2015) p.1187.

62 For further reading, see Lécuyer (2006).

63 Bensaude (2015) p.1179. The author made references to three cases, namely CA Paris, 21 January 1997, *Société Nu Swift PLC v. Société White Knight et autres*, Rev. Arb. 1997, p.429, CA Paris, 6 May 2004, *Carthago Films v. Babel Productions*, Rev. Arb. 2006, p.661, and CA Paris, 18 February 1986, *G. Aïta v. A. Ojjeh*, Rev. Arb. 1986, p.583. In all three cases the court awarded the aggrieved parties damages ("*les dommages-intérêts*"). See also Seraglini & Ortscheidt (2013) p.867. Additionally, Lécuyer in Lécuyer (2006) pp.585-589 further explains what types of sanctions are available (analyzing damages ("*les dommages-intérêts*"), fines ("*l'amende civile*"), irrecoverable costs ("*les frais irrépétibles*") and costs ("*les dépens*")).

64 See section 5.4.

65 Although an agreement to arbitrate is essential in the consensual paradigm of the arbitral tribunal's mandate, whenever the challenge is directed at the scope of the agreement to arbitrate it fits better under the category of the excess of jurisdiction rather than under the mandate issue. Consequently, it would trigger the appli-

the scope of the parties' initial agreement to arbitrate. French international arbitration law proves to be a very progressive regime when it comes to requirements regarding an agreement to arbitrate, both when it comes to the requirements (i) as to the form of an agreement to arbitrate and (ii) as to the scope of the agreement to arbitrate.

Pursuant to Article 1507 of the CCP: "*an arbitration agreement shall not be subject to any requirements as to its form.*"[66] According to Bensaude, "*an agreement to arbitrate may exist whenever evidence is provided that there is a 'common intent of the parties' to arbitrate their disputes.*"[67] It means that virtually all agreements to arbitrate will bind the parties, no matter in what form they were drafted, as long as some evidence exists showing the parties' intent to arbitrate.[68] It goes without saying that an agreement to arbitrate can take the form of an arbitration clause (referring to arbitration of future disputes) or of a submission agreement (being an agreement to arbitrate already existing disputes).[69]

The same liberal approach is offered to the interpretation of the scope of the arbitration agreement and the parties' "common intent to arbitrate".[70] For this reason, "*the language of the clause [is] critical.*"[71] In other words, parties should take their time in carefully drafting their agreement to arbitrate, especially if they want to narrow the adjudicative powers of the tribunal. For example, as aptly concluded, "*[a] broadly worded clause will generally be found to cover both contract and tort claims arising out of or in connection with the contract at issue.*"[72]

Additionally, one should also take into account the impact that arbitral rules[73] may have on the scope of the tribunal's powers. Considering that "*the language of the clause is critical*",[74] reference to the rules may give an indication of the intent to be bound by the content of such rules.

---

cation of Art. 1520(1) of the CCP instead of Art. 1520(3) of the CCP. See further, *e.g.*, section 6.1.1 (and the second main question therein). See also Giraud (2017) pp.68-72.

66 ("*La convention d'arbitrage n'est soumise à aucune condition de forme.*").

67 Bensaude (2015) p.1136 with a reference to Cour de Cassation Civ 1ère, 20 December 2000, *Prodexport v. FMT Productions*, Rev. Arb. 2003, p.1342.

68 It holds true in cases of international agreements to arbitrate. In the domestic context, French (domestic) arbitration law is much less lenient. See Art. 1443 of the CCP in particular. Some of the domestic arbitration law provisions are applicable to international arbitration by virtue of Art. 1506 of the CCP. This way principles of separability and competence-competence are introduced. Apart from mentioning the fact that these domestic provisions do not have much impact on the notion of the tribunal's mandate, as such they will not be discussed further.

69 Giraud (2017) p.74 ("*Par l'emploi de la formule générique « convention d'arbitrage », la jurisprudence vise tant le compromis que la clause compromissoire.*").

70 Bensaude (2015) p.1180.

71 Bensaude (2015) p.1181.

72 Bensaude (2015) p.1181 with reference to CA Paris, 19 May 2005, *SA Sucres et denrées v. Société Talsy Shipping Co Ltd.*, Rev. Arb. 2006, p.927.

73 That is procedural rules of arbitral institutions or the UNCITRAL Rules.

74 See fn.71.

At all times, a broad definition of the arbitral mandate will require the tribunal to adjudicate the dispute.[75] Therefore, an agreement to arbitrate should explicitly call for a judicial determination of the dispute, *i.e.* a final and binding resolution of the dispute between the parties by the arbitral tribunal.[76] Consequently,

> it may be said that where a third party is appointed by disputants merely to express an opinion or to give recommendations or proposals which are not binding, such third party is not an arbitrator; thus, persons are not arbitrators unless they are appointed to adjudicate, and so resolve a dispute.[77]

Overall, an agreement to arbitrate is an essential element to conduct an arbitral process and a primary source of the arbitral tribunal's mandate.[78] Although, in an international context, the legal requirements are rather relaxed, the result of the agreement to arbitrate should "*be an adjudication, which is binding upon the parties in the same manner as a court judgment.*"[79]

4.2 *Relevance of parties' submissions: reference of a dispute and other requests of the parties*

As already highlighted above "*[...] the mandate of the arbitrators is defined by the arbitration agreement and limited by the subject matter of the dispute as framed by the parties' claims even if the issue to be decided is not mentioned in the terms of reference.*"[80] It entails that (i) the initial agreement to arbitrate serves only as a provisional determination of the arbitral tribunal's adjudicative mandate, because it is narrowed further down by the actual claims submitted to the tribunal. At the same time, however, (ii) the parties' subsequent submissions may also play a role in a potential modification of claims introduced at the beginning in the agreement to arbitrate.

75 For further reading, see section 5.1. See also Giraud (2017) pp.102-103.

76 For further reading, see Oppetit (1998) pp.72-81, Rouche et al. (2009) pp.21-22, Carducci, *The Arbitration Reform in France: Domestic and International Arbitration Law* (2012) p.127, Loquin (2015) pp.5-12.

77 Rouche et al. (2009) p.22.

78 See also fn.65. Arguably, there might be a slight difference in interpreting the pre- and post-dispute agreements to arbitrate (thus arbitration clauses and submission agreements), because after the dispute arises, the parties are more conscious in delineating the tribunal's adjudicative authority.

79 Rouche et al. (2009) p.16.

80 Derains & Kiffer, *National Report for France* (2013) Chapter VII(2)(B)(a)(3). See also CA Paris, 27 November 2008, *Société GFI informatique SA v. Société Engineering Ingegneria Informatica SPA et autre*, Rev. Arb. 2009, p.229, where it was concluded that "*[t]he arbitrator's mandate, is defined by the agreement to arbitrate and limited primarily by the subject-matter of the dispute, as determined by the claims of the parties.*" ("*La mission de l'arbitre, définie par la convention d'arbitrage, est délimitée principalement par l'objet du litige, tel qu'il est déterminé par les prétentions des parties.*").

The first point is rather clear-cut, because it merely points out that the parties' *petita* restrict the scope of the tribunal's powers. Put differently, the tribunal will only be competent to decide on the claims that have been brought by the parties. These should generally be brought at the earliest stage of the proceedings.[81] Importantly, however, claims submitted should fit within the scope of the agreement to arbitrate,[82] unless there is a clear indication that parties intend to modify their earlier agreement to arbitrate.[83]

The second point is a bit more sensitive in nature. It reflects the instances where the parties amend (or expand) their initial claims and inevitably influence the limits given to the adjudicative mandate in the first place.[84] Such amendments or expansions might raise legitimate concerns, because these may contradict the consensual character of the tribunal's mandate.[85] For this reason, changes should always be subjected to the acceptance of all entities involved. At times, however, new submissions presented without any objection by the opposite side might be considered as tacitly accepted by the opposite side and be considered as permission for the tribunal to act in this modified scope.

In the proceedings under the ICC Arbitration Rules, the Terms of Reference ("*l'acte de mission*") constitute an additional element on the procedural map. The ICC Terms of Reference stress the importance of well-defined and structured claims at the initial stage of the proceedings. Consequently, it gives a clear framework for the tribunal's adjudicative mandate[86] and imposes an obligation on the parties to prepare their claims carefully. After the Terms of Reference are signed, they can be changed only with the authorization of the arbitral tribunal.[87] Occasionally, however, it may happen that the claims as introduced in the Terms of Reference are broad or leave a backdoor open for the alteration of claims. This scenario will be further discussed below.[88] Briefly speaking, such a drafting strategy may result in difficulties with challenging the excess of the tribunal's mandate.

---

81 Other (subsequent) parties' submissions throughout the arbitral process are also of relevance. Especially if claims are being modified or added, which is discussed in the second part of section 4.2.

82 Giraud (2017) p.70.

83 The modification on the level of the agreement to arbitrate might be relevant not only to the dispute at hand but also to any other future dispute arising under this agreement to arbitrate. It also distinguishes this hypothetical from the modifications of the relief sought.

84 It will also be discussed further in section 6.1.

85 Giraud (2017) p.132 ("*Il pourrait être objecté que la modification des contours du litige par la soumission d'une demande nouvelle contredit le caractère conventionnel de la mission arbitrale.*").

86 It is even further evidenced by the French name of the Terms of Reference: "*l'acte de mission*".

87 See Art. 23(4) of the (draft) 2021 ICC Rules, Art. 23(4) of the 2017 ICC Rules, Art. 23(4) of the 2012 ICC Rules. It is logical the consequence of the consensual character of the mandate: after the Terms of Reference are signed, the parties *and* the tribunal accept the shape of the mandate as certain. Therefore, if any of the parties wishes to change the scope of the mandate, the tribunal needs to accept a modification. See also section 6.1.5.

88 See section 6.1.5.

4.3 *Mandatory rules of law of (French international) public policy and their impact*

Arbitration, being a creature of contractual origins, is always subject to the underlying principles of justice that are at the core of any legal system. These principles are expressed by the mandatory rules of law of a public policy character. Under French international arbitration law, not all violations of public policy rules may constitute a ground for recourse. Pursuant to Article 1520(5) of the CCP, an arbitral award may be set aside only if "*recognition or enforcement of the award is contrary to international public policy.*"[89] Further, the concept of international public policy entails both procedural and substantive public policy.

In principle, procedural public policy is related to the due process considerations[90] and substantive public policy will be violated in cases, for example, of bribery, corruption or money laundering.[91] Additionally, a public policy violation needs to cause an actual harm to the party alleging violation[92] and traditionally it was necessary that the violation was "*flagrant, effective and concrete*".[93] This standard greatly limited the French courts intervention. The more recent case law, however, departs from the requirement that the violation needs to be *flagrant.*[94] Consequently, although the threshold for violation of the (French) international public policy remains high, the French courts reclaim a greater control over the arbitral awards when scrutinizing if the award violates the international

89 ("*La reconnaissance ou l'exécution de la sentence est contraire à l'ordre public international.*"). It means that the violation of policy has to be the consequence of the recognition or enforcement and not of the award itself.

90 See Art. 1510 of the CCP.

91 See, *e.g.*, CA Paris, 21 February 2017, *République du Kirghizistan v. M. Belokon*, Rev. Arb. 2017, p.336, CA Paris, 16 January 2018, *Société MK Group v. SARL Onix et autre*, Rev. Arb. 2018, p.295. For further reading, see also Bensaude (2015) pp.1166-1167 (in the context of the enforcement of the awards) and pp.1183-1185.

92 CA Paris, 21 January 1997, *Société Nu Swift PLC v. Société White Knight et autres*, Rev. Arb. 1997, p.429.

93 CA Paris, 18 November 2004, *SA Thalès Air Défense v. GIE Euromissile*, Rev. Arb. 2005, p.752 ("*Considérant que la violation de l'ordre public international au sens de l'article 1502-5° du NCPC doit être flagrante, effective et concrète, que le juge de l'annulation peut certes, dans le cadre de ses pouvoirs de nature disciplinaire, porter une appréciation en droit et en fait sur les éléments qui sont dans la sentence déférée à son contrôle, mais pas statuer au fond sur un litige complexe qui n'a jamais encore été ni plaidé, ni jugé devant un arbitre concernant la simple éventualité de l'illicéité de certaines stipulations contractuelles*"). Cour de Cassation Civ 1ère, 4 June 2008, Société SNF SAS v. Société Cytec Industries BV, Rev. Arb. 2008, p.473.

94 See *e.g.* CA Paris, 20 January 2015, *SA Telecel Faso v. SA Alcatel Lucent International*, Rev. Arb. 2015, p.273 (referring to *manifest* and *concrete* violation of international public policy) or CA Paris, 14 April 2015, *République Hellénique v. Société Bombardier Inc.*, Rev. Arb. 2015, p.645 (referring to *effective* and *concrete* standard), CA Paris, 21 February 2017, *République du Kirghizistan v. M. Belokon*, Rev. Arb. 2017, p.336 (referring to *manifest, effective* and *concrete* requirements); same CA Paris, 16 January 2018, *Société MK Group v. SARL Onix et autre*, Rev. Arb. 2018, p.295. For further reading see also Racine (2016) pp.601-602.

public policy.[95] The outstanding question is how public policy rules affect the concept of the mandate. In principle, they are relevant, because they impose on the tribunal a duty to follow them. In that sense, it is a duty autonomous from the contractual framework for the tribunal's mandate. Consequently, public policy rules may have an impact on several aspects of the tribunal's adjudicative mandate. For example, the tribunal will not be able to resolve non-arbitrable disputes. It will also need to comply with due process rules.[96] Furthermore, French international public policy may have an impact on the process of (mis)application of law, or even its manifest disregard. These issues will be addressed further in the part below.[97]

5 THE FRENCH CONCEPT OF THE ARBITRAL TRIBUNAL'S MANDATE AND TESTING ITS EXCESS AT THE POST-AWARD STAGE

For as long as the general notion of the arbitral tribunal's mandate has been present in international arbitration, only very few jurisdictions have decided to introduce an "excess of mandate" ground to their post-award challenge mechanism.[98] It has already been highlighted above that, under the French international arbitration law, such a recourse is possible and can be found in Article 1520(3) of the CCP, which reads that the award may be set aside if "*the arbitral tribunal ruled without complying with the mandate conferred upon it.*"[99] The problem lies, however, with defining the notion of the mandate itself and determining when it is exceeded.

Indeed, on its face, the third prong of Article 1520 of the CCP seems to be an elusive concept. Perhaps even more so in the present version of the provision, when one looks at the verbs used and the use of the verb *confier* in particular. A thorough analysis has initially been presented by Giraud in his work where he analyzed the verbs used in Article 1520(3) of the CCP: *statuer* (Eng. "*to rule*"), *se conformer* (Eng. "*to comply*") and *confier* (Eng. "*to entrust, to confide*"). When comparing the 1981[100] and 2011[101] versions of the French

95 CA Paris, 21 February 2017, *République du Kirghizistan v. M. Belokon*, Rev. Arb. 2017, p.336 (referring to *manifest*, *effective* and *concrete* requirements); CA Paris, 16 January 2018, *Société MK Group v. SARL Onix et autre*, Rev. Arb. 2018, p.295.

96 See Art. 1510 of the CCP.

97 See section 6 at large. Generally, public policy will not be discussed in every subsection of section 6. It will be considered only in parts where its application is relevant.

98 France, the Netherlands and Sweden. See Art. 1065(1)(c) and Art. 1065(4) of the Dutch Code of Civil Procedure and Section 34(3) of the Swedish Arbitration Act respectively.

99 ("*Le tribunal arbitral a statué sans se conformer à la mission qui lui avait été confiée*").

100 Art. 1502(3) of the Old CCP ("*L'appel de la décision qui accorde la reconnaissance ou l'exécution n'est ouvert que dans les cas suivants [...] si l'arbitre a statué sans se conformer à la mission qui lui avait été conférée*").

101 Art. 1520(3) of the CCP ("*Le recours en annulation n'est ouvert que si [...] [l]e tribunal arbitral a statué sans se conformer à la mission qui lui avait été confiée*").

international arbitration law, the third out of these verbs has replaced the verb *conférer* (Eng. "*to confer*") which was used in the 1981 version of the French international arbitration law. These two words are often considered as synonyms.

On top of that, Giraud highlights that neither commentators, nor courts have attributed any meaning to this change.[102] At the same time, however, he suggested that the use of *conférer* focuses more on the formal aspect of the tribunal's mandate, whereas the use of the verb *confier* puts in the spotlight the relation of trust between the person who *entrusts* and the person who *is entrusted with*. His observations are correct and, arguably, such a change may affect the types of arguments brought against the award in the setting-aside proceedings as well as the way the provision is being interpreted, because it gives room to rely on the concept of trust, which is subtle.

Accordingly, the notion of breach of trust may not necessarily be limited to the contractual framework (*e.g.* a written agreement[103]), but opens the possibility to invoke other expectations from the tribunal.[104] Consequently, it may influence how the courts will approach the excess of mandate challenge in the future. It is so particularly considering that it may be (and it is) overly tempting for the award-debtor to interpret the excess of mandate ground excessively broad and to use it as a ground that accommodates many different procedural and substantive challenges. In turn, this may endanger the efficiency and the finality of the arbitral process.[105]

The analysis below relies greatly on the recent noteworthy study of Giraud, who undertook a similar exercise of searching for the meaning of the arbitral tribunal's mandate, its limits and possible venues for challenge at the post-award stage.[106] In his analysis, he decided to use two terms in order to structure the analysis of the mandate, one with a broad meaning and the second with a narrow scope. Giraud, therefore, suggests that the mandate can be understood both in a broad sense as a responsibility (or function) ("*la*

102 Giraud (2017) p.31.

103 As to the importance of the constraints in writing, see section 4; also Giraud (2017) p.133.

104 One should also reflect that the most common English translation for the French word "*mission*" is an the English "*mandate*", where it could be easily possible to translate it as the English "*mission*". Arguably, it would go in line with the "trust paradigm" explained above. Notably, as such (*i.e.* "mission") it was used by Craig in his article Craig, *The arbitrator's mission and the application of law in international commercial arbitration* (2010).

105 In similar vein, it has been argued by Poudret and Besson in Poudret & Besson (2007) p.741, that "*the mission of the arbitrator defines both his duties and powers so that this ground for setting aside could include all failures regarding the first and all excesses in respect of the second. Conceived in such a wide manner, it would not only have the same purpose as the other violations […], but it could excessively weaken the award.*" See also Gaillard & Savage, *Fouchard Gaillard Goldman on International Commercial Arbitration* (1999) pp.937-938.

106 For further reading, see Giraud (2017). His reflections, however, are (mostly) limited to French domestic and international arbitration law. The research at hand aims to scrutinize the "excess of mandate" challenges from a comparative law perspective. For further reading, see Chapter VII.

mission-office")[107] and in a narrow sense as a contract ("*la mission-contrat*").[108] At the same time, he argues that none of those definitions alone fits the notion of the mandate envisaged by Article 1520(3) of the CCP. Instead, he suggests that the concept of the mandate in Article 1520(3) of the CCP envisages a correlation of the two, namely it addresses the adjudicative responsibility (or function) ("*la mission-office*") that is shaped by the parties' agreement ("*la mission-contrat*").[109]

Consequently, one should reflect on the concept of the mandate under French international arbitration law in its broad (section 5.1) and narrow sense (section 5.2) and the one which is reflected under Article 1520(3) of the CCP (section 5.4). Additionally, since the adjudicative mission of the arbitral tribunal is invariably shaped by the parties' consent, one should read the following sections together with the part above, namely the one on the consensual framework of the arbitral tribunal's mandate (section 4). Moreover, it is necessary to briefly discuss the time limits in exercising adjudicative duties (section 5.3) and – more loosely related to the concept of the mandate – the possibility to contract out of the setting-aside recourse against the award (see section 5.5).

5.1 *The functional aspect of the arbitral tribunal's mandate*

As highlighted above, the main issue at hand is the problem of a precise delineation of the scope of the tribunal's mandate (and the meaning of the mandate for the purposes of Article 1520(3) of the CCP in particular).[110] Arguably, if one takes a functional aspect of the tribunal's undertakings as a defining, underlying element of the mandate, one will conclude that the mandate of the arbitral tribunal is to finally resolve the dispute(s) between the parties.[111]

This broad type of definition brings *the adjudication of the dispute* to the core of the tribunal's mandate. At the same time, definitions often require the tribunal to follow applicable procedural and substantive rules. Therefore, for example, some authors suggested

107 Giraud (2017) pp.55-58 and pp.94-103.

108 Giraud (2017) pp.58-72 and pp.104-114.

109 Giraud (2017) p.135 ("*La mission générale de l'arbitre est une mission unique, offrant deux aspects hiérarchisés: la mission-office de l'arbitre, mission première, est modulée par la mission-contrat, subsidiaire, qui rassemble les éléments déterminés conventionnellement par les parties. Au sein de ce cadre, la mission visée à l'indice 3 des articles 1492 et 1520 du Code de procédure civile désigne le point particulier de rencontre entre ces deux missions. Elle correspond à la portion de mission juridictionnelle modelée par la mission conventionnelle. En d'autres termes, c'est la coloration de la mission-office par la mission-contrat.*").

110 See also section 4.

111 For a discussion on tasks undertaken by the arbitral tribunal, see, *i.a.*, Lévy & Robert-Tissot (2013) pp.861-952.

that "*in a broad sense, the arbitrator's brief is to reach a fair decision in accordance with the rules governing the procedural and substantive aspects of the case.*"[112]

Others elaborated that *'la mission de l'arbitre'* refers to the tribunal's

> [...] contractual obligation towards the parties to make a conclusive determination of the disputes submitted to it for resolution, in an award made in proceedings in which the parties' agreement as to the applicable rules of procedure and substantive rules of law have been respected, and any relevant mandatory or supple[men]tory provisions have been applied[113]

or that "*the mission of the arbitrator defines both his duties and powers [...].*"[114]

These broad definitions, when applied under the Article 1520(3) of the CCP challenge, expose the tribunal's mandate to too many ineligible attacks, when one considers, *e.g.*, a tribunal's alleged non-compliance with procedural or substantive rules.[115] Notably, however, the definition of the mandate as a responsibility or function may be useful (for the purpose of the excess of mandate challenge) whenever temporal limits to the arbitral tribunal's mandate are at stake.[116]

5.2 *The contractual framework of the arbitral tribunal's mandate*

The narrow interpretation of the arbitral tribunal's mandate focuses on the contractual framework for its powers and duties. It has been stated that: "*the mandate of the arbitrators is defined by the arbitration agreement and limited by the subject matter of the dispute as framed by the parties' claims.*"[117] Similarly, other authors observe that the arbitrators exercise the adjudicative mandate that has its origins in the parties' contract.[118] In other words, the mandate is confined to the parties' agreement to arbitrate, the Terms of Reference ("*l'acte de mission*"), as well as to the claims and defenses which the parties decide to bring before

---

112 Gaillard & Savage, *Fouchard Gaillard Goldman on International Commercial Arbitration* (1999) pp.937-938.

113 Rouche et al. (2009) p.247.

114 Poudret & Besson (2007) p.741 ("*The mission of the arbitrator defines both his duties and powers so that this ground for setting aside could include all failures regarding the first and all excesses in respect of the second. Conceived in such a wide manner, it would not only have the same purpose as the other violations studied until now, but it could excessively weaken the award. Even if only serious failures are taken into account – those violating the fundamental rights of the defence or the requirements of international public policy – such a ground for setting aside nevertheless has a wide scope and is frequently raised.*").

115 For further reading, see section 6.

116 Giraud (2017) pp.56-57. See also section 5.3.

117 Derains & Kiffer, *National Report for France* (2013) Chapter VII(2)(B)(a)(3).

118 See Seraglini & Ortscheidt (2013) p.22 ("*[...] l'arbitre exerçant une mission juridictionelle qui a une origine conventionelle*").

the tribunal.[119] These elements have already been explained above, thus a cross-reference should suffice.[120]

The agreement to arbitrate as the contractual element shaping the scope of the submitted dispute is not the only contractual component surrounding the execution of the tribunal's adjudicative mandate. Since resolving disputes is a service rendered to the parties, Giraud reports that on top of the agreement to arbitrate, several other contractual ties bind the parties and arbitrator and are relevant in the fulfillment of the adjudicative function of the arbitrator. He therefore lists the contract of the arbitrator,[121] the contract between the parties and the arbitral institution and the contract between the arbitrators and the arbitral institution.[122] Each of these contractual ties are relevant for exercising the tribunal's (adjudicative) mandate, yet, each creates a different set of rights and obligations between the different actors involved.[123] It further implicates a duality of liability. It means that, on the one hand, the tribunal is provided with arbitral (judicial-like) immunity. On the other hand, it might face civil liability claims in cases of failure to comply with its contractual obligations.[124]

In addition, it is necessary to highlight that the arbitral tribunal's adjudicative mandate may be constrained in time, which has to be also analyzed in the contractual dimension of the arbitral tribunal's mandate. This issue will be discussed more closely in the section that follows.[125]

All in all, if one considers the plethora of issues related to the contractual dimension of the arbitral tribunal's mandate, one will find that in fact the contractual definition of the mandate is inadequate for the purpose of the "excess of mandate" challenge, because the test of Article 1520(3) of the CCP does not focus on the contractual constraints alone. Instead, by and large, it relates to the resolution of the dispute as constrained by the parties' submissions. For this reason, both dimensions of the mandate should be considered in correlation only.[126]

---

119 The contractual framework was discussed in detail in the previous sections.

120 See section 4.1 and section 4.2.

121 Occasionally itself considered to fall under the term "mandate". Its legal character is also uncertain. For further reading, see Schöldstrom (1998).

122 Giraud (2017) pp.88-94.

123 For further reading, see Giraud (2017) pp.104-115.

124 See Giraud (2017) pp.115-121.

125 For further reading, see section 5.3.

126 See further section 5.4.

5.3 *The time limits for the execution of the arbitral tribunal's mandate*

The temporal framework for the arbitral tribunal's mandate is provided in the French Code of Civil Procedure. According to French international arbitration law in Articles 1456(1) and 1457(1) of the CCP, (i) the tribunal is constituted when all arbitrators accept their mandate[127] and (ii) the mandate shall be carried out until completed.[128] Consequently, the tribunal is able to exercise its powers over parties and carry out its obligation only during the duration of the mandate. It further implies that any powers may not be exercised when the mandate is concluded. In fact, the initial proposal of the *Comité Français de l'Arbitrage* for the reform of French arbitration law expressly provided that an award may be set aside when "*the tribunal ruled without complying with the mandate conferred upon it or ruled after its mandate has expired.*"[129]

In summary, the arbitral tribunal's mandate, in its broad meaning, entails the reference to the adjudicative function of the arbitral panel, which in turn, is timely framed. This is arguably one of the dimensions of the parties' agreed limitations to the tribunal's adjudicative function. It is therefore observed that after the deadline passes the tribunal's adjudicative mandate ceases to exist. Put differently, in the words of one commentator: "*[a] tribunal that fails to render its award within the applicable deadline, if any, [...] fails to comply with its mission [...].*"[130] Notably, Giraud reports that failure to comply with the agreed time limit by a few days or even hours will lead to a successful challenge of the

127 Art. 1456(1) of the CCP reads that: "*[t]he constitution of an arbitral tribunal shall be complete upon the arbitrators' acceptance of their mandate. As of that date, the tribunal is seized of the dispute.*" ("*Le tribunal arbitral est constitué lorsque le ou les arbitres ont accepté la mission qui leur est confiée. A cette date, il est saisi du litige*").

128 Art. 1457(1) of the CCP reads that: "*[a]rbitrators shall carry out their mandate until it is completed, unless they are legally incapacitated or there is a legitimate reason for them to refuse to act or to resign.*" ("*Il appartient à l'arbitre de poursuivre sa mission jusqu'au terme de celle-ci à moins qu'il justifie d'un empêchement ou d'une cause légitime d'abstention ou de démission.*").

129 ("*[L]e tribunal arbitral a statué sans se conformer à la mission qui lui avait été conférée ou après l'expiration de cette mission*"). See Art. 1518 of the Proposal in CFA, *Texte proposé par le Comité Français de l'Arbitrage pour une réform du livre IV NCPC* (2006) p.516. *Cf* with Section 34(2) of the old Swedish Arbitration Act ("*if the arbitrators have made the award after the expiration of the period decided on by the parties, or where the arbitrators have otherwise exceeded their mandate*"). Translation as available at http://sccinstitute se/media/37089/the-swedish-arbitration-act.pdf [last accessed 28 April 2018] and Section 32(2) of the (new) Swedish Arbitration Act ("*if the arbitrators have made the award after the expiration of the time limit set by the parties*"). Translation as available at https://sccinstitute.com/media/408924/the-swedish-arbitration-act_1march2019_eng.pdf [last accessed 28 April 2019].

130 Bensaude (2015) p.1182. Importantly, however, Art. 1463(2) of the CCP (which is applicable to international arbitration) reads that: "*[t]he statutory or contractual time limit may be extended by agreement between the parties or, where there is no such agreement, by the judge acting in support of the arbitration.*" ("*Le délai légal ou conventionnel peut être prorogé par accord des parties ou, à défaut, par le juge d'appui.*").

award.[131] Additionally, he concludes that it entails that the contractual dimension of the mandate is protected, but, at the same time and by all means, a more flexible solution would be desirable.[132] This is indeed what should be preferred.

There are strong arguments in favour of excluding the availability of the challenge in the context of delays, in particular minimal ones. When both dimensions of the mandate are put on a scale, the adjudicative one should prevail. One should observe and prioritize the essential duty of the tribunal, namely to resolve the dispute. The temporal aspect, albeit extremely important, does not affect the tribunal's findings themselves. Arguably, the decision on the parties' claims has already been undertaken during the tribunal's deliberations and as such may serve the sole purpose why arbitration was ever commenced. A delay in the tribunal communicating its (otherwise much sought) decision should not by itself invalidate it.

Arguably, setting aside the tribunal's decision due to a delay puts too much weight on the contractual aspect of the mandate. Nothing in Article 1520(3) of the CCP directly refers to the consequences of time delays. Importantly, the current shape of Article 1520(3) of the CCP is a departure from the first draft proposed by the *Comité Français de l'Arbitrage* explained at the outset,[133] which could suggest a more lenient and flexible position of the French legislator.

This is not to say that delays in rendering an arbitral award should be treated lightly.[134] Again, arguably, the delays in producing the award are good examples where the remedies against the arbitrators (for breach of contractual duties) and not against the award itself should be sought.

5.4 *The concept of the mandate (and of its excess) under Article 1520(3) of the CCP*

As highlighted above and underlined by Giraud, neither "the broad"[135] nor "the narrow"[136] definition of the mandate fits the needs of the excess of mandate challenge.[137] This is why,

131 Giraud (2017) p.394. See also Cour de Cassation Civ 1ère, 6 December 2005, *L. et B. Juliet v. X. et autres*, No. 03-13.116, Rev. Arb. 2006, p.126 and CA Paris, 18 June 2013, *M. Bruno Polge et autre v. M. Philippe Chaumeau et autres*, Rev. Arb. 2013, p.811.

132 Giraud (2017) p.394 ("*Une telle sanction protège la dimension contractuelle de l'arbitrage. Toutefois, cette radicalité de droit positif surprend dans une matière habituée à des solutions souples et pragmatiques, et une évolution est souhaitable.*").

133 See fn.129.

134 Especially considering the pursuit of efficiency imposed on all actors (and arbitrators in particular) in international arbitration.

135 See section 5.1.

136 See section 5.2.

137 Giraud (2017) p.135.

the abovementioned author offered two definitions of the mandate: (i) the general one and (ii) the one tailored to the purposes of Article 1520(3) of the CCP.

The first proposes that: "*the mandate of the arbitrator is a function entrusted by two or more parties to one or more individuals to resolve a dispute, while deciding on the basis of two conflicting legal claims presented by the parties and in accordance with the procedural rules and rules of law chosen by them [the parties].*"[138]

Conversely, under the second definition, it is suggested that "*the mandate of the arbitrator referred to in the third prong [of Article 1520 of the CCP] identifies the contractual elements that are directly relevant in the exercise of the adjudicative mandate.*"[139] Put differently, Giraud argues that the arbitral tribunal's mandate, understood as a responsibility (or function), is subsequently limited by the contractual framework of the mandate,[140] and should be applied as such for the purposes of Article 1520(3) of the CCP.[141]

The tailored definition (proposed as aligned with Article 1520(3) of the CCP), therefore, stresses the importance of the contractual restraints on the adjudicative mandate given to the tribunal by the parties. In other words, one could say that the challenge against the tribunal's mandate can only be successful if it focuses on violations of *contractual restraints* imposed by the parties that expressly relate to deciding on claims, *i.e.*, resolving the dispute brought before arbitrators. Therefore, in the context of the excess of mandate challenge, the parties' *petita* are inevitably in the spotlight. Usually, if the tribunal's decision is not aligned with the relief sought by the parties (*petita*), it is discussed in three variations, namely (i) *ultra*, (ii) *extra* and (iii) *infra petita*. In principle, therefore, each of these might in turn trigger the Article 1520(3) challenge. This will be reviewed further under the following section.[142]

Since *infra petita* is covered separately below,[143] it is sensible to highlight the difference between *ultra* and *extra petita*.

Giraud observes that

> the arbitrator adjudicating extra petita grants something that had not been requested. By definition, the parties have not envisaged that. The violation of the adversarial process is then quasi systematic. This argument must be nuanced

138 Giraud (2017) p.134 ("*La mission de l'arbitre est l'office confié par deux ou plusieurs parties à une ou plusieurs personnes physiques de trancher un litige, en statuant entre deux prétentions juridiques antagonistes, dont les contours sont déterminés par les parties, et selon les modalités procédurales et les règles de droit qu'elles choisissent.*").

139 Giraud (2017) p.134 ("*La mission de l'arbitre visée à l'indice 3 désigne les éléments conventionnels participant directement de l'exercice de la mission juridictionnelle.*").

140 See section 5.2.

141 See Giraud (2017) pp.134-135.

142 See further section 6. As to the *infra petita*, see particularly section 6.1.6.

143 See section 6.1.6.

in the case of ultra petita. The initial request has certainly been exceeded, but the principle of the request was envisaged by the parties. In such a case, only the modalities (the amount in case of granting damages) envisaged differ from those in the award. Then the violation of the adversarial process seems less automatic.[144]

Additionally, and importantly, the *ultra petita* challenge will be considered separately in comparison to the request of each party (for example in the case of counterclaims).[145]

All in all, one should always take into account both the functional and the contractual aspect of the mandate in the context of the Article 1520(3) test.

5.5 (Contractual) waiver of the right to set an arbitral award aside

As mentioned in the previous section,[146] the 2011 reform introduced a new mechanism within the framework of French international arbitration law that allows the parties to opt out contractually from bringing setting-aside actions.[147]

Pursuant to Article 1522 of the CCP: "*[b]y way of a specific agreement the parties may, at any time, expressly waive their right to bring an action to set aside.*"[148] This mechanism can be used only under the international regime.[149] Additionally, it needs to be sufficiently specific to be considered as the provision contracting out of the setting-aside review. It means that, for example, Article 35(6) of the 2017 ICC Rules will not satisfy the conditions to be considered as a valid waiver.[150] Notably, as pointed out by Gaillard: "*[...] unlike the law in Switzerland, Belgium or Sweden – where such waiver is available only when none of the parties has its domicile, habitual residence or business establishment in that country –*

---

144 Giraud (2017) p.269 ("*Il convient de distinguer l'extra de l'ultra petita. L'arbitre qui statue extra petita octroie quelque chose qui n'avait pas été demandé. Par définition, les parties n'en ont pas discuté. La violation du contradictoire est alors quasi systématique. Ce raisonnement doit être nuancé en cas d'ultra petita. La demande initiale a certes été dépassée, mais le principe de cette demande a été discuté par les parties. Dans ce cas, seules ses modalités – son montant, dans le cas de l'octroi de dommages intérêts – ont varié entre les débats et la sentence. La violation du principe de la contradiction apparaît alors moins mécanique.*").

145 Giraud (2017) p.269, with a reference to CA Paris, 14 December 2000, *SA Lapeyre et autres v. Sauvage*, Rev. Arb. 2001, pp.805-810, confirmed Cour de Cassation Com., 9 July 2002, No. 01-01750.

146 See section 2.1.

147 For further reading, see, *i.a.*, Seraglini & Ortscheidt (2013) pp.856-863.

148 ("*Par convention spéciale, les parties peuvent à tout moment renoncer expressément au recours en annulation.*").

149 Namely, in domestic system, see Art. 1491 of the CCP.

150 See Scherer, *The fate of parties' agreements on judicial review of awards: a comparative and normative analysis of party-autonomy at the post-award stage* (2016) p.441. The rule remain unchanged under Art. 35(6) of the (draft) 2021 ICC Rules.

French law does not limit the parties' right to waive an action to set aside."[151] Importantly, contracting out of the setting-aside mechanism will not entail that the defensive mechanism at the enforcement stage will also be foreclosed.[152] Put differently, if the (international) award that was rendered in France consequently is to be enforced in France, the resisting party will be able to invoke the same grounds as they would have in the setting-aside procedure when appealing the enforcement order. The time limits to appeal are similar to the ones of the setting-aside proceedings, namely "*one month following notification of the award bearing the enforcement order*"[153] or three months when a foreign party is involved.[154]

6 Application of the excess of mandate ground to selected decisions of the arbitral tribunal

The previous sections aimed at introducing a (working) definition of the arbitral tribunal's mandate and at explaining the key elements limiting the possible scope of the mandate. Briefly speaking, the analysis above stresses the importance of contractual limitations that are directly relevant for the tribunal's responsibility to resolve the dispute.[155] In turn, it is necessary to test what categories of the tribunal's decisions may amount to being undertaken in excess of the mandate. For the purpose of this exercise, different types of decisions have been catalogued. Therefore, the excess of mandate challenge analysis will be applied to decisions on claims (section 6.1), remedies (section 6.3) and other decisions accessory to the parties' main submissions (section 6.4). At the same time, reflections on the process of application of law will be offered (section 6.2).

6.1 Decisions on parties' claims

Claims that are brought by the parties outline the tribunal's mandate.[156] They may have a different source, however. Generally, one of the most obvious ones is the contract to which

151 Gaillard, *France Adopts New Law on Arbitration* (2011) p.2; Clay, *Code de l'arbitrage commenté* (2015) p.227.

152 Carducci, *The Arbitration Reform in France: Domestic and International Arbitration Law* (2012) p.155 ("*[i]f the parties have expressly waived their right to file a recours en annulation against the award, they may have instead filed an appeal against the court's ordonnance d'exequatur of the award.*").

153 Art. 1522(3) of the CCP ("*L'appel est formé dans le délai d'un mois à compter de la notification de la sentence revêtue de l'exequatur.*").

154 See Bensaude (2015) p.1175. Also Derains & Kiffer, *National Report for France* (2013) VII(2)(B)(b) ("*If foreign parties are involved, the time limit is increased by two months by virtue of Art. 643(2) CCP.*").

155 See sections 4.1 and 4.2.

156 See sections 5.4 and 4.2.

an agreement to arbitrate applies. As a result, a contract (for example its infringement) may be a reason for bringing contractual claims (section 6.1.1) or counterclaims (section 6.1.2). The situation may get more complicated when claims are based on torts (section 6.1.4) or a set-off (based either on a contract or on tort) is sought (section 6.1.3). Some difficulties may arise also in cases where new claims (or counterclaims) are submitted (section 6.1.5) and when some claims (or counterclaims) are left unresolved (section 6.1.6). Under this section it will be reviewed whether a tribunal exceeds its mandate while rendering a decision on a specific claim, or more explicitly if the tribunal is allowed to address specific categories of claims depending on their source.

6.1.1 Decision on contractual claims

A contractual claim is perhaps the most basic demand that can be sought by a claimant.[157] In the simple scenario where a buyer and a seller conclude a contract of sale (including an arbitration clause) and the buyer fails to pay, it is most likely that the seller will file a claim based on a contractual obligation for payment. In principle, the resolution of contractual claims is the underlying reason why an agreement to arbitrate is introduced in the first place. As such, it is possible that the tribunal's decision on a contractual claim is challenged (albeit unlikely to be successful) under the excess of mandate ground for setting aside. There are three potential ways to challenge the tribunal's decision on contractual claims, which arguably fit into the definition of excess of mandate. The first is a classic example of the excess of mandate, namely the challenge of the tribunal's decision that goes beyond the scope of the parties' requests.[158] The second deals with the requalification of the claim by the arbitrators. The third refers to the challenge against the fact that the tribunal has awarded claims as requested (by the parties) which did not, however, conform to the scope of the initial agreement to arbitrate.

The first notion, namely the *ultra* (or *extra*) *petita* notion requires, by and large, to compare the request sought by a party with the decision by the tribunal on that request. If the latter is somewhat larger than or different from the former, then the tribunal exceeds its mandate. For the purpose of this section, however, the reflections are limited to the *basis* of the claim, therefore a contract (and not, for example, the amount of damages granted).

157 The distinction is made between claims and counterclaims. On the one hand, claims are always introduced initially by the claimant at the outset of the dispute. Counterclaims, on the other hand, are usually brought by the respondent (it may so happen that the claimant also submits counterclaims as a response to the respondent's counterclaims). Since both types of claims are considered as legally independent they will be discussed separately. Most of the analysis of this section, however, will be equally applicable to counterclaims. For further reading, see also sections 6.1.2 and 6.1.4-6.1.6 (including *infra petita* considerations).

158 Either in the form of *ultra* or *extra petita*. See section 5.4. For further reading on parties' submissions, see section 4.2.

The second hypothetical concerns the scenario where the tribunal requalifies the basis for the claim.[159] For example, if claimant requests the tribunal to declare the contract avoided because of non-payment, but the tribunal finds that the contract is avoided because of *force majeure*,[160] it may be sensible to scrutinize the award for the excess of mandate challenge.[161] That being said, one should consider three scenarios: (i) the tribunal chooses one of the legal theories presented by the parties, (ii) the tribunal requalifies the basis for the claim on its own motion, or (iii) the tribunal aims to give sense to claimant's claims that are vague or ambiguous.

The tribunal, in principle, does not exceed its mandate when claimant in its request introduces a few alternatives (or independent) grounds for its claim. In this instance, it is reasonable to conclude that the tribunal's mandate is shaped by all bases on which claimant's case is brought and it is up to the tribunal to choose one (if any). At all times, however, the parties' requests are subject to restrictions prescribed in the agreement to arbitrate. Therefore, it may so happen that some of the (alternative) claims fall outside the scope of the initial agreement to arbitrate and the tribunal is unable to decide on the issue if its jurisdiction in this respect is challenged by the respondent.[162]

Requalification of the (basis of the) claim on the tribunal's own motion might be considered as an excess of mandate violation because the tribunal does not act on the basis of the request. Rather, it exercises independent legal research that would justify granting the relief sought.[163] Consequently, the tribunal effectively advocates for the position of claimant rather than acts as a neutral adjudicator. In practice, however, the circumstances of the violation may not be as obvious. Instead of surprising parties with a requalification of the claim on the face of the award,[164] it is more likely that the tribunal would invite the

159 Requalification may take place either from one contractual ground to another or from a contractual basis to a non-contractual one (*e.g.* torts or unjust enrichment).

160 For example, when the debtor is excused because of economic sanctions.

161 Another example is requalifying the claim from a contractual one to a non-contractual one. One could imagine that a Memorandum of Understanding includes a penalty clause, which is triggered when a party fails to conclude certain contracts. When a dispute arises, the claimant brings a claim based on a penalty clause. Despite the claim, the tribunal grants a request on the basis of the failure to negotiate in good faith. For further reading on the tribunal's decision based on pre-contractual liability, see also section 6.1.4.

162 It will be discussed at the later stage of this section (section 6.1.1).

163 By and large, this issue will be related to the issue of *iura novit arbiter*, which will be discussed elsewhere. See section 6.2.3.

164 See, *e.g.*, CA Paris, 25 March 2010, *Société Commercial Caribean Niquel v. Société Overseas Mining Investments Ltd*, Rev. Arb. 2011, p.442, confirmed Cour de Cassation Civ 1ère, 29 June 2011, Rev. Arb. 2011, p.678. In this case the tribunal substituted the compensation for lost profit with the (not invoked) compensation for the loss of the chance. The court found that "*this substitution is not a mere method for evaluating the damage, but modifies the basis for compensation of OMI.*" (Translation after Dimolitsa, *The Raising Ex Officio of New Issues of Law* (2014) p.26). Consequently, the tribunal violated the parties' right to be heard. The commentators highlighted, however, that the tribunal's approach (*i.e.* requalification) was aimed at the efficiency of the proceedings. See Park, *Arbitration in Autumn* (2011) p.293 ("*Emphasizing procedural fairness over efficiency, the Paris Cour d'appel affirmed the parties' right to comment on new legal theories even at the*

parties for an extra round of submissions with a hint of what theories the tribunal wishes to be additionally informed on or even would request the parties to take a position on the theories introduced by the tribunal.[165] As a result, it may be difficult to show (therefore challenge) the excess of mandate, because the tribunal will be able to substantiate its conclusions on supplementary submissions. In any event, a tribunal's attempt to "improve" the qualification of claimant's claim may raise justified concerns regarding due process and equal treatment of the parties.[166]

Yet another question relates to the effect that vague or ambiguous claims have on the scope of the tribunal's mandate.[167] Although claims should accurately outline the dispute that needs to be resolved, occasionally a claimant tries to introduce claims in an ambiguous way in order to leave room for some modification at a later stage in the proceedings. Such a tactical maneuver may have consequences for the tribunal's mandate. One may assume that (similar to the first scenario above) the tribunal will ask the parties for guidance as to the exact scope of the submissions. This offers a perfect occasion for the respondent to object to any loose-end claims that it finds should not be admitted by the tribunal. It is also an opportunity for the claimant to clarify the meaning of its claims. Notwithstanding the parties' efforts to help the tribunal with explaining ambiguous claim(s) (and therefore with defining the limits to the tribunal's mandate), the tribunal will need to interpret the claims submitted. Arguably, its decision on the remaining ambiguities should not be reviewed[168] and should survive the excess of mandate challenge as long as it does not go beyond the scope of the underlying agreement to arbitrate if contested by the respondent.

---

addition of cost and delay."), Dimolitsa, *The Raising Ex Officio of New Issues of Law* (2014) pp.26-27 ("*From a pragmatic point of view, however, the attitude of the arbitrators, who apparently after due consideration of time parameters did not wish to reopen the proceedings when evaluating the damage, is understandable. Moreover, dealing with lost profit or loss of chance implies consideration of the same facts, and in both cases the underlying rules on contractual liability are the same. If the lost profit were retained as a basis of the evaluation of the damage, any compensation might be dismissed, which would be an unfair result once CCN's liability had already been accepted. Finally (and this is not the least of the present reflections, having also in mind Swiss case law), the loss of chance is a percentage of the lost profit, and the amount of compensation awarded to OMI on the basis of the loss of chance was actually lesser than the one claimed. From another point of view, it may though be said that the lost profit and the loss of chance are two different legal notions that bring into play different rules of evaluation of the damage and alter the subject matter of proof (objet de la preuve).*").

165 Allowing parties to comment on the tribunal's findings and new legal theories is of paramount importance for the well-being of the award at the post-award stage. In all cases, the parties' right to be heard needs to be respected. See Chainais (2011) pp.449-467, Giraud (2017) pp.278-280, Dimolitsa, *The Raising Ex Officio of New Issues of Law* (2014) pp.25-27.

166 These may be brought under Art. 1520(4) of the CCP. See also Art. 1510 of the CCP.

167 In this case it is in principle a claim (and not the basis for the claim) that is difficult to interpret.

168 There should be no review on the merits, see section 3.2.

Additionally, arguably, many of the problems with vague claims may be avoided in ICC arbitration once the ICC Terms of Reference are established.[169]

The second main question introduced above deals with a problem occurring when the request of a party goes beyond the initial agreement to arbitrate and the tribunal agrees to grant the request nonetheless. It should be pointed out that only the agreement to arbitrate has a consensual element where the parties *mutually* agreed to resolve their disputes in arbitration. A request of a party, conversely, is a unilateral declaration obligating the tribunal to decide on it. Since the parties' consent is *essential* for the tribunal to go forward, allowing the claim that goes beyond the parties' authorization (as introduced in the agreement to arbitrate) should (and would) be challengeable if timely contested by the respondent. Importantly, however, "*[...] the language of the clause will be critical.*"[170] It entails that broadly drafted clauses (for example institutional model clauses)[171] can be interpreted as accommodating any type of contractual claim. At the same time, meticulously formulated (narrow) clauses should effectively prohibit the tribunal from dealing with the claim that goes beyond the agreement to arbitrate.

That being said, one should note that this notion brings additional controversies with the delineation between the scope of the tribunal's jurisdiction and the mandate and, consequently, whether an award is to be challenged on the basis of excess of jurisdiction or of a mandate.[172] Occasionally it is argued that when the tribunal grants relief sought that allegedly goes beyond the scope of the agreement to arbitrate, it is acting in excess of jurisdiction and not of mandate.[173] For example, Bensaude argues that "*a tribunal that issues an award on matters falling outside the terms of a restrictive arbitration clause runs*

169 See Art. 23 of the (draft) 2021 ICC Rules, Art. 23 of the 2017 ICC Rules and Art. 23 of the 2012 ICC Rules. The question is whether the ICC Terms of Reference will be respected as a definite outline of the claims. See, for example, Loquin (2015) pp.429-430 and the case law therein, suggesting that the ICC Terms of Reference are not a definite limitation to the tribunal's adjudicative powers and as such parties may modify claims afterwards. See also Giraud (2017) pp.260-263.

170 Bensaude (2015) p.1181.

171 See, *e.g.*, the ICC Model Clause ("*All disputes arising out of or in connection with the present contract shall be finally settled under the Rules of Arbitration of the International Chamber of Commerce by one or more arbitrators appointed in accordance with the said Rules.*") or the UNCITRAL Model Clause ("*Any dispute, controversy or claim arising out of or relating to this contract, or the breach, termination or invalidity thereof, shall be settled by arbitration in accordance with the UNCITRAL Arbitration Rules*").

172 The question will be whether a challenge should be brought under Art. 1520(1) or (3) of the CCP. Arguably, this distinction may have further implications, for example, on the actions that parties should undertake to be able to rely on the objection at the post-award stage. Generally, parties should act as soon as they learn about a possible violation. See Art. 1466 of the CCP.

173 A tribunal may face this type of critique particularly in a multi-contract scenario, where different claims refer to different contractual relationships between the parties. An extra layer of difficulties is added when different contracts include different dispute resolution mechanisms. These instances will be discussed further in the following sections (see section 6.1.2 and section 6.1.3 in particular) and will this applies to contractual claims as well.

the risk that the award will not be enforced in light of art. 1520(1)."[174] This is possibly a more convincing way to approach this specific violation by the arbitral tribunal.

Conceivably, however, there is room to argue that such a violation may trigger Article 1520(3) of the CCP as well. Even though the tribunal complies with the parties' submissions, one should not forget that under Article 1520(3) of the CCP[175] the tribunal's mandate may be violated if the tribunal fails to respect the *contractual constraints* imposed by the parties on the tribunal's adjudicative function. One may thus conclude that going beyond the agreement to arbitrate is in violation of the mandate. Although the better view is to apply Article 1520(1) of the CCP, at the end of the day, the reviewing court may step in and modify the legal basis for the challenge. As suggested by Derains and Kiffer: "*if a party fails to specify the grounds for the action or chooses the wrong grounds, the courts [in the setting-aside action] may be inclined to re-characterize the basis of the action rather than declaring it inadmissible.*"[176] Therefore, an award-debtor seeking a challenge may hope that this rather academic dispute will not affect his chances of success, if a tribunal indeed decided on a claim beyond the agreement to arbitrate.

All in all, it is rather unlikely that the tribunal's decision on a contractual claim will go beyond the scope of its mandate. Similarly, the enforcement of this type of decision will rather survive a review in terms of French international public policy (unless the contractual claims were inarbitrable from the very beginning).[177]

6.1.2 Decision on contractual counterclaims

As aptly suggested by Pavić, "*when facing a claim before an arbitral tribunal, the defendant has three options at his disposal. One is, naturally, to deny the claimant's allegations. The other, a more 'offensive' tactic, would be to submit a counterclaim, and the third, a 'defensive' option, to raise a set-off defense.*"[178] It entails that when the dispute arises and the respondent is faced with a claim, on occasion, it may be eager to countersue.[179] If it does so, the tribunal would be required to determine if it is possible to entertain such a (counter)claim. Indeed, the tribunals are often faced with counterclaims ("*la demande reconventionnelle*"), which

174 See Bensaude (2015) p.1181 with the reference to CA Paris, 22 May 2003, *SA Ess Food v. Société Caviartrade*, Rev. Arb. 2003, pp.1252-1265.

175 See the definition given by Giraud (2017) p.134 ("*La mission de l'arbitre visée à l'indice 3 désigne les éléments conventionnels participant directement de l'exercice de la mission juridictionnelle.*"). For further reading, see the discussion above in section 5.4.

176 Derains & Kiffer, *National Report for France* (2013) Chapter VII(2)(B)(a) and the case law therein. See also Seraglini & Ortscheidt (2013) p.881.

177 See section 4.3.

178 Pavić (2006) p.102.

179 Berger in Berger, *Set-off in International Economic Arbitration* (1999) p.60 notes that "*[a] counterclaim [...] is a procedural instrument to raise an independent substantive claim, i.e. a means of recourse for the respondent to take initiative and attack the claimant in order to obtain a separate judgment.*"

can be distinguished from claims brought by the claimant and which may influence the scope of the tribunal's mandate.

Essentially, a counterclaim should be recognized as an independent claim, which means that it is not affected by the withdrawal of the initial claim and should lead to a separate tribunal's decision.[180] A counterclaim "*[...] aims at [the] obtaining of its credit rather than the extinction of the mutual claim.*"[181] Further, the value of a counterclaim can be higher than the initial claim.[182] That being said, it should be noted that the findings of the previous section will be applicable to counterclaims by analogy.[183] It means, in principle, that a respondent should be able to bring contractual counterclaims in the same way as a claimant is able to bring its claims. The situation gets slightly more complicated, however, in a multi-contract matrix.

When several contractual ties bind the parties, one should reflect on a number of paradigms, namely whether a counterclaim arises out of (i) the same contract, (ii) different contracts,[184] or (iii) an extra-contractual relationship between the parties. Since the third instance[185] is discussed elsewhere, only the first two will be addressed at this point.

Generally, if one considers that parties in arbitration should have equal rights, then contractual counterclaims arising out of the same contract as the initial contractual claim should fit comfortably within the scope of the agreement to arbitrate.[186] Arguably, therefore, a contractual counterclaim (arising out of the same contract) should be considered as nothing else than any other contractual claim (apart from being brought by the respondent). Consequently, for the purpose of the research at hand, the counterclaim will share all the characteristics of contractual claims as explained above[187] and a tribunal's decision on contractual counterclaims arising out of the same contract should survive the excess of mandate challenge.

The extension of the agreement to arbitrate to related contracts will also be generally possible based on the theory of "group of contracts".[188] What will be therefore tested therein is the economic link between the contracts. As reflected by Leboulanger: "*[i]n many cases, the different kinds of agreements seem to give rise to an indivisible transaction, an economical*

180 Conversely to set-off. See section 6.1.3.

181 Fortún (2010) p.454.

182 Pryles & Waincymer, *Multiple Claims in Arbitration Between the Same Parties* (2009) p.448. For further reading, see also, *i.a.*, Karrer, *Jurisdiction on set-off defences and counterclaims* (2001), Pavić (2006).

183 See section 6.1.1.

184 This can be complicated further if each contract includes different dispute resolution mechanisms.

185 See section 6.1.4.

186 See Pryles & Waincymer, *Multiple Claims in Arbitration Between the Same Parties* (2009) p.449 ("*It is the connection to the contract and not who makes the claim that matters [...]*").

187 See section 6.1.1.

188 The "group of contracts" theory has been particularly developed in France. For further reading, see, *i.a.*, Leboulanger (1996) pp.43-97, Mantilla Serrano (2010) pp.19-22. See also Cour de Cassation Civ 1ère, 27 March 2007, *Alcatel Business Systems (ABS) v. société Amkor Technology et autres*, Rev. Arb. 2007, p.785.

and operational unit "hidden" behind a multi-contract façade, that actually amounts to one fundamental single relationship."[189] Consequently, it is likely that the parties' underlying intention was to accommodate all possible claims arising out of their economic transaction, which possibly contains more than one contractual relation. Put differently, if the contracts are interrelated, it may be sensible to treat them as a single legal relationship.[190] It would be especially the case if parties decided to draft their agreement to arbitrate in broad terms (containing the wording such as "*any dispute arising out of or in connection with this contract*" or the like).

French case law demonstrates, for example, that

> where a chain of contracts operates successive transfer of merchandise property, the arbitration agreement contained in one of these contracts is transmitted together with the contractual rights at issue, unless evidence is provided that there was reasonable ignorance of the arbitration clause on the part of the party against whom that clause is invoked.[191]

At the same time, however, it has been observed that "*[...] an award may be found unenforceable under art. 1520(1) where an arbitral tribunal settles in a single arbitration a dispute concerning two separate contracts that respectively contain different arbitration clauses providing for arbitration at different seats.*"[192] Even in case of the different dispute resolution mechanisms, however, it might occasionally be reasonable to accept both claims and counterclaims notwithstanding conflicting dispute resolution regimes.[193]

One should conclude that the French courts will always try to give effect to the parties' initial intent revealed in the agreement to arbitrate. It means that parties should draw up their agreement to arbitrate with care, especially if they intend to settle only a narrow category of disputes in arbitration. If the agreement to arbitrate is broad and contractual

---

189 Leboulanger (1996) p.46.

190 See, *i.a.*, Leboulanger (1996) pp.43-97.

191 Bensaude (2015) p.1180, with a reference to Cour de Cassation Civ 1ère, 27 March 2007, *Alcatel Business Systems (ABS) v. Société Amkor Technology et autres*, Rev. Arb. 2007, p.785. See also Clay, *Code de l'arbitrage commenté* (2015) pp.184-185, Carducci, *The Arbitration Reform in France: Domestic and International Arbitration Law* (2012) p.151.

192 Bensaude (2015) p.1181, with a reference to CA Paris, 16 November 2006, *Société Empresa de Telecomunicaciones de Cuba SA v. SA Telefonica Antillana et SNC Banco Nacional de Commercio Exterior*, Rev. Arb. 2008, p.109. Here again, the scope of the agreement to arbitrate, therefore a basis for the tribunal's decisional power, is addressed under Art. 1520(1) of the CCP. Taking into account the definition of the mandate for the purposes of Art. 1520(3) of the CCP (see section 5.4), arguably, the scope may be also addressed under Art. 1520(3) of the CCP. For the arguments, see section 6.1.1.

193 For the arguments favoring a tribunal's jurisdiction over counterclaims even in cases of conflicting dispute resolution mechanisms, see Karrer, *Jurisdiction on set-off defences and counterclaims* (2001) pp.177-178.

counterclaims are properly submitted, the tribunal will not exceed its mandate when deciding on respondent's claims, even when those are based on a separate contract.

6.1.3 Decision on set-off

Although the notion of set-off might be problematic in international commercial arbitration,[194] it seems that nowadays a broad recognition of the set-off as a defensive tool has been established.[195] The set-off as discussed under this section will, in principle, entail the notion of "*compensation légale*".[196] Mourre succinctly observes that "*[s]et-off is a defence to the whole or a portion of a claim based on a defendant's claim to money which entails the mutual extinction of both claims, in full or in part.*"[197] Consequently, in order to successfully apply a set-off defense, the parties' obligations need to be mutual, of the same kind, due and payable and certain.[198] Moreover, set-offs may not exceed the value of the original claim (thus on which it is dependent), which means that "*contrary to a counterclaim, the respondent can recover nothing for himself.*"[199] It also entails that "*[...] there is no need for separate awards on claim and set-off defence. The other corollary of that is that if the claim is not made out or is withdrawn, there is no need to adjudicate upon the set-off.*"[200] Finally (and importantly), it should be noted that for the purpose of this study, set-off would be considered as a party's substantive right (*compensation légale*), thus a mechanism of a substantive rather than of a procedural nature.[201] The outstanding question herein is whether (and if so, how) the tribunal exceeds its mandate when granting set-off. This

194 See Pryles & Waincymer, *Multiple Claims in Arbitration Between the Same Parties* (2009) p.448.

195 See, *e.g.*, Pryles & Waincymer, *Multiple Claims in Arbitration Between the Same Parties* (2009) p.453, Berger, *Set-off in International Economic Arbitration* (1999) p.60 ("*It can be used only 'as a shield not as a sword"*).

196 In the French system an additional mechanism of *compensation judiciaire* exists. It has been aptly described as "*a procedural mechanism, which requires a judge to declare the set-off; in other words proceedings must be brought. Where the debts are connected (for example, arise out of the same contract) the judge is obliged to declare the set-off. Where the debts are not connected the judge has a discretion to declare the set-off. If he does, he will have jurisdiction to hear the set-off claim as an exception to the usual jurisdictional rules.*" See Rogers (2006) pp.131-132. In addition, parties may also agree to include contractual set-off ("compensation conventionelle") provisions in their contract. For further reading, see also Pichonnaz & Gullifer (2014) pp.28-30.

197 Mourre, *The Set-off Paradox in International Arbitration* (2008) p.387.

198 See Rodner (2011) p.553 and pp.554-557. Similarly, *i.a.* Mourre, *The Set-off Paradox in International Arbitration* (2008) pp.387-388, Schöll (2006) p.99.

199 Berger, *Set-off in International Economic Arbitration* (1999) p.60. Similarly, Pryles & Waincymer, *Multiple Claims in Arbitration Between the Same Parties* (2009) pp.453-454.

200 Pryles & Waincymer, *Multiple Claims in Arbitration Between the Same Parties* (2009) p.454.

201 Berger, *Set-off in International Economic Arbitration* (1999) p.72. Rules applicable to set-off may differ depending on the jurisdiction. Sometimes it is perceived as a procedural tool (*e.g.* the English concept of statutory set-off), otherwise it constitutes the substantive right of the party (*e.g.* the French concept of *compensation légale*). For further reading, see, *e.g.* Scherer, *The Award and the Courts, Set-Off in International Arbitration* (2015) pp.455-456.

should be analyzed particularly (i) in the multi-contract scenario[202] and (ii) in the case of setting-off the claim without a party's request.

Before going further into details, in principle, the problems that an international arbitral tribunal may encounter with regard to set-off are related mainly to its jurisdiction or determination of applicable law (and not the excess of mandate).[203] Therefore, these issues do not immediately fit within the scope of the inquiry at hand. As pointed out above, objections regarding the alleged excess of the scope of the agreement to arbitrate are usually well suited to the challenge of the tribunal's jurisdiction (thus the challenge under Article 1520(1) of the CCP). At the same time, however, they may also fit the excess of mandate challenge. Possibly the best and most commonly used solution for the award-debtor is to invoke the excess of jurisdiction challenge with a conditional challenge of the mandate.[204] That being said, one should briefly reflect on set-offs arising out of a multi-contract situation and on how it impacts the tribunal's mandate.

When the set-off is based on a different contract than the initial claim, two main hypotheticals are possible: (i) only the contract from which the initial claims stem from has an arbitration clause or (ii) both contracts have dispute resolution clauses. This multi-contractual puzzle has already been discussed in the context of contractual counterclaims and those considerations generally apply here as well.[205] Therefore, the idea of single economic transaction and the theory of the "group of contracts" will be relevant.[206] The notion of set-off, however, adds another twist to it. In other words, although it is true that the expression of the common intention of the parties is essential, it is equally important to remember that set-off constitutes a substantive defense against the initial claim brought. Therefore, it should, in principle, be possible to include set-off claims, even if the set-off arises out of a different contract. One should bear in mind that

> [b]eing a substantive defence which denies the existence of the claim, the set-off has the same quality as any other substantive defence. The tribunal should therefore be authorized to decide on all defences which are raised against the claim ('le juge de l'action est le juge de l'exception'), and consequently on the merits of the set-off.[207]

202 In essence, there should be no doubt that set-off based on the same contract as the initial claim should be granted.

203 See, *e.g.* Scherer, *The Award and the Courts, Set-Off in International Arbitration* (2015), Rodner (2011), Berger, *Set-off in International Economic Arbitration* (1999).

204 The intertwinement between both challenges has been addressed above, see section 6.1.1.

205 See section 6.1.2.

206 See section 6.1.2. See also Pryles & Waincymer, *Multiple Claims in Arbitration Between the Same Parties* (2009) p.491.

207 Berger, *Set-off in International Economic Arbitration* (1999) pp.72-73.

That being said, it is necessary to be cautious with general conclusions. Although "*[t]he extension of jurisdiction to the defense of setoff, does not extend the jurisdiction to other matters arising out of the related contracts*",[208] allowing for set-off in cases where two contracts include dispute resolution clauses is a delicate matter. It is so, because one may reasonably conclude that two resolution clauses entail that parties intended to introduce separate mechanisms for each of the contracts. Indeed, it would be particularly true when the dispute resolution clauses are different (for example, an arbitration clause and a choice of court clause).[209]

Nonetheless, Karrer suggests that

> set-off should be possible pending an arbitration even if the obligation that is used for the set-off is not subject to the arbitration agreement under which the first obligation is sought to be enforced, and even if the party setting off could have brought it as a claim only before a different arbitral tribunal or a state court as provided in the agreement from which it arises.[210]

He justifies his opinion arguing that (amongst other things) "*[c]ontracts are primarily designed to prevent disputes or to resolve them amicably, and exercising a right to set-off is a perfectly acceptable way to extinguish obligations.*"[211] Arguably, his argument is more convincing in the context of (or against) the excess of mandate challenge. As explained above, a tribunal's mandate, primarily, gives the parties the expectation that the disputes between them will be resolved. In this context, it is a more than sensible solution to admit set-off as a way of speeding up the process of resolving the conflicts between parties. Ultimately, the tribunal's mandate is to resolve the dispute between parties and, by acting on set-offs, the tribunal will precisely fulfill its adjudicative function.[212] That being said, it

---

208 Rodner (2011) p.562.

209 Even where both contracts call for the same dispute resolution mechanism (*e.g.* an ICC arbitration), parties may have intended to appoint different arbitrators for different disputes.

210 Karrer, *Jurisdiction on set-off defences and counterclaims* (2001) p.177.

211 Karrer, *Jurisdiction on set-off defences and counterclaims* (2001) p.177.

212 See also Pichonnaz & Gullifer (2014) p.59 ("*[...] the best practice is for an arbitral tribunal also to adjudicate the cross-claim, despite the absence of [an] original jurisdiction. One reason is linked to the efficiency of arbitral proceedings but, moreover, it takes into account the fact that refusing to take account of a set-off of a substantive nature, which has possibly already been triggered outside of court proceedings, places too much weight on the right of the cross-debtor to have his arguments heard by the judge who would have had jurisdiction. By relying on set-off, the cross-creditor has, at least de facto, renounced the original jurisdiction. Finally, an arbitral tribunal avoids the schizophrenic situation of rendering an award which is already inadequate as a matter of substantive law, since the main claim may have already been reduced by the effect of (extrajudicial) set-off.*").

is necessary to add that the tribunal's decision will not be ironclad in the context of the potential excess of jurisdiction challenge.[213]

The second point concerns the eventuality of a set-off deduction from the initial claim made by a tribunal *ex officio*. This is, of course, an obvious example of *extra petita* and thus excess of mandate.[214] Arguably, however, the situation may change when the tribunal is given *amiable composition* authority or if the tribunal finds that in specific circumstances set-off operates *ipso iure*.[215] In these instances it is possible to conclude that set-off is inherently entwined with providing a just determination of a dispute. If this argument is accepted, the tribunal's decision would survive the challenge.

6.1.4 Decision on claims/counterclaims based on torts or pre-contractual liability

Although most of the disputed claims are contractual, it does not exclude the possibility that also *non*-contractual liability may cause a party to bring a claim (or counterclaim) in arbitration. Nowadays there is a growing acceptance that non-contractual claims would fit comfortably within the scope of the broad agreement to arbitrate. As pointed out by Bensaude, "*[a] broadly worded clause will generally be found to cover both contract and tort claims arising out of or in connection with the contract at issue.*"[216] Therefore, the principal test therein would be that they are sufficiently connected with the contract or transaction.[217] This question, however, yet again deals more with the scope of the agreement to arbitrate. Consequently, it is an issue closer related to the tribunal's jurisdiction than to its mandate. As such, it has already been addressed above and will not be dealt with again.[218]

Yet another way in which parties may be eager to attack the tribunal's decision on claims based on torts exceeding the tribunal's mandate is when the tribunal requalifies the basis for the claim from contractual to tortious.[219] This issue, however, has been also addressed above.[220] In principle, by requalifying the claim the tribunal may be found to

213 Thus under Art. 1520(1) of the CCP.

214 See also section 6.1.1.

215 In any event the tribunal should consult the parties about its findings.

216 Bensaude (2015) p.1181.

217 See for example, Poudret & Besson (2007) p.267 ("*[...] the jurisdiction of an arbitrator to rule on tort claims depends on the wording of the arbitration agreement and should ordinarily be recognised, unless such agreement is clearly confined to disputes concerning the performance of the contract. The expression "disputes resulting from the contract" is ambiguous in this respect and should be replaced by "disputes in relation to" or "in connection with the contract", which definitely allows the arbitrator to rule on tort claims.*"). Similarly, Berger, *Set-off in International Economic Arbitration* (1999) p.65 ("*This wording [i.e. 'dispute which has arisen out of or in connection with the contract'] covers not only contractual claims. Thus from this procedural standpoint, the cross-claim can also be of a tortious nature.*").

218 See sections 6.1.1 and 6.1.3.

219 Or any other non-contractual basis for a claim. Of course, it can also go the other way around, *i.e.*, a change from a non-contractual basis to a contractual one.

220 See section 6.1.1.

assist one of the parties in its inquiry and in obtaining the request sought. It means that the tribunal exposes itself to allegations of bias in helping to achieve one party's goal in arbitral proceedings against the other party's goal. As already explained, in reality, a requalification of a claim is much more subtle and most likely involves an invitation from the tribunal to the parties to discuss its suggestions. On the one hand, it can be argued that the tribunal is appointed for its expertise and its advice might be very useful (especially for example if given to both parties). Additionally, it touches upon the notion of *iura novit arbiter*[221] and the tribunal's powers to apply relevant legal mechanisms and theories to the facts and circumstances presented by the parties. On the other hand, however, if a tribunal's requalification "strengthens" the arguments of one party only, it may create an appearance of bias (especially if parties are not given sufficient opportunity to address the tribunal's changes) and violation of *principe de la contradiction*.[222] Consequently, the tribunal will no longer (properly) exercise its mandate. Instead, it will violate it.[223] Arguably, as long as the *principe de la contradiction* is preserved, the tribunal's actions will not be easily open for challenge under Article 1520(3) of the CCP.

Other conclusions, mentioned above,[224] will apply here by analogy. Therefore, (i) in cases where parties present alternative claims, the tribunal will not exceed its mandate when choosing a non-contractual cause of action rather than a contractual one, and (ii) in cases of ambiguous or vague claims, a tribunal should have a final say in interpreting them, especially if parties fail to address the ambiguity or fail to clarify their positions. It entails that parties should not be given an opportunity to object to the tribunal's interpretations at the post-award stage, provided that it decides within the scope of the agreement to arbitrate.[225]

6.1.5 Decision on new claims/counterclaims and change of claims/counterclaims

Since the arbitral tribunal's mandate is shaped by the agreement to arbitrate and is further limited by the parties' requests, reformulation of the initial parties' requests inevitably affects the limits of the mandate. Consequently, there are several issues that need to be addressed accordingly.[226] First, it is possible that a new claim/counterclaim (or a changed claim/counterclaim) goes beyond the scope of the agreement to arbitrate. This type of contention has already been addressed above.[227] Second, there is a possibility the new

221 "An arbitrator knows the law". For further reading, see section 6.2 and the literature therein.

222 See Art. 1510 and Art. 1520(4) of the CCP. See also CA Paris, 25 November 1997, *Société VRV v. Pharmachim*, Rev. Arb. 1998, p.684.

223 Arguably, however, due process violations would be better addressed under 1520(4) of the CCP.

224 Section 6.1.1.

225 It is also very well possible that the tribunal rejects the claim if it is exceedingly vague. See also section 6.1.1.

226 See also Giraud (2017) pp.256-268.

227 See sections 6.1.1 and 6.1.3. Also Giraud (2017) pp.258-260.

claim/counterclaim does not exceed the framework of the agreement to arbitrate but goes beyond the dispute initially submitted to the tribunal. Third, the question arises whether the tribunal may exceed its mandate while acting on a new, changed or late claim/counterclaim.

As pointed out by some scholars "*[...] the fact that the new claims fall within the ambit of the arbitration agreement is not necessarily sufficient. It may be contended that the new claims go beyond the dispute or difference referred to the arbitration already commenced and thereby require the commencement of a new arbitration.*"[228] The difficulties that arise from a submission of a new claim/counterclaim are related to the consensual character of the tribunal's adjudicative mission.[229] The moment in which the tribunal accepts its mandate,[230] a new contractual multiparty relationship is created. From this point in time the parties and the tribunal have defined and accepted the scope of the mandate. It further entails that the introduction of the new claim/counterclaim may disturb the balance that has been agreed upon. As it is rather undisputed that the introduction of new claims/counterclaims may alter the scope of the mandate of the arbitral tribunal, one should reflect whether a party has a power to unilaterally stretch the boundaries of the mandate initially agreed upon by all involved.[231]

In principle, it would be possible for the party to submit a new claim/counterclaim, provided that the tribunal agrees to accept it and therefore to accept alteration of the mandate.[232] It also entails that it would be rather difficult to argue successfully that the tribunal exceeded its mandate, because it went beyond what was *initially* submitted to it.[233] It would be particularly true when the initial parties' submissions or Terms of Reference as in the ICC system are drafted in a particularly broad fashion. In this way, parties may

228 Pryles & Waincymer, *Multiple Claims in Arbitration Between the Same Parties* (2009) p.470.

229 Giraud (2017) p.132 ("*Il pourrait être objecté que la modification des contours du litige par la soumission d'une demande nouvelle contredit le caractère conventionnel de la mission arbitrale.*").

230 Art. 1456(1) of the CCP.

231 Yet another question is how far the party autonomy can go to modify the tribunal's mandate. In other words, how far the tribunal's (initial) mandate may be modified by the parties' agreement during the proceedings.

232 Whether the tribunal has a power to accept new claims will be discussed immediately below.

233 See Derains & Kiffer, *National Report for France* (2013) Chapter VII(2)(B)(a)(3) ("*the mandate of the arbitrators is defined by the arbitration agreement and limited by the subject matter of the dispute as framed by the parties' claims even if the issue to be decided is not mentioned in the terms of reference. The agreement of the parties plays a predominant role.*"); also Bensaude (2015) p.1183 ("*The arbitral tribunal's substantive mission is defined by the subject matter of the parties' dispute, which is itself determined by the parties' submissions during the course of the arbitration [...]. As a consequence, claims that are not expressly set out in [the] terms of reference do not necessarily fall outside the arbitrators' mission [...].*"), with a reference to CA Paris, 29 September 2011, *M. René Scolardi et autres v. SASU Techman* Head, Rev. Arb. 2011, p.1093, Cour de cassation Civ 1ère, 20 June 2012, *Chaudronnerie Mécanique Algéroise v. Adlor Sofal Nemoneh*, No. 10-21375, and Cour de Cassation Civ 1ère, 6 March 1996, *Société Farhat Trading Company v. Société Daewoo*, Rev. Arb. 1997, p.69.

leave themselves room for the introduction of a new claim/counterclaim within the meaning of what was already submitted and thus, within the meaning of the tribunal's initial mandate.

Moreover, the tribunal will not exceed its mandate when admitting new claims. By and large, it will be able to find a power to admit late claims in the institutional rules governing the proceedings.[234] One should note, however, that the wording of each set of rules differs, which means that also the scope of the tribunal's powers to accept certain category of claims (*e.g.* claims/counterclaims/set-offs) may be different.[235] Also in *ad hoc* arbitration, the tribunal should be allowed to decide on late claims. Overall, it is most likely that the tribunal accepts new claims/counterclaims only when it finds it relevant to reach a just result as to the dispute between the parties and having in mind all the circumstances of the case.[236] Depending on the applicable procedural rules, the issue is, thus, much more one of due process than of mandate.

6.1.6 Decision not covering all claims/counterclaims

In general terms, a decision that does not address all parties' claims/counterclaims (decision *infra petita*) violates their expectations, which means that the arbitral panel can be considered to fail to comply with the mission entrusted to it. Therefore, it is necessary to reflect (i) if such a failure on the side of the tribunal meets the threshold set by Article 1520(3) of the CCP, or (ii) to the contrary, the decision is not reviewable and deserves to be *res iudicata*, thus to be finally adjudged.

An *infra petita* award would not be easily susceptible to the excess of mandate challenge under French international arbitration law.[237] As concluded by Bensaude: "*[a]wards that are infra petita do not run foul of art. 1520(3), because in such a situation, the claim may be again submitted to the tribunal.*"[238] The reference therein is given to the rule provided

234 See, *e.g.*, Art. 23(4) of the (draft) 2021 ICC Rules, Art. 23(4) of the 2017 ICC Rules, Art. 23(4) of the 2012 ICC Rules, Art. 22 of the 2010 UNCITRAL Rules, Art. 20 of the 1976 UNCITRAL Rules.

235 *Cf*, *e.g.*, Art.23(4) of the 2017 ICC Rules, Art. 22 of the 2010 UNCITRAL Rules and the powers available under Art. 22.1(i) of the 2014 LCIA Rules or Art. 22.1(i) of the 2020 LCIA Rules.

236 Arguably, if the tribunal does not allow a new claim, the issue will remain outstanding between the parties, waiting to be submitted before another tribunal.

237 Even though it can be considered as non-compliance with the mandate. See Loquin (2015) p.431 ("*L'omission de statuer n'est pas en revanche un moyen d'annulation de la sentence arbitrale et cela, même s'il est vrai, qu'en ne statuant pas sur toutes les demandes des parties, le tribunal ne respecte pas la mission qui lui a été conférée.*"). See also Giraud (2017) pp.154-156.

238 Bensaude (2015) p.1182, Racine (2016) pp.546-547 and p.590. See also, *i.a.*, CA Paris, 27 June 2002, *SA Compagnie commerciale Comecim v. Société Theobroma NV*, Rev. Arb. 2002, p.793 ("*Le recours en annulation de l'article 1502-3° NCPC ne peut être exercé contre une sentence ayant statué infra petita, les cas d'ouverture de ce recours devant s'interpréter restrictivement, d'autant plus que l'impossibilité de réunir à nouveau le tribunal arbitral pour compléter éventuellement la sentence n'est pas démontrée.*"), CA Paris, 12 September 2002, *Société Enterprise de la Céramique Sanitaire Ouest (ECO) v. Société Eurotech SPA*, Rev. Arb. 2002, p.1044 ("*L'omission de statuer sur certains chefs de demandes n'entre dans aucun des moyens d'annulation*

in Article 1485(2) of the CCP according to which: "*[...] on application of a party, the tribunal may interpret the award, rectify clerical errors and omissions, or make an additional award where it failed to rule on a claim. The arbitral tribunal shall rule after having heard the parties or having given them the opportunity to be heard.*"[239] Consequently, the first step that an aggrieved party should undertake is to refer the point that has not been decided back to the tribunal. Importantly, the tribunal may only then decide on *infra petita* and cannot reopen the case and decide all issues anew.[240]

Arguably, only when the tribunal refuses to take any action to remedy the alleged *infra petita* occurrence, may the party request the court to set the award aside. One should note, however, that "*[...], the tribunal's failure to decide upon each and every legal or factual argument raised by the parties in the course of an arbitration is not sufficient to trigger the application of art. 1520(3).*"[241] Additionally, it is likely that the tribunal's omission needs to be so grievous as to violate (French) international public policy.[242] Even if successful, it is most likely that the challenge will affect only part of the award.[243] Further, it leads to the conclusion that arbitral awards, in principle, benefit from the presumption that the arbitral mandate has been fulfilled in full. As noted by Born "*[t]he presumption is that arbitrators did not decide matters infra petita, but rather decided all the disputes submitted to them (including by impliedly rejecting claims and defenses not specifically addressed)*".[244]

The presumption that the tribunal's mandate has been completed entails that *all* the disputes and claims of the parties have been considered and decided upon by the tribunal.

---

des articles 1502 et 1504 NCPC, l'auteur du recours n'établissant pas, au demeurant, une impossibilité de saisir à nouveau le tribunal arbitral [...]"), CA Paris, 23 June 2005, *Société British Motors et autre v. Société Bentley Motors Limited*, Rev. Arb. 2005, p.798 ("*L'infra petita ne constitue pas une cause d'annulation de la sentence mais une omission de statuer qui peut toujours être réparée.*").

239 ("*[...] À la demande d'une partie, le tribunal arbitral peut interpreter la sentence, réparer les erreurs et omissions matérielles qui l'affectent ou la completer lorqu'il a omis de statuer sur un chef de demande. Il statue après avoir entendu les parties ou celles-ci appelées.*"). The application of this rule is possible by virtue of Art. 1506 of the CCP. Perhaps, however, it would be better if the translation exposes more that, on the reading of the provision alone, the "error" and/or "omission" is substantial. Consequently, one may suggest that the provision in fact reads that: "*[...] on application of a party, the tribunal may interpret the award, rectify substantial errors and omissions which affect the award, or make an additional award where it failed to rule on one of the heads of a claim. The arbitral tribunal shall rule after having heard the parties or having given them the opportunity to be heard.*"

240 See Derains & Kiffer, *National Report for France* (2013) Chapter V(7)(A)(a): "*However, even in that case the arbitrators do not have the power to modify their decision on the issues already decided.*" The authors argue that no modification should be allowed in the context of domestic arbitration. It is argued that the same holds true in an international arbitration context. Consequently, if the tribunal failed to decide upon a substantial defense submitted, it would be, arguably, impossible to bring the case back to a tribunal and request it to adjudicate the omitted claim without revisiting its previous conclusions.

241 Bensaude (2015) p.1182, also Gaillard & Savage, *Fouchard Gaillard Goldman on International Commercial Arbitration* (1999) p.940. See also the case law referred to in fn.238.

242 For further reading, see section 4.3.

243 See also section 3.3.

244 Born, *International Commercial Arbitration* (2014) p.3294.

In fact, it will be even strengthened if the tribunal concludes its award with the magical formula "*rejecting any and all other claims*" or the like. In this case, arguably, a party that wishes to challenge the award on the excess of mandate ground will have a difficult task.

6.2 *Process of application of law by the arbitral tribunal*

The arbitral tribunal's fulfillment of its adjudicative mandate inherently entails that it will reach its decision in accordance with a certain set of legal rules. Consequently, the process of application of law by the tribunal can be broken down into a series of decisions on particular issues. First, the tribunal may need to decide what method would be appropriate to determine the applicable law (section 6.2.1) and decide on the basis of the selected law accordingly (section 6.2.2). When the applicable law is selected, the tribunal will be required to apply the selected law to the facts of the case (section 6.2.3) and carefully approach the question of the applicable mandatory rules of law (section 6.2.4). Occasionally, the tribunal may be given the additional power of rendering its decision based on equity or reached *ex aequo et bono* (section 6.2.5). It is therefore of essence, to explain in what instances (if any) the tribunal will exceed its mandate by applying these standards and when its decision is open to the Article 1520(3) challenge.

6.2.1 Decision on the method of determining applicable law

It is by far the most preferable solution for the parties to make an explicit choice of law in their contract.[245] In case of the parties' default, however, the tribunal may be required to search for an applicable law. In principle, two methods are available for arbitrators to determine the applicable law: (i) a conflict of laws (private international law) analysis[246] or (ii) a direct choice of law ("*voie directe*"). Irrespective of which method the tribunal chooses, this step is an important one and may have a great impact on the outcome of the

245 There are possibly (at least) two separate choices that need to be made: (i) the choice of law applicable to the agreement to arbitrate and (ii) the choice of law applicable to the merits of the dispute. Arguably, for the purpose of the excess of mandate challenge, it is not necessary to distinguish them at this stage, because they only affect the tribunal's later decision on applicable law. The distinction may be relevant in the phase of applying the chosen law. Consequently, the law chosen to be applicable to the merits of the case may influence its outcome, whereas the law chosen to apply to the agreement to arbitrate may have an impact on the tribunal's jurisdiction (and not necessarily on the mandate).

246 When the tribunal decides to follow the conflict of laws analysis, it would be, in fact, required to explain as well why it finds specific conflict of laws rules to be applicable (for example conflict of laws rules available at the seat of arbitration) which adds yet another layer of complexity to the scenario. It falls outside the scope of the research at hand, however.

case.[247] At the same time, it is unlikely that its decision on the method of determining the applicable law is open to the excess of mandate challenge.

The challenge will have little chance of success, because French international arbitration law gives the tribunal a lot of freedom in the process of applying the law.[248] In particular, pursuant to the first paragraph of Article 1511 of the CCP, "*[t]he arbitral tribunal shall decide the dispute in accordance with the rules of law chosen by the parties or, where no such choice has been made, in accordance with the rules of law it considers appropriate.*"[249] This provision allows the tribunal to select the applicable law directly without invoking a conflict of laws analysis.[250] "*To satisfy in practice the requirements of art. 1511, the arbitral tribunal needs merely to state in the award that the rules of law selected and applied by the tribunal are 'appropriate in the circumstances'.*"[251] In addition, some of the (leading) institutional rules exempt the tribunal from undertaking a conflict of laws analysis.[252] Consequently, one may conclude that determining appropriate applicable rules of law is inherently within the scope of the tribunal's adjudicative mandate.

Arguably, the only exception where the tribunal's decision on the method of determining applicable law is exposed to a challenge is in the situation where the parties, instead of

---

247 See, *e.g.*, Craig, *The arbitrator's mission and the application of law in international commercial arbitration* (2010) p.260: "*It is certain that the arbitrator's discretion to choose the applicable law in the absence of choice by the parties gives him the widest power to influence the outcome of the case on the merits by the choice of a national law that he feels appropriate to the subject and providing a legal basis for the outcome he sees as desirable.*"

248 The question if the freedom of arbitrators using the *voie directe* approach is "absolute" (see Poudret & Besson (2007) pp.586-588 or "complete" (see Mayer, *Reflections on the International Arbitrator's Duty to Apply the Law – The Freshfields Lecture 2000* (2001) p.238) falls outside of the scope of this research. For further reading, see, *i.a.*, the discussion in Poudret & Besson (2007) pp.586-588, Gaillard & Savage, *Fouchard Gaillard Goldman on International Commercial Arbitration* (1999) pp.876-877.

249 ("*Le tribunal arbitral tranche le litige conformément aux règles de droit que les parties ont choisies ou, à défaut, conformément à celles qu'il estime appropriées.*").

250 Bensaude (2015) p.1157, Mayer, *The Laws or Rules of Law Applicable to the Merits of a Dispute and the Freedom of the Arbitrator* (2011) pp.54-55, Poudret & Besson (2007) pp.586-88.

251 Bensaude (2015) p.1157. The tribunal, however, will be still free to undertake a conflict of laws analysis, see, *e.g.*, Rouche et al. (2009) pp.144-145 ("*It often happens, however, that arbitrators, even though they have very wide discretion in the manner in which they determine the substantive law, give reasons for their decisions which reveal that they are very cautious, perhaps because they are anxious that any court called upon to order enforcement of their award should be satisfied that serious thought and research were devoted to the question. For this reason, it is not unusual for arbitrators sitting in France to take the French conflict of laws route, or to make a comparative law approach to various systems of conflict of laws, in order to ascertain common provisions; sometimes they refer, in support of their finding, to general principles of the conflict of laws which they believe exist.*").

252 See, *e.g.*, Art. 21(1) of the (draft) 2021 ICC Rules, Art. 21(1) of the 2017 ICC Rules, Art. 21(1) of the 2012 ICC Rules, Art. 35(1) of the 2010 UNCITRAL Rules, Art. 17(1) of the 1998 ICC Rules. See, however, Art. 33(1) of the 1976 UNCITRAL Rules, which requires this additional step of conflict of laws analysis when determining the applicable law.

including a choice of law clause, opt for selecting (only) applicable conflict of laws rules.[253] Such a choice, similarly to the choice of applicable law,[254] should be respected by the tribunal. Thus, if the tribunal does not follow the parties' choice (of applicable conflict of laws rules), but rather applies a different set of (conflict of laws) rules,[255] its decision might be considered to be in the excess of mandate conferred upon it in the same way as if it does not follow the parties' choice of law.[256] Nonetheless, the wrong application of the chosen a conflict of laws rules is not reviewable.[257]

6.2.2 Decision on applicable law

As already discussed in the previous section, it is preferred that parties designate which law is to be applied to the merits of the dispute.[258] In fact, in the context of the French international arbitration regime, this statement needs to be qualified to the extent that the explicit choice of the parties does not only entail the choice of *law* but also the choice of *rules of law*. It will be discussed further in this section. But first, one should reflect on the underlying question, *i.e.* when does the tribunal exceed its power (i) when a choice of law[259] exists and (ii) in the absence of any choice by the parties.

The disregard of the parties' choice of law to be applied would, in general, meet the requirements of invoking the excess of mandate challenge, because it directly violates contractual constraints imposed on the tribunal's adjudicative powers.[260] It is necessary to

253 See also Mayer, *The Laws or Rules of Law Applicable to the Merits of a Dispute and the Freedom of the Arbitrator* (2011) p.58.

254 Bensaude (2015) p.1157 ("*Where the parties have agreed on rules of law to govern the merits of their dispute, the arbitral tribunal must apply those rules of law in its awards*").

255 Or if it opts for the *voie direct* approach.

256 See also section 6.2.2.

257 See section 3.2. See also Derains & Kiffer, *National Report for France* (2013) Chapter VII(2)(B)(a)(3) ("*However, an error of law in applying the law agreed upon by the parties is not seen as a breach of the arbitrator's mandate.*").

258 See section 6.2.1. As highlighted in the previous section (see fn.245), there are two outstanding questions with regard to the applicable law, namely (i) what law applies to the agreement to arbitrate and (ii) what law applies to the merits of the case. The first question, however, relates more to the jurisdiction of the tribunal and need not to be discussed further at the moment. As such it will be reviewable under Art. 1520(1) of the CCP. Notably, Bensaude observes that "*when evaluating an appeal or a request for setting aside based on [Art.] 1520(1), the Court of Appeal will not refer to any national law other than the mandatory rules of French law and French international public policy.*" For further reading, see Bensaude (2015) pp.1179-1180. Additionally, "*under French international arbitration law, the law chosen by the parties to apply to the merits of a dispute is no indication of a choice of law to govern either the arbitration agreement or procedure, unless this has been expressly agreed upon by the parties*" See Bensaude (2015) pp.1156-1157, with a reference to Cour de Cassation Civ 1ère, 10 May 1988, *Wasteels v. Société Ampafrance*, Rev. Arb. 1989, p.51. On the law applicable to the agreement to arbitrate in general, see also Loquin (2015) pp.127-147.

259 The term "choice of law" here includes both parties' choice of law and their choice of rules of law.

260 Bensaude (2015) p.1157 ("*Where the parties have agreed on rules of law to govern the merits of their dispute, the arbitral tribunal must apply those rules of law in its awards.*"), Loquin (2015) p.437 ("*Lorsque les parties ont choisi les règles de droit applicables au litige conformément à l'article 1511 CPC, la mission du tribunal*

distinguish, however, the scenario where parties expressly designate a specific law to govern their contract and one where their choice is implied. The latter is more problematic, since it is feasible that parties will submit contradicting statements, with respect to which law they intended to be applicable.[261] Consequently, it would be up to the tribunal to examine all relevant circumstances and decide which law has been impliedly chosen. Since contractual interpretation is one of the essential prerogatives of the arbitral tribunal, it will enjoy a general protection of the "no review on the merits" principle.[262] Therefore, in cases where the choice of law is (allegedly) implied, but parties at the moment of the dispute are not in agreement (or not anymore) of what the choice really was, the tribunal's decision on applicable law would be likely to survive the challenge at the post-award stage.[263]

The tribunal's decision should also stand when parties did not choose any law to govern the contract. In this instance, it is likely (again) that they will submit opposite views as to which law should apply and the tribunal will have to determine which law is "appropriate".[264] More often than not, it will entail that the tribunal will follow one of the parties' suggestions. Occasionally, however, the tribunal may wish to apply the law[265] that has not been introduced by the parties. If that happens it is important that the tribunal consults the parties and gives them an opportunity to address its new idea. As explained by Bensaude: "*[s]hould the arbitral tribunal consider that it may be appropriate to apply rules of law that have not been suggested by any party, the tribunal must first request the parties' comments on such rules of law before taking a decision, in order to comply with the requirements of due process [...].*"[266] In case of such a violation, however, a party might be

---

arbitral est d'appliquer au litige ces règles. La non-application du droit choisi est considérée par la jurisprudence comme une violation de sa mission par le tribunal arbitral."). See also Derains & Kiffer, *National Report for France* (2013) Chapter VII(2)(B)(a)(3) ("*The same is true for the parties' choice of the applicable substantive law. Respect for this choice is also considered part of the arbitrator's mandate.*"). Mayer, *The Laws or Rules of Law Applicable to the Merits of a Dispute and the Freedom of the Arbitrator* (2011) p.48 ("*Under French law, if the arbitrator [...] applies a law different from that which was agreed upon in the terms of reference, the arbitrator's award could either be annulled or unrecognized for failure to conform to the mission of the arbitrator [...]*"). See, however, CA Paris, 10 March 1988, *Société Crocodile Tourist Project Company (Egypte) v. Aubert, ès qual. et autres*, Rev. Arb. 1989, p.269 and CA Paris, 29 April 2003, *SA Impregilo v. Secrétariat aux communications et transports maritimes de la Jamahiriya arabe libyenne populaire et socialiste*, Rev. Arb. 2004, p.130.

261 It would be the same case, when an express choice exists but its validity or scope is contested by one of the parties. See Mayer, *The Laws or Rules of Law Applicable to the Merits of a Dispute and the Freedom of the Arbitrator* (2011) pp.48-49. See also Mayer, *La liberté de l'arbitre* (2013) pp.350-351.

262 See section 3.2. Also *e.g.* Loquin (2015) p.437 ("*En revanche, le principe de non révision exclut le contrôle de la bonne application des règles de droit choisies par le parties.*").

263 If, however, both parties plead their case on the basis of the same law then the tribunal should also not deviate from it.

264 Of course, if the parties reach an agreement as to which law should apply, this choice should bind the tribunal.

265 Or rules of law pursuant to Art. 1511(1) of the CCP. It will be discussed below under this heading.

266 Bensaude (2015) p.1157.

better suited with an Article 1520(4) challenge which directly addresses due process issues. "*[U]ltimately, the arbitrators' choice of law must appear neither partial nor arbitrary.*"[267]

Finally, one should highlight that the French international arbitration regime explicitly grants the possibility *to decide the dispute in accordance with the rules of law.*[268] Such a wording of a statutory fallback mechanism is truly remarkable, because it gives a great flexibility to opt not only for national laws but also for a-national rules of law. It further means that, for example, rules of the enigmatic *lex mercatoria* or of the UNIDROIT Principles may become a perfectly valid choice.[269] In addition, one cannot stress enough that not only parties may choose a non-national set of rules, but also the tribunal is able to select these rules if it considers them appropriate. In turn, the tribunal has a great power in designating which rules should apply and, therefore, one may conclude that the tribunal's decision on applicable law will not be exposed to the Article 1520(3) challenge.

6.2.3 Ascertaining the content of applicable law by the arbitral tribunal

In principle, the essential element of fulfilling the tribunal's mandate is to interpret the contract between the parties and the legal issues surrounding their dispute. Consequently, the decision-making process undertaken by the tribunal, in most instances, entails the application of law and determination of its content.[270] Considering, therefore, that the process of applying the law to the facts of the case is inherent to the exercise of the arbitral tribunal's mandate,[271] one should reflect if it is exposed to the challenge of Article 1520(3) of the CCP (excess of mandate), especially in cases where the tribunal is considering (i) to rely on its own legal knowledge and research or (ii) to seek an equitable solution.

Regarding the first point, one should reflect whether the tribunal's mandate to apply the law[272] is unfettered (*e.g.*, by relying on the principle *iura novit arbiter*) or limited to

---

267 Mayer, *The Laws or Rules of Law Applicable to the Merits of a Dispute and the Freedom of the Arbitrator* (2011) p.57.

268 Art. 1511(1) of the CCP.

269 See, *e.g.*, Bensaude (2015) p.1157, Audit (2014) p.10. See also CA Paris, 25 February 2020, *Prakash Steelage Ltd v. Uzuc SA*, n°17/18001.

270 "Law" should be, again, understood as both (applicable) national law and (applicable) rules of law. See also section 6.2.2. In the alternative, the tribunal would have to decide on its own sense of justice and act as *amiable compositeur* (see section 6.2.5, where this will be discussed further). Theoretically other solutions (such as flipping the coin) are also possible, albeit unlikely.

271 See also section 4.

272 Yet another question is whether ascertaining the content of the applicable law is the tribunal's duty. For further reading, see CA Paris, 25 November 1997, *Société VRV v. Pharmachim*, Rev. Arb. 1998, p.684 (where the court held that if the dispute is to be decided in accordance with French substantive law, the tribunal is required to ascertain the content of the law). See also Giovanni (2010) p.500, Dimolitsa, *The equivocal power of the arbitrators to introduce ex officio new issues of law* (2009) p.434. Arguably, it falls outside the scope of the research at hand, however. Yet, if one considers that "*the mission of the arbitrator defines both his duties and powers*" (see fn.114), there is room for the argument that failing to ascertain the content of the applicable law amounts to a failure to comply with the tribunal's mandate. At the same time, however,

legal theories raised by the parties only.[273] The tribunal should be, in principle, allowed to bring its own legal findings to the parties. Dimolitsa is correct in saying that the discretion to introduce new issues of law (*i.e.* new legal theories)

> is the normal consequence of the power to ascertain the law and falls within the legitimate freedom of the arbitrator, as a judge, in applying law and proceeding to the fair resolution of the dispute. It can only be excluded by an explicit agreement of the parties limiting the arbitrators' jurisdictional mission to the legal arguments they will invoke.[274]

At the same time, it is to be noted that new legal theories should not come as a surprise to the parties.[275] "*Providing an opportunity for the litigants to comment on the law remains vital both to the arbitrator getting it right and to the parties' sense of being treated justly.*"[276] Moreover, the newly introduced theories should not lead to granting the request beyond what was sought (a classic case of *ultra petita*).[277]

Pursuant to Article 1520(3) of the CCP, as mentioned before, the award may be set aside if "*the arbitral tribunal ruled without complying with the mandate conferred upon it.*" Consequently, as to the second point, if one considers that the mandate conferred on

---

it will entail the review of the merits of the tribunal's decision and will effectively free the parties from educating the tribunal as to the content of the applicable law. That being said, the tribunal should know the applicable public policy rules that might affect the fate of the award at the post-award stage. See further section 6.2.4.

273 In addition, one may distinguish if the tribunal adds new legal theories *ex officio* or requalifies already existing ones (*i.e.* the ones submitted by the parties). For further reading on requalification, see, *i.a.*, Giraud (2017) pp.277-282.

274 Dimolitsa, *The equivocal power of the arbitrators to introduce ex officio new issues of law* (2009) p.431. See also Giraud (2017) p.282 ("*Par ailleurs, l'arbitre voit sa liberté de relever d'office des moyens de droit limitée par la volonté des parties. Ainsi, dans l'hypothèse où les parties ont prévu que l'arbitre ne puisse appliquer d'autres règles de droit que celles qu'elles ont limitativement énumérées, l'arbitre viole sa mission s'il applique une règle non autorisée.*").

275 ILA, *ILA Report on Ascertaining the Contents of the Applicable Law in International Commercial Arbitration* (2008) p.20. See also Cour de Cassation Civ 1ère, 14 March 2006, *Conselho Nacional de Carregadores v. Charasse Société Groupe Antoine Tabet v. République du Congo*, Rev. Arb. 2006, p.653.

276 Park, *The Predictability Paradox - Arbitrators and Applicable Law* (2014) p.64, see also Dimolitsa, *The Raising Ex Officio of New Issues of Law* (2014) p.25 ("*[...] the French Courts, they also welcome the arbitrators' freedom to raise ex officio new issues of law or to attribute another legal qualification to the facts of the case, without however referring to the maxim jura novit curia. They require conversely, always – irrespective of any criterium of surprise for the parties – the rigorous respect of the principle audi alteram partem (principe de la contradiction) 'in such a way that nothing from what served as a ground of the tribunal's decision has escaped the debate of the parties'.*"). See also Giraud (2017) pp.277-282 for a discussion on the requalification of the legal basis for the claim.

277 Giovanni (2010) p.497 ("*There is unanimous consent among ordinary courts that the international arbitrator is bound by the prayers for relief set forth by the parties*"). Dimolitsa, *The equivocal power of the arbitrators to introduce ex officio new issues of law* (2009) p.438. See also section 4 and section 6.1.1 on the general analysis as to a decision granting claim (including requalification).

a tribunal requires the application of the law, it would be fair to conclude that the tribunal's decision *not* based on law should be open for a challenge.[278] This would be the case when the tribunal renders a decision based on equity without being authorized to do so and as such it is addressed by both French international arbitration law[279] and institutional rules.[280] These instruments are adamant that the power of *amiable compositeur* has to be explicitly given by the parties to arbitration. Nonetheless, even if not given, convincing the setting-aside court that the tribunal usurped the power of *amiable compositeur* might not be easy whenever the tribunal's decision has a reference to the rules of law.

Additionally, one should note that if the award has a reference to the law or rules of law, the (courts') analysis is restricted. Namely, as always, the starting point of the court's analysis is the underlying principle that the arbitral awards are not subject to a merits review by the setting-aside court.[281] It means that if the parties ask the tribunal to apply the law in resolving the dispute, any error in interpretation of the law the tribunal may commit will escape post-award scrutiny as long as it does not violate the French concept of international public policy.[282]

Before concluding, one should note that Article 1511(2) requires that "*[i]n either case, the arbitral tribunal shall take trade usages into account.*"[283] Also, institutional rules use similar non-permissive language.[284] Dimolitsa even argues that

> [i]ntroducing issues emerging from the contract or from trade usages that are deemed inherent in the contractual agreement may be conceived as an obligation rather than a discretion of the arbitrators, and this not only when the applicable arbitration rules provide that "in all cases" the tribunal shall take into account the terms of the contract and relevant trade usages [...].[285]

At the same time, however, Bensaude highlights that: "*despite the use of the words 'shall' and 'in all cases' in art. 1511, there is no French case law annulling an award on the basis that a tribunal failed to take trade usages into account.*"[286] Irrespective of whether it is a duty or discretion, arguably, "*[b]y raising new issues from the contract that relate to their*

278 See also section 6.2.5.

279 Art. 1512 of the CCP.

280 See, *e.g.*, Art. 21(3) of the (draft) 2021 ICC Rules, Art. 21(3) of the 2017 ICC Rules, Art. 21(3) of the 2012 ICC Rules, Art. 35(2) of the 2010 UNCITRAL Rules.

281 See section 3.2.

282 See section 4.3.

283 ("*Il tient compte, dans tous les cas, des usages du commerce.*").

284 See Art. 21(2) of the 2012 ICC Rules, Art. 35(3) of the 2010 UNCITRAL Rules, Art. 17(2) of the 1998 ICC Rules, Art. 33(3) of the 1976 UNCITRAL Rules.

285 Dimolitsa, *The equivocal power of the arbitrators to introduce ex officio new issues of law* (2009) p.430.

286 Bensaude (2015) p.1157.

mandate, arbitrators substantially act within their contractual mission and abide by party autonomy, as specifically expressed therein, with regard to the legal relationship at hand."[287]

In conclusion, it is essential for the tribunal not to alter the parties' *petita*[288] and to ensure that parties are heard in all legal issues presented (including those introduced by the tribunal).[289] Consequently, its decision should stand.[290] Furthermore, only violation of French international public policy and non-authorized use of the power of *amiable compositeur* may allow a party to annul the decision ascertaining the content of the applicable law under Article 1520(3) of the CCP.

6.2.4 Application of mandatory rules of law by the arbitral tribunal

Much has already been said about the interface between the arbitral tribunal's mandate and the process of application of the law. In principle, the tribunal needs to follow the parties' submissions, but in the absence of any parties' guidance it will have ample freedom in applying the law. Mandatory rules of law, however, have a unique status which, arguably, shifts the balance in what the tribunal is expected to do. Consequently, it is necessary to reflect whether (i) the tribunal can disregard the parties' choice of law (where, for example, the sole purpose was to oust it from applying certain mandatory rules of law), (ii) the tribunal can invoke mandatory rules of law *ex officio*, and (iii) recourse is available when the tribunal misapplies mandatory rules of law.

Before going further, it is necessary to highlight that mandatory rules of law are embedded in any national legal order. As aptly explained by Waincymer "*[a] mandatory rule is one that purports to apply irrespective of the wishes of the parties.*"[291] They are designed to protect the essential elements of legal system(s).[292] Importantly, in international arbitration "*[t]here may be mandatory rules in a number of jurisdictions that must be taken*

---

287 Dimolitsa, *The equivocal power of the arbitrators to introduce ex officio new issues of law* (2009) p.430. The author qualifies that although the tribunal always knows the contract it may not (always) be familiar with trade usages. In that case it should invite the parties to "submit evidence". Dimolitsa, *The equivocal power of the arbitrators to introduce ex officio new issues of law* (2009) pp.430-431.

288 *Ultra* or *extra petita*. See section 5.4 and section 6.1.1.

289 See, *e.g.*, Dimolitsa, *The Raising Ex Officio of New Issues of Law* (2014) p.23 ("*There is a great discussion about the risk for the arbitrators to give thus the impression that they favour one party. We think that such a risk is debatable. It seems quite improbable that an arbitrator may be considered as partial by inviting all parties to discuss a legal issue the arbitrator raised ex officio – an act that does not prejudge the final solution of the dispute – if such invitation is specific and punctual, while the arbitrator's overall behaviour during the entire procedure does not give rise to any blame. To the extent known, there is no example in case law of refusing enforcement or setting aside an award for impartiality of an arbitrator based on such a reason.*").

290 Dimolitsa, *The Raising Ex Officio of New Issues of Law* (2014) p.28.

291 Waincymer (2009) p.1.

292 Siwy (2012) p.166 ("*The distinguishing feature of mandatory rules, which separates them from rules aimed at balancing the interests of the parties, is the interest served by such mandatory rules: Mandatory rules serve over-individual public purposes or national or economic policies.*"). Although the author does not discuss the French legal system, the argument would be equally valid in the French context.

into account [...]."[293] For this reason, one should recognize a dichotomous divide of mandatory rules. Put differently, it is necessary to distinguish the rules that are "mandatory" only when a certain law (of which they are part of) applies ("simple" mandatory rules[294] or rules of *ordre public interne*[295]) from the "overriding" mandatory rules that safeguard public interest[296] and "*that parties cannot contract away (lois d'application immediate) [...].*"[297] This distinction may play a considerable role in the tribunal's exercise of ascertaining the (mandatory rules of) law. Therefore, one should bear it in mind while testing the hypotheses below.

The first two questions have some common denominator in the tribunal's due diligence. In the first two hypotheses, therefore, the tribunal undertakes its own legal research if any mandatory rules come into play and may affect the award. In the first out of two, however, the tribunal focuses more on mandatory rules that might possibly be relevant but do not form part of the legal rules chosen by the parties to apply. In the second scenario, one would observe if the tribunal is able to invoke mandatory rules of law that form a part of the law chosen by the parties.

In the first scenario, it is sensible to make use of the distinction between the "simple" and the "overriding" mandatory rules. One can easily imagine that parties from countries A and B designate the law from country C to govern their contractual relations. Perhaps the choice is made in order to avoid any "home field" advantage only. It is possible, however, that occasionally parties deliberately use their choice of law solely to avoid the application of mandatory rules.

As briefly mentioned above, the parties' freedom of choosing the governing law finds its limits when faced with "overriding" mandatory rules. As some authors concluded,

> [...], arbitration cannot be used as an instrument to evade mandatory rules that would have been applicable to a business transaction in the absence of the parties' choice of law and that are considered as public policy rules in the other jurisdiction. Mandatory public policy rules are thus a limit to the parties' freedom of choice.[298]

In similar vein, the ILA Committee explained that

293 Capper et al. (2014) p.35.
294 Radicati di Brozolo (2012) p.50.
295 ILA, *ILA Report on Ascertaining the Contents of the Applicable Law in International Commercial Arbitration* (2008) p.21.
296 Radicati di Brozolo (2012) p.50.
297 ILA, *ILA Report on Ascertaining the Contents of the Applicable Law in International Commercial Arbitration* (2008) p.21.
298 Capper et al. (2014) p.35.

> [a]lthough commercial arbitration is a means of privately resolving disputes, it operates within a public legal system defined by international conventions and national laws. These conventions and laws acknowledge that public policy constrains contractual and arbitral freedom, and may impose limitations or restrictions that the parties cannot agree to disregard.[299]

Similarly, Mayer reflected that "*a mandatory rule (loi de police in French) is an imperative provision of law which must be applied to an international relationship irrespective of the law that governs that relationship.*"[300] In other words, it means that "*[...] fraudulent evasion of the law, together with the non application of foreign mandatory rules (lois de police) and the violation of international public policy, [are] among the grounds allowing the arbitrators to disregard the parties' choice of law.*"[301]

Having said what the effect of the "overriding" mandatory rules is, one should consider what happens when the tribunal disregards the parties' choice of law in order to apply the "simple" mandatory rules. In this instance, due process is of utmost importance. Therefore, arguably, if the tribunal invites the parties to comment on the application of "simple" mandatory rules of law,[302] its decision should survive at the post-award stage unless it violates French international public policy.

The second scenario envisages the situation where the tribunal on its own initiative introduces mandatory rules of law it considers applicable. At the same time, it will be presumed that parties did not discuss these mandatory rules in their submissions.[303] Finally, it goes without saying that the tribunal should give the parties an opportunity to express their views on its legal findings. In principle, the tribunal will be well within the limits of its mission when addressing public policy rules of the applicable law and other potentially applicable "overriding" mandatory rules.

In fact, it is rather uncontroversial nowadays to accept the tribunal's power to investigate the applicability of "overriding" mandatory rules of law even when parties fail to submit any arguments on the topic.[304] Put differently, "*[i]n order to fulfil their duty to render a*

299 ILA, *ILA Report on Ascertaining the Contents of the Applicable Law in International Commercial Arbitration* (2008) p.21.

300 Mayer, *Mandatory rules of law in international arbitration* (1986) p.275.

301 Poudret & Besson (2007) p.607.

302 Even if they do not form part of the law chosen by the party, but are somewhat related to the contract and may influence its fate (and the fate of a prospective award).

303 The mandatory rules of the law applicable to the merits will need to be taken into account always. On top of that, one might need to investigate other mandatory rules of law which are of "overriding" nature. For this reason, one might need to consult the law of the seat, the law of the country of (potential) enforcement or otherwise.

304 It is important for these rules to be of public policy nature, in order for the tribunal to enjoy inherent and unrestricted freedom to apply them. As explained earlier in this section, the mandatory rules of public policy character without any reservation restrain the parties' autonomy. As explained in Poudret & Besson

final and enforceable award, the arbitrators may have to consider such mandatory [public policy] rules even in the event that none of the parties refer to them."[305] Therefore it is often stated that "*[...] it is clear that the public policy nature of a provision implies that it must be applied ex officio.*"[306]

In addition, if one accepts that the tribunal has an obligation or a responsibility to render an enforceable award, it is only reasonable to conclude that the application of mandatory rules of a public policy character is not only its power but also that it constitutes a core part of fulfilling the mission to finally resolve the disputes between parties.[307] In other words, the tribunal's *ignorance* of public policy rules (rather than its voluntary compliance with them) is more likely to violate the adjudicative mission of the arbitrator.[308] In these instances, however, the tribunal's violation will be tested against French international public policy instead of Article 1520(3) of the CCP.[309] Consequently, the standard of review is heightened (standard of *manifest*, *effective* and *concrete* violation)[310]

(2007) p.607: "*[i]t is [...] evident that all mandatory laws or rules of internal public policy cannot prevail over the freedom of choice accorded to the parties by the lex arbitrii. Only international public policy can have the effect of restricting such freedom because only a violation thereof can lead, under most laws, to a setting aside of the award or a refusal of recognition.*"

305 Capper et al. (2014) p.35.

306 Poudret & Besson (2007) p.613. See also Derains & Kiffer, *National Report for France* (2013) Chapter V(4) ("*[...] however, if the jurisdictional issue turns on the question of subject-matter arbitrability, which is outside the parties' autonomy, the arbitrators must examine it ex officio. [...]*"), Dimolitsa, *The equivocal power of the arbitrators to introduce ex officio new issues of law* (2009) p.426 ("*The power of arbitrators to introduce ex officio new issues of law refers to legal issues and arguments on the merits not invoked by the parties. As to the term 'power' it is used in contract to the obligation that arbitrators do have to raise issues of transnational public policy or may consider that they have before a dispute implicating 'public policy rules' ('lois de police').*").

307 The argument would be even stronger in the case where the tribunal is required by the institutional rules to "*make every effort to make sure that the award is enforceable at law.*" See, *e.g.*, Art. 41 of the 2012 ICC Rules.

308 See, however, the "minimalist" approach developed in CA Paris, 18 November 2004, *SA Thalès Air Défense v. GIE Euromissile*, Rev. Arb. 2005, p.752, where the court held that there is no reason to allow the award-debtor to raise a defense based on mandatory competition law rules in order to challenge the award, when it failed to bring such a defense before the arbitrators. Considering the finality of the award and a principle of no review on the merits, the court concluded that when there is no fraud nor manifest violation of mandatory rules the award cannot be set aside. Similarly, Cour de Cassation Civ 1ère, 4 June 2008, Société SNF SAS v. Société Cytec Industries BV, Rev. Arb. 2008, p.473. See also Radicati di Brozolo (2005) pp.529-560. It does not change the fact, however, that "*[t]o the extent that the mandatory rules of the seat are considered to be part of ordre public of that state, arbitrators should – solely for practical reasons and without any dogmatic justification – examine whether the disregard of such rules could lead to the setting aside of the award. In practice, this will mostly be the case if mandatory rules of procedure are violated [...].*"). See Siwy (2012) p.182.

309 See also section 4.3.

310 See *e.g.* CA Paris, 21 February 2017, *République du Kirghizistan v. M. Belokon*, Rev. Arb. 2017, p.336, CA Paris, 16 January 2018, *Société MK Group v. SARL Onix et autre*, Rev. Arb. 2018, p.295. See also fn.94.

and disregard of mandatory rules (French or foreign) that do not amount to international public policy might not suffice to annul the award.[311]

A final reflection has to be given on the tribunal's wrongful application of public policy rules. As previously explained, the setting-aside court should not get involved in the review of the merits of the case.[312] Therefore, one should have in mind that "*[...], an error of law in applying the law agreed upon by the parties is not seen as a breach of the arbitrator's mandate.*"[313] The ultimate test, however, is whether the tribunal violated French international public policy while misapplying mandatory rules of law. As suggested above, it is more likely that abstaining from applying overriding public policy rules rather than their erroneous interpretation may infringe the French concept of international public policy.[314] Therefore, the tribunal's decision on the application of mandatory rules has high chances in surviving the Article 1520(3) of the CCP challenge.

6.2.5 Decision reached as *amiable compositeur* or on equity

The instances where the tribunal is allowed *not* to apply the legal rules, but rather to follow its own (and more elusive) concepts of justice and equity, are rather exceptional. There are a number of notions that refer to this general power of the tribunal, with *amiable compositeur* and *ex aequo et bono* being the most popular ones. For the purpose of the research at hand, however, the distinction is not as relevant.[315] Therefore, under this section what happens to the decisions *not* based on legal rules will be considered.[316] In the context

311 Especially considering the principle of no review on the merits (see section 3.2). Generally, however, the tribunal should make sure that the applicable (foreign) public policy rules are respected considering that it might affect the likelihood of enforceability of the award (and the tribunal should make sure that the award is enforceable).

312 Section 3.2.

313 Derains & Kiffer, *National Report for France* (2013) Chapter VII(2)(B)(a)(3).

314 The violation of French international public policy needs to be flagrant, effective and concrete (CA Paris, 18 November 2004, *SA Thalès Air Défense v. GIE Euromissile*, Rev. Arb. 2005, p.752) in order to effect in the annulment of the arbitral award. See also section 4.3. This is not to say that the wrongful application of mandatory rules will never be susceptible to setting aside. Arguably, however, this will seldom occur, because the violation of the legal rule would have to be manifest. See fn.308.

315 For further reading on decisions not based on law, see, *e.g.*, Rubino-Sammartano, *Amiable Compositeur (Joint Mandate to Settle) and Ex Bono et Aecquo (Discretional Authority to Mitigate Strict Law): Apparent Synonyms Revisited* (1992) pp.5-16, Yu (2000) pp.79-98, Maniruzzaman, *The Arbitrator's Prudence in Lex Mercatoria: Amiable Composition and Ex Aecquo Et Bono in Decision Making* (2003) pp.1-8. In the context of the French system, see in particular Loquin (1980) pp.1-385. See also Giraud (2017) pp.292-303.

316 See fn.315. Also, CA Paris, 28 November 1996, *Société CN France v. Société Minhal France*, Rev. Arb. 1997, p.380 ("*[...] la clause d'amiable composition est une renonciation conventionnelle aux effets et au bénéfice de la règle de droit, les parties perdant la prérogative d'en exiger la stricte application et les arbitres recevant corrélativement le pouvoir de modifier ou de modérer les conséquences des stipulations contractuelles dès lors que l'équité ou l'intérêt commun bien compris des parties l'exige*").

of this chapter, these decisions will be considered under the general notion of *amiable compositeur*.[317]

Pursuant to Article 1512 of the CCP, "*[t]he arbitral tribunal shall rule as amiable compositeur if the parties have empowered it to do so.*"[318] It means that "*[i]n order to decide a dispute as amiable compositeur, an arbitral tribunal must ensure, at the outset, that the parties have empowered it to do so. The expression of the parties' intentions must be clear and unambiguous, even though it may be implied; no special form is required.*"[319] The same clear authorization from the parties for the tribunal to act as *amiable compositeur* is also required by the leading institutional rules.[320]

In consequence, the basic answer to the question when the tribunal's decision can be challenged for failure to comply with the mandate is rather simple: it may happen when the tribunal acts as *amiable compositeur* without the parties' authorization[321] or the tribunal does not adhere to its power of *amiable compositeur*.[322] Such an answer, however, requires a few additional reflections. Accordingly, one should further discuss (i) the impact of the 'no review on the merits' principle on the challenge of the decision as *amiable compositeur*, (ii) the use of equity in cases where the tribunal is required to apply the law, and likewise (iii) the possibility to apply the law while acting as *amiable compositeur*.

The first point, albeit important, need not to be discussed at length.[323] Setting-aside procedures are not designed to challenge the merits of the award and it holds true also in the context of the Article 1520(3) challenge. It means that invoking this ground might be

---

317 Bensaude (2015) p.1158 ("*An arbitrator is empowered to rule as amiable compositeur when vested with the powers to decide the parties' dispute either in amiable composition, ex aequo et bono or in an equitable manner (équité). French courts generally understand these concepts to have similar meanings in the context of international arbitration.*").

318 ("*Le tribunal arbitral statue en amiable composition si les parties lui ont confié cette mission*"). It would be perhaps better to include the reference to the mandate in the English translation as well. See for example the one offered by Bensaude in Bensaude (2015) p.1157, who suggested that "*[t]he arbitral tribunal shall decide as amiable compositeur if the parties have entrusted the tribunal with such mission.*" It is so, because, arguably, the French text gives an indication that the mandate to decide as *amiable compositeur* should be considered as a distinctive type of the tribunal's mandate.

319 Rouche et al. (2009) p.150.

320 See, *e.g.*, Art. 21(3) of the 2017 ICC Rules, ("*The arbitral tribunal shall assume the powers of an amiable compositeur or decide ex aequo et bono only if the parties have agreed to give it such powers*"), the same in Art. 21(3) of the (draft) 2021 ICC Rules, Art. 21(3) of the 2012 ICC Rules, Art. 17(3) of the 1998 ICC Rules, Art. 35(2) of the 2010 UNCITRAL Rules ("*The arbitral tribunal shall decide as amiable compositeur or ex aequo et bono only if the parties have expressly authorized the arbitral tribunal to do so.*"), Art. 33(2) of the 1976 UNCITRAL Rules ("*The arbitral tribunal shall decide as amiable compositeur or ex aequo et bono only if the parties have expressly authorized the arbitral tribunal to do so and if the law applicable to the arbitral procedure permits such arbitration.*").

321 Lévy & Robert-Tissot (2013) pp.900-901.

322 In essence, however, it is a tribunal's power and not an obligation to not apply the law. See Loquin (2015) p.434 ("*Il est bien établi en jurisprudence que l'amiable compositeur a la faculté, et non l'obligation, de juger en équité*").

323 For further reading, see section 3.2.

particularly difficult against decisions as *amiable compositeur*. In essence, if the tribunal is allowed to act as *amiable compositeur*, its decision escapes any scrutiny, because there is no benchmark, apart from French international public policy, on which the setting-aside judge can rely while reviewing a tribunal's equitable solution.[324] As pointed out by Bensaude, "*[i]n all cases, an arbitral tribunal vested with powers of amiable compositeur must abide by due process and other fundamental rules of procedural international public policy*".[325] Therefore, unless the tribunal's decision violates the French concept of international public policy, its decision would likely survive.

The second point that needs to be discussed is the arbitral tribunal's ability to reach an available equitable solution while applying the rules of law. Mayer suggests that, at times, implementation of legal rules and reaching an equitable decision might be conflicting notions.[326] In these instances where the tribunal prefers an equitable decision, the tribunal's award will be exposed to the challenge that the tribunal usurped a power to decide as *amiable compositeur*. However, it would only be successful when the tribunal admits that it considered a legal (*i.e.* based on the rules of law) solution, disregarded it and opted for an equitable one. As explained by Loquin "*[t]his is not an error of law in itself, nor the use of equity infra legem that are sanctioned [thus available for challenge under Article 1520(3) of the CCP], but the deliberate abandonment of law.*"[327]

Indeed, because of the flexibility of the French system of international arbitration, even when applying the rules of law, the tribunal has ample freedom to render equitable decisions. It entails that there is room for "*the use of equity infra legem*".[328] It is particularly true when parties did not select any applicable rules of law. Consequently,

---

324 Arguably, although errors in application of law are not the basis for setting aside as well, the court has an "easier" task in assessing the tribunal's decision-making process when it is able to analyze the legal basis of the tribunal's decision and how the tribunal applied it. If, however, it assesses the tribunal's decision on equity it will be unable do the same exercise.

325 See Bensaude (2015) p.1158. See also Dimolitsa, *The Raising Ex Officio of New Issues of Law* (2014) p.26 ("*It is confirmed in Buildinvest vs. Guy Roy that the powers of amiable compositeur do not dispense the arbitrators from their obligation to give parties the opportunity to be heard on the new issues of law that they have raised ex officio.*"). See CA Paris, 18 September 2012, *S.A. Buildinvest et autres v. M. Guy Roy*, Rev. Arb. 2012, p.867, Poudret & Besson (2007) p.477.

326 Mayer, *Reflections on the International Arbitrator's Duty to Apply the Law – The Freshfields Lecture 2000* (2001) p.241 ("*[t]he mission of an arbitrator is [...] much more ambiguous than that of a judge. Conflicting considerations may play a role. More specifically, there may be a conflict between on the one hand the method consisting in implementing the legal syllogism on the basis of the applicable rule of law, and on the other hand two different concerns: the search for the most equitable solution, and the endeavour to favour the solution that conforms most closely with the true will of the parties.*").

327 Loquin (2015) p.433 ("*Ce n'est donc pas l'erreur de droit en soi, ni le recours à l'équité infra legem qui sont sanctionnés, mais l'abandon délibéré du droit.*").

328 Loquin (2015) p.433.

> [...] an arbitral tribunal already enjoys a large measure of freedom as a result both of its status and power to determine the appropriate 'rules of law' as the substantive law. [...] [A]n arbitral tribunal, or at least an international one, may decide disputes on the basis of rules of law which are not strictly defined and which include flexible and malleable princip[l]es derived from many sources. In such circumstances, it might seem unnecessary to provide for 'amiable composition', when it is possible to find a just and fair solution with an intelligent and sensitive use of the above general principles and usages.[329]

Therefore, even when equipped with the default tools of Article 1511 of the CCP only, the tribunal should be able to reach a just result which would be, in principle, non-reviewable under Article 1520(3) of the CCP.

Finally, as to the third point, the mere reference to the law in the tribunal's decision does not amount to a failure to comply with a mission of *amiable compositeur.*[330] It has already been suggested that acting as *amiable compositeur* is a power and not the tribunal's duty.[331] Bensaude explains that:

> [a] tribunal vested with such powers [of amiable compositeur] may refer to rules of law and adopt such rules if the tribunal considers these rules to provide a fair solution. The tribunal's reasoning should not be limited only to the strict application of rules of law, but should also indicate or at least implicitly suggest that the decision reached by the tribunal complies with that tribunal's own sense of fairness.[332]

Therefore, as long as the tribunal is in search for an equitable solution, there is no reason to prohibit it to seek inspirations in (or refer to) rules of law.[333]

---

329 Rouche et al. (2009) p.149.

330 CA Paris, 6 May 1988, *Société Unijet S.A. v. S.A.R.L. International Business Relations Ltd (I.B.R.),* Rev. Arb. 1989, p.83.

331 See Loquin (2015) p.434 ("*Il est bien établi en jurisprudence que l'amiable compositeur a la faculté, et non l'obligation, de juger en équité*"). Also referred to in fn.322. It should be considered, however, a power but also a mission. See Loquin (2015) p.326 ("*L'amiable composition est en effet une mission en no pas seulement un pouvoir.*").

332 Bensaude (2015) pp.1158-1159, with a reference to CA Paris, 15 March 1984, *Soubaigne v. Limmareds Skogar,* Rev. Arb. 1985, p.285. Also, *e.g.,* Craig, *The arbitrator's mission and the application of law in international commercial arbitration* (2010) p.268 ("*[t]he mission of the amiable compositeur does not exclude application of rules of law.*"). Poudret & Besson (2007) p.743 ("*[The tribunal does not exceed its mission] when the amiables compositeurs apply rules of law since the role of moderator which is given to them by the parties does not prohibit them from applying the law if it can lead to a solution which seems fair.*").

333 Cour de Cassation Civ 2ème, 15 February 2001, *Halbout et société Matenec HG v. Epoux Hanin,* Rev. Arb. 2001, p.135 (the arbitral tribunal acting as *amiable compositeur* cannot justify its decision only with the strict reference to the rules of law and with no reference to notion of equity).

Conversely, "*the strict application of the parties' contractual terms or legal provisions, with no reference to the powers of amiable compositeur and no consideration of fairness, could jeopardise the enforcement or the validity in France of an award rendered by an amiable compositeur.*"[334] Therefore, "*if a tribunal merely applied the law, without taking into account "equitable" considerations, then they would violate their mandate.*"[335]

It is also possible that parties designate the law (or rules of law) applicable to the dispute and, at the same time, give the tribunal power to act as *amiable compositeur*. "*In that case, the arbitral tribunal will first seek a solution to the dispute by interpreting and applying the contract terms according to the applicable law and then would depart from this application, by exercise of its powers as amiable compositeur only if it would find that strict application of the law would lead to an inequitable result.*"[336]

All in all, there is nothing else but to conclude, after Loquin, that "*[t]he setting-aside judge must simply check that the arbitrator has respected the mission that the parties had conferred. This control does not imply control of the correctness of the grounds, but only a check for the existence of grounds in equity.*"[337]

6.3 Decisions on remedies

The analysis undertaken would be incomplete if it does not include the discussion on the most common remedies available to the parties in international commercial arbitration. This is so because granting (or rejecting) the relief sought is an ultimate goal of the tribunal's

334 Bensaude (2015) pp.1158, Craig, *The arbitrator's mission and the application of law in international commercial arbitration* (2010) p.269. See CA Paris, 3 July 2007, *Leizer v. Bachelier*, n°RG 2006/00011, Rev. Arb. 2007, p.827 ("*L'arbitre n'a pas statué en amiable compositeur dès lors qu'il a fait application des clauses contractuelles sans jamais confronter à l'équité les résultats obtenus alors pourtant qu'une partie l'y invitait implicitement, ce dont il n'a pas tenu compte la mission de juger en amiable compositeur n'étant jamais évoquée dans la sentence*").

335 Born, *International Commercial Arbitration* (2014) p.2775. See also CA Paris, 15 January 2004, *Société Centrale Fotovista v. Vanoverbeke et autres*, Rev. Arb. 2004, p.907 ("*Considérant que le tribunal arbitral avait ainsi pour mission de trancher en amiable composition le litige concernant l'absence d'accord des parties sur la cession du capital de la société Edelcolor, que l'arbitre ayant statué en appliquant la règle de droit français sans s'expliquer à aucun moment au cours des quatorze pages de sa sentence sur la conformité à l'équité de la décision ainsi motivée, la sentence est annulée sans qu'il soit besoin d'examiner les autres arguments à l'appui du moyen*").

336 Craig, *The arbitrator's mission and the application of law in international commercial arbitration* (2010) p.269. Also, Bensaude (2015) p.1159 ("*In rare cases, parties agree that certain rules of law shall apply to the merits of their dispute, and vest the tribunal with the powers of amiable compositeur. In such cases, the tribunal should first apply the rules of law chosen by the parties to the dispute and thereafter compare the solution reached at law with fairness, and decide in accordance with its own sense of fairness. This comparison may be implied from the content of the award.*").

337 Loquin (2015) p.435 ("*Le juge de l'annulation doit simplement vérifier que l'arbitre a respecté la mission que les parties lui avaient conférée. Ce contrôle n'implique en rien un contrôle du bien-fondé des motifs, mais seulement un contrôle de l'existence de motifs d'équité.*").

mandate. What follows is that any decision by the arbitral tribunal on remedies is an unequivocal result of exercising its adjudicative mandate. Therefore, it is necessary to reflect whether decisions on damages (section 6.3.1), specific performance (section 6.3.2) and modifications of the contract (section 6.3.3) can be challenged under Article 1520(3) of the CCP.

6.3.1 Decision on damages

A decision on damages would be often one of the last steps of the decision-making process undertaken by the tribunal and, arguably, one of the most anticipated by the parties. In principle, it would be one of the basic powers of the tribunal, whose mission would be to remedy loss incurred. Put differently, granting damages will be, more often than not, inherently embedded in the tribunal's mandate. At the same time, however, one should contemplate whether the tribunal fails to comply with its mission when it grants (i) an amount higher (or lower) than requested, (ii) a remedy different than that sought (*i.e.* damages instead of specific performance), (iii) damages notwithstanding the parties' explicit limitation in the agreement to arbitrate, or (iv) damages unknown to French law (*e.g.* punitive damages).

The first hypothesis is rather straightforward. If the value of the damages granted by the tribunal exceeds the value of the damages sought, the tribunal will not comply with the constraints of its mandate. In turn, such a decision will be susceptible to the Article 1520(3) challenge. One should add, however, that it is likely that the court will set aside the part of the award which goes beyond the parties' *petita.*[338]

That being said, one should reflect what happens if a party in its request for relief uses a formula rather than an exact amount to explain its request. This may give room for ambiguity but may occasionally not be avoided.[339] For example, in a simplified hypothesis, a party asks the tribunal to award the amount resulting from the equation 2+2=5 in damages. In most instances, considering that arbitration is an adversarial process, such a mistake should be detected by the counterparty. The problem arises if it is not.

In this instance, the tribunal, which is already at the deliberation stage of the proceedings, will have to decide what to do. One reasonable solution for the tribunal would be to reopen the case on the issue. At the same time, however, it might not be procedurally efficient (and cost effective). Another option is to determine independently which side of the equation is the correct party's *petita.*[340] As long as in example, the answer is rather

338 Bensaude (2015) pp.1182-1183 ("*Awards that are ultra petita do provide a basis under art. 1520(3) for appeal of an order of enforcement of a foreign award or the setting aside of an international award rendered in France, but only with respect to that part of the award that is ultra petita [...].*").

339 See also section 6.1.1.

340 Considering that nobody challenges that the formula is incorrect, the tribunal will not know which side of it is the correct one (intended one).

obvious, and correction of the calculation mistake should not cause any difficulties, it may so happen that the formulas are much more elaborate and even the analysis of other materials submitted does not help resolve the dilemma. Arguably, however, if the tribunal awards a higher amount from the example (*i.e.* "5") its award should survive the challenge. The same is most likely to happen if it corrects the value and awards the lower amount (*i.e.* "4" in the example). In any event, the more sensible solution would be, for example, to render a partial final award on all claims but for the ambiguous one.

The second scenario envisages a situation where a party asks for damages, but the tribunal decides to grant specific performance instead (or the other way around). In principle, this should amount to a failure of compliance with the tribunal's mandate (especially when the tribunal "surprises" parties), unless the tribunal possesses a *carte blanche* to grant any remedy it considers appropriate in the circumstances of the case.[341] Additionally, it is the parties who are responsible for the shape of the submissions, however good, bad or ugly. Consequently, it is not the tribunal's task to restructure the parties' *petita*, because a change in the remedy sought would inevitably lead to favoring one party (the one who benefits from the change). This analysis shares characteristics with the reflections on the requalification of the legal basis for the claim that has been discussed above.[342] The former differs from the latter, because it truly touches the parties' *petita*, and as such the tribunal's mandate, which it then unilaterally rewrites. Such a behavior of the arbitral tribunal should be sanctioned by Article 1520(3) of the CCP.

The next, the third hypothesis is quite similar to the second one. If, however unlikely, the parties limit the remedial powers of the arbitral tribunal in their agreement to arbitrate by eliminating the power to grant damages, the tribunal should comply with those constrains.[343] It further means that the tribunal's decision to grant damages in this instance might be challenged at the post-award stage. At the same time, however, such a clause might be considered as inoperative and effectively frustrate the arbitral process.

The fourth and last point that needs to be briefly addressed refers to the recognition of the award granting punitive damages.[344] The starting presumption is that the parties expressly allowed the tribunal to grant punitive damages or have chosen the law that permits such a remedy and that punitive damages were requested by the parties. Still, the tribunal, as a part of its mission, should be interested in the well-being of the arbitral award

341 Of course when a party submits alternative claims, the tribunal would be able to select from different options.

342 See section 6.1.1.

343 Arguably, in cases of limitation of damages clauses the situation would be different (included in the contract, but outside the agreement to arbitrate), because the addressee would be different (parties and not the arbitral tribunal). Consequently, these clauses do not directly refer to the tribunal's powers. Instead they are directed towards parties and define the shape of their rights. As such it is the exclusive competence of the tribunal to interpret the contract.

344 For further reading, see, *i.a.*, Parker (2013) pp.389-432, Wester-Ouisse & Thiede (2012) pp.115-122, West Janke & Licari (2012) pp.775-804, Rowan (2010) pp.513-516, Borghetti (2009) pp.55-73.

and reflect if its award survives the prospective challenges at the post-award stage. For this reason, the recurring concern is whether punitive damages violate French international public policy. This issue has been addressed by the *Cour de Cassation* in the *Fountaine Pajot* case, where the court found that "*a foreign judgment ordering a party to pay punitive damages is not in principle contrary to international public policy.*"[345] The court also held, however, that international public policy may be violated if the punitive damages are disproportionate.[346] Therefore, notably, depending on the circumstances of the case, even the tribunal's decision on punitive damages may survive the challenge at the post-award stage if *Fountain Pajot* decision is to be applied to arbtiration.[347]

Overall, the tribunal's remedial powers are rather broad and usually it should be anticipated that they are within the limits of its mandate.

6.3.2 Decision on specific performance

If damages for breach of contract are insufficient, specific performance might serve well as a useful remedy for the parties to seek in arbitration. Some scholars point out that "*specific performance is a widely accepted remedy in civil law countries.*"[348] Of course, its availability will depend on the applicable law or the parties' authorization.[349] In principle, however, it does not raise additional questions in the context of the research at hand. For this reason, reflections put forward in the context of the discussion on damages would apply by analogy.[350] Therefore, as long as the tribunal's decision fits in the framework delineating its mandate,[351] its decision will survive a challenge.

In other words, one may conclude that the tribunal's decisions on specific performance will be set aside only when they have not been requested or the tribunal's remedial powers have been limited by the parties' agreement or the overriding rules of public policy of the applicable law.

---

345 Cour de Cassation Civ 1ère, 1 December 2010, *Les époux X v. Société Fountaine Pajot*, No. 09-13303, Bull.civ. I, No 248 ("*qu'une décision étrangère condamnant une partie à paiement de dommages-intérêts punitifs n'est pas, par principe, contraire à l'ordre public international de fond*").

346 Cour de Cassation Civ 1ère, 1 December 2010, *Les époux X v. Société Fountaine Pajot*, No. 09-13303, Bull.civ. I, No 248 ("*Mais attendu que si le principe d'une condamnation à des dommages-intérêts punitifs, n'est pas, en soi, contraire à l'ordre public, il en est autrement lorsque le montant alloué est disproportionné au regard du préjudice subi et des manquements aux obligations contractuelles du débiteur*"). One should note that in the *Fountaine Pajot* case the court found the 1:1 ratio between compensatory and punitive damages disproportionate.

347 It is still yet to be seen how the case law develops in this regard.

348 Lew et al., *Comparative International Commercial Arbitration* (2003) p.650. See also Blackaby et al. (2015) p.519.

349 Blackaby et al. (2015) p.519.

350 See section 6.3.1.

351 See section 4.

6.3.3 Decision on contract adaptation and filling of gaps in the contract

The idea that the arbitrators have a power to adapt a contract, or to fill in the contractual gaps has not always been welcomed in France. In principle, the difficulty had arisen because a contract adaptation and gap filling exercise has been considered a creative mechanism as opposed to the adjudicative function of the tribunal. Nowadays, however, the discussion seems to be rather obsolete because the prevailing opinion amongst the authorities is that the tribunal should be equipped with contract adaptation tools.[352] In any event, being mindful that Article 1520(3) of the CCP makes, arguably, a reference to the *adjudicative* mandate of the arbitral tribunal,[353] one may wonder if contract adaptation fits within the scope of a tribunal's mandate and consequently whether it can be reviewed under the abovementioned provision.

Some explanations on contract adaptation should be added, nonetheless. Therefore, one should briefly address (i) the distinction between the *arbitrage jurisdictionnel* and *arbitrage contractuel* as developed in France together with (ii) a rationale for such a distinction (creative v. jurisdictional powers of the tribunal). Moreover, it is necessary to highlight (iii) the importance of the applicable law and contractual provisions; the last point (iv) deals with a tribunal's power to adapt the contract under the mandate of *amiable compositeur.*

As to the first and second points, the distinction between *arbitrage jurisdictionnel* and *contractuel* attracted a fair amount of attention some years ago. The arguments have been brought forward explaining that the task of an arbitrator (in *arbitrage jurisdictionnel*) is the same as the one of a judge, consequently entailing that "*arbitration is generally seen as a judicial dispute settlement mechanism which replaces state courts.*"[354] Conversely, in case of *arbitrage contractuel,*

> the arbitrator is requested not to settle a dispute, but rather to add or integrate an element into the contract that the parties were not willing or were not in the position to include directly at the time they entered into the agreement. The legal basis of such determination is a mandate to the third party by both parties.[355]

352 Gaillard & Savage, *Fouchard Gaillard Goldman on International Commercial Arbitration* (1999) p.29. ("*Nowadays, commentators are largely in favor of arbitrators being empowered, in French law, to adapt a contract.*").

353 See section 4.

354 Kröll, *Contractual gap-filling by arbitration tribunals* (1999) p.12. ("*To put it in the words of Kassis, 'L'arbitre tranche un différend, et sa mission est exactement la même que celle d'un juge.' This means that arbitration is generally seen as a judicial dispute settlement mechanism which replaces state courts.*").

355 Carducci, *The Arbitration Reform in France: Domestic and International Arbitration Law* (2012) p.127. See also, Gaillard & Savage, *Fouchard Gaillard Goldman on International Commercial Arbitration* (1999) p.25 ("*Strictly speaking, "the fixing of a price by third parties does not, in principle, constitute a judicial act:" there*

In the opinion of some, therefore, it was irreconcilable for the tribunal, whose mandate was to resolve the dispute, to get involved in an "*exclusively creative act.*"[356]

In principle, there is some merit in the argument recognizing the different set of responsibilities imposed on arbitrators when asked to fill the contractual gaps. It is emphasized that the adjudicative function of the tribunal "*is [...] normally restricted to the determination of pre-existing rights*",[357] whereas a gap-filling exercise "*in its proper sense is characterised by arbitrators adding provisions to the contract at their discretion. They take up the creative task of rule-making and of regulating the parties' relationship.*"[358] In any event, as observed by David: "*[t]he arbitrator may be given by the parties the task of settling a legal dispute or intervening in the regulation of a contractual relationship. In both cases the situation is, in essence, the same.*"[359] It is argued therefore, that if parties are willing to extend the traditionally understood adjudicative function of the arbitral tribunal they should be free to do so.[360] Such an extension should not be considered to be against the French concept of international public policy.

Importantly, as to the third point, the power to fill the gap does depend on a number of factors, the first one being the distinction between "initial" and "supervening" gaps.[361]

---

is no "dispute" or, more precisely, there is neither a prior "claim" by one party, nor an assessment of that claim by a third party. Such factors would be characteristic of a judicial act and therefore also of the role of an arbitrator. The latter could not, in that capacity, be required to extend or modify a contract."), and Motulsky (2010) p.47.

356 Motulsky (2010) p.47. See also Gaillard & Savage, *Fouchard Gaillard Goldman on International Commercial Arbitration* (1999) p.27. Notably the authors of Gaillard & Savage, *Fouchard Gaillard Goldman on International Commercial Arbitration* (1999) add on p.27 that: "*These reservations [...] generally related to the initial determination by a third party of the price of goods, which Article 1592 of the French Civil Code inaccurately describes as an "arbitration.*"

357 Kröll, *Contractual gap-filling by arbitration tribunals* (1999) p.12. See also Loquin (2015) p.436 ("*L'acte jurisdictionnel implique au contraire la sanction de droit déjà né, après verification de son existence.*").

358 Kröll, *Contractual gap-filling by arbitration* tribunals (1999) p.12. See also Loquin (2015) p.436 ("*La creation d'une obligation nouvelle par un tiers appartient normalement au seul domaine du mandate commun, et suppose non pas l'existence d'un désaccord, mais bien contraire l'accord des parties sur cette creation.*").

359 David (1985) p.410.

360 Parenthetically, one should note the tribunals' reluctance to accept the power to adapt the contract. See Gaillard & Savage, *Fouchard Gaillard Goldman on International Commercial Arbitration* (1999) pp.25-26 ("*[a]rbitrators will generally be reluctant to accept the doctrine of change in circumstances even in long-term, non-speculative contracts. Instead, they will often consider that parties to international contracts are, generally speaking, experienced professionals well able to protect themselves in their agreements from changes in circumstances. [next para] Even when acting as amiables compositeurs, arbitrators are generally reluctant to interpret clauses giving them powers to rule in equity as enabling them to fill gaps left in the contract or to adapt the contract to future circumstances. Some arbitrators do, however, consider that their amiable compositeur status allows them to attenuate the overly harsh consequences of a strict application of the contract, and recent French case law has accepted this practice.*").

361 See Berger, *Power of Arbitrators to Fill Gaps and Revise Contracts to Make Sense* (2001) p.3 ("*Initial gaps are those deliberately left open by the parties during of the drafting the contract. In this case, the arbitrator is not regarded as competent to fill the gap. Supervening gaps occur after the conclusion of the contract and are unforeseen at the moment. Here, the arbitrator may be authorized to fill the gap if the conditions of the*

The second one is whether hardship clauses or other clauses allowing the tribunal to address the issue of changed circumstances exist, or, in the alternative, the tribunal undertakes contract adaptation based on its understanding of the agreement to arbitrate.[362] The third one is whether the tribunal can find a source of such a power in *lex arbitri* or the law applicable to the merits of the case.[363] In any event, it all leads to the question of the parties' common intention, and as such is rather more a jurisdictional than a mandate question. For this reason, it may be occasionally difficult to choose the appropriate ground for challenge.[364]

Finally, the fourth point of inquiry to be discussed is, namely the tribunal's power of gap-filling in case of a mandate as *amiable compositeur*. As explained above, the power of *amiable compositeur* gives much more leeway for the tribunal to decide the case.[365] It does not give the power to create new contractual ties between parties *per se*. It is, therefore, again a question of the parties' common intention. As explained by Bensaude, "*[a]lthough the tribunal may moderate the effects of the parties' contractual agreement, such power is not without limit. The arbitral tribunal cannot go so far as to create a new contract that was not envisaged by the parties.*"[366]

---

applicable procedural and substantive law are met."). A similar distinction has been explained by Poudret & Besson (2007) p.20: ("*As has been noted, namely by Jarrosson, it is important to distinguish whether the third party is requested to fill a true gap in an incomplete contract – in which case we have seen that his decision will have a constitutive effect – or whether he only has to fill gaps concerning secondary points. In the latter situation the third party does not complete the contract instead of the parties, but resolves a dispute by way of interpretation, thereby exercising a jurisdictional task as an arbitrator. The same can be the case when a contract is adapted in order to take a change of circumstances into account. Contrary to Fouchard, Gaillard and Goldman, we do not think that the arbitrator's jurisdiction depends on whether the contract contains an adaptation clause*").

362 Gaillard & Savage, *Fouchard Gaillard Goldman on International Commercial Arbitration* (1999) p.25 ("*Most of the controversy surrounding this issue centers on arbitrators' powers to add to a contract, or to adapt it to a change in circumstances, in the absence of a clause expressly allowing them to do so. The position varies according to the attachment of the applicable law to the pacta sunt servanda principle, and to whether or not that law grants the courts the power to substitute themselves for the agreement between the parties.*").

363 See fn.362. For further reading, see also Berger, *Power of Arbitrators to Fill Gaps and Revise Contracts to Make Sense* (2001) pp.10-12.

364 Gaillard & Savage, *Fouchard Gaillard Goldman on International Commercial Arbitration* (1999) p.28. ("*The only question which may arise is whether the parties did actually confer a power of adaptation on the arbitrators. This is a matter of interpretation of the parties' common intention. If such an intention does exist, one has to accept both that it is legitimate, and that there is nothing improper about calling the intended procedure arbitration. After all, in such cases the arbitrators will be required to determine which of the conflicting positions is well-founded, and therefore to resolve a dispute.*").

365 See section 6.2.5.

366 Bensaude (2015) p.1158, Robert (1993) pp.160-161. See also CA Paris, 4 November 1997, *Société Taurus Films v. SARL Les Films du jeudi*, Rev. Arb. 1998, p.699 ("*La mission d'amiable compositeur, qui a pour fondement la renonciation des parties à se prévaloir d'une exécution stricte des droits qu'elles tiennent du contrat, donne à l'arbitre le pouvoir notamment de modérer les effets du contrat dans la recherche d'une solution juste et conforme à l'équité en écartant au besoin l'application de certains droits nés de la convention,*

Overall, however, it is argued that since arbitration is an adversarial process, it is likely that parties submit concurring views on how the contract should be adapted and, in turn, the "creative" powers given to the tribunal by the parties will be an "extension" or a gloss of the tribunal's adjudicative and interpretative powers.[367] Therefore, in principle, a decision on contract adaptation will be susceptible to the Article 1520(3) challenge and, consequently, failure to comply with the mission will take place in the similar instances as already mentioned in the section on damages.[368]

6.4 *Decisions accessory to the parties' main submissions and the merits of the case*

Under this section, a few additional comments will be made on decisions that are more of procedural nature, which are added to the parties' main submissions. What follows, therefore, is a discussion on the availability of the challenge against the tribunal's decision on interest (section 6.4.1), costs (section 6.4.2) and procedural issues (section 6.4.3). These issues are characterized by the fact that the tribunal may find the source of said powers in law and as such may be occasionally more inclined to step in and modify the parties' request.

6.4.1 Decision on interest

Decisions on interest in international arbitration can be financially significant. At the same time, French international arbitration law is silent on the question whether the tribunal has the power to award interest. It also holds true for the leading institutional arbitration rules.[369] In general, it is also not mentioned in the agreements to arbitrate concluded between parties in international arbitration. Sometimes it is suggested that the power to award interest is inherent to the arbitral process unless prohibited.[370]

---

sous réserve de ne pas en modifier l'économie en substituant aux obligations contractuelles des obligations nouvelles ne répondant pas à l'intention commune des parties.").

367 In the alternative, one should argue either (i) that the mission for the purpose of Art. 1520(3) of the CCP has to be broader than only an adjudicative one (in order to entertain the tribunal's "creative" mission) or (ii) that the tribunal exceeds its jurisdiction (thus Art. 1520(1) of the CCP should apply) when it undertakes "creative" tasks. As explained in this section, it is generally acceptable for the tribunal to take up contract adaptation requests.

368 See section 6.3.1 (by and large, where the relief granted is different or higher than that requested or is against the explicit limitation to the tribunal's powers).

369 No rule in the 2017 ICC Rules and the 2010 UNCITRAL Rules is dedicated to the issue of interest. *Cf* with Art. 26.4 of the 2014 LCIA Rules or Art. 26.4 of the 2020 LCIA Rules.

370 ILA, *ILA Report on Inherent Powers of Arbitral Tribunals* (2014) p.10.

There are a number of outstanding issues with regard to the process of deciding on interest. For example, the tribunal has to establish which law applies,[371] what the starting date for accruing interest is, the relevant rate and type of interest (simple or compound). Its conclusions, therefore, in many places can go wrong.[372] It is argued, however, that the challenge against the decision on interest will be available in the same instances as already discussed in other sections, *i.a.* under the section on damages.[373] It means that the tribunal's decision may be subject to challenge in cases where (i) an interest rate is different (usually higher) than sought, (ii) an interest type is different than sought, (iii) granting interest is prohibited by the agreement to arbitrate, (iv) interest on the claim has not been requested at all, or (v) the interest granted is considered usury under French law. These instances will be explained briefly below.

As to the first point, when the interest rate is different than sought,[374] there should be no doubt that the tribunal decided *ultra petita* and as such failed to comply with its mandate. The same should be the case if, for example, the tribunal decides to fix the starting date for the accrual of interest earlier than it was requested.[375]

Similarly, as mentioned in the second hypothesis, if the tribunal decides to award interests of a different type than sought (for example a compound interest instead of a simple one) it may face a challenge under Article 1520(3) of the CCP. It will generally only happen when the rate was not discussed during the proceedings and cannot be based on the parties' submissions.[376]

As to the third point, if, however unlikely, parties prohibit the tribunal to award interest, the tribunal should respect these limits to its powers. It goes in line with the conclusions of the ILA Report mentioned above.[377] Arguably, these restrictions would also apply even in cases where statutory provisions enable the tribunal to grant damages.

371 In principle, there are different theories regarding whether the interest issue has a substantive or procedural character which may affect what law will be chosen by the arbitrator. This line of argumentation has already been discussed above in section 6.2.1 and section 6.2.2. See also Born, *International Commercial Arbitration* (2014) pp.3102-3112.

372 See also Giraud (2017) pp.268-275.

373 See section 6.3.1. See also fn.371.

374 See Giraud (2017) p.269 ("*Par ailleurs, constitue une situation d'ultra petita le fait pour l'arbitre d'appliquer un taux d'intérêt différent de celui plaidé.*").

375 CA Paris, 28 June 1988, *Total Chine v. E.M.H.*, Rev. Arb. 1989, p.328.

376 Giraud (2017) pp.274-275 ("*Il en va autrement en matière d'anatocisme. En effet, l'article 1154 du Code civil ne prévoit pas que le juge puisse accorder d'office la capitalisation des intérêts. Statuera ultra petita l'arbitre qui prononce l'anatocisme des intérêts alors que le contrat ne le prévoit pas et qu'aucune partie n'en a fait la demande. Toutefois, la discussion, par les parties, au cours de la procédure arbitrale, du taux d'intérêt applicable fera obstacle au recours reprochant à l'arbitre d'avoir statué ultra petita en ordonnant l'anatocisme.*"). The author refers as well to CA Paris, 16 January 2003, *Thales Electronics v. Ingénierie des technologies nouvelles*, 2001/11782, Rev. Arb. 2003, p.249. See also Cour de Cassation Civ 1ère, 12 October 2011, *Société Groupe Antoine Tabet v. République du Congo*, Rev. Arb. 2012, p.91.

377 See fn.370.

Fourthly, when parties do not express limitations to the tribunal's powers to grant interest, the tribunal's decision on granting interest may survive even when a party did not request them. It will depend on the applicable law. Without going further into details, it is sufficient to highlight that if French law is applicable to the issue of interest, the tribunal would be able to grant it (at the statutory rate), even in the absence of the parties' request. It is argued that the tribunal may exercise the power to award statutory interest by relying on Article 1153(1) of the Civil Code[378] and that interest is accessory to the main claim.[379] Therefore, when there is no doubt that the tribunal may decide on the main claim, it will be also able to determine the applicable interest.[380] Again, it is necessary to stress that such a position may change if a different law is applicable. Arguably, however, the tribunal's decision granting statutory interest not requested, which is based on a statutory provision of foreign law will stand at the post-award stage in France and would not violate French international public policy.

The fifth point, and "*[o]f note, [award] ordering payment of an interest rate that is considered usury under French law, does not violate French international public policy*".[381] It all leads to the conclusion that the tribunal's decision on interest fits well in the tribunal's mandate.

6.4.2 Decision on costs

Yet another issue that is accessory to the main claims brought by the parties is the costs of the proceedings. The outstanding question is therefore, whether the tribunal's decision on costs may fail to comply with the tribunal's mandate. The traditional analysis should apply with a review of the law, the arbitration agreement and the parties' request. In principle, one should note that French international arbitration law does not include any provision as to the tribunal's authority to decide on costs. Consequently, the power would be dependent on the agreement to arbitrate and the parties' request.

Although parties may not expressly address the issue in their agreements to arbitrate, whenever they do refer to the institutional rules such a tribunal's power will be likely discussed therein.[382] Notably, the complexity of said provisions in institutional rules may

378 ("*En toute matière, la condamnation à une indemnité emporte intérêts au taux légal même en l'absence de demande ou de disposition spéciale du jugement. Sauf disposition contraire de la loi, ces intérêts courent à compter du prononcé du jugement à moins que le juge n'en décide autrement.*").

379 See fn.380. See also ILA, *ILA Report on Inherent Powers of Arbitral Tribunals* (2014) p.10 ("*[T]he Iran-US Claims Tribunal [...] found the power to award interest 'inherent in the Tribunal's authority to decide claims' [...].*").

380 For further reading, see Giraud (2017) pp.272-275.

381 Bensaude (2015) p.1185.

382 See, *e.g.*, Art. 38 of the (draft) 2021 ICC Rules, also Art. 38 of the 2017 ICC Rules, in particular Art. 38(4) which gives the tribunal prerogative to allocate the costs ("*The final award shall fix the costs of the arbitration and decide which of the parties shall bear them or in what proportion they shall be borne by the parties.*").

differ, which further entails the different scope of the tribunal's powers. Occasionally it is also suggested that the tribunal has an inherent power to award costs.[383] Finally, the discussion should be based on the parties' submissions. Under certain circumstances, however, the tribunal's decision on costs even in the absence of the parties' request may survive the challenge. It will be briefly highlighted below.

In principle, a decision on costs shares features of the decision on interest discussed above and the conclusions considered above (on decisions *ultra* or *extra petita*) may be applicable by analogy.[384] It further means that challenges against the mandate can be categorized as follows: (i) the tribunal divided the costs between the parties differently than has been expressly agreed between the parties, and (ii) the tribunal granted costs not requested.

Importantly, however, one should observe that a broad discretion in awarding costs is one of most important procedural (managerial) powers of the tribunal, because it is one of the few mechanisms that allows the tribunal to discipline (and eventually punish) parties for their behavior throughout the proceedings. Such a power to discipline parties is also expressly provided in some institutional rules.[385] Similarly, the ICC Task Force "*has highlighted the relevance of cost decision-making to case management, and particularly the use of cost allocation as a means of incentivizing efficient and cost-effective procedural conduct and sanctioning inefficient and improper conduct.*"[386] Therefore, arguably, although the parties' agreement should be a starting point for the tribunal to decide on costs, its decision on costs also needs to take into account other circumstances of the case. It entails that costs allocations that are different than the one agreed by the parties may still survive the challenge providing that, for example, the tribunal wishes to discipline a party for a bad faith conduct. It is also possible that a similar rationale may be the basis for the tribunal's decision granting costs not requested. It all leads to conclusion that the

---

The same rules were included in the 2012 ICC Rules (See Art. 37 of the 2012 ICC Rules, in particular Art. 37(4)) See also Arts. 40-42 of the 2010 UNCITRAL Rules, in particular Art. 42 of the 2010 UNCITRAL Rules ("*1. The costs of the arbitration shall in principle be borne by the unsuccessful party or parties. However, the arbitral tribunal may apportion each of such costs between the parties if it determines that apportionment is reasonable, taking into account the circumstances of the case. 2. The arbitral tribunal shall in the final award or, if it deems appropriate, in any other award, determine any amount that a party may have to pay to another party as a result of the decision on allocation of costs.*").

383 Indeed, if one thinks of *ad hoc* proceedings, where no fallback mechanism is given (which is opposite to institutional arbitration), one would observe that, arguably, the tribunal will be an ultimate decision maker with regard to the costs. Otherwise, the process regarding costs will be easily frustrated, with difficulties in collecting arbitration costs.

384 See section 6.4.1. It also mirrors the reflections on the decision on damages (section 6.3.1).

385 See, *e.g.*, Art. 38(5) of the (draft) 2021 ICC Rules, Art. 38(5) of the 2017 ICC Rules and Art. 37(5) of the 2012 ICC Rules, which state that: "*In making decisions as to costs, the arbitral tribunal may take into account such circumstances as it considers relevant, including the extent to which each party has conducted the arbitration in an expeditious and cost-effective manner.*"

386 ICC Commision, *Report on Decisions on Costs in International Arbitration* (2015) p.18.

setting-aside court would likely respect the tribunal's findings on costs and leave the decision on costs intact.

6.4.3 Decision on procedure

Under the French international arbitration regime, the tribunal's procedural decisions (that do not follow parties' choice) may be challenged on the basis of the tribunal's failure to comply with its mandate.[387] Again, the starting point is (i) a traditional analysis of the law, the agreement to arbitrate and the parties' submissions, which will be discussed at first together with (ii) the prospective clash between party autonomy to shape the proceedings and the tribunal's managerial powers to conduct proceedings efficiently. Furthermore, a few reflections need to be added regarding (iii) the requirement of establishing that harm has been caused to the parties by the tribunal's decision on procedure and (iv) the impact of the challenge against violation of due process and the violation of French international public policy. Finally, what follows is (v) a short analysis of the tribunal's powers to grant a judicial penalty ("*astreinte*").

The initial analysis should start with French international arbitration law. Pursuant to Article 1509(1) of the CCP "*an arbitration agreement may define the procedure to be followed in the arbitral proceedings, directly or by reference to arbitration rules or to procedural rules.*"[388] Only if the agreement to arbitrate does not provide otherwise, "*the arbitral tribunal shall define the procedure as required, either directly or by reference to arbitration rules or to procedural rules.*"[389] It therefore entails that the tribunal will be obliged to rely on the content of the agreement to arbitrate as to the scope of its procedural powers, be it as it may, based on institutional rules, national (even foreign) laws[390] or the parties' imagination. Only if the parties have not reached any agreement on the issue, the tribunal may step in.[391] Similarly, Bensaude explained it as follows:

387 Racine (2016) p.591.

388 ("*La convention d'arbitrage peut, directement ou par référence à un règlement d'arbitrage ou à des règles de procédure, régler la procédure à suivre dans l'instance arbitrale.*").

389 Art. 1509(2) of the CCP ("*Dans le silence de la convention d'arbitrage, le tribunal arbitral règle la procédure autant qu'il est besoin, soit directement, soit par référence à un règlement d'arbitrage ou à des règles de procédure.*").

390 French law accepts the concept of delocalized arbitration, which entails that the award rendered by the tribunal seated in France that is governed by a different procedural law will not be considered against French international public policy.

391 Clay, *Code de l'arbitrage commenté* (2015) p.189. ("*Premièrement, il existe une hiérarchie dans le choix des règles de procédure applicables à l'arbitrage: c'est d'abord aux parties qu'il revient de faire ce choix, et ensuite, à défaut, aux arbitres. Deuxièmement, ce choix, libre, peut être opéré soit de manière directe, soit de manière indirecte, et il s'impose aux parties. Troisièmement, ce choix peut porter sur un règlement d'arbitrage ou sur des règles de procédure à la normativité incertaine à une véritable lex arbitrii.*").

> [w]here the parties agree upon rules to govern the arbitral proceedings, the arbitral tribunal must conduct the proceedings in accordance with those rules. In all cases, the parties' agreement will bind the tribunal, so long as that agreement is express and sufficiently specific. [...] If the arbitrators breach the parties' procedural agreement, the award may be denied enforcement or set aside in France for failure of the tribunal to comply with its mission (see art. 1520(3)). Failing an express and specific agreement of the parties on any part of the procedure, the tribunal may freely establish procedural rules without reference to any national procedural law or preexisting set of arbitration rules.[392]

Likewise, Loquin observes that "*[t]he [French] Supreme Court held that 'in the presence of specific procedural rules fixed in the arbitration clause, arbitrators could not depart from those rules without disregarding the law that the parties were given and which was binding on them'*."[393]

As to the second point, indeed, it is reasonable to expect that the tribunal follows the parties' wishes that are introduced in the agreement to arbitrate or the initial submissions (up to the moment of drafting the Terms of Reference, if applicable). It is so, because these guidelines made by the parties are made before the tribunal accepts its mandate and, as such, it knows what "rules of the game" it is expected to follow.[394] The situation becomes complicated, however, when a party (or parties) decides to modify the agreement as to the procedure *during* the arbitral process that is *after* the tribunal had already accepted its mandate. There, the legitimate concerns arise. In similar vein, Giraud observes that "*[w]hen the disagreement relates to rules for which nothing had been defined at the time of acceptance by the arbitrators of their mission, the tension between the will of the parties and the jurisdictional aspect of arbitration is the biggest.*"[395] The author distinguishes three hypotheses: (i) one party wishes to modify the procedural rule, (ii) both parties agree to alter the rules of the procedure, and finally (iii) it is the tribunal that imposes change in the proceedings against the will of both parties'.

The first situation is rather simple, because the tribunal is not bound at all to follow one party's wish. In other words, disregarding (in the sense of deciding not to follow) the unilateral party's request should not be perceived as a failure to comply with the mandate.

392 Bensaude (2015) p.1151.

393 Loquin (2015) p.437 ("*La Cour de cassation a jugé « qu'en présence de règles de procédure précises fixées par la clause compromissoire, les arbitres ne pouvaient s'écarter de ces règles sans méconnaître la loi que les parties s'étaient donnée et qui s'imposait à eux ».*").

394 See also Giraud (2017) pp.196-197.

395 Giraud (2017) p.197 ("*Lorsque le désaccord porte sur des règles pour lesquelles rien n'avait été défini au moment de l'acceptation par les arbitres de leur mission, la tension entre la volonté des parties et l'aspect juridictionnel de l'arbitrage est maximale.*").

The second scenario is the most difficult one. In this case, the tension between party autonomy and the jurisdictional mandate of the arbitral tribunal is at its peak. Giraud observes that:

> [t]he second case is more complex, where the parties, by mutual agreement, intend to impose on the arbitrator's compliance with new procedural rules. The arbitrator then already accepted his mission without these new procedural provisions; he is not, at first sight, contractually bound [to follow modifications]. But is he then authorized to refuse? Does the mission of the arbitrator imply acceptance of any procedural modification by the parties during the proceedings? Mr. Jarrosson expressed "caution" about automatic welcoming of any voluntary agreement of the arbitrating parties. The arbitrator must indeed have leeway to carry out his adjudicative mission. He must therefore be able, in this case, to refuse to comply with this change without this constituting a violation of his mission.[396]

This is a reasonable position. One should bear in mind that the legal tie of the tribunal's mandate is no longer between the parties, but it is between three equal entities, the arbitral tribunal included. For this reason, the principle of party autonomy should ultimately find its limit in not allowing the parties to frustrate the arbitral process, if the tribunal refuses to follow procedural modifications of the parties after it accepts its mandate.[397] It is particularly so, because the only (legal) mechanism it has to resist the parties' usurpation would be to resign its mandate,[398] which most likely would frustrate the proceedings even

396 Giraud (2017) p.197 ("*La seconde hypothèse est plus complexe, lorsque les parties, d'un commun accord, entendent imposer à l'arbitre le respect de nouvelles règles de procédure. L'arbitre a alors déjà accepté sa mission, sans ces nouvelles dispositions procédurales; il n'est à première vue pas tenu contractuellement. Mais cela l'autorise-t-il pour autant à refuser? La mission de l'arbitre implique-t-elle son acceptation de toute modification procédurale par les parties au cours de l'instance? M. Jarrosson exprime sa « circonspection » quant à un accueil automatique de tout accord de volonté des parties au litige. L'arbitre doit en effet disposer d'une marge de manœuvre pour mener à bien sa mission juridictionnelle. Il doit donc pouvoir, dans cette hypothèse, refuser de se conformer à ce changement sans que cela constitue une violation de sa mission.*"). See also Schütze (2013) p.106, discussing the application of Art. 19 of the 2012 ICC Rules and limits to party autonomy and references to Art. 22(1) of the 2012 ICC Rules (conducting the proceedings in a cost-effective manner) and Art. 25(1) of the 2012 ICC Rules (requirement to establish facts of the case in as short a time as possible). In the 2017 version of the ICC Rules the same articles apply.

397 Importantly, see Art. 1464 of the CCP, which reads: "*Both parties and arbitrators shall act diligently and in good faith in the conduct of the proceedings.*" ("*Les parties et les arbitres agissent avec célérité et loyauté dans la conduite de la procedure.*"). The translation offered in Bensaude (2015) p.1152 better exposes the requirement to act expeditiously ("*The parties and the arbitrators shall act with celerity and loyalty in the conduct of the proceedings.*"). As explained by Bensaude, "*[t]his provision imposes on the parties and the arbitrators to act 'loyally' and 'swiftly' in the arbitration proceedings.*" See also Clay, *Code de l'arbitrage commenté* (2015) p.92.

398 See Art. 1457 of the CCP.

more. Of course, at the same time, the tribunal's persuasive skills (rather than legal tools) will be essential: "*[d]ialogue and awareness of its adjudicative function are two useful tools for the arbitrator to maintain flexibility in the conduct of the arbitration proceedings.*"[399]

The third scenario envisages a situation where the tribunal imposes a certain procedural rule which neither of the parties wishes to follow.[400] Arguably, however, it is correct to allow the tribunal to lead and manage the proceedings as it finds appropriate to reach its underlying goal of resolving the parties' dispute. It should again be able to follow its understanding of the adjudicative mandate as well as to engage in a dialogue with parties as mentioned above. At the same time, it is necessary to add that in any case, the tribunal, while imposing its will, cannot afford to violate the principle of due process and the fundamental rules of French international public policy.

Additionally, one should observe the adequate argument brought by scholars:

> [t]he majority opinion submits that the arbitrator or arbitrators may not veto a procedural agreement which has been properly concluded by the parties but may only resign if they feel unable to accomplish their task. De lege lata, we feel that this majority opinion is correct in view of the principle of party autonomy. De lege ferenda, we are of the opinion that the Swedish solution is preferable and that the arbitrators should by law have the power to set aside agreements which are an obstacle to the smooth conduct of the proceedings, without having to threaten to resign in order to make their point.[401]

Leaving aside the clash between party autonomy and the adjudicative function of the arbitral tribunal, it is also necessary to highlight that a party that wishes to invoke the ground of failure of the tribunal to comply with its mission on the procedural grounds needs to establish that the procedural decision caused harm to that party. As explained by Loquin, "*[a]n action for annulment of the award may be received in respect of this complaint [i.e. not following parties' procedural agreement], but only as long as the violation of the will of the parties caused a harm [to] any of them.*"[402]

Importantly, Loquin also adds that

> [t]he harm referred [to] should not be confused with violation of due process defence which falls under Article 1492-4°of the Civil Procedure Code. It is

399 Giraud (2017) pp.197-200. See also ILA, *ILA Report on Inherent Powers of Arbitral Tribunals* (2014) p.19.

400 The rule, however, is not in opposition to the rules of the proceedings introduced before acceptance of the mandate. See also fn.397.

401 Poudret & Besson (2007) pp.462-463.

402 Loquin (2015) p.437 ("*Un recours en annulation de la sentence pourra être reçu au titre de ce grief, mais seulement à la condition que la violation de la volonté des parties cause à l'une d'entre elles un préjudice.*").

> other than that resulting from the infringement of the right to defend, which explains its rarity. This can be for example failure to respect [the] time limit for presenting parties' submissions or filing written statements, contractually fixed by the parties to arbitration.[403]

It consequently leads to the fourth point of inquiry, thus the interface between different prongs of the setting-aside procedure.

Violating French international public policy and the violation of due process, thus grounds separate from failure to comply with the tribunal's mission, will be particularly relevant in the context of the tribunal's decision on procedure. As already pointed out earlier,[404] the annulment court may decide to requalify the challenge and assign it with a different setting-aside ground. It means that even if a challenging party invokes Article 1520(3) of the CCP as the ground for annulment, the court may very well consider that the challenge is valid, albeit under a different ground. Therefore, for example, one should highlight that "*misinterpretation of documentary evidence must not be confused with the violation of the mission of the arbitrators since the latter only concerns the jurisdictional powers and not the decision on the merits.*"[405] At the same time, even if the challenge against the procedural decision is not requalified, the tribunal should be always cautious to decide in accordance with French international public policy. As has been argued, "*[i]n any event, all procedural decisions made by the tribunal must be made in conformity with French procedural international public policy, such as the principles of due process and equality among the parties.*"[406]

Finally, it is necessary to point out that whenever the tribunal is seated in France, it will have a rather unique procedural power, namely *astreinte*.[407] "*Astreinte is a periodic penalty payment which can be imposed by a court on a debtor who has not executed his duty.*"[408] It has been observed that

> [t]here is controversy as to whether arbitrators can attach penalties to their procedural orders. It has been argued that their lack of imperium and the absence of statutory basis prevents them from doing so. However, we consider

---

403 Loquin (2015) p.437 ("*[...] Le prejudice visé ne doit pas être confondu avec violation des droits de la défence qui relève de l'article 1492-4° du Code de procédure civile. Il est autre que celui résultant de l'atteinte aux droits de la défense, ce qui explique sa rareté. Il peut s'agir par exemple du non-respect d'un délai de remis des conclusions ou d'une pièce du dossier, fixé contractuelement par les parties à l'arbitrage.*").

404 See section 3.1.

405 Poudret & Besson (2007) p.742.

406 Bensaude (2015) p.1151.

407 See Art. 1468 of the CCP.

408 Borghetti (2009) p.57. The author also adds that "*[t]he latter has to pay, in addition to his initial debt and possible damages set by the court, a certain sum (usually calculated on a daily basis) until he fulfils his duty.*"

> that where the arbitration agreement is drafted in terms sufficiently broad so as not to exclude that option (such as "all disputes arising out of the present contract"), there is no reason why international commercial arbitrators should not attach penalties to their injunctions, provided that the measures are incorporated, in the interests of enforcement, in an interim award. The French courts have held this approach to be valid.[409]

Other scholarly writing considered that "*[the] power [to grant astreinte] results from the jurisdiction and not from the imperium*"[410] and that, more importantly,

> [t]he arbitrator, similarly to the state judge, may order *astreinte* ex officio without acting ultra petita. The new Article 1468 [of the CCP] [which is applicable in international arbitration] does not envisage any restrictions to the arbitral tribunal's power to impose *astreinte*. It is for the arbitral tribunal to determine 'if there is need' to impose *astreinte*.[411]

In the end, it means that the tribunal's decision disciplining the party will fit within the tribunal's procedural powers.[412] All in all, as long as Article 1520(3) of the CCP may be invoked to challenge the procedural decision of the arbitral tribunal, one should note that it will not be easily accepted by the setting-aside court.

7 Concluding remarks

The position of France as leading forum for international arbitration remains impregnable. The new statutory framework for international arbitration refreshed and modernized the model introduced at the beginning of the 1980s without disturbing the core principle of the system, namely its pro-arbitration stand. In addition, judges continue to respect the parties' choice to outsource the resolution of their disputes to arbitration and to defer to the tribunal's decisions at the post-award stage. Therefore, the courts will adhere to the

409 Gaillard & Savage, *Fouchard Gaillard Goldman on International Commercial Arbitration* (1999) p.697.

410 Loquin (2015) p.282 ("*Ce pouvoir relève de la juridiction et non de l'imperium.*").

411 Loquin (2015) p.283 ("*L'arbitre, comme le juge étatique, peut d'office ordonner une astreinte sans juger ultra petita. Le nouvel article 1468 CPC ne prévoit aucune restriction au pouvoir du tribunal arbitral de prononcer une astreinte. Il appartient au tribunal arbitral d'apprécier « s'il est besoin » de prononcer une astreinte.*").

412 For further reading, see, *e.g.*, Mourre, *Judicial Penalties and Specific Performance in International Arbitration* (2011) pp.355-378, Racine (2016) pp.448-449. See also CA Paris, 7 October 2004, *Société Otor Participations et autres v. Carlyle Holdings 1 et autre*, Rev. Arb. 2005, p.737 ("*Le prononcé d'astreintes ou d'injonctions constitue un prolongement inhérent et nécessaire à la fonction de juger pour assurer une meilleure efficacité au pouvoir juridictionnel et ne caractérise ainsi aucun dépassement de la mission de l'arbitre.*").

no review on the merits principle, will remedy (if possible) the tribunal's wrongdoings by annulling the award only the part of the award that is flawed and by sanctioning abusive use of the setting-aside proceedings.

The provision that is invoked for the excess of mandate challenge reads that the award can be set aside when "*the tribunal ruled without complying with the mandate conferred upon it.*" Essentially it means that the setting-aside court needs to test what the mandate given to the tribunal was and check if the tribunal respected its constraints. The outstanding question is *who* conferred the mandate upon the tribunal: the parties or the State. In fact, both the parties and the State shape the mandate. The parties have a much closer impact on the shape of the arbitral tribunal's mandate, because they designate the tribunal's powers and responsibilities in the agreement to arbitrate and (individually) in their respective prayers for relief. The State, however, influences the mandate as well, because it allows the parties to delegate the dispute resolution and rendering of justice to the independent, non-state service provider with the commandment not to violate international public policy. Consequently, it entails that the mandate is delineated by the agreement to arbitrate, the parties' requests and the French concept of international public policy.

Because both the parties and the State are relevant in shaping the mandate, different definitions explaining the meaning of the arbitral tribunal's mandate can be introduced. In this chapter it has been argued that the mandate in its broader sense explains the functional aspect of the tribunal's responsibility. In other words, the broad definition of the tribunal's mandate focuses on the adjudicative role of the tribunal, therefore, the power that is delegated to the tribunal (indirectly) by the State. Conversely, the narrow definition of the mandate stresses the importance of the parties' constraints imposed on the tribunal's powers. None of these two definitions alone serves well for the purpose of Article 1520(3) of the CCP. For this reason, both of them need to be taken into account. Effectively, the mandate under Article 1520(3) of the CCP should be understood as to refer to the limits dictated by the parties but only on the adjudicative powers of the arbitral tribunal.

Notably, the excess of mandate provision has been slightly redrafted during the reform of French arbitration law. In the French text of the new provision the verb *confier* (Eng. to entrust, to confide) has been used and replaced the verb *conférer* (Eng. to confer) that had been used previously. Both of them have been usually translated in English as *to confer* and have been used accordingly.[413] Neither scholars nor judges had found this change relevant (yet).[414] One should reflect nonetheless if the change does not shift the balance of the teleological meaning of the provision by accentuating more the trust that is given to the tribunal by the parties (and the State) rather than the formal (contractual) framework

413 See Annex 1.

414 Giraud (2017) p.31.

on which the tribunal's mandate has been established.[415] Additionally, one should note that in the original French text the term "mission" rather than "mandate" has been used. Arguably, "mission that is entrusted" stresses more the adjudicative function than the phrasing "the mandate that is conferred upon". Accordingly, if such an argument survives, it is the adjudicative function of the tribunal that is of key importance rather than the (contractual) limitations envisaged by the parties themselves. It would be particularly relevant in the case of the procedural decisions of the tribunal, where the goal of resolving disputes between the parties would eventually trump the parties' will to shape the proceedings freely and, on occasion, carelessly.

The application of the excess of mandate ground to the selected tribunal's decisions resulted in several observations. In general, decisions on claims will fit under this challenge whenever the tribunal's decision is rendered *ultra petita* or *extra petita*. In other words, the decision that grants something more (*ultra petita*) or something different from what was claimed (*extra petita*) should be successfully annulled at the post-award stage. Notably, however, only the part of the award that goes beyond the request is most likely to be set aside by the court. One should add that the *infra petita* award (therefore the award where not all claims have been decided upon) are not susceptible to the excess of mandate ground because of the remedial power given by Article 1485(2) of the CCP.

The multi-contract universe (or instances where tort claims are brought) gives rise to another issue. When the claims presented before the tribunal arise from a different contract, the problem of delineating the mandate is closely intertwined with the notion of the scope of the tribunal's jurisdiction. Sometimes, based on facts, it is difficult to distinguish whether it is the mandate of the jurisdiction that is exceeded and consequently, whether the challenge should be based on Article 1520(1) or Article 1520(3) of the CCP. More often than not, however, these scope questions fit better under the excess of jurisdiction ground (*i.e.* Article 1520(1) of the CCP).

Similarly, issues relating to set-offs give rise to jurisdictional questions (and not to those on mandate). On occasion, however, they may be qualified as a mandate question. Again, in the multi-contract scenario, where the set-off claimed is based on a different contract than the initial claim, the tribunal will be faced with a difficult balancing exercise. On the one hand, it has to recognize that its mandate is primarily shaped by the parties' *common* intention, which means that they may have wished to resolve disputes arising out of different contracts separately (by including different dispute resolution clauses for example). On the other hand, set-off is considered a material defense and if it is brought to the tribunal, it means that a party makes use of its prerogative to apply all available defenses. Depending on the circumstances of the case it is argued that at least in some instances (for example where claims are sufficiently related) the tribunal's decision granting

415 See further section 5.

set-off should survive the challenge. It is likely, however, that such a decision will risk being set aside.

Another problem appears when the tribunal decides to requalify the parties' claim. Since the parties' claims shape the limits to its function, by requalifying it the tribunal will alter its mandate. If it does so, however, without asking the parties to comment on the suggested requalification, it may violate due process and, consequently, trigger the application of Article 1520(4) of the CCP even though it can be argued that by requalifying the claim it fails to comply with its original task. In any event, it has been explained that the French courts will subsume the challenge to the appropriate legal ground if they find another ground to be better suited than the excess of mandate.

The process of the application of law, arguably, does not give rise to many excess of mandate issues. It is so, because of the great default power given to the tribunal under Article 1511 of the CCP. Pursuant to this Article, "*[t]he arbitral tribunal shall decide the dispute in accordance with the rules of law chosen by the parties or, where no such choice has been made, in accordance with the rules of law it considers appropriate.*" It essentially means that the application of law is inherent to the tribunal's adjudicative function. Remarkably, the tribunal is *even* allowed to apply not only the law, but also the rules of law on its own motion. Consequently, only decisions that acknowledge the parties' choice of applicable law and nevertheless disregard it might be successfully challenged or decisions that violate the French concept of international public policy. At this point it should be added therefore that the tribunal's compliance with the overriding rules of public policy constitutes a core part of its mandate. Therefore, in case of a clash between overriding rules of public policy and parties' arrangements (that are contrary to these overriding rules of public policy), a tribunal's decision that defers to the public policy rules would have more chances to survive.

The tribunal will have a unique set of powers when it is given the mandate of *amiable compositeur.* According to Article 1512 of the CCP, the tribunal may rule as *amiable compositeur* only when expressly empowered by the parties. It means that the non-authorized use of such powers or violation of the French concept of international public policy will be the only arguments that would explain the successful application of Article 1520(3) of the CCP.

Overall, the tribunal's remedial powers are broad and, in principle, it should be anticipated that they would fit within the limits of the tribunal's mandate. Essentially, the tribunal will have the power to grant damages, to grant specific performance or to adapt the contract. Consequently, it entails that a decision on remedies may be only set aside if not requested (or is different from that requested) or falling outside the scope of a tailored (narrow) agreement to arbitrate or the applicable law (which limits the tribunal's power to grant specific performance for example). In other words, the tribunal's decisions on remedies may be challenged under similar circumstances as decisions on claims (usually it will be the same decision). Therefore, in principle, only decisions *ultra* and *extra petita* will be challengeable.

The decisions accessory to main claims such as a decision on interest or costs should also survive the excess of mandate challenge. Notably, a decision on interest may be enforced even if not requested, considering that the applicable law allows for the addition of interest in statutory rate *ipso iure*. A decision on costs shows similarities with a decision on interest. Importantly, however, they are one of a few disciplinary mechanisms against the parties available to the tribunal. For this reason, these decisions should be approached by the setting-aside court with leniency. In other words, if the tribunal's decision on costs is not aligned with the parties' requests, because of a bad faith conduct it should not be set aside at a post-award stage even if it does not comply with the prayers for relief. Often, such a power to discipline is given by the institutional rules.

Finally, decisions on the procedure are sometimes brought under the excess of mandate challenge. As highlighted above these objections are better suited under Article 1520(4) or 1520(5) of the CCP, namely the challenge of due process or violation of French international public policy. As noted, invoking the excess of mandate ground is rarely successful because the party needs to show that the (procedural) decision caused harm to that party.

In any event, if the parties frame their agreement as to the proceedings, the tribunal will be generally obliged to follow it. It becomes more complicated, however, when the procedural rules are being remodeled after the tribunal had accepted its mandate. Put differently, if the parties decide to change "the rules of the game" while playing it, tension is brought between party autonomy and the tribunal's legitimate expectations as to how it can exercise its adjudicative function. For this reason, the better view is to allow the arbitrators the freedom to disregard the parties' (procedural) agreements that are made after the establishment of the mandate. It also means that failure to comply with the amendments of the procedural aspect of the mandate that have been made after the tribunal accepted the mandate, should not succeed at the post-award stage. Of course, such a far-reaching freedom should only be used when dialogue with parties fails and when the proposed procedural agreement seriously hampers the efficiency of the proceedings and the successful completion of the underlying aim of dispute resolution.

All in all, it seems that the French courts to date do their best to ensure that only grievous examples of non-compliance with the mandate are set aside at the post-award stage. One should be aware, however, that the ground remains open for (broadening) interpretation that potentially might interfere with the autonomy of international arbitration.

IV England and the Arbitration Act of 1996

1 Introduction

English arbitration law is currently structured upon the Arbitration Act of 1996 (hereafter also referred to as the "Act" or the "Arbitration Act"),[1] which has been drafted by the Departmental Advisory Committee on Arbitration Law (also referred to as the "DAC").[2] The DAC introduced in the 1996 English arbitration regime rather an elaborate mechanism for challenging an arbitral award, which will be explained in detail below. At the outset it should be noted, however, that the "excess of mandate" is *not* one of the grounds listed in this challenge procedure. Nonetheless, it does not mean that the tribunal's transgressions will escape the courts' scrutiny. In fact, it only shows that the concept of "excess of mandate" is scattered and, consequently, it might be necessary to invoke all three challenge provisions to determine whether the tribunal has exceeded its "mandate". The three relevant challenge provisions are provided below.

Section 67 of the Act provides that:

> (1) A party to arbitral proceedings may (upon notice to the other parties and to the tribunal) apply to the court—
> (a) challenging any award of the arbitral tribunal as to its substantive jurisdiction; or
> (b) for an order declaring an award made by the tribunal on the merits to be of no effect, in whole or in part, because the tribunal did not have substantive jurisdiction.
> A party may lose the right to object (see section 73) and the right to apply is subject to the restrictions in section 70(2) and (3).
> (2) The arbitral tribunal may continue the arbitral proceedings and make a further award while an application to the court under this section is pending in relation to an award as to jurisdiction.
> (3) On an application under this section challenging an award of the arbitral tribunal as to its substantive jurisdiction, the court may by order—

1 Whenever reference is made to the older Acts, the term will be preceded by the date of enactment of the Act, for example, the Arbitration Act of 1950 will be mentioned as the 1950 Act. In the historical part, in order to avoid confusion, the Act will be sometimes referred to as the 1996 Act.

2 For further reading on the historical overview, see section 2.

(a) confirm the award,
(b) vary the award, or
(c) set aside the award in whole or in part.
(4) The leave of the court is required for any appeal from a decision of the court under this section.

Pursuant to Section 68 of the Act:

(1) A party to arbitral proceedings may (upon notice to the other parties and to the tribunal) apply to the court challenging an award in the proceedings on the ground of serious irregularity affecting the tribunal, the proceedings or the award.
A party may lose the right to object (see section 73) and the right to apply is subject to the restrictions in section 70(2) and (3).
(2) Serious irregularity means an irregularity of one or more of the following kinds which the court considers has caused or will cause substantial injustice to the applicant—
(a) failure by the tribunal to comply with section 33 (general duty of tribunal);
(b) the tribunal exceeding its powers (otherwise than by exceeding its substantive jurisdiction: see section 67);
(c) failure by the tribunal to conduct the proceedings in accordance with the procedure agreed by the parties;
(d) failure by the tribunal to deal with all the issues that were put to it;
(e) any arbitral or other institution or person vested by the parties with powers in relation to the proceedings or the award exceeding its powers;
(f) uncertainty or ambiguity as to the effect of the award;
(g) the award being obtained by fraud or the award or the way in which it was procured being contrary to public policy;
(h) failure to comply with the requirements as to the form of the award; or
(i) any irregularity in the conduct of the proceedings or in the award which is admitted by the tribunal or by any arbitral or other institution or person vested by the parties with powers in relation to the proceedings or the award.
(3) If there is shown to be serious irregularity affecting the tribunal, the proceedings or the award, the court may—
(a) remit the award to the tribunal, in whole or in part, for reconsideration,
(b) set the award aside in whole or in part, or
(c) declare the award to be of no effect, in whole or in part.
The court shall not exercise its power to set aside or to declare an award to be of no effect, in whole or in part, unless it is satisfied that it would be

inappropriate to remit the matters in question to the tribunal for reconsideration.
(4) The leave of the court is required for any appeal from a decision of the court under this section.

Finally, Section 69 of the Act reads:

(1) Unless otherwise agreed by the parties, a party to arbitral proceedings may (upon notice to the other parties and to the tribunal) appeal to the court on a question of law arising out of an award made in the proceedings.
An agreement to dispense with reasons for the tribunal's award shall be considered an agreement to exclude the court's jurisdiction under this section.
(2) An appeal shall not be brought under this section except—
(a) with the agreement of all the other parties to the proceedings, or
(b) with the leave of the court.
The right to appeal is also subject to the restrictions in section 70(2) and (3).
(3) Leave to appeal shall be given only if the court is satisfied—
(a) that the determination of the question will substantially affect the rights of one or more of the parties,
(b) that the question is one which the tribunal was asked to determine,
(c) that, on the basis of the findings of fact in the award—
(i) the decision of the tribunal on the question is obviously wrong, or
(ii) the question is one of general public importance and the decision of the tribunal is at least open to serious doubt, and
(d) that, despite the agreement of the parties to resolve the matter by arbitration, it is just and proper in all the circumstances for the court to determine the question.
(4) An application for leave to appeal under this section shall identify the question of law to be determined and state the grounds on which it is alleged that leave to appeal should be granted.
(5) The court shall determine an application for leave to appeal under this section without a hearing unless it appears to the court that a hearing is required.
(6) The leave of the court is required for any appeal from a decision of the court under this section to grant or refuse leave to appeal.
(7) On an appeal under this section the court may by order—
(a) confirm the award,
(b) vary the award,
(c) remit the award to the tribunal, in whole or in part, for reconsideration in the light of the court's determination, or

> (d) set aside the award in whole or in part.
> The court shall not exercise its power to set aside an award, in whole or in part, unless it is satisfied that it would be inappropriate to remit the matters in question to the tribunal for reconsideration.
> (8) The decision of the court on an appeal under this section shall be treated as a judgment of the court for the purposes of a further appeal.
> But no such appeal lies without the leave of the court which shall not be given unless the court considers that the question is one of general importance or is one which for some other special reason should be considered by the Court of Appeal.

At the outset, it seems that the concept of "excess of powers" of Section 68(2)(b) of the Act (as one of the serious irregularities) is the closest to the "excess of mandate" challenge. Consequently, an analysis of the "excess of powers" ground will be a primary objective of this chapter. Focusing, however, only on this notion would lead to incomplete results, because some of the tribunal's actions in relation to the exercise of the tribunal's powers might escape the excess of powers challenge while they can trigger other grounds available under the English Arbitration Act (for example arbitral awards *infra petita* may trigger a different heading of "serious irregularities"; a challenge of substantive jurisdiction or an appeal on point of law can also be relevant to determine how the tribunal exercised its powers). For this reason, and as explained above, it is better to have a closer look at all three avenues of the English challenge procedure (*i.e.* substantive jurisdiction (Section 67 of the Act), (selected) serious irregularities (Section 68 of the Act) and appeal on point of law (Section 69 of the Act) to determine which proviso(s) can be used (and in what circumstances) to test the tribunal's exercise of its adjudicative mission.

At first, it is necessary to sketch a brief overview of how the setting-aside system of the English arbitration regime evolved. Since the earliest legislation on arbitration has already been introduced in the seventeenth century,[3] it is important to show the development (and provide an understanding) of the concept of judicial control over the arbitral award with special focus on the actions against the tribunal's breach of mandate.

Secondly, following the historical summary, general information on the currently available recourse methods in the English system will be provided. Three sections will follow, each explaining one of the three types of challenges that will be studied (namely violation of substantive jurisdiction, serious irregularity and appeal on point of law). The outline of these sections will be similar thus they are discussed here jointly. At the beginning

---

3 See Lew & Holm, *Development of the Arbitral System in England* (2013) p.2 ("*Statute 9 & 10 Will. 3, c.15 which has sometimes been referred to as the first arbitration act or the Arbitration Act of 1698*"). For the ease of reference, the term "1698 Arbitration Act" will be used. See also Mustill & Boyd (1989) pp.436-440.

of each of these sections the standard of the court's review will be discussed. Having established how the court may approach the challenge, due regard needs to be given to the meaning and the application of each offensive ground prescribed by Sections 67 to 69 of the Arbitration Act.

The focus will particularly remain, however, on the concept of serious irregularity, because grounds such as excess of powers and failure to deal with all the issues that were brought before the tribunal are listed as a serious irregularity. Pursuant to Section 68(2) of the Arbitration Act "*serious irregularity means an irregularity [...] which the court considers has caused or will cause substantial injustice to the applicant.*" In addition, it needs to be pointed out that Section 68 of the Act (along with Section 67) is a mandatory provision from which parties cannot contractually deviate.

The sections explaining the grounds available to challenge the award will lead further to the introduction of a three-headed concept for a challenge. Some reflections as to the relevance of a three-headed concept for the review of the tribunal's adjudicative powers under the English arbitration regime will be presented. Arguably, each of the provisions on the challenge might be relevant while reviewing the arbitral tribunal's undertakings.

Thirdly, different tribunal's actions will be tested against the challenge. Ultimately (and similarly to other chapters), the analysis of hypothetical scenarios seeks to clarify when it is appropriate to apply the challenge procedure to the tribunal's actions that are beyond its authority. The tribunal's actions have been selected to comprehensively illustrate what the tribunal must do in order to effectively fulfill its adjudicatory function. Therefore, the list includes the tribunal's decisions on different types of claims, different types of remedies and on the process of application of law. Moreover, the list entails the tribunal's decisions that are supplementary to its decisions on the main claims such as, for example, decisions on interest and costs. The conclusions offered should clarify how the tribunal's mandate can be tested when the international commercial arbitration is seated in England and governed by the English Arbitration Act.

2 Historical overview of the development of judicial scrutiny over arbitral awards under English arbitration law

Before giving a more elaborate analysis of the 1996 Act and the three-headed concept created therein (see section 3), a few historical highlights regarding the judicial control of arbitral awards will be addressed.[4] Therefore, the overview below will be divided into the

4 The analysis aims to give only a brief overview, thus, on occasion it may come across as oversimplified. Additionally, it will not deal with, albeit important, recourse against the tribunal's "mistake of law". For further reading on history of arbitration in England and judicial supervision of the English courts, see, *i.a.*, Mustill & Boyd (1989) pp.431-458, Tweeddale & Tweeddale (2007) pp.477-492, Lew & Holm, *Development*

period before the 1889 Act (section 2.1), that before the 1996 Act (section 2.2) and it will be concluded with a brief comment on the preparations of the 1996 Act (section 2.3).

2.1 *Judicial control of arbitral awards before the 1889 Act*

In order to understand the peculiarities of English arbitration it is necessary to briefly examine the English arbitration regime predating the 1889 Act where in fact three autonomous arbitration systems existed, each of them having a different scope of judicial control. Therefore one should look at the scrutiny over (i) voluntary arbitration,[5] (ii) a reference to arbitration ordered by a court[6] and (iii) a reference to arbitration in accordance with the 1698 Act.[7]

In principle, voluntary arbitration largely escaped the court's scrutiny, because "*[…] the arbitration proceeded independently of the courts, and the powers of judicial intervention were more narrow than in the case where the submission was a rule of court [thus, reference to arbitration ordered by a court], although not wholly non-existent.*"[8] In the context of voluntary arbitration it has been also argued that:

> [j]udicial control over a voluntary reference out of Court was clumsy and unsystematic. Misconduct by the arbitrator was never recognised as a defence to an action on the award or on the penal bond. Nor was there ever a jurisdiction

of the Arbitral System in England (2013) pp.1-18. For the historical perspective, see also Russell (1849), Cave & Wetton (1935), Ellenbogen (1952), Blanco White & Walton (1957), Walton & Vitoria (1982).

5 Voluntary arbitration has been aptly summarized in Mustill & Boyd (1989) p.434: "*We have already referred to the fact that the form of arbitration in use at the beginning of the seventeenth century was a voluntary submission out of the court, secured by a penal bond. This procedure was, subject to a potentially fatal weakness, namely that the arbitrator's authority was conceived to be a mandate revocable at the will of either party, at any time before award. This meant that a party could frustrate the reference simply by withdrawing the authority of the arbitrator. The revocation was treated as a breach of contract, for which damages would lie, and an action could also be brought on the bond. But these did not always permit a complete remedy. A revocation did not attract the penalties appropriate to a contempt of court, since the submission was a private contract; and the position was not improved by an insertion in the submission of an agreement not to revoke it, since the mandate was regarded as being intrinsically revocable.*" See also Lew & Holm, *Development of the Arbitral System in England* (2013) p.2 ("*[…] the voluntary process relied heavily on the good faith of parties. An arbitral award was not equated to a judgment: a party wishing to enforce an arbitral award had to bring new proceedings at court for breach of contract.*"

6 Mustill & Boyd (1989) p.433 ("*A reference in a pending cause. The submission to arbitration came after, not before, the involvement of the Court in the dispute.*").

7 Mustill & Boyd (1989) p.433 ("*Here the submission was consensual, and preceded the involvement of the Court. The effect of an order making the submission a rule of court was not to turn the arbitration into action, but to attach to the submission certain characteristics which were similar to those possessed by a reference in a pending cause.*"), see also *i.a.* Tweeddale & Tweeddale (2007) p.482.

8 Mustill & Boyd (1989) p.434.

> in a court of common law to set aside an award for misconduct. The only available remedy was a bill in equity.[9]

For the purpose of the research at hand, however, all the more interesting is the review mechanism with the other two types of arbitration.

This (second) method of arbitration was called "*a reference in a pending cause*".[10] In a nutshell, "*[i]n the absence of an arbitration agreement, high court judges had an inherent jurisdiction to refer the matter to arbitration with the consent of the parties. Arbitration pursuant to an order of the court remained under close supervision and control of the court.*"[11] It was available to the parties even before the 1698 Act and is important because the arbitral tribunal's powers relied on the powers of the court.[12] In turn, the court could rely on its inherent jurisdiction to supervise arbitration,[13] thus also to set the arbitral award aside.[14]

Russell in the first edition of his treatise collected and categorized when the award can be set aside. He explained that the award may be challenged (i) "*where the conduct of the arbitrator [is] corrupt or irregular*" (ii) "*when the award [is] a mistaken decision in law or fact*", (iii) "*when the award is a nullity*", (iv) "*when the award is not final*", (v) "*when the award is uncertain*", (vi) "*when the arbitrator has exceeded his authority*", (vii) "*where [the] party or witness [is] in fault, or [a] new matter [is] discovered*".[15]

The enactment of the 1698 Act "*allowed for enforcement of a written submission to arbitration that was expressly made a rule of court, thus affording voluntary arbitration some of the procedural advantages enjoyed by court-based arbitrations.*"[16] More importantly,

---

9 Mustill & Boyd (1989) p.435; see also Russell (1849) p.434 ("*When the submission was by agreement out of court, the courts of common law had no authority to set aside an award until the statute 9 & 10 Will. III c. 15.*").

10 Mustill & Boyd (1989) p.433.

11 Lew & Holm, *Development of the Arbitral System in England* (2013) p.2.

12 Mustill & Boyd (1989) pp.432-433 ("*[a]lthough the Court delegated part of its functions to the arbitrator, it retained the remainder. No statutory powers were needed to enable the Court to intervene in case of error or misconduct; it possessed these powers inherently, because the arbitrator's mandate from the court was limited to the conduct of the reference in a proper manner.*").

13 Mustill & Boyd (1989) p.433. Notably, however, some authors suggest that "*prior to 1698 there were almost no grounds on which a court could review an arbitrator's award. On questions of law and fact the decision of the arbitral tribunal was final. The court would not even review the merits of the award where questions of natural justice were raised.*" For further reading, see Tweeddale & Tweeddale (2007) pp.482-483; the authors made reference *i.a.* to *Matthew v. Ollerton* (1693) 4 Mod 226, where "*the courts refused to overturn an award made by the arbitrator who was in fact one of the parties in dispute.*"

14 Mustill & Boyd (1989) p.437.

15 For further reading, see Russell (1849) pp.442-449.

16 Lew & Holm, *Development of the Arbitral System in England* (2013) p.3. As pointed out by a number of scholars, the advantage being that qualifying non-compliance with a submission agreement expressly made a rule of court a contempt of court. See Mustill & Boyd (1989) p.433 ("*The Statute went on to provide that parties who wished to submit a dispute to arbitration could agree that their submission to arbitration should be made a rule of any court of record of their choice. Upon production of such an agreement, the Court would by summary process make the submission a rule. Failure to comply with the submission would render the*

however, it also included the statutory provision on the setting-aside procedure, where, in the relevant part, it has been stated that the award could be set aside if "*procured by corruption or undue means*".[17] As long as challenge on the ground of corruption is rather clear for the contemporary reader, the setting aside of the award "procured by undue means" requires perhaps few words of explanation.

Russell explains that:

> [i]t is evident that the term 'undue means' signifies something different from corruption, for although there be no ground for imputing improper motives to the arbitrator, the court will set aside the award as procured by 'undue means,' if the course pursued on [ ] the reference ha[s] been inconsistent with natural justice; as for instance, if the witnesses have been examined in the absence of the parties, or the plaintiff [is] not allowed a proper opportunity of discussing his case.[18]

In similar vein, the authors of the thirteenth edition of *Russell on Arbitration* concluded that: "*[t]he latter phrase was interpreted to mean some act contrary to natural justice, and included misconduct when such misconduct was contrary to natural justice.*"[19] Therefore, one can conclude that two types of judicial supervision over the arbitral awards developed simultaneously and this development had its consequences on the period that followed.[20]

---

offender liable to process for contempt of court."), Tweeddale & Tweeddale (2007) p.482 ("*[...] where the arbitration submission was made a rule of court then a breach of the submission agreement would amount to a contempt of court.*"), Lew & Holm, *Development of the Arbitral System in England* (2013) pp.2-3 ("*The 1698 Act provided that where an arbitration was conducted under the inherent jurisdiction or by consent of the court, a failure by a party to perform the award amounted to contempt of court.*").

17 Pursuant to *9 & 10 W. III. c. 15, s.2* "*And be it further enacted by the authority aforesaid, that any arbitration or umpirage procured by corruption or under means, shall be judged and esteemed void and of none effect, and accordingly be set aside by any Court of law or equity [...].*" Reference made after Cave & Wetton (1935) p.172.

18 Russell (1849) p.449. Yet, the same author also acknowledged that "*The restriction, however, imposed by the language of the Act has subsequently been much disregarded, for the courts will listen to application to set aside awards under the statute on other grounds than the two enumerated in the section; [...] And Lord Eldon, C., observing on the Act in one instance, remarked, 'There is one case in which the courts have not considered themselves strictly bound by the words of the statute. The Act is silent as to mistake or error of the arbitrators, yet it is now settled that an award may be set aside for mistake or error, if admitted by the arbitrators.'*"

19 Cave & Wetton (1935) p.173.

20 It is necessary to note the importance of the Common Law Procedure Act of 1854. Since this statute, the courts were empowered not only to set the award aside but also to remit the case back to the tribunal. See Lew & Holm, *Development of the Arbitral System in England* (2013) p.3. As argued by Mustill and Boyd, this statutory competence to remit was available for the courts both in cases of (i) submissions by rule of court in a pending action and (ii) submissions in accordance with the 1698 Act. For further reading, see Mustill & Boyd (1989) p.443.

2.2 *Judicial review of arbitral awards before the 1996 Act*

There is a huge gap in time between the 1889 Act and the 1996 Act. During these years a number of changes to the English arbitration regime had taken place, starting with the 1889 Act through the 1934 Act and the 1950 Act. The last one was also amended by the 1979 Act.[21] For the purpose of the research at hand, however, it is only relevant for how the grounds to set the award aside developed throughout the years.[22] Yet, a division has to be made for awards being set aside (i) according to the statutory provision and (ii) pursuant to the court's inherent jurisdiction.

With regard to the statutory grounds for setting aside, the 1889 Act replaced two grounds available under the 1698 Act.[23] The new model was proposed with the 1889 Act.[24] Pursuant to Section 11(2) of the 1889 Act, "*[w]here an arbitrator or umpire has misconducted himself, or an arbitration has been improperly procured, the Court may set the award aside.*"[25] It has been further amended by the 1934 Act, which supplemented the wording with the expression "*or the proceedings*"[26] and later became Section 23(2) of the 1950 Act, which reads: "*[w]here an arbitrator or umpire has misconducted himself or the proceedings, or an arbitration award has been improperly procured, the High Court may set the award aside.*"[27] The distinction (between the misconduct of the arbitrator and misconduct of the proceedings) was said to have no practical significance though it attracted "*speculation as to the difference between the two forms of words.*"[28]

Essentially, it has been argued that "*little would be gained by attempting a complete definition of the behavior which constitutes 'misconduct'*".[29] In any event, of particular allure

---

21 Few other Acts relating to arbitration were enacted during this period. They are not, however, of immediate relevance for this research and will not be discussed. For further reading, see, *e.g.*, Mustill & Boyd (1989) pp.436-458, Tweeddale & Tweeddale (2007) pp.485-489, Lew & Holm, *Development of the Arbitral System in England* (2013) pp.3-8.

22 In general, the grounds for setting aside are the same grounds that can be invoked to remit the award to the tribunal. Walton & Vitoria (1982) p.396.

23 Thus "an award procured by corruption" and "an award procured by undue means". See section 2.1 above.

24 Blanco White & Walton (1957) p.289 ("*The power to set aside for 'misconduct' generally was new with the 1889 Act: the previous Act, referred only to 'arbitration or umpirage procured by corruption or undue means'. Misconduct inconsistent with 'natural justice' was regarded as coming within these words, but cases decided before 1889 must nevertheless be regarded as unreliable upon this point. At common law, there was an inherent jurisdiction to set aside already referred to. [The reference in section 23 (2) to misconduct of the proceedings was new in 1934: it appears to have been, in substance, declaratory].*").

25 As referred to by Cave & Wetton (1935) p.172.

26 According to Cave & Wetton (1935) p.172, "*the word in italics ['or the proceedings'] were added by s.15 of the Arbitration Act, 1934.*" The reading of Mustill & Boyd (1989) p.447 seems to suggest that the 1934 Act supplemented the meaning of this section with the words "*or the reference*" which were in turn substituted by the 1950 Act with the words "*or the proceedings*".

27 Section 23(2) of the 1950 Act.

28 Mustill & Boyd (1989) p.552.

29 Mustill & Boyd (1989) p.550.

to Mustill and Boyd was the formulation introduced by Atkin J, namely "*such a mishandling of the arbitration as is likely to amount to some substantial miscarriage of justice.*"[30] Obviously the understanding of the term "misconduct" changed over the years.[31] In a nutshell, however: "*[t]he term 'misconduct' here would appear to be used in its widest sense, perhaps even including a mistake (in law or fact) admitted by the arbitrator.*"[32]

It makes the concept elusive and as argued by Mustill and Boyd:

> [t]he task of formulating a general definition is made the more difficult by the fact that various types of conduct which have prompted the Court to remit or set aside an award can equally be categorized as misconduct or as separate ground giving the Court jurisdiction to intervene. For example, excess of jurisdiction and defects in the form of the award are probably best regarded as separate grounds for invoking the jurisdiction of the Court, but there is substantial authority for the view that they also amount to misconduct.[33]

Although there are arguments favoring inclusion of "excess of jurisdiction" within the scope of the statutory concept of misconduct, traditionally, this ground had an independent standing among other grounds based on the court's inherent jurisdiction.[34] These grounds naturally evolved as to their scope, which became more and more limited.[35]

On top of that the 1979 Act:

> [...] limited the much criticized and outdated case stated procedure and the setting aside of awards for errors of fact or law on the face of the award. These antiquated procedures were replaced by a limited appeal procedure 'on any question of law arising out of an award on an arbitration agreement' provided that all the parties consented to this or leave of court was obtained.[36]

---

30 Mustill & Boyd (1989) p.550, with a reference to *Williams v. Wallis and Cox* [1914] 2 KB 478 at [485].

31 Compare for example Cave & Wetton (1935) pp.177-187 and Walton & Vitoria (1982) pp.406-425 or Mustill & Boyd (1989) pp.550-553.

32 Walton & Vitoria (1982) p.395.

33 Mustill & Boyd (1989) p.551.

34 Walton & Vitoria (1982) p.395 ("*the court has further an inherent power to set aside an award which is bad on its face as not complying with the requirements of finality and certainty. The inherent power to set aside also extends to an award which exceeds the arbitrator's jurisdiction [...].*"). Importantly, one of the examples of the award having "patent defects" (being bad on its face) that was suggested in Mustill & Boyd (1989) p.557 (with a reference to the relevant case law), was when "*the award fails to deal with all the issues, the matter will be remitted so that the arbitrator can fill the gaps.*"

35 Compare for example Cave & Wetton (1935) pp.187-216 and Walton & Vitoria (1982) pp.426-430 or Mustill & Boyd (1989) pp.553-562.

36 Lew & Holm, *Development of the Arbitral System in England* (2013) p.7. For the procedure of appeal on point of law under the 1996 Act, see section 6 below.

Notably, therefore, the excess of jurisdiction ground remained, arguably, the most relevant independent ground based on the court's inherent jurisdiction.[37] An award in excess of jurisdiction was summarized in the following words:

> [a]n award will be entirely void if the parties never made a binding arbitration agreement; if the matters in dispute fell outside the scope of the agreement; if the arbitrator was not validly appointed, or lacked the necessary qualifications; or if the whole of the relief granted lay outside the powers of the arbitrator.[38]

In any event, an important, and arguably still valid question, has been posed by Mustill and Boyd:

> [a] particular difficulty arises where the contract prescribes the remedy which must be granted in the event of a breach. In such a case if the arbitrator, having found a breach, mistakenly proceeds to award a remedy other than the one prescribed by the contract, is this outside his jurisdiction, so as to render the award void, or is it simply a mistake of law, which like a mistake as to the primary rights and obligations under the contract, does not amount to an excess of jurisdiction?[39]

The authors are of the opinion that

> [i]t seems that the latter is the correct view, and that there is no distinction to be drawn in this connection between a mistake as to primary rights and obligations and a mistake as to the remedies prescribed by the contract. If, however, he applies the correct remedy, but does so in an incorrect way – for example by miscalculating the damages which the submission empowers him to award – then there is no excess of jurisdiction. An error, however gross, in the exercise of his powers does not take an arbitrator outside his jurisdiction and this is so whether his decision is on a matter of substance or procedure.[40]

These conclusions should be applauded and would be equally applicable to the 1996 Act regime.

37 See also Mustill & Boyd (1989) pp.554-555 and pp.558-561. Also Walton & Vitoria (1982) pp.427-428.

38 Mustill & Boyd (1989) p.554.

39 Mustill & Boyd (1989) p.554.

40 Mustill & Boyd (1989) pp.554-555.

All in all, since the court was able to rely on both broad statutory grounds as well as on its inherent jurisdiction while setting the award aside, it is understandable why the users of arbitration were critical towards the system.[41]

2.3 *The 1996 Act: work in progress*

One of the reasons why the most recent reform of the English arbitration law has been introduced was "*the wide discontent over the extent to which the judiciary could interfere in arbitrations [...]*".[42] Additionally, it has been recognized that English arbitration law was not readily comprehensible for the users of arbitration in England.[43] Consequently, the DAC took up the challenge, which is expressed in the very first words of the 1996 Act, namely "*to restate and improve the law relating to arbitration pursuant to an arbitration agreement*".[44]

Additionally, the DAC in its report observed that:

> [n]owadays the Courts are much less inclined to intervene in the arbitral process than used to be the case. The limitation on the right of appeal to the Courts from awards brought into effect by the Arbitration Act 1979, and changing attitudes generally, have meant that the Courts nowadays generally only intervene in order to support rather than displace the arbitral process. We are very much in favour of this modern approach and it seems to us that it should be enshrined as a principle in the Bill.[45]

---

41 The criticism was perhaps directed more to the intrinsic involvement of the courts throughout the whole arbitral process and not only its post-award stage. See, *e.g.*, Lew & Holm, *Development of the Arbitral System in England* (2013) p.7 ("*The criticisms were directed especially at the case stated procedure set out in section 21 of the 1950 Act. Incessant referrals to the courts on points of law led to delays in arbitration proceedings*"). In any event, arguably, the setting-aside procedure was in itself less accessible to foreign parties or non-English lawyers considering the complexity of the system.

42 Karali & Ballantyne (2009) p.352. The authors use these words in relation to the 1979 Arbitration Act, it holds true for the situation before the 1996 Act nonetheless. See also Lew & Holm, *Development of the Arbitral System in England* (2013) p.8 ("*[d]espite the progressive changes to English arbitration law, there remained significant views in England and abroad that there was excessive judicial scrutiny of and interference in arbitral proceedings. This was considered to have had an adverse effect on London as a centre for international arbitration.*").

43 See sections 2.1 and 2.2 above. Also Tweeddale & Tweeddale (2007) p.480 (in particular) with a reference to the Saville LJ speech on the 1996 Act: "*Our law has built up over a very long time indeed. In the main the developments have come from cases, but in addition, from as early as 1698, Parliament has passed legislation dealing with the law of arbitration. To a large degree this legislation has been reactive in nature, putting right perceived defects and deficiencies in the case law. Thus it is not easy for someone new to English arbitration to discover the law, which is spread around a hotchpotch of statutes and countless cases.*"

44 See Preamble of the 1996 Arbitration Act.

45 *Report on the Arbitration Bill* (1996) para 22. Similarly, Mustill & Boyd (1989) pp.569-570.

With these words the DAC confirmed that the supportive approach of the courts towards arbitration should be transformed into the leading principle of the new arbitration statute.[46]

In order, however, to achieve this goal, the DAC did not want to implement the Model Law in *verbatim*.[47] Instead, the DAC decided to use the Model Law as a reference point, while constructing an autonomous draft Bill, which later became a legal act (now) known as the English Arbitration Act 1996.In the context of the setting-aside mechanism, differences between the Model Law and the Arbitration Act are visible. The DAC, instead of following the text of the Model Law (and the New York Convention) created a unique system of review that took into account the previous development of English law and tailored the entrenched principles of the court's supervision to the new pro-arbitration reality. In turn, pursuant to the 1996 Act, recourse against an arbitral award can be made in cases where the tribunal did not have substantive jurisdiction, serious irregularity occurred or, under limited circumstances, a party to the arbitral proceedings brings an appeal on point of law. These challenges will be analyzed in detail below.

3 The three-headed concept for the challenge procedure

As indicated in the introduction, a party that wishes to attack an arbitral award before English courts has, generally, three options: it can either (i) submit a challenge on the basis of lack of substantive jurisdiction of the arbitral tribunal, (ii) submit a challenge on the basis that serious irregularities occurred, or (iii) appeal on point of (English) law. Based on the brief overview that follows, it is concluded that all three concepts are relevant to test if the tribunal acted within the framework of its adjudicative powers.

The first ground for challenge introduced in the Arbitration Act is a lack of substantive jurisdiction. Pursuant to Section 67(1) of the Act a party to arbitral proceedings may apply to the court either (under (a)) for setting aside any award of the arbitral tribunal as to its substantive jurisdiction or (under Section (b)) for an order declaring an award made by the tribunal on the merits to be of no effect, because the tribunal did not have substantive jurisdiction. It is necessary to add that Section 67 of the Act is a mandatory provision of the Act and parties may not contractually deviate from its content.[48]

46 See, however, the Lord Thomas of Cwmgiedd lecture of 2016 criticizing the deference of the courts towards arbitral awards because of its effect on the non-development of common law. For further reading, see https://www.judiciary.gov.uk/wp-content/uploads/2016/03/lcj-speech-bailli-lecture-20160309.pdf [last accessed 30 April 2018].

47 DAC, *Report on the Arbitration Bill* (1996) para 4.

48 See Section 4(1) of the Act: "*The mandatory provisions of this Part are listed in Schedule 1 and have effect notwithstanding any agreement to the contrary.*"

The notion of substantive jurisdiction is strongly intertwined with Section 30 of the Act, which sets out when the tribunal is competent to rule on its own jurisdiction.[49] For the research at hand Section 30(1)(c) of the Act is of relevance, which reads that the tribunal may rule on its own substantive jurisdiction, that is, as to "*whether matters have been submitted to arbitration in accordance with the arbitration agreement.*" In fact, Merkin and Flannery made a comparison between the Act and the Model Law and suggested that Article 34(2)(a)(iii) of the Model Law falls within the scope of the understanding of substantive jurisdiction explained in Section 30(1)(c) of the Act.[50] It further entails that when challenging the arbitrators' powers one should take a look not only at Section 68 of the Act, but also consult Section 67 of the Act. This is particularly important because these sections provide the court not only with different standards of review but also with different remedies when faced with a challenge.[51] Importantly, Section 30 of the Act, however, is not listed in Schedule 1 of the Act. Therefore, it is not a mandatory provision and can be shaped differently by the will of the parties.[52]

The second challenge prescribed in Section 68(1) of the Arbitration Act refers to serious irregularity and reads that a party to arbitral proceedings may apply to the court on the ground of serious irregularity affecting the tribunal, the proceedings or the award. It further explains the meaning of serious irregularity in Section 68(2) of the Act and provides an exhaustive list of what constitutes serious irregularities.[53] Amongst others, the tribunal exceeding its powers in a different way than by exceeding its substantive jurisdiction[54] and the tribunal's failure to deal with all the issues that were brought before it,[55] amounts to serious irregularity.[56] Each of these concepts will be explained further in the sections that

49 Section 30 of the Act recognizes positive competence-competence within the English system of international arbitration. The relevance of the definition of substantive jurisdiction for the purpose of Section 67 of the Act (as introduced in Section 30 of the Act) has been explained under Section 82(1) of the Act which reads that: "*'substantive jurisdiction', in relation to an arbitral tribunal, refers to the matters specified in section 30(1)(a) to (c), and references to the tribunal exceeding its substantive jurisdiction shall be construed accordingly.*"

50 Merkin & Flannery, *Arbitration Act 1996* (2014) p.294 ("*There are two sources of jurisdictional challenges within the Model Law [...]. The second is Art. 34(2), which provides that the courts of the seat may set aside an award if the applicant proves that: [...] (3) the award deals with a dispute not contemplated by, or not falling within, the terms of the submission to arbitration [...]. It can be seen that (3) [...] fall[s] within section 30(1)(c) [...].*"). For further reading on Art. 34(2)(a)(iii) of the Model Law, see Chapter II. Similar observations have been made in the context of Section 103(d) of the Act, which implements the New York Convention grounds for refusal of recognition and enforcement of the arbitral award. See Merkin & Flannery, *Arbitration Act 1996* (2014) pp.399-400.

51 See Annex 2.

52 See DAC, *Report on the Arbitration Bill* (1996) para 139.

53 See section 5.1.

54 Section 68(2)(b) of the Act. See also section 5.2.2.

55 Section 68(2)(d) of the Act. See also section 5.2.3.

56 Two additional concepts will be introduced, *i.e.* breach of general duties of the tribunal (Section 68(2)(a) of the Act) and uncertainty or ambiguity as to the effect of the award. See section 5.2.1 and section 5.2.4.

follow.[57] Section 68 of the Act, similarly to Section 67 of the Act, constitutes a mandatory part of the Act.[58]

Finally, and under very limited circumstances, a party seeking recourse against an arbitral award may file an appeal on a point of law (Section 69 of the Act). It can be brought only with the agreement of all the parties to the proceedings or with the leave of the court.[59] In a nutshell, the leave can be granted only in exceptional circumstances,[60] and only regarding questions of English law.[61] The appeal on point of law is a non-mandatory provision and as such can be derogated by the parties' agreement. An *opt-out* mechanism has been implemented for the purpose of the Section 69 appeal. It means that the parties may agree to exclude this recourse, but if they *did* not agree otherwise, it is at the parties' disposal at the post-award stage.[62] *Prima facie* it seems that both the mandatory challenge procedure as well as the appeal on point of law may be relevant to test the tribunal's violations as to the way it exercised its functions. It remains yet to be seen, however, what the importance of each of the challenges is in general and as applied to individual cases.[63]

4 TESTING THE SCOPE OF THE SUBSTANTIVE JURISDICTION: THE IMPORTANCE OF THE CONTRACTUAL FRAMEWORK FOR THE ARBITRAL TRIBUNAL'S POWERS

The substantive jurisdiction of the arbitral tribunal relates to the concept of competence-competence. In other words, it refers to the tribunal's authority to decide on its own jurisdiction and how it exercised this authority. Section 30(1) of the Act, however, has a broader scope which allows one to conclude that the concept of substantive jurisdiction (and in consequence a challenge against substantive jurisdiction) is also relevant to the issue at hand.[64] At the outset, the approach that the courts take when faced with the challenge of substantive jurisdiction will be explained (section 4.1). Subsequently, the limits to the substantive jurisdiction will be analyzed as long as they are relevant in the context of the tribunal's adjudicative competence (section 4.2).

57 See section 5.
58 See fn.48.
59 Section 69(2) of the Act.
60 Section 69(3) of the Act.
61 Section 82(1) of the Act.
62 Section 69(1) of the Act. See also section 6.
63 See section 6.
64 Thus to the overarching research question: when does the tribunal exceed its mandate?

4.1 *The court standard of review when faced with the challenge*

When a challenging party satisfies all the formal requirements imposed, the court will have to reflect on how to approach the parties' objections based on Section 67 of the Act. It should first consider if it is allowed to be involved in any reassessment of the facts already established by the arbitral tribunal or whether it should only apply a deferential test to review the arbitral award (section 4.1.1). Additionally, when faced with a challenge the court will have to determine how to remedy the alleged wrongdoings of the tribunal (section 4.1.2).

4.1.1 The scope of the court's review

By and large, in jurisdictions with a modern arbitration structure, courts are asked to act in a pro-arbitration fashion. This entails *inter alia* that national courts will support an arbitral tribunal throughout the process. It also means that courts (usually) should treat the tribunal's findings with a considerable degree of deference. If, however, objections raised by a party refer to the very existence of the substantive jurisdiction of the arbitral tribunal, the court may have to reflect twice if deference to the analysis conducted by the tribunal itself is the best option as to how to proceed. Instead of limiting itself to the examination of the arbitral award and the findings therein, national courts may consider reevaluating evidences (that underlie the challenge) presented already to the tribunal. Notably therefore, English courts when faced with the Section 67 objections opt for reopening the case and rehearing it.[65]

Rehearing the case from scratch before the English court entails that all the factual evidences and legal pleadings that have been initially brought to the attention of the arbitral tribunal would be assessed yet again by the court.[66] In principle, even new evidences or arguments might be admissible, if they fit within the scope of the same ground of objection

65 See Merkin & Flannery, *Arbitration Act 1996* (2014) pp.296-298, Sutton et al. (2007) para 8-060, Joseph (2010) p.481. See also, *e.g.*, *Gulf Azov v. Baltic Shipping* [1998] C.L.C. 1240, where the court held that: "*[a]lthough there might be some prejudice to the expeditious and economical disposal of the application by permitting oral evidence, the justice of the matter required the court to accede to Azov's application that oral evidence should be permitted on the s. 67 application. The parties might have come to court by agreement under s. 32 of the 1996 Act, or if the arbitral tribunal had given its permission, because the issue was not simply the width of the arbitration clause (on which the arbitrator's decision might have been accepted) but whether Azov was party to the agreement. However the court, on a challenge under s. 67, should not be placed in a worse position than the arbitrator for the purpose of determining that challenge even if there had already been a full hearing before arbitrators since there were substantial issues of fact as to whether Azov was party to the agreement. The court was not required to review the challenge to the arbitrator's award through the eyes of the arbitrator or on his findings of fact.*" As one may observe, however, the issue at hand was the very existence of the agreement to arbitrate between the parties.

66 See, *e.g.*, DAC, *Report on the Arbitration Bill* (1996) para 143 ("*A challenge to jurisdiction may well involve questions of fact as well as questions of law. Since the arbitral tribunal cannot rule finally on its own jurisdiction, it follows that both its findings of fact and its holding of law may be challenged.*"). See also fn.72.

raised already before arbitrators.[67] New grounds of objection will, however, be barred by virtue of Section 73(1) of the Act.[68]

As highlighted by some authorities, apart from trying the case anew, regrettably

> [...] judges are only paying lip service to the idea that the award ought to have any persuasive value; in many cases (and unlike many other countries, where the award is given much more respect), the award appears to be largely ignored (or at least hardly referred to at all in some of the judgments).[69]

There is no easy answer on how the court should approach the challenge of an arbitral tribunal's jurisdiction and whether full retrial as exercised by English courts is appropriate. On the one hand, as aptly pointed out "*[i]t does no favours for the reputation of arbitration if awards are made (and subsequently enforced) against parties that had never agreed to arbitrate in the first place*"[70] and that is why, "*[t]he process is not, therefore, a mere judicial review but a complete retrial.*"[71] On the other hand, retrial raises a number of concerns regarding efficiency[72] and costs.[73] Since the arguments are strong on both ends, arguably,

---

67 *Primetrade AG v. Ythan Ltd.* [2005] 2 C.L.C 911 at [62]. If, however, they cannot be entertained by the objections raised already before arbitrators being entirely new objections they will not be admitted by the court: see *Athletic Union of Constantinople v. National Basketball Association and Ors* [2002] 1 Lloyd's Rep. 305, 2001 WL 825340 and *JSC Zestafoni G Nikoladze Ferroalloy Plant v. Ronly Holdings Ltd* [2004] 1 C.L.C. 1146.

68 Therefore non-admissible unless a party proves that it did not know or could not have reasonably known about this (new) ground for challenge. For further reading, see, *i.a.*, *Athletic Union of Constantinople v. National Basketball Association and Ors* [2002] 1 Lloyd's Rep. 305, 2001 WL 825340.

69 Merkin & Flannery, *Arbitration Act 1996* (2014) p.298. See *e.g. Gulf Azov v. Baltic Shipping* [1998] C.L.C. 1240, *Peterson Farms Inc v. C&M Farming Ltd* [2004] EWHC 121 (Comm), [2004] 1 Lloyd's Rep 503. Similarly (at the enforcement stage) *Dallah Real Estate and Tourism Holding Company v. The Ministry of Religious Affairs, Government of Pakistan* [2010] UKSC 46.

70 Merkin & Flannery, *Arbitration Act 1996* (2014) p.296. See also Grierson & Taok (2011) p.416.

71 Merkin & Flannery, *Arbitration Act 1996* (2014) p.296.

72 See, *e.g.*, Paulsson J., *Arbitration-Friendliness: Promises of Principle and Realities of Practice* (2007) pp.489-490 ("*The major, and well-documented, difficulty with the section 67 process is that it is a rehearing rather than a review of the tribunal's conclusion. This is obviously inefficient. It also creates pressure for the courts (as is now increasingly wont) to override the competence-competence principle by determining jurisdictional issues first, without referring the case to arbitration. According to this logic, requiring a court hearing before an arbitration can commence helps avoid one after it has finished.*"). See also Harris et al., *The Arbitration Act 1996* (2014) p.329 ("*On the other hand, in Ranko Group v. Antarctic Maritime SA* (1998) LMLN 492 *the court said it would be most unfortunate if parties could contest jurisdiction before an arbitrator and then, on a later application under this section, seek to introduce a raft of new evidence which could and should have been put before the arbitrator in the first instance.*").

73 One of the consequences of the full review is that considerable costs might be involved in hearing the case on jurisdiction before two different *fora*. See Merkin & Flannery, *Arbitration Act 1996* (2014) pp.296-297.

the standard of full review should be carried out by the courts sensibly and with (at least some) degree of flexibility when faced with the Section 67 challenge.[74]

One should imagine the case where a party had an undisrupted and complete opportunity to introduce all its evidences and arguments against the tribunal's jurisdiction before the tribunal (which it fully presented under protest) and such a party, notwithstanding the arbitral process, subsequently presents a Section 67 challenge before the court seeking a full rehearing with a possibility to present new arguments or evidences (even within the scope of the same ground of objection as previously raised in arbitration).[75] Merkin and Flannery are right in saying that in these circumstances, and if the full rehearing standard remains inflexible, giving a challenging party an opportunity to fight two equally complex legal battles does not represent the most just result.[76] In other words, if the challenging party has had ample opportunity to present its case before the arbitral panel, there is no reason why the court should not defer to the arbitral tribunal's findings (instead of relying on the parties' pleadings anew) and benefit from an arbitral award on jurisdiction as a starting point for its own (*i.e.* court's) analysis.

The hypothetical sketched above is most likely to occur when the scope of the agreement to arbitrate (rather than its existence or validity) is being challenged. It is so, because the question regarding what matters has been submitted to arbitration in accordance with the arbitration agreement is likely to be intertwined with the merits of the case and as such decided upon as late as in the final award. Therefore, the better view is that deference should be given to the tribunal's analysis regarding the scope of the arbitration agreement. Ultimately one should observe that disregarding a tribunal's analysis will also conflict with the underlying principle pursuant to Section 1(a) of the Act, which reads that "*the object of arbitration is to obtain the fair resolution of disputes by an impartial tribunal without unnecessary delay or expense*".[77]

4.1.2 Remedies at the court's disposal

The Arbitration Act spells out a number of tools that are imminently at the court's disposal when faced with a challenge of the arbitral tribunal's substantive jurisdiction. In a nutshell,

74 It is sometimes argued that because English courts retry the case with regard to substantive jurisdiction, it is prudent for the parties to challenge the substantive jurisdiction before the court (sometimes already) at the outset of the case (even before the constitution of the tribunal) to save unnecessary time and expenses which may occur if the jurisdictional issues are being tried twice. It interferes with the underlying principle of (positive) competence-competence, however. In any event, if one wishes to invite the court to determine a tribunal's substantive jurisdiction early in the proceedings, adequate mechanisms are available in the Act. See Section 31 and Section 32 of the Act.

75 Merkin & Flannery, *Arbitration Act 1996* (2014) p.297.

76 Merkin & Flannery, *Arbitration Act 1996* (2014) p.297.

77 See Section 1(a) of the Act.

the court will be able to (i) confirm the *jurisdictional* award,[78] (ii) vary it,[79] (iii) set it aside in whole or in part.[80] In the alternative the court will be able to (iv) declare an award made by the tribunal on the *merits* to be of no effect, in whole or in part, because the tribunal did not have substantive jurisdiction.[81] There is a palpable distinction made by the drafters of the Act between options open to the court depending on whether a party challenges a *jurisdictional* award or an award on *the merits*. As long as the first three measures mentioned above can be used by the court against a jurisdictional award,[82] only the fourth, at least theoretically, remains available for the award on the merits.[83] Each of the mechanisms will be briefly analyzed below.

The two first remedies, namely confirmation and variation of the award are fairly self-explanatory. The first allows the court to accept and confirm the jurisdictional findings of the arbitral tribunal, whereas the second permits the court to change the content of the (jurisdictional) award.[84] Additionally, pursuant to Section 71(2) of the Act, "*[w]here the award is varied, the variation has effect as part of the tribunal's award.*"

Some authorities discourage the courts from using their power to vary the award in the international context, because "*this may appear to be an unwarranted intrusion on the tribunal's function. In all cases where the court is considering varying an award, we would suggest that it be remitted to the tribunal for reconsideration, perhaps with a direction that the tribunal make the necessary changes.*"[85] In the context of Section 67 challenges, however sound their argument is in other respects, remission might not be applicable, because courts deciding jurisdictional objections (pursuant to Section 67 of the Act) are not vested with the power to remit the award back to the tribunal.[86]

---

78 Section 67(3)(a) of the Act.

79 Section 67(3)(b) of the Act.

80 Section 67(3)(c) of the Act.

81 Section 67(1)(b) of the Act.

82 Namely, options pursuant to Section 67(3)(a)-(c) of the Act.

83 See Section 67(1)(b) of the Act.

84 Any part of the arbitral award may be varied. In other words, variation can easily entail variation of the award on costs or change of the scope of the accepted/declined jurisdiction. It should be also noted that the court does not have power to remit the case to arbitrators. If, however, an arbitral award declining jurisdiction is being set aside by the court (thus the jurisdiction is being reinstated), it is likely that the tribunals will respect the court's analysis and follow the court's guidance. Arguably, this could be considered as a *de facto* remission.

85 Merkin & Flannery, *Arbitration Act 1996* (2014) p.350.

86 In Harris et al., *The Arbitration Act 1996* (2014) p.328 (following *Hussmann (Europe) Ltd v. Pharaon (formerly trading as Al Ameen Development and Trade Establishment)* [2003] 1 C.L.C. 1066) it has been argued that there is no need for a power to remit under Section 67 of the Act, because "*[...] the arbitration simply carries on or revives as necessary. Although a valid final award on the merits will exhaust arbitrators' jurisdiction, there is no reason in principle why an invalid final award, in excess of jurisdiction, should lead to the same result when once it has been declared to be of no effect by the courts. It follows that after an award has been set aside or declared to be of no effect the arbitral tribunal remains seized of the matter.*" See also *Hussmann (Europe) Ltd v. Pharaon (formerly trading as Al Ameen Development and Trade Establishment)* [2003] 1

The last two remedies available for courts, namely an order to set the jurisdictional award aside and an order to declare an award made by the tribunal on the merits to be of no effect, deserve separate attention. While reading Section 67 of the Act one may wonder why two distinct powers have been introduced by the drafters of the Act. Since the DAC Report does not offer any guidance in this respect,[87] ultimately, it is necessary to determine whether the difference between these two orders in any way affects the fate of the arbitral award (irrespective of whether it is a jurisdictional or final decision on the merits).

In the words of one authority:

> [i]t did not seem that there was any difference of principle in those remedies. Section 67(3)(c) of the 1996 Act contemplated that setting aside, in whole or in part, was a possible remedy for a successful challenge to the tribunal's substantive jurisdiction. It might be that where the whole of an award had been declared to be 'of no effect' (s.67(1)(b)), there was no need for any setting aside, but the one was not inconsistent with the other. It was an award 'on the merits' which might be ordered to be of no effect, which suggested that an award which went only to jurisdiction was simply to be set aside. While the declaration 'of no effect' might usefully emphasise the retrospective aspect of such an order, there was no difference in principle in either order so far as concerned its effect on the continuing status of an arbitration where there had been a final award on the merits which had lacked substantive jurisdiction.[88]

In any event, even if the outcome of these remedies remains the same, the better view is for the parties wishing to challenge the award to follow the instructions prescribed by Section 67 of the Act. It means that when they apply against a jurisdictional award or an award on the merits, they should bring their application for a correct order, namely (respectively) for an order to set aside or an order to declare the award on the merits to be of no effect.

C.L.C. 1066 at [82-84]. Notably, Merkin & Flannery, *Arbitration Act 1996* (2014) p.301 seem to observe to the contrary by stating that "*it is also unclear why the drafters of the section did not include the power for the court to remit the award to the arbitrators. Such a power would seem sensible in cases where, for example, the effect of the court's ruling on jurisdiction is such as to result in a different costs order.*"

87 For the DAC commentary on Section 67 of the Act, see DAC, *Report on the Arbitration Bill* (1996) paras 275-277.

88 *Hussmann (Europe) Ltd v. Pharaon (formerly trading as Al Ameen Development and Trade Establishment)* [2003] 1 C.L.C. 1066 at [2]; see also Sutton et al. (2007) para 8-068 and para 8-165; Merkin & Flannery, *Arbitration Act 1996* (2014) on p.320 briefly summarize that a theoretical difference between the setting-aside order and the order declaring the award to be of no effect may exist, "*based on the fact that an award made without jurisdiction may be regarded as a nullity, and it may be more appropriate to declare it to be of no effect.*"

Yet another issue that needs to be briefly addressed is the role of the tribunal in the case when the award (even final) has been set aside or declared to be of no effect. It has been pointed out that:

> [w]hilst the effect of an order to set aside an award clearly deprives that award of all legal effect, such an order does not mean that the entire arbitral process is thereby frustrated. No distinction is drawn between an order setting aside an award as to jurisdiction and an order setting aside a final award on the merits. In both cases, the arbitration may be able to carry on or revive as necessary unless of course the sustained jurisdictional objection relates to the identity or manner of appointment of the tribunal or validity of the agreement to arbitrate.[89]

Additionally, Wolfson and Charlwood observe that

> [t]he setting aside of an award on jurisdiction does not render the tribunal *functus officio* if they are in a position to continue and make a final award on the merits. Similarly, a tribunal may continue to make a further award following a declaration of no effect in relation to an award on the merits, made in excess of jurisdiction.[90]

All in all, it should be noted that English courts have a number of remedies when faced with the Section 67 challenge. Distinctively, however, they (formally) lack power to remit the award back to the tribunal. In any event, courts should use the tools available to tailor the remedy in a pro-arbitration fashion. They can do so by setting aside (declare to be of no effect) only the narrow parts of the award and use their power to confirm or (at most) vary healthy portions of the award.[91]

4.2 *Limits to the scope of the arbitral tribunal's substantive jurisdiction*

According to the definition of substantive jurisdiction as provided in Section 30(1)(c) of the Act, the tribunal may rule on its own substantive jurisdiction as to *what matters have been submitted to arbitration in accordance with the arbitration agreement.* In other words, the question of the scope of the parties' submissions, which is of relevance for the research

89 Sutton et al. (2007) para 8-068.

90 See also Wolfson & Charlwood (2013) p.557.

91 Merkin & Flannery, *Arbitration Act 1996* (2014) p.301 ("*There is also no reason why a judgment may not combine some or even all of those results, if the part of the award is set aside, part varied and part confirmed.*").

at hand, fits comfortably within the Section 67 scrutiny. Therefore, an analysis of the scope of an agreement to arbitrate (section 4.2.1) and the parties' submissions (section 4.2.2) needs to be offered. Finally, the highlights with respect to the public policy rules need to be briefly discussed (section 4.2.3).

4.2.1 The agreement to arbitrate and its scope

Indisputably, the first and the main source of any tribunal's powers is the parties' consent expressed through their agreement to arbitrate. Consequently, if an arbitral tribunal exceeds restrictions imposed by the parties, they may have a legitimate reason to seek recourse against the arbitral tribunal's undertakings. For this reason, a few basic notions regarding an agreement to arbitrate and its scope will be concisely addressed below.

The starting point for the analysis of what constitutes an agreement to arbitrate is the definition that is expressly provided in Section 6(1) of the Act which reads that "*[i]n this Part an "arbitration agreement" means an agreement to submit to arbitration present or future disputes (whether they are contractual or not).*"[92] It is shaped in terms similar to Article 7(1) of the Model Law[93] and following the DAC suggestions it is "*a more informative definition than that in Section 32 of the 1950 Act*".[94]

In a nutshell, the Arbitration Act allows the parties to conclude an agreement to arbitrate both in the form of an arbitration agreement concluded before any dispute arises (usually in the form of an arbitration clause included in the contract)[95] and in the form of an agreement submitting already existing disputes to a tribunal's determination (often called submission agreements).[96] Additionally, it should be noted that parties may decide to alter their initial scope of the arbitration clause by concluding a submission agreement.[97]

Another point that explicitly stands out on the face of Section 6(1) of the Act is that not only contractual, but also non-contractual disputes can be referred to arbitration. The

92 Section 6(1) of the Act. Pursuant to Section 6(2) of the Act, "*[t]he reference in an agreement to a written form of arbitration clause or to a document containing an arbitration clause constitutes an arbitration agreement if the reference is such as to make that clause part of the agreement.*" Subsection (2) therefore deals with the incorporation of the arbitration agreement by reference. It will not be, however, subject to any further analysis here. For further reading, see, *i.a.*, Merkin & Flannery, *Arbitration Act 1996* (2014) pp.31-34, DAC, *Report on the Arbitration Bill* (1996) para 42.

93 DAC, *Report on the Arbitration Bill* (1996) para 41, Harris et al., *The Arbitration Act 1996* (2014) p.50, Veeder (1997) Ch.II.1.a.

94 DAC, *Report on the Arbitration Bill* (1996) para 41. Section 32 of the (English) Arbitration Act 1950 reads that: "*[i]n this Part of this Act, unless the context otherwise requires, the expression "arbitration agreement" means a written agreement to submit present or future differences to arbitration, whether an arbitrator is named therein or not.*"

95 Veeder suggests that these agreements to submit future disputes to arbitration are sometimes called "agreements to refer", see Veeder (1997) Ch.II.1.a.

96 Also referred to as "ad hoc agreements", see Sutton et al. (2007) para 2-003 and para 2-006.

97 See, *e.g.*, discussion on the issue in *LG Caltex Gas Co Ltd & Anr v. China National Petroleum Corp & Anr* [2001] 1 WLR 1892 at [44-68].

term "dispute" has been further explained in Section 82(1) of the Act as including "any difference."[98] It has been consequently suggested that because of the reference to "any difference", the meaning of "dispute" is broader.[99]

Additionally, following the concept of the "one-stop method of adjudication",[100] parties are in fact presumed to submit all disputes between them to be decided by arbitrators. In similar vein, as pointed out by one authority "*[f]ollowing the decision in Premium Nafta Products Ltd v. Fili Shipping Ltd, the parties will be presumed (unless there is a clear indication otherwise) to have intended that all and any disputes arising out of their commercial relationship will be covered by the arbitration agreement, whether contractual or not.*"[101] This issue will be further discussed below.[102]

Finally, it should be highlighted that reference to the institutional rules in the agreement to arbitrate plays an important role and should be consulted while determining the scope of the arbitrators' powers.[103] In addition, it has been argued that "*[w]here there is a reference to arbitration rules, the general principle is that (unless the contract specifies otherwise) the version of the rules current when the arbitration is commenced is the applicable version, even though there have been changes since the arbitration agreement was made.*"[104] The above leads to the conclusion that nowadays courts would employ a rather liberal interpretation of an agreement to arbitrate, initiating their analysis from the point that parties wish to have all their disputes resolved before one forum and accepting that the tribunal's powers may be included also within institutional rules.[105]

---

98 Section 82(1) of the Act reads that: "*[i]n this Part [...] "dispute" includes any difference*". The term "difference" instead of "dispute" has been used in the definition of the arbitration agreement under Section 32 of the Arbitration Act 1950.

99 Harris et al., *The Arbitration Act 1996* (2014) p.52 ("*'Dispute' includes 'any difference' between the parties by virtue of the definition in s.82(1) and thus has a broader meaning than previously.*").

100 This is the term used by Lord Hope of Craighead in *Premium Nafta Products Ltd v. Fili Shipping Ltd* [2007] UKHL 40 at [27] (also known as *Fiona Trust v. Privalov*).

101 Merkin & Flannery, *Arbitration Act 1996* (2014) p.26, see also section 6.1.

102 See sections 6.1.1 to 6.1.6.

103 Some model arbitration clauses are rather explicit on that point. *See, e.g.*, the LCIA Recommended Clause for future disputes (in its 2014 version), which reads that "*[a]ny dispute [...] shall be [...] resolved by arbitration under the LCIA Rules, which Rules are deemed to be incorporated by reference into this clause.*"

104 Merkin & Flannery, *Arbitration Act 1996* (2014) p.34, with a reference to *Jayaar Impex Ltd v. Toaken Group Ltd* [1996] 2 Lloyd's Rep. 437; *China Agribusiness Development Corporation v. Balli Trading* [1998] 2 Lloyd's Rep. 76; *Ranko Group v. Antarctic Maritime SA, The Robin* [1998] ADRLN 35. The authors recognize, however, that it is common and prudent for the parties to agree subsequently on the most up to date version of the rules.

105 See, *e.g.*, Art. 22 of the 2014 LCIA Rules, Art. 22 of the (draft) 2021 ICC Rules, Art. 22 of the 2017 ICC Rules, Art. 22 of the 2012 ICC Rules.

4.2.2 Relevance of parties' submissions

When discussing the limits to the tribunal's jurisdiction, one should always reflect not only on the importance of the agreement to arbitrate but also on the importance of the parties' subsequent submissions. In fact, pursuant to Section 30(1)(c) of the Act, it is the *matters that have been submitted to arbitration in accordance with the arbitration agreement* that matter in determining the scope of the tribunal's jurisdiction.

In principle, parties are obliged to introduce their claims at the outset of the proceedings in their initial statements. For this reason, one should consult the notice of arbitration and the response to the notice of arbitration[106] in order to determine what matters are submitted to arbitration. It has been noted, however, that "*[t]he process of analysis of the scope of the reference is usually confined to the document or documents described above, considered objectively, and in their proper context, with the full background matrix in mind.*"[107] On this occasion authors made a reference to one case where the tribunal was allowed to decide the issues not formally submitted in the notice of arbitration, but unresolved and known, and where the language of the notice of arbitration was open enough to accommodate such claims.[108] Therefore, as long as the scope of reference should be, in principle, set out at the outset of the proceedings, one should be careful in considering it as a definitive one.

Under certain circumstances, however, the limits imposed might have a definitive character. This would be the case, for example, with the ICC Terms of Reference.[109] The character of the restrictions might play a role in cases where new claims or the amendments for claims are introduced which will be further analyzed below.[110] In any event, it should be concluded that all the parties' submissions need to be thoroughly analyzed when assessing the tribunal's jurisdiction.

4.2.3 Overriding and mandatory rules of public policy

The two preceding sections of this chapter have been dedicated to explaining the importance of the parties' consent in the context of the scope of the tribunal's authority. Yet, it should not be forgotten that the parties' autonomy is not unlimited. Pursuant to Section 1(b) of the Act "*the parties should be free to agree how their disputes are resolved, subject only to*

---

106 Under different institutional rules it may be called differently. See, *e.g.*, 'Request of Arbitration' under the 2014 LCIA Rules, the 2012 ICC Rules, and the 2017 ICC Rules. 'Notice of Arbitration' under the 1976 UNCITRAL Rules and the 2010 UNCITRAL Rules.

107 Merkin & Flannery, *Arbitration Act 1996* (2014) p.109.

108 See *Lesser Design & Build Ltd v. University of Surrey* (1991) 56 BLR 57. The notice of arbitration referred to "*a dispute [...] regarding* inter alia *the following*" and "*for the avoidance of doubt, the sums claimed [...]* include *all sums for which it has not yet been reimbursed*"; emphasis after Merkin & Flannery, *Arbitration Act 1996* (2014) p.109.

109 Occasionally it is also argued that the ICC Terms of Reference would constitute a submission agreement. See Merkin & Flannery, *Arbitration Act 1996* (2014) p.26.

110 See section 6.1.5.

such safeguards as are necessary in the public interest." In effect, it should not come as a surprise that the autonomy of the parties to shape the tribunal's powers according to their will is confined by the fundamental rules of justice. Consequently, the overriding legal rules of public policy may very well influence the range of the arbitral tribunal's authority for example with the notion of the arbitrability of the claims.[111]

5 SUBSTANTIAL INJUSTICE AND THE CONCEPT OF "SERIOUS IRREGULARITIES" AND ITS RELEVANCE FOR TESTING THE MANDATE

The second, and perhaps the most relevant, tool that is available to test the arbitral tribunal's authority before English courts is the Section 68 challenge which allows parties to object to an arbitral award that has been flawed with serious irregularities. The analysis below is divided in five sections. At first it is necessary to discuss the courts' standard of review as conditioned upon the concept of serious irregularities (section 5.1). Finally, selected examples of serious irregularities relevant to the "excess of mandate" review will be explained (section 5.2). It should also be noted that Section 68 of the Act is mandatory.

5.1 The court's standard of review as conditioned upon the seriousness of irregularity

As explained above, pursuant to Section 68(1) of the Act a party to arbitral proceedings may challenge an award based on the occurrence of serious irregularity affecting the tribunal, the proceedings or the award. Additionally, the framework of Section 68(1) of the Act is supplemented by a definition of serious irregularity and the list of serious irregularities introduced in Section 68(2) of the Act, which reads that "*serious irregularity means an irregularity of one or more of the following kinds which the court considers has caused or will cause substantial injustice to the applicant [...].*"[112] The application of said Section is mandatory and cannot be contracted out.

In a nutshell, the test of serious irregularity is a vital mechanism for objection at the post-award stage of the proceedings. It has been developed, however, to be a means of

111 According to some authorities, Section 1(b) of the AA is not related to the concept of arbitrability. See *Fulham FC v. Richards & Anr* [2008] 1 Lloyd's Rep. 616 as reported in Merkin & Flannery, *Arbitration Act 1996* (2014) p.10. For the explanation of "limits to arbitration agreements" see, Merkin & Flannery, *Arbitration Act 1996* (2014) p.110 ("*Obviously, no arbitration clause can be regarded as unlimited in scope. Even the most widely drafted clauses will not be taken to clothe the tribunal with jurisdiction to entertain criminal complaints, or indeed contracts with a criminal objective, or contracts that are void for illegality or otherwise contrary to public policy.*").

112 The list of serious irregularities follows the definition. The relevant irregularities are further discussed in section 5.2.

recourse limited to the list of irregularities provided on the face of Section 68 of the Act (section 5.1.1). Moreover, it has been restricted by the notions (i) of seriousness of alleged irregularity and (ii) of substantial injustice caused to the applicant (section 5.1.2). These statutory filters frame the courts' approach allowing them to accept challenges only against the most grievous and unjust tribunal's actions (section 5.1.3). Each point introduced here will be further explained in the sections below, together with reflections on remedies available to the courts when confronted with challenges (section 5.1.4). Notably, the standard of the court's review and remedies available differ when compared with the challenge under Section 67 of the Act.[113]

5.1.1 The scope of the court's review limited to the irregularities listed

The first proposition that should be advanced when discussing the standard of the court's review under Section 68 of the Act is that the list of serious irregularities (introduced therein) outlines the framework within which courts may operate.[114] It means that the court would only focus on violations which have been captivatingly described by Merkin and Flannery with the use of a car analogy: "*[...] section 68 is only concerned with what we may term serious mechanical breakdowns, as opposed to substantive legal errors (driving on the wrong side of the road or through a red light), or jurisdictional breakdowns (arriving at the wrong destination or carrying the wrong passenger).*"[115]

Additionally, the list of irregularities is exhaustive and limits the scope of the court's inquiry. In the words of the DAC:

> [t]he Clause we propose is designed not to permit such interference, by setting out a closed list of irregularities (which it will not be open to the Court to extend), and instead reflecting the internationally accepted view that the Court should be able to correct serious failure to comply with the 'due process' of arbitral proceedings [...].[116]

---

113 See section 4.1 above.

114 See Section 68(2) of the Act; also, section 5.2 of this chapter. It has been also pointed out that Section 68 of the Act did not have a precise counterpart in older legislation. For further reading, see Merkin & Flannery, *Arbitration Act 1996* (2014) pp.304-307.

115 Merkin & Flannery, *Arbitration Act 1996* (2014) p.304.

116 DAC, *Report on the Arbitration Bill* (1996) para 282. The phrase "such interference" should be understood as interference in the arbitral process agreed by the parties. For the concise comment on Section 68 of the EAA, see *Petroships Pte Ltd v. Petec Trading and Investment Corporation and Ors* [2001] 2 Lloyd's Rep. 348 at [351]. See also Merkin & Flannery, *Arbitration Act 1996* (2014) p.306 explaining that "irregularities" may relate to the arbitral procedure or award.

It has been further explained that: "*The list of grounds is exhaustive and deliberately so, since the DAC thought that the courts should not be free to invent more.*"[117]

There should be therefore no doubt that the courts have no ability to freely construe what constitutes a serious irregularity. Instead they should seek guidance in the predetermined list of irregularities in Section 68(2) of the Act. That is also to the detriment of applicants should fit their objections within one of the grounds listed in the Section discussed here.[118] Therefore the applicants may not employ the Section 68 mechanism for reviewing the tribunal's findings of facts or law.[119]

5.1.2 The two-step test exercised by the courts faced with challenge

Having in mind the pro-arbitration stand of the English Arbitration Act, courts tend to use the sifting mechanism designed and introduced in the Act and consequently deter from intervening in the arbitral process. In fact Section 68 of the Act caters the courts with two filters used in order to minimize their (the courts) involvement in arbitration: the first one bars the irregularity challenge upon its seriousness and the second requires the serious irregularity to result in substantial injustice caused to the applicant.

The two filters are intertwined since they are in fact two subsequent steps of the same instrument used by courts to test irregularities that (allegedly) occurred during arbitration. As aptly put:

> Section 68 involves what has been described as a two-stage investigation, viz, (1) has there been an irregularity of at least one of the nine kinds identified in the section and (2) whether the incidence of such irregularity has caused or will cause substantial injustice. If the court decides that there has not been an irregularity of that kind, there is no need to investigate the issue of substantial injustice.[120]

Put differently, only if the court is satisfied that (i) an irregularity occurred and (ii) it is serious,[121] will the court initiate the second part of the test, namely an assessment whether

---

117 Harris et al., *The Arbitration Act 1996* (2014) p.335.

118 One should note that "irregularities" are not mutually exclusive. Additionally, if the challenge is not brought within the Section 68(2) framework, the objection may be found as lacking legal standing; see the example of the challenge against the award with a blatant (yet not admitted) error that a tribunal refuses to correct (*i.e.* 2+2=5). For further reading, see Merkin & Flannery, *Arbitration Act 1996* (2014) pp.305-306.

119 Merkin & Flannery, *Arbitration Act 1996* (2014) p.304

120 Sutton et al. (2007) para 8-072, see also Merkin & Flannery, *Arbitration Act 1996* (2014) p.306.

121 See, *e.g.*, *Bromley Park Garden Estates Limited v. Gary Christopher Mallen, Bruce Maunder Taylor* [2009] EWHC 609 (Ch), 2009 WL 648823 at [15-16] ("*The Court should not lightly find that there has been an irregularity in the conduct of an arbitration: a challenge under section 68 is only available in extreme cases, where the arbitrator has gone so wrong in his conduct of the arbitration in one of the respects listed in section 68,*

serious irregularity led to (or will lead to) substantial injustice upon the applicant.[122] It all leads to the conclusion that the two-level test brings a very high threshold for challenge.[123]

Before going further into details as to the threshold of the test,[124] two brief notes deserve to be mentioned. At first, it should be pointed out that even if the court is satisfied that substantial injustice was caused to the applicant, it does not automatically mean that the challenge will be successful. Instead, the court, before granting a relief, will need to balance the injustice that occurred during the arbitration against the possible injustice caused by its own decision (thus by deciding to set aside the arbitral award).[125] The second reflection has been aptly summarized by commentators: "*[i]t is also important to note that the courts will not allow a challenge under s.68 to be a vehicle for abuse by, for instance, allowing it to stand as a substitute for what should be an appeal on a point of law under s.69.*"[126]

In any event, applicants wishing to challenge the award on the basis of serious irregularity carry a heavy burden of proof in order to succeed, thus they should draft their application carefully so that the court is satisfied that the irregularity was serious and caused a substantial injustice.

---

that justice calls for it to be corrected. However, where an irregularity has occurred, it is a 'serious irregularity' for section 68 purposes if, had it not occurred, the arbitrator might realistically have reached a conclusion significantly more favourable to the applicant."), *Compania Sud-Americana de Vapores S.A. v. Nippon Yusen Kaisha* [2009] EWHC 1606 (Comm), 2009 WL 2392365 at [61] ("*[...] the question is whether, but for the irregularity which caused the arbitrators to reach (by a majority) a conclusion unfavourable to CSAV, they might not have reached that conclusion. To put it another way, might what CSAV was deprived of have made a difference.*"). Also *Zermalt Holdings v. Nu-Life Upholstery Repairs* [1985] 2 EGLR 14 as referred to in *ABB AG v. Hochtief Airport GMBH, Athens International Airport S.A.* [2006] EWHC 388 (Comm), 2006 WL 755473 at [64] ("*... As a matter of general approach, the courts strive to uphold arbitration awards. They do not approach them with a meticulous legal eye endeavouring to pick holes, inconsistencies and faults in awards and with the objective of upsetting or frustrating the process of arbitration. Far from it. The approach is to read an arbitration award in a reasonable and commercial way, expecting, as is usually the case, that there will [be] no substantial fault that can be found with it.*").

122 See also section 5.1.3.

123 See, *i.a.*, *Lesotho Highlands Development Authority v. Impregilo SpA & Ors* [2005] UKHL 43 (hereafter "Lesotho Highlands"). For further reading, see section 5.1.3.

124 See section 5.1.3.

125 See *CNH Global N.V. v. PGN Logistics Limited, Graglia SRL, Wincanton Trans European Ltd.* [2009] EWHC 977 (Comm), 2009 WL 2848157 at [38] ("*A reversal of this procedural irregularity would then cause that substantial injustice – namely, the substantial injustice which was itself caused by the howler. In my judgment it cannot be possibly arguable that it would cause substantial injustice to the Claimant if the procedural irregularity were reversed and the correction of the howler prevented, if doing so would cause, on the one hand, a substantial injustice to the Defendant and, on the other, a wholly undeserved windfall to the Claimant.*") and *CNH Global N.V. v. PGN Logistics Limited, Graglia SRL, Wincanton Trans European Ltd.* [2009] EWHC 977 (Comm), 2009 WL 2848157 at [43] ("*I have no doubt whatever that this case falls slap within the limit of s.68, that limit being that the court will not intervene to set aside what would otherwise be a procedural irregularity, where such irregularity has not caused substantial injustice to the applicant because to remove it would cause substantial injustice to the other party.*").

126 Harris et al., *The Arbitration Act 1996* (2014) p.336.

5.1.3 The high threshold for the irregularity to amount to substantial injustice

As hinted in the section above, the threshold for serious irregularity to amount to substantial injustice has been put very high.[127] As explained in the DAC Report, "*[...] Clause 68 is really designed as a long stop, only available in extreme cases where the tribunal has gone so wrong in its conduct of the arbitration that justice calls out for it to be corrected.*"[128]

Authorities seem to unanimously agree that the substantial injustice test only allows for the minimal intervention of the courts. For example, the salient argument was brought by the DAC in its report, where the committee concluded that

> [t]he test of 'substantial injustice' is intended to be applied by way of support for the arbitral process, not by way of interference with that process. Thus it is only in those cases where it can be said that what has happened is so far removed from what could reasonably be expected of the arbitral process that we would expect the Court to take action.[129]

Similarly it has been concluded that: "*[t]he preliminary requirement of substantial injustice does not entail the court having a general supervisory role over arbitrations; it can be called upon to intervene only if there is clear and substantial injustice.*"[130] On top of that, it has been argued that "*[t]he court's power is essentially designed to be supportive of arbitration in the sense of maintaining its good reputation by being available to rectify glaring and indefensible irregularities that occasion injustice. The limitations on the power restrain the court from interfering with the arbitral process on any lesser occasion.*"[131]

This high threshold has also been recognized by the courts.[132] In the seminal decision of *Lesotho Highlands Development v. Impregilo SpA*,[133] which was welcomed with approval

127 See section 5.1.2.

128 DAC, *Report on the Arbitration Bill* (1996) para 280.

129 DAC, *Report on the Arbitration Bill* (1996) para 280. For a rare example of successful challenge under Section 68 of the Act, see *K v A* [2019] EWHC 1118 (Comm).

130 Merkin & Flannery, *Arbitration Act 1996* (2014) p.306, see also DAC, *Report on the Arbitration Bill* (1996) para 280.

131 Harris et al., *The Arbitration Act 1996* (2014) p.335; additionally, authors brought up an example of the pre-Act judgment (*Indian Oil Corporation v. Coastal (Bermuda) Ltd.* [1990] 2 Lloyd's Rep. 407), where the court remitted the award for further consideration of an argument not pursued before arbitrators with a comment that under the 1996 Act regime such a remedy would not be possible.

132 *Petroships Pte Ltd v. Petec Trading and Investment Corporation and Ors* [2001] 2 Lloyd's Rep. 348; *Warborough Investments Ltd v. S Robinson & Sons (Holding) Ltd* [2003] EWCA Civ 751; *Bulfracht (Cyprus) Ltd v. Boneset Shipping Co Ltd, The MV Pamphilos* [2002] 2 Lloyd's Rep. 681; *Pacol Ltd. v. Joint Stock Co Rossakhar* [2000] 1 Lloyd's Rep. 109 (see in particular [115] where Colman J concludes that setting aside appropriate if serious irregularity so severe that would full rehearing of the case); *Buyuk Camlica Shipping Trading and Industry Co Inc v. Progress Bulk Carriers Ltd* [2010] EWHC 442 (Comm) at [47] see also fn.137 below.

133 *Lesotho Highlands Development Authority v. Impregilo SpA & Ors* [2005] UKHL 43.

by the arbitral community,[134] Lord Steyn concluded that "*[a] major purpose of the Act was to reduce drastically the extent of intervention of courts in the arbitral process.*"[135]

Additionally, his Lordship adequately highlighted general principles that underlie the Section 68 challenge by noting that:

> First, unlike the position under the old law, intervention under section 68 is only permissible after an award has been made. Secondly, the requirement is a serious irregularity. [...] Plainly a high threshold must be satisfied. Thirdly, it must be established that the irregularity caused or will cause substantial injustice to the applicant. This is designed to eliminate technical and unmeritorious challenges. [...]. Fourthly, the irregularity must fall within the closed list of categories set out in paragraphs (a) to (i).[136]

Currently, the courts continue to approach the serious irregularities challenge narrowly.[137] For this reason, it seems now well established that the threshold for the serious irregularity to amount to substantial injustice is indeed very high. Ultimately, it also disciplines the parties and reminds them about their bargain to have their disputes arbitrated (with all its consequences).

5.1.4 Remedies at the court's disposal

The final point that requires further exploration relates to remedies that the court can use when dealing with the Section 68 challenge. Pursuant to Section 68(3) of the Act the court may (i) remit the award for reconsideration,[138] (ii) set the award aside[139] or (iii) declare the award to be of no effect.[140] Each of these remedies can be applied to an award in whole or only to its defective part. Most importantly, however, the same Section reads that *[t]he court shall not exercise its power to set aside or to declare an award to be of no effect, in whole or in part, unless it is satisfied that it would be inappropriate to remit the matters in question to the tribunal for reconsideration.*" Such a design of the remedial tools fits perfectly

134 See, *i.a.*, Merkin & Flannery, *Arbitration Act 1996* (2014) pp.306-307 ("*The decision in that case affirmed many previous judicial pronouncements to the effect that the section 68 threshold is a very high one, that being consonant with the philosophy behind the Act of minimal judicial intervention.*"); Park, *The Nature of Arbitral Authority: A Comment on Lesotho Highlands* (2005) p.484 ("*In rejecting arguments that an error about the currency of an award represented an excess of jurisdiction, their Lordships confirmed a healthy appreciation that arbitrators do not exceed their powers simply by making a mistake*").

135 *Lesotho Highlands Development Authority v. Impregilo SpA & Ors* [2005] UKHL 43 at [26].

136 *Lesotho Highlands Development Authority v. Impregilo SpA & Ors* [2005] UKHL 43 at [28].

137 *Bandwidth Shipping Corp v. Intaari* [2008] 1 Lloyd's Rep. 7, *ABB AG v. Hochtief Airport GmbH and Ors* [2006] 2 Lloyd's Rep. 1, *Terna Bahrain Holding Co WLL v. Al Shamsi* [2013] 1 Lloyd's Rep. 86 at [85].

138 Section 68(3)(a) of the Act.

139 Section 68(3)(b) of the Act.

140 Section 68(3)(c) of the Act.

with the principle of minimal court intervention in the arbitral process, because (i) it points out the presumption of the remission of the award back to the tribunal, (ii) it allows for preserving the healthy part of the award not affected by the alleged default. In addition, it clarifies and structures the remedial powers of the courts.[141]

Arguably, since the remission for reconsideration "*is the primary remedy following a successful application under section 68 [...]*",[142] it leads to the conclusion that it is a remedy that underlies the framework of the court's remedial powers in the context of any serious irregularity challenge.[143]

In addition, it has been observed that:

> [t]he proviso to section 68(3) codifies the principle developed under the 1950 Act that, faced with a choice of remitting or setting aside the award, the court is to remit whenever it can and set aside only where remission would not be appropriate. The cases demonstrate that setting aside the award is appropriate where irregularity is so severe that there has to be a full rehearing, or where it is otherwise inappropriate to allow the original arbitrators to reconsider their award owing, for example, to incompetence or bias.[144]

Importantly, once the award is remitted for reconsideration, the jurisdiction of the tribunal (that became *functus officio* when the award was made) will be revived to the extent of the remission.[145] The tribunal shall make a fresh award within three months of the date of remission or in the time directed by the court.[146] Exceptionally, if the court considers

141 Harris et al., *The Arbitration Act 1996* (2014) p.335 ("*By contrast with the previous position [i.e. under the 1950 Act], where the court could remit an award for reconsideration whenever it thought fit, and where the setting aside of the award was linked to the difficult concept of the arbitrator's 'misconduct', this section gives considerably more definition and structure to the court's power to intervene on the basis of irregularity.*").

142 Wolfson & Charlwood (2013) p.557. See also *The Secretary of State for the Home Department v. Raytheon Systems Limited* [2015] EWHC 311 (TCC) at [3] ("*It is clear that remission is the "default" option and the Court cannot set aside unless it would be "inappropriate" to remit.*"), *K v A* [2019] EWHC 1118 (Comm).

143 Harris et al., *The Arbitration Act 1996* (2014) p.353 suggest, however, that "*remission is likely to be the usual remedy under susbss.(2)(d) [failure to deal with all issues], (f) [uncertainty or ambiguity as to the effect of the award], (h) [failure to comply with the requirements as to the form of the award]. Setting aside may be appropriate under the other subsections*".

144 Merkin & Flannery, *Arbitration Act 1996* (2014) p.320. See also Wolfson & Charlwood (2013) p.557 ("*Where remission would be inappropriate includes cases of bias or incompetence on the part of the tribunal.*").

145 Merkin & Flannery, *Arbitration Act 1996* (2014) p.320, with a reference to *Glencore International AG v. Beogradaska Plovidba, The Avala* [1996] 2 Lloyd's Rep. 311 ("*If the award is remitted for reconsideration, it is likely that the same arbitrators will be retained for, although a tribunal becomes functus officio once the award is made, its jurisdiction is revived by remission, albeit to the extent of the remission, so that no new matters can be argued.*").

146 See Section 71(3) of the Act.

remission to the same tribunal inappropriate, it may decide to remit the case to a newly constituted tribunal.[147]

The second characteristic does not require much explanation. It is sufficient to point out that, if possible, the court will exercise its remedial powers only to the part of the award affected by the serious irregularity. In other words, the court will not intervene in the healthy part of the award.

If the award cannot be cured from the serious irregularity, the court will have two additional tools at its disposal: setting aside the award or declaring it to be of no effect. These remedies have already been discussed in the context of the challenge of the substantive jurisdiction and will not be analyzed in detail here.[148] In a nutshell, they should be used only if the award is so faulty that other remedies will not rectify it. The DAC's intentions for the introduction of two separate remedies are unclear.[149] In the context of serious irregularities challenge, however, authors do not attach much importance to the difference between setting aside the award and declaring it to be of no effect,[150] concluding that they practically lead to the same results.[151]

All in all, having in mind the principle of minimal court intervention with the arbitral process, the courts should always consider remitting the award back to arbitrators as a primary remedy and ordering the setting aside only as a last resort.[152] Even then, however, it is likely that only the part in default (rather than the whole award) will be affected by the courts' rectifying order.

147 *The Secretary of State for the Home Department v. Raytheon Systems Limited* [2015] EWHC 311 (TCC).

148 See section 4.1.2.

149 No explanation is given in the DAC Report.

150 See Merkin & Flannery, *Arbitration Act 1996* (2014) p.320; the authors conclude that as long as in the context of the challenge of the substantive jurisdiction, one can see at least some theoretical arguments why two remedies should be introduced. These (theoretical) arguments do not apply to the Section 68 challenge. See also Wolfson & Charlwood (2013) p.557.

151 *Hussmann (Europe) Ltd v. Pharaon (formerly trading as Al Ameen Development and Trade Establishment)* [2003] 1 C.L.C. 1066 at [81] ("*In the present case, there has been no order of setting aside, but instead a declaration of no effect. It does not seem to us, however, that there is any difference of principle in those remedies.*").

152 For the list of issues taken into account in assessing the appropriate remedy, see *The Secretary of State for the Home Department v. Raytheon Systems Limited* [2015] EWHC 311 (TCC) at [4] ("*What the Court needs to do in deciding whether to remit or set aside is to consider all the circumstances and background facts relating to the dispute, the award, the arbitrators and the overall desirability of remission and setting aside, as well as the ramifications, both in terms of costs, time and justice, of doing either. A review of "appropriateness" encompasses a pragmatic consideration of all the circumstances and relevant facts to determine what it is best to do but it necessarily covers the interests of justice as between the parties.*").

5.2 *Selected "irregularities" relevant in the context of the arbitral tribunal going beyond the parties' requests*

The closed catalogue of Section 68 of the Act refers to nine irregularities. Not all of them, however, are relevant to the research at hand.[153] Therefore, the following subsections will be devoted to selected irregularities that are arguably the most relevant in the context of the tribunal going beyond the parties' requests.[154] The first section will explain the tribunal's breach of general duties (section 5.2.1) whereas the second section will deal with the excess of the arbitral tribunal's powers (section 5.2.2). It will be followed by sections on failure to deal with all submitted issues (section 5.2.3) and on ambiguity as to the effect of the award (section 5.2.4).

5.2.1 Breach of general duties of the arbitral tribunal

The first of the notions labeled as a serious irregularity according to Section 68(2)(a) of the Act, is the tribunal's failure to comply with Section 33 of the Act, which defines the tribunal's general duty.[155] These duties are described in fairly general terms,[156] which attracts disappointed parties to challenge the award on that basis.[157] It does not change the fact, however, that "*[...] applicants seeking to challenge awards under this provision would do*

153 Only four from the list of serious irregularities have been selected considering their relevance for the research at hand. These are (i) breach of general duties of the tribunal, (ii) excess of powers, (iii) failure to deal with all issues that were brought before the tribunal, and (iv) uncertainty or ambiguity as to the effect of the award. For the whole list of grounds see Section 68(2) of the AA. Also see section 1 of this chapter.

154 One might also consider that Section 68(2)(g) of the Act could be of relevance since it refers to the notion of public policy. In particular, it reads that serious irregularity may occur if "*the award being obtained by fraud or the way in which it was procured being contrary to public policy.*" The authors of *Russel on Arbitration*, however, highlight that "*[a]lthough the second part of the sub-section, 'an award procured contrary to public policy' is wider on its face than the first part, 'an award obtained by fraud' the courts have in fact interpreted the twin concepts consistently.*" (for further reading, see Sutton et al. (2007) paras 8-099 to 8-101). Moreover, according to Merkin & Flannery, *Arbitration Act 1996* (2014) p.316: "*to be contrary to public policy, the impugned conduct had to involve more than inadvertence and generally had to involve behavior that could readily be described us unconscionable or reprehensible.*" (see also, *i.a.*, *Double K Oil Products 1996 Limited v. Neste Oil OYJ* [2010] 1 Lloyd's Rep. 141; [2009] EWHC 3380 (Comm) at [33]). Although duly noted, it has been decided to leave this irregularity among the concepts of Section 68(2) *not* discussed under this heading as they are less important in the context of the research at hand.

155 Section 33 of the Act provides that: "*(1) The tribunal shall (a) act fairly and impartially as between the parties, giving each party a reasonable opportunity of putting his case and dealing with that of his opponent, and (b) adopt procedures suitable to the circumstances of the particular case, avoiding unnecessary delay or expense, so as to provide a fair means for the resolution of the matters falling to be determined. (2) The tribunal shall comply with that general duty in conducting the arbitral proceedings, in its decisions on matters of procedure and evidence and in the exercise of all other powers conferred on it.*" For further reading, see Merkin & Flannery, *Arbitration Act 1996* (2014) pp.124-133.

156 These duties have been aptly summarized in Harris et al., *The Arbitration Act 1996* (2014) p.340: "*[t]his includes matters such as bias, procedural unfairness and breach of natural justice.*"

157 Merkin & Flannery, *Arbitration Act 1996* (2014) p.307 ("*Section 68(2)(a) is perhaps the most significant provision in this list (and probably the most often relied upon by upset losers).*").

well to bear in mind that the three principles of party autonomy, judicial minimalism and finality of award will combine to support the award, and the tribunal, in all cases except the most egregious."[158]

One of the duties imposed by Section 33 of the Act is a duty of fairness. The Section 68(2)(a) challenge might (since it is often relied upon) arguably be relevant for the research at hand to the extent that it deals with the tribunal's power to act judicially and to draw its own conclusions on the facts. Parties regularly challenge the award as "unfair", because of the way the tribunal interpreted the facts which could not have been anticipated during the course of the arbitration.[159] At this point, however, it is sufficient to note that there is no simple equality between the duty of fairness and the arbitral tribunal's power to make findings of fact,[160] nor is there a breach of fairness if the tribunal provided an opportunity to submit arguments on "all of the *essential* building blocks in the tribunal's conclusion."[161]

Nonetheless, a number of reported examples[162] of the (usually futile) challenges illustrate that the parties challenged the award when *i.a.* the tribunal had made secondary findings of fact without seeking submissions[163] or had cited authorities without seeking submissions.[164] Also when the tribunal took a course not put forward by any of the parties, but which lies somewhere in between was not sufficient to challenge the award, provided that the findings are not based on propositions which the parties have not had an opportunity to deal with.[165] The courts where not convinced that challenge should be admitted when the tribunal had taken account of its own expertise in analyzing the

158 Merkin & Flannery, *Arbitration Act 1996* (2014) p.308 see also section 5.1.

159 See fn.160.

160 As highlighted by Colman J in *Bulfracht (Cyprus) Ltd v. Boneset Shipping Co Ltd, The MV Pamphilos* [2002] 2 Lloyd's Rep. 681 at [687] ("*It has to be emphasized, however, that the duty to act fairly is quite distinct from the autonomous power of the arbitrators to make findings of fact. Thus, whereas it may normally be contrary to the arbitrator's duty to fail to give the parties an opportunity to address them on proposed findings of major areas of material primary facts which have not been raised during the hearing or earlier in the arbitral proceedings, it will not usually be necessary to refer back to the parties for further submissions every single inference of fact from the primary facts which arbitrators intend to draw, even if such inferences may not have been previously anticipated in the course of the arbitration.*").

161 See *OAO Northern Shipping Co. v. Remol Cadores de Marin SL* [2007] EWHC 1821 (Comm) at [22] ("*In such cases, whilst it is not necessary for the tribunal to refer back to the parties each and every legal inference which it intends to draw from the primary facts on the issues placed before it, the tribunal must give the parties "a fair opportunity to address its arguments on all of the essential building blocks in the tribunal's conclusion."*").

162 See Merkin & Flannery, *Arbitration Act 1996* (2014) p.308 and p.311; Harris et al., *The Arbitration Act 1996* (2014) pp.342-343.

163 *Bulfracht (Cyprus) Ltd v. Boneset Shipping Co Ltd, The MV Pamphilos* [2002] 2 Lloyd's Rep. 681.

164 *Sanghi Polyesters Ltd v. The International Investor KCSC* [2000] 1 Lloyd's Rep. 480 at [26-28].

165 *Weldon Plant Ltd v. Commission for the New Towns* [2000] 2 T.C.L.R. 785 at [35]; but see *Lorand Shipping Ltd v. Davof Trading (Africa) BV MV "Ocean Glory"* [2014] EWHC 3521 (Comm). See also, *Ameropa SA v. Lithuanian Shipping Co of Lithuania* [2015] EWHC 3847 (Comm).

evidence.[166] Naturally, these types of challenges are very fact specific and no universal conclusion can be drawn from the examples addressed.

In any event,

> collectively, the cases demonstrate that the courts will allow tribunals a significant degree of leeway in determining what is required in order to ensure that there is no transgression of the obligation of fairness, and that the tribunals that refuse to spare the rod to spoil the child will not be in danger of their award being overturned, provided that they have taken into account all the circumstances and carefully weighed all the relevant factors before taking their decision.[167]

Tribunals should not surprise the parties with their conclusions and should not reach their decision on the underlying dispute based on findings which parties could not address.

For example, in one case the award was remitted for reconsideration, since

> the arbitrator had been guilty of an irregularity in reaching a conclusion [...] which was contrary to the common position the parties had adopted in the arbitration and in failing to give the parties notice that he was minded so to hold and an opportunity to address him on the point.[168]

In another case the court decided that the tribunal did not comply with its duty of fairness when the tribunal awarded interest at a rate higher than claimed without giving the parties an opportunity to address the appropriateness of the new rate and without indicating why it had chosen a higher rate.[169] One can thus conclude that, while tribunals deserve a high degree of leeway for their appreciation of facts, they should be very careful in building their decision on what parties were actually able to address during the proceedings.

All in all, arbitrators should be capable of using their own expertise and draw independent conclusions on the facts before them. In turn, these undertakings of the tribunal would generally not be found as unfair or excessive ones, unless they surprise

166 *Checkpoint ltd v. Strathclyde Pension Fund* [2003] EWCA Civ 84; *Warborough Investments Ltd v. S Robinson & Sons (Holding) Ltd* [2003] EWCA Civ 751; *Alphapoint Shipping Ltd v. Rotem Amfert Negev Ltd, The Agios Dimitrios* [2005] 1 Lloyd's Rep. 23.

167 Merkin & Flannery, *Arbitration Act 1996* (2014) p.310.

168 *Omnibridge Consulting Ltd v. Clearsprings (Management) Ltd* [2004] EWHC 2276 (Comm) at [43].

169 *Van der Giessen-de-Noord Shipbuilding BV v. Imtech Marine & Offshore BV* [2009] 1 Lloyd's Rep. 273 at [28]. See also section 6.4.1.

parties or leave them no opportunity to address "essential building blocks in the tribunal's conclusions."[170]

5.2.2 Excess of powers

Pursuant to Section 68(2)(b) of the Act, serious irregularity may also occur if the tribunal exceeds its powers in a way other than by exceeding its substantive jurisdiction.[171] Such a concept of "excess of powers" on its face value is arguably capacious, even though it is included in the closed list of serious irregularities.[172] It does not, however, change the fact that courts approach it very cautiously and in line with the principle of minimal court intervention. A few points deserve further attention: (i) the excess of powers challenge should not be confused with the concept of jurisdictional challenge (the tribunal's substantive jurisdiction),[173] (ii) the discussed challenge can be mounted only against the powers that the tribunal never possessed, and finally (iii) the Section 68(2)(b) challenge is not a vehicle for reviewing the merits of the case.

The first feature of the discussed challenge is rather clear from the wording of Section 68(2)(b) of the Act, which qualifies the excess of powers as an irregularity distinct from the excess of substantive jurisdiction.[174] Put differently, there is a reason why these two different concepts have been introduced in the Act and applicants should be careful in respecting the statutory distinction.[175] As stated by scholars: "*[t]he distinction between*

170 See fn.161.

171 Section 68(2)(b) of the Act also includes a cross-reference to Section 67 of the Act, thus to the challenge on substantive jurisdiction.

172 See section 5.1.1.

173 Even though the excess of powers test depends as well on the analysis of the agreement to arbitrate and parties' submissions. For further reading, see section 4.2. In addition, sources of the arbitral tribunal's powers can be found in the Arbitration Act. See, *e.g.*, Section 48 of the AA.

174 See fn.176.

175 On the one hand, Lord Steyn in *Lesotho Highlands Development Authority v. Impregilo SpA & Ors* [2005] UKHL 43 at [30] suggests that the "excess of powers" ground (*i.e.* Section 68(2)(b) of the AA) was modelled on Art. V(1)(c) of the NYC ("*Specifically, it is likely that the inspiration of the words 'the tribunal exceeding its powers (otherwise than by exceeding its substantive jurisdiction)' in section 68 are the terms of article V(1)(c) of the New York Convention and the jurisprudence on it. The context is that article V(1)(a) stipulates that the invalidity of the arbitration agreement is a ground for non-enforcement of an award: it involves the competence of the arbitrator. Article V(1)(c) relates to matters beyond the scope of the submission to arbitration. It deals with cases of excess of power or authority of the arbitrator.*") On the other hand, if one looks at the construction of the substantive jurisdiction provided in Section 30(1)(c) of the AA (which stipulates that the tribunal may decide on its substantive jurisdiction including "*what matters have been submitted to arbitration in accordance with the arbitration agreement*"), one would see closer similarities between the language of this Section 30(1)(c) of the Act and the language of Art. V(1)(c) of the NYC, which in turn, might suggest that the New York Convention's ground (c) is closer to the concept of substantive jurisdiction, rather than to "serious irregularity". Merkin and Flannery similarly suggest that Section 103(2)(d) of the AA (which implements Art. V(1)(c) of the NYC into English Law) "*is concerned with substantive jurisdictional matters, not procedural matters, which fall within section 103(2)(c) or within the general public policy rules, rather than this provision.*" See Merkin & Flannery, *Arbitration Act 1996* (2014) p.400, with a reference to

jurisdictional and non-jurisdictional issues is normally clear enough. An arbitrator who exceeds his powers in conducting an arbitration is not to be regarded as having exceeded his jurisdiction: the former relates to procedure, and the rules on jurisdiction are inapplicable."[176] It is particularly true if the challenge of the substantive jurisdiction relates to the validity or existence of the agreement to arbitrate.

Occasionally, however, one may find that there is a fine line between a factual underpinning of the jurisdictional challenge regarding the scope of the tribunal's jurisdiction and the excess of powers challenge, because both will rely on an interpretation of the agreement to arbitrate, the parties' submissions and mandatory rules of law.[177] In any event, the Section 67 challenge can be invoked when the tribunal granted relief over a matter which was not within its jurisdiction (*e.g.* narrow arbitration clause provided for arbitrating technical disputes, but the tribunal also decided on the issue of avoidance of contract),[178] whereas the excess of powers challenge will be available only for the irregularities that involve the exercise of a tribunal's power which was never allowed, for example, the use of a remedial power by the tribunal that it never had (such as the power to grant specific performance or interests). That being said, it leads to the second point of interest, namely to the meaning of "excess".

By and large, the simple textual interpretation of Section 68(2)(b) of the Act should suggest that there needs to be an *excess* of powers in order to successfully challenge this type of serious irregularity. It means that the tribunal's powers have to be truly missing in order to invoke this ground.[179] Therefore parties should first review the contents of the agreement to arbitrate, the applicable rules and the English Arbitration Act to check if the tribunal truly does not have a specific power.[180] Regularly, however, applicants attempt to

"the only English authority on this provision [Section 103(2)(d) of the AA]", namely *Minmetals Germany GmbH v. Ferco Steel Ltd* [1999] C.L.C. 647, [1999] 1 All E.R. (Comm) 315. The decision of the court in and of itself, however, is less straightforward to classify Section 103(2)(d) of the Act as "substantive jurisdictional matters". All in all, it is sensible to include *ultra petita* decisions within the scope of the "excess of powers" challenge, considering that *infra petita* decisions are on the same list of irregularities that might cause "substantial injustice". If the *ultra petita* decisions are subsumed under jurisdictional challenge then there will be dissonance in the treatment of *ultra* and *infra petita* awards. For further reading, see section 5.2.3 and section 6 in general.

176 Merkin & Flannery, *Arbitration Act 1996* (2014) p.112.

177 See section 4.2. Arguably, the applicable "mandatory rules of law" might be different in the context of "jurisdiction" and "powers".

178 For further reading on the Section 67 challenge, see section 3 of this chapter. See also Merkin & Flannery, *Arbitration Act 1996* (2014) p.110.

179 See *CNH Global N.V. v. PGN Logistics Limited, Graglia SRL, Wincanton Trans European Ltd.* [2009] EWHC 977 (Comm) 2009 WL 2848157, where the court was satisfied that the tribunal acted in the "excess of powers", because it had used the power it never possessed. At the same time, however, the court concluded that the excess *did not* amount to a substantial injustice.

180 The Arbitration Act, on this point, is very "user friendly" by, in general, introducing margin notes entitling specific Sections with the word "power" in them. Arguably, it might give some indication of the powers that are available and, in turn, may be exceeded. For party-agreed limits, see section 4.2.

bring other objections (regarding the allegedly erroneous use of powers) under the umbrella of the alleged excess of powers. Courts have repeatedly rejected such arguments.[181]

The landmark decision *Lesotho Highlands* offers some guidelines on the issue. Their Lordships concluded that:

> [i]n order to decide whether section 68(2)(b) is engaged it will be necessary to focus intensely on the particular power under an arbitration agreement, the terms of reference, or the 1996 Act which is involved, judged in all the circumstances of the case. In making this general observation it must always be borne in mind that the erroneous exercise of an available power cannot by itself amount to an excess of power. A mere error of law will not amount to an excess of power under section 68(2)(b).[182]

A similar view has been expressed by scholars. Merkin and Flannery note that:

> [b]efore a losing party decides upon invoking section 68(2)(b), it should 'focus intensely' on the particular power involved, whether derived from the arbitration agreement, the terms of reference or the Act, set against the background of all the circumstances of the case. It should also bear in mind that the erroneous exercise of an available power cannot itself amount to an excess of power.[183]

Also Harris and others underline that "*[i]t is now abundantly clear that an excess of jurisdiction will only occur where the arbitrator can be said to have exercised a power he did not have rather than wrongly exercised a power he did have.*"[184]

The last reflection addresses applications against an allegedly incorrect decision as to the facts or the law. Occasionally parties do invoke that by erroneous application of law a tribunal exceeds its powers. It is important to note, however, that courts are impervious to arguments aiming at the review of the merits of the tribunal's decision. Once again, the seminal decision of *Lesotho Highlands* is a good reference point.

---

181 With a more general reference to Section 68 of the Act, see, *e.g.*, *Sonatarch v. Statoil Natural Gas* [2014] 2 Lloyd's Rep. 252 at [11] ("*The focus of the enquiry under Section 68 is due process and not the correctness of the Tribunal's decision.*").

182 *Lesotho Highlands Development Authority v. Impregilo SpA & Ors* [2005] UKHL 43 at [32].

183 Merkin & Flannery, *Arbitration Act 1996* (2014) p.312.

184 Harris et al., *The Arbitration Act 1996* (2014) p.345. See also Sutton et al. (2007) para 8-074 ("*Implementing this firm policy, the House of Lords drew a clear distinction between whether the tribunal purported to exercise a power which it did not have or whether it erroneously exercised a power that it did have. Only the former could give rise to a challenge under s.68. Provided that the tribunal is exercising a power which it does have, as opposed to one which it does not have, it does not matter how significant the error is: no relief will be afforded under s.68. The issue is not whether the tribunal has come to the right conclusion; the sole issue is whether it committed a serious irregularity resulting in a substantial injustice.*").

In this decision, it was emphasized that:

> Section 68(2)(b) does not permit a challenge on the ground that the tribunal arrived at a wrong conclusion as a matter of law or fact. It is not apt to cover a mere error of law. This view is reinforced if one takes into account that a mistake in interpreting the contract is the paradigm of a 'question of law' which may in the circumstances specified in section 69 be appealed unless the parties have excluded that right by agreement. In cases where the right of appeal has by agreement, sanctioned by the Act, been excluded, it would be curious to allow a challenge under section 68(2)(b) to be based on a mistaken interpretation of the underlying contract. Moreover, it would be strange where there is no exclusion agreement, to allow parallel challenges under section 68(2)(b) and section 69.[185]

Also in another case, it was confirmed that the principle described in *Lesotho Highlands* also applies to cases when non-English law is being used by the tribunal.[186] Therefore, the error in applying English or foreign law will not amount to excess of powers.[187] Such a conclusion is also endorsed in academic writings.[188]

5.2.3 Failure to deal with all the issues that were brought before the arbitral tribunal

The next point that deserves attention is the tribunal's failure to address all issues before it.[189] According to Section 68(2)(d) of the Arbitration Act, "*failure by the tribunal to deal with all the issues that were put to it*" might constitute a serious irregularity. There are a considerable number of decisions that provide guidance as to how this provision should be interpreted.[190] The reflections presented here, however, would be restricted to presenting

185 *Lesotho Highlands Development Authority v. Impregilo SpA & Ors* [2005] UKHL 43 at [31].

186 *B v. A* [2010] 2 Lloyd's Rep. 681.

187 See *B v. A* [2010] 2 Lloyd's Rep. 681 (regarding the arguments concerning the misapplication of foreign law), *Lesotho Highlands Development Authority v. Impregilo SpA & Ors* [2005] UKHL 43 (discussing arguments on error in application of English law).

188 Merkin & Flannery, *Arbitration Act 1996* (2014) p.312 ("*It does not permit a challenge on the ground that the tribunal arrived at the wrong conclusion as a matter of law or fact.*"); Harris et al., *The Arbitration Act 1996* (2014) p.345 ("*This subsection cannot be used to mount a challenge on the ground that a tribunal has arrived at a wrong conclusion as a matter of fact or law [...]*"). Craig, *The arbitrator's mission and the application of law in international commercial arbitration* (2010) p.266 ("*Errors in the performance of the mission are not reviewable, but failure to respect the mission may be a cause for annulment.*").

189 See Section 68(2)(d) of the Act.

190 They are conveniently summarized by Akenhead J. in *The Secretary of State for the Home Department v. Raytheon Systems Ltd* [2014] EWHC 4375 (TCC) at [33]; see also previous summaries at *i.a. Primera Maritime (Hellas) Ltd & Ors v. Jiangsu Eastern Heavy Industry Co Ltd & Anor* [2013] EWHC 3066 (Comm) at [8]; *Petrochemical Industries Co v. Dow Chemical* [2012] 2 Lloyd's Rep. 691 at [16].

the most important features of the Section 68(2)(d) review.[191] Therefore the analysis will focus on the test developed in *Petrochemical Industries Co v. Dow Chemical*[192] which is four-fold and enables one to approach a challenge in a systematic way. In this case, Andrew Smith J contemplated that "*the general question whether there was a serious irregularity within subsection 68(2)(d) in turn raises [...] more specific questions.*"[193] He then continued by listing four questions namely (i) whether the relevant point or argument was an "issue" within the meaning of sub-section [68(2)(d)]; (ii) if yes, whether it was "put to" the tribunal; (iii) whether the tribunal failed to "deal with" it; (iv) if all of the above is answered in the affirmative, whether the failure has caused or will cause substantial injustice.[194] Since the fourth question has been dealt with already above,[195] at this point it is necessary to briefly examine the first three questions.

The first question deals with difficulties as to what constitutes an "issue" for purposes of Section 68(2)(d) of the Act. There is neither a statutory definition of an "issue" nor is there an easy answer to this question. Merkin and Flannery argue that "*[...] 'issue' does not mean each and every point in dispute; it means (one of) the very disputes the arbitration has to resolve.*"[196] Similarly, it has been suggested that "*the tribunal only has to decide matters relevant to its ultimate decision. Ground (d) is therefore designed to cover those issues the determination of which is essential to a decision on the claims or specific defences raised.*"[197] In the same way, it has been decided that "*the 'issue' referred to in section 68(2)(d) must be an important or fundamental issue for only a failure to deal with such could be capable of causing substantial injustice.*"[198] Finally, "*a matter will constitute an "issue" where the whole of the applicant's claim could have depended upon how it was resolved, such that "fairness demanded" that the question be dealt with.*"[199]

As to the second question of the *Petrochemical Industries* test, it seems the court will look at all parties' submissions to determine whether an issue has been brought before the

191 For further reading, see, *i.a.*, Harris et al., *The Arbitration Act 1996* (2014) pp.345-347, Merkin & Flannery, *Arbitration Act 1996* (2014) pp.313-315, Sutton et al. (2007) paras 8-093 to 8-097.

192 *Petrochemical Industries Co v. Dow Chemical* [2012] 2 Lloyd's Rep. 691 at [15] followed *i.a. Primera Maritime (Hellas) Ltd & Ors v. Jiangsu Eastern Heavy Industry Co Ltd & Anor* [2013] EWHC 3066 (Comm) at [7].

193 *Petrochemical Industries Co v. Dow Chemical* [2012] 2 Lloyd's Rep. 691 at [15].

194 *Petrochemical Industries Co v. Dow Chemical* [2012] 2 Lloyd's Rep. 691 at [15]; followed in *Primera Maritime (Hellas) Ltd & Ors v. Jiangsu Eastern Heavy Industry Co Ltd & Anor* [2013] EWHC 3066 (Comm) at [7].

195 See section 5.1.3.

196 Merkin & Flannery, *Arbitration Act 1996* (2014) p.313; see *Checkpoint Ltd v. Strathclyde Pension Fund* [2003] EWCA Civ 84 at [49] ("*[...] 'issues' certainly means the very disputes which the arbitration has to resolve.*").

197 Sutton et al. (2007) para 8-094.

198 *Fidelity Management SA & Ors v. Myriad International Holdings BV & OR* [2005] EWHC 1193 (Comm) at [10].

199 *The Secretary of State for the Home Department v. Raytheon Systems Ltd* [2014] EWHC 4375 (TCC) at [33(g)(iii)], with a reference to *Petrochemical Industries Co v. Dow Chemical* [2012] 2 Lloyd's Rep. 691 at [21].

tribunal. In *Petrochemical Industries Co v. Dow Chemical*, the court was satisfied that the issue was "put to" the tribunal when it was introduced in the exchange of pre-hearing memorials and closing submissions, notwithstanding the fact that it was not listed on the agreed list of issues (introduced shortly before the hearing),[200] and it was addressed as an aspect of a different question during oral pleadings.[201] Additionally, in *The Secretary of State for the Home Department v. Raytheon Systems Ltd* it has been noted (with reference to *Petrochemical Industries Co v. Dow Chemical*) that "*the issue must have been put to the tribunal as an issue and in the same terms as is complained about in the Section 68(2) application.*"[202]

The third prong of the *Petrochemical Industries* test addresses the question whether the tribunal "dealt with" the issues presented.[203]

In a nutshell, if the tribunal *does* address the issues presented (in any form), it will make Section 68(2)(d) of the Act inapplicable.[204] "*[O]nce it is recognised that the tribunal has 'dealt with' the issue, the sub-section does not involve some qualitative assessment of how the tribunal dealt with it. Provided that the tribunal has dealt with it, it does not matter whether it has done so well, badly or indifferently*".[205] Additionally, Section 68(2)(d) of the Act does not require "*a tribunal to set out each step by which they reach their conclusion or deal with each point made by a party in an arbitration. Any failure by the arbitrators in that respect is not a failure to deal with an issue that was put to it*"[206] nor does it require to "*answer every question that qualifies as an 'issue'. It can deal with an issue by making clear that it does not arise in view of its decisions on the facts or their legal conclusions.*"[207]

Importantly,

> [n]either the parties nor the court should have to indulge in speculation as to whether a tribunal might have dismissed and not dealt with a particular issue because it was wholly devoid of merit: if the determination of an issue is crucial

200 In this specific case it was not listed by either of the parties: *Petrochemical Industries Co v. Dow Chemical* [2012] 2 Lloyd's Rep. 691 at [23].

201 See *Petrochemical Industries Co v. Dow Chemical* [2012] 2 Lloyd's Rep. 691 at [22-25].

202 *The Secretary of State for the Home Department v. Raytheon Systems Ltd* [2014] EWHC 4375 (TCC) at [33(g)(v)].

203 *Petrochemical Industries Co v. Dow Chemical* [2012] 2 Lloyd's Rep. 691 at [27]. See also *The Secretary of State for the Home Department v. Raytheon Systems Ltd* [2014] EWHC 4375 (TCC) at [33]; *Schwebel v. Schwebel* [2010] EWHC 3280 (TCC) at [23]. For further reading, see Sutton et al. (2007) para 8-094, Merkin & Flannery, *Arbitration Act 1996* (2014) pp.313-315.

204 *Primera Maritime (Hellas) Ltd & Ors v. Jiangsu Eastern Heavy Industry Co Ltd & Anor* [2013] EWHC 3066 (Comm) at [40].

205 *Primera Maritime (Hellas) Ltd & Ors v. Jiangsu Eastern Heavy Industry Co Ltd & Anor* [2013] EWHC 3066 (Comm) at [40].

206 *Hussmann (Europe) Ltd v. Al Ameen Development & Trade Co & Ors.* [2000] C.L.C. 1243 at [56].

207 *Petrochemical Industries Co v. Dow Chemical* [2012] 2 Lloyd's Rep. 691 at [27]. See also *Buyuk Camlica Shipping Trading and Industry Co Inc v. Progress Bulk Carriers Ltd* [2010] EWHC 442 (Comm) at [30].

> to the result then, however unmeritorious the arguments in favour of that issue might be, the tribunal is bound to deal with it in its award in such a way as to make it evident to the parties that it has indeed dealt with it.[208]

The general point therefore is that the tribunal's conclusions on the key issues would make application of Section 68(2)(d) of the Act rather moot.

5.2.4 Uncertainty or ambiguity as to the effect of the award

Uncertainty or ambiguity as to the effect of the award may amount to serious irregularity.[209] In very limited circumstances it may be relevant in order to determine whether the tribunal decided on the issues presented to it. In all cases, however, it should be considered that it is the *effect* of the award that has to cause uncertainty and not the reasoning of the award. It was explained in the DAC Supplementary Report that the intention of the drafters was to allow recourse in cases where "the result of the award was uncertain or ambiguous."[210] As put by scholars: "*[...] the Act is concerned only with the ability of the winning party to enforce the award. What is required [...] is that the obligations of the parties under the award [...] are free from ambiguity. In other words the ambiguity must refer to the dispositive part of the award.*"[211] It goes without saying that all preliminary steps, thus *i.a.* requesting the tribunal to clarify its award, should be exercised before filing the Section 68(2)(f) application.[212]

6 "Appeal on point of law": a limited safeguard of the system and the arbitral tribunal's discretion to apply the law

After carefully weighing a number of arguments and a fair amount of criticism, the DAC decided that appeal on point of law, under limited circumstances should remain a viable recourse in the 1996 Arbitration Act regime. Thus, pursuant to Section 69(1) of the Act, "*[u]nless otherwise agreed by the parties, a party to arbitral proceedings may (upon notice to the other parties and to the tribunal) appeal to the court on a question of law arising out of an award made in the proceedings.*" The detailed procedure on how to appeal on a point of law has been further explained under subsequent subsections of Section 69 of the Act.

208 As aptly summarized in Harris et al., *The Arbitration Act 1996* (2014) p.347. See also *Buyuk Camlica Shipping Trading and Industry Co Inc v. Progress Bulk Carriers Ltd* [2010] EWHC 442 (Comm) at [38].
209 Section 68(2)(f) of the Act.
210 DAC, *Supplementary Report on the Arbitration Act 1996* (1996) para 35.
211 Merkin & Flannery, *Arbitration Act 1996* (2014) p.315.
212 See Section 57(3)(a) of the AA. See also Merkin & Flannery, *Arbitration Act 1996* (2014) pp.239-241 and p.315.

The mechanism will be briefly summarized in this part of the chapter.[213] Therefore, the standard of the court's review (section 6.1) and selected (essential) features of the test (section 6.2) will be explained. It should be always borne in mind that Section 69 of the Act is non-mandatory.[214]

6.1 *The court's standard of review when faced with challenge*

In line with the underlying principle of the Act, courts do minimize their interference with the arbitral process. In the context of the appeal on point of law, review is based on factual findings made in the arbitral award (section 6.1.1) and courts have a number of remedies available in order to limit the instances when the award can be set aside (section 6.1.2).

6.1.1 Review based on factual findings made in the arbitral award

As explained above, the appeal can be mounted only upon the express (written) agreement of all the other parties to the proceedings or with the leave of the court.[215] Section 69 of the Act gives a clear indication that the court's review should be based on the tribunal's conclusions on facts.[216]

As further explained by the DAC in its report:

> [t]here have been attempts, both before and after enactment of the Arbitration Act 1979 to dress up questions of fact as questions of law and by that means to seek an appeal on the tribunal's decision on the facts. Generally these attempts have been resisted by the Court, but to make the position clear, we propose to state expressly that consideration by the Court of the suggested question of law is made on the basis of the findings of fact in the award.[217]

Arguably, also when the appeal is brought with the agreement of all other parties to the proceedings,[218] the courts should defer to the factual findings of the tribunal. After all, the Section 69 mechanism is designed to test the tribunal's conclusions of law, not on fact.

213 Since the process of application of law is the core function of the arbitral tribunal, the availability of appeal on point of law might be potentially relevant in the context of the "excess of mandate" type of challenge. This is why it needs to be briefly discussed.

214 See Schedule 1 of the Act.

215 See Section 69(2) of the Act.

216 Section 69(3)(c) of the Act (*"leave for appeal shall be given only if the court is satisfied [...] that, on the basis of the findings in the award [...]."*).

217 DAC, *Report on the Arbitration Bill* (1996) para 286(iii).

218 Section 69(2)(a) of the Act.

6.1.2 Remedies at the court's disposal

According to Section 69(7) of the Act, in an appeal under this Section the court may by order confirm the award,[219] vary the award,[220] remit the award to the tribunal, in whole or in part, for reconsideration in the light of the court's determination,[221] or set aside the award in whole or in part.[222] Additionally, following the reading of the same subsection "*[t]he court shall not exercise its power to set aside an award, in whole or in part, unless it is satisfied that it would be inappropriate to remit the matters in question to the tribunal for reconsideration.*" Put differently, remission should be the primary remedy used when faced with a faulty arbitral award. Since all of the tools available to the courts have been already explained in previous parts, they will not be analyzed further at this point.[223]

6.2 *Distinctive features of the Section 69 challenge*

A few additional features of a Section 69 appeal should be mentioned. Therefore, a brief comment on the opt-out character of the appeal (section 6.2.1) will be given among the comment that appeal can be mounted only on a point of law (section 6.2.2) and only on a point of English law (section 6.2.3).

6.2.1 The opt-out character of the system

One should note that Section 69(1) of the Act provides that "*unless otherwise agreed by the parties, a party to arbitral proceedings may […] appeal […] on a question of law […].*" In a nutshell, it means that parties can agree to exclude the appeal mechanism from the matrix of their relations. Such an agreement, however, should be in writing.[224] In any event, institutional rules that "*contain exclusion provisions count as an effective waiver for this purpose, as in, e.g. the LCIA or ICC Rules.*"[225] Arguably, not all of the institutional rules'

219 Section 69(7)(a) of the Act.

220 Section 69(7)(b) of the Act.

221 Section 69(7)(c) of the Act. Notably, the wording is slightly different than a similar provision under Section 68 of the Act. *Cf* Section 68(3)(a) of the Act.

222 Section 69(7)(d) of the Act.

223 For further reading, see sections 4.1.2 and 5.1.4 of this chapter.

224 See Section 5 of the Act.

225 Merkin & Flannery, *Arbitration Act 1996* (2014) p.322. As argued by said authors on p.323, not all *formulae* used in (other) international rules (*e.g.* the UNCITRAL Rules) will work as an effective exclusion (see the comparison below). See Art. 26.8 of the 2020 LCIA Rules. *Cf* Art. 26.8 of the 2014 LCIA Rules ("*[…] the parties also waive irrevocably their right to any form of appeal, review or recourse to any state court or other legal authority, insofar as such waiver shall not be prohibited under any applicable law.*"); also in Art. 26.9 of the 1998 LCIA Rules ("*the parties also waive irrevocably their right to any form of appeal, review or recourse to any state court or other judicial authority, insofar such waiver may be validly made.*"); Art. 34.6 of the 2012 ICC Rules ("*By submitting the dispute to arbitration under the Rules, the parties undertake to carry out any award without delay and shall be deemed to have waived their right to any form of recourse insofar as*

wording will be considered sufficiently strong to circumvent the application of Section 69 of the Act.[226] Finally, in accordance with the final sentence of Section 69(1) of the Act, "*[a]n agreement to dispense with reasons for the tribunal's award shall be considered an agreement to exclude the court's jurisdiction under this section.*" All in all, if parties wish to exclude an option to appeal, they should be careful as to the wording (or the reference) they use.

6.2.2 Appeal on point of law not fact

It is self-evident that Section 69 serves only as a means of recourse against the legal findings of the arbitral tribunal.[227] According to Section 69(4) "*an application for leave to appeal under this section shall identify the question of law to be determined and state the grounds on which it is alleged that leave to appeal should be granted.*"[228] Consequently, under no circumstances should it effectively serve against the tribunal's factual findings. As observed in *Russel on Arbitration*, "*the tribunal's findings of fact are conclusive. The appeal is only concerned with a question of law and must not encroach upon the facts.*"[229] In fact, pursuant to Section 69(3)(c) of the Act, the leave to appeal can only be given by the court "*on the basis of the findings of fact in the award [...].*" As held in *Demco Investments & Commercial S.A. & Others v. Se Banken Forsakring Holding Aktiebolag*, "*[t]here is no room for any appeal under section 69 against the findings of fact in the Award itself since these have to be accepted for the purpose of any application for permission to appeal.*"[230]

It is acknowledged that the distinction between point of facts and law can occasionally be difficult.[231] For the purposes of the research at hand, it is sufficient to conclude that the better approach for the courts is to undertake the restrictive "*view of what is a properly reviewable finding of law*"[232] and that

such waiver can validly be made."); *cf* Art. 32.2 of the 1976 UNCITRAL Rules ("*The award [...] shall be final and binding on the parties. The parties undertake to carry out the award without delay*"); or Art.34.2 of the 2010 UNCITRAL Rules ("*All awards [...] shall be final and binding on the parties. The parties shall carry out all awards without delay.*").

226 See fn.225; also Sutton et al. (2007) para 8-122 and Merkin & Flannery, *Arbitration Act 1996* (2014) p.323. For an argument supporting the notion that the wording of the UNCITRAL Rules should suffice, see Dedezade (2006) p.60.

227 See Section 69(1) of the Act.

228 Section 69(4) of the Act.

229 Sutton et al. (2007) para 8-125.

230 *Demco Investments & Commercial S.A. & Others v. Se Banken Forsakring Holding Aktiebolag* [2005] EWHC 1398 (Comm), 2005 WL 1534592 at [35]. For further reading, see also the explanatory note in DAC, *Report on the Arbitration Bill* (1996) para 286(iii).

231 For further reading, see, *i.a.*, Sutton et al. (2007) paras 8-124-8-126, Merkin & Flannery, *Arbitration Act 1996* (2014) pp.324-327, Harris et al., *The Arbitration Act 1996* (2014) pp.362-364.

232 Sutton et al. (2007) para 8-126.

> the court's function under section 69 is not to embark on any investigation into the facts or the evidence, and (jurisdictional challenges apart) it would be in an extreme case only where the court might be justified in opening any issues of fact, and certainly not for the purposes of attempting to decide whether any particular factual finding was without any evidential basis.[233]

6.2.3 Appeal on point of English law only

As discussed in the preceding section,[234] upon application for leave to appeal, an applicant will be required to identify the question of law justifying the application.[235] The reference, however, is restricted only to a question of English law as defined in Section 82(1) of the Act.[236] Therefore, English courts will not take upon them the exercise of reviewing the tribunal's findings on foreign law, "*even if the tribunal proceeds on the basis that for all practical purposes English law is the same as the foreign governing law.*"[237]

7 THE APPLICATION OF A THREE-HEADED CONCEPT TO SELECTED ISSUES THAT MIGHT FALL OUTSIDE THE ARBITRAL TRIBUNAL'S AUTHORITY

As explained above, all three challenges available under the English arbitration regime are at least to some degree relevant in the context of determining of the scope of the arbitral tribunal's authority.[238] Consequently, it is necessary to take them all into account while reviewing if the tribunal was empowered to grant decisions on the parties' claims (section 7.1), remedies requested (section 7.3) or decisions accessory to the parties' claims (section 7.4). Similarly, it is also relevant to assess the way in which the tribunal has applied the law (section 7.2). Unquestionably, certain tribunal's decisions will meet the threshold to be included in more than one of the above categories. Each category shares, however, some common features according to which the analysis will be conducted.

233 Merkin & Flannery, *Arbitration Act 1996* (2014) p.326.

234 Section 6.2.2.

235 Section 69(4) of the Act.

236 Section 82(1) of the Act in relevant part reads that "*'question of law' means – (a) for a court in England and Wales, a question of the law of England and Wales, and (b) for a court in Northern Ireland, a question of the law of Northern Ireland*".

237 Sutton et al. (2007) para 8-124.

238 See section 3.

7.1 Decisions on parties' claims

The first category of the tribunal's decisions deals with the origin of the parties' claims. It means that it is necessary to discuss in what instances the tribunal exceeds its adjudicative authority when the claim in question has its roots in contract (section 7.1.1) or in tort (section 7.1.4). Additionally, one should distinguish the tribunal's decisions on counterclaims (sections 7.1.2, 7.1.4 and 7.1.5), as well as decisions on set-off (section 7.1.27.1.3). Finally, it is important to consider what happens with decisions on new claims/counterclaims (section 7.1.5) and decisions that do not cover all claims submitted (section 7.1.6). Broadly speaking, most of the tribunal's decisions being analyzed in this section would be qualified as decisions as to the scope of the parties' submissions and thus suitable for a recourse under Section 67 of the Act (challenge of substantive jurisdiction). This will be discussed in greater detail below.

7.1.1 Decision on contractual claims

By and large, it is rather uncontroversial to say that if the parties contract for arbitration, their underlying intention is to have (at least) their contractual disputes resolved by the arbitral tribunal. For this reason, in principle, an arbitral tribunal will be the most competent body to render a decision on contractual claims[239] and consequently a challenge against such a decision would be rather futile. This conclusion, however, is not unqualified and deserves further analysis. It is therefore necessary to establish what prongs of the three-headed concept can be used (and in what circumstances) to object to decisions on contractual claims.

As pointed out in the introduction to this section, the mechanism set out in Section 67 of the Act would be, in principle, the most appropriate tool against the decision on contractual claims. It is so, because an underlying rationale for any objection one may have against a decision on a contractual claim is whether this claim decided upon fell within the scope of the submission to arbitration. Under the English arbitration regime this question is quite straightforward.

In order to determine if a decision exceeds the scope of the submission to arbitration, it is necessary to apply by reference Section 30(1)(c) of the Act.[240] Put differently, one should test the tribunal's decision against "*the matters that have been submitted to arbitration in accordance with the arbitration agreement*". Such an exercise is two-fold, because one should establish (i) whether the matters have been submitted to the tribunal

239 Being claims based on contract and brought by claimant. It distinguishes this category from decisions on counterclaims that are (generally) submitted by the respondent. For further reading, see sections 6.1.2, 6.1.4, 6.1.5 and 6.1.6.

240 See also section 4.2.2.

and (ii) whether they (the matters) were in accordance with the arbitration agreement. Consequently, the tribunal may exceed its substantive jurisdiction if it awards (i) a claim that has not been submitted or (ii) a claim that has not been in accordance with the arbitration agreement (even though properly submitted).

Generally, the first scenario presented above is a rather simple one: only contractual claims submitted by the claimant can be granted by the tribunal. In other words, there is no (and there should not be any) overarching tribunal's power to award to the claimant relief that it did not seek.

One should reflect further, however, what happens if claims submitted are vague or difficult to identify.[241] In these instances, the tribunal, having in mind its general duty to act fairly and give the parties a reasonable opportunity to put their case,[242] should invite all parties for additional submissions.[243] The rationale is to assist the arbitral panel in understanding what the definite scope of the claimant's submission is. Respondent should use this opportunity to protest if it considers that the claim in question (ambiguous or difficult to identify) should not be admitted by the tribunal.[244] In the end, however, it should be the tribunal's prerogative to interpret any remaining ambiguity as to the claims as long as its interpretation of claimant's submission to arbitration does not exceed the scope of an underlying arbitration agreement.[245] It seems that, at the post-award stage, the Section 67 challenge can be triggered if respondent considers that the tribunal's conclusions on ambiguous claims lead to an award that goes, in respondent's opinion, beyond the scope of the claimant's submissions.[246] Importantly, English courts faced with a challenge of the interpretation of the ambiguous claim will be able to decide the scope

241 One should observe that, for example, according to the LMAA 2012 Rules (similarly the 2006 LMAA Rules) in Schedule 2, submissions *must "set out the position of the parties in respect of the issues that have arisen between them as clearly, concisely and comprehensively as possible"*.

242 Section 33(1)(a) of the Act; reiterated for example in Art. 14.1(i) of the 1998 LCIA Rules, Art. 14.4(i) of the 2014 LCIA Rules, Art. 14.1(i) of the 2020 LCIA Rules.

243 The tribunal should proceed similarly when it considers requalification of the basis for the claim. For further reading, see section 6.1.4.

244 In principle, objections should be raised as soon as possible after the matter alleged to be beyond its jurisdiction is raised. See Section 31(2) of the Act. Additionally, one should observe that, for example, pursuant to Art. 23.3 of the 2014 LCIA Rules: "*An objection that the Arbitral Tribunal is exceeding the scope of its authority shall be raised promptly after the Arbitral Tribunal has indicated its intention to act upon the matter alleged to lie beyond its authority.*" See also 23.3 of the 2020 LCIA Rules. For the consequences of the untimely protest, see Section 73(1) of the Act.

245 On a similar note, it might also be difficult to conclusively asses the scope of the submission if claimant decides to modify, amend or add new claims in the course of the proceedings. For further reading on new/changed claims, see section 6.1.5.

246 For example, respondent alleges that the tribunal wrongly interpreted the (ambiguous) relief sought. By doing so the tribunal admitted claims that were never brought. Arguably, such an objection might be raised even if the relief granted fits within the framework of the underlying agreement to arbitrate.

question (pursuant to Section 67 of the Act) anew.[247] Notwithstanding, the better approach would be to give (at least some) deference to the tribunal's interpretation.[248]

The second scenario introduced above deals with the situation where *the claimant's submissions* go beyond the agreement to arbitrate and are nonetheless granted by the arbitral panel. Considering that the modern (model) arbitration clauses are to the effect to entertain many possible disputes,[249] arguably, any claimant's submission should fit the scope of the underlying arbitration agreement. Additionally, taking into account the effect of the seminal decision of *Premium Nafta Products Ltd v. Fili Shipping Ltd*,[250] parties are presumed to opt to have all their disputes resolved by a single adjudicative body. Such a "one-stop method of adjudication" would further entail that any contractual claim submitted by claimant will be in conformity with the underlying arbitration clause. Obviously, parties are free to draft a narrow arbitration clause, where only limited contractual claims can be brought to the tribunal's attention. These restraints should be, however, explicit and clear. It is necessary to point out that it is of utmost importance for respondent to timely contest submissions that are not in accordance with the arbitration agreement. Otherwise it may lose the right to object at the post-award stage or even be considered to have impliedly consented to the extension.

It is rather unlikely that Section 68 of the Act (a recourse against serious irregularities) will be applied to challenge the decision on contractual claims, because it is not designed to tackle the scope questions. That being said, if a tribunal, for example, violates its duty of fairness[251] or renders the decision (on a contractual claim) that is uncertain or ambiguous as to its effect,[252] invoking the serious irregularity challenge might indeed be possible.

To bring an appeal on point of law would be even more farfetched. Assuming that parties did not opt out from the application of Section 69 of the Act, the decision accepting a claim based on contract would have to be obviously wrong, raise a question of general

247 See section 4.1.1. Also *i.a.* Merkin & Flannery, *Arbitration Act 1996* (2014) pp.296-300.

248 See also section 4.1.1.

249 See, *e.g.*, the 2014 LCIA Model Clause ("*Any dispute arising out of or in connection with this contract, including any question regarding its existence, validity or termination, shall be referred to and finally resolved by arbitration under the LCIA Rules, which Rules are deemed to be incorporated by reference into this clause.*"); the Standard 2017 ICC Arbitration Clause ("*All disputes arising out of or in connection with the present contract shall be finally settled under the Rules of Arbitration of the International Chamber of Commerce by one or more arbitrators appointed in accordance with the said Rules.*").

250 *Premium Nafta Products Ltd v. Fili Shipping Ltd* [2007] UKHL 40.

251 For example, by not giving an opportunity to object to the scope of the ambiguous claim as illustrated in the first scenario. See also section 5.2.1.

252 See section 5.2.4.

public importance and at least be open to serious doubts.[253] It is difficult to envisage such a hypothetical.[254]

All in all, parties alleging that the tribunal did not have the authority to decide the contractual claim submitted by claimant will have the highest chances of success by using the Section 67 mechanism. However, these objections have a standing mostly (if not only) when the underlying agreement to arbitrate is explicitly narrow (thus to exclude all or some types of contractual claims). In cases where the tribunal granted a relief which was not sought Section 68(2)(b) will also be relevant.[255]

7.1.2 Decision on contractual counterclaims

Counterclaims are claims that are submitted by a respondent in opposition to a claimant's initial claims. Nonetheless, at the same time, they are independent from the latter, which entails that they usually lead to a separate tribunal's decision,[256] which may exceed the claimant's primary claim.[257] The main element under this section is that counterclaims are (by and large) brought by the respondent.[258] One should add that, in principle, observations made with regard to decisions on contractual claims will be applicable also to decisions on contractual counterclaims.[259] A few additional points, however, should be added.

As pointed out, the Section 67 challenge will apply in the same manner as it applies to decisions on contractual claims.[260] Therefore, in a nutshell, as long as the tribunal decides

253 See also section 6.

254 It is necessary to highlight once again that, under section 6.1.1, the distinctive feature of the tribunal's decision that is being analyzed is that the tribunal grants a claim submitted by claimant *that is based on contract*. Therefore, by no means should it be understood that any decision on a contractual claim may not be appealed on point of law. It is only unlikely that an appeal can be substantiated on the fact that the tribunal wrongly applied the law because it granted a *contractual* claim.

255 See also section 5.2.2 and section 6.3.1. When the relief granted exceeded or was different to the one sought (*ultra* or *extra petita*) Section 68(2)(b) of the AA is triggered. One argument for this application of the post-award review mechanism is a systemic one. Arguably, considering that *infra petita* is included in the list of serious irregularities, *ultra petita* awards should be a part of the same list. See also fn.175. Additionally, it would be the case, if one follows Lord Steyn's suggestion and align the reading of Section 68(2)(b) of the Act with the interpretation of Art. V(1)(c) of the NYC. See *Lesotho Highlands Development Authority v. Impregilo SpA & Ors* [2005] UKHL 43 at [30]. At the same time, however, one might consider that the Act provides that the question regarding "what matters have been submitted to arbitration in accordance with the arbitration agreement" is one of the issues related to the substantive jurisdiction. See Section 30(1)(c) of the AA. Consequently, one might consider Section 67 of the Act as a better fit (unless it is obvious that the issue at stake relates to the limitation of the remedial authority imposed in the agreement to arbitrate). In principle, the better view is to employ Section 68(2)(b) of the Act.

256 Fountoulakis (2011) p.121.

257 Pryles & Waincymer, *Multiple Claims in Arbitration Between the Same Parties* (2009) p.448.

258 Claimant, of course, may counter the counterclaims.

259 See section 6.1.1.

260 See section 6.1.1.

on submitted (counter)claims that were within the scope of the initial agreement to arbitrate, its decision should survive the challenge.[261] Additionally, however, one should reflect on instances where multiple contractual relationships exist between claimant and respondent. In these cases, it is much more likely that respondent may wish to bring its counterclaim that is based on a different contract than the one used by claimant to commence an arbitral process. It consequently leads to the question whether an underlying agreement to arbitrate would cover (counter)claims that are rooted in a separate contract.[262]

The most common approaches would consider that broadly drafted agreements to arbitrate entail claims based on different contracts if they are brought *in connection with* or *relating to* the "main" contract. It would be, thus, respondent's task to convince the tribunal of the admissibility of such counterclaims. The tribunals and the courts might be, however, reluctant to accept these arguments.[263] Arguably, if the ties between two contracts are strong, the counterclaim (arising out of a different contract) that is made *in connection with* or *relating to* the "main" contract should be accepted.[264]

Arguably, testing a decision on counterclaims against the background of Section 68 of the Act will slightly differ (from the review of a decision on the parties' claims). The question that stands out relates to the parties' opportunity to present their case. If the tribunal in its conclusions does not take account of the claims brought by respondent or even does not allow respondent to submit its claims in the first place, it may raise doubts as to equality of arms. Consequently, respondent may consider invoking Section 68(2)(a) of the Act.[265] In any event, however, it all comes down to the scope of the agreement to arbitrate: if the parties' initial consent is limited, disallowing filing of any cross-actions, there should be no question regarding the tribunal's fairness.

---

261 In the majority of cases broad arbitration clauses should cover any contractual counterclaims within its scope. As observed by the authors in Pryles & Waincymer, *Multiple Claims in Arbitration Between the Same Parties* (2009) p.449: "*A properly drawn agreement would allow for both claims and counterclaims under the contract that contains the arbitration clause.*"

262 In other words, it is a contract that is distinct from the one of which the agreement to arbitrate forms part.

263 See, for example, *Metal Distributors (UK) Ltd v. ZCCM Investment Holdings PLC* [2005] EWHC 156 (Comm); [2005] 2 Lloyd's Rep. 37 and *Econet Satellite Services Ltd v. Vee Networks Ltd* [2006] EWHC 1664 (Comm); [2006] 2 Lloyd's Rep. 423. In both cases the tribunal rejected its jurisdiction over counterclaims and/or set-offs. It is important to observe, however, that in the first case ([2005] EWHC 156 (Comm)) the arbitration clause was rather narrow and in the second case the 1976 UNCITRAL Rules were applicable (including Art. 19(3) which allows for counterclaims and set-offs only when they arise out of the same contract). Additionally, these cases predated the *Fiona Trust* case which formulated a strong presumption favoring a broad interpretation of the agreement to arbitrate. See also section 4.2.1.

264 See, *e.g.*, *Norscot Rig Management PVT Ltd v. Essar Oilfields Services Ltd* [2010] EWHC 195, [2010] 2 Lloyd's Rep. 209 (the case (post-*Fiona Trust*) where the tribunal's decision to accept jurisdiction over set-offs and counterclaims arising out of the related contract was subsequently upheld (and the Section 67 challenge dismissed)). At the same time, however, there should be no competing *fora* for the resolution of a dispute, *i.e.* two contracts should not include competing arbitration or dispute resolution clauses.

265 See section 5.2.1.

Similar to a decision on contractual claims, it would be difficult to appeal on point of law against contractual counterclaims if the nature of the objection focuses on the *contractual character* of the counterclaim.[266]

7.1.3 Decision on set-off

Deciding on set-off claims might be a particularly complex topic in international commercial arbitration. On the one hand, the general presumption in most legal regimes is that set-off is a form of defense against the initial claim. On the other hand, the concept of set-off as developed in other jurisdictions considerably differs.[267] The differences are particularly noticeable in England, where the notion of set-off evolved independently from its continental counterparts.[268] In international commercial arbitration, however, the first step of inquiry is to determine what law applies to set-off related issues.[269]

In cases where the seat of arbitration is in England, the possible challenge against the decision on set-off is likely to be based either on Section 67(1), Section 68(2)(a) or 68(2)(d) of the Act. It is simply because the underlying concern may focus either on the scope of the agreement to arbitrate or the overarching notion of procedural fairness and a party's right to present its case.

The objection available under Section 67 of the Act questions whether the tribunal's decision on set-off fits within the scope of an agreement to arbitrate.[270] This might depend

266 See also section 6.1.1.

267 An important note has been put forward by Pryles and Waincymer in Pryles & Waincymer, *Multiple Claims in Arbitration Between the Same Parties* (2009) p.461 ("*[...] we merely wish to reiterate that there is no simple solution to the question of admissibility of set-off claims. It should not automatically be allowed simply because all legal families entitle them as "defences"*.).

268 A detailed analysis of the legal character of set-off claims falls outside the scope of this research. By and large, under English law one may recognize that the term "set-off" refers to (i) statutory set-off, (ii) abatement, and (iii) equitable set-off, and (iv) contractual set-off. For further reading, see, *i.a.*, Wood (1989), Aeberli (1992), Berger, *Set-off in International Economic Arbitration* (1999), Rogers (2006) pp.129-133, Fountoulakis (2011) pp.100-123. The distinction between different types of set-off may be relevant in the context of admitting set-off as a defense. The main (noticeable) difference is between "statutory set-off" and "equitable set-off". The former operates as a judicial remedy and does not require connectivity between the primary claim and the set-off claim (therefore sometimes it is labeled as an "independent set-off"). See, *e.g.*, *Aectra Refining & Manufacturing Inc. v. Exmar NV* [1994] 1 WLR 1634 at [1650] ("*Independent set-off [...] is not a substantive defence to the claim, but a procedure for taking and account of the balance between the parties.*"). The latter (*i.e.* equitable set-off) has characteristics of a substantive defense. See, *e.g.*, Berger, *Set-off in International Economic Arbitration* (1999) p.58. Notably, Berger in Berger, *Set-off in International Economic Arbitration* (1999) p.57 highlighted that "*[t]oday, the distinction between equitable set-off and set-off at law is said to be blurred. However, like the 'compensation légale' and 'compensation judiciaire' of French law, the two institutions have to be distinguished in terms of both prerequisites and legal nature.*"

269 Considering it is a substantive defense, the issue would be determined in accordance with applicable substantive law. Consequently, the particularities of English law might not be relevant.

270 It also operates under the general assumption that a party (usually the respondent) submitted a set-off claim. It goes without saying that the tribunal should not be able to decide on set-off *ex officio*, except in highly unusual circumstances when expressly authorized by the parties. See also reflections on the scope

on the legal nature of the set-off applied by the party, especially in the context of an independent set-off and an equitable set-off.[271]

As mentioned above independent set-off usually arises in a multi-contract reality and it may concern unrelated contracts. Bearing in mind that the tribunal's adjudicative powers are intrinsically dependent on the scope of the agreement to arbitrate, it is often argued that the tribunal's jurisdiction needs to expressly encompass any prospective counterclaim that may arise for the purpose of statutory set-off. Additionally, under the English legal regime statutory (independent) set-off is not considered as a substantive defense, but rather as procedural in nature.[272] Consequently, arbitral tribunals are not readily eager to accept jurisdiction in the case of independent set-off.[273] Even if arbitral jurisdiction over the counterclaims for the purpose of a statutory set-off (thus brought under a different factual basis than the main claim) is accepted by the arbitral panel, it is likely to be subsequently overturned by the English courts.[274]

Contrary to statutory set-offs, it is often accepted for the international arbitral tribunal to entertain its jurisdiction over the counterclaims submitted for the purpose of an equitable

---

question in section 6.1.1. For general comments, see also Merkin & Flannery, *Arbitration Act 1996* (2014) p.111, Harris et al., *The Arbitration Act 1996* (2014) p.162.

271 See fn.268. Also Berger, *Set-off in International Economic Arbitration* (1999) p.57. It would seldom happen that the tribunal would not have jurisdiction to decide on the two other types of set-offs recognized in the English system, *i.e.*, abatement or contractual set-offs. Abatement serves as a narrow defense, which requires connectivity and as such is based on the same contract. Having its basis in the same contract and being a defense, arguably, it would rarely go outside the tribunal's jurisdiction. It should be also noted that parties may decide to expand or limit their entitlement to a set-off by including a specific set-off provision in the contract. Consequently, it would be evident on the face of the contract what parties intended and thus in what instances the tribunal may decide on set-off. See also Pryles & Waincymer, *Multiple Claims in Arbitration Between the Same Parties* (2009) p.457 ("*Where debts are connected, a cross entitlement is often a pure defence and does not even need to be treated as a set-off. Consider for example, a case of a buyer and seller who have an ongoing two way commercial relationship with regular two way payment obligations. The supplier sues the buyer for outstanding payment but the buyer says the claim fails to take into account agreed allowances for faulty goods. This need not be separately pleaded as a set-off if the claimant is only entitled to a net amount under their agreement. It is simply an allegation that the net position as claimed is wrong. This is at times described as contractual set-off. If it is expressly or impliedly agreed to in this way it would easily fall within any arbitration agreement covering the primary claim.*").

272 See above. Also Pryles & Waincymer, *Multiple Claims in Arbitration Between the Same Parties* (2009) p.459 ("*An independent set-off at common law is allowed for where it is capable of being ascertained with suitable precision, described as liquidated. This would also include some damages claims, for example, where they arise out of an express contractual provision setting up a damages formula, such as in the case of late performance in construction contracts. Such an independent set-off need not arise out of related transactions and is seen as purely procedural, requiring the imprimatur of legal proceedings. As such it cannot be invoked unilaterally. It is sometimes described as statutory set-off.*").

273 Sutton et al. (2007) para 6-016. Scherer, *The Award and the Courts, Set-Off in International Arbitration* (2015) p.464 ("*[English common law] favors arbitral jurisdiction over set-offs that arise from the same or related facts as the main claim ('transaction set-off') while disfavoring such jurisdiction over set-offs that are factually unrelated to the main claim ('independent set-off'). Arbitral tribunals applying English law as the lex arbitri have followed the courts in acceding to this dichotomy*").

274 Scherer, *The Award and the Courts, Set-Off in International Arbitration* (2015) pp.464-465.

set-off.[275] Of course, it does, yet again, depend on the content of the agreement to arbitrate. For this reason, if the agreement to arbitrate is a narrow one, a court will likely accept an argument that the tribunal does not have jurisdiction over a set-off arising out of a different contract.[276] At the same time, however, equitable set-off works as a (substantive) defense, hence rejecting it or disallowing a set-off to be submitted may affect a party's right to present its case.

On this point it has been concluded in *dictum* that:

> [p]rovisionally, I would be minded to think that an arbitrator does or should have jurisdiction to allow a 'transaction' set-off, even though that set-off arises under another contract [...] As it seems to me, the investigation and determination of the availability and amount of such a set-off do not involve the arbitrator arrogating to himself a jurisdiction over separate contracts which he does not have (albeit that considerations of issue estoppel may well arise); instead these steps form part of the process of arriving at a conclusion of whether a defence is properly available in respect of the contract to which the arbitrator alone has jurisdiction.[277]

Put differently, "*as a matter of principle, an arbitrator should have jurisdiction to deal with an equitable set-off because such a set-off is a defence.*"[278]

As highlighted above, when attempting to challenge the tribunal's decision on set-off, not only the Section 67 mechanism is of value. Therefore, it is necessary to reflect on the Section 68 objection. In principle, Section 67 of the Act will be (more often) applied by a party that seeks to annul the award accepting jurisdiction over the set-off defense,[279] whereas Section 68 of the Act would be commonly invoked when a party remains unsatisfied with a decline of the set-off, thus rejecting its defense.

As explained elsewhere,[280] Section 68 of the Act could be used as a filter to sift serious irregularities that cause substantial injustice. Therefore, arguably, the possibility to bring a set-off defense might be an essential feature of the concept of fair trial. Consequently, "*[...] if a tribunal makes an award for a sum to be immediately payable without properly*

275 See, *e.g.*, Scherer, *The Award and the Courts, Set-Off in International Arbitration* (2015) p.464.

276 See for example *Econet Satelite Services Ltd. v. Vee Networks Ltd* [2006] EWHC 1664 (Comm); [2006] 2 Lloyd's Rep. 423, where the court upheld the tribunal's decision declining jurisdiction over a set-off because of the scope of the agreement to arbitrate.

277 *Ronly Holdings Ltd v. JSC Zestafoni G Nikoladze Ferroalloy Plant* [2004] EWHC 1354 (Comm) at [33].

278 Friedman (2011) p.501 and also p.500.

279 Bringing an action regarding the tribunal's negative ruling (thus one rejecting jurisdiction over set-off) is of course possible. See, *e.g.*, *Econet Satelite Services Ltd. v. Vee Networks Ltd* [2006] EWHC 1664 (Comm); [2006] 2 Lloyd's Rep. 423.

280 See section 5.

considering a claimed right of set-off, the award may be subject to challenge."[281] In this instance a tribunal's decision on set-off might thus be susceptible to arguments that the tribunal violated its general duty of fairness[282] or failed to deal with all the issues brought before it.[283] In principle, a tribunal will have to weigh all the arguments submitted and carefully explain why the solution that it chose (*i.e.* accepting or rejecting a set-off defense) better serves an efficient dispute resolution and the finality of the award.[284]

Similar to decisions analyzed previously,[285] a decision on set-off is a decision on specific parties' submissions. In turn, parties are better off challenging substantive jurisdiction of arbitral tribunals or serious irregularity rather than appealing on point of law. Nonetheless, in cases where an appeal is available, one may wonder if, in some instances, awarding independent set-off will not trigger the possibility of a legal appeal.[286]

All in all, a tribunal required to decide on set-off will find itself between Scylla and Charybdis, because however it decides, its conclusions might be the target of a potential challenge at the post-award stage. On the one hand, being on the safe side, it is likely that tribunals will restrain themselves to decisions fitting within the scope of the agreements to arbitrate. On the other hand, however, there are strong arguments favoring the tribunal's efforts to resolve any and all disputes between parties by way of accepting set-off defenses even if it is not *per se* in accordance with an agreement to arbitrate. Therefore, the tribunal should look favorably on set-off submissions, but accept them only after full analysis of their factual underpinning.

7.1.4 Decision on claims/counterclaims based on torts and pre-contractual liability

A closer look at the statutory definition of an arbitration agreement introduced in the English Arbitration Act "*[...] makes [it] clear that a non-contractual dispute can be referred to arbitration.*"[287] Pursuant to Section 6(1) of the Act "*[...] 'an arbitration agreement' means an agreement to submit to arbitration present or future disputes (whether they are contractual or not).*" Yet, (at least) two questions remain unanswered: (i) does the scope of every single

281 Sutton et al. (2007) para 6-017. An argument has been advanced in the context of contractual set-offs; it will hold true also for other types of (substantive) set-off.

282 Section 68(2)(a) of the Act.

283 Section 68(2)(d) of the Act.

284 See, *e.g.*, Pryles & Waincymer, *Multiple Claims in Arbitration Between the Same Parties* (2009) p.488 ("*We believe that in addition to considering whether all claims should be allowed, tribunals must also consider how to conduct proceedings even if some claims are rejected. They must still consider the appropriate elements of due process within each arbitral process, at least with an eye to what is happening with the other. In either circumstance tribunals also have to consider the potential impact on enforceability of their decisions as to admissibility.*").

285 See section 6.1.1 and section 6.1.2.

286 Still, however, it would be probably easier to apply Section 67 of the Act instead.

287 Merkin & Flannery, *Arbitration Act 1996* (2014) p.26.

agreement to arbitrate envisage claims regarding the extra-contractual liability of the parties[288] and (ii) is it possible to challenge the tribunal's decision that requalifies contractual claims as tortious? In a nutshell, similarly to the other scope questions, Section 67 of the Act would be the most useful provision for parties seeking to challenge the scope, whereas arguably Section 68(2)(b) of the Act will serve its purpose under the second hypothetical.

As to the first question, for a long time the question whether an agreement to arbitrate covered claims having their basis outside the contract was highly dependent on the exact wording of the agreement to arbitrate. Even broadly drafted clauses were no guarantee that the tribunal would enjoy jurisdiction over all of the claims submitted. This situation changed with the seminal decision of House of Lords in *Premium Nafta Products Ltd v. Fili Shipping Ltd.*[289]

Premium Nafta's contribution was to applaud the notion of "one-stop arbitration", where all disputes between the parties are resolved before the same arbitral panel.[290]

In the opinion of Lord Hoffmann:

> [...] the construction of an arbitration clause should start from the assumption that the parties, as rational businessmen, are likely to have intended any dispute arising out of the relationship into which they have entered or purported to enter to be decided by the same tribunal. The clause should be construed in accordance with this presumption unless the language makes it clear that certain questions were intended to be excluded from the arbitrator's jurisdiction. As Longmore LJ remarked, [...]: 'if any businessman did want to exclude disputes about the validity of a contract, it would be comparatively easy to say so.'[291]

In other words, if parties decide to include an agreement to arbitrate in their contract, their presumed intention (unless clearly indicated otherwise) is to cover any and all their disputes (irrespective of whether they are contractual or not) before the arbitral tribunal.[292]

Occasionally a generous interpretation of the narrow agreement to arbitrate could also lead to a conclusion that the non-contractual claims are so closely related to the contract

288 For the purpose of this section, claims and counterclaims will be discussed together. Here, the analysis is not focused on the question *who* brings the claim, but rather on what is the *basis* for the argument (namely torts).

289 *Premium Nafta Products Ltd v. Fili Shipping Ltd* [2007] UKHL 40.

290 Merkin & Flannery, *Arbitration Act 1996* (2014) p.110 ("*Much work, and no doubt many potential billable hours, were finally swept away and replaced by the sense and sensibility of the Court of Appeal in Fiona Trust, led by Longmore LJ, in a pragmatic and praiseworthy attempt (largely successful) to ensure that parties (particularly international commercial parties) are almost always to be treated as having bargained to bring all their disputes under the one roof, namely that provided by the arbitration agreement and the arbitral tribunal*").

291 *Premium Nafta Products Ltd v. Fili Shipping Ltd* [2007] UKHL 40 at [13].

292 Merkin & Flannery, *Arbitration Act 1996* (2014) p.26.

that the initial agreement to arbitrate may extend to connected non-contractual claims.[293] On a similar note, it has been argued that "*[w]hatever the wording of the arbitration agreement, noncontractual claims may of course become part of the reference if they are included in a pleading and no point is taken by the other party, even if there had originally been no contractual relationship between the parties.*"[294]

In sum, on the one hand, following a broad, arbitration-friendly interpretation of an underlying agreement to arbitrate, the English courts will hold the parties to their contractual arbitration bargain. On the other hand, however, excessive expansion of the meaning of the agreement to arbitrate might impede what parties have actually agreed upon. That being said, the better view is for the tribunal to always consult the initial agreement to arbitrate and not to be overly eager to rely only on the presumption of a "one stop arbitration" even if in most instances courts will likely accept arbitral jurisdiction over tort claims if it is not evident at face value that there is an agreement to arbitrate.

The second instance that requires analysis concerns the tribunal's requalification of the claims submitted. One should reflect if a tribunal acts within its powers when, after reviewing the parties' submissions, it decides to grant the relief sought, but on a non-contractual basis instead of a contractual one. Such a scenario may occur if (i) a party submits two alternative bases for its claim, or (ii) a tribunal introduces a new basis for the party's claim on its own motion.[295]

If a party seeks a specific relief and argues that it should be granted because there is a contractual basis as well as one of a tortious nature, the tribunal should be free to choose which path to follow.[296] In this case it will simply explain which theory submitted convinces it most and will decide accordingly. The tribunal's decision should survive the challenge.

If, however, the tribunal requalifies a claim on its own motion, it risks that the challenge against its award may be successful. Changing the basis for the claim from contractual to tortious should not be treated lightly, because, it will effectively mean that the tribunal

293 Sutton et al. (2007) para 2-004 ("*Provided the terms of the arbitration agreement are broad enough to encompass such claims they can in principle be the subject of an arbitration. Whether they do so in any particular case requires an examination of the arbitration agreement but the courts have generally given a broad interpretation to the scope of arbitration agreements in this regard. In this context it may be possible to conclude that the non-contractual claims are so intimately connected with a contract that even an arbitration clause designed primarily for contractual claims will extend to connected non-contractual claims. In Asghar v. Legal Services Commission claims for conspiracy, misfeasance in public office and inducement to commit breach of conduct were all found to be within the arbitration agreement because 'the resolution of the contractual claims cannot sensibly or practically be divorced from the resolution of the non-contractual claims.'*") The reference is made to *Asghar v. Legal Services Commission* [2004] EWHC 1803 at [18].

294 Sutton et al. (2007) para 2-004.

295 The tribunal bases this on its own legal expertise. For further reading on the tribunal's process of application of the law, see section 6.2. See also section 5.2.1.

296 Occasionally its decision might be burdened with its own consequences *e.g.* when the tribunal opts to follow a tort theory, but the scope of the agreement to arbitrate is not broad enough for the panel to enjoy jurisdiction over such a claim.

substitutes the parties' pleadings with its own and, in turn, will step into the shoes of one party's counsel rather than remain an impartial adjudicative body. Therefore, if the tribunal decides to change a justification for the remedy granted from contractual to non-contractual, it may find itself in breach of the duty of fairness[297] or in excess of its powers.[298] That being said, arguably, the tribunal may try to minimize the chances for a prospective challenge by inviting parties to address its recommendation for changing the basis for the claim. This way it will make sure that parties had a full opportunity to present their case. Under no circumstances should it "surprise" the parties with its legal conclusions.[299]

Parties seeking to challenge a tribunal's decision because the relief sought is not based on contract would have a difficult task trying to convince the court that appeal on a point of law is justified.

The reflections above lead to the conclusion that Section 67 of the Act is best suited to be used against the tribunal's decision based on torts claims. Occasionally, however, since serious irregularities may occur also when the tribunal is exercising its power over tort claims, Section 68 may be also relevant. In any event, the threshold for a successful challenge remains high.

7.1.5 Decision on new claims/counterclaims and change of claims/counterclaims

As explained earlier, the parties' submissions shape the tribunal's jurisdiction and its powers.[300] In principle, parties are obliged to introduce their claims at the outset of the proceedings in their initial statements.[301] It may happen, however, that during the proceedings parties wish to amend their original submissions.[302] They may do so by limiting the scope of the relief previously sought. They may also decide to the contrary, namely to change or to expand the content of their underlying request. The question that follows is whether the arbitral panel can enjoy jurisdiction and powers over the changed or late claims and accept them as such. Allowing for a change of claims or admitting new claims may in turn trigger a challenge based on Section 67[303] or 68(2)(a),[304] 68(2)(b),[305] or 68(2)(c)[306] of the Act at the post-award stage. Appeal on a point of law is unlikely to be applicable.

297 Section 68(2)(a) of the Act.
298 Section 68(2)(b) of the Act.
299 For a discussion on the arbitral tribunal "surprising" the parties with new legal theories, see section 5.2.1 and section 6.2. "Surprise" decisions will be susceptible to challenge under Section 68(2)(a) of the Act (breach of general duties of the tribunal).
300 See section 4.2.2.
301 See section 4.2.2.
302 The terms "new claims", "changed claims" and "late claims" will be used interchangeably for the purpose of this study.
303 (Challenge of substantive jurisdiction).
304 (Breach of general duties of the arbitral tribunal).
305 (Excess of powers of the arbitral tribunal).
306 (Failure to conduct the proceedings in accordance with the procedure agreed by the parties).

The brief analysis below would thus focus on the issues of (i) jurisdiction and (ii) the tribunal's powers.

The Act does not offer a special rule as to how to proceed with new or amended claims. Therefore, a traditional scope analysis (pursuant to Section 30(1)(c) of the Act) should be employed in order to determine whether the tribunal can accept jurisdiction and allow new claims or the change of claims.[307] Consequently, the new claims should be tested against the scope of the agreement to arbitrate. Broadly drafted arbitration clauses, however, will be of little assistance on how to deal with late submissions, which means that they will also not provide any specific guidelines for the amendment of claims. The issue is often addressed by the institutional rules, if applicable.[308] The institutional rules give the arbitral tribunal discretion to decide whether new claims will be admitted or not.[309] That being said, the rules vary as to how far the tribunal's power to accept new claims goes.[310] In any event, the question rarely occurs if the tribunal (in institutional international arbitration) has jurisdiction to allow late claims, as long as they fit within the scope of an agreement to arbitrate.[311] Arguably, where all parties agreed to allow new claims that fall outside the initial jurisdiction of the tribunal, one may conclude that parties consented to the extension of the tribunal's jurisdiction.

The second issue does not relate to the tribunal's jurisdiction, but rather to the tribunal's managerial powers. As such, it is necessary to reflect if admitting late claims affects the fairness of the arbitral process. It has been accurately concluded by Derains in the context of amendments to the claims and new claims:

307 See, *i.a.*, section 6.1.1 of this chapter.

308 See, *e.g.*, Art. 22.1(a) of the 1998 LCIA Rules, Art. 22.1(i) of the 2014 LCIA Rules, Art. 22.1(i) of the 2020 LCIA Rules, Art. 23.4 of the 2012 ICC Rules, Art. 23.4 of the 2017 ICC Rules, Art. 20 of the 1976 UNCITRAL Rules, Art. 22 of the 2010 UNCITRAL Rules.

309 Similarly, Derains, *Amendments to the Claims and New Claims: Where to Draw the Line?* (2004) p.71 ("*as a matter of principle, new claims filed in the course of the proceedings are admissible, under the control of the arbitrators.*").

310 *Cf* Art. 22.1(i) of the 2014 (or 2020) LCIA Rules and Art. 23.4 of the 2017 ICC Rules. For example, Derains in Derains, *Amendments to the Claims and New Claims: Where to Draw the Line?* (2004) p.71 concluded with reference to the 1998 LCIA Rules that "*[w]hat is the borderline after which a new claim or counterclaim should be declared inadmissible, unless its admission is accepted by the other side? Under the LCIA Rules, the arbitrator's power is unlimited. [...]*", whereas with regard to the 1998 ICC Rules he stated that "*[t]he ICC Rules [...] have a more objective approach. Their emphasis is put on the possible effect of the new claim on the conduct of the proceedings.*" Although Derains discussed previous versions of the rules, his conclusions hold true to the new ones as well.

311 In cases of ad hoc arbitration, it is better if all parties (and the tribunal) agree to an extension of claims. In any event, even if there is no consensus, there is a strong argument favoring the tribunal's jurisdiction over the late claims that it is universally accepted practice to give a tribunal discretion to accept or reject the late claim.

> [i]n reality, the two aspects must be successively taken into consideration by the arbitrators. The effect on the conduct of the proceedings of admitting the new claim should be the leading criterium. In case the new claim is filed at a time, which allows the other side to respond to it without delaying the schedule agreed or imposed by the arbitrators. There is no[] reason not to admit it, even if such claim could have been submitted before. On the contrary, in case the admission of the new claim has a delaying effect on the proceedings, consideration of fairness justify that the arbitrators allow the claim if they are satisfied that the claim reasonably could not have been submitted before.[312]

All in all, challenging a decision on new or changed claims would be possible if a party can convince the court that the tribunal did not give it a reasonable opportunity to present its case.[313]

Additionally, as highlighted above in most instances where the arbitral process is conducted under the auspices of an arbitral institution, the tribunal will have a discretionary power to accept late claims.[314] Consequently, the challenges based on alleged excess of powers[315] or failure to conduct the proceedings in accordance with the proceedings agreed will likely be unsuccessful.[316] The situation differs when parties explicitly excluded late submissions or when agreed rules for the ad hoc arbitration proceedings are silent on the matter of late claims.[317]

The overarching conclusion is that the Section 68 objections are most appropriate when a successful recourse is sought against the tribunal's decision on new or changed claims. The threshold to be satisfied is, however, high.[318]

7.1.6 Decision not covering all claims/counterclaims

These days arbitration is a sophisticated process where parties are able to produce lengthy submissions before the arbitral panel. For strategic or tactical reasons, they may also draft the relief sought broadly so that it may be difficult to distill its true meaning. It may so happen, that different alternative or secondary claims are introduced which makes the relation between the different claims not so easy to grasp. Faced with these circumstances,

312 Derains, *Amendments to the Claims and New Claims: Where to Draw the Line?* (2004) p.71.

313 Section 33(1)(a) of the Act. See also section 5.2.1 of this chapter.

314 See fn.310.

315 Section 68(2)(b) of the Act.

316 Section 68(2)(c) of the Act.

317 Arguably, however, even when ad hoc proceedings are conducted and nothing has been said about late submissions, the general notion of procedural fairness and pervasive practice of international commercial arbitration (that in principle allows tribunals to deal with late claims) might lead to the conclusion that the tribunal would be entitled to decide on late claims. See also fn.311.

318 See section 5.1.3.

arbitrators might be tempted to use, consciously or not, heuristics in reaching their conclusions.

In cases where an arbitral award does not fully reflect the relief sought by the parties, the tribunal's decision will be considered as *infra petita*. The English Arbitration regime addresses *infra petita* in Section 68(2)(d) of the Act. Pursuant to said provision, the award can be challenged when the tribunal failed "*to deal with all the issues that were put to it*". Much has already been said in section 5.2.3 of this chapter and reference therein is in place.[319]

The most relevant features of the challenge that deserve to be reiterated are the following: (i) not all arguments put forward before the tribunal can be considered as issues for the purposes of the Section 68(2)(d) application,[320] (ii) if the tribunal in its award dealt with the issue in any way (however good, bad, or ugly)[321] it will make Section 68(2)(d) of the Act inapplicable, and (iii) the court will seek to exercise its remedial powers only on the part of the award which is affected by serious irregularity, usually preferring remission back to the tribunal instead of the (partial) setting aside of the award.[322] That being said, two further reflections should follow: (i) one refers to the eventuality of the *res iudicata* effect of the *infra petita* award and (ii) another deals with the possibility of setting aside the *infra petita* award.

On the one hand, if one considers that the *infra petita* award does not fully address the relief sought, it is possible to argue that the outstanding issues are still unresolved thus it cannot be considered *res iudicata*. On the other hand, the contention that (even) the *infra petita* award has a *res iudicata* effect is particularly alluring in cases where the tribunal acknowledges a claim not decided upon in any form in its reasoning or if it opts to conclude its decision with *formulae* such as "*rejects any and all other claims*" or the "*award is in full and final settlement of all claims between the parties*". If the tribunal, however, does address the claim in any way, a challenging party might face difficulty with substantiating its Section 68(2)(d) objection.[323] In any event, if the court is satisfied with a challenge, it will use its

319 See section 5.2.3.

320 Merkin & Flannery, *Arbitration Act 1996* (2014) p.313 ("*There is a distinction between failing to deal with major issues and failing to deal in the award with every argument in detail that was put to the arbitrators: the latter allegation will fail unless the claimant can show that, on a fair reading of the award, key issues were not considered at all. Furthermore, an 'issue' for the purpose of section 68(2)(d) is one that is of decisive effect on the outcome, and not an incidental or peripheral matter, whose resolution is largely immaterial to the overall result or that falls away in the light of other holdings.*").

321 The formula was used, albeit in a different context, in the U.S. Supreme Court decision of *Oxford Health Plans LLC v. Sutter*, 133 S. Ct. 2064, 2070-71, 186 L. Ed. 2d 113 (2013).

322 For further reading, see section 5.1.4 and section 5.2.3. See also *e.g. The Secretary of State for the Home Department v. Raytheon Systems Limited* [2015] EWHC 311 (TCC) at [3] ("*It is clear that remission is the "default" option and the Court cannot set aside unless it would be "inappropriate" to remit.*"').

323 If tribunal does not refer to a claim (that is of such an importance that it can be classified as an issue) at all, it will be a clear-cut Section 68(2)(d) scenario. See section 5.2.3.

remedial powers to ensure that the relief sought has been addressed in full.[324] Otherwise the tribunal's (allegedly) *infra petita* decision would, arguably, stand and have a *res iudicata* effect.[325]

As to the second reflection, it has been suggested by some authors, with reference to Section 68(2)(d) of the Act, that "*this provision reflects the previous common law position that an award which does not deal with all the issues may be remitted back to the arbitrators with a direction to remedy the deficiency.*"[326] In most instances, remission would be the most appropriate tool if a party is able to show that some prayer for relief has not been dealt with. However, setting aside is also available in *infra petita* situations and it might be a particularly relevant remedy in cases where the award has a *res iudicata* effect. Nonetheless, the setting-aside mechanism should, in any event, be reserved for a very limited catalogue of cases. The question (that needs to be addressed on a case-by-case basis) regards the fate of the award after being set aside, namely is it possible that the same tribunal is asked for reconsideration[327] or should the award be set aside to be resolved by a different arbitral tribunal.[328] It means that the reviewing court will likely undertake a careful analysis as to what solution is better for the case before it and will assess whether the original tribunal is able to resume and incorporate the court's observations or whether it is better for a new tribunal to have a fresh look at the outstanding issues.[329]

7.2 *The process of application of law by the arbitral tribunal*

The process of application of law by arbitrators is an inherent exercise on the way to grant a relief requested. By and large, the tribunal would first need to determine what conflict of laws rules are applicable (section 7.2.1) before deciding what law applies (section7.2.2). Once the tribunal identifies the governing law, it will face the task of ascertaining the content of the applicable law (section 7.2.3) and its mandatory rules (section 7.2.4). Occasionally, however, the arbitral panel may be entrusted with rendering a decision not based on a national system of law (section 7.2.5). The underlying question is whether the tribunal has the power to apply the law, and if so, how this process can be supervised by the English courts.

---

324 Again, by "relief sought being addressed in full" one should understand all major items of the relief that can be categorized as "issues". See also section 5.2.3.

325 Arguably, it will hold true even if the tribunal conclude its award with a closing *formula* ("*rejects any and all other claims*") without realizing that some issues remain unresolved.

326 Merkin & Flannery, *Arbitration Act 1996* (2014) p.313.

327 *Ascot Commodities NV v. Olam International Ltd.* [2002] C.L.C. 277. See also *Brockton Capital LLP v. Atlantic-Pacific Capital Inc* [2014] 2 Lloyd's Rep. 275 at [34].

328 *The Secretary of State for the Home Department v. Raytheon Systems Limited* [2015] EWHC 311 (TCC).

329 For a detailed analysis seeking the most appropriate remedy, see *The Secretary of State for the Home Department v. Raytheon Systems Limited* [2015] EWHC 311 (TCC) at [2-12].

An appropriate reference point to start the analysis with is Section 46 of the Act.[330] The first part of this Section reads that: "*[t]he arbitral tribunal shall decide the dispute (a) in accordance with the law chosen by the parties as applicable to the substance of the dispute, or (b) if the parties so agree, in accordance with such other considerations as are agreed by them or determined by the tribunal.*"[331] Additionally, pursuant to the second subsection: "*[f]or this purpose the choice of the laws of a country shall be understood to refer to the substantive laws of that country and not its conflict of laws rules.*"[332] Finally, according to the last proviso: "*[i]f or to the extent that there is no such choice or agreement, the tribunal shall apply the law determined by the conflict of laws rules which it considers applicable.*"[333] In a nutshell, therefore, this provision empowers the tribunal to decide on applicable law. It is necessary, however, to reflect further on the question when the tribunal's conclusions are open for recourse.

It is argued that the process of application of law will not, in any way, affect the tribunal's substantive jurisdiction, which means that the Section 67 challenge would be inapplicable for the purpose of this section. Therefore, only the Section 68 (challenge based on serious irregularities) and the Section 69 (appeal on point of law) mechanisms will be taken into account.

7.2.1 Determining the method of selection of applicable law

Although not always necessary, determining the applicable conflict of laws rules is the first step of the legal analysis undertaken by the arbitral tribunal. This decision of the arbitral tribunal will have, potentially, far-reaching consequences.[334]

Starting with the assumption that the parties did not include a choice of law clause in their contract, it is considerably clear that the tribunal has a power to determine what conflict of laws rules applies.[335] Pursuant to Section 46(3) of the Act, "*[i]f or to the extent that there is no such choice or agreement [regarding the law applicable to the substance of the dispute], the tribunal shall apply the law determined by the conflict of laws rules which it considers applicable.*" The tribunal will be able to rely on this fallback solution introduced in the Act and, ultimately, enjoy broad discretion while assessing the appropriate conflict

330 This section, albeit with some significant amendments, has been modeled on Art. 28 of the Model Law. For further reading on the Model Law, see Chapter II.

331 Section 46(1) of the Act.

332 Section 46(2) of the Act.

333 Section 46(3) of the Act.

334 The choice of applicable conflict of laws rule has a direct impact as to what law applies.

335 Arguably, the Act does not allow the tribunal to directly choose the applicable law. It means that the tribunal should always make a conflict of laws analysis (unless otherwise agreed by the parties). Consequently, if the tribunal relies on the *voie directe* methodology, its decision might be annulled based on the tribunal's failure to comply with its general duties (Section 68(2)(a) of the Act) or on the excess of powers (Section 68(2)(b) of the Act).

of laws rules.[336] Nonetheless, one should follow questions formulated by Merkin and Flannery and reflect whether (i) a party has a remedy when it considers that the arbitrators' choice of the relevant conflict of laws rule is incorrect and whether (ii) any remedy is available in cases where the tribunal's application of a conflict of laws rule leads to the choice of an incorrect substantive law.[337]

The most appropriate remedy to consider in cases of alleged incorrectness of legal findings is the one provided in Section 69 of the Act. Having posed the two questions mentioned above, scholars consequently argued that recourse will not be possible under the first scenario,[338] but can eventually be available only under the second hypothetical[339] if the parties left open the possibility to appeal on point of law.

As to the first question, it appears that the default mechanism prescribed by Section 46(3) of the Act effectively makes the tribunal's choice of conflict of laws rules unreviewable, since "*[...] it is difficult to understand how their [tribunal's] determination of the applicable conflict of law rules (as opposed to the determination of the applicable law) could be held to constitute an error of English law, giving rise to a right of appeal under section 69.*"[340] With regard to the second question, however, under a unique set of circumstances it might be possible to attack errors in choosing the substantive law according to the conflict of laws rules. It has been argued that such a recourse might be possible if (i) the parties have not waived the opportunity to appeal on a point of law, (ii) arbitrators decided that the English conflict of laws rules apply, or (iii) when applying these rules "*the arbitrators choose an applicable law that is not a reasonably probable consequence of the application of the conflict of law rules [...] [T]his is presumably an error of law only, and may be attacked [...] under the error of law provisions in Section 69.*"[341] Even if recourse is available, one should not forget that the threshold imposed by the requirements of Section 69 is very high.

Arguably, Section 68(2)(b) of the Act might also be relevant when a decision on the applicable conflict of laws rules is rendered. One has to imagine then that the underlying contract includes a choice of law provision, but the tribunal, disregarding it, selects a different legal regime based on its own conflict of laws analysis. Acting in this way, the tribunal will usurp a power it never possessed.[342] As such, it would likely be qualified as

336 See also DAC, *Report on the Arbitration Bill* (1996) para 225.

337 Merkin & Flannery, *Arbitration Act 1996* (2014) p.207.

338 A scenario where the choice of a conflict of laws rule is incorrect.

339 A scenario where the application of a (correct) conflict of laws rule leads to the application of incorrect law.

340 Merkin & Flannery, *Arbitration Act 1996* (2014) p.207.

341 Merkin & Flannery, *Arbitration Act 1996* (2014) p.207, with a reference to *CGU International Insurance plc v. AstraZeneca Insurance Co Ltd* [2007] 1 Lloyd's Rep. 142.

342 The power which, at the same time, does not affect the tribunal's substantive jurisdiction. See also section 5.2.2 of this chapter.

serious irregularity amounting to substantial injustice. All in all, one should conclude that the chances for a decision on applicable conflict of laws rules to be challenged are scant.

Importantly, however, arbitrators are required to substantiate their decision with a conflict of laws analysis. Therefore, the provision, arguably, limits their power to exercise other methods of identifying the applicable law, *e.g.* the direct approach.[343] In turn, if the tribunal (not authorized by the parties and using default mechanisms only) does not rely on the conflict of laws methodology when reaching its conclusion on applicable law, this decision may also be susceptible to attacks on the excess of powers ground. Yet another layer is added when the tribunal considers that English conflict of laws rules apply. This has already been discussed above.[344] In a nutshell, and at least in theory, these decisions can be exposed to the appeal on a point of law (if available). In any event the mere (simple) error in the choice of law analysis may not be sufficient ground to succeed in annulment proceedings,[345] even if appeal on a point of law is attainable.

7.2.2 Decision on applicable law

At the initial stage of the proceedings, as a result of the analysis described in the previous section or by following the parties' choice, the tribunal will need to decide what law applies to the merits of the case. Its conclusions on applicable law will affect the outcome of the dispute. For this reason, the process of choosing the applicable law is the subject of ongoing scrutiny by practitioners and academics.[346] The outstanding question herein, however, is whether the tribunal's decision on applicable law can be made in excess of its authority and be challenged as such.

By and large, one should reflect if the possibility for recourse exists when (i) parties included a choice of law clause in their contract and when (ii) they did not include such choice.[347] Arguably, a challenge is only available under the first hypothesis, where the parties

343 Since, however, the tribunal can apply *any* conflict of laws rules it considers appropriate, the results of its analysis will be effectively the same as if it chooses the direct approach method. For the discussion on a direct approach, see also Chapter III.

344 See section 6.2.1.

345 It has been argued by Craig in Craig, *The arbitrator's mission and the application of law in international commercial arbitration* (2010) p.261, albeit as a notion attributable to international arbitration in general, that "*[i]f the practice of international arbitration shows broad flexibility, if not laxity in the choice-of-law process, this must be attributed in some part to the fact that a mere error by the arbitrator in the choice of law is not subject to judicial review under most modern arbitration laws in effect at the most frequently chosen neutral venues for international arbitration.*" This conclusion would be also valid for the English arbitration regime. Even if a Section 69 appeal is available, the standards that need to be satisfied are high.

346 For further reading, see, *i.a.*, ILA, *ILA Report on Ascertaining the Contents of the Applicable Law in International Commercial Arbitration* (2008).

347 There are several variations of these main scenarios (for example, express choice of applicable conflict of laws rules or different choice of law clauses in the main contract and the arbitration agreement, on the one hand, or the parties' choice of law is implied or pleaded before the tribunal, on the other hand). Effectively, however, for the purpose of the research at hand mainly these two hypotheticals are of relevance.

incorporated a choice of law provision in their contract, but the tribunal did not respect the parties' clear direction and decided on its own concept of what law is applicable. Similarly, under the second hypothesis, where no choice of law clause exists, parties may still agree on applicable law at the outset of the proceedings. The tribunal's decision's ignoring the parties' directive in this instance may be open to recourse. As already illustrated above,[348] in these cases the tribunal takes over a power (*i.e.* to determine the applicable law) that the parties did not intend to give away. For this reason, the excess of power challenge might be available.[349]

In circumstances where parties failed to address the issue of applicable law in their contract, the arbitral panel may rely on the default mechanism of Section 46(3) of the Act. It reads that "*[i]f or to the extent that there is no such choice or agreement, the tribunal shall apply the law determined by the conflict of laws rules which it considers applicable.*" Consequently, it means that arbitrators may rely on this provision when deciding what law applies.[350] This has been discussed in the preceding section.[351]

It is necessary to add that the tribunal's discretion under Section 46(3) of the Act is limited to the application of *law* and not rules of law (*e.g. lex mercatoria*), which means that the application of rules of law *ex officio* might also trigger the "excess of powers" challenge.[352]

7.2.3 Ascertaining the content of the applicable law by the arbitral tribunal

One of the implications of the fact that arbitration is a creature of contract is that "*in a dispute that is to be decided in accordance with law, arbitrators should identify, ascertain the contents of and apply the applicable law.*"[353] This statement entails that it is not always necessary for the tribunal to ascertain the contents of the applicable law. If, however, the dispute brought before the tribunal is of a legal nature, the tribunal should undertake the task of determining the contents of the law.[354] For the purpose of the research at hand, it

348 See section 6.1.1 of this chapter.

349 Of course, if the parties do not agree as to the validity or the scope of the choice of law clause and submit different pleadings on the issue, the tribunal would be fully vested with the power to decide on the applicable law.

350 Still, the best approach is for the tribunal to invite the parties to submit their arguments on conflict of laws rules or on applicable law. If the parties' submissions point out the same law to be applied, it should be conclusive for the tribunal. If the parties' arguments on applicable law differ, they would still be of value for the tribunal. It does not change the fact that the tribunal should not surprise the parties with its choice of law analysis, without allowing them the opportunity to advance their views.

351 See section 6.2.1.

352 Section 68(2)(b) of the Act. See also Section 68(2)(a) of the Act (the tribunal's failure to comply with its general duties).

353 ILA, *ILA Report on Ascertaining the Contents of the Applicable Law in International Commercial Arbitration* (2008) p.19.

354 This is not to unequivocally qualify the tribunal's task as a "duty". See, however, in the context of international commercial arbitration in general, ILA, *ILA Report on Ascertaining the Contents of the Applicable Law in*

is only relevant to question if the tribunal's exercise of applying the law can be challenged before the English courts.[355]

The method selected for the analysis requires testing the tribunal's action against the mechanisms prescribed in Sections 67-69 of the Act. As pointed out in the introduction to this section,[356] it is unlikely that the mere process of ascertaining the content of the law would affect the scope of the tribunal's jurisdiction.[357] Consequently, arguably, the Sections 68 and 69 mechanisms remain viable. Naturally, the "obvious" choice to challenge the tribunal's legal conclusions is appeal on a point of law.[358] Even so, the scope of this remedy is very limited since it allows for recourse only on a point of English law and only when additional requirements are fulfilled.[359] Therefore a tribunal's analysis of the content of non-English law will fall beyond the scope of application of Section 69 of the Act. It leaves the question whether ascertaining the content of law may be qualified as a serious irregularity amounting to substantive injustice (*i.e.* the Section 68 challenge).

Yet, before going further, it is necessary to take a look at Section 34 of the Act which gives to the tribunal a discretion "*to decide all procedural and evidential matters, subject to the right of the parties to agree any matter*".[360] These matters, among other things, include "*whether and to what extent the tribunal should itself take the initiative in ascertaining the facts and the law*".[361] "*This provision enables tribunals to act in an inquisitorial manner. Once again, it removes the possibility of debate as to whether arbitrators could so act.*"[362] It consequently means that, the tribunal may actively participate in the process of identifying the content of the applicable law.[363] In turn, "*the arbitrator – in conducting his/her independent legal research – can reach – a new qualification of the facts of the case in his/her*

International Commercial Arbitration (2008) p.19 ("*This [identifying and ascertaining the contents of the applicable law] is one of an arbitral tribunal's duties in fulfilling its mandate [...].*").

355 The starting assumption here is that the applicable law is fully identified (either by the choice of law clause or the tribunal's determination). Therefore, what matters is the approach that the tribunal chooses when addressing the *content* of the applicable law.

356 See section 6.2.

357 One may argue that actions resulting from ascertaining the content of the applicable law on its own motion may influence the scope of the tribunal's jurisdiction if the tribunal, for example, after consulting the applicable law, finds on its own motion that a party is entitled to interest (which it did not request) and consequently grants it. Such a relief sought, however, is a result of (at least) two decisions undertaken: (i) determining that interests are available and (ii) granting them. The aim here is to treat these decisions separately. For this reason, it is concluded that the mere process of establishing what the law contains, in itself, will not affect the tribunal's jurisdiction. See also *B v. A* [2010] 2 Lloyd's Rep. 681. For decisions on interest, see section 6.4.1.

358 For further reading, see section 6.

359 See section 6.2.

360 Section 34(1) of the Act.

361 Section 34(2)(g) of the Act.

362 (Harris, Planterose, & Tecks, The Arbitration Act 1996, 2007) p.175. Also Giovanni (2010) pp.499-500.

363 Arguably, the tribunal's interpretation of Section 34(2)(g) of the Act can be subjected to appeal on point of law analysis (if available).

conclusion that has not been argued by the parties."[364] At the same time, however, "*a tribunal must be mindful of its s.33 duties, particularly, for example, by giving all the parties an opportunity of commenting on any evidence it obtains or any law it thinks applies.*"[365]

In principle, and following the preceding paragraph, one may conclude that the process of ascertaining the content of the applicable law will escape the judicial scrutiny of Section 68 of the Act. There are, however, several instances (rare and largely dependent on the factual underpinning) that might constitute an exception to the rule. The first irregularity that needs to be acknowledged is surprising the parties with the tribunal's legal conclusions.[366] When the tribunal applies a rule or a principle which has not been invoked by any of the parties, at the same time barring their opportunity to express their position on the tribunal's findings,[367] the tribunal will effectively risk violating the duty of fairness as a result of which the decision can be challenged under Section 68(2)(a) of the Act.[368] Additionally, Section 34 of the Act leaves no doubt that parties may deviate from the basic rule prescribed therein.[369] Therefore, arguably, if they explicitly define way to establish the content of the applicable law, the tribunal should follow parties' guidelines.[370] It holds true also to the parties' choice of law.[371] Failing to do so, the tribunal's decision may face the challenge on the basis of the excess of powers[372] or failure to conduct the proceedings in accordance

364 Giovanni (2010) p.502. See also section 6.1.4.

365 (Harris, Planterose, & Tecks, The Arbitration Act 1996, 2007) p.175.

366 See also section 5.2.1 and section 6.1.4 (regarding requalification of the claim).

367 See, however, Dimolitsa, *The Raising Ex Officio of New Issues of Law* (2014) p.27 ("*The English courts do also require that the parties be provided the opportunity to address all issues that may be relevant to the resolution of a dispute on application of the principle of fairness [...]. The English courts are however less severe in their requirement to respect the parties' right to be heard, since they examine in addition, on application of Section 68 of the Arbitration Act 1996, whether such 'irregularity' caused 'substantial injustice' to the applicant; this unavoidably entails though an extensive examination of the award on the merits.*" See also the reference to *F Ltd v. M Ltd* [2009] EWHC 275 (TCC). For a rare example of a successful Section 68 challenge, see also *K v A* [2019] EWHC 1118 (Comm) where the case was remitted to the tribunal.

368 See also fn.365.

369 Pursuant to Art. 34(1) of the Act, "*[i]t shall be for the tribunal to decide all procedural and evidential matters, subject to the right of the parties to agree any matter.*" One should note that, generally, institutional rules reinforce the tribunal's ability to ascertain the law. See, *e.g.*, Art. 22.1(iii) of the 2014 LCIA Rules, Art. 22.1(iii) of the 2020 LCIA Rules. The 2014 LCIA Rules are also explicit (Art. 22.1 of the 2014 LCIA Rules) that the parties need to have a reasonable opportunity to state their views for the tribunal to exercise its power of ascertaining the content of law. See also Art. 22.3 of the 2014 LCIA Rules, Art. 22.3 of the 2020 LCIA Rules.

370 According to authorities, however, it rarely happens. See ILA, *ILA Report on Ascertaining the Contents of the Applicable Law in International Commercial Arbitration* (2008) p.16 ("*Parties are unlikely to include in their contract any express provision on how arbitrators are to determine the contents of applicable law.*").

371 See section 6.2.2.

372 Section 68(2)(b) of the Act. If parties specifically introduced the framework as to how the tribunal should address the law, going beyond it might be considered as using the power it never possessed.

with the parties' agreement.[373] Finally, committing an error of law does not qualify as excess of powers.[374]

To conclude, in words of the ILA Committee on International Commercial Arbitration:

> [...] save in the exceptional cases where the parties have dealt with the matter, the arbitrators will need to decide how to approach the contents of law question, without any general rules to guide them. The freedom of the arbitrators in this respect will be largely unfettered. The issue is by and large procedural and thus governed by broad discretionary powers of arbitral tribunals. Orders and awards of tribunals will not be subject to judicial review in setting aside and enforcement proceedings, save for violation of impartiality, due process, excess of mandate and public policy [...].[375]

7.2.4 Application of mandatory rules of law by the arbitral tribunal

By and large, the compliance with mandatory rules of law might be crucial for the survival of an arbitral award at the post-award stage, because these rules are designed to act as a safety net of the legal system. Accordingly, parties may not derogate from them and may not modify their scope. At the same time, courts will try to make sure that these rules are recognized. Therefore, the tribunal's willingness to abide by mandatory rules should not be surprising.[376] Nonetheless, in some instances parties may be willing to seek recourse against the tribunal's decision reflecting on mandatory rules.

At the outset, however, it is necessary to highlight two nuances that accompany the process of the application of mandatory rules of law by the tribunal. Although they fall outside the scope of the research at hand, they should at least be identified, since they may be relevant for the scenarios discussed. It is sometimes recognized that two types of mandatory rules exist,[377] *i.e.* "simple" mandatory rules[378] and "overriding" mandatory

---

373 Section 68(2)(c) of the Act. Taking into account that the underlying theme of Section 34 of the Act is a procedure, an agreement on the tribunal's approach to law might be also considered as an agreed conduct of the proceedings.

374 See *Lesotho Highlands Development Authority v. Impregilo SpA & Ors* [2005] UKHL 43 at [32].

375 ILA, *ILA Report on Ascertaining the Contents of the Applicable Law in International Commercial Arbitration* (2008) p.16.

376 Sometimes it is argued that the tribunal has a duty to render an enforceable award. Not all agree. Even if, however, such a "duty" does not exist in a legal sense, it is sensible for the arbitral panels to respect the systemic safeguards introduced as mandatory rules. See, *e.g.*, Mayer, *Reflections on the International Arbitrator's Duty to Apply the Law – The Freshfields Lecture 2000* (2001) p.247.

377 A similar distinction has been recognized by ILA, *ILA Report on Ascertaining the Contents of the Applicable Law in International Commercial Arbitration* (2008) p.21.

378 Radicati di Brozolo (2012) p.50. "Simple" mandatory rules have been characterized as "*rules that in each legal system cannot be derogated from by agreement if the relationship is governed by that law.*" The author additionally concludes that "*in arbitration these rules lose their mandatory character because the parties are permitted to contract out of them by an appropriate choice of a different state law to govern the merits of the*

rules.[379] Consequently, only the latter will have a public policy character.[380] Having this in mind, it is now time to turn to the outstanding question, namely whether the tribunal's decision reflecting on mandatory rules is challengeable in setting-aside proceedings.

The scenarios where parties might (be tempted to) initiate actions for annulment are the following: (i) the parties intended (in their agreement to arbitrate or at the outset of the proceedings) to opt out from the application of a certain mandatory law and the tribunal ignored their choice,[381] (ii) parties did not submit arguments regarding (applicable) mandatory rules, but the tribunal reflected these (mandatory) rules in its award regardless, and finally (iii) parties seek recourse against the allegedly "wrong" application of mandatory laws. Similarly to previous sections, prospective annulment actions may be based either on Section 68 or Section 69 of the Act.[382] It does not change the fact, however, that the chances of success are rather low.

The first two scenarios mentioned above are fairly similar.[383] On the one hand, the tribunal should respect the parties' choice of law or legal rules applicable to the dispute and constraints of their legal pleadings, on the other hand, it is increasingly relevant for the tribunals to render enforceable awards[384] and to serve justice instead of only providing the service of resolving problems with contractual interpretation. In other words:

---

dispute or even by choosing non-national rules." This argument is only partly true, because contracting out of one set of mandatory rules would easily lead to falling within the scope of "simple" mandatory rules of a system of law or legal rules selected by the parties. In other words, "choice of a different state law" would effectively mean that a different set of mandatory norms would likely influence the arbitral dispute. Of course the author qualifies that parties are able to make an "appropriate choice", it does not change the fact that, although it is possible to contract around specific "simple" mandatory rules assigned to the particular national system, the parties will not be able to contract out of "simple" mandatory rules at large. Put differently, the only thing parties are (arguably) able to do is to choose which set of "simple" mandatory rules would apply to their contractual relationship and not rule them out completely (possibly save for non-national legal rules which may be short in mandatory components). Therefore, even "simple" mandatory rules may still be relevant in international arbitration.

379 Radicati di Brozolo (2012) p.50. These rules are explained as safeguards to public interests. For this reason, they will apply to the dispute, even if the law applicable to the contract is different. As such they will have an "overriding" effect.

380 See fn.379.

381 It may take, at least theoretically, different forms: (i) parties select a specific legal regime, but exclude the application of a certain mandatory rule, (ii) parties in order to circumvent application of mandatory rules of system A select system B, or (iii) parties define the way the law has to be applied. Under this scenario mostly the second form is analyzed. The first form would be ineffective, because the parties cannot contractually opt out of the mandatory rules of applicable law and the third form touches upon *ex officio* application of the mandatory rules of law, which is reflected upon under a different scenario explained under this section.

382 Section 67 of the Act would not be relevant if the mere process of application of law is being challenged. See above, *i.a.* fn.357.

383 It is so, because they are the consequence of the tribunal's balancing exercise.

384 See, for example, Art. 41 of the 2012 ICC Rules or Art. 32.2 of the 2014 LCIA Rules, Art. 32.2 of the 2020 LCIA Rules.

> arbitrators will have to bear in mind something akin to a professional duty not to become accomplices of a violation or circumvention of the law. While it is true that arbitrators are primarily at the service of the parties, it is now recognized that they are not their mere servants and that in some way they are also under a broader duty to see that justice is done.[385]

Consequently, it would be sensible for the tribunal to investigate whether mandatory rules are of relevance for the dispute at hand.

In principle, the first two scenarios focus on the concept of the tribunal taking the initiative to apply the mandatory rules of law rather than the process of the actual application of legal rules.[386] In turn, it is argued that the tribunal's account of mandatory rules will not trigger Section 69 of the Act (appeal on point of law). There is limited room, however, to challenge the tribunal's undertaking under Section 68 of the Act (serious irregularity).

For example, if the parties choose to contractually opt out from a certain legal regime, but the tribunal brings into equation the (mandatory) legal rules of this system, it might be possible to invoke the excess of powers ground for the non-compliance with Section 46(1)(a) of the Act.[387] Arguably, the challenge might have some prospects of success, because taking the initiative of ascertaining the law is a matter of procedure[388] and ascertaining the content of the law not chosen by the parties (thus non-applicable) goes beyond what parties contracted for. Such an argument might eventually survive, however, only if the tribunal bases its decision on "simple" mandatory rules that had been ruled out by the parties in their choice of law clause.[389] The strength and appeal of the argument decreases dramatically, in cases where the tribunal ignores the initial choice of law, because it finds that mandatory rules of *public policy character* may be in play.[390] It brings back the notion of the tribunal's determination to render an enforceable award. Other considerations regarding the possibility to challenge the tribunal's decision based on the breach of duty of fairness and the like would not deviate much from what has already been established in previous sections. Therefore, a cross-reference should suffice.[391]

---

385 Radicati di Brozolo (2012) p.68, see also Mayer, *Reflections on the International Arbitrator's Duty to Apply the Law – The Freshfields Lecture 2000* (2001) p.247.

386 On this topic see also section 6.2.3.

387 Namely, the provision pursuant to which the tribunal shall decide the dispute in accordance with the law chosen by the parties.

388 Section 34(2)(g) of the Act. For further reading, see section 6.2.3.

389 See also the elaborate analysis provided in fn.378.

390 Obviously, the award does not have to conform to all public policy rules in the world. It has already been acknowledged, that determining with which public policy rules to comply is not an easy task. Further analysis, however, falls outside the scope of this research.

391 For further reading, see sections 6.2.1-6.2.3.

If parties fail to address the otherwise applicable mandatory rule in their submissions, it means that the tribunal may rely on the default mechanism of Section 34(2)(g) of the Act.[392] Consequently, the tribunal's decision ascertaining the applicability of mandatory rules, taken on its own initiative, may be challenged similarly to other legal rules ascertained. It has already has been the subject of the analysis in section 6.2.3. In a nutshell, it would be generally possible to challenge the award if the tribunal surprises parties with its conclusions.

Finally, under the third illustration it is necessary to address to what extent allegedly "wrong" decisions on mandatory law are reviewable. It has been mentioned in the previous section[393] that incorrect decisions on facts or law are not reviewable under the excess of powers challenge.[394] They would be a classic examples of the Section 69 application with arguably moderate (thus "higher" than other instances discussed herein) chances of success, since determining the flaw in the tribunal's interpretation of mandatory laws might be considered as a question of general public importance.[395] Such recourse is, of course, only available in cases where English law is applicable and all other conditions of Section 69 of the Act are fulfilled. Therefore, errors in the application of mandatory rules that underlie legal regimes other than English law will not suffice to use the Section 69 appeal.

In the end the tribunal is better off with applying relevant public policy rules, since it is unlikely that its decision would annulled because of its willingness to comply with the underlying principles of public policy status. As aptly put: "*[a]rbitrators must respond not only to the legitimate expectation of the parties, but also to that of the states which allow them the power to decide even disputes in which the general interest is at stake.*"[396]

7.2.5 Decision based on equity or reached *ex aequo et bono*

It is remarkable when parties decide to entrust the tribunal to rule on the parties' dispute by applying principles of equity. Because of the far-reaching consequences of such a power,[397] the drafters of the Model Law[398] as well as many national legislators often

392 Pursuant to Art. 34(2)(g) of the Act the tribunal shall decide procedural matters (unless parties agree otherwise), including "*whether and to what extent the tribunal should itself take the initiative in ascertaining the facts and the law*".

393 See section 5.2.2.

394 See, *e.g.*, *Lesotho Highlands Development Authority v. Impregilo SpA & Ors* [2005] UKHL 43 at [31].

395 Section 69(3)(c)(ii) of the Act.

396 Poudret & Besson (2007) p.610.

397 This in fact led some scholars to conclude "a note of caution" regarding "*consequences of an agreement other than one which requires the tribunal to decide in accordance with law*". See Harris et al., *The Arbitration Act 1996* (2014) p.245.

398 Pursuant to Art. 28(3) of the Model Law, "*[t]he arbitral tribunal shall decide ex aequo et bono or as amiable compositeur only if the parties have expressly authorized it to do so.*" See also Chapter II.

address it explicitly in their respective legal acts.[399] It has been argued with regard to English law that

> [t]he 1996 Act brought English law into line with the approach in many other jurisdictions by permitting the parties to choose to have their dispute resolved by considerations other than the rules of a particular national law. It is now clear that if the parties choose to have the tribunal decide the dispute "ex aequo et bono" or as an "amiable compositeur" or on the basis of non-national law principles or indeed on the basis of any other considerations, that choice will be binding so long as it is ascertainable.[400]

The concept allowing the parties to opt for their disputes to be resolved based on principles of equity has been introduced in Section 46(1)(b) of the Act which reads that the arbitral tribunal shall decide the dispute *if the parties so agree, "in accordance with such other considerations as are agreed by them or determined by the tribunal"*.[401] This provision, despite being inspired by the Model Law, considerably differs from it.[402]

The DAC in its report explains that:

> subsection (1)(b) recognises that parties may agree that their dispute is not to be decided in accordance with a recognised system of law but under what in this country are often called 'equity clauses', or arbitration 'ex aequo et bono', or 'amiable composition', i.e. general considerations of justice and fairness, etc. It will be noted that we have avoided using this description in the Bill just as we have avoided using the Latin and French expressions found in the Model Law. There appears to be no good reason to prevent parties from agreeing to equity clauses.[403]

Arguably, a challenge to the tribunal's decision based on equity might be available if (i) the tribunal renders an equitable decision without explicit authorization or (ii) by usurping

---

399 Also institutional rules require express authorization. See, *e.g.*, Art. 22.4 of the 2014 LCIA Rules, Art. 22.4 of the 2020 LCIA Rules (including a written requirement for the authorization), Art. 21(3) of the 2012 ICC Rules, Art. 21(3) of the 2017 ICC Rules, Art. 21(3) of the (draft) 2021 ICC Rules. Art. 22.4 of the 2020 LCIA Rules

400 Sutton et al. (2007) para 2-091; see also para 4-142 therein.

401 The scope of application of this provision, in principle, does not refer only to *ex aequo et bono* or *amiable compositeur* but also entails application to *lex mercatoria* or religious laws. For the research at hand, mostly decisions based on equity would be of relevance. See also Harris et al., *The Arbitration Act 1996* (2014) p.245, Merkin & Flannery, *Arbitration Act 1996* (2014) pp.205-207.

402 See Art. 28(3) of the ML. Also Chapter II.

403 DAC, *Report on the Arbitration Bill* (1996) para 223.

the role of *amiable compositeur* while relying on the fallback mechanism in the absence of an express choice of law.[404] Additionally, it is argued that only Section 68 of the Act, and the excess of powers ground in particular, would be relevant for parties seeking recourse.[405]

Deciding *ex aequo et bono* without the parties' authorization is a classic example of the excess of powers, because it implies that the tribunal makes use of a power it was never conferred.[406] It should not require further explanation. The second example provided above is a slight variation of the decision without the parties' authorization. In this case, the tribunal may try to shield its decision on equity based on the default mechanism that allows it to decide on the applicable law in the absence of the parties' choice.[407] This argument, however, would be insufficient because Section 46(3) of the Act indeed entitles the tribunal to act if parties did not decide on the applicable law, but, at the same time, it limits the tribunal's choice to *the law determined by the conflict of laws rules which [the tribunal] considers applicable.* Consequently, the tribunal cannot take the initiative and decide on general considerations of justice and fairness. For it will again constitute an excess of powers.

7.3 Decisions on remedies

Parties, while bringing their cases before the arbitral tribunal, will inevitably seek a relief. Consequently, the tribunal will have to decide whether the parties' requests are appropriate. In principle, the tribunal's decision would either concern claims for damages (section 7.3.1), specific performance (section 7.3.2), contract adaptation and filling the gaps (section 7.3.3).

At the outset it is necessary to highlight that the structure of the Arbitration Act provides many fallback mechanisms, including the tribunal's default powers regarding remedies. Consequently, pursuant to Section 48 of the Act, unless otherwise agreed by the parties the tribunal may: (i) *make a declaration as to any matter to be determined in the*

---

404 For the purpose of this section, the differences between the concepts of equitable findings, deciding *ex aequo et bono* or acting as *amiable compositeur* will be assumed to have the same meaning. For this reason the terms will be used interchangeably.

405 Deciding on equity does not raise any doubts on jurisdiction. Accordingly, since no legal rule would be applied by the tribunal there can be no appeal on point of law as prescribed by Section 69 of the Law. The DAC in its report (DAC, *Report on the Arbitration Bill* (1996) para 223) unequivocally concludes that "*[...] it is to be noted that in agreeing that a dispute shall be resolved in this way, the parties are in effect excluding any right to appeal to the Court (there being no "question of law" to appeal).*" Similarly Harris et al., *The Arbitration Act 1996* (2014) p.245 ("*Since such an approach applies no system of law, it follows that no question of law would arise for decision, [...] or appeal, (s.69).*").

406 See also section 5.2.2.

407 Assuming, at the same time, that the tribunal is not granted with the authority to decide on equity.

proceedings,[408] (ii) *order the payment of a sum of money, in any currency,*[409] (iii) *order a party to do or refrain from doing anything,*[410] (iv) *order specific performance of a contract (other than a contract relating to land),*[411] or (v) *order rectification, setting aside of cancellation of a deed or other document.*[412] Although this catalogue is not exclusive,[413] it gives a clear indication of what are the basic remedial tools at the tribunal's disposal (unless parties agree otherwise).

7.3.1 Decision on damages

Arguably, damages are by far the most common relief sought. Therefore, one could reasonably expect that the tribunal should be able to grant damages and its power to award damages should not be subject to challenge as such. Instances related to damages which require further analysis are the following: (i) parties in their agreement excluded damages (or particular type of damages) from the list of remedial powers available to the arbitral tribunal which, nonetheless, did not stop the tribunal from granting them upon request, (ii) parties in their agreement allowed the tribunal to grant the type of damages that would be otherwise unavailable under the applicable law (for example, punitive damages), (iii) the tribunal granted damages higher than sought, or (iv) the tribunal granted a remedy different than sought.

It is clear that if parties designed their agreement to arbitrate narrowly, the tribunal should respect it.[414] Two variations could be put forward: (i) parties submit a request for damages, ignoring their initial agreement to arbitrate or (ii) the tribunal awards damages without seeking the parties' submissions. In the case of the latter situation the tribunal will commit a flagrant violation of the parties' trust and its conclusions would be open for challenge of the substantive jurisdiction under Section 67 of the Act.[415] The former, however, is more fact specific.

When the parties' submissions go beyond the matrix of the initial agreement to arbitrate it is possible to argue, on the one hand, that the parties' intention is to extend the scope of the original agreement and consequently the original jurisdiction of the arbitral tribunal

408 Section 48(3) of the Act.

409 Section 48(4) of the Act.

410 Section 48(5)(a) of the Act.

411 Section 48(5)(b) of the Act.

412 Section 48(5)(c) of the Act.

413 Merkin & Flannery, *Arbitration Act 1996* (2014) p.214.

414 If the agreement is silent on the possibility to award damages (or in the words used in Section 48(2) of the Act "*unless otherwise agreed by the parties*"), the tribunal should be able to grant damages if requested. In similar vein, Harris in Harris et al., *The Arbitration Act 1996* (2014) p.250 argues that: "*The Section [48 of the Act] also sets out the powers which the tribunal is to have if the parties do not agree otherwise. They correspond to certain of the more familiar powers of the courts. An agreement 'otherwise' may be in respect of some or all of the powers.*"

415 For further reading, see also section 3.

to award damages. On the other hand, one should reflect whether parties had a sufficient (and equal) opportunity to address the claim for damages (submitted by one of them). If they had an opportunity to rebut the claim, but failed to raise an objection, the tribunal may assume that such a conduct led to an implied consent or waiver.[416] Consequently, the tribunal's decision on damages that answers the relief sought (which, however, is beyond the scope of the initial agreement to arbitrate) may be then tested against the excess of powers ground.[417] In any event, the chances for success are rather scant. Additionally, one may imagine that the annulment ground of Section 68(2)(a) of the Act (referring to the general duties of the tribunal)[418] might be available if the tribunal does not give the parties the opportunity to address the claim for damages. It is argued that granting damages (even against the scope of the initial agreement to arbitrate) will be insufficient to appeal on a point of law.[419]

Another issue relates to the question whether parties are able to alter the scope of the arbitral tribunal's powers to the extent that the tribunal can exercise them differently than the court in court proceedings or even allow it to grant remedies known in other jurisdictions, for example, punitive damages.[420] Since the initial line of Section 48(1) of the Act reads "*the parties are free to agree on the powers exercisable by the arbitral tribunal as regards remedies*", it is reasonable to conclude that the parties' liberty to choose available remedies is unconstrained.[421] Consequently, it seems possible that, with the parties' express authorization, the tribunal's decision on punitive damages should survive the challenge.

Similarly, it has been concluded that:

416 Or, in the alternative, it may work as a waiver. If, however, a party objected (to the tribunal's power to grant damages) but was unsuccessful, it will still be able to raise this objection at the post-award stage.

417 Section 68(2)(b) of the Act. For further reading, see section 5.2.2. Arguably, the power to grant damages is included in the catalogue of remedial powers of the tribunal (which parties can freely shape, see Section 48(1) of the Act). For this reason, it will not constitute a jurisdictional issue, but it will fit the scope of the "excess of powers" ground precisely (which is designed to deal with the tribunal's undertakings that go beyond the parties' consent, but are not related to the tribunal's jurisdiction, see Section 68(2)(b) of the Act). If this argument is rejected, however, it may very well be that the challenge should be brought against the tribunal's jurisdiction (Section 67 of the Act) because it relates to the scope of the agreement to arbitrate.

418 See Section 33(1)(a) of the Act in particular.

419 It is necessary to recognize that appeal might be unavailable in cases where a party brings a challenge based on the argument that the tribunal decided on damages. By no means should it be understood that the award on damages may not be, when all conditions are met, brought under Section 69 of the Act. On a similar note see fn.254.

420 See DAC, *Report on the Arbitration Bill* (1996) para 234 ("*Given that the parties are free to agree on the remedies that a tribunal may order, there is nothing to restrict such remedies to those available at Court.*"); Harris et al., *The Arbitration Act 1996* (2014) p.249. See also Rowan (2010).

421 Harris et al., *The Arbitration Act 1996* (2014) p.249 ("*[Section 48 of the Act] essentially provides that the parties are at liberty to agree what powers the tribunal should exercise.*").

> [i]n the light of s.48 of the Arbitration Act 1996 it seems likely that [the court] would [enforce the award] if the parties had expressly agreed to give the tribunal power to award exemplary damages or had chosen an applicable substantive law that permits the award of exemplary damages in the circumstances of the particular case. The court would, however, look very closely at the agreement and would seek to construe it narrowly.[422]

Conversely, the tribunal's decision without the parties' express authorization, will likely be subject to a (successful) recourse. Indeed,

> [i]f a tribunal purported to award exemplary damages in the absence of express agreement between the parties that it should do so, and in circumstances where under English law there is no entitlement to them, the award would be vulnerable to challenge for both serious irregularity under s.68 and for error of law pursuant to s.69 of the Arbitration Act 1996.[423]

The appropriate ground of Section 68 of the Act in this instance would be excess of the tribunal's powers.[424]

Finally, one should observe that recourse against an *ultra* or *extra petita* decision should be available at all times. If the amount of damages granted is higher or a remedy different than was actually requested by the parties, the tribunal exceeds its powers prescribed by the agreement to arbitrate, thus the vehicle of Section 68(2)(b) would be an option.[425]

7.3.2 Decision on specific performance

As aptly summarized by Harris and others, "*[s]pecific performance is a discretionary remedy by which a party in breach of contract is ordered to complete its performance.*"[426] It serves as particularly useful in cases where monetary compensation would not be an adequate remedy. For the purpose of the study at hand, however, the decision on specific performance would not differ much from the decision on damages.[427] Therefore, in principle, the decision

---

422 Sutton et al. (2007) para 6-106.

423 Sutton et al. (2007) para 6-106.

424 Section 68(2)(b) of the Act.

425 Sometimes it might also be argued that granting relief above the reference made (higher than requested) is susceptible to challenge under Section 67 of the Act, because it goes beyond the matters that have been submitted to arbitration. See, *e.g.*, granting interest before the date claimed as in *Westland Helicopters Ltd v. Sheikh Salah Al-Hejailan* [2004] EWHC 1625 (Comm) at [56]. See, however, the comments and arguments in section 5.2.2 and section 6.1.1.

426 Harris et al., *The Arbitration Act 1996* (2014) p.251. For a brief take on specific performance, see also Blackaby et al. (2015) p.519.

427 See section 6.3.1.

on specific performance would be mainly challengeable under the excess of powers ground if (i) it is explicitly excluded from the scope of the agreement to arbitrate or (ii) while relying on the default mechanism of Section 48(5)(b)[428] it concerned a contract relating to land or (iii) it is rendered *ultra petita*. The reflections provided in the section above would be equally applicable here (in the particular scenarios (i) and (iii)). Therefore, a few points directed specifically to the second scenario (ii) will be raised below.

It is important to note that if parties wish to limit the tribunal's powers to grant specific performance, they should make their intentions clear. Otherwise Section 48(5)(b) of the Act will apply. In turn, the tribunal will be entitled *to order specific performance of a contract (other than a contract relating to land)*. As explained by the DAC, "*[w]e have excluded specific performance of land contracts, so as not to change the law in this regard.*"[429] Without going further into details, it is sufficient to add that a *contract relating to land* is *one which creates or transfers an interest in land.*[430] "*[W]hen considering whether the claim fell within the land exclusion, the proper approach is to characterise not the whole contract, but the obligation of which specific performance is sought.*"[431]

Some authors, however, raise the argument that "*[g]iven the availability of quick registration and enforcement in the High Court of English arbitral awards under section 66, we are not certain that the exclusion of contracts 'relating to land' has any justification any more.*"[432] Additionally, the inclusion of the LCIA 2014 Rules would effectively expand the tribunals' powers over contracts relating to land, since according to Article 22.1(vii) of the 2014 LCIA Rules the tribunal shall have the power to *order compliance with any legal obligation, payment of compensation for breach of any legal obligation and specific*

428 Section 48(5)(b) of the Act reads that "*[t]he tribunal has the same powers as the court [...] to order specific performance of a contract (other than a contract relating to land) [...]*".

429 DAC, *Report on the Arbitration Bill* (1996) para 234.

430 See *Telia Sonera Ab v. Hilcourt (Docklands) Limited* [2003] EWHC 3540 (Ch) at [29-31]; see also Sutton et al. (2007) para 6-108 ("*Power to order specific performance. Section 48(5)(b) of the Arbitration Act 1996 provides that the tribunal has the same power as the court to order specific performance of a contract other than a contract relating to land. A contract relating to land is one which creates or transfers an interest in land. In the event of a failure to comply with the tribunal's award, the coercive powers of the court may be available once steps have been taken to enforce the award.*"), Harris et al., *The Arbitration Act 1996* (2014) pp.251-252 ("*The position prior to this Act, that specific performance was not available in respect of a contract relating to land, is preserved, (see the Arbitration Act 1950, s.15). However, it has been held that the expression 'contract relating to land' in subs.48(5)(b) is confined to contracts for the creation or transfer of an interest in land; and the proper approach is to characterize not the whole contract but the obligation of which specific performance is sought, which effectively means reading the words 'if and so far as it relates to land' in the parenthesis in the subsection [...].*").

431 Merkin & Flannery, *Arbitration Act 1996* (2014) p.217.

432 Merkin & Flannery, *Arbitration Act 1996* (2014) p.217.

performance of any agreement (including any arbitration agreement or any contract relating to land) [...]."[433]

All in all, the challenge against the decision on specific performance may be available in the three instances mentioned above. In principle, a tribunal's decision may be tested on the ground of excess of powers. It is difficult to imagine how it would affect the tribunal's substantive jurisdiction or how it would be appealable on point of law.

7.3.3 Decision on contract adaptation and filling of gaps in the contract

The tribunal's power to fill the gap in the contract might not be self-evident. Essentially, the problem arises when the gap-filling exercise is perceived as the tribunal's "creative" competence instead as a variation on its (contract) interpretative tool. Although the analysis herein should be confined to testing the alleged transgression of the tribunal's powers, a few preliminary and, perhaps self-evident, remarks on the sources of the contract adaptation powers should be introduced.

It has been concluded by Berger that

> in order to determine the power of an international arbitrator to adapt or supplement a contract in an individual case, one has to refer simultan[e]ously to three different legal sources: the arbitration agreement, the law applicable to the arbitration (*lex arbitri*) and the law applicable to the substance of the dispute (*lex causae*).[434]

For the purpose of the research at hand, the two first sources, albeit in reverse order, are taken into account.[435]

433 See also Gerbay et al. (2015) pp.249 ("*Article 22.1(vii) enumerates the contractual remedies an arbitrator may order. In the 1998 version of the LCIA Rules, this subsection provided solely for the remediation of a contract to the extent there was mutual mistake. Under the 2014 Rules, the Tribunal is specifically empowered to order specific performance and compensation for breach.*"). See also Art. 22.1(ix) of the 2020 LCIA Rules.

434 Berger, *Power of Arbitrators to Fill Gaps and Revise Contracts to Make Sense* (2001) pp.7-8; others disagree, suggesting that the law applicable to the substance is only relevant for the content and limits to the gap-filling power rather than its existence, see Frick (2001) p.194 ("*In our opinion, whether or not the conditions for an adaptation are met depends on the applicable substantive law. Whether or not the power of the arbitrator in this respect is curtailed, is a separate, procedural question.*"). In the context of testing the tribunal's powers before the English courts, this distinction might be relevant, because allowing the tribunal to rely on the (foreign) substantive law (*i.e.* law applicable to the merits) will effectively make its possible decision on contract adaptation non-reviewable by English courts, even in the absence of the parties' express consent to adapt the contract and (only) with an implied approval of the English Arbitration act as to the gap-filling powers of the tribunal.

435 Without a doubt, the law applicable to the substance of the dispute will have an impact on shaping the tribunal's powers. In any event, it is concluded that no matter how influential, it will not be open for the review mechanisms of English courts during the setting-aside procedure. See also fn.434.

The reversal in the analysis is caused by the fact that under the old English arbitration regime it has long been debated whether parties could authorize the tribunal to adapt the contract.[436] Following the 1996 Arbitration law reform, however, it seems less controversial to conclude that according to the 1996 Act, although impliedly, parties would be able to give the tribunal the power to fill in the gaps in the contract.[437] For example some authors concluded that "*[...] it is generally accepted in modern times that an arbitral tribunal has implied consent to 'fill gaps' by making a determination as to the presumed intention of the parties in order to make a contract operable.*"[438] Furthermore, as pointed out by Poudret and Besson "*[...] Kröll considers that pursuant to the Arbitration Act 1996, s.46(1)(b) the parties can confer such power on an arbitrator by express provision even though a court might not have such power.*"[439] Additionally, one should also be able to rely on Section 48(1) of the Act, which gives the parties a broad discretion to individually fashion remedies at the tribunal's disposal.[440] Notably, however, a power to fill gaps and revise contractual provisions has not been expressly included in the list of the default powers of Section 48 of the Act.[441] It might arguably lead to the conclusion that the English Arbitration regime tolerates contract adaptation by the tribunal if mandated by the parties, but it would be less congenial to the tribunal's decision made in the absence of some kind of parties' authorization.[442] Consequently, one should consider whether a tribunal's decision can be

436 Since the tribunal's powers could only mirror the ones of the court and since the gap-filling request may take place even where there is no "dispute" between the parties. For further reading, see Kröll, *Contractual gap-filling by arbitration tribunals* (1999).

437 In this respect, most of the authors seem to rely on (and to follow with approval) the major study of Kröll, namely Kröll, *Ergänzung und Anpassung von Verträgen durch Schiedsgerichte* (1998). See, *e.g.*, Poudret & Besson (2007) p.21 ("*[...] In all the countries considered here [thus including England], an arbitrator should be empowered to deal with such questions in the same way as all other disputes arising from a contract, but only within the limits of the law applicable to the merits.*"); Lew et al., *Comparative International Commercial Arbitration* (2003) p.652, fn.143, with a reference to Kröll, *Contractual gap-filling by arbitration tribunals* (1999) p.305 ("*see also Kröll, ibid, 305, who concludes that the English and the German arbitration laws also provide for the power of the tribunal to fill gaps and adapt the contract.*"), Berger, *Power of Arbitrators to Fill Gaps and Revise Contracts to Make Sense* (2001) p.16, with a reference to Kröll, *Contractual gap-filling by arbitration tribunals* (1999) p.305 ("*As Stefan Kröll has stated in his study on gap-filling and contract adaptation by arbitrators: 'last doubts of a legal or procedural nature against the arbitrators' authority [to fill gaps and adapt a contract under English law] should have been dissipated with the new [1996] Arbitration Act'.*"), Kröll, *Contractual gap-filling by arbitration tribunals* (1999). See also Blackaby et al. (2015) pp.524-527.

438 Blackaby et al. (2015) pp.524-525. See also the reference made to *Mamidoil-Jetoil Greek Petroleum Company SA v. Okta Crude Oil Refinery AD* [2001] EWCA Civ 406, 2001 WL 272881 at [69].

439 Poudret & Besson (2007) pp.20-21, with a reference to Kröll, *Contractual gap-filling by arbitration* tribunals (1999) pp.14-16.

440 A discretion going, arguably, as far as to allow the tribunal to grant remedies (even) unknown to the English legal system. See also section 6.3.1.

441 In any event, as pointed out above this list is not exhaustive and, as such, it is not a conclusive evidence of the unavailability of the gap-filling mechanism. See section 6.3 above.

442 Either in the form of the adaptation clause or otherwise.

challenged in the case where there is (i) an express agreement allowing the tribunal to adapt the contract, (ii) where the contract is silent on the matter, or (iii) where the tribunal adapts the contract when such a possibility is excluded by the parties.

By and large, the tribunal's decision adapting the contract based on the parties' express agreement will escape the scrutiny of the national courts.[443] If, however, a contract does not include any adaptation or hardship clause, the tribunal's actions might be contested on the basis of excess of the tribunal's powers.[444] Even then, starting with a presumption that contract adaptation has been requested by one of the parties, the tribunal's decision might still survive the challenge if, for example, it relied on the law applicable to the merits as the source of the power.[445]

Also, although highly dependent on the facts of the case, the tribunal may conceive that a broadly drafted arbitration clause entails the power of adapting contractual relations if, for example, it is included in a long-term contract. Accordingly, the tribunal may rely on the implied authorization measured by "*the significance and purpose of the agreement and the large number of 'open' contract clauses contained therein*".[446] Indeed, more often than not, however, the absence of a clear authorization would be rather a sign that parties did not intend to give the power to a tribunal and, subsequently, "*adaptation and supplementation may not be imposed on them by arbitrators*".[447]

It goes without saying that the tribunal shall comply with the parties' express prohibition to exercise certain remedial powers (such as the power to fill the gap in the contract).

All in all, it is reasonable for prudent parties to expressly vest the tribunal with gap-filling power. However, without such an authorization a tribunal's decision may not be lost when brought before the English court. At the same time, a gap-filling exercise may very well amount to serious irregularity (*i.e.* the Section 68 challenge) such as excess of powers,[448] depending on the factual underpinning of the case.

443 Not reviewable with regard to the tribunal's authority to fill the contractual gaps. Conversely, if the tribunal fills the gaps against the parties' express prohibition of this power, it will constitute the excess of powers.

444 Section 68(2)(b) of the Act. In turn, the Section 67 challenge will not be available.

445 See above fn.434.

446 Berger, *Power of Arbitrators to Fill Gaps and Revise Contracts to Make Sense* (2001) pp.8-9. The author immediately adds that "*[a]bsent such an implied authority, international arbitral tribunals are reluctant to accept such a far-reaching competence. This reluctance is based on a reasonable interpretation of the contract and the increased responsibility of businessmen for their contractual relations. This responsibility is derived from the presumption of the professional competence of the parties to international business contracts which is generally regarded by international arbitrators as a principle of transnational commercial law. This presumption serves an important function in this context. It is regarded by the arbitrators as a yardstick for the distribution of risks in the contract. Based on this presumption, international arbitrators assume that it is up to the parties to take precautions in their contract against unforeseen circumstances. If no such clauses are inserted into the contract, arbitrators are reluctant to overrule the principle of pacta sunt servanda in favour of contract adaptation and gap-filling.*"

447 Berger, *Power of Arbitrators to Fill Gaps and Revise Contracts to Make Sense* (2001) p.9.

448 Especially in cases when the parties explicitly prohibit arbitrators to fill the gaps.

7.4 *Decisions accessory to the parties' main submissions and the merits of the case*

A few remarks should be added with regard to decisions auxiliary to the parties' main claims. The English Arbitration Act in its architecture includes relevant tools for the tribunal to decide on interests (section 7.4.1), on costs (section 7.4.2) as well as on different procedural issues including provisional measures (section 7.4.3). The mechanisms introduced, however, are rather detailed and will not be discussed here elaborately. Instead, the analysis will only concern the avenues available for the challenge of the tribunal's decision on specific issues.

7.4.1 Decision on interest

A decision on interest in terms of its value may be substantial, which in turn encourages the parties to challenge it at the post-award stage. A number of problems can arise from the tribunal's decision on interest that need to be decided on a case-by-case basis, including questions, *inter alia*, on whether a decision on interest should be governed by procedural law of the seat or whether it should be governed by the substantive law applicable to the merits of the case or whether a claim for interest may form an independent claim or always share the fate of a decision on the main claim. The same goes for the tribunal's powers to decide on *pre*-award and *post*-award interest, the accrual of interest,[449] and the tribunal's power to consider interest as damages.[450] Before going further, it is necessary to point out that the English default mechanism is rather detailed. Thus, if parties wish to deviate therefore from how far the tribunal can go with awarding interest, they should do so explicitly. Depending on the circumstances, it seems that all challenges might be available for the tribunal's decision on interest.

As mentioned above, the fallback mechanism, pursuant to Section 49 of the Act, reads as follows:

> (1) The parties are free to agree on the powers of the tribunal as regards the award of interest.
> (2) Unless otherwise agreed by the parties the following provisions apply.
> (3) The tribunal may award simple or compound interest from such dates, at such rates and with such rests as it considers meets the justice of the case

449 With regard to accrual of interest, the position has changed *vide* the 1950 Act. See Harris et al., *The Arbitration Act 1996* (2014) p.255 ("*Another significant change is that interest no longer automatically accrues on sums awarded, as it did under s.20 of the 1950 Act. So arbitrators have to remember to consider awarding such interest: in our view they should generally do so.*"). Also Reisberg & Pauley (2013) p.26.

450 For further reading, see, *e.g.*, Merkin & Flannery, *Arbitration Act 1996* (2014) pp.218-221, Harris et al., *The Arbitration Act 1996* (2014) pp.254-258, Sutton et al. (2007) paras 6-115 to 6-128.

(a) on the whole or part of any amount awarded by the tribunal, in respect of any period up to the date of the award;
(b) on the whole or part of any amount claimed in the arbitration and outstanding at the commencement of the arbitral proceedings but paid before the award was made, in respect of any period up to the date of payment.
(4) The tribunal may award simple or compound interest from the date of the award (or any later date) until payment, at such rates and with such rests as it considers meets the justice of the case, on the outstanding amount of any award (including any award of interest under subsection (3) and any award as to costs).
(5) References in this section to an amount awarded by the tribunal include an amount payable in consequence of a declaratory award by the tribunal.
(6) The above provisions do not affect any other power of the tribunal to award interest.

Merkin and Flannery commented that:

> [o]f course, if claimant does not make any claim for interest, the arbitrators are not empowered to award interest, as it does not form a part of the reference. If a claim for interest is subsequently added, and the respondent does not object, then the tribunal's jurisdiction may be regarded as having been extended accordingly. Similarly, if the tribunal's final award does not provide for interest, but a claim for interest was made prior to the award, the tribunal has jurisdiction to rectify that omission by a later award, under section 57(3); if, on the other hand, the question of interest was not raised, 57(3) cannot rescue the claimant.[451]

These arguments, which also rely on the cases mentioned below, inevitably lead to the challenge under Section 67 of the Act, namely the challenge of the substantive jurisdiction. It consequently shows that such a challenge against the decision on interest is possible.

At the same time, one should observe, however, that the possibility of the challenge under these factual circumstances is closely related to the question whether a claim for interest is framed in the request for arbitration and the temporal aspect of *when* it is submitted rather than whether the tribunal has the power to award interest.[452] Indeed, it seems that parties occasionally submit their claim for interest at the later stage of the proceedings instead of doing it at the initial phase and, consequently, the jurisdiction questions arise. In these instances, parties should be reminded that if no objection has

451 Merkin & Flannery, *Arbitration Act 1996* (2014) pp.218-219.

452 For a discussion on new claims, see section 6.1.5.

been advanced by them in due course (against such a late claim), they might be estopped from bringing the challenge pursuant to Section 73(1) of the Act.

In the case of *Westland Helicopters*, the court concluded, for example, that since no objection on a point of jurisdiction over the independent claim on interest was brought before the tribunal, a party was precluded from raising this ground of objection after the award was made.[453] It was still possible, however, to object (under Section 67 of the Act) to the award awarding interest for the period before the indicated period (thus longer) for which interest was sought.[454] Additionally, one should also take account of the *functus officio* considerations. It has been held in *Pirtek (UK) Ltd v. Deanswood Ltd, Gordon Harris* that the arbitrator exceeded his jurisdiction, when he awarded interest based on submissions made after the award on the main claim was granted.[455] Importantly, in this case, no claim for interest was pursued prior to the award being rendered.[456]

In principle, an award on interest may amount to serious irregularity causing substantial injustice.[457] It is thus possible to imagine that the duty of fairness has been violated (when the tribunal does not give the parties sufficient opportunity to address the claim on interest),[458] or that the award is *infra petita* by not including the claim on interest,[459] or that the award on interest was somewhat ambiguous as to its effect.[460]

It is difficult, albeit not impossible, to envisage a case where the tribunal would exceed its powers while awarding interest. As always, it is important to note that in order to be the basis of a successful Section 68 challenge the alleged excess needs to cause substantial injustice.[461] An "excess of powers" that causes substantial injustice might in theory occur, if the request for interest is sought in disregard of the explicit choice of the parties in the original agreement to arbitrate (where they expressly agree that the tribunal may *not* award interest or a specific type of interest)[462] and the tribunal, relying on its default competences stemming from Section 49 of the Act, consequently grants the claim for interest sought. Conversely, where the initial agreement to arbitrate is "only" silent as to the interest, Section

453 See *Westland Helicopters Ltd v. Sheikh Salah Al-Hejailan* [2004] EWHC 1625 (Comm) at [54-57].

454 See *Westland Helicopters Ltd v. Sheikh Salah Al-Hejailan* [2004] EWHC 1625 (Comm) at [57].

455 *Pirtek (UK) Ltd v. Deanswood Ltd, Gordon Harris* [2005] EWHC 2301 (Comm), [2005] EWHC 2301 (Comm) 2005 WL 3278910.

456 *Pirtek (UK) Ltd v. Deanswood Ltd, Gordon Harris* [2005] EWHC 2301 (Comm), [2005] EWHC 2301 (Comm) 2005 WL 3278910 at [10] and at [34-36].

457 For further reading, see section 5 above.

458 Section 68(2)(a) of the Act. See *Van der Giessen-de-Noord Shipbuilding BV v. Imtech Marine & Offshore BV* [2009] 1 Lloyd's Rep. 273 at [28-31]. Also, section 5.2.1 of this chapter.

459 Section 68(2)(d). See section 5.2.3.

460 Section 68(2)(f) of the Act. See section 5.2.4.

461 See section 5.1.3. Also *CNH Global N.V. v. PGN Logistics Limited, Graglia SRL, Wincanton Trans European Ltd.* [2009] EWHC 977 (Comm) 2009 WL 2848157, where the "excess of powers" *did not* amount to a substantial injustice.

462 See also *Lesotho Highlands Development Authority v. Impregilo SpA & Ors* [2005] UKHL 43.

49 of the Act is, arguably, a very powerful device within the tribunal's powers for making decisions on interest, which in turn makes it (the decision) to a large extent resistant to the excess of powers challenge.[463]

Finally, one can not completely exclude the possibility that the decision on interest may be open for an appeal on point of law.[464] An example of this is difficult to find nonetheless.

On occasion it has been concluded that decision on interest is "*an inherent element of a tribunal's adjudicatory authority and is implicitly contained within the terms of agreements to arbitrate, at least absent contrary indication by the parties.*"[465] Considering the powers prescribed in Section 49 of the Act, it may not be easy to convince the court that the tribunal's decision on interest should be set aside.

7.4.2 Decision on costs

The English Arbitration Act offers a very detailed framework as to the costs of arbitration proceedings. In fact, seven Sections of the Act are devoted solely to the question of assessing the costs of arbitration.[466] Since the default mechanism is extensively developed, it diminishes the chance of a decision on costs being subject to challenge. In any event, it seems that a decision on costs mainly triggers a challenge as to serious irregularity. Similar to other decisions, recourse against the decision on costs depends on (i) the will of the parties outlined in the agreement to arbitrate, and (ii) how they frame their submissions, and (iii) how far the tribunal relies on the fallback mechanism.

If the parties frame how the tribunal should tackle the issue of costs, the tribunal should inevitably follow their instructions. Very often, with regard to costs, institutional rules supplement the parties' choice expressed in the agreement to arbitrate.[467] If not, the tribunal may rely on a default rule prescribed in Section 61 of the Act:

> (1) The tribunal may make an award allocating the costs of the arbitration as between the parties, subject to any agreement of the parties.

---

463 Section 68(2)(b) of the Act. For further reading, see also 5.2.2 of this chapter.

464 For further reading, see also section 6.

465 Born, *International Commercial Arbitration* (2014) p.3103, also ILA, *ILA Report on Inherent Powers of Arbitral Tribunals* (2014) p.10.

466 See Sections 59-65 of the Act. The structure of the Act has been explained by a number of scholars and will not be elaborated upon here. For further reading, see DAC, *Report on the Arbitration Bill* (1996) paras 265-272, Merkin & Flannery, *Arbitration Act 1996* (2014) pp.244-261, Harris et al., *The Arbitration Act 1996* (2014) pp.291-316, Sutton et al. (2007) paras 6-129 to 6-161. As highlighted by Merkin and Flannery in Merkin & Flannery, *Arbitration Act 1996* (2014) p.245, the statutory costs provisions are not mandatory (with the exception of Section 60 of the Act). See, however, Harris et al., *The Arbitration Act 1996* (2014) p.291.

467 See, *e.g.*, Art. 28 of the 2014 LCIA Rules, Art. 28 of the 2020 LCIA Rules, Art. 38 of the (draft) 2021 ICC Rules, Art. 38 of the 2017 ICC Rules, and Art. 37 of the 2012 ICC Rules.

> (2) Unless the parties otherwise agree, the tribunal shall award costs on the general principle that costs should follow the event except where it appears to the tribunal that in the circumstances this is not appropriate in relation to the whole or part of the costs.

In principle, parties should claim their costs, if they wish these to be awarded to them. If they do not do so, the tribunal is, arguably, not under any obligation to award costs. At the same time, however, the tribunal should have the power to sanction bad faith conduct in its award on costs. In these cases, the tribunal may rely on Section 61(2) of the Act[468] or on the institutional rules, for example on Article 28.4 of the 2014 LCIA Rules.[469]

In any event, an apt argument has been put forward by some scholars who concluded that: "*[w]hichever way the tribunal orders costs, it must act fairly and give both sides an opportunity to address it on matters and of quantum, and not proceed to determine costs in a manner that come as a surprise to the loser (or even the winner) upon reading the award.*"[470] It means that a decision on costs may be open to the Section 68(2)(a) of the Act challenge (failure to comply with the tribunal's general duties). Additionally, similar to the decision on interest the decision on costs may be subjected, for example, to *infra petita*.[471] As hinted above, arguably, the excess of powers challenge might be rarely useful considering how elaborately the Arbitration Act deals with the costs issues. Recourse against the tribunal's substantive jurisdiction or appeal on point of law would be also rather unsuccessful.[472]

7.4.3 Decision on procedure

As already explained above on a number of occasions, the Arbitration Act is very detailed and provides the tribunal with a great deal of procedural powers.[473] Since they are of

468 "*Unless the parties otherwise agree, the tribunal shall award costs on the general principle that costs should follow the event except where it appears to the tribunal that in the circumstances this is not appropriate in relation to the whole or part of the costs.*" For further reading, see also Merkin & Flannery, *Arbitration Act 1996* (2014) p.249.

469 Pursuant to Art. 28.4 of the 2014 LCIA Rules "*[...] [t]he Arbitral Tribunal may also take into account the parties' conduct in the arbitration, including any co-operation in facilitating the proceedings as to time and cost and any non-co-operation resulting in undue delay and unnecessary expense. Any decision on costs by the Arbitral Tribunal shall be made with reasons in the award containing such decision.*" Additionally, Art. 28.4 of the 2020 LCIA Rules includes a direct reference not only to parties but also to their "authorised representatives". See also *e.g.* Art. 38.5 of the 2017 ICC Rules and Art. 37.5 of the 2012 ICC Rules.

470 Merkin & Flannery, *Arbitration Act 1996* (2014) p.248.

471 See Section 68(2)(d) of the Act. Also, section 5.2.3 of this chapter.

472 See the reflections put forward above under section 6.4.1.

473 See, *i.a.*, Section 37 of the Act (granting the tribunal power to appoint experts, legal advisers or assessors) and Section 38 of the Act (referring to general powers exercisable by the tribunal, *e.g.*, allowing the tribunal to order security for cost).

procedural character, it is unlikely that they would trigger the Section 67 challenge.[474] Therefore, more often than not, they are eventually open for a challenge for serious irregularity.[475]

One of the grounds listed as a serious irregularity under Section 68 is tailored precisely to the non-compliance with the parties' procedural requests. Pursuant to Section 68(2)(c) of the Act the award may be successfully challenged when the court is satisfied that the "*failure by the tribunal to conduct the proceedings in accordance with the procedure agreed by the parties*" will amount to a serious irregularity causing substantial injustice. At the same time, however, scholars observe that "*[i]n practice, this head will be of little significance, as the arbitrators are free to determine the procedure in the absence of any agreement to the contrary, and (except in relation to institutional arbitrations) there is rarely any such agreement.*"[476] For this reason, other grounds listed under Section 68 will be of relevance and the "excess of powers" ground will be at the top of the list.[477]

Again, considering that the tribunal has many procedural powers under the Arbitration Act itself and that these are further supplemented by the powers included in the applicable institutional rules, the use of the "excess of powers" challenge is limited. The relevant question that arises in the context of the procedural decisions is who bears the ultimate power of managing the proceedings. Put differently, the question is whether the parties' joint procedural request would be controlling for the tribunal or, conversely, whether the tribunal will have a power to disregard it if it considers that it will affect its adjudicative function.

An important shift in this regard has been made in the recent change to the LCIA Rules. According to the 1998 version of the Rules,[478] the tribunal should follow the parties' directives and "*[i]n principle [it] cannot override procedural agreements of the parties*" (with the exception of the violation of mandatory rules of law).[479] The 2014 modification tips the scales in favor of the arbitral tribunal. Pursuant to Article 14.2 of the 2014 LCIA Rules, "*[t]he parties may agree on joint proposals for the conduct of their arbitration for consideration by the Arbitral Tribunal. They are encouraged to do so in consultation with the Arbitral Tribunal and consistent with the Arbitral Tribunal's general duties under the Arbitration Agreement.*" Consequently, it gives the tribunal the so much needed control

474 The Section 67 challenge is limited to the challenge of substantive jurisdiction. It is not designed to tackle procedural irregularities. See section 3.

475 For the requirements that need to be fulfilled, see section 5 above.

476 Merkin & Flannery, *Arbitration Act 1996* (2014) p.312.

477 Another ground that might be relevant is the one prescribed under Section 68(2)(a) of the Act (failure to comply with the general duty of the tribunal).

478 See Art. 14 of the 1998 LCIA Rules.

479 Konrad & Hunter (2013) p.456.

over the arbitral process, making the parties' joint requests a suggestion or a proposal rather than mandatory directives.[480] Indeed,

> [i]n deciding whether to accept the parties' agreement, or reject or modify it, the Arbitral Tribunal should evaluate the parties' request in light of the Arbitral Tribunal's own obligations and duties and after considering the position of the Arbitral Tribunal itself. In carrying out this evaluation it will be helpful if the Tribunal is able to identify the reasons why the parties have reached their agreement, insofar as the Tribunal is able to do so.[481]

All in all, considering the broad spectrum of procedural freedom given to a tribunal and the high threshold that needs to be met in order to successfully challenge an arbitral award, in most instances the procedural decisions will survive.

8 Concluding remarks

In general, the 1996 Act is a true milestone for the development of English law. Among other things, it truly brought the post-award judicial control closer to the internationally recognized standards. The developed tradition of the supervision based on the statutory grounds and the courts' inherent jurisdiction could easily become a burden in structuring the new system. Yet, the drafters were able to take into account previous achievements and, at the same time, introduce the versatile yet comprehensible system of judicial review in the 1996 Act.

The setting-aside system under the Act is based on three pillars, namely a challenge of the tribunal's substantive jurisdiction, a challenge of the serious irregularities causing substantial injustice and, finally, an appeal on point of law. Each of these grounds for recourse, although to a different degree, proved relevant for testing the tribunal's use of its adjudicative powers. Also, each of them has its autonomous features. To name a few, on a comparative basis, only the challenge of substantive jurisdiction and the challenge of serious irregularity are mandatory provisions thus parties are not able to freely exclude from the post-award judicial review on these grounds. Importantly, the English system of appeal on point of law, although non-mandatory is designed as an opt-out system, which means that parties are well advised to be explicit if they intend to contract out from a judicial control on point of law. Another important comparative point is the difference in

480 Arguably, the 2020 amendment of the LCIA Rules reinforces tribunal's prerogatives even further, see Arts. 14.1, 14.2, 14.5, 14.6 of the 2020 the LCIA Rules.

481 Gerbay et al. (2015) p.206.

the standard of the court's review with regard to objections regarding the tribunal's substantive jurisdiction and the serious irregularities. In the case of the former, it seems that the court is able to review the case *de novo* including having a full hearing and (even) admission of new evidence, whereas in the case of the serious irregularities courts apply a much higher degree of deference towards the tribunal's decisions. Last, but not least, the way the courts may approach each of the available challenge routes differs because different remedies will be at court's disposal. Notably, not only traditional remission and setting aside are possible, but also confirmation of the award, variation of the award or declaration of the award to be of no effect. The availability of remedies depends on which head of the challenge is being invoked. However, the court reviewing the tribunal's substantive jurisdiction has, at least in theory, been deprived of the power to remit it back to the tribunal. It could, arguably, prove to be useful in cases where the court reviews *the scope* of the tribunal's substantive jurisdiction, thus in the single instance of the substantive jurisdiction challenge that is of interest for the research at hand.

As pointed out above, the substantive jurisdiction challenge is only relevant for the research at hand to the extent it is invoked against *the scope* of the substantive jurisdiction (thus not when the validity, the existence of the agreement to arbitrate, nor the constitution of the arbitral tribunal are at stake). By and large, the scope of the tribunal's substantive jurisdiction is determined by the underlying agreement to arbitrate (along with arbitration rules, if applicable), the subsequent parties' submissions and the statutory rules that protect the public interest at large. Importantly, pursuant to Section 30(1)(c) of the Act, the scope of the tribunal's substantive jurisdiction is primarily predetermined by the *parties' submissions* (or put differently, by the matters that have been submitted to arbitration). Only if a matter is truly submitted does it deserve to be checked against the matrix of the agreement to arbitrate.

The test of serious irregularities is different. The irregularity may affect *the tribunal, the proceedings* or the award. It shows that, arguably, this test can be traced back to the (pre-1996 Act) review of whether the arbitrator misconducted *himself* or *the proceedings*. In turn, it implies that the test of the serious irregularities is closely connected with the service of justice, thus, by and large, with the concept of due process. Instead of the broad definition that could have been freely shaped by the courts, the 1996 Act provides that "only" nine notions can be effectively considered by the courts as a serious irregularity. It means that this exhaustive list remarkably limits the scope of the court's review. Additionally, the successful application for the setting aside on the ground of serious irregularity is conditioned not only upon the fact that the irregularity needs to be serious, it also has to cause a substantial injustice to the applicant and the setting aside should not itself cause the substantial injustice.

Out of the nine irregularities listed, arguably, three are of particular importance when testing the tribunal's adjudicative powers. Of course the most important is the notion of "excess of powers" which is accompanied by the failure to comply with the duty of fairness and failure to deal with all the issues brought before the tribunal. The Act in itself makes a clear distinction of the difference between the excess of powers and excess of jurisdiction. In practice, however, it is sometimes difficult to properly categorize the objection. Acknowledging that it can be considered as an overly simplistic view, it is argued that parties may find inspiration in the Act itself to determine which of the tribunal's powers do not affect the tribunal's jurisdiction. An overlook of the content of the Act would suggest that the tribunal has a power for example to order a specific performance, the power to award interest and the like. In turn, if the parties decide to limit these powers and, in turn the tribunal exceeds them, it will be appropriate to remedy these tribunal's actions with the excess of powers challenge. Otherwise, however, the Act proves to be a comprehensive source of the tribunal's powers.

Additionally, it goes without saying that the tribunal should act fairly, which means that, amongst other things, it should not surprise parties with its conclusions. Put differently, it should give the parties the opportunity to address the "*essential building blocks*" of its own conclusions.

Finally, the tribunal should *deal* with all the issues brought before it. One of the main difficulties regarding this ground lies in the definition of the notion "*issues*". As put by one authority: "*a matter will constitute an "issue" where the whole of the applicant's claim could have depended upon how it was resolved, such that "fairness demanded" that the question be dealt with*".[482] Also, arguably, "the issue" should be distinguished from "the matter" that is a relevant concept for the substantive jurisdiction challenge.

The DAC left an appeal on point of law as a statutory ground for challenge notwithstanding criticism from the international arbitration community. As highlighted this opt-out system is rather limited in its scope of application. Even if applicable, however, it will be subject to a number of strict requirements. Consequently, in the case of testing the tribunal's adjudicative powers it will rarely be of relevance.

The application of this three-headed concept of a challenge proved that all of the three heads (however, the mandatory ones in particular) are relevant when testing different decisions of the arbitral tribunal.

By and large, decisions on contractual and non-contractual claims and counterclaims will most likely trigger the challenge of substantive jurisdiction since the claims indeed are *matters* brought before the tribunal and thus define the scope of the tribunal's substantive jurisdiction. It does not change the fact that, on occasion, the tribunal's decision on claims (in a broad sense) can be flawed with a serious irregularity causing substantive injustice.

482 See fn.199.

In principle, the process of determining the applicable law (including conflict of laws rules) and ascertaining the content of the applicable law will naturally attract an appeal on point of law. As pointed out, however, its scope of application is rather limited. Since it is unlikely that the *process* of applying the law affects the tribunal's jurisdiction, parties will be left with the challenge of serious irregularities.

It has already been suggested that the possibility to grant a remedy should be considered a *power* of the tribunal. Consequently, in cases where the tribunal granted a remedy that was not at its disposal, such a decision should be set aside on the "excess of powers" grounds.[483] Since, however, the Act includes many fallback mechanisms, it arguably means that parties should first expressly limit the tribunal's powers to grant certain types of remedies in their agreement to arbitrate in order to rely on Section 68(2)(b) of the Act. As always, it may be relevant to test the tribunal's decision upon the (most invoked) ground of the breach of duty of fairness and possibly failure to deal with all essential issues.

Finally, the conclusion regarding decisions on remedies is equally applicable to decisions accessory to the main submissions. Therefore, in short, they may be flawed with serious irregularities and the excess of powers. However, taking into account a number of default powers prescribed by the Act, the challenge will rarely be successful.

483 And should not be a challenge of the substantive jurisdiction under Section 67 of the Act.

V The United States and the Federal Arbitration Act of 1925

1 Introduction

The U.S. arbitration law is a complex legal system that provides a perfect setting for the study of the "excess of mandate" type of challenge – the challenge that across the ocean would be, by and large, understood under the notion of "excess of powers" rather than the "excess of mandate".[1] In turn, the subject of the present inquiry is the meaning of the concept "excess of powers" by the arbitral tribunal in the U.S.[2]

Before addressing the underlying question (*i.e.* with respect to concept of the "excess of powers"), the intricacies of the arbitration architecture in the U.S. need to be highlighted. Therefore, at first, the legal framework of arbitration will be discussed in general terms. It means that reference will be made to the Federal Arbitration Act of 1925 (hereafter the "FAA")[3] as well as to state laws governing arbitration. In particular, it seems of relevance to discuss the relation between Chapter 1 of the FAA and state arbitration statutes regarding the grounds for vacating an arbitral award.[4] A brief comment will follow on how the judicial system in the U.S. functions and how the U.S. Supreme Court (in this chapter also referred to as the "Supreme Court" or "the Court") (re)shapes the structure of commercial arbitration in the U.S.

The American notion of "excess of powers" has been introduced in Section 10(a)(4) of the FAA according to which:

> the United States court in and for the district wherein the award was made may make an order vacating the award upon the application of any party to the

1 As explained in Chapter I, "excess of mandate" and "excess of powers" are different models of the "excess of mandate" type of challenge. These will be the subject of a separate comparative law analysis in Chapter VII.

2 It should be acknowledged that in the U.S. consumer arbitration, labor arbitration and securities arbitration are areas of the arbitration system distinct from commercial arbitration. The scope of the research at hand is limited, however, to commercial arbitration. In any event, some principles developed in other specialized arbitration systems have been successfully transplanted into commercial arbitration. For that reason, some reference to the "non-commercial arbitration" cases may be occasionally made.

3 *9 U.S.C. § 1 et seq.*

4 When discussing the arbitration system in the U.S. one should note that the statutory language of the FAA (and state laws) refers to vacatur of the arbitral award. For the purpose of the research at hand, it will be considered that the vacating procedure is an extraordinary means of recourse against an arbitral award recognized elsewhere as a setting-aside procedure or annulment procedure.

> arbitration [...] where the arbitrators exceeded their powers, or so imperfectly executed them that a mutual, final, and definite award upon the subject matter submitted was not made.

This provision, drafted in rather broad terms, aches for further analysis.

First, the court standard of review should be briefly discussed. Other questions that need to be answered accordingly are the following: should the court be allowed to confirm the arbitral award in part and should the court take into account the correlation between an arbitral award rendered and alleged "excess of powers" (and if so, to what extent)? In other words, can the tribunal "exceed its powers" in other ways than by producing the award?

After explaining the general features of vacating arbitral awards, the core issue (*i.e.* the "excess of powers" challenge) needs to be properly addressed. The study undertaken will be three-fold. As a starting point, the limits to the arbitral tribunal's powers and lines for their demarcation will be defined. Further, this research will focus on the meaning of both the notion of "excess of powers" and the concept of "imperfect execution of powers upon the subject matter submitted" and how the courts interpret these notions. It consequently means that the "excess of powers" challenge in a broad sense will be considered to comprise the notions of "excess of powers" and "imperfect execution of powers upon the subject matter submitted". Further, it is necessary to briefly reflect on the (alternative) argument suggesting that the New York Convention grounds rather than the grounds prescribed in Chapter 1 of the FAA should be applicable to international awards rendered in the U.S.[5]

What naturally follows from the judicial interpretation of the statutory concepts in the common law jurisdictions is the introduction of the body of common law that expands the understanding of the provisions of law (if needed). In the context of the "excess of powers" challenge in the U.S., the doctrine of the "manifest disregard of the law" that has been judicially created on the federal level should not be passed by and unnoticed. The additional question, however, would be whether the "manifest disregard of the law" doctrine is independent from grounds prescribed in Section 10 of the FAA or whether it may fit within the ambit of the "excess of powers" challenge.

The next section of this chapter will be dedicated to the application of the "excess of powers" challenge to selected issues that arguably may fall outside the scope of the arbitral tribunal's powers. The section is divided thematically into four parts: the first will be devoted to the arbitral tribunal's decisions on parties' claims (including, *i.a.*, contractual claims, set-off claims and tort claims); the second will explain the process of application of law by the arbitral tribunal (starting from the application of relevant choice of law rules through the decision on applicable law, and finishing with ascertaining the content of the

5 Whether this line of argumentation is accepted, see Chapter II and Chapter VI.

applicable law by the arbitral tribunal); the third part focuses on the excess of the arbitral tribunal's powers when awarding different types of remedies (such as damages, punitive damages, specific performance, contract adaptation and filling the gaps); the fourth and final part is devoted to arbitral tribunals' decisions on interest and costs which are decisions accessory to the parties' main submissions. The decision on the procedure should also be taken into account.

The concluding remarks will give a general overview of the approach taken by the courts when testing the award for the alleged excess of the tribunal's powers, especially taking into account that the "excess of powers" ground is said to be the most frequent statutory ground for vacating arbitration awards.[6]

The research at hand recognizes the importance of the recently finalized Restatement (Third) of International Commercial Arbitration (also referred to as the "Restatement on International Arbitration" or the "Restatement").[7] It is a major project undertaken by the American Law Institute that started in December 2007 and concluded in the mid 2019.[8] The Restatement provides a profound and systematic analysis of the system of international commercial (and investment) arbitration as it developed in the U.S. It is not, however, source of law thus it does not bound the U.S. courts. It may only operate as a (strong) persuasive authority.[9]

2 The legal context of international commercial arbitration in the United States

Before discussing in detail how the "excess of powers" of the arbitral tribunal is tested in the U.S., a brief outline of the U.S. legal landscape has to be given. It should be noted that the issues addressed here remain subject to the ongoing debate and as such they may come

6 *136 A.L.R. Fed. 183 (Originally published in 1997) ("The most frequent ground for vacating arbitration awards is that the arbitrators exceeded their powers permitting the vacating of the award under § 10(a)(4) and more awards have been vacated on this ground than under all the other re[a]sons for vacating awards combined.")*. See also Brewer & Mills (2009) p.46, Mills & Brewer (2013) p.121.

7 Due notice is also made to a bill of the Arbitration Fairness Act of 2018 (hereafter the "AFA") that has been referred to a Senate Committee on the Judiciary on 22 March 2018 (see S.2591 - Arbitration Fairness Act of 2018 115th Congress (2017-2018) available at https://www.congress.gov/bill/115th-congress/senate-bill/2591 [last accessed 23 April 2019]. It is, however, uncertain whether the bill would be enacted by the Congress, taking into account that it has been already introduced for a discussion at least six times (in 2007, 2009, 2011 and 2013, 2015, 2017) and it was repeatedly rejected. In any event it should be noted that the AFA is aimed at protecting consumers and employees and invalidating predispute arbitration agreements concluded with them. Further, the AFA does not contain any amendments to Section 10 of the FAA (grounds for vacatur). In consequence, it has *no* direct influence on commercial arbitration, especially in the context of the "excess of powers" challenge which is the subject of the research at hand.

8 See https://www.ali.org/projects/show/international-commercial-arbitration/ [last accessed 23 April 2019].

9 Occasionally, the reference can be made to the earlier drafts of the Restatement.

across as oversimplified. The aim of this section, however, is just to sketch a general picture that would explain *i.a.* what the legal bases are for the architecture of (international) arbitration in the U.S. (see section 2.1 and section 2.2), how the judicial system of the U.S. functions (section 2.3), and finally the role of the U.S. Supreme Court in (re)designing of the system of arbitration (section 2.4).

2.1 *The Federal Arbitration Act of 1925 and its supremacy*

The FAA is often reported as "*a response to the judiciary's long standing refusal to enforce executory agreements to arbitrate.*"[10] Taking into account the "judicial hostility" against arbitration that existed in the U.S. until the beginning of the twentieth century,[11] enactment of the FAA in 1925 is considered to be a breakthrough,[12] because it provided a much-needed statutory framework for the enforcement of arbitration agreements and arbitral awards.[13]

Additionally, it is frequently suggested that the FAA was designed by Congress as a procedural device to enforce arbitration in federal courts,[14] which was intended to apply in an interstate context.[15] Consequently, a number of authors reject the idea that the FAA was ever considered to be a body of substantive law. As put forward by Horton, "*the legislative record repeatedly disavows the idea that the statute [the FAA] creates federal substantive law capable of binding states.*"[16] Nonetheless, after a series of Supreme Court decisions, starting with *Moses H. Cone Memorial Hospital v. Mercury Construction Corp.* (hereafter "Moses H. Cone Memorial Hospital")[17] and *Southland Corp. v. Keating* (also

10 See, *i.a.*, Burns (2010) p.1817; Horton (2013) p.1219. See also *H.R. Rep. No. 68-96, at 1-2 (1924).*

11 "Judicial hostility" was taken in by American courts from the English jurisprudence which heavily influenced the development of the U.S. legal system. As explained by Horton in Horton (2013) p.1225: "*In seventeenth-century England, judges invented special rules to stunt arbitration's development. Under the ouster doctrine, they invalidated agreements to arbitrate because mere individuals were not competent... [to] diminish the statutory judicial power. Likewise, the revocability doctrine allowed either party to retract their assent to arbitrate until the arbitrator ruled.*" See also Haydock & Henderson (2002) pp.145-148. It is also mentioned by Burns in Burns (2010) p.1817 that "*U.S. courts criticized the common law rule, but they refused to overturn it without legislative action*"; similarly, Horton (2013) p.1225 (saying that American courts were invoking these doctrines under frequent protest).

12 See, *e.g.*, Rutledge et al. (2009) p.877.

13 Rutledge et al. (2009) p.878 ("*[...] the FAA provided [...] that arbitration agreements are enforceable (subject only to generally applicable contract defences) and that arbitral awards are judicially enforceable (subject to limited number of non-merits defences).*") For a summary of arguments favoring enforcement of agreements to arbitrate presented before the Congress, see also Moses, *Statutory Misconstruction: How the Supreme Court Created a Federal Arbitration Law Never Enacted by Congress* (2006) pp.101-109.

14 See, *i.a.*, Schwartz (2004) p.8, also Moses, *Statutory Misconstruction: How the Supreme Court Created a Federal Arbitration Law Never Enacted by Congress* (2006) pp.101-113, and Burns (2010) p.1818.

15 *H.R. Rep. No. 68-96, at 1 (1924)*, Bermann et al. (2009) p.1335, also Burns (2010) p.1818.

16 Horton (2013) p.1227.

17 *Moses H. Cone Memorial Hospital v. Mercury Construction Corp.*, 460 U.S. 1, 103 S. Ct. 927 (1983).

referred to as "Southland"),[18] the FAA was no longer a procedural vehicle enacted by the Congress in 1925. As such "*[the FAA] has now been pressed into service as a body of substantive law that binds state courts as well, requiring that arbitration agreements be enforced on the same footing as other contracts.*"[19] It means that, irrespective of the Congress' intentions in 1925, nowadays the FAA applies in state courts and preempts state law that is in conflict with the spirit of the FAA, namely with a federal policy favoring arbitration.[20] For this reason, it may be, by and large, considered superior to (and overriding) state legislation, especially in the context of international arbitration.

The FAA consists of three chapters: Chapter 1 introduces general provisions regarding (among others) enforcement of arbitration agreements, the appointment of arbitrators, and vacatur and the enforcement of arbitral awards,[21] whereas Chapters 2 and 3 contain implementing legislation for the New York Convention (Chapter 2)[22] and the Inter-American Convention on International Commercial Arbitration (hereafter the "Panama Convention") (Chapter 3). In this paper, however, mainly Chapter 1 of the FAA will be discussed in detail.[23]

2.2 *State laws and their (marginal) significance*

In a nutshell, one may *not* disregard the importance of state law.[24] Two separate legal regimes on a state level need to be distinguished: firstly an intrastate ("domestic") arbitration statute that may be of relevance and secondly an interstate (or even international) arbitration law (if enacted) on a state level that can also add a layer of confusion as to the question which law applies. These two legal frameworks might be particularly important in cases where state law has been explicitly chosen by the parties as the governing law or in cases

18 *Southland Corp. v. Keating*, 465 U.S. 1, 104 S. Ct. 852 (1984).

19 Park, *Amending the Federal Arbitration Act* (2002) p.2.

20 For further analysis of the FAA's preemption, see section 2.4. For further analysis of the pro-arbitration policy, see section 3.1.

21 *9 U.S.C. § § 1-16.*

22 For further reading, see also Chapter VI; the Panama Convention escapes the focus of this research.

23 For a comprehensive analysis of the "excess of mandate" type of challenge under the New York Convention, see Chapter VI. See, however, the Restatement's take on the post-award relief against arbitral awards (in principle, suggesting to follow the New York Convention grounds). For further reading, see section 5.3.

24 It is so, notwithstanding the fact that, by and large, state legislation may be preempted if it conflicts with the FAA, it is not entirely clear, however, when this may happen. Bermann in Bermann, *'Domesticating' the New York Convention: the Impact of the Federal Arbitration Act* (2011) p.330 points out that "*the fact remains that many US states have also enacted legislation governing arbitration in both interstate and foreign commerce. Moreover, this legislation differs in many important respects both from the FAA and indeed from state to state. While the FAA enjoys supremacy over state arbitration law in the event of conflict between them, it does not preempt the field. Unfortunately, it remains to this day unclear when exactly state law that is different from federal law is also in conflict with federal law.*" See also sections 2.1 and 2.4 of this chapter.

where an enforcement of a foreign arbitral award is not possible under the New York Convention nor under the Panama Convention.[25] Therefore, apart from the framework set out on the federal level by the FAA, state legislation on arbitration can also be significant with regard to international arbitration.

It should be noted that intrastate ("domestic") arbitration statutes are usually modeled either on the Uniform Arbitration Act of 1955 (hereafter the "UAA"),[26] or on the Revised Uniform Arbitration Act of 2000 (hereafter the "RUAA")[27] whereas separate international arbitration statutes on a state level can be based for example on the Model Law on International Commercial Arbitration.[28] It is argued, however, that in the context of the analyzed ground for vacatur it is nearly impossible for the intrastate ("domestic") statute that is based on the UAA or the RUAA to be conflicting with (and thus preempted by) the FAA. It is simply because the wording of the provisions is almost identical.[29] The situation may change if the state introduces an independent legal regime that governs international arbitration in the said state. Still, however, it is highly unlikely that even the corresponding provision of the Model Law[30] that has completely different wording from the FAA, would be inconsistent with the spirit of the FAA.[31] Consequently, it is considered that state law rarely differs and thus will rarely matter with regard to vacatur of the arbitral awards.

25 In the case of the enforcement of arbitral awards that are subject to neither the New York nor Panama Convention some argue that Chapter 1 of the FAA shall apply, others that state law should be the governing law. This question, among others, has been the subject of analysis in the Restatement (Third) of International Commercial Arbitration. For further reading, see Bermann et al. (2009) pp.1338-1339 or Bermann, *Restating the U.S. Law of International Commercial Arbitration* (2009) p.196.

26 In order to provide the users of arbitration with consistency, the National Conference of Commissioners on Uniform State Laws prepared the model bill that could be used by a state legislator wishing to introduce state arbitration acts. http://www.uniformlaws.org/LegislativeFactSheet.aspx?title=Arbitration%20Act%20(1956) [last accessed 23 April 2018].

27 See http://www.uniformlaws.org/LegislativeFactSheet.aspx?title=Arbitration%20Act%20(2000) [last accessed 23 April 2018].

28 See California, Connecticut, Florida, Georgia, Illinois, Louisiana, Oregon, Texas. See the list available at http://www.uncitral.org/uncitral/en/uncitral_texts/arbitration/1985Model_arbitration_status.html [last accessed 23 April 2018]. For further reading on the Model Law, see Chapter II.

29 See § 12(a)(3) of the UAA ("*[t]he arbitrators exceeded their powers)* or Section 23(a)(4) of the RUAA ("*an arbitrator exceeded the arbitrator's powers*") as compared to Section 10(a)(4) of the FAA ("*where the arbitrators exceeded their powers, or so imperfectly executed them that a mutual, final, and definite award upon the subject matter submitted was not made*"). One may also argue that the wording of the UAA and RUAA is even more narrow. In any event, and considering the emphatic, federal policy favoring arbitration it is likely that the wording of these statutes would be interpreted in line with the FAA.

30 Art. 34(2)(a)(iii) of the Model Law provides with a completely different model of the "excess of mandate" type of challenge ("*the award deals with a dispute not contemplated by or not falling within the terms of the submission to arbitration, or contains decisions on matters beyond the scope of the submission to arbitration, provided that, if the decisions on matters submitted to arbitration can be separated from those not so submitted, only that part of the award which contains decisions on matters not submitted to arbitration may be set aside*"). For further reading, see Chapter II.

31 Arguably, Art. 34(2)(a)(iii) of the ML limits instances for recourse against an arbitral award more than the FAA does. See also Chapter II and Chapter VII and also section 5.3.

Nonetheless, as argued by some authors, "*the practitioner should always keep this dual system [i.e. state and federal law] in mind, both because of the potential forum-selection benefits and for the occasional case where state practice becomes relevant.*"[32] Notably it may dramatically change if the Carbonneau draft proposal for the new federal arbitration law was to be enacted.[33] According to the Preamble of the (Carbonneau draft) FAA proposal, "*[...] the present statute is commanded by a strong national policy favoring arbitration and the arbitrability of disputes.*"[34]

As explained by Carbonneau:

> [...] the emphatic of strong federal policy on arbitration has been replaced by a 'strong national policy favoring arbitration,' thereby underscoring that the proposed law, if enacted, will become the national American law on arbitration. It would govern at all levels of the U.S. legal system and would not have any state law statutory rivals.[35]

Such an undertaking would effectively simplify the U.S. law on arbitration by framing it only on one legislative (national) level.[36]

2.3 *The role of the courts and the organization of the judicial system in the United States*

A few words of introduction addressing the organization of the U.S. judiciary need to be added. Farnsworth aptly points out that

> [t]he judicial system [in the U.S.] is the best starting point for an inquiry into the sources of law for, though decisional law stands below legislation in the hierarchy of authorities, and case law is subject to change by statute, the judiciary has been the traditional fountainhead of law in America as in other common law countries.[37]

In other words, it cannot be forgotten, however, that the system of arbitration in the U.S. (*i.e.* a common law country) is not based only on the statutory provisions but also on

32 Rutledge et al. (2009) p.879.

33 One should note, however, that the Carbonneau draft is a private initiative, and – as such – not currently considered as a basis for a legislative reform.

34 Carbonneau, Toward a New Federal Law on Arbitration (2014) p.101. See also pp.143-147 therein.

35 Carbonneau, Toward a New Federal Law on Arbitration (2014) pp.144-145.

36 Arguably, the Restatement efforts are also directed at simplifying the U.S. arbitration regime.

37 Farnsworth, *An Introduction to the Legal System of the United States* (2010) p.43.

federal common law. For this reason, in the context of arbitration one should take into account that the structure of the vacating mechanism of the FAA has been supplemented *i.a.* by the judicially developed doctrine of *manifest disregard of the law*.[38] The interpretation and the impact of this doctrine will be addressed later in this chapter.[39]

The judicial system of the U.S. is organized nationwide into two prongs: a system of state courts and a system of federal courts. It means that, as long as federal law may be considered superior and may preempt the application of state law in case of a conflict, the state court decisions are independent and generally not subject to review by the federal courts. Instead, the state judiciary provides for its own independent mechanism of appeal to the highest appeal court of the said state.[40] The federal court system, on the other hand and as it is relevant for arbitration, consists of the U.S. District Courts, the U.S. Court of Appeals and the U.S. Supreme Court.

The division of competence on state and federal level in the context of international arbitration, nonetheless, is not clear-cut.[41] The argument advanced by many authors is that "*[i]ndeed, by all outward appearances, it [the FAA] was subject to an important limit: it was a procedural rule that governed federal courts and thus neither applied in state court nor preempted conflicting state law.*"[42] Surprisingly, however, the FAA does not create subject matter jurisdiction for the federal court and, as such, parties that seek to proceed before the federal court are required to assert a separate jurisdictional basis for the federal court.[43] Conversely, in the light of *Southland* and its progenies state courts can (and do) apply the FAA notwithstanding the original intention of the Congress. It is argued that in the context of the vacatur of the arbitral award, the FAA may only be applied by the federal court as Section 10 of the FAA has been considered as a procedural vehicle rather than the substantive law provision.[44] Still, even if it so happens that the state court applies the FAA, it will do so in a fashion that accommodates federal policy favoring arbitration.[45]

---

38 The phrase first appeared in *dictum* of the case *Wilko v. Swan*, 346 U.S. 427, 74 S. Ct. 182 (1953) (*overruled on other grounds by Rodriguez de Quijas v. Shearson/Am. Express, Inc.*, 490 U.S. 477, 109 S. Ct. 1917 (1989)). Currently, the availability of the manifest disregard challenge is, however, uncertain. For further reading, see section 6.1.1.

39 See section 6.2 of this chapter.

40 Farnsworth, *An Introduction to the Legal System of the United States* (2010) pp.44-45.

41 This is especially the case after *Southland*. For more, see section 2.4. See also Bermann, *'Domesticating' the New York Convention: the Impact of the Federal Arbitration Act* (2011) p.329.

42 Horton (2013) p.1226.

43 Burns (2010) p.1819.

44 Conversely to Section 2 of the FAA, which is said to be a substantive law provision.

45 See also section 3.1. Additionally, one should observe that the Restatement, while defining what the "court" entails (for the purposes of the Restatement) concludes that "*The vacatur, confirmation, recognition, and enforcement of international awards are not entrusted exclusively to federal courts. FAA Chapters Two and Three contemplate that vacatur, confirmation, and enforcement of Convention awards may be sought in state or other nonfederal courts, as evident from the removal provisions found in § § 205 and 302 (incorporating § 205 for actions under the Panama Convention). In connection with agreements to arbitrate governed by*

2.4 *The role of the United States Supreme Court in (re)structuring the system of arbitration*

The important point that needs to be highlighted under this section is the process of the "federalization" of arbitration law in the U.S. Reference should be made to the already mentioned *Moses H. Cone Memorial Hospital* and *Southland* cases which are a part of the so-called "second trilogy", *i.e.* a part of three U.S. Supreme Court decisions that are considered to "federalize" arbitration law, by showing domination of federal law over state law and preempting the latter.[46] To use the words of Brunet: "*[...] the Supreme Court has shaped a Federal Arbitration Act ('FAA') that routinely trumps state laws dealing with arbitration and created a situation in which applications of state arbitration law are the exception.*"[47] As explained by one scholar, "*ironically, FAA preemption, though seen as illegitimate, is now well-established.*"[48] Therefore, without going into the details of the ongoing debate regarding the intentions of the Congress in 1925 and the Supreme Court interpretation of the FAA, the superior character of the FAA should be taken as a starting point for the analysis of the "excess of powers" challenge.[49] In consequence, one may argue that, by and large, only grounds for vacatur arising out of the FAA (and not state legislation) are of relevance.[50]

FAA Chapter One, the Supreme Court has stated that FAA § 2 creates 'a substantive rule applicable in state as well as federal courts.' Southland Corp. v. Keating, 465 U.S. 1, 16 (1984). Relatedly, several state courts have regarded agreements to arbitrate that are subject to the New York Convention as requiring enforcement as a matter of treaty obligation. See F.A. Richard & Assocs., Inc. v. Gen. Marine Catering Co., 688 So. 2d 199, 203 (La. Ct. App. 1997) (compelling London arbitration). Thus, Convention awards and non-Convention awards are subject to confirmation, recognition, and enforcement in all courts throughout the United States and its territories." See the Restatement (second tentative draft) p.36.

46 Authors generally refer to *Moses H. Cone Memorial Hospital, Southland* and *Dean Witter Reynolds Inc. v. Byrd*, 470 U.S. 213 (1985). See, *e.g.*, Carbonneau, *Carbonneau on Arbitration: Collected Essays* (2010) p.54, Stipanowich (2011) p.325, Bermann, *United States: Arbitration* (2014) p.493.

47 Brunet (2007) p.326.

48 Horton (2013) p.1228.

49 Although taking into account that the core of the preemption debate refers (mainly) to the validity of an arbitration agreement, thus section 2 of the FAA (sometimes introduced as "front end" issues), it has been also suggested that challenges against arbitral awards as prescribed by Section 10 of the FAA (being part of so-called "back-end" issues) would be also (exclusively) controlled by the FAA. For illustrative purposes, see "The Preemption Continuum" and "Preemption Venn Diagram" in Hayford, *Federal Preemption and Vacatur: The Bookend Issues under the Revised Uniform Arbitration Act* (2001) p.74 and p.77.

50 It would be even more evident if one takes into account Carbonneau's draft proposal for the new federal arbitration law and its "national policy favoring arbitration". For further reading, see section 2.2 of this chapter.

3 Court standard of review of arbitral awards

The vacatur procedure is an extraordinary means of recourse against an arbitral award. By and large, it further entails that it is governed by the rules prescribed by the FAA rather than the general rules of American civil procedure. In this section, the court standard of review of arbitral awards will be analyzed.

In the case where the court finds itself competent to review the arbitral award based upon a challenge of excess of powers, it needs to follow a pro-arbitration stand that usually entails deference to the original arbitral decision (section 3.1) and no review on the merits (section 3.2). Even if the court is satisfied with the objections against the award, it will still aim at (at least) the partial confirmation of the healthy part of the award (section 3.3).

3.1 Pro-arbitration stand in the context of vacatur

The pro-arbitration policy was the underlying reason why the FAA was introduced in the first place. Having in mind the "judicial hostility towards arbitration" at the beginning of the twentieth century,[51] the FAA proved to be one of the first legal instruments worldwide that effectively guaranteed that the arbitral award will be respected in its shape and will be judicially enforced. Consequently, the ultimate goal of the court is to confirm the arbitral decision unless the FAA grounds for vacatur are met; a closer look at Section 9 of the FAA proves that the court *must* confirm the arbitral award unless it is (in exceptional circumstances) vacated, modified or corrected.[52]

The FAA's philosophy favors the enforcement of arbitral award. In the words of *Domke on Commercial Arbitration*, "*when arbitration awards are reviewed by courts under [Section] 10(a) [of the FAA], they are construed liberally rather than technically or exactly, and every reasonable assumption is made in their favor.*"[53] Additionally, Born argues that, "*U.S. courts have consistently interpreted the provision of the FAA concerning vacatur and confirmation of awards in a robustly pro-enforcement fashion.*"[54] This "robust pro-enforcement fashion" entails that courts generally rely on the findings of the arbitral tribunal and refrain from

51 See section 2.1.

52 Section 9 of the FAA reads that "*[...] any party to the arbitration may apply to the court [...] for an order confirming the award, and thereupon the court must grant such an order unless the award is vacated, modified, or corrected as prescribed in sections 10 and 11 of this title.*"

53 Domke et al., *Domke on Commercial Arbitration* (2013) § 39:13. See also *Halliburton Energy Servs., Inc. v. NL Indus.*, 553 F. Supp. 2d 733, 754 (S.D. Tex. 2008) ("*In deciding whether an arbitration panel exceeded its authority as a basis for vacatur under the FAA, the district court resolves all doubts in favor of arbitration*").

54 Born, *International Commercial Arbitration* (2014) p.3181.

the review on the merits employed on ordinary appeal.[55] Therefore, it has been concluded that,

> [s]ince the goal of arbitration is to provide the parties an alternative to a lengthy and costly litigation process, a court reviewing an arbitration award is more deferential to the arbitrator's decision than an appellate court would be in reviewing a decision of a trial court. Thus, a court will not overturn an arbitral award for serious factual or legal errors.[56]

Courts continuously support this line of argumentation. The Supreme Court held that "*[u]nder the FAA, courts may vacate an arbitrator's decision 'only in very unusual circumstances.'*"[57] Accordingly, courts explained that, "*[a] reviewing court examining whether arbitrators exceeded their powers 'must resolve all doubts in favor of arbitration'*"[58] and that "*judicial review of commercial arbitration awards is narrowly limited [...] [the] federal court should defer to [the] arbitrator's decision whenever possible.*"[59] Similarly, it was also held that "*[...] any judicial review of an arbitration award is 'extremely limited,' and is, in fact, 'among the narrowest known to the law'*"[60] and that "*review of the arbitration award itself 'is very deferential'.*"[61]

3.2 *The scope of the court's review*

As hinted to in the previous section, no review of the merits shall be at the disposal of the parties during vacatur.[62] It has been pointed out that "*[t]he scope of judicial review sanctioned by §10(a) of the FAA is extremely narrow*"[63] and the pro-arbitration policy limits the ambit

55 See section 3.2, however.

56 Domke et al., *Domke on Commercial Arbitration* (2013) § 38:1. Similarly Holtzmann et al., (2013) Chapter VII(2)(a) ("*In light of the strong public policy favoring arbitration, courts are highly deferential to arbitrators' decisions*"); *136 A.L.R. Fed. 183 (Originally published in 1997)* ("*The grounds upon which a Federal District Court may vacate an arbitration award are, therefore, much narrower than the grounds upon which an appellate court can overturn a decision of a Federal District Court and the courts have, correspondingly, shown little inclination to vacate arbitration awards on any ground [...]*").

57 *Oxford Health Plans LLC v. Sutter*, 133 S. Ct. 2064, 186 L. Ed. 2d 113 (2013) (hereafter "Oxford Health") (referring to *First Options of Chicago*).

58 *Action Industries, Inc. v. U.S. Fidelity & Guar. Co.*, 358 F.3d 337,343 (5th Cir. 2004).

59 *B.L. Harbert Intern., LLC v. Hercules Steel Co.*, 441 F.3d 905, 909 (11th Cir. 2006).

60 *Long John Silver's Restaurants, Inc. v. Cole*, 514 F.3d 345, 349 (4th Cir. 2008).

61 *PoolRe Ins. Corp. v. Organizational Strategies, Inc.*, 783 F.3d 256, 262 (5th Cir. 2015).

62 See, *e.g.*, *Med. Shoppe Int'l, Inc. v. Turner Investments, Inc.*, 614 F.3d 485 (8th Cir. 2010) ("*Court of Appeals would not review merits of arbitrator's conclusions since franchisees did not allege grounds enumerated in Federal Arbitration Act (FAA).*").

63 Domke et al., *Domke on Commercial Arbitration* (2013) § 39:13.

of review of the award.[64] Further, it is argued that "*[...] the grounds for vacatur of an arbitral award under s[ection] 10 of the FAA are directed to procedural issues and do not allow a substantive review of the arbitrator's decision on the merits.*"[65] Finally, the Restatement reads that "*under no circumstance, should a court take a judicial review as an opportunity to revisit the merits of the underlying dispute.*"[66] It should be mentioned, however, that if a challenge is targeted at the validity or existence of an agreement to arbitrate, a court will give no deference to an arbitral tribunal's decision and will pursue an independent determination on the issue.[67]

Although no reassessment of the merits of the arbitral award can be made,[68] one should know that courts will still exercise a fully independent determination on whether the grounds for vacatur exist. In other words, although the court should refrain from judging whether the tribunal's interpretation of facts or of law is correct, it will examine *de novo* the content of the award in order to establish whether a party's objections (*e.g.* that the tribunal exceeded its powers) are valid; no other conclusions affecting the arbitral decision can be reached by the court at that point. It is reasonable to allow the court to have a second look at the tribunal's findings, but with the clear goal to only check whether a party's challenge is valid.

Occasionally courts were tempted to examine (at least partly) the merits of the award, while considering objections on the non-statutory grounds, *i.e.* on the basis of 'violation of public policy', an arbitral award being 'irrational', in 'manifest disregard of the law' or 'not drawing its essence from the agreement'.[69] Even in these instances, however, it has been reported that "*US courts have consistently held that they cannot be invoked to challenge mere errors of fact or law, but rather should be limited to extreme circumstances, such as where the arbitrator knew of a binding rule of law but consciously chose to disregard it.*"[70] After the Supreme Court decision in *Hall Street*,[71] availability of these grounds became uncertain.[72] In general, it should be concluded that under no circumstances shall the court

64 Domke et al., *Domke on Commercial Arbitration* (2013) § 39:1 ("*Any discussion of judicial review of commercial arbitration awards must take into account the strong federal policy favoring arbitration reflected in the [FAA]. The key to effectuating this policy as reflected in § 10(a) of the FAA, is by limiting judicial review of arbitration awards.*").

65 Rutledge et al. (2009) p.930.

66 The Restatement (second tentative draft) p.105. See also *Med. Shoppe Int'l, Inc. v. Turner Investments, Inc.*, 614 F.3d 485, 488 (8th Cir. 2010) ("*Courts have no authority to reconsider the merits of an arbitration award, even when the parties allege that the award rests on factual errors or on a misinterpretation of the underlying contract.*").

67 For further reading, see section 7.1 of this chapter.

68 Unless parties agreed to have an appeal mechanism included in their arbitration agreement.

69 See also section 6.

70 Rutledge et al. (2009) p.930.

71 *Hall Street Assocs, LLC v. Mattel, Inc.*, 552 U.S. 576, 128 S. Ct. 1396, 170 L. Ed. 2d 254 (2008) (hereafter "Hall Street").

72 For further reading, see section 6.2.

find itself competent to correct errors of law or fact made by arbitrators, thus it shall refrain from reviewing and revising the merits of the case.

3.3 *The remedial powers of the courts*

In principle, the U.S. courts are well-equipped with remedial powers when faced with the arbitral award at the post-award stage. These include (i) the power to correct and modify the award[73] and (ii) the power to remand the award back to the tribunal.[74] What can be readily observed is that there is no power to rescue a healthy part of the award in cases where it can be severed from the part affected by flaw. Nonetheless, one will find that the remedial powers of the courts in the U.S. are to the same (if not greater) effect.

The first power of the courts that will be analyzed is prescribed under Section 11 of the FAA, which allows the court to correct or modify[75] the award "*upon the application of any party to the arbitration*".[76] It can be done in three cases.[77] Particularly relevant in the context of excess of powers is, however, Section 11(b) of the FAA that reads that the modification or correction can be made "*where the arbitrators have awarded upon a matter not submitted to them, unless it is a matter not affecting the merits of the decision upon the matter submitted.*"[78]

Notably, as explained by the Restatement,

> [a]n alternative route to the same result [as in Section 11(b)] is a partial confirmation and partial vacatur of the award. Although the FAA does not by its terms contemplate partial confirmation or vacatur, courts faced with awards that resolve matters not submitted to arbitration sometimes confirm in part and vacate in part, rather than purport to correct the award as such. The Restatement expressly acknowledges a court's power to do so.[79]

Therefore, the Restatement, while acknowledging that the FAA does not include partial confirmation and partial vacatur as a remedial power of the court, proposes that Section 11

73 See Section 11 of the FAA.

74 See Section 10(b) of the FAA.

75 As reported in the Restatement there is no practical distinction between "correction" and "modification" and they are used interchangeably. See the Restatement (third tentative draft) p.74.

76 Section 11 of the FAA.

77 Apart from Section 11(b) of the FAA which is explained, other instances include "*evident material miscalculation*" or "*evident material mistake in the description of any person, thing, or property*" in the award (see Section 11(a) of the FAA) and imperfections "*in matter of form not affecting the merits of the controversy*" (see Section 11(c) of the FAA).

78 Section 11(b) of the FAA.

79 The Restatement (third tentative draft) p.75.

of the FAA fulfills the same function (as a partial vacatur).[80] More importantly, however, the Restatement is adamant that the vacating court may make use of its Section 11 powers *ex officio* (or *sua sponte* as considered by the Restatement).[81] This is, arguably, in contrast with the wording of Section 11 itself, where "the application of any party to the arbitration" is required.[82] Considering the deference that is given to the tribunal's findings, however, parties are well advised to initiate the Section 11 mechanism themselves.

The second power of the court is prescribed in Section 10(b) of the FAA. It reads that "*[i]f an award is vacated and the time within which the agreement required the award to be made has not expired, the court may, in its discretion, direct a rehearing by the arbitrators.*" This provision allows the court to use the power to remand the award back to the tribunal. As one may see, according to the text of Section 10(b) the remand is possible once the award is vacated. Nonetheless, the Restatement concludes that the remand is an important tool to salvage the award *before* it is vacated. As pointed out "*[c]ourts in the United States [...] have followed the practice [of remanding] as an alternative to vacatur in limited settings, such as when the award's language leaves the court uncertain of the award's import.*"[83] Importantly, "*[r]emand is usually surgically framed. Thus, one court remanded when only a portion of the remedy given exceeded the tribunal's mandate, but the tribunal's help was required to identify exactly the portion to be confirmed.*"[84] Finally, the Restatement reports that similar to the case of the Section 11 mechanism, a court can remand the award on its

80 See the Restatement (third tentative draft) p.78 ("*A court's power to correct and modify coexists with its power to vacate or deny confirmation under [the New York Convention grounds]. FAA § 10 (enumerated vacatur grounds) and § 11 (grounds for correction and modification) are part of the same post-relief architecture and were crafted together. Although the Restatement contemplates partial vacatur [...], FAA § 10 does not. Rather, FAA § 11 seems to have been intended to perform that function.*"). See also the Restatement (third tentative draft) p.75 ("*[w]hile a court may, in keeping with the FAA vocabulary, describe its narrowing of the award's scope as a 'correction' or 'modification,' the relief granted is in effect partial vacatur [...].*").

81 See the Restatement (third tentative draft) p.77 ("*In the context of a proceeding to vacate or confirm a U.S. Convention award, a court may elect sua sponte to correct or modify an award. A court may do so whether or not a party preserved its rights to seek such relief and whether or not such relief was first sought before the arbitral tribunal. The parties may not by agreement preclude correction or modification by a court.*"). Also the Restatement (third tentative draft) p.79 ("*Sound policy favors that courts retain considerable flexibility in selecting the appropriate form of relief following issuance of an award, consistent with the relief actually requested. In the context of a post-award action to vacate or confirm a U.S. Convention award, little would be gained by precluding a court from correcting or modifying an award of its own initiative 'so as to effect the intent thereof and promote justice between the parties.' See FAA § 11(c). For similar reasons, courts may reform an award whether or not a party first sought such relief from the arbitral tribunal and notwithstanding an agreement purporting to limit a tribunal's options to vacatur or confirmation in the event of defects. In practice, such agreements are not often encountered.*").

82 See Section 11 of the FAA.

83 The Restatement (third tentative draft) p.82.

84 The Restatement (third tentative draft) p.83, with a reference to *Clarendon Nat'l Ins. Co. v. TIG Reinsurance Co.*, 990 F. Supp. 304 (S.D.N.Y. 1998).

own motion (when faced with the award at the post-award stage).[85] In the end, one should note, that the remedial powers available to the U.S. courts are unique on their face. In any event, they allow the courts to approach the award with the pro-enforcement fashion at the post award stage. As concluded by the Restatement: "*[s]ound policy favors that courts retain considerable flexibility in selecting the appropriate form of relief following issuance of an award, consistent with the relief actually requested.*"[86]

4 Limits to the arbitral tribunal's powers

To proceed with the further analysis on the "excess of powers" ground for challenge, one should start with establishing the framework upon which the arbitral tribunal's powers are based. It remains undisputed that in determining the limits to the scope of the powers of the arbitral tribunal one should identify the parties' consent. In a nutshell, it means that it is the agreement between the parties that shapes an arbitral tribunal's powers (see section 4.1). Nonetheless, in establishing the limits, one might also need to confer with the parties' subsequent submissions (see section 4.2) and the statutory rules of a public policy character (see section 4.3).

4.1 Agreement to arbitrate

In the commercial context, a valid agreement to arbitrate is all it takes to require the parties to make their disputes subject to the arbitral tribunal's (rather than a court's) final determination. Pursuant to Section 2 of the FAA:

> [a] written provision in any maritime transaction or a contract evidencing a transaction involving commerce to settle by arbitration a controversy hereafter arising out of such contract or transaction, or the refusal to perform the whole or any part thereof, or an agreement in writing to submit to arbitration an existing controversy arising out of such a contract, transaction, or refusal, shall

---

85 See the Restatement (third tentative draft) p.82 ("*In the context of a proceeding to vacate or confirm a U.S. Convention award, a court may elect sua sponte to remand an award to the arbitrators. To allow courts to remand to the arbitrators adds flexibility, and often efficiency, to the administration of justice. Entrusting the arbitrators to refine the award in appropriate instances also comports with the parties' choice of arbitration to resolve their dispute. It follows that the parties should not be empowered by agreement to restrict a court's access to the remand option. Equally, a court retains the prerogative to remand an award even if neither party has first sought post-award relief from the arbitral tribunal or otherwise preserved its right to seek remand to the arbitrators.*").

86 The Restatement (third tentative draft) p.79.

> be valid, irrevocable, and enforceable, save upon such grounds as exist at law or in equity for the revocation of any contract.

What is important for the study at hand is that the FAA, similar to other modern arbitration statutes, recognizes as valid agreements both arbitration clauses (being agreements to arbitrate before any dispute or "controversy" arises) and submission agreements[87] (*i.e.* the agreements to arbitrate already existing disputes).[88] In consequence, both types of agreements are able to frame what the tribunal is entitled to do and if the tribunal trespasses these limits, it may face a successful challenge against its decision on the basis of the excess of powers defense;[89] both scholars and judges seem to support this conclusion.[90]

Since an agreement to arbitrate limits the arbitral tribunal's powers, parties shall draft it cautiously.[91] An agreement should express the clear and unmistakable intention of the parties in what they entrust the tribunal to do.[92] Particularly in cases where the parties wish to narrow the scope of what the tribunal can or should do, the intent should be articulated unambiguously.[93] As some authorities suggest, it is the case because the courts

---

87 The term submission agreements is used by some authorities (see, *e.g.*, Rutledge et al. (2009) pp.882-890); others, however, are simply referring to them as "submissions" (see, *e.g.*, Domke et al., *Domke on Commercial Arbitration* (2013) § 8:4). In order to distinguish submission agreements from submissions (thus parties' motions and filings), "submission agreement" will be the term used for the reference to the agreement to arbitrate already existing dispute(s).

88 Other issues regarding the formal and substantive validity of agreements to arbitrate fall outside the scope of this research. For further reading, see, *e.g.*, Domke et al., *Domke on Commercial Arbitration* (2013) part III in general.

89 Notably, since the FAA does not include a separate "excess of jurisdiction" recourse, the concept "excess of powers" entails excess of jurisdictional powers as well as other powers given to the tribunal. See, *i.a.*, section 7.1. See also the Restatement's take on the "excess of powers" ground, section 5.3.

90 See, *e.g.*, Born, *International Commercial Arbitration* (2014) pp.3287-3288, Domke et al., *Domke on Commercial Arbitration* (2013) § 39:6, also *Kimm v. Blisset, LLC*, 388 N.J. Super. 14, 25, 905 A.2d 887, 894 (App. Div. 2006) ("*[...] the arbitrator's powers are limited by the agreement of the parties and an arbitrator may not exceed the scope of the powers granted to him or her by the parties.*").

91 For example it is suggested in Domke et al., *Domke on Commercial Arbitration* (2015) § 8:4 that "*a submission to arbitrate [i.e. submission agreement] must embrace everything necessary to give the arbitrators jurisdiction over the parties and the matter in dispute although it will be presumed that the parties intended to grant to the arbitrators such powers as are reasonably necessary to settle the dispute fully.*".

92 See, *e.g.*, *Seagate Tech., LLC v. W. Digital Corp.*, 854 N.W.2d 750, 765 (Minn. 2014) ("*In addition, we reiterate that the scope of [the] arbitrator['s] authority is a matter of contract [...] and parties are always free to fashion arbitration agreements in ways that limit the arbitrator's power to award certain types of relief.*").

93 One should know that the interpretation of the clauses may differ between circuits. See Domke et al., *Domke on Commercial Arbitration* (2015) § 8:14 ("*The Ninth and Second Circuits have held that a clause that covers disputes "arising out of" or 'arising under,' but omits reference to claims 'relating to' an agreement, covers only those disputes relating to the interpretation and performance of the contract itself. Thus, a misappropriation of trade secrets claim does not relate to the interpretation or performance of the contract; it is an independent wrong from any breach of the licensing and nondisclosure agreements and is therefore nonarbitrable. By contrast, the Eleventh and Seventh Circuits have rejected this approach and have held that the terms 'arising out of,' 'arising under,' and 'arising hereunder' are sufficiently broad to encompass all claims that are germane to the subject matter of the contract, and not merely those that sound in contract.*").

may even be willing to expand the scope of the initial intent of the parties after the decision of the Supreme Court in *Mastrobuono v. Sherman Lehman Hutton Inc.*[94] and the general pro-arbitration and pro-enforcement trend in case law.[95] The only way to avoid the risk of scope-broadening by courts is a precise drafting of the agreement to arbitrate.[96]

Precision is also required with respect to the question of the tribunal's competence to determine its own competence.[97] It has been suggested that "*parties would be well advised to indicate whether threshold jurisdictional questions should be referred initially to the arbitral tribunal or United States courts.*"[98] After *First Options of Chicago v. Kaplan*[99] it would be presumed that it is a court that decides on the underlying question of whether the parties agreed to arbitrate at all. Therefore, if the parties fail to *clearly and unmistakably* designate the power to the arbitral tribunal to establish its own jurisdiction, arguably the tribunal will not be capable (will not have power) to decide this issue.[100] One should note, however, that *generally* the incorporation of arbitral rules that provide for the tribunal's competence-competence will suffice to express the clear and unmistakable intention of the parties to grant the tribunal the power to resolve the issue of its own competence.[101] The issue, however, is a bit more complex when the validity or existence of the arbitration agreement is at stake.[102]

Finally, it should also be stated that arbitral rules, as one of the components of the agreement to arbitrate, may also (indirectly) constitute the framework for the arbitral tribunal's powers and obligations (other than the power to decide on its own competence). If the parties do not include any specific deviation from the rules in their agreement to arbitrate, then the tribunal itself will be safe to make use of any power prescribed by the

94 *Mastrobuono v. Sherman Lehman Hutton Inc.*, 514 U.S. 52, 115 S. Ct. 1212 (1995) (also referred to as "Mastrobuono").

95 Rutledge et al. (2009) p.886 ("*Thus, in an attempt to broaden the power of arbitrators, the Mastrobuono court essentially revised the nature of the proceeding the parties initially agreed upon. In light thereof, it may be that US courts are willing to prioritize the power and utility of arbitration proceedings over and above the nature of the agreement itself.*"). See also section 3.1.

96 Rutledge et al. (2009) p.886 ("*parties may hedge this risk of scope-broadening by clearly and precisely defining the scope of their arbitration clause*").

97 Especially considering the question whether it is an exclusive competence given to the tribunal. It will be particularly relevant in the context of the competence regarding the issues relating to the scope, the validity and the existence of the agreement to arbitrate. For further reading, see section 7.1.1 and section 7.1.2.

98 Rutledge et al. (2009) p.883.

99 *First Options of Chicago, Inc. v. Kaplan*, 514 U.S. 938, 115 S. Ct. 1920, 131 L. Ed. 2d 985 (1995).

100 See also section 7.1.

101 Rutledge et al. (2009) p.892; for examples of the competence-competence provisions see, *i.a.*, Art. 18 of the 2016 JAMS Rules, Art. 19 of the 2014 ICDR Rules, R-7 of the 2013 AAA Rules.

102 See section 7.1 and, *i.a.*, Bermann, *The "Gateway" Problem in International Commercial Arbitration* (2012), Born, *International Commercial Arbitration* (2014) pp.1125-1208 (discussing the division of competence between courts and tribunals regarding jurisdictional threshold issues in the U.S.).

arbitral rules.[103] In cases where the rules allow the tribunal to do so, it will also be empowered to interpret the rules.[104]

4.2 *Parties' (subsequent) submissions*

The FAA offers no guidance as to whether the parties' submissions should be taken into account when determining whether the tribunal exceeds its powers. Section 10(a)(4) of the FAA is silent on the point of the excess of powers and only makes some reference to the "subject matter submitted" in connection with the "imperfect execution of the tribunal's powers".[105] Nonetheless, when seeking the limits to the tribunal's powers, one should *not* disregard the parties' subsequent submissions.

The importance of the parties' submissions in determining the scope of the arbitral tribunal's powers entails that any party's filing should be taken into account. It further means that every parties' motion, starting from the initial one (usually called "Request for Arbitration",[106] "Notice of Arbitration"[107] or "Demand for Arbitration"[108]) to the last one should be taken into consideration as long as it (the filing) includes any reference to claims or demands of the parties.[109] According to some scholars, "*[t]he parameters of the exceeded powers inquiry are defined by the submission of issues to the arbitrator and by the arbitrator's authority as set forth in the arbitration agreement.*"[110] Additionally, it is argued that "*[a] tribunal exceeds its authority by ruling on an issue not presented by the parties in the arbitration even if the issue or dispute that it addresses is within the scope of the parties' arbitration agreement.*"[111] It has been similarly viewed by the courts which held that the tribunal will exceed its powers if it decides on issues not presented to it. In one case a district court held that "*[...] relief [granted by the tribunal] exceeded the arbitrators' powers because it was not sought by either party, and was completely irrational because it wrote*

---

103 For example, to grant provisional measures, to award interest or costs. See also section 7.5.

104 See *Ecopetrol S.A. v. Offshore Exploration & Prod. LLC*, 46 F. Supp. 3d 327, 344 (S.D.N.Y. 2014) ("*Accordingly, the arbitral panel was vested with the authority to interpret and apply the rules governing the parties' arbitration.*").

105 The notion of the "imperfect execution of powers" will be further discussed in section 5.2.

106 In accordance with, *i.a.*, Art. 4 of the (draft) 2021 ICC Rules, Art. 4 of the 2017 ICC Rules.

107 See, *e.g.*, Art. 2 of the 2014 ICDR Rules.

108 Pursuant to *i.a.* R-4(a) of the AAA Rules.

109 Especially taking into account that parties may wish to modify or expand their submissions. See Oehmke & Brovins (2014) § 146:3 ("*Parties may expand the scope of arbitrable issues explicitly by stipulation, implicitly if both parties present evidence on an issue and seek a ruling, or when one party submits new issues to the arbitrator and the other party fails to object.*").

110 Domke et al., *Domke on Commercial Arbitration* (2015) § 39:6.

111 Born, *International Commercial Arbitration* (2014) pp.3291-3292. See also Domke et al., *Domke on Commercial Arbitration* (2015) § 39:6.

material terms of the contract out of existence."[112] In another case it has been held that "*[a]rbitrators have the authority to decide only those issues actually submitted by the parties.*"[113]

One may, thus, conclude that when testing the arbitral tribunal's powers, one should not be satisfied with only the framework of the arbitration agreement; instead, one should seek further guidance in the parties' submissions of claims and mandatory rules of a public policy character.[114]

4.3 *Mandatory rules of public policy character*

As hinted in the previous section, public policy may also condition the scope of the arbitral tribunals' powers. Public policy is usually considered a non-statutory addition to the statutory excess of powers test provided in Section 10 of the FAA.[115] Since the parties' contract does not exist in a legal void, the tribunal may be required to consider the mandatory rules of public policy character in the matrix of its award. It further entails that (i) on the one hand, the tribunal might have a(n) (implied) power to decide upon the claims that escape the scope of the initial agreement to arbitrate (*e.g.* statutory claims)[116] and (ii) on the other hand, it can be argued that the existence of mandatory rules of a public policy character imposes a duty on the arbitrators to apply and enforce these rules even if they have not been raised by the parties (for example the application of patent law or antitrust law).[117]

Although there is no *statutory* basis to annul the award on the basis of violation of public policy,[118] it is well settled that such a judicially created ground for vacatur exists.[119] Therefore, the consequences of noncompliance with the mandatory rules of a public policy character is substantial, because the court may vacate the award if it is convinced that public policy was violated.[120]

112 *PMA Capital Ins. Co. v. Platinum Underwriters Bermuda, Ltd.*, 400 F. App'x 654, 656 (3d Cir. 2010).

113 *AGCO Corp. v. Anglin*, 216 F.3d 589, 593 (7th Cir. 2000).

114 See section 4.3.

115 See also section 6.1.2 and section 6.2. See, however, section 5.3 and the Restatement's interpretation of the "excess of powers" ground.

116 Either by rejecting them as nonarbitrable or accepting them even if they have been originally contracted out or have not been expressly agreed upon by the parties. It is argued that mandatory rules of public policy character are so basic and essential that they have to be taken into the decision-making process.

117 The application of the mandatory rules by the arbitral tribunal will be further discussed in section 6.2.4.

118 See, however, the Restatement's interpretation of the "excess of powers" ground. See section 5.3.

119 Rutledge et al. (2009) p.932. See also section 6.1.2.

120 It can be argued that the public policy test – as a non-statutory ground for vacatur – did not survive the Supreme Court's ruling in *Hall Street*; notwithstanding it is only possible to conclude that the possibility to invoke public policy is a fundamental component of arbitration law and works as a safety valve for the

It should be highlighted, however, that challenge on the basis of public policy is exceptionally narrow and needs to satisfy the following test:

> (1) the decision must violate some explicit public policy that is well-defined and dominant, and this dominant policy is to be ascertained by reference to laws and legal precedents rather than general considerations of supposed public interest and (2) the conflict between the public policy and the arbitration award must be explicit and clearly shown.[121]

In other words, only the most severe violations of public policy would satisfy the vacating courts, thus: "*public policy can generally be invoked only where recognition of a decision would 'undermine the public interest, the public confidence in the administration of the law or security for individual rights' or be 'repugnant to fundamental notions of what is decent and just in the State where enforcement is sought.'*"[122] The mandatory rules of a public policy character should be taken into account when determining the scope of the arbitral tribunal's powers.[123] If the parties' claims clearly and unequivocally infringe public policy and the tribunal awards these claims (irrespectively of whether consciously or carelessly), it will act beyond its powers prescribed by law, even if no contractual limits have been trespassed.[124]

5 The United States standards for excess of arbitral tribunal's powers

The tribunal's going beyond the powers that have been given it by the parties is one of the reasons why the arbitral award can be challenged. The FAA envisages two separate concepts that relate to the notion of the tribunal's powers: the excess of powers (section 5.1) and the imperfect execution of these powers (section 5.2). In addition, a brief reflection on the Restatement's views on the post-award relief needs to be given (section 5.3).

---

arbitral tribunal's grievous wrongdoings. Consequently, public policy cannot be removed from the legal framework. See also section 6.1.2 and Marcantel (2009), the Restatement (second tentative draft) p.291.

121 Domke et al., *Domke on Commercial Arbitration* (2013) § 38:24, also Born, *International Commercial Arbitration* (2014) p.3314 and the Restatement (second tentative draft) p.291.

122 Born, *International Commercial Arbitration* (2014) p.3314.

123 The Restatement (second tentative draft) p.291.

124 If one wishes to follow the division between "substantive" and "procedural" public policy, arguably both limit the scope of the tribunal's powers.

5.1 *The concept of the "excess of powers"*

The concept of the "excess of powers" is an important element of the structure of the FAA since it appears, at least according to some authorities, to be the most frequently used (statutory) ground when an award-debtor wishes to challenge an arbitral award before a national court.[125] The FAA does not, however, give any definition of what constitutes the arbitral tribunal's powers and "*as such, the statutory phrase, 'exceeding their powers', is an empty vessel into which content must be poured by judicial determinations of what are the powers of the arbitrators.*"[126] When answering this inquiry, courts rely on the three pillars mentioned in the previous sections, namely (i) the agreement to arbitrate, (ii) the parties' submissions, and (iii) the mandatory rules of a public policy character.[127] Importantly, one should also review the alternative reading of the post-award architecture[128] and the "excess of powers" provision made by the Restatement.

Firstly, the starting point for the analysis of a court faced with the vacatur challenge is rather straightforward: the underpinning of arbitration is the parties' consent; consequently, if any restrictions to the (usually broad) arbitral tribunal's powers exist, they will stem from limits expressed by the parties in their agreement.[129] Therefore, it has been suggested that "*[t]he measure as to whether the arbitrator did or did not exceed the powers contractually granted is to compare the arbitration agreement (and related documents) against the award.*"[130] Courts seem to follow this method. It has been held for example that "*[b]ecause [the arbitrator] acted contrary to the express arbitrator- and forum-selection clauses in the arbitration agreements to which PoolRe was a party, we affirm the district court's holding that [the arbitrator] exceeded his authority under [the FAA].*"[131] Another court explained that "*[w]here the arbitrator goes beyond that self-limiting agreement between consenting*

125 See fn.6 above.

126 The Restatement (second tentative draft) p.287.

127 See, *e.g.*, *Liebman v. Better Way Wholesale Autos, Inc.*, No. 3:15CV1263 (JBA), 2017 WL 1088078, at *3 (D. Conn. Mar. 21, 2017) ("*For the Arbitrator to have exceeded his authority he must have either (1) considered issues outside those submitted to him by the parties for consideration, or (2) reached issues prohibited by law or the parties' agreement.*") For further reading, see sections 4.1-4.3.

128 See section 5.3.

129 See also section 4.1 and also Oehmke & Brovins (2014) § 146:1 ("*The paramount point to be remembered is that the power and authority of an arbitrator derives totally from the parties contract; this prohibits the arbitrator from substituting a unique brand of industrial or commercial justice for what has been contractually agreed to by the parties. An arbitrator is empowered to decide all issues of fact and law that are submitted and to fairly remedy the problem, unless contractually proscribed by the arbitration contract*").

130 See Oehmke & Brovins (2014) § 146:1.

131 *PoolRe Ins. Corp. v. Organizational Strategies, Inc.*, 783 F.3d 256, 265 (5th Cir. 2015). See also *Ancor Holdings, LLC v. Peterson, Goldman & Villani, Inc.*, 294 S.W.3d 818, 829 (Tex. App. 2009), *Morgan Stanley & Co., LLC v. Core Fund*, 884 F. Supp. 2d 1229, 1231 (M.D. Fla. 2012), *Murtagh v. Emory Univ.*, 321 Ga. App. 411, 414, 741 S.E.2d 212, 215 (2013), reconsideration denied (Apr. 11, 2013) ("*Under the FAA, an arbitrator of a contract dispute issues an unauthorized award or exceeds his powers to resolve the dispute only when the arbitrator's award contradicts the express language of the parties' agreement.*").

parties, it acts inherently without power, and an award ordered under such circumstances must be vacated."[132]

Importantly, however, it should be noted that, according to some authorities, the contractually defined powers of the arbitrators do not refer only to the adjudicatory function of the tribunal,[133] but also to the tribunal's "managerial" role.[134]

The Restatement suggests that

> [i]f the parties do not agree to arbitrate a dispute or a particular claim in the dispute, then the tribunal does not have the power to adjudicate that dispute or claim. Similarly, if the parties agree to certain procedures and the tribunal materially deviates from those procedures, the tribunal exceeds its powers.[135]

Additionally Carbonneau observes that

> [u]nder traditional principles of law, excess of arbitral authority refers to circumstances in which the arbitrators ruled on matters not submitted thereby exerting excessive authority. [...] From a less traditional angle, excess of arbitral authority can – in theory – cover a multitude of 'sins' – from overbearing procedural decisions and the prejudicial treatment of a party to the exclusion of evidence and testimony to manifest disregard of the law. Possible infractions are copious and frequently overlap.[136]

The "traditional angle" better serves the purpose of the interpretation of the "excess of powers" ground.

Arguably, Section 10(a)(4) of the FAA should be interpreted as covering only "adjudicatory powers" (and not the "managerial" ones) of the arbitral tribunal. It is so, because this provision refers to powers both (i) in case of the excess and (ii) imperfect execution of powers. If one agrees that "powers" in both legs of this proviso refer to the same concept, one needs to conclude that by "imperfect" execution of powers also has to

132 *Porzig v. Dresdner, Kleinwort, Benson, N. Am. LLC*, 497 F.3d 133, 140 (2d Cir. 2007). See also *Ray v. Chafetz*, No. CV 16-428 (CKK), 2017 WL 663527 (D.D.C. Feb. 17, 2017) ("*To succeed on claim that an arbitrator exceeded his powers under the Federal Arbitration Act (FAA), as basis for vacatur of [the] arbitration award, a party must demonstrate that the arbitrator strayed from interpretation and application of the agreement and effectively dispensed his own brand of industrial justice*"), *Axia Netmedia Corp. v. Massachusetts Tech. Park Corp.*, 973 F.3d 133 (1st Cir. 2020).

133 It refers to the power to decide upon matters submitted by the parties.

134 That is the role of conducting and managing the arbitral process.

135 The Restatement (second tentative draft) p.284. See also Chapter II and Chapter VI.

136 Carducci, *The Arbitration Reform in France: Domestic and International Arbitration Law* (2012) pp.517-518.

be meant to embody the adjudicative function of the tribunal, simply because (arguably), no imperfect execution of the "managerial" powers of the tribunal will have a bearing on the rendition of the "mutual, final and definite" award. Consequently, it is only reasonable to conclude that Section 10(a)(4) of the FAA refers to the power of the tribunal to finally resolve the dispute and bind parties by that decision.

It is acknowledged, however, that lack of appropriate recourse against the procedure chosen by the tribunal lures parties to expand the understanding of Section 10(a)(4) of the FAA. Also the Restatement prefers to include (material) incompliance with the agreed procedure within the scope of Section 10(a)(4) of the FAA. It would be, arguably, much easier had this provision referred only to the "excess of powers" without a complementing concept of imperfect execution of powers. In any event, the better view would be to interpret Section 10(a)(4) of the FAA as designed to cover only (or at least mainly) the adjudicative power of the tribunal. This is, however, not the prevailing view.[137]

Secondly, parties' submissions also serve a purpose in delineating the tribunal's powers.[138] It has been confirmed by courts on several occasions. In one case the court concluded that "*[o]ur inquiry under Section 10(a)(4) [of the FAA] is whether the arbitrator had the authority, based on the arbitration clause and the parties' submissions, to reach a certain issue, not whether the arbitrator correctly decided the issue.*"[139] Another court stated that "*Section 10(a)(4) of the FAA empowers a court to vacate an arbitration award if the arbitrators "exceeded their powers," but the provision applies narrowly and only if the arbitrators decide an issue not submitted by the parties or grant relief not authorized in the arbitration agreement.*"[140]

Thirdly, the importance of the public policy rules should not be passed unnoticed.[141] It has been underlined by the Restatement that "*[a]lthough FAA §10 does not expressly list public policy as a ground for vacating an arbitral award, such a ground is a necessary part of a national arbitration.*"[142] What is more, "*an award whose recognition or enforcement would violate public policy is by definition an award in excess of an arbitral tribunal's powers.*"[143]

Fourthly, it is necessary to highlight that, under the Restatement interpretation of the FAA, the "excess of powers" ground would be available against "non-convention awards".[144]

137 See also further under this section and section 7.5.3.

138 See also section 4.2.

139 *Ancor Holdings, LLC v. Peterson, Goldman & Villani, Inc.*, 294 S.W.3d 818, 829 (Tex. App. 2009). See also *Axia Netmedia Corp. v. Massachusetts Tech. Park Corp.*, 973 F.3d 133 (1st Cir. 2020).

140 *Morgan Stanley & Co., LLC v. Core Fund*, 884 F. Supp. 2d 1229, 1231 (M.D. Fla. 2012).

141 See section 4.3 and Domke et al., *Domke on Commercial Arbitration* (2013) § 39:6.

142 The Restatement (second tentative draft) p.291.

143 The Restatement (second tentative draft) p.286.

144 It means that international awards that are rendered by the tribunals seated in the U.S. would be generally subject to post-award relief based on the New York Convention (or Panama Convention) grounds unless

As such, according to the Restatement, the capacity of the "excess of powers" is large enough to fit the whole range of concepts that are used under the New York Convention regime.[145] These include (i) the invalidity of the agreement to arbitrate,[146] (ii) the "excess of mandate" type of challenge,[147] (iii) the procedure was not in accordance with the parties' agreement,[148] (iv) the subject matter is not arbitrable,[149] and (v) an award violates public policy.[150] Such a broad interpretation brings some difficulties, however.

For example, as mentioned above, entertaining the non-compliance with parties' procedural agreements might not easily fit under Section 10(a)(4) of the FAA, if one acknowledges that it includes two concepts (excess of powers and imperfect execution of powers) and not only the "excess of powers". Similarly, including the concept of inarbitrability and public policy within the meaning of the "excess of powers" ground makes it sometimes available only upon the application of the party and sometimes available for the court on an *ex officio* basis. It creates a potential risk of developing two standards of application of the same provision. By filling Section 10(a)(4) of the FAA with so many different concepts, the Restatement shows how capacious it is.

In any event, all authorities seem to agree that the underlying, pro-enforcement philosophy behind the FAA,[151] will permit the vacatur only in exceptional cases. Therefore, it is necessary to highlight that under no circumstances should the court find itself competent to engage in the contract interpretation when evidence (even remote) exists that the tribunal's findings stem from the contract and the parties' agreement. For example, in *BG Group v. Argentina*, the Supreme Court held that "*arbitrators' decision, in concluding that [the] foreign investor in [an] Argentinian entity was excused from having to comply with local court litigation requirement, did not stray from interpretation and application of arbitration provisions in treaty, and could not be disturbed by court.*"[152]

Similarly, in *Oxford Health*, the Supreme Court concluded that

> [n]othing we say in this opinion should be taken to reflect any agreement with the arbitrator's contract interpretation, or any quarrel with Oxford's contrary reading. All we say is that convincing a court of an arbitrator's error – even his

the award is not susceptible of being enforced under these Conventions. The reason for such an interpretation is to align the U.S. vacatur system with the internationally recognized concepts of the New York Convention. See further section 5.3.

145 For further reading, see the Restatement (second tentative draft) pp.283-297.

146 See Art. V(1)(a) of the NYC.

147 See Art. V(1)(c) of the NYC.

148 See Art. V(1)(d) of the NYC. The Restatement qualifies this ground as "*the arbitral procedure is contrary in a material respect to the agreement of the parties*". See the Restatement (second tentative draft) p.283.

149 See Art. V(2)(a) of the NYC.

150 See Art. V(2)(b) of the NYC.

151 See section 3.1.

152 *BG Grp., PLC v. Republic of Argentina*, 134 S. Ct. 1198, 188 L. Ed. 2d 220 (2014).

> grave error – is not enough. So long as the arbitrator was "arguably construing" the contract – which this one was – a court may not correct his mistakes under §10(a)(4). […] The arbitrator's construction holds, however good, bad, or ugly.[153]

Therefore, the interpretation of the parties' contract is the responsibility of the arbitrators and

> [...] a court may not rely on a finding that [the arbitrator] misapprehended the parties' intent, because § 10(a)(4) [of the FAA] bars that course, and permits courts to vacate an arbitral decision only when the arbitrator strayed from his delegated task of interpreting a contract, not when he performed the task poorly.[154]

Consequently, deference to the arbitrators' decision proves to be imposed on a high level.[155]

5.2 *The notion of "imperfect execution of powers upon the subject matter submitted"*

The FAA in Section 10(a)(4) offers, as a ground complimentary to the excess of powers challenge, the concept that an arbitral award can be vacated in case of the imperfect execution of the arbitral tribunal's powers.[156] Pursuant to the second part of Section 10(a)(4) of the FAA the award may be vacated if the arbitrators "*so imperfectly executed them [i.e. powers] that a mutual, final, and definite award upon the subject matter submitted was not made.*" By and large, it should be pointed out that (i) the imperfect execution of the tribunal's powers is impeccably linked to the formation of the arbitral award and its finality; (ii) courts faced with the challenge discussed here would be rather likely to remand the award back to arbitrators instead of vacating it; and finally, (iii) even if the court would be satisfied that the powers were so imperfectly executed that the decision upon the subject

153 *Oxford Health Plans LLC v. Sutter*, 133 S. Ct. 2064, 2070-71, 186 L. Ed. 2d 113 (2013); also, *i.a.*, *Johnson v. Directory Assistants Inc.*, 797 F.3d 1294, 1301-02 (11th Cir. 2015), *BNSF R. Co. v. Alstom Transp., Inc.*, 777 F.3d 785, 788 (5th Cir. 2015). For further reading, see section 7.

154 *Wolf v. Sprenger + Lang, PLLC*, 86 A.3d 1121, 1134 (D.C. 2013), as amended (Jan. 30, 2014).

155 For further reading, see, *i.a.*, section 3.1 and Domke et al., *Domke on Commercial Arbitration* (2015) § 38:14.

156 As noted previously (see fn.29), it is worth mentioning that the notion of imperfect execution of powers is not included neither in the UAA nor the RUAA. Some states, however, expanded the model solution and brought "imperfect execution" back to the text of their state arbitration laws (see, *e.g.*, *Delaware Arbitration Act, 10 Del. C. 1953, § 5714(a)(3)*).

matter submitted has not been made, it would not hesitate to enforce the healthy part of the award.

Pursuant to the second part of Section 10(a)(4) of the FAA, the tribunal's powers are executed imperfectly if the dispute submitted has not been resolved by the tribunal in its award. As highlighted above, it is necessary to establish that a certain issue in dispute has been submitted before arbitrators *and* that the tribunal failed to address it. Notably, however, it is required that the arbitral award that is being tested be *mutual, final* and *definite*.

In words of one authority, for the award to be considered as *mutual* and *final* it

> must fully resolve a single issue, or all issues as to a given party, that were submitted for arbitration [...] Arbitrators must resolve all issues submitted to arbitration, and determine each issue fully so that no further litigation is necessary to finalize [the] obligation of parties under the award. An award is not final if it merely 'kicks the can' to the court to determine an issue that the arbitrators should have resolved.[157]

The award is *definite* when it is unambiguous and ready for confirmation and enforcement.[158] One can add that, due to an overriding pro-arbitration policy,[159] even partial or interim arbitral awards can be considered mutual and final if they definitely dispose of some independent claims.[160] In other words, interim orders or partial awards

---

157 Oehmke & Brovins (2014) § 147:2, See Domke et al., *Domke on Commercial Arbitration* (2015) § 39:6. See also *PNGI Charles Town Gaming, L.L.C. v. Mawing*, 603 F. App'x 137, 139 (4th Cir. 2015), where the court observed that the award that the award can only be vacated as a not final and definite award "*when the arbitrator either failed to resolve an issue presented to him or issued an award that was so unclear and ambiguous that a reviewing court could not engage in meaningful review of the award.*" For further reading on parties' submissions, see section 4.2 of this chapter. See also section 3.3 for the information on the court's broad remedial powers. In principle, in cases where the award is unclear and ambiguous it will be remanded back to the tribunal. See, as well, the Restatement (third tentative draft) p.82.

158 See fn.157.

159 See section 3.1.

160 Oehmke & Brovins (2014) § 147:4, section 4.2. See also, *i.a.*, *Compania Chilena De Navegacion Interoceanica, S.A. v. Norton, Lilly & Co.*, 652 F. Supp. 1512, 1515 (S.D.N.Y. 1987) ("*Contrary to defendant's argument, "an 'interim' award that finally and definitively disposes of a separate, independent claim may be confirmed notwithstanding the absence of an award that finally disposes of all the claims that were submitted to arbitration. The $48,010 award in the instant case, based solely on defendant's accounting, is separate from plaintiff's other claims, which will require the consideration of more extensive evidentiary sources. The arbitration panel explicitly indicated the separate nature of the $48,010 award by describing it as a Partial Final Award.*"), *Crawford Grp., Inc. v. Holekamp*, No. 406-CV-1274 CAS, 2007 WL 844819, at *5 (E.D. Mo. Mar. 19, 2007) ("*[...] in determining whether an award is final, a court must consider the language of the award and the intention of the arbitrators. As noted above, the Court finds that the language of both the interim award and the final award indicate that the interim award reached a final determination on the merits with respect to the most significant issues. Thus the Court finds that the arbitrators intended the interim award to be final as to the substantive issues in this matter.*"), *Ecopetrol S.A. v. Offshore Exploration & Prod. LLC*, 46 F. Supp.

may also survive the challenge of the second part of Section 10(a)(4) of the FAA if the court becomes satisfied that the tribunal included, in a partial award, its ultimate and final decision on certain matters submitted.

If, however, a court has difficulty with determining whether the subject matters submitted have been finally and unambiguously decided upon, it will still use the federal pro-arbitration policy as its signpost. Consequently, it will rather remand the award back to the tribunal for the corrections than use its authority to vacate. According to the Restatement, "*[i]n the domestic setting, this vacatur ground overlaps to a substantial degree with the power of a court to remand a matter to the tribunal to complete or clarify the award.*"[161] As one court held: "*while I have the authority to vacate the arbitrator's award under 9 U.S.C. § 10(a)(4), I find that remanding the matter back to the arbitrator is more appropriate as I conclude that the arbitrator failed to make a final determination on a material, threshold issue.*"[162]

In the case when an arbitral award cannot be corrected by the court itself or sent back to the tribunal for corrections, the court faced with a challenge will still be able to confirm or enforce the healthy part of the award.[163] In other words, if a claim is finally and definitely addressed and can be separated from the claims that are being questioned it can (and will likely) be confirmed.[164]

3d 327, 336 (S.D.N.Y. 2014) ("*an award which finally and definitely disposes of a separate independent claim may be confirmed although it does not dispose of all claims that were submitted to arbitration. In other words, an award is final if it resolves the rights and obligations of the parties definitively enough to preclude the need for further adjudication with respect to the issue submitted to arbitration.*").

161 The Restatement (second tentative draft) p.288.

162 *Fisher v. Gen. Steel Domestic Sales, LLC*, 2011 U.S. Dist. LEXIS 125826, *10, 2011 WL 5240372 (D. Colo. Oct. 31, 2011). Similarly, in *Olympia & York Florida Equity Corp. v. Gould*, 776 F.2d 42, 45 (2d Cir. 1985) it was also concluded that "*[t]he Award was thus ambiguous and did not constitute 'a mutual, final, and definite award upon the subject matter submitted' within the meaning of 9 U.S.C. § 10(d). While this defect may not bring the Award within the provisions of 9 U.S.C. § 11(c) empowering the district court to make an order modifying or correcting an award where it 'is imperfect in matter of form not affecting the merits of the controversy,' there is sufficient evidence of lack of a 'mutual, final, and definite award' within § 10(d) to warrant a remand to the arbitrators to enable them to state what their true intention was if Gould, having elected to purchase, should hereafter default.*"

163 See section 3.3.

164 See, *e.g.*, *Zephyros Mar. Agencies, Inc. v. Mexicana De Cobre, S.A.*, 662 F. Supp. 892, 894 (S.D.N.Y. 1987) ("*[...] an interim award that finally and definitely disposes of a separate, independent claim may be confirmed notwithstanding the absence of an award that finally disposes of all claims that were submitted to arbitration.*") See also *Compania Chilena De Navegacion Interoceanica, S.A. v. Norton, Lilly & Co.*, 652 F. Supp. 1512 (S.D.N.Y. 1987).

5.3 The Restatement's take on the post-award challenge architecture

Since the Restatement's views on the post-award architecture and the interrelation between different Chapters of the Federal Arbitration Act might influence the applicability of Chapter 1 of the FAA to the vacatur of international arbitration awards rendered in the U.S., it is necessary to give a brief overview of the Restatement's position.[165]

Although initially "confirmation and vacatur" and "recognition and enforcement" of the awards were to be discussed under two separate chapters of the Restatement, the decision was made to consolidate both under the overarching concept of the "post-award relief".[166] Consequently, "*the draft [Restatement] adopted the position that the grounds for vacating or denying confirmation of U.S. Convention awards are those specified in the Conventions, not the grounds set forth in FAA Section 10.*"[167] If this version is accepted, then the U.S. vacatur system for international awards would effectively mirror the Model Law system and make the analysis of this chapter largely obsolete.[168] At the same time, however, "*[t]he majority of the circuits that have addressed the issue [namely the issue whether to apply the New York Convention grounds or Section 10 of the FAA] have used the FAA § 10 grounds.*"[169]

Applying Section 10 of the FAA for the purpose of vacatur is a more sensible solution. The New York Convention has not been designed to be applicable at the challenge stage. Additionally, there is a question on the applicability of Article V(1)(e) of the New York Convention if the Convention grounds are used for vacatur purposes.[170] Additionally, one may wonder if the vacatur grounds as prescribed in Section 10 of the FAA might not develop to be even narrower than the ones envisaged by the New York Convention, especially considering the developed and strong policy favoring arbitration.[171]

All in all, from the general perspective of the post-award review not much will change. Indeed

> [a]n initial question is whether the choice among the two sets of grounds even matters. Certainly the verbal formulation of the grounds for denying recognition

165 For an overview, see also Bermann, *'Domesticating' the New York Convention: the Impact of the Federal Arbitration Act* (2011) pp.317-332.

166 For a more elaborate explanation, see the Restatement (second tentative draft) pp.xvii-xviii.

167 The Restatement (second tentative draft) p.xvii.

168 For further reading on the New York Convention and the Model Law system, see Chapter II and Chapter VI respectively.

169 The Restatement (second tentative draft) p.155 and the case law therein.

170 Art. V(1)(e) of the NYC reads that the award may be refused recognition and enforcement in cases where "*[t]he award has not yet become binding on the parties, or has been set aside or suspended by a competent authority of the country in which, or under the law of which, that award was made.*"

171 See section 3.1.

or enforcement under the New York and Panama Conventions differs from the verbal formulation of the grounds for vacating awards under the FAA. But courts and commentators have tended to construe the grounds similarly.[172]

At the same time, it will matter, when one interprets the "excess of powers" ground based on the Restatement's conclusions.[173] Should one try to invoke Chapter 1 of the FAA for the purpose of vacatur, as traditionally envisaged, the better view therefore is to construe it in a more narrow fashion than the Restatement.

6 The impact of non-statutory grounds on the Federal Arbitration Act framework: "manifest disregard of the law" and other concepts

By and large, the vacatur is limited to the ground listed in the FAA. Occasionally, however, the courts have been willing to develop additional non-statutory grounds for vacatur. In this section it is necessary to briefly explain these grounds (see section 6.1). Subsequently, one should try to establish if they indeed fall outside the ambit of Section 10 of the FAA or whether they can be depicted as a "judicial gloss" on the statutory grounds for vacatur provided by Section 10 of the FAA and it should be observed if these (non-statutory) concepts in any way influence the understanding of the "excess of powers" challenge (see section 6.2).

6.1 *Judicially created non-statutory grounds for vacatur*

Without a doubt, the most (in)famous and most often discussed non-statutory ground is the manifest disregard of the law. It is therefore important to briefly explain what the manifest disregard of the law entails and also if the test is still available after the *Hall Street* decision (section 6.1.1). Nonetheless, it should not be forgotten that over the years courts also vacated the award when it was "contrary to public policy" (section 6.1.2), "arbitrary and capricious" or "completely irrational" (section 6.1.3).

6.1.1 Decision in manifest disregard of the law

The first judicially created ground that should be scrutinized is the manifest disregard of the law. It is usually said that the manifest disregard of the law is rooted with the Supreme

172 The Restatement (second tentative draft) p.152.

173 See section 5.1.

Court decision in *Wilko v. Swan*, where it was held in *dictum* that "*the interpretations of the law by the arbitrators in contrast to manifest disregard are not subject, in the federal courts, to judicial review for error in interpretation.*"[174] This wording has been accepted as allowing the review of the arbitral award on the basis of manifest disregard of the law. Both federal and state courts welcomed with open arms such an opportunity to evaluate if an arbitral award can be vacated "*where the arbitrators consciously choose to disregard a clearly applicable legal princip[le]*".[175]

It can be reasonably concluded that

> [t]he principle of vacating an arbitration award because of a manifest disregard of the law is an important safeguard of the integrity of alternate dispute resolution mechanisms, because judicial approval of arbitration decisions that so egregiously depart from established law that they border on the irrational would undermine society's confidence in the legitimacy of the arbitration process.[176]

Instances, however, where the manifest disregard may apply are exceptional.[177]

By and large, the test for the manifest disregard of the law as applied by the federal courts is two-fold.[178] First, one should determine if the applicable legal principle is well-defined and clearly applicable to the case at hand; secondly, it should be concluded if the arbitrator knowingly ignored to apply such a well-defined legal principle.[179] Only

174 *Wilko v. Swan*, 346 U.S. 427, 436-437 (1953) (*overruled on other grounds Rodriguez de Quijas v. Shearson/Am. Express, Inc.*, 490 U.S. 477 (1989)). The Restatement points out, however, that "*[...] the authorities cited by the Wilko Court suggest that what the Court meant by 'manifest disregard' may have been different from the modern understanding of the phrase – i.e., that an arbitral tribunal manifestly disregards the law if it knowingly refuses to follow a controlling legal rule. See 346 U.S. at 437 n.24. Those authorities, including three Supreme Court cases that predated enactment of the FAA, provide evidence that the modern view of manifest disregard was not what the Court was describing in Wilko.*" For further reading, see the Restatement (second tentative draft) p.295 and the literature therein (*i.a.* Scodro (2005)).

175 Domke et al., *Domke on Commercial Arbitration* (2013) § 38:23; also Carbonneau, *The Rise in Judicial Hostility to Arbitration: Revisiting Hall Street Associates* (2013) p.604 ("*The classical formulation is that it [manifest disregard] pertains to a situation in which the arbitrators describe the applicable law cogently and knowledgeably and then deliberately ignore it in reaching their determination*").

176 Domke et al., *Domke on Commercial Arbitration* (2013) § 38:23. See also Restatement (second tentative draft) p.297.

177 Carbonneau, *The Rise in Judicial Hostility to Arbitration: Revisiting Hall Street Associates* (2013) p.604.

178 Some scholars highlighted that the wording of a manifest disregard test varies slightly among the circuits but generally the two-prong test is applicable. See Domke et al., *Domke on Commercial Arbitration* (2013) § 38:23.

179 Holtzmann et al., (2013) Chapter VII(2)(a)(8), see also Born, *International Commercial Arbitration* (2014) p.3345, Domke et al., *Domke on Commercial Arbitration* (2013) § 38:23 and the questions therein: "*courts generally apply the following two part test in determining if the award should be vacated for manifest disregard of the law: (1) Did the arbitrator know of the governing legal princip[le] yet refused to apply it or ignored it all together? and (2) Was the law ignored by the arbitrators well-defined, explicit and clearly applicable to*

when the court finds that the answer to both questions is in the affirmative may it vacate the award on the basis of manifest disregard.[180] In effect, courts construe the manifest disregard test in an extremely narrow fashion.[181] In similar vein, it has been argued that "*[...] the manifest disregard standard is akin to public policy analysis, requiring that the tribunal have been aware of controlling legal authority and deliberately chos[e] to disregard it – hence, the phrase 'manifest disregard of the law'.*"[182] Consequently, no court will vacate the award on the basis of a simple misapplication of law, even if the legal error committed by the arbitrator is obvious.[183]

The application of the manifest disregard test became somewhat problematic after the Supreme Court's decision in *Hall Street*.[184] The Supreme Court had to decide the split between the circuits with regard to the contractual extension for the grounds for vacatur as prescribed by the FAA.[185] In its holding the Court concluded that the grounds stated in

---

the case?" See also *e.g. Prestige Ford v. Ford Dealer Computer Servs., Inc.*, 324 F.3d 391, 395 (5th Cir. 2003), *Long John Silver's Restaurants, Inc. v. Cole*, 514 F.3d 345, 349-50 (4th Cir. 2008) ("*[...] an arbitrator does not act in manifest disregard of the law unless: (1) the applicable legal principle is clearly defined and not subject to reasonable debate; and (2) the arbitrator refused to heed that legal principle.*").

180 Domke et al., *Domke on Commercial Arbitration* (2013) § 38:23, see also Holtzmann et al., (2013) Chapter VII(2)(8), the Restatement (second tentative draft) p.292.

181 Born, *International Commercial Arbitration* (2014) p.3341, Domke et al., *Domke on Commercial Arbitration* (2013) § 38:23, also *i.a. Prestige Ford v. Ford Dealer Computer Servs., Inc.*, 324 F.3d 391, 395-96 (5th Cir. 2003) ("*[...] the 'manifest disregard' standard is an extremely narrow, judicially-created rule with limited applicability.*").

182 Born, *International Arbitration: Law and Practice* (2012) p.330.

183 See, *e.g.*, *Huntington Hosp. v. Huntington Hosp. Nurses' Ass'n*, 302 F. Supp. 2d 34, 40-41 (E.D.N.Y. 2004) ("*Vacating an award on the ground of manifest disregard of the law is severely limited. For an award to be vacated on this ground there must be more than a showing that the arbitrator made an error or misstated the applicable law. Instead, it must be shown that the error made was obvious and capable of being readily and instantly perceived by the average person qualified to serve as an arbitrator. Additionally, it must be shown that the arbitrator knew of the governing legal principle but chose to ignore it. The limited nature of the manifest disregard ground has been demonstrated by the Second Circuit which has recently described this ground as 'a doctrine of last resort – its use limited only to those exceedingly rare instances where some egregious impropriety on the part of the arbitrators is apparent, but where none of the provisions of the [Federal Arbitration Act] apply.'*"), *Josephthal & Co. v. Cruttenden Roth Inc.*, 177 F. Supp. 2d 232, 238 (S.D.N.Y. 2001) ("*An award may not be vacated under this subsection on the grounds that the arbitrators' opinion fails to interpret correctly the law applicable to the issues in dispute in the arbitration proceeding, or misinterprets the underlying contract, even if that misinterpretation is 'clearly erroneous.'*"), *Gwynn v. Clubine*, 302 F. Supp. 2d 151, 161 (W.D.N.Y. 2004) ("*Application of the doctrine requires more than 'simple error in law or a failure by the arbitrators to understand or apply it; and, it is more than an erroneous interpretation of the law.' Id. To vacate an arbitration award for manifest disregard of the law, the court must find 'something beyond and different from a mere error in the law or failure on the part of the arbitrators to understand or apply the law.'*").

184 *Hall Street*, 552 U.S. 576, 128 S. Ct. 1396, 170 L. Ed. 2d 254 (2008).

185 Carbonneau, *The Rise in Judicial Hostility to Arbitration: Revisiting Hall Street Associates* (2013) p.593, see also Domke et al., *Domke on Commercial Arbitration* (2013) § 38:23. For more literature on opt-in agreements extending the scope of the review, see for example Marcantel (2009) p.600.

Section 10 of the FAA are exclusive grounds to vacate an arbitral award,[186] therefore they cannot be supplemented by contract.[187] It further meant, arguably, that if the statutory grounds for vacatur enumerated in the FAA were to be exclusive, it would entail that non-statutory grounds such as manifest disregard would cease to apply.[188]

Irrespective of its holding, however, the *Hall Street* Court, engaged in the discussion what the manifest disregard of the law could actually mean by stating that

> [m]aybe the term 'manifest disregard' was meant to name a new ground for review, but maybe it merely referred to the § 10 grounds collectively, rather than adding to them. Or, as some courts have thought, 'manifest disregard' may have been shorthand for § 10(a)(3) or § 10(a)(4), the paragraphs authorizing vacatur when the arbitrators were 'guilty of misconduct' or 'exceeded their powers.'[189]

In other words, the Supreme Court indicated three ways how the manifest disregard standard could be construed: either (i) as an independent ground for vacatur, (ii) as a "judicial gloss" on Section 10 of the FAA collectively, or (iii) as a "shorthand" for individual statutory grounds (arbitrator's misconduct or excess of powers).[190] Consequently, if one reads the manifest disregard as a judicial interpretation of statutory grounds (either of Section 10 in general or subsection (a)(3) or (a)(4) individually), it would mean that the manifest disregard doctrine may survive the *Hall Street* holding. After the *Hall Street*

186 *Hall Street*, 552 U.S. 576, 128 S. Ct. 1396, 170 L. Ed. 2d 254 (2008) ("*grounds stated in the Federal Arbitration Act (FAA) either for vacating, or for modifying or correcting, arbitration award constitute the exclusive grounds for expedited vacatur and modification of arbitration award pursuant to provisions of the FAA [...]*"). Acknowledged *i.a.* by the courts in *Citigroup Global Markets, Inc. v. Bacon*, 562 F.3d 349, 355 (5th Cir. 2009) ("*The answer seems clear. Hall Street unequivocally held that the statutory grounds are the exclusive means for vacatur under the FAA*"), *Cat Charter, LLC v. Schurtenberger*, 646 F.3d 836, 843 (11th Cir. 2011) ("*The Supreme Court has made clear that the statutory grounds justifying vacatur found in 9 U.S.C. § 10(a) are exclusive.*").

187 Cullemark (2014) p.167.

188 *Citigroup Global Markets, Inc. v. Bacon*, 562 F.3d 349, 358 (5th Cir. 2009) ("*In the light of the Supreme Court's clear language that, under the FAA, the statutory provisions are the exclusive grounds for vacatur, manifest disregard of the law as an independent, nonstatutory ground for setting aside an award must be abandoned and rejected.*").

189 *Hall Street*, 552 U.S. 576, 585, 128 S. Ct. 1396, 1404, 170 L. Ed. 2d 254 (2008).

190 The idea of the manifest disregard doctrine being a "shorthand" description of statutory grounds has been criticized as having no basis in either legislative history or the statutory language. See Carbonneau, *The Rise in Judicial Hostility to Arbitration: Revisiting Hall Street Associates* (2013) p.605.

decision, circuits split[191] and doctrinal debate[192] ignited yet again on the question of the future of the manifest disregard of the law. To date, no further guidance from the Supreme Court has been given since it refused to clarify if the manifest disregard test is still available in deciding *Stolt-Nielsen* by concluding that "*[w]e do not decide whether 'manifest disregard' survives our decision in Hall Street [...] as an independent ground for review or as a judicial gloss on the enumerated grounds for vacatur set forth at 9 U.S.C. §10.*"[193]

Currently, the question whether the manifest disregard of the law doctrine together with other non-statutory grounds for vacatur (i) can be reconciled with the exclusivity of the FAA challenges or (ii) whether they simply cannot apply anymore, still stands and aches to be addressed by the Supreme Court. Without going into details at this point,[194] it should be noted that the prevailing opinion is that the manifest disregard of the law doctrine after *Hall Street* is not a ground for vacatur *under the FAA* and it usually has been argued that if it is available at all, it has to fit within the excess of powers challenge.[195] A reasonable alternative is to recognize the doctrine as a variation of public policy.[196]

In any event, it should not be forgotten that

> it is clear that an award cannot be vacated on manifest disregard grounds merely because the reviewing court is convinced that the award is wrong, or even clearly wrong, about the law. In one lower court's colorful explanation: Arbitrators do not act as junior varsity trial courts where subsequent appellate review is readily available to the losing party.[197]

---

191 For example, courts of the Fifth, Eighth and Eleventh Circuit concluded that manifest disregard is no longer a viable ground for vacatur. The Fourth Circuit accepted the application of the manifest disregard irrespective of whether it is interpreted as an independent ground or just a judicial gloss on the FAA's statutory grounds, the Second and Ninth Circuits are of the opinion that the manifest disregard of the law test still exists as a "*judicial gloss on the FAA's statutory grounds*". For further reading, see Born, *International Commercial Arbitration* (2014) p.3343; also *i.a.* Cullemark (2014) pp.170-171 or Marcantel (2009) p.633.

192 See, *i.a.*, Smit, *Hall Street Associates v. Mattel: A Critical Comment* (2006), Ellis (2009), Gross (2009), Marcantel (2009), Burns (2010), Carbonneau, *The Rise in Judicial Hostility to Arbitration: Revisiting Hall Street Associates* (2013), and Cullemark (2014).

193 *Stolt-Nielsen S.A. v. AnimalFeeds Int'l Corp.*, 559 U.S. 662, 672, 130 S. Ct. 1758, 1768, 176 L. Ed. 2d 605 (2010) (hereafter "Stolt-Nielsen").

194 For further reading, see section 6.2.

195 The Restatement (second tentative draft) p.292 ("*The Restatement takes the position that manifest disregard of the law is not a ground for vacating or denying recognition or enforcement of an award under FAA § 10. Because the FAA § 10 grounds are exclusive, manifest disregard of the law, if it is available at all, must fall within the excess-of-powers ground stated in § 10(a)(4).*"). See also Born, *International Commercial Arbitration* (2014) p.3344 ("*Even if the manifest disregard doctrine retains vitality, the doctrine provides very little, if any, basis for annulment beyond that provided by the FAA's "excess of authority" provision (in § 10(a)(4) of the FAA).*").

196 Rau, *Fear of Freedom* (2006) pp.500-501. See section 6.2.

197 Born, *International Commercial Arbitration* (2014) p.3344.

6.1.2 Violation of public policy

An allegation that the arbitral award is contrary to the public policy is another reason that the parties seeking vacatur invoke. Similar to the manifest disregard, courts will be rather resistant to accept the allegation that the award violates public policy. As explained in one of the previous sections, the challenge on this non-statutory ground would only be successful if the court is satisfied that the unambiguous, well-defined and dominant public policy is being violated.[198] The existence of the public policy exception, however, became questioned (together with other non-statutory grounds) as an aftermath of the *Hall Street* holding.[199]

In any case, the public policy exception *needs* to survive the *Hall Street* holding, because it is an essential element of the arbitration system and the last resort safeguard protecting the legitimacy of the arbitral process.[200] Similarly, the Restatement acknowledges that "*[a]lthough FAA § 10 does not expressly list public policy as a ground for vacating an arbitral award, such a ground is a necessary part of a national arbitration law.*"[201] Rau also recognizes that "*[...] vacatur for violation of "public policy" is a necessary fail safe, universally understood in every existing legal system as a ground (whether 'statutory' or 'non-statutory') for refusing to honor an award. However rarely successful, it must somehow be made to fit within the architecture of our law of arbitration.*"[202] Consequently, the better view is to allow the courts to rely on public policy as a safety valve irrespective of whether it is a gloss on the excess of powers or as an independent ground for recourse.

6.1.3 Arbitrary, capricious and completely irrational awards: the award that fails to draw its essence from the underlying contract

The last non-statutory grounds that need to be briefly addressed are the vacatur in cases where the award is "arbitrary and capricious" or "completely irrational", or "fails to draw its essence from the contract". All of them originate from labor arbitration[203] and all of

198 See section 4.3. See also, the Restatement (second tentative draft) p. 291 and *i.a. Huntington Hosp. v. Huntington Hosp. Nurses' Ass'n*, 302 F. Supp. 2d 34, 41 (E.D.N.Y. 2004) ("*Courts have come to recognize a limited public policy exception to the general rule in favor of confirmation of an arbitrator's award. The public policy exception is narrow, and requires an award to be vacated only if the arbitrator's interpretation of the contract violates some explicit public policy that is well-defined and dominant.*").

199 Marcantel (2009). For other examples see Rau, *Fear of Freedom* (2006) and fn.103 therein.

200 Marcantel makes a strong case by arguing that the use of the public policy exception is an inherent power of the courts derived from their social contract powers. For further reading, see Marcantel (2009) *i.a.* pp.608-611 and pp.635-638.

201 The Restatement (second tentative draft) p.291. As mentioned in the Restatement, however, one court decided to exclude the possibility to vacate on public policy grounds, see *Frazier v. CitiFinancial Corp.*, 604 F.3d 1313, 1324 (11th Cir. 2010), where the court held that "*[its] judicially-created bases for vacatur are no longer valid in light of Hall Street.*"

202 Rau, *Fear of Freedom* (2006) pp.501-502.

203 Domke et al., *Domke on Commercial Arbitration* (2013) § § 39:10-39:12, also Oehmke & Brovins (2014) § 148:1.

them are likely to share the fate of all judicially created grounds: in other words, it is highly uncertain if these grounds for vacatur remain viable.[204]

Before analyzing all of the grounds, one should be reminded that a court should under no circumstances conduct *de novo* review of the merits of the arbitral awards.[205] It has been held that it is possible to vacate an arbitral award under the "arbitrary and capricious" standard only if the award exhibits a wholesale departure from the law, or is not grounded in the contract which provides for the arbitration.[206] As long as there is a proper basis for the award, it will be confirmed.[207] Some authors observed that the "complete irrationality" test is similar in nature and a thrust to the "arbitrary and capricious test" and "*[t]hus an award could not stand if it did not meet the test of fundamental rationality.*"[208] Others suggested that "*complete irrationality is an extremely narrow, limited and highly-deferential standard for vacatur not found in the FAA [...]*" and that "*one articulation of the irrationality test is when an award is unfounded in reason and fact.*"[209] Finally, the award fails to draw its essence from the contract if "*it is contrary to plain contractual language, or where the arbitrator has construed the contract in a way that is implausible or irrational.*"[210]

In summary, it is very difficult to successfully challenge the award on these non-statutory grounds because of the deferential standard of review and federal pro-arbitration policy.[211] In addition to their questionable value, it is also uncertain if these grounds can still be used against arbitral awards at the post-award stage.

6.2 *Attempts to judicially expand the "excess of powers" challenge on the federal level*

As highlighted earlier in this chapter,[212] the concept of the excess of powers resembles an "empty vessel" that has to be filled with meaning by the courts.[213] Accordingly, parties fighting awards in courts were eagerly willing to provide arguments to courts that *even* common law grounds to vacate in fact fit within the scope of the FAA as an addition to

204 Arguably, the public policy ground for vacatur should be the exception to the post-*Hall Street* regime. See section 6.1.1 and for further reading, see also sections 6.1.1 and 6.2 and Reuben (2009) pp.1141-1142.

205 See section 3.1; also Oehmke & Brovins (2014) § 148:3, Domke et al., *Domke on Commercial Arbitration* (2013) § 39:12.

206 *Brown v. Rauscher Pierce Refnes, Inc.*, 994 F.2d 775, 781 (11th Cir. 1993).

207 Oehmke & Brovins (2014) § 148:2, see also Domke et al., *Domke on Commercial Arbitration* (2013) § 39:10.

208 Domke et al., *Domke on Commercial Arbitration* (2013) § 39:11.

209 Oehmke & Brovins (2014) § 148:2; as indicated by the authors, "*mere errors of law do not make an award irrational.*" See Oehmke & Brovins (2014) § 148:2.

210 Oehmke & Brovins (2014) § 148:3.

211 See section 3.1.

212 See section 5.1.

213 See also the Restatement (second tentative draft) p.287.

the open-ended phrasing used in Section 10(a)(4) of the FAA.[214] The notion that the "vessel" of the excess of powers can be "filled with" concepts of non-statutory grounds became particularly accurate when the Supreme Court in its opinion in *Hall Street* proposed that the manifest disregard can be perceived as judicial shorthand for statutory grounds for vacatur.

The *Hall Street* Court's suggestion regarding the inclusion of the manifest disregard standard into the FAA's framework was two-fold: this doctrine could be perceived either as the characterization of the FAA's statutory grounds collectively or as the interpretation of Section 10(a)(3) or Section 10(a)(4) of the FAA.[215] Since the first contention is rather far-fetched,[216] the second one (*i.e.* manifest disregard as a variation of the excess of powers challenge) deserves more attention. The idea that the manifest disregard of the law is a leg of the excess of powers challenge has been occasionally used before *Hall Street*.[217] After *Hall Street*, however, it became an essential argument in favor of keeping the manifest disregard alive.[218] Also the Restatement acknowledges that *if (and only if)* the manifest disregard of the law is still available "*at all, [it] must fall within the excess-of-powers ground stated in § 10(a)(4).*"[219] In the alternative, not mentioned by the *Hall Street* court but acknowledged by the Restatement, manifest disregard might be classified as a special case of public policy.[220]

If one argues that the manifest disregard is still viable under Section 10(a)(4) of the FAA, one must acknowledge this statutory ground's limitations. Under no circumstances should the "manifest disregard of the law" doctrine and the "excess of powers" challenge be reconciled at the cost of expanding the understanding of the latter. It also goes without

214 Similarly, broad discretion can be observed in the language of Section 10(a)(3) of the FAA ("*where the arbitrators were guilty of misconduct in refusing to postpone the hearing, upon sufficient cause shown, or in refusing to hear evidence pertinent and material to the controversy; or of any other misbehavior by which the rights of any party have been prejudiced [...]*").

215 *Hall Street*, 552 U.S. 576, 585, 128 S. Ct. 1396, 170 L. Ed. 2d 254, 2008, A.M.C. 1058 (2008). The court also recognized that it may be considered as a non-statutory ground for vacatur; then, however, it does not fit in the FAA framework.

216 Conceptually it does not fit in with any existing illustration of the manifest disregard doctrine.

217 Without success, however. See, *e.g.*, *136 A.L.R. 183 § 24*; occasionally parties had argued that other non-statutory grounds for vacatur also constitute a judicial interpretation of the excess of powers challenge.

218 It has been accepted by some circuits. See fn.191.

219 It should not be forgotten, however, that the primary position of the Restatement is that "*manifest disregard of the law is not a ground for vacating or denying recognition or enforcement of an award under FAA § 10.*" See the Restatement (second tentative draft) p.292. Also, *i.a.*, Born, *International Commercial Arbitration* (2014) p.3344.

220 The *Hall Street* court could not classify manifest disregard under the public policy exception, since the latter is also a non-statutory ground for vacatur. As argued previously, it needs to survive the *Hall Street* holding, to ensure the legitimacy of arbitration as a system. See section 6.1.1. The Restatement's take on the post-award relief would allow the inclusion of the manifest disregard under the public policy ground for recourse. It can happen if one accepts that the New York Convention grounds apply for the purpose of vacating international awards. See section 5.3.

saying that even if we conclude that the manifest disregard of the law doctrine is a "judicial gloss" on the excess of powers, no review of the arbitral tribunal's legal conclusions will be available.[221]

An alternative, *i.e.* classifying manifest disregard of the law "as a special case of public policy", is far more appealing.[222] Under such a notion, the manifest disregard of the law doctrine only provides that "*an arbitrator may not direct the parties to violate the law*".[223]

As observed by Rau:

> [m]ost of the isolated holdings in which a finding of 'manifest disregard' has actually led to vacatur can be fitted within this rationale. And it is evident that this leg of the analysis conflates 'manifest disregard' and the notion of vacatur on grounds of 'public policy' as now understood by the Supreme Court – in the process, rendering the former essentially irrelevant.[224]

The manifest disregard of the law doctrine is better off being subsumed under the public policy exception rather than under the excess of powers ground for vacatur. First of all, the standard of review against public policy is more deferential than one employed in testing excess of powers challenge. Secondly, although the manifest disregard loses its independence, it will make it possible to further shape and provide the necessary structure for the elusive public policy ground – the only non-statutory ground that needs to survive the *Hall Street* aftermath, the only one that is fitted to be used against fundamental wrongdoings of an arbitral tribunal and the only one that in extreme rare circumstances may limit the arbitral tribunal's powers beyond the contractual framework set by the parties.

---

221 See section 3.1.

222 According to the Restatement this is the view adopted in the Seventh Circuit. See the Restatement (second tentative draft) p.292 ("*Under the Seventh Circuit's alternative definition, manifest disregard is a special case of the public policy ground for vacating or denying recognition or enforcement of awards*"); also Born, *International Commercial Arbitration* (2014) p.3344 ("*[...] the manifest disregard standard is akin to a form of public policy analysis [...]*"), p.3346 ("*Indeed, as noted above, one post-Hall Street decision effectively equated the doctrine with notions of public policy [...]*"), with a reference to the pre-*Hall Street* decision of *George Watts & Son, Inc. v. Tiffany & Co.*, 248 F.3d 577, 580 (7th Cir. 2001).

223 *George Watts & Son, Inc. v. Tiffany & Co.*, 248 F.3d 577, 580 (7th Cir. 2001).

224 Rau, *Fear of Freedom* (2006) pp.500-501. A similar conclusion can be found in the Restatement (second tentative draft) p.292 ("*As such, manifest disregard of the law has no independent substantive force as a ground for denying recognition or enforcement of non-Convention awards.*"). See also fn.220.

7 Application of the United States standard of excess of powers to selected issues that might fall outside the arbitral tribunal's authority

Decisions undertaken by the arbitral tribunal can be divided into certain categories based on their common denominator. This division becomes helpful for the analysis of which of the tribunals' decisions go beyond the powers vested upon them. The sections may intertwine (*e.g.* decisions on parties' claims would be (irreconcilably) decisions on remedies that parties request). Nevertheless, carrying out the analysis of excess of powers from different angles might be useful for a more profound understanding of the issue.

Since the whole arbitration process starts with the underlying question of whether the tribunal has jurisdiction based upon a valid arbitration agreement, it would be a starting point (section 7.1). If the tribunal's decision on its jurisdiction stands, the vacating court may still be asked to review the arbitral tribunal's determinations on the parties' respective claims (section 7.2). This section will address the issue of the availability of particular claims in arbitration in more abstract terms, whereas sections on decisions on remedies (section 7.4) and on decisions accessory to the parties' main submissions (section 7.5) will follow. A tribunal's determination of the applicable law will be discussed in detail in section 7.3.

7.1 Decisions on jurisdictional/threshold issues

By and large, according to the principle of competence-competence the tribunal is inherently competent to decide on its own jurisdiction. Generally, this concept has been recognized by major arbitration-friendly jurisdictions as one of the key features of arbitration.[225] In tandem with the principle of severability[226] it serves well as a safeguard of a tribunal's authority to have a first (and usually the final) say on issues that are detrimental to the tribunal's jurisdiction. In the U.S, however, the traditional paradigm of competence-competence has been shifted by the introduction of the notion of "gateway issues".[227] The meaning of the term "gateway issues" in this chapter would "*encompass only those threshold issues that a court, if asked to do so, will decide at the outset, but excluding those that courts reserve for initial determination, along with the merits, to the*

225 Depending on the jurisdiction, it takes up different forms, *i.e.* negative competence-competence and positive competence-competence.

226 The principle of severability entails that the agreement to arbitrate (arbitration clause) will be treated as a contract independent from the main contract. For further reading, see *i.a.*, the Restatement (fourth tentative draft) pp.46-57.

227 And no default (positive) competence-competence rule is provided in the FAA. See, *e.g.*, Born, *International Commercial Arbitration* (2014) p.1127.

arbitral tribunal itself'.[228] As aptly put by Bermann "*[g]raphically, it is easy to picture a "portal" through which a party seeking arbitration must pass before arbitration may commence, in the event that its opponent raises certain objections to arbitral jurisdiction at the outset.*"[229]

Generally, the salient question there is who has the authority to decide these objections: a court or an arbitral tribunal.[230] For the purpose of the current study, it is more appropriate, however, to ask what happens *if* the tribunal decides on a certain threshold issue and whether its decision can be subsequently (and successfully) challenged on the basis of excess of powers. In turn, if vacatur is possible what is the appropriate standard of review of the tribunal's decision on threshold issues?[231] Additionally possible threshold issues enjoy a slightly different treatment from the court at the post-award stage, which will be explained further below.

It should be noted that threshold issues are sometimes discussed altogether, not only under the term "gateway issues" but also under the broad notion of "arbitrability", understood "*as if to denote every condition or requirement that must be met in order for an arbitration to go forward.*"[232] The term "arbitrability", however, should be reserved to entail

228 Bermann, *The "Gateway" Problem in International Commercial Arbitration* (2012) p.8; the author recognized a narrow and broad definition of gateway issues. The concept of the gateway issues used in this chapter represents the narrow meaning of the term; the broad definition includes "*any feature of a dispute, the parties to it, or the contract from which it arises that, when raised by a party resisting arbitration, can potentially keep an arbitration from going forward.*" see Bermann, *The "Gateway" Problem in International Commercial Arbitration* (2012) p.7.

229 Bermann, *The "Gateway" Problem in International Commercial Arbitration* (2012) p.8.

230 A more detailed analysis of who defers to whom, falls outside the scope of this research. The basic question in the competence-competence discussion in the U.S. boils down to the point who has the first and/or final authority to decide the "gateway issues". The question here is when does the tribunal exceed its powers *if* it decides the "gateway issues". For further reading, see, *i.a.*, Rau, *Arbitral Jurisdiction and the Dimensions of "Consent"* (2008), Bermann, *The "Gateway" Problem in International Commercial Arbitration* (2012), Born, *International Commercial Arbitration* (2014) pp.1125-1208.

231 It should be also noted that both positive and negative jurisdictional decisions made by an arbitral tribunal are subject to the subsequent court's review. It means that the vacating court has competence to rule on the tribunal's decision rejecting its jurisdiction over the dispute. As argued by Born in Born, *International Commercial Arbitration* (2014), p.3212: "*Similarly § 10(a)(4) of the [FAA] applies equally to both positive and negative jurisdictional awards.*" For further reading, see therein pp.3211-3213.

232 See Bermann, *The "Gateway" Problem in International Commercial Arbitration* (2012) pp.10-13. The term arbitrability, as developed in the U.S., is then further divided into "substantive arbitrability" and "procedural arbitrability". Whereas the authority to address the "substantive arbitrability" questions is initially for the court to decide, the authority regarding the questions of "procedural arbitrability" is for the tribunal to decide. The Restatement, for example, explains that this division corresponds to the division between questions of "jurisdiction" and "admissibility". See further the Restatement (fourth tentative draft) pp.63-64. The "procedural admissibility" would entail "'*procedural' questions which grow out of the dispute and bear on its final disposition*". See *Howsam v. Dean Witter Reynolds, Inc.*, 537 U.S. 79, 84, 123 S. Ct. 588, 592, 154 L. Ed. 2d 491 (2002). Importantly, the Supreme Court also found that the 18 months litigation requirement before the commencement of the arbitration was a procedural question for the tribunal to decide. See *BG Grp., PLC v. Republic of Argentina*, 134 S. Ct. 1198, 188 L. Ed. 2d 220 (2014).

only the reference to the question what disputes can be subjected to the arbitrators' determination. Alas, the term can also appear in its broad sense in some extracts from court decisions.

Objections that may be characterized as gateway questions, include the question of the validity or existence of an agreement to arbitrate (section 7.1.1), the scope of the arbitration agreement (section 7.1.2), arbitrability of claims[233] (section 7.1.3), and class arbitration (section 7.1.4). These matters are extremely delicate, since they touch upon the very existence of the parties' consent to arbitrate (in case of objections towards validity or existence of the agreement to arbitrate and to some extent when the scope of the agreement to arbitrate is in question)[234] or public policy (in the case of arbitrability of claims or class arbitration).

7.1.1 Decision on the validity and existence of an agreement to arbitrate

Decisions on the validity or existence of an agreement to arbitrate lead to the very core question, whether the parties consented to arbitrate their disputes. Consequently, if a party argues that no agreement to arbitrate had ever been concluded, the existence of adjudicatory powers of the tribunals is subject (at the very least) to a legitimate concern. For this reason, it is only logical to accept the premise that the tribunal's decision on the validity or existence of an agreement to arbitrate should not escape judicial scrutiny.[235]

That being said, it should be noted that, under the U.S. statutory framework the tribunal's considerations on the validity or existence of an agreement to arbitrate will be subject to judicial review pursuant to Section 10(a)(4) of the FAA. Few elements of this judicial test, however, need to be highlighted and analyzed further: (i) if the very existence (or validity) of the arbitration agreement is at stake, the court will likely pursue an independent and full (instead of deferential) review on the point of the parties' underlying consent to arbitrate; (ii) arguably, the explicit authorization to decide upon all matters related to the arbitration agreement (including, but not limited to its existence and validity) may alter how profound a review the court would exercise; (iii) similarly, the parties'

---

233 This is understood as what categories of claims are capable of being arbitrated, thus can be lawfully brought before the tribunal for its final determination. See, *i.a.*, Born, *International Commercial Arbitration* (2014) pp.943-1045.

234 The consent is a cornerstone of arbitration. Consequently, if a party argues before a court that no agreement to arbitrate had ever been concluded (therefore no consent to confer a tribunal with the adjudicatory powers have ever been granted), a legitimate concern arises regarding why the court should give a deference to the arbitral panel.

235 The analysis reflects what happens with the jurisdictional challenges at the post-award stage. It is noted, however, that the court may be involved with the jurisdictional issues pending arbitration, for example, when the dispute has been brought to the court notwithstanding the agreement to arbitrate or when a motion for an order to compel arbitration is filed. For further reading on interlocutory judicial resolution, see *i.a.*, Born, *International Commercial Arbitration* (2014) pp.1148-1151 and pp.1198-1204.

agreements surrendering jurisdictional issues to the arbitrators' *final* determination will further modify the degree of the court's analysis.

The starting point for the court faced with a challenge of an arbitral tribunal's decision on jurisdiction, would be to review it *de novo*.[236] In other words, no deference needs to be given to the tribunal's jurisdictional findings and conclusions when the existence or validity of an arbitration agreement is challenged at the vacatur stage.[237] The origins of the court's full review can be traced down to the Supreme Court's decision in *First Options of Chicago*.[238] In its holding the Supreme Court concluded that the "*question whether arbitrators or courts have primary power to decide if parties agreed to arbitrate merits of dispute depends on whether parties agreed to submit question to arbitration.*"[239] In its opinion the Court further explained that "*[if] [...] the parties did not agree to submit the arbitrability question itself to arbitration, then the court should decide that question just as it would decide any other question that the parties did not submit to arbitration, namely, independently.*"[240] Additionally, the Court concluded that "*courts should not assume that the parties agreed to arbitrate arbitrability unless there is 'clea[r] and unmistakabl[e]' evidence that they did so.*"[241]

In other words, a default position is that it would be the court, not the arbitral tribunal, who will have the power to answer the questions related to arbitrators' jurisdiction, in the absence of clear and unmistakable evidence that the parties agreed to vest the tribunal with the competence to answer all questions related to the validity or existence of an agreement to arbitrate. Consequently, the tribunal's decision on the validity or existence of an agreement to arbitrate, granted without the parties' express authorization, would likely be subject to a successful vacatur on the basis of the "excess of powers" ground.[242]

---

236 Born, *International Commercial Arbitration* (2014) p.3208.

237 Born, *International Commercial Arbitration* (2014) p.3208. Born recognizes, however, that the vacatur courts, while formally distancing themselves from accepting the preclusive effect of the tribunal's conclusions on its jurisdiction, they (*i.e.* the courts) tend to follow (or at least give some weight to) the tribunal's factual and legal findings regarding the existence or validity of the arbitration agreement. See Born, *International Commercial Arbitration* (2014) pp.3208-3210.

238 *First Options of Chicago*, 514 U.S. 938, 115 S. Ct. 1920, 131 L. Ed. 2d 985 (1995).

239 *First Options of Chicago*, 514 U.S. 938, 115 S. Ct. 1920, 131 L. Ed. 2d 985 (1995).

240 *First Options of Chicago*, 514 U.S. 938, 943, 115 S. Ct. 1920, 1924, 131 L. Ed. 2d 985 (1995).

241 *First Options of Chicago*, 514 U.S. 938, 944, 115 S. Ct. 1920, 1924, 131 L. Ed. 2d 985 (1995).

242 It does not mean, however, that every arbitral tribunal's decision on the validity or existence of the agreement to arbitrate will automatically lead to its vacatur at the post-award stage. The vacating court may very well be convinced that this decision was inherently for the tribunal to make. See, *e.g.*, Born, *International Commercial Arbitration* (2014) p.1164 ("*Thus, at least in international cases, parties virtually always agree to 'arbitrate arbitrability': the arbitrators' competence-competence to consider and resolve jurisdictional disputes is presumptively an integral and fundamental part of their adjudicatory mandate. Although it is beyond the scope of this Treatise, the same conclusion should apply in domestic U.S. matters. The competence-competence to consider jurisdictional challenges is an inherent aspect of any adjudicatory body, and there is no suggestion in the FAA or in U.S. judicial authority that, absent a First Options agreement, arbitrators in the United*

In any event, parties may try to shield themselves from the full review of the court on the jurisdictional/threshold issues by explicitly delegating the power to resolve these issues to arbitrators. Parties can do so by including a clear and unambiguous delegation clause in their agreement to arbitrate or, in the alternative, they can refer to the institutional rules that ensure that the tribunal has the power to decide all questions related to its jurisdiction.[243] It has been noted that

> because the United States has taken a unique position regarding the extent of an arbitral tribunal's initial competence-competence, parties would be well advised to indicate whether threshold jurisdictional questions should be referred initially to the arbitral tribunal or United States courts. Major arbitral institutions offer model arbitration clauses that are ordinarily expected to withstand judicial challenge.[244]

Arguably, delegation would work satisfactorily in the case of the question of the validity of the agreement to arbitration,[245] but it will not withhold the court at the post-award stage from pursuing an independent review if the very existence of the agreement to arbitrate is at issue.[246]

States lack the authority to consider jurisdictional challenges; [...] it is clear that any such suggestion would be unfounded.").

243 See, *e.g.*, Art. 6(3) and 6(5) of the (draft) 2021 ICC Rules, Art. 6(3) and Art. 6(5) of the 2017 ICC Rules, Art. 21(1) of the 1976 UNCITRAL Rules, Art. 23(1) of the 2010 UNCITRAL Rules, Art. 18 of the 2016 JAMS Rules and R-7(a) of the 2013 AAA Rules ("*The arbitrator shall have the power to rule on his or her own jurisdiction, including any objections with respect to the existence, scope, or validity of the arbitration agreement or the arbitrability of any claim or counterclaim.*"). In the context of AAA Rule, see *Blanton v. Domino's Pizza Franchising LLC*, 962 F.3d 842, 844-45 (2020) ("*That brings us to the question in this case. In his arbitration agreement, Piersing agreed that "[t]he American Arbitration Association ('AAA') will administer the arbitration and the arbitration will be conducted in accordance with then-current [AAA Rules]." [...] The question for us is whether that's "clear and unmistakable" evidence that Piersing agreed to arbitrate "arbitrability." [...] There are good reasons to think it is. To start, the AAA Rules clearly empower an arbitrator to decide questions of "arbitrability"—for instance, questions about the "scope" of the agreement.*"). See, however, criticism in the Restatement (fourth tentative draft) pp.66-71.

244 Rutledge et al. (2009) p.883. One should carefully observe developments in *Henry Schein* saga, *Henry Schein, Inc. v. Archer & White Sales, Inc.*, 139 S. Ct. 524, 527, 202 L. Ed. 2d 480 (2019); *Archer & White Sales, Inc. v. Henry Schein, Inc.*, 935 F.3d 274 (5th Cir. 2019), cert. granted, 207 L. Ed. 2d 1050 (June 15, 2020), and cert. denied, 207 L. Ed. 2d 1053 (June 15, 2020).

245 See the Restatement (fourth tentative draft) p.71 ("*We may assume that if the unconscionability issue is amenable to delegation, so too are other challenges to an arbitration agreement's validity.*"). The conclusion is based on the Supreme Court's decision in *Rent-A-Center, West, Inc. v. Jackson*, 130 S. Ct. 2772, 2774, 561 U.S. 63, 63 (U.S. 2010) ("*Under the FAA, where an agreement to arbitrate includes an agreement that the arbitrator will determine the enforceability of the agreement, if a party challenges specifically the enforceability of that particular agreement, the district court considers the challenge, but if a party challenges the enforceability of the agreement as a whole, the challenge is for the arbitrator.*").

246 Born, *International Commercial Arbitration* (2014) p.3215. Born explains that "*where a party denies that it has concluded any agreement at all, there cannot be 'clear and unmistakable' evidence of an agreement to*

As highlighted, generally, courts will be satisfied to respect the arbitrators' decision on the validity of the agreement to arbitrate if the power over jurisdictional/threshold questions has been given to the tribunal by the incorporation of the institutional rules.[247] If the clear and unmistakable evidence of delegation of powers exists, then the level of scrutiny of the court's review changes drastically. In other words, if the court is satisfied that parties agreed to pass the competence over jurisdictional/threshold issues to the tribunal, the vacating court will pursue only a deferential review of the arbitral tribunal's decision as opposed to the full test in the absence of a delegation clause.[248] If the delegation provides that the tribunal's determination of the jurisdictional/threshold issues is to be treated as final, the degree of the court's deference is even higher.[249]

Finally, it should be pointed out that under no circumstances will the court surrender its power to independently and fully determine if the agreement to arbitrate ever existed. Consequently, parties cannot contractually alter the scope of the court's review on this issue. It is reasonable to conclude that if the initial consent to arbitrate is being questioned, the court will undertake the full test on that point no matter how clear and unmistakable an agreement to arbitrate is or whether the agreement leaves the tribunal with the power of a final determination.[250]

7.1.2 Decision on the scope of an agreement to arbitrate

The scope of an agreement to arbitrate qualifies in the U.S. for the category of jurisdictional/threshold issues. Under the FAA default mechanism it is also, presumptively,

---

arbitrate arbitrability issues; any such evidence, in the form of the putative arbitration agreement, is necessarily disputed and cannot satisfy First Options' requirement for 'clear and unmistakable' evidence."

247 See, in general, Born, *International Commercial Arbitration* (2014) pp.1167-1170. See, however, the Restatement (fourth tentative draft) pp.67-69 ("*[T]he majority of lower courts, when asked to determine the effect of arbitral rules and more specifically whether they constitute the 'clear and unmistakable evidence' contemplated by First Options, have concluded that they do. [...] The Restatement rejects the majority line of cases as based on a misinterpretation of the institutional rules being applied.*"). The broadly drafted agreements to arbitrate, in principle, will not be sufficient to show "clear and unmistakable" evidence to surrender disputes related to the validity or existence of the agreement to arbitrate. See, *e.g.*, Born, *International Commercial Arbitration* (2014) pp.1170-1171.

248 See Born, *International Commercial Arbitration* (2014) p.1169 ("*Most lower courts have held that the First Options analysis requires evidence of an agreement to arbitrate jurisdictional issues, not a waiver of judicial review of arbitral decisions regarding jurisdictional issues. Under these decisions, once such an agreement to arbitrate particular jurisdictional disputes exists, then the arbitrators' jurisdictional decisions are subject to judicial review only under the FAA's de minimis manifest disregard standard, in the same way as awards resolving other arbitrable disputes.*").

249 Born, *International Commercial Arbitration* (2014) p.3214, Bermann, *The "Gateway" Problem in International Commercial Arbitration* (2012) pp.36-40.

250 Even though the court reviews the issue of the existence of an agreement to arbitrate independently and fully, it does not change the fact that in line with the federal pro-arbitration policy the court will likely reject frivolous challenges against the tribunal's decision on the issue. See section 3.1.

for the court and not for the tribunal to decide.[251] At the same time, however, "*it is [...] clear that the presumption that scope disputes are for judicial decision is a rebuttable one under the First Options analysis – which leaves the parties free to agree that particular objections will be submitted to arbitration.*"[252] Therefore, if parties, in their agreement, are keen to (expressly) delegate the disputes over the scope of the agreement to arbitrate, the courts are likely to defer to their bargain. By and large, one should also observe that the incorporation of (most of) the institutional rules or even broadly drafted agreements to arbitrate[253] might suffice as evidence of the parties' consent to surrender the scope issues to the tribunal's determination.[254] Consequently, if an arbitral tribunal decides on the scope of the agreement to arbitrate, its decision on the issue deserves a high degree of judicial deference.[255]

Generally, incorporation of the institutional rules will give the tribunal competence to decide on its own jurisdiction.[256]

As accurately reported by the Restatement:

> there appears to be a consensus that parties can validly delegate to an arbitral tribunal primary authority over whether a given dispute falls within the scope of an arbitration agreement (assuming its existence and validity are not questioned). Courts that are prepared to treat the incorporation by reference of a competence-competence clause as "clear and unmistakable evidence" under First Options have little hesitation in doing so in the context of a dispute over

---

251 *First Options of Chicago*, 514 U.S. 938, 115 S. Ct. 1920, 131 L. Ed. 2d 985 (1995). Born, *International Commercial Arbitration* (2014) pp.1181-1183.

252 Born, *International Commercial Arbitration* (2014) p.1183.

253 For instance with a formula such as "*Any and all disputes arising out of or in connection with...*".

254 Even if no express delegation of powers to an arbitral tribunal exists in the agreement to arbitrate. In cases of broad agreements to arbitrate the scope question might not be mentioned. Nonetheless, based on the comprehensive wording of the agreement to arbitrate it might be implied that it is a question for the tribunal to decide. Arguably, only when the agreement to arbitrate is narrowly drafted, may the court question the parties' intention to delegate the scope question to arbitrators. This would be particularly important for the interlocutory judicial revision of the agreement to arbitrate. See fn.235. Arguably, however, it might also affect the standard of the post-award review which is discussed at hand.

255 See Born, *International Commercial Arbitration* (2014) p.3298 ("*Where parties have concluded a valid agreement to arbitrate, the arbitral tribunal's decision on the scope of that agreement should be accorded substantial deference. That is particularly true where parties have agreed to institutional arbitration rules granting arbitrators authority to determine their own jurisdiction, but the same conclusion is also implicit in an agreement to arbitrate.*").

256 See, *e.g.*, Art. 19 of the 2014 ICDR Rules, Art. 18 of the 2016 JAMS Rules, Art. 6 of the (draft) 2021 ICC Rules, Art. 6 of the 2017 ICC Rules, Art. 6 of the 2012 ICC Rules, Art. 21(1) of the 1976 UNCITRAL Rules, Art. 23(1) of the 2010 UNCITRAL Rules. See, however, applicable in domestic context, R-7(a) of the 2013 AAA Rules ("*The arbitrator shall have the power to rule on his or her own jurisdiction, including any objections with respect to the existence, scope, or validity of the arbitration agreement or the arbitrability of any claim or counterclaim.*").

> whether a dispute falls within the scope of an arbitration agreement. [...] This result is not particularly surprising since whether a given dispute falls within the scope of an arbitration agreement is ultimately a question of contract interpretation [...], and it is not unreasonable to suppose that primary authority of a question of that type is delegable to the arbitrators.[257]

It should be pointed out, however, that – on the one hand – globally recognized rules, such as the ICC Rules or the UNCITRAL Rules, introduce a rather broad notion of competence-competence, without mentioning that the tribunal is competent to decide on the scope of the agreement to arbitrate. Arguably, it shows that these rules acknowledge, as a default tenet, that the decision on the scope of an agreement to arbitrate is inherently for the tribunal to make. Major American arbitral institutions – on the other hand – fathom the structure of the arbitral system in the U.S. and prefer to leave no doubt that the decision on the scope of an agreement to arbitrate fits comfortably within the limits of the tribunal's adjudicatory powers. As such these set of rules include jurisdictional delegation clauses on the issues regarding the scope of the agreement to arbitrate.[258]

In any event, as argued by Born, "*[i]n the case of scope objections [...] most institutional rules should be interpreted as granting arbitrators the authority to finally resolve such disputes.*"[259] Consequently, if the vacating court accepts that, by reference to the institutional rules, the power to decide the scope of an agreement to arbitrate has been transferred to the tribunal, it will exercise a deferential test of the arbitral tribunal's decision. Moreover, if the court is satisfied that the parties agreed that the tribunal will decide the scope of an agreement to arbitrate, the *excess* of powers objections will likely fail.

Arguably, also broadly drafted agreements to arbitrate entail that the scope disputes can be decided by an arbitral tribunal (as discussed, subject to the subsequent judicial

257 The Restatement (fourth tentative draft) pp.69-70.

258 See, *e.g.*, Art. 19 of the 2014 ICDR Rules ("*The arbitral tribunal shall have the power to rule on its own jurisdiction, including any objections with respect to the [...] scope [...] of the arbitration agreement(s) [...]*"), R-7(a) of the 2013 AAA Rules ("*The arbitrator shall have the power to rule on his or her own jurisdiction, including any objections with respect to the [...] scope [...] of the arbitration agreement*"). In the context of AAA Rule, see *Blanton v. Domino's Pizza Franchising LLC*, 962 F.3d 842, 844-45 (2020) ("*That brings us to the question in this case. In his arbitration agreement, Piersing agreed that "[t]he American Arbitration Association ('AAA') will administer the arbitration and the arbitration will be conducted in accordance with then-current [AAA Rules]." [...] The question for us is whether that's "clear and unmistakable" evidence that Piersing agreed to arbitrate "arbitrability." [...] There are good reasons to think it is. To start, the AAA Rules clearly empower an arbitrator to decide questions of "arbitrability"—for instance, questions about the "scope" of the agreement.*"). One should carefully observe developments in *Henry Schein* saga however. See *Henry Schein, Inc. v. Archer & White Sales, Inc.*, 139 S. Ct. 524, 527, 202 L. Ed. 2d 480 (2019); *Archer & White Sales, Inc. v. Henry Schein, Inc.*, 935 F.3d 274 (5th Cir. 2019), *cert. granted*, 207 L. Ed. 2d 1050 (June 15, 2020), and *cert. denied*, 207 L. Ed. 2d 1053 (June 15, 2020).

259 Born, *International Commercial Arbitration* (2014) p.1184.

control upon vacatur).[260] Therefore, only in the case of a narrowly drafted agreement to arbitrate,[261] may a vacating court become satisfied that no authorization to decide the scope issues has ever been granted. If that happens, the vacating court will take the default position that the scope question is presumptively for the court to decide. Consequently, if the vacating court becomes satisfied that no authorization to decide the scope issues has ever been granted, it will be entitled to an independent and full review of this threshold issue. It should be noted, however, that a tribunal's initial decision on the scope of the agreement to arbitrate does not exist in a void. Therefore, the vacating court will vacate not on the basis of an abstract decision on the scope of the agreement, but rather it will vacate the part of the award that addresses the issue or dispute that has not been (in the court's opinion) part of the initial consent to arbitrate.[262]

All in all, it is more than reasonable to let the tribunal decide the issues regarding the scope of the agreement to arbitrate (with the reservation that the existence or validity of the agreement to arbitrate is not disputed), since "*these disputes are [...] inescapably intertwined with the substantive interpretation of the underlying contract and the parties' right thereunder – matters which are plainly for the arbitral tribunal to resolve under the parties' arbitration agreement.*"[263] In other words, determining the issue of the scope of the agreement to arbitrate might be a task too closely related to the merits of the dispute for the court to interfere with the arbitral process. It is therefore sensible to allow the tribunal to first determine this issue.

7.1.3 Decision on arbitrability of claims

Yet another jurisdictional/threshold decision that may be challenged during vacatur proceedings is the decision on arbitrability of claims (or the decision on subject-matter arbitrability), *i.e.* the decision determining whether certain categories of claims (for example, anti-trust claims) may be disposed in arbitration at all. Generally, the analysis from the

260 Born, *International Commercial Arbitration* (2014) p.1187 ("*where commercial parties have admittedly entered into a valid, broadly-drafted arbitration agreement, whose continued validity is not disputed, then it is most consistent with their expectations, and with an efficient arbitral process, for the arbitral tribunal to resolve disputes about the scope of its jurisdiction.*").

261 See, *e.g.*, *Granite Rock Co. v. Int'l Bhd. of Teamsters*, 561 U.S. 287, 308, 130 S. Ct. 2847, 2862, 177 L. Ed. 2d 567 (2010) ("*The issue is whether the formation-date defense that Local raised in response to Granite Rock's no-strike suit can be characterized as 'arising under' the CBA. It cannot for the reasons we have explained, namely, the CBA provision requiring arbitration of disputes 'arising under' the CBA is not fairly read to include a dispute about when the CBA came into existence.*"). For further reading, see, *e.g.*, the Restatement (fourth tentative draft) p.134, Born, *International Commercial Arbitration* (2014) pp.1185-1188.

262 Taking into account the federal pro-arbitration policy, it is suggested that only part of the award would be vacated.

263 Born, *International Commercial Arbitration* (2014) p.1188. See also the Restatement (fourth tentative draft) p.70 ("*This result is not particularly surprising since whether a given dispute falls within the scope of an arbitration agreement is ultimately a question of contract interpretation [...], and it is not unreasonable to suppose that primary authority of a question of that type is delegable to the arbitrators.*").

previous two sections can be applied here in *verbatim*. Therefore, without the parties' express authorization, the vacating court will give no deference to the tribunal's decision on arbitrability and thus proceed with an independent analysis. If, however, parties did authorize the tribunal to decide on the issue of the arbitrability of claims,[264] the vacating court will test the award with some degree of deference.[265] Since the consent of the parties would not be an issue, the arguments that might be eventually raised to evidence the excess of powers objections will be built up upon the notion that the tribunal's decision (i) went beyond the parties' submissions or (ii) violated public policy.

Parenthetically, it is necessary to mention that instances where decisions on arbitrability are challenged upon vacatur rarely occur, because a decision on arbitrability *per se* would be rather of declaratory character and, arguably, would not be rendered as a self-standing award. Instead, the decision on arbitrability is a prerequisite for the tribunal to grant particular relief to a party.[266] Therefore, the challenging party will be aiming at vacating the decision on a specific claim of which the arbitrability is questionable, rather than the decision on arbitrability of said claim (which is accessory to the main decision).

Arguably, the only instances where a decision on arbitrability might stand as an independent award and in turn be challenged on vacatur is the tribunal's decision rejecting a claim as nonarbitrable or the tribunal's ruling rejecting jurisdiction based on the nonarbitrability (inarbitrability) of a certain claim.

If it is argued that a decision rejecting a claim as nonarbitrable went beyond the scope of the parties' submissions, it means that a proper defense against a nonarbitrable claim has not been raised and the tribunal decided to refuse to grant a nonarbitrable claim on its own motion.[267] The tribunal's decision to this effect squarely points to the fact that the

264 Either in the text of the comprehensive arbitration clause (see, *e.g.*, the JAMS Model Arbitration Clause ("*Any dispute, controversy or claim arising out of or relating to this contract, including the formation, interpretation, breach or termination thereof, including whether the claims asserted are arbitrable [...]*")), or by reference to the rules that expressly provide for the tribunal's competence over the arbitrability of claims (see, *e.g.*, R-7(a) of the 2013 AAA Rules ("*The arbitrator shall have the power to rule on his or her jurisdiction, including any objections with respect [...] to the arbitrability of any claim or counterclaim.*")).

265 Especially taking into account that the vast majority of claims after the Court's seminal decision in *Mitsubishi Motors Corp. v. Soler Chrysler-Plymouth, Inc.*, 473 U.S. 614 (1985) (after: "Mitsubishi Motors") are considered arbitrable in the U.S. For further reading, see the Restatement (second tentative draft) p.241, also *e.g.* Moses, *Statutory Misconstruction: How the Supreme Court Created a Federal Arbitration Law Never Enacted by Congress* (2006) p.144 ("*After Mitsubishi, however, the Court continued to add more new rooms to its FAA structure, holding other kinds of statutory rights to be arbitrable, including those under the Racketeer Influenced and Corrupt Organizations Act (RICO), the Age Discrimination in Employment Act (ADEA), and the Carriage of Goods by Sea Act (COGSA). It is unlikely that many statutes remain today that the Court would not find arbitrable.*").

266 For example, respondent's anti-trust counterclaim is arbitrable and valid thus the tribunal agrees to award damages based on that counterclaim.

267 On the tribunal's considerations on arbitrability raised by the tribunal on its own motion, Born in Born, *International Commercial Arbitration* (2014) p.1044 aptly concluded that "*The arbitral tribunal's adjudicative mandate is to resolve the disputes that are submitted to it in accordance with applicable law – including*

panel had major policy concerns relating to the claim presented.[268] Consequently, the tribunal considered that the award granting (and not rejecting) the claim would put the enforceability of the award at risk. If, however, a court decides to vacate such a tribunal's decision[269] as going beyond the scope of the submission, it would, at the same time, unequivocally conclude that the tribunal was wrong and thus the claim (being arbitrable) should be arbitrated. It is difficult to imagine how the tribunal's decision rejecting a claim as nonarbitrable would violate public policy.[270]

The scenario, where the tribunal decides to reject its jurisdiction because it finds the claims inarbitrable (for example because claims are of a criminal nature) is similar to the one explained immediately above with the only difference that it affects the tribunal's *jurisdictional* findings. The court – as is the case with any other tribunal's jurisdictional decision (positive or negative) – will be able to step in and vacate the award.[271] It seems unlikely, however, that the court would be convinced with arguments that the tribunal has exceeded its powers.[272]

7.1.4 Decision on class arbitration

The Supreme Court's decision in *Stolt-Nielsen* cast a shadow on the availability of class actions in arbitration.[273] At this point it suffices to say that the tribunal can accept jurisdiction over a class action only when the parties in their agreement to arbitrate expressly consent to class arbitration. In fact, however, express waivers of class actions rather than a willingness to give a tribunal the power to decide on class claims occur more often. Therefore, if no agreement on class actions has been reached, a decision accepting

---

applicable mandatory law – and to render an award on such matters that is binding and enforceable. Where the parties' contract raises issues of illegality, violations of public policy or mandatory law, or performance of administrative functions, then the tribunal's mandate must necessarily include consideration of those issues insofar as they would affect its decision or the enforceability of its award. For an obvious example, the parties' request that the tribunal decide whether to grant a patent or declare a party bankrupt should not prevent the tribunal from considering sua sponte whether or not such claims are arbitrable; equally, if granting one party's substantive claims (or defenses) would violate applicable mandatory criminal, competition, intellectual property, other laws, then the tribunal both can and must consider those mandatory law issues on its own motion. Of course, as discussed elsewhere, it is an essential element of the arbitrators' mandate and the parties' procedural rights that any sua sponte consideration of nonarbitrability or similar issues by a tribunal be accompanied by notice to the parties and an opportunity to be heard on the issue."

268 Before deciding on the issue, a tribunal would likely give the parties an opportunity to address their concerns. That makes it even more difficult to imagine that a decision would go beyond the parties' submissions. See also fn.267.

269 This is a tribunal's (*ex officio*) decision rejecting the claim as being nonarbitrable.

270 This goes squarely to the application of mandatory rules *ex officio*. See further section 6.2.4.

271 See fn.231.

272 See fn.267.

273 *Stolt-Nielsen*, 559 U.S. 662, 130 S. Ct. 1758, 176 L. Ed. 2d 605 (2010).

jurisdiction over such actions will be vacated as a decision in excess of the tribunal's powers.[274]

7.2 Decisions on parties' claims

Decisions on parties' claims in an abstract sense focus mostly on the *basis* for the claims rather than on remedies sought by the parties.[275] Not all claims, however, may fall under the scope of the arbitral tribunal's powers based on their underlying legal nature. Therefore, it is necessary to establish if the tribunal exceeds its powers if it decides on contractual claims (see section 7.2.1) and contractual counterclaims (see section 7.2.2). Additionally, decisions on set-off defenses (section 7.2.3) have their unique features that should be highlighted. Also, decisions on claims that are of a non-contractual basis, *i.e.* based on torts (section 7.2.4), need to be subsequently analyzed. Finally, it might be necessary to determine if it is possible to challenge a tribunal's decisions on the introduction of new claims (and counterclaims) or changes to the existing ones (section 7.2.5), as well as a tribunal's decision that does not cover all claims (or counterclaims) (section 7.2.6).

7.2.1 Decision on contractual claims

At face value, a tribunal's decision on contractual claims appears to be the most basic reason why the tribunal has been requested to act in the first place. The decision on contractual claims covers the claims that arise out of contract and that are brought by claimant (as opposed to counterclaims that are brought by respondent in response to the claimant's initial claims).[276] In general, it should be considered that the decision on contractual claims would be rarely vacated by the court because (i) claims arising out of contract would be anticipated by most of the (model) agreements to arbitrate, (ii) the decision answers claimant's direct request, and (iii) it is unlikely that contractual claims will infringe public policy.

A quick look at institutional model clauses proves that the claims arising out of or in connection to the contract are unambiguously designated to be settled in arbitration.[277]

274 For further reading, see, *i.a.*, Strong (2013), Pharaon (2015).

275 See section 7.4.

276 For further reading, see section 7.2.2.

277 See, *i.a.*, the ICDR Model Clause ("*Any controversy or claim arising out of or relating to this contract, or the breach thereof*"), the JAMS Model Arbitration Clause ("*Any dispute, controversy or claim arising out of or relating to this contract, including the formation, interpretation, breach or termination thereof [...]*"), the 1976 UNCITRAL Model Arbitration Clause ("*Any dispute, controversy or claim arising out of or relating to this contract, or the breach, termination or invalidity thereof [...]*"), the 2010 UNCITRAL Model Arbitration Clause for Contracts ("*Any dispute, controversy out of or relating to this contract, or the breach, termination or invalidity thereof [...]*"), the 2012 and the 2017 Standard ICC Arbitration Clause ("*All disputes arising out of or in connection with present contract [...]*"). See also *In re Arbitration Between Gen. Sec. Nat. Ins.*

This means, that the general assumption of users of arbitration is to submit all the contractual matters before the tribunal for its final determination. Of course, parties are free to tailor their agreement to arbitrate differently than the model solutions and, in turn, designate different or more limited powers towards the arbitral tribunal. Nonetheless, as noted above, contractual claims are in the very core of the arbitral system and it is very unlikely that the parties will limit their consent to arbitration by excluding *contractual* claims.[278] It is possible, however, that parties in their agreement will entrust the tribunal only with a specific category of contractual claims (*e.g.* claims on damages or compensation for breach of contract) or, in contrast, they will exclude certain contractual claims from the tribunal's powers (*e.g.* claims over the validity or existence of the main contract). In these instances, the tribunal needs to respect the limitations imposed. Otherwise, the award might suffer in the vacatur proceedings based on the "excess of powers" ground.[279]

Furthermore, the parties' submissions shape the scope of the tribunal's powers. For this reason, claimants' contractual claims introduced in the documents initiating the arbitral process[280] and motions made at the early stage of the proceedings[281] frame what contractual claims should be scrutinized by the tribunal. It further means that the tribunal is not entitled to render, on its own motion, a decision on other contractual claims that have not been brought by claimant before the tribunal. That being said, two issues need to be highlighted, namely, (i) what happens if the contractual claims brought are not clear in themselves and (ii) what happens if the contractual claims go beyond the initial agreement to arbitrate.[282]

If the contractual claims are not clear, claimant risks of not being awarded what it asked for. If the claims are ambiguous, however, they would be an easy target for respondent to rebut and/or for the tribunal to call for clarification during *e.g. a* preliminary hearing.[283] If the claims are not rebutted nor the tribunal's call for clarification answered, the tribunal who accepted jurisdiction over these claims will have to address the claims in the way it interprets them.[284] Unusually, some authors argue that "*[t]hough the amount which is being*

Co. & AequiCap Program Administrators, 785 F. Supp. 2d 411, 418 (S.D.N.Y. 2011) ("*As a threshold matter, arbitration provisions that specify that 'any disputes' shall be determined by arbitration are typically deemed to be 'broad' arbitration provisions.*").

278 Parties are more often tempted to exclude claims based *e.g.* on torts. For reflections on decisions based on torts, see section 6.1.4.

279 The vacatur court, however, will exercise a deferential test over the tribunal's decision. See sections 3.1 and 7.1.2 of this chapter.

280 For example, Notice of Arbitration under the ICDR Rules, Request for Arbitration under the JAMS Rules, Demand for Arbitration under the AAA Rules.

281 See, *e.g.*, Terms of Reference under the ICC Rules. For the claims submitted at the later stage of the proceedings, see section 7.2.5.

282 As will be explained below, it would likely take the form of the "scope" question.

283 See, for example, R-21(a) of the AAA Rules.

284 It is equally possible that the tribunal will simply reject ambiguous claims.

sought as the relief by the party-claimant need not necessarily be included in the submission, in certain instances it may be advisable to mention it, thus framing the issue as far as the demand for a money-award is concerned."[285] By doing so, claimant will limit the discretion of the tribunal regarding the amount awarded by the tribunal. In reviewing the decision on contractual claims (that are alleged to be unclear), the vacating court will likely defer to the tribunal's interpretation.[286]

As a default rule, if claimant requests the tribunal to decide on the issues that go beyond the scope of the parties' initial agreement to arbitrate, the tribunal should reject the claim as being placed beyond the parties' consent. Nevertheless, in the event that the participating respondent fails to raise that the tribunal has no power over these claims, it may very well be found to have impliedly consented to expand the initial scope of the agreement to arbitrate. In turn, a tribunal's decision might conceivably survive the challenge at the vacatur stage. It should be noted, however, that in this instance the challenge would likely be framed as the jurisdictional/threshold issue (namely the "scope" question) and, consequently, be subject to a *de novo* review by the vacatur court.[287]

The public policy considerations on contractual claims come down to the question whether the claims are arbitrable. Since the question of arbitrability has been discussed above,[288] it should be highlighted that it is unlikely that the contractual claims will infringe public policy.

7.2.2 Decision on contractual counterclaims

The decision on counterclaims deserves separate attention, because it may not always be allowed for the tribunal to decide on counterclaims. Generally, they need to be characterized as a category of offensive actions brought by respondent in response to claims initiating arbitral proceedings.[289] Additionally, counterclaims are, by and large, remote from the claimant's claim and therefore shall lead to the arbitral tribunal's separate and independent determination.[290] In effect, even if the initial claimant's claims are rejected or even withdrawn, the tribunal's decision on counterclaims will be standing out. In this section,

285 Domke et al., *Domke on Commercial Arbitration* (2015) § 8:4.

286 Irrespective of whether it is claimant or respondent who challenges the award. If the tribunal gave the party a reasonable opportunity to address its concern and it failed to do so, it should not be allowed to raise its arguments as late as at the post-award stage.

287 See further section 7.1.2.

288 Section 7.1.3 of this chapter.

289 Fortún (2010) p.453. The theoretical possibility exists, where it is a claimant who brings a counter-counterclaim in response to the respondent's counterclaim. It should not, however, affect the analysis undertaken in this section. If the tribunal accepts to hear counterclaims it is only reasonable that it will also accept to hear the claimant's counter-counterclaims, taking into account the principle of equal treatment of the parties.

290 Pryles & Waincymer, *Multiple Claims in Arbitration Between the Same Parties* (2009) p.448, Fortún (2010) p.453.

only the decision on counterclaims that have their source in the contract will be discussed, since the focus here should be directed on the most basic notion of the decision on counterclaims that can arise out of contractual relations.[291] As long as some parts of the analysis mirror the conclusions from the previous section,[292] few additional reflections will be introduced.[293]

Similar to the considerations mentioned above,[294] a tribunal first needs to seek a power to award contractual counterclaims in the agreement to arbitrate.[295] Typically, model arbitration clauses should be interpreted in a way that they allow contractual counterclaims to be introduced. It is so, because they use the general notion of "*controversy or claim arising out of or relating to this contract*".[296]

Arguably, it is the relation between the (counter)claim and the contract that matters.[297] Consequently, if the clause is drafted broadly, it should allow both parties to bring their claims before the tribunal. In other words, it might be considered that *counterclaims* are nothing more than *claims* falling within the scope of the arbitration agreement.[298]

In a comparable fashion, when faced with the agreement to arbitrate stating that "*any controversy between us arising out of or relating to this contract or the breach thereof or arising out of transactions with you shall be settled by arbitration*", one court concluded that

291 In the following sections the point of interest will be shifted to the non-contractual basis for the claims and to the question if such a basis can alter the scope of the tribunal's power to grant a specific counterclaim. In these instances, however, claims and counterclaims will be discussed jointly since they can both be considered, for the purpose of the analysis, as the same type of *offensive* claim with the only difference lying in who is bringing the claims. Therefore, the claims can only be brought by claimant, whereas counterclaims are generally brought be respondent (it is still possible that claimant in its answer to counterclaims presents additional counter-counterclaims. See fn.289). See sections 6.1.4-7.2.6 of this chapter.

292 See section 7.2.1.

293 Occasionally, a party may wish to file a conditional counterclaim. It is argued that the analysis of this section will also apply to them.

294 See section 7.2.1.

295 See, *i.a.*, Pavić (2006) pp.104-106.

296 For examples of model arbitration clauses, see fn.277.

297 And not the relation between the claim and counterclaim.

298 Pryles and Waincymer in Pryles & Waincymer, *Multiple Claims in Arbitration Between the Same Parties* (2009) p.449 also suggest that "*[i]t is the connection to the contract and not who makes the claim that matters [...].*" Nonetheless, they immediately raise their concerns that "*[...] although there can still be consent issues as to the constitution of the tribunal which should hear the case.*" The authors further explain *i.a.* that there may be some "fairness considerations" with regard to the tribunal's composition under "some procedural systems", where counterclaims do not have to be notified prior to the tribunal's composition. In that case the claimant might not be able to select the most suitable arbitrator to hear both claims and counterclaims. In the U.S. context, however, taking into account the rules of the major American arbitral institutions, it should be conceivably concluded that these doubts will generally not apply. See, *e.g.*, Art. 3.2 of the 2014 ICDR Rules and Art. 5.1(e) the 2016 JAMS Rules which allow claimant to respond to respondent's counterclaims.

> [i]t is not an unreasonable construction of the terms of the provision for the arbitrators to consider the counterclaims for defamation and damage as a result of an unfounded suit on the breach of the customer agreement. A restrictive reading of the broad language of the arbitration clause would be contrary to the law favoring arbitrability of disputes.[299]

Also in a different case, another court found that "*The arbitration was certainly broad enough to comprehend the issues raised by [former employees]. It was [the employer] that filed the cross-claims in the first place, and there is nothing unusual or heterodox about the counterclaims.*"[300] Therefore, one may conclude that, more often than not, the tribunal will find adjudicative authority over contractual counterclaims in the underlying agreement to arbitrate.

Usually, even if institutional model clauses are not used, parties do refer to the institutional rules. If they do so, these rules will complement the parties' consent expressed in the agreement to arbitrate. In consequence, it is likely that a respondent will have an opportunity to bring its counterclaims and it will be, by all means, in the tribunal's powers to render the decision on respondent's request.[301] As it was in the context of claimant's contractual claims, the tribunal's decision on counterclaims can only follow the respondent's request as actually submitted. Another point is that the counterclaims should be brought only against claimant.

An additional problem arises in the multiple contract reality. There, it is possible that counterclaims brought by respondent find their support in a different contract from the one used by claimant to evidence the initial claims.[302] In this case, it all boils down to the question of the scope of the agreement to arbitrate, which, as discussed, is usually for the tribunal to decide.[303] When the agreement to arbitrate is drafted broadly, respondent will have sufficient chance to prove that its counterclaim, based on a different contract *arises out of* or *relates to* the contract on which the initial claim was brought. If the claim is accepted, however, depends on the tribunal's determination. By and large, if the scope question is within the tribunal's capacity to decide, then the vacating court will respect the

---

299 *Ritterman v. Amari*, 1989 U.S. Dist. LEXIS 13569, *6 (S.D.N.Y. Nov. 14, 1989).

300 *Johnston Lemon & Co. v. Smith*, 886 F. Supp. 54, 55-56 (D.D.C. 1995) aff'd, 84 F.3d 1452 (D.C. Cir. 1996). In its holding, the court argued that "*(1) [the] arbitration panel did not exceed its powers or scope of arbitration by awarding damages on various tort counterclaims asserting unfairness of [the] firm's pursuit of [the] indemnification claim against employees after prior arbitration had concluded with rulings in their favor on [a] similar indemnification claim*".

301 See, *e.g.*, Art. 5.1(b) of the 2016 JAMS Rules, Art. 3.2 of the 2014 ICDR Rules.

302 Although the contract is different, it may very well be between claimant and respondent.

303 See section 7.1.2.

tribunal's findings on the construction and interpretation of the (scope of the) agreement to arbitrate.[304]

Finally, one should note that, like the decision on contractual claims, the decision on contractual counterclaims may be reviewed on public policy grounds only when the counterclaim granted was in fact nonarbitrable.[305] It is difficult to imagine how the tribunal's choice to accept or reject contractual counterclaims would amount to the violation of public policy, especially taking into account how extremely narrow the public policy test is.[306] Notably, considering the Restatement's take on the post-award relief under the FAA,[307] public policy challenges will also be considered under the "excess of powers" ground.[308]

7.2.3 Decision on set-off

In contrast to a traditional counterclaim that works as an attacking tool, set-off is, by and large, considered as a respondent's defensive mechanism.[309] It cannot be stressed enough that these two concepts cannot be mixed.[310] Some of the set-off's traits should be, thus, briefly highlighted.[311] First of all, as mentioned above, a counterclaim has a destiny independent from the initial claimant's claim, whereas the set-off claim shares the fate of the primary claim.[312] Therefore, if, for example, the primary claim falls outside the scope of the agreement to arbitrate, so does the set-off claim.[313] Secondly, the amount of the set-off claim cannot exceed the amount of the primary claim.[314] Thirdly and finally, the set-off claim has to be of monetary character.

Traditionally, also in the context of set-off claims, it is necessary to reflect on the question (i) how these claims fit into the scope of the agreement to arbitrate and (ii) what

304 Even if a vacating court will not be satisfied that parties *clearly and unmistakably* agreed to have the arbitrators decide the scope question and, in consequence, proceed with the independent review of the agreement to arbitrate, generally, it will reach the same conclusion as the tribunal did, since the broadly drafted clauses are presumed to include counterclaims that especially take into account federal policy favoring arbitration. See, *e.g.*, fns.299 and 300.

305 See section 7.1.3.

306 See section 4.3 and section 6.1.1.

307 See section 5.3.

308 For further reading, see section 6.1.2. The Restatement's take on the "excess of powers" ground is considered for the purposes of the post-award relief against "non-convention awards". See section 5.1 and section 5.3.

309 In principle, set-off will be considered as a substantive defense. Therefore, the initial question would be to determine the law applicable to the issue of set-off. Consequently, U.S. law will not necessarily will be the law that applies to the issue of set-off. For a brief analysis of U.S. law on set-off, see Rodner (2011) p.551.

310 See, *i.a.*, Berger, *Set-off in International Economic Arbitration* (1999) pp.58-61, Fortún (2010) pp.453-454, Pryles & Waincymer, *Multiple Claims in Arbitration Between the Same Parties* (2009) pp.448-449.

311 For further reading on set-off in international commercial arbitration see, *i.a.*, Fountoulakis (2011), Pichonnaz & Gullifer (2014).

312 The primary claim being usually the claimant's initial claim. It is possible, however, that a set-off defense is raised by claimant in response to respondent's counterclaim.

313 Berger, *Set-off in International Economic Arbitration* (1999) pp.60-61.

314 Berger, *Set-off in International Economic Arbitration* (1999) p.61.

is the relevance of the parties' relief sought.[315] An answer to these questions will help to determine when the tribunal's decision can be found to be in excess of powers.

In order to answer the first question, one should imagine (at least) three scenarios: in the first, the simplest one, the tribunal decides on a set-off claim that has its standing in the same contract as the primary claim; in the second one, the claimed set-off is based on torts related to the same contract; in the last, and the most difficult one, the tribunal accepts the set-off defense emerging from a different contract (different from the contract that is the basis for the primary claim) or even torts related to a different contract.[316]

The first two out of three scenarios are rather straightforward. In the first hypothesis, irrespectively of how broad or narrow an agreement to arbitrate is, the tribunal should be able to also decide on the subject of said set-off claim, especially taking into account that both concurring claims (the primary claim and the set-off) arise out of the same contract and that the set-off claim shares the fate of the primary claim. The second hypothesis depends on the wording of the agreement to arbitrate. The traditional broad wording of agreements to arbitrate (such as "*controversy or claim arising out of or relating to this contract*")[317] may allow for the tribunal to reach a decision on set-off also if it is based on a tort claim. If parties drafted their agreement narrowly (limiting the tribunal panel's considerations to only contractual claims), the tribunal would violate the limits of its powers if it grants set-off on the basis of a tort.[318]

The third scenario is more difficult. By and large, the narrowly drafted, traditional agreement to arbitrate (*e.g.* "*claim arising out of this contract*") would not encompass set-off claims arising out of a different contract. Arguably, the broad wording of the agreement to arbitrate ("*controversy or claim arising out of or relating to this contract*") might entail that set-off claims based on different contracts or tortious liability related to different contracts if there is evidence that these claims are sufficiently linked (*i.e. arise out of* or *relate to*) to the primary contract.

315 It is difficult to imagine how the tribunal's decision on set-off could violate federal public policy. Although not discussed under this section, it is always necessary, on a case-by-case basis, to determine if a specific tribunal's decision infringes the underlying values of the American legal system. On that note, in one case a court held that "*dismissal of [a] counterclaim, even if granted as sanction for [a] company's destruction of evidence, did not warrant vacating [the] arbitration award.*" See *AmeriCredit Fin. Servs., Inc. v. Oxford Mgmt. Servs.*, 627 F. Supp. 2d 85 (E.D.N.Y. 2008).

316 Arguably, not only the decision accepting the claim but also the tribunal's negative determination on set-off can be challenged in vacatur proceedings. If, however, the tribunal found that the specific set-off cannot be dealt with under the underlying agreement to arbitrate, it is unlikely that the vacating court would vacate such a decision on the basis of excess of powers. As mentioned previously (section 7.1.2), the vacating court will not overturn the decision on the scope *per se* but rather annul these elements of the decision that go beyond the parties' consent.

317 For other examples, see fn.277.

318 One should note that it will exceed the powers because it was based on a tort claim and not because it dealt with a set-off defense. For further reading on decisions on tort claims, see section 6.1.4.

In case of multiple contracts, however, one twist can shatter the arbitral tribunal's power over set-off claims based on other contracts: when these contracts have its own arbitration or forum selection clause, there is an obvious obstacle in the way of determination of the parties' intent to arbitrate.[319] If the parties included different dispute resolution mechanisms in their contracts (even related ones), the tribunal's decision on set-off claims that fits within the scope of a different agreement to arbitrate[320] might raise legitimate concerns regarding the arbitral panel's powers to decide on the claims.

That being said, and coming to the second question introduced at the outset, it is also necessary to remember the defensive character of set-off claims. It means that set-off arguments will be submitted by the parties themselves in defense of the initial claims. Consequently, there are strong arguments, usually advocated by Swiss scholars, to let the tribunal decide on these types of set-offs. First of all, respondent should have a right to oppose and present material defense reducing its outstanding obligations. Second of all, having in mind procedural efficiency, it might be justified to resolve all the parties' disagreements at once rather than to tolerate the state of a permanent legal battle between the parties.

Likewise, Karrer reflected that

> [...] the parties must be presumed to prefer the dispute about the set-off defence to be resolved by the arbitral tribunal already in place. After all, the claimant started the arbitration before that arbitral tribunal, and the respondent who is setting off prefers to use the second obligation the other way, as a defence in the existing arbitration, or the respondent would not have raised it there and would have commenced arbitration elsewhere. All this makes good sense to me, and the claimant's insistence that the obligation used as a set-off defence should be brought before a different arbitral tribunal that first must be set up appears abusive of the legal process. The legal process should bring peace quickly and efficiently and should not be an all-out battle.[321]

Additionally, a very cogent argument has been advanced by Blessing: "*[t]he Tribunal could not confine itself [to] adjudicating the claims arising under one contract only, while closing*

319 See, however, Karrer, *Jurisdiction on set-off defences and counterclaims* (2001) p.177, who discusses the issue in general ("*(...) in my opinion, it would be very difficult to say that the existence of incompatible arbitration or choice-of-forum clauses makes it impossible to set off obligations which otherwise could be set off one against another. (...) Contracts are primarily designed to prevent disputes or to resolve them amicably, and exercising a right to set-off is a perfectly acceptable way to extinguish obligations.*"). See also Pryles & Waincymer, *Multiple Claims in Arbitration Between the Same Parties* (2009) pp.488-492.

320 Therefore the agreement to arbitrate that is different from the one which sets up the tribunal's jurisdiction.

321 Karrer, *Jurisdiction on set-off defences and counterclaims* (2001) p.177.

its eyes in respect of certain justified set-off claims (although those originated from different contracts with different arbitration clauses)."[322]

Being extremely cautious over each individual case's factual underpinning, it is a sensible solution to allow the tribunal to decide on set-off when it constitutes a truly substantive defense to a primary claim, even if it has a different basis than the primary contract, thus, even if, arguably, they go within the scope of the competing agreement to arbitrate.

Importantly, some of the institutional rules in the U.S. seem to accept the notion that set-offs may not necessarily be covered by the agreement to arbitrate (as opposed to counterclaims) for the tribunal to decide upon them. For example, the 2014 ICDR Rules provide that "*[a]t the time Respondent submits its Answer, Respondent may make any counterclaims covered by the agreement to arbitrate or assert any setoffs [...].*"[323] One should note that it is a significant change in the rules, considering that in their 2010 edition they provided that respondent "*may make counterclaims or assert setoffs as to any claim covered by the agreement to arbitrate[...].*"[324]

All in all, it is important for the parties to request set-offs. Under no circumstances should the tribunal *ex officio* extinguish the claimant's claim against a non-requested set-off claim. Such a tribunal's decision would likely be found in excess of powers and violating the equal treatment of the parties.

7.2.4 Decision on claims/counterclaims based on torts and pre-contractual liability

Award-debtors, although contemporarily with lesser frequency, may try to argue that a decision based on torts exceeds the tribunal's powers. This argument may be based either (i) on the notion that the agreement to arbitrate did not foresee claims based on torts. In the alternative, (ii) one may also suggest that the excess can be illustrated by the case where the tribunal decides to requalify the parties' claims (by awarding the relief sought but changing the basis for the claim from contractual to tortious).

Nowadays it is rather uncontroversial that an arbitral tribunal should enjoy the possibility to address all the parties' claims at once. The practical argument is the one of the reasonable expectations of the parties to settle the whole conflict (all disputes) between

322 Blessing did not discuss the U.S. arbitration system. The argument remains strong, nonetheless. The original reference made by Fortún in Fortún (2010) p.459.

323 Art. 3.2 of the 2014 ICDR Rules. See also Art. 5.1(b) of the 2016 JAMS Rules that mentions that the Statement of Defense should include a brief statement describing the nature and circumstance of any setoffs asserted or counterclaims advanced by the respondent against the claimant. The AAA Rules do not design specific rules to deal with set-off claims. They refer only to counterclaims (R-5 of the 2013 AAA Rules). To the contrary, for example, Art. 19(3) of the 1976 UNCITRAL Rules explicitly allowed only set-off claims that have arisen out of the same contract as primary claim.

324 See Art. 3.2 of the 2010 ICDR Rules.

them in order to be able to move on with their business relationship.[325] This means that a broad agreement to arbitrate presumptively covers not only contractual differences but also other disputes that may arise in the context of the underlying contractual relationship. It should also be noted that such an agreement would address claims irrespective of by whom they are introduced. It further entails that both claims and counterclaims can be of a tortious nature.[326] Courts have generally rejected challenges against the tribunal's awards based on torts, finding that tort claims have been covered by the agreement to arbitrate.[327]

Additionally, it is necessary to reflect on the issue of a tribunal's requalification of the basis of the party's claim. To illustrate such an instance, one should imagine that a party requested the tribunal to award damages supporting this claim on the underlying contract; the tribunal awarded damages, but at the same time rejected the contractual foundations of the claim. Instead, it went to find that the damages are in fact justified but on the basis of extra-contractual rather than the contractual liability. In the case when a party submitted two alternative bases for the claim of damages, there is no reason why the tribunal's decision should be successfully vacated.

If, however, the tribunal rejects the basis for the claim submitted and nonetheless grants the claim substantiating it, on its own motion, on torts, such an action gives rise to legitimate concerns. As long as it is fair to say that such an award should be vacated, the question remains if the challenge should be based on the excess of powers ground.

Arguably, not only claims in themselves limit the tribunal's powers, but also the remaining content of the parties' submissions, including the parties' legal reasoning for the claims. In the alternative, however, the hypothetical touches upon the notion of *iura novit arbiter* in international arbitration and the extent for the tribunal to introduce its own legal theories while deciding the claims.[328] In any event, even in case of rejection of the argument that the tribunal's decision was an act beyond its power, it is likely that it will also amount to violation of due process if the parties are not heard about the tribunal's

325 The concept is sometimes called the "one-stop shop for arbitration". For further reading on this subject, see Chapter IV.

326 Berger, *Set-off in International Economic Arbitration* (1999) p.65. Although the arguments are not made in the American arbitration context, they will be equally applicable.

327 See, *i.a.*, the court in *Jih v. Long & Foster Real Estate, Inc.* (1992, DC Md) 800 F. Supp. 312 decided that the "*arbitration panel did not exceed [its] authority because damages awarded, though potentially based on a tort theory of liability, were inextricably tied up with the merits of the underlying dispute*" (as reported in *EST, LLC v. Smith*, No. 5:08-CV-32, 2011 WL 2118984, at *6 (W.D.N.C. May 24, 2011). See also *Federated Dep't Stores, Inc. v. J.V.B. Indus., Inc.*, 894 F.2d 862, 869 (6th Cir. 1990) ("*We hold that the arbitration clause [...] is broad enough to encompass a tort claim originating in an alleged breach of the contracts.*"), *Johnston Lemon & Co. v. Smith*, 886 F. Supp. 54 (D.D.C. 1995) aff'd, 84 F.3d 1452 (D.C. Cir. 1996) (the "*arbitration panel did not exceed its powers or scope of arbitration by awarding damages on various tort counterclaims asserting unfairness of [the] firm's pursuit of [the] indemnification claim against employees after prior arbitration had concluded with rulings in their favor on [a] similar indemnification claim*").

328 See also section 6.2.3.

new theory, because the tribunal, while changing the basis for the claim, effectively argues for one of the parties. Considering, how broad the concept of the "excess of powers" is being interpreted by the Restatement, arguably, such a due process violation will also be considered under Section 10(a)(4) of the FAA.[329]

7.2.5 Decision on new claims/counterclaims and change of claims/counterclaims

It goes without saying that bringing new claims[330] or amending already presented claims might reshape the arbitral tribunal's adjudicatory powers. Nonetheless, in order to protect the procedural integrity of an arbitration, it is not always acceptable to let the parties proceed as they will (that is to redraft the scope of their submissions). Generally, the usual test of the vacatur court, *i.e.* comparing the award with an agreement to arbitrate, parties' submissions and public policy, equally applies to a tribunal's decision as discussed in this section. What needs to be determined is, however, whether the tribunal initially has a power to decide on extended/amended claims and what happens in instances where these claims are perceived as being (i) within and (ii) beyond the initial agreement to arbitrate.

The FAA does not provide any guidance with regard to the question of the admissibility of new claims or the amendment of existing ones. Generally speaking, the same contention applies to broadly drafted arbitration clauses. Nonetheless, usually the issue is addressed by the arbitration rules which provide that, after the tribunal is constituted, the tribunal has to agree on the admission of new claims.[331] One could argue that the request for the tribunal's consent effectively denotes its power to decide on the issue.

Additionally, the institutional rules further assist in determining the second issue of interest, namely, to what extent parties can expand their initial claims. The ICDR and the JAMS Rules are very explicit in saying that amendment or addition to the initial claims *cannot* go beyond the initial agreement to arbitrate,[332] whereas the AAA Rules do not address the relevance of the initial agreement to arbitrate in the context of the change of

329 See section 5.1 and section 5.3.

330 Under this section, the term "claims" should be interpreted broadly so that it entails both "offensive" counterclaims and "defensive" counterclaims.

331 See, *e.g.*, Art. 9 of the 2014 ICDR Rules ("*Any party may amend or supplement its claim, counterclaim, setoff, or defense unless the arbitral tribunal considers it inappropriate to allow such amendment or supplement […]*"), Art. 6.1 of the 2016 JAMS Rules ("*Claims or counterclaims within the scope of the arbitration clause may be added or amended prior to the establishment of the Tribunal, but hereafter only with the consent of the Tribunal.*"), Art. 6.1 of the 2016 JAMS Rules, and R-6(b) of the 2013 AAA Rules ("*After the arbitrator is appointed, however, no new or different claim may be submitted except with the arbitrator's consent.*"). See also, Art. 20 of the 1976 UNCITRAL Rules, Art. 22 of the 2010 UNCITRAL Rules, Art. 23(4) of the 2017 ICC Rules, and Art. 23(4) of the 2012 ICC Rules.

332 Art. 9 of the 2014 ICDR ("*A party may not amend or supplement a claim or counterclaim if the amendment or supplement would fall outside the scope of the agreement to arbitrate*") and Art. 6.1 of the 2016 JAMS Rules ("*However, a claim or defense may not be amended in such a manner that the amended claim or the amended defense falls outside the scope of the arbitration clause or the parties' separate arbitration agreement*").

claims or the introduction of new ones.[333] As mentioned earlier on several occasions, the institutional rules do influence the shape of the tribunal's powers. Therefore, although the tribunal will still be able to determine the scope question (*i.e.* whether new/changed claims fit within the framework of the agreement to arbitrate),[334] it would need to follow the guidelines of the institutional rules that limit the scope of its powers ultimately to the ambit of the agreement to arbitrate, prohibiting the tribunal to admit claims that go beyond the initial consent to arbitrate. Failing to do so would expose the arbitral award to vacatur on grounds of excess of powers.

7.2.6 Decision not covering all claims/counterclaims

In the *infra petita* situation, *i.e.* when the tribunal has not decided in its award on all claims or issues submitted to it, there is no concern as to the scope of the agreement to arbitrate nor is there a problem with public policy violations. The only thing that matters is that the tribunal failed to address all the claims/counterclaims presented before it. Since the FAA does not provide for a separate ground for vacatur regarding *infra petita* decisions, the question that follows is whether such a tribunal's decision can be challenged on the excess of powers ground.

Hypothetically, one could reflect that it is justified to vacate the decision, especially when it does not address all of the counterclaims or material defenses. If the tribunal omitted certain parts of the parties' submissions, it could be questioned whether (i) the panel deliberately decided *not* to render a decision on a certain claim or (ii) whether it was an accident. That could be particularly important for the fate of an *infra petita* award.

If the tribunal knowingly chose not to decide on a claim (or counterclaim), one may wonder if it had a power to do so. On the one hand, parties have genuine expectations towards the tribunal to have all of their claims answered, since it is the underlying reason why the tribunal is specifically contracted. On the other hand, if a specific claim has been omitted in the award, but it is clear that it has been taken into account during the deliberations, it might be conceivable that by not including the claim the tribunal impliedly rejected it.[335] Such a conclusion would be particularly true if the tribunal firmly states that it "*rejects any and all other claims*" or that "*it was in full and final settlement of all claims between the parties.*"[336] In this context, such an *infra petita* award would be in fact considered

333 The AAA Rules do address, however, the difference between the change of the value of the claim, which practically does not ask for the tribunal's permission (as it does not affect its adjudicatory powers) and change of the claims themselves or introduction of new claims that requires the tribunals' ruling. See R-6(a) and R-6(b) of the 2013 AAA Rules. These are, however, domestic rules.

334 Subject to its general competence of the scope question, see section 7.1.2.

335 Arguably, however, an implied rejection of claims is not an ideal solution, especially if it has been introduced as a party's material defense.

336 See, *e.g.*, *Gonzalez v. Shearson Lehman Bros.*, 794 F. Supp. 53, 55 (D.P.R. 1992) ("*[...] the record of the proceedings reflects that the arbitrators, although silent in their award regarding the counterclaim, did consider*

complete and as such it will also entail a *res iudicata* effect, preventing parties' from bringing omitted claims before another arbitral tribunal or before the court.

Conversely, if it is clear from the award that the tribunal indeed failed to address all the issues, namely, intended to answer all issues raised, but was not successful, the award cannot be considered as complete. It is possible, however, that it will also be concluded with an closing statement that it "*rejects any and all other claims*", which would make it difficult to prove that the omissions were not intended. Nonetheless, if the court finds that a material defense of a party has not been considered, it might use its remedial powers to save the award.[337]

On the one hand, Born prefers that

> awards should generally be subject to annulment on infra petita grounds, including when [...] arbitration legislation contains no express provision to that effect. That is because an arbitral tribunal's failure to consider issues presented to it in fact amounts to an excess of authority, even if it appears only to be the reverse, because it effectively rewrites the tribunal's mandate, which is an act beyond the arbitrators' competence; that is particularly true when a tribunal fails to consider defenses or counterclaims related to relief that it does grant.[338]

On the other hand, the Restatement offers remedies in order to heal the *infra petita* awards and make them in turn effectively confirmed. In the view of the Restatement:

---

and render a decision on the claim. The chairman stated that the arbitrators had reviewed all the papers filed by the parties, which presumably included respondents' counterclaim. Respondents testified in some detail as to their alleged damages arising out of their counterclaim. As a result, the explicit statement in the award that it was in full and final settlement of all claims between the parties must be viewed as a statement that it included a decision on petitioners' counterclaim – in respondent's favor.").

337 See section 3.3. See, however, the Restatement (third tentative draft) pp.83-84 ("*Courts occasionally remand awards because a matter that was properly submitted to the tribunal and is essential to the completeness of the award appears not to have been decided in the award. [...] Reference in this context is usually made to overlooked claims rather than overlooked defenses. However, a tribunal's utter and inexplicable failure to address a matter such as the statute of limitations, a jurisdictional argument, or even an essential substantive defense, if properly invoked, may justify remand for supplementation of the award. [...] On the other hand, it is critical in this regard that the court remand only if there is a real and genuine omission. Before finding a lacuna that might justify remand, a court will carefully consider whether remand for supplementation is unnecessary, and indeed improper, because a decision on the ostensibly omitted matter is implicit in the award's reasoning. In cases of doubt, the court may ask a tribunal to indicate more clearly what in fact it decided in the award; that response will determine whether further action by the tribunal is required.*"). For further reading on remand, see the Restatement (third tentative draft) pp.80-85.

338 Born, *International Commercial Arbitration* (2014) p.3294.

> [i]ndeed, an 'incomplete' award might be characterized as a partial award – an award that resolves some but not all issues in dispute – and be enforceable as such. A party faced with an incomplete award may nevertheless ask a court to remand it to the arbitrators [...], and, in appropriate circumstances, a court may be entitled to provide a remedy using its powers of correction [...].[339]

The better view is the one of the Restatement. Having in mind the exclusive character of the grounds for vacatur, it is argued that *infra petita* is not one of them and it should not be subsumed by the excess of powers ground. Taking into account the federal pro-arbitration policy it is preferred to partially enforce the award or remand the award to the tribunal rather than to vacate the award. If the tribunal intentionally omitted some claims, it could mean that they should be considered as not admitted, if, however, the omission happened by mistake, it is difficult to attribute the intention to "rewrite the mandate" to the arbitral panel.

7.3 *Process of application of law by the arbitral tribunal*

The process of application of law by the tribunal is a complex one. Since the beginning of an arbitration until the very moment of the issuance of the award, the tribunal has a power but also a duty to follow the applicable rules of law. Albeit not all of its decisions on applicable law can be found in the award, each of these decisions undoubtedly structures final determinations of the tribunal made in the award. The process of application of law can be divided into steps that will be analyzed below: first, the tribunal needs to determine the method of selecting the applicable law (section 7.3.1) and consequently choose the applicable substantive law (section 7.3.2). While ascertaining the content of the applicable law (section 7.3.3), the tribunal might face problems related to the mandatory rules of law (section 7.3.4) and its ability to decide on principles of equity (section 7.3.5).

7.3.1 Determining the method of selection of applicable law

This section is intended to briefly reflect on two methods of selecting the applicable law, namely (i) on the choice of the applicable conflict of laws rules and (ii) on the direct determination of the applicable law. Generally, such a first step is only necessary when no choice of law clause can be found in the contract. In the absence of the parties' choice of law, the tribunal will be, by and large, entitled to determine on its own motion what law

339 The Restatement (second tentative draft) p.201. See also the Restatement (third tentative draft) p.79 ("*Remand is also the appropriate mechanism by which to perfect an award that demonstrably has failed to address a claim or defense that was properly before the tribunal. In such a case, a court lacks authority to decide the omitted matter itself, while vacatur may also be inappropriate or unavailable.*"). See also p.82 therein.

is the most "appropriate". Conversely, if parties have expressly indicated the applicable law, the tribunal should follow the parties' choice of law.[340]

Assuming that the parties have not included a choice of law clause, then the tribunal needs to initiate an inquiry in order to determine what law applies. Since the FAA does not provide any fallback mechanism (nor limitations) for determining the applicable law, the tribunal, arguably, will have extensive freedom in the approach it takes for the determining the *method* to select the applicable law. On that note, in fact, the conflict of laws rules analysis is not the easiest one and thus the tribunal may decide not to opt for this path at all, especially taking into account that it has another approach at its disposal, namely, the direct application of law without any reference to the applicable conflict of laws rules. Conceivably, a number of institutional rules accommodate the tribunals with such a power to decide on the applicable law without the need of any recourse to the conflict of laws rules.[341] In any event, the decision on the applicable conflict of laws rules (if any) or the direct selection of the applicable law should be, in principle, considered as embedded in the process and, therefore, within the boundaries of the tribunal's powers save for an agreement of the parties to the contrary as explained above.[342] This implies that the tribunal's determination of the method of selecting the applicable law would likely survive the excess of powers challenge.[343]

7.3.2 Decision on applicable law

As pointed out in the previous section, the tribunal, prior to its decision on the merits of the case, needs to determine what law applies. If no choice of law provision exists, the tribunal has to either employ a conflict of laws analysis or decide directly what the governing law is.[344] Irrespective of its choice, the tribunal's selection will inevitably affect its decision on the parties' claims. As always, however, it is necessary to reflect if it is possible to challenge (if at all) the tribunal's decision on applicable law by invoking the excess of

340 Silberman & Ferrari (2010) p.323 ("*where parties make an express choice of national law to govern the substance of their dispute and the arbitrators fail to honor that choice – by applying general principles of commercial law or disregarding a choice to apply a particular substantive legal regime – that action should be considered outside the scope of the arbitrators' authority and regarded as an excess of power by the arbitrators.*").

341 See, *e.g.*, Art. 31.1 of the 2014 ICDR Rules, Art.19.1 of the 2016 JAMS Rules.

342 Parties may also designate the choice of law rule (instead of the applicable law) in their contract. This should bind the tribunal as well.

343 See, *e.g.*, *Abu Dhabi Inv. Auth. v. Citigroup, Inc.*, 557 F. App'x 66, 67 (2d Cir.) cert. denied, 135 S. Ct. 137, 190 L. Ed. 2d 45 (2014).

344 Most likely the tribunal will directly choose the applicable law. See section 7.3.1. Also see Craig, *The arbitrator's mission and the application of law in international commercial arbitration* (2010) p.259.

powers ground.[345] Since the decision on applicable law is closely related to the conflict of laws analysis, the reflections from this and the previous section should be read together.[346]

On a general note, at the outset of the dispute, a tribunal may be faced either (i) with an express choice of law provision provided in a contract or (ii) find the necessary guidance in the parties' pleadings on applicable law. Only if it cannot distill the parties' intentions from these sources will it initiate the procedure to find an "appropriate" law.[347]

In case the parties' intent has been explicitly articulated, it goes without saying that the tribunal should follow the parties' agreement (on applicable law).[348] Consequently, an express choice of law should be considered as a bar for the tribunal to decide to the contrary.[349] In the absence of the parties' express choice, the parties' submissions frame the issue at hand. The most anticipated scenario is that the parties submit opposing views as to what law applies.[350] If that happens, on the one hand, it is reasonable to expect the tribunal to follow one of the parties' views and not to seek the applicable law independently.[351] On the other hand, the institutional rules (*e.g.* the ICDR Rules or the JAMS Rules)[352] give a broad discretion for the tribunal to determine the "appropriate" law. Therefore, arguably, the tribunal's decision that does not follow the parties' submissions (and is based on the tribunal's own legal findings) might still survive the challenge. The better view for the tribunal is, however, to follow the parties' lead and restrict its choice of law to law(s) suggested by the parties. In any event, the tribunal's choice of law will likely survive the "excess of powers" challenge.[353]

345 At this point, it is also necessary to recognize that the tribunal might need to grant two separate decisions, namely (i) on the law applicable to the agreement to arbitrate and (ii) on the law applicable to the merits of the dispute. Such a distinction might be relevant because it might affect the court's approach to the excess of powers challenge. Arguably, the analysis dealing with the law applicable to the agreement to arbitrate will relate to the tribunal's jurisdiction, whereas the decision on the law applicable to the merits will be a first step of the decision on the merits. Consequently, the scope of the court's review might differ. See also Silberman & Ferrari (2010) p.318.

346 See section 7.3.1.

347 See section 7.3.1.

348 See also the Restatement (second tentative draft) pp.219-220.

349 See section 7.3.1.

350 If parties are unanimous on the subject of governing law, they do not leave any leeway for the tribunal to decide otherwise.

351 Since the U.S. is a common law system where the principle of *iura novit arbiter* does not apply. See Rutledge et al. (2009) p.920. Also ILA, *ILA Report on Ascertaining the Contents of the Applicable Law in International Commercial Arbitration* (2008).

352 Art. 31 of the 2014 ICDR, Art. 19 of the 2016 JAMS Rules. Importantly, the ICDR Rules allows also for application of "Rules of Law" and not only law.

353 Importantly, the court standard of review for a decision on applicable law might differ, depending on if it deals with law applicable to the agreement to arbitrate or to the merits of the case. See fn.345.

7.3.3 Ascertaining the content of applicable substantive law by the arbitral tribunal

The tribunal's ultimate task, when asked to decide upon the legal principles, is to subsume legal norms to the facts of the case and render the award. One view is that the tribunal should follow the parties' legal reasoning or face the challenge that it exceeds its powers by deciding differently than parties have pleaded. In the alternative, since the parties choosing arbitration are contracting (among other things) for the finality of the tribunal's decision, the process of application of law by the tribunal should be, by and large, non-reviewable.[354] Put differently, (alleged) errors in application of law should not lead to a successful vacatur on the "excess of powers" ground.[355] In any case, some reflections on the process of determining the content of the applicable law need to be put forward.

First of all, as highlighted earlier,[356] parties may rely on a general choice of law clause in order to evidence which law applies. If that happens, the tribunal would be, in principle, bound to follow the parties' selection. Parties, however, should *not* assume that the mere reference to the general choice of law clause in the main contract would suffice to impose the limits on the tribunal's powers prescribed by said law (for example, restriction on the power to award punitive damages, which is prohibited by the law applicable to the dispute).[357] In other words, an express (albeit general) choice of law provision limits the tribunal's determinations as to the question which law applies, but does not force the tribunal to follow substantive limitations (that could be found in applicable law) on its otherwise broad authority. In order to put restrictions on the tribunal's powers, parties need to invoke these constraints explicitly in their agreement.

Secondly, in the context of ascertaining the contents of the applicable law it is impossible not to mention the doctrine of manifest disregard of the law. As discussed above,[358] it is (was) one of the most frequently used non-statutory grounds to challenge the award. Nonetheless, since the Supreme Court's decision in *Hall Street* it became uncertain whether the doctrine can still be used.[359] The manifest disregard standard goes beyond the notion of simple error in interpreting the law. In order to satisfy the court, the challenging party must not only prove that there was a clear and well-defined legal rule, but also it

354 See also section 3.2.

355 *Josephthal & Co. v. Cruttenden Roth Inc.*, 177 F. Supp. 2d 232, 238 (S.D.N.Y. 2001) ("*An award may not be vacated under this subsection on the grounds that the arbitrators' opinion fails to interpret correctly the law applicable to the issues in dispute in the arbitration proceeding, or misinterprets the underlying contract, even if that misinterpretation is 'clearly erroneous.'*"), *Seed Holdings, Inc. v. Jiffy Int'l AS*, 5 F. Supp. 3d 565, 585 (S.D.N.Y. 2014) ("*Arbitration awards are not reviewed for errors made in law or fact [...] Rather, an award may only be vacated on extremely limited grounds.*").

356 See section 7.3.2.

357 See *Mastrobuono*, 514 U.S. 52, 63-64, 115 S. Ct. 1212, 1219, 131 L. Ed. 2d 76 (1995).

358 See section 6.1.1.

359 See section 6.1.1.

needs to show that the tribunal consciously decided to ignore this rule in its decisional process. In one pre-*Hall Street* decision one court held that "*arbitrators exceed their powers in this regard not when they merely interpret or apply the governing law incorrectly, but when the award is completely irrational, or exhibits a manifest disregard of the law.*"[360] In the post-*Hall Street* reality, it is even more difficult to substantiate the challenge on the manifest disregard ground. Therefore, arguably, even when the tribunal ignores a legal rule, the award is likely to survive vacatur, unless the disregarded rule is of a public policy character. The exception to the rule would be manifest disregard of mandatory rules of public policy.[361]

Although the process of ascertaining the contents of the applicable law might escape from a thorough judicial scrutiny, it is necessary to point out that

> [...] while it may well be true that, except for extreme cases of willful disregard of law amounting to irrationality, there is little possibility of holding the arbitrator to the application of substantive legal principles, the wide leap in reasoning that leads to the conclusion that the state and federal arbitration statutes absolve the arbitrator from the use of law is not justified.[362]

Finally, one may wonder whether the tribunal needs to follow the parties' legal pleadings when deciding on the dispute. Rutlege and others mention that "*[c]onsistent with its common law tradition, the general expectation and practice in US arbitration is for the parties to provide the tribunal with the applicable legal authorities and written argument applying those authorities to the specific facts of the case.*"[363] Conceivably, a tribunal's decision that is based on its own legal arguments or theories may still survive the excess of powers challenge as long as the tribunal gives the parties an equal opportunity to submit their comments on the legal rules that the tribunal finds relevant.

7.3.4 Application of mandatory rules of law (of public policy character) by the arbitral tribunal

Presumably there are only three hypothetical instances where the process of the application of mandatory rules of law (of a public policy character)[364] by an arbitral tribunal may be challenged on the basis of excess of powers: (i) the parties tried to limit the application of legally prescribed restrictions and the tribunal did not conform, (ii) the parties did not

360 *Schoenduve Corp. v. Lucent Technologies, Inc.*, 442 F.3d 727, 731 (9th Cir. 2006).

361 See section 6.2.4.

362 Domke et al., *Domke on Commercial Arbitration* (2015) § 30:5.

363 Rutledge et al. (2009) p.920.

364 These are the rules that parties may not contract out. See, *e.g.*, Radicati di Brozolo (2012) pp.50-51 who discusses *i.a.* the "overriding" character of some mandatory rules.

raise arguments based on mandatory provisions and the tribunal applied them irrespectively, and (iii) the tribunal violated public policy by misapplying mandatory norms.[365]

In a nutshell, each of these arguments is fallacious and is rarely successful. The ultimate notion that underlines the rebuttal of all of these assertions is the tribunal's duty of care for the well-being of the award at the post-award stage.[366] In fact, it is more likely that the court would vacate the award if the tribunal follows the parties' ill-founded restrictions on the application of mandatory rules (and thus refrains from applying the mandatory rules), rather than punish the tribunal for trying to respect and apply the most fundamental concepts of law.[367]

In response to the first and second challenges, as explained above,[368] it should be noted that it is in the very nature of mandatory rules of public policy that parties may not contract out of them. It further means that the tribunal should determine their impact on the dispute even if parties seek to avoid it. It has been argued by Craig, with the reference to the *Mitsubishi* case, that "*[...] case law in the United States [...] not only finds that mandatory law issues are arbitrable, but that the arbitrators have a duty to examine the effect of mandatory law on contractual obligations.*"[369]

In addition, as pointed out by the International Law Association in its report of 2008:

> In disputes implicating rules of public policy or other rules from which the parties may not derogate, arbitrators may be justified in taking measures appropriate to determine the applicability and contents of such rules, including by making independent research, raising with the parties new issues (whether legal or factual), and giving appropriate instructions or ordering appropriate

---

365 Two qualifications need to be done: (i) misapplication should be considered as an error in determining the contents of law; therefore, it cannot be framed within the "excess of powers" challenge since, arguably, the concept of *an error* in interpretation does not fit comfortably within the scope of the definition of *an excess*. For this reason, only public policy considerations are in place (see section 4.3). See, however, the Restatement's take on post-award relief, section 5.1 and section 5.3 (which will bring the public policy violations back to the scope of Section 10(a)(4) of the FAA). Additionally, and arguably, (ii) for the purpose of this study (and in the context of U.S. law), the distinction between procedural and substantive rules of public policy character is not relevant.

366 Without going into details whether the tribunal has the duty to render an enforceable award or not, the tribunal should be at least sensible of what may happen with the award after its production.

367 Arguably, if the tribunal follows the parties' wishes and refrains from applying clear-cut legal concepts of public policy character, it might face a challenge on the basis of the manifest disregard of the law. See also section 6.1.1.

368 See fn.364.

369 Craig, *The arbitrator's mission and the application of law in international commercial arbitration* (2010) p.278. Importantly, in this passage, Craig discusses the "law of mandatory application (*lois de police*)" which he defines on p. 277 in these words: "*Laws of mandatory application are those which by the subject matter that they address and the intent of the legislature, pre-empt, in the territory of their application, any agreement by the contracting parties to the contrary.*"

> measures insofar as they consider this necessary to abide by those rules or to protect against challenges to the award.[370]

The last challenge tries to accommodate an argument that the tribunal violates public policy when it (mis)applies mandatory rules of a public policy character. Generally, however, it has been considered that

> [...] an incorrect application of mandatory law rules is not fundamentally different from mis(application) of other rules of law by the arbitral tribunal and that only in cases involving serious errors of mandatory law, leading to results that significantly undermine or frustrate statutory objectives in a socially-unacceptable manner, may an award be annulled. Other errors of law, including mandatory law, do not ordinarily provide a basis for annulment.[371]

Consequently, the tribunal's exercise of the power to apply mandatory rules of law will greatly escape the "excess of powers" review.

7.3.5 Decision based on equity or reached *ex aequo et bono*

Allowing the tribunal to decide on the basis of the general concept of equity and justice instead of applying the rules of law requires an ultimate trust from the parties. It has been pointed out that

> [p]arties are free to grant the arbitrators the power to decide their dispute in accordance with general principles of equity (ie ex aequo et bono). In the absence of such agreement by the parties, and particularly where the parties have agreed to a particular substantive governing law, the arbitrators are generally obligated to apply a specific system of law.[372]

That is why the only reasonable view and the only instance when the tribunal has the power to decide on the basis of equity is when parties expressly vest it with the authority to do so.

---

370 ILA, *ILA Report on Ascertaining the Contents of the Applicable Law in International Commercial Arbitration* (2008) Recommendation 13, p.23.

371 Born, *International Commercial Arbitration* (2014) p.3330. See, however, Born, *International Commercial Arbitration* (2014) pp.3330-3331 ("*Nonetheless, there are commentators who urge, and national courts which apply, more extensive judicial review of arbitrators' mandatory law and public policy decisions, on the grounds that this is necessary in order to safeguard underlying public values.*").

372 Rutledge et al. (2009) p.920.

Although the statutory framework set out in the FAA is silent on the issue of deciding *ex aequo et bono*, the rules of leading arbitration institutes introduce a clear-cut rule that puts emphasis on the parties' express authorization being necessary for the tribunal to decide on the case based on equity.[373]

Additionally, one of the leading commentators argue that the rationale behind the unauthorized determination of *ex aequo et bono* is similar to the classic approach to the manifest disregard of the law (*i.e.* the one that "*pertains to a situation in which the arbitrators describe the applicable law cogently and knowledgeably and then deliberately ignore it in reaching their determination*").[374] The comparison is very well founded. Arguably, however, having in mind the uncertain fate of the manifest disregard after *Hall Street*, the challenging party would be better off with substantiating its objections with the excess of powers ground and not the manifest disregard.[375] In any event, parties considering a challenge of the award on the basis of the non-authorized application of the *ex aequo et bono* standard will carry a heavy burden of proof.[376]

373 Art. 31.3 of the 2014 ICDR Rules ("*The tribunal shall not decide as amiable compositeur or ex aequo et bono unless the parties have expressly authorized it to do so.*"); Art. 31.1 of the 2016 JAMS Rules ("*The Tribunal will decide a dispute ex aequo et bono or as amiable compositeur only if the parties have expressly authorized it to do so.*").

374 Carbonneau, *The Rise in Judicial Hostility to Arbitration: Revisiting Hall Street Associates* (2013) p.604 ("*In effect, manifest disregard is roughly equivalent to a finding that the arbitrator engaged in amiable composition without the disputing parties' authorization. Amiable composition is a civil law concept that originated in French arbitration law, allowing arbitrators to rule in equity when the application of the governing law would yield an unjust or inappropriate outcome given the circumstances of the case. An arbitrator may rule as an amiable compositor only if the parties specifically grant the arbitrator such authority. Granting the arbitrators the power to rule as amiable compositors can act as a 'safety valve' for commercial parties seeking to avoid legal conclusions that are antagonistic to their business interests. An arbitral award that recognizes the governing law but deliberately ignores it can be vacated for manifest disregard of the law.*"). See also Craig, *The arbitrator's mission and the application of law in international commercial arbitration* (2010) pp.271-272.

375 For further reading on excess of powers and manifest disregard of the law, see sections 5.1 and 6.1.1.

376 See, *e.g.*, the Restatement (second tentative draft) p.218 ("*However, a party challenging an award on this basis bears a serious burden. It must show that, despite an express prohibition, the tribunal clearly and unambiguously adopted and applied ex aequo et bono standards, and that the resulting departure from the agreed-upon manner of proceeding was material within the meaning of Comment d, supra. A party cannot meet this burden merely by arguing that the tribunal, while purporting to decide the dispute by reference to the chosen law, in fact interpreted or applied that law so as to reach a result dictated by ex aequo et bono reasoning rather than by application of the chosen law. The body of law that the parties adopted to govern the contract, or that the tribunal chose to apply in the absence of a choice by the parties, will in any event commonly include general principles of equity, good faith, and commercial reasonableness that may resemble, but still not constitute, ex aequo et bono reasoning, thus making it difficult to find that the tribunal decided the dispute ex aequo et bono rather than by reference to the chosen law.*").

7.4 *Decisions on remedies*

Generally speaking, the basic rationale for the parties to bring their dispute before the tribunal is to seek relief. It can take the form of different types of remedies. The most traditional forms of remedies will be discussed below. Damages, which are the basic form of the remedy under U.S. contract law, should be analyzed first (section 7.4.1 and section 7.4.2).[377] Then an analysis of specific performance (section 7.4.3) and contract adaptation (section 7.4.4) will follow. In principle, however, as briefly explained by Born, the tribunal is given a broad spectrum of remedial powers[378] and awards are rarely annulled for excess of authority based on the way the tribunal uses its remedial authority; notably, it holds true even if the "*award of relief [...] violates contractual limitations.*"[379]

7.4.1 Decision on damages in general

As mentioned above, seeking damages is the basic form of relief in U.S. contract law. For that reason the likelihood that parties will request the tribunal to grant damages is rather high. Consequently, a party's *request* usually entails that the tribunal has a power to grant the remedy sought. There are, however, instances that need to be analyzed further: (i) parties in their agreement to arbitrate state that the tribunal cannot grant damages and the tribunal granted them irrespectively,[380] (ii) the tribunal awards damages higher than requested, and (iii) the tribunal grants damages when a different type of relief (for example specific performance) was sought.

It is difficult to envisage the first scenario happening in practice.[381] On the one hand, an agreement to arbitrate is an ultimate benchmark for the tribunal with regard to the

---

377 Of course, law different from U.S. contract law can be applicable to the issue of damages. This would have to be resolved by the applicable law analysis. For further reading, see section 7.3.1 and section 7.3.2.

378 See also *Timegate Studios, Inc. v. Southpeak Interactive, L.L.C.*, 713 F.3d 797, 803 (5th Cir. 2013) ("*In this case, the arbitration clause is quite broad and contains no limits relevant to the instant dispute: 'any dispute ... shall be submitted to binding arbitration.' [...] Moreover, 'the arbitrator's selection of a particular remedy is given even more deference than his reading of the underlying contract.' [...] 'The remedy lies beyond the arbitrator's jurisdiction only if 'there is no rational way to explain the remedy handed down by the arbitrator as a logical means of furthering the aims of the contract.'*'").

379 This would then likely entail the erroneous "substantive" decision freed from judicial review. See Born, *International Commercial Arbitration* (2014) pp.3305-3306 ("*A recurrent issue concerns the consequences of an arbitral tribunal's award of relief that violates contractual limitations (e.g., an award of consequential damages or lost profits, notwithstanding contractual provisions forbidding such relief). In general, most national courts have (correctly) concluded that these types of awards do not constitute an excess of authority, but instead involve erroneous substantive decisions, not subject to judicial review.*"). Notably and importantly, the supporting case law is from the U.S.

380 It is far less difficult to foresee parties prohibiting the tribunal to grant reliefs other than damages. Holtzmann and Donovan in Holtzmann et al., (2013) Chapter VII(2)(a)(6) conclude that "*courts have also found arbitrators to have exceeded their powers when they granted remedies prohibited by the agreement.*"

381 It is possible, however, in cases of insurance disputes, for example, that the authority has capped on a certain amount. See, *e.g.*, *Brijmohan v. State Farm Ins. Co.*, 92 N.Y.2d 821, 699 N.E.2d 414 (1998) ("*[The a]rbitrator*

scope of its powers and thus the tribunal should respect limitations to its powers. On the other hand, however, the general (but explicit) limitation to the power to grant damages might make an agreement to arbitrate inoperative to the extent that no other remedies might be available to the parties.[382] Arguably, if this is the case, upon one party's request for damages, a tribunal might try to circumvent the initial restrictions in order to rescue an agreement to arbitrate from its created limits and explore the parties' underlying intent to arbitrate. It would be, however, highly controversial for the tribunal to cure a prospectively pathological clause.[383] If an agreement to arbitrate does not entail any express limit to the tribunal's powers, it is argued that the tribunal has a certain leeway to accept (or even tailor) reliefs sought.[384]

As argued by commentators:

> [a]n arbitrator is not required to read a contract literally. While the arbitrator may not award relief expressly forbidden by the agreement of the parties, the court cannot vacate the award just because the relief granted is not found in the language of the contract. In other words, subject to the terms of the empowering clause, arbitrators have latitude in crafting arbitration awards as wide as their latitude in deciding cases.[385]

Also institutional rules expressly limit the tribunal's broad discretion to grant any remedies to the contents of the parties' intentions expressed in the parties' agreement.[386] Notably,

exceeded his authority by awarding $75,000 in uninsured motorist (UM) benefits, where the policy's arbitration clause provided that the arbitrator would not render an award that exceeded the policy limits and a declarations page showed that the UM limits were only $10,000, even though the insurer did not produce the declarations page or otherwise object until the confirmation hearing").

382 Yet, the agreement is controlling (thus damages may not be granted) if the tribunal possesses the alternative remedial powers. See also *Seagate Tech., LLC v. W. Digital Corp.*, 854 N.W.2d 750, 765 (Minn. 2014) ("*In addition, we reiterate that the scope of arbitrator authority is a matter of contract and parties are always free to fashion arbitration agreements in ways that limit the arbitrator's power to award certain types of relief.*").

383 See, *e.g.*, *Augusta Capital, LLC v. Reich & Binstock, LLP*, No. 3:09-CV-0103, 2009 WL 2065555, at *4 (M.D. Tenn. July 10, 2009) ("*The Court finds that the arbitration panel in this case exceeded its powers by fashioning a remedy that added to, altered and/or modified the terms and conditions of the parties' agreement in violation of Section 12.2(a) of that agreement.[...] [B]y limiting the terms of Section 7.5 to make them 'less harsh,' the arbitration panel exceeded its authority specifically set forth in Section 12.2 of the agreement. Therefore, in fashioning the remedy, the arbitrators exceeded their powers [...]*").

384 See fn.378 and fn.379. See also *Axia Netmedia Corp. v. Massachusetts Tech. Park Corp.*, 973 F.3d 133, 142–43 (1st Cir. 2020).

385 Domke et al., *Domke on Commercial Arbitration* (2015) § 38:14. For further reading, see also Cole (2016) pp.223-224.

386 See, *e.g.*, Art. 31.1 of the 2016 JAMS Rules ("*The Tribunal may grant any remedy or relief, including, but not limited to, specific performance of a contract, which is within the scope of the agreement of the parties and permissible under the law(s) or rules of law applicable to the dispute [...]*"); in a domestic context R-47(a) of the 2013 AAA Rules ("*The arbitrator may grant any remedy or relief that the arbitrator deems just*

the Restatement makes an important distinction between contractual limitation to the tribunal's remedial authority and contractual limitation on the available contractual remedies.[387] Only in the case of the former the award may be vacated on the "excess of powers" ground. The latter would work only as a restriction imposed on the parties themselves rather than on a tribunal. Consequently, the court will not review the merits of the case. As concluded by the Restatement: "*[...] if the parties intended to preclude or limit the recovery of certain remedies, a broad arbitration clause would give the tribunal the authority to rule on the enforceability of the remedy limitation, and a court will not review the tribunal's decision.*"[388]

The second scenario is rather evident. The tribunal should not exceed the amount of damages sought by the parties. If a tribunal renders an *ultra petita* decision, it should expect that it will be successfully vacated pursuant to Section 10(a)(4) of the FAA. It should be noted, however, that, if possible, the vacating court may decide to vacate not the entire award but only the part that goes beyond the parties' requests.[389] It is also necessary to highlight that the tribunal, while awarding damages, should take into account the limits for damages that could be prescribed by applicable law. In one case it was reported that "*[a]n award violates public policy when it exceeds the maximum amount of recovery allowed by law.*"[390]

Under the third scenario the tribunal effectively modifies the relief sought by the parties. By doing so (unless a party submitted alternative claims) it will exceed its powers and will put its award at risk. The tribunal will violate its task to answer the relief sought and instead will impose its own vision of a just solution.

7.4.2 Decision on punitive damages

By and large, a feature of the arbitration system in the U.S. is the possibility to grant punitive damages. It has been pointed out, however, that "*although punitive damages are regularly awarded in domestic arbitrations in the US, such awards are quasi-inexistent in the international arena*"[391] and that "*[o]verall, it appears that punitive damages awards in arbitration are essentially an American phenomenon.*"[392] Leaving aside the question of

---

and equitable and within the scope of the agreement of the parties, including, but not limited to, specific performance of a contract.").

387 See the Restatement (second tentative draft) pp.195-198 and pp.200-201.

388 The Restatement (second tentative draft) p.196.

389 See section 3.3; the vacating court may also come to the conclusion that the *ultra petita* holding is nothing more than mere miscalculation and use its competence based on Section 11 of the FAA to make an order modifying or correcting the award.

390 Domke et al., *Domke on Commercial Arbitration* (2013) § 39:9, referring to *Matter of Carty (Nationwide Ins. Co.)*, 149 A.D.2d 328, 539 N.Y.S.2d 374 (1st Dep't 1989).

391 Petsche (2013) p.89.

392 Petsche (2013) p.91.

constitutionality of punitive damages[393] and their availability in both a tort and contractual context,[394] the issue at hand is whether the tribunal's decision on punitive damages can be successfully challenged on the basis of the excess of powers ground. Not surprisingly, the analysis should reflect on international and not on domestic commercial arbitration.[395]

In international commercial arbitration, as has been suggested above, the notion of the tribunal granting punitive damages is rather theoretical. Nonetheless, for illustrative purposes, one should assume a hypothetical dispute between foreign parties with the tribunal having its seat in New York. Following a challenge on the tribunal's decision awarding punitive damages, the vacating court would exercise the regular three-step test for an excess of powers review.

The first step, therefore, would be to assess the scope of an agreement to arbitrate and how the parties address the issue of punitive damages (if they do so at all). Sometimes parties argued that the limitation to award punitive damages was introduced by the choice of law selection that does not allow the tribunal to grant certain types of damages (*i.e.* punitive). As noted above, however, and following the *Mastrobuono* decision, parties may not rely on their choice of law clause in order to evidence that they intended to follow the restrictions on the tribunal's authority envisaged by the chosen law.[396] Arguably, parties may try to rely on the content of the institutional rules which, in the international context, accommodate an express provision banning the use of punitive damages (unless agreed otherwise).[397]

The better view is to follow the suggestion aptly pointed out by Farnsworth:

> [i]f you [i.e. the drafter of an agreement to arbitrate] would strip the arbitrators of the power to award punitive damages, you should – in so many words – either ban 'punitive' (or 'exemplary') damages or allow only 'compensatory'

---

393 Farnsworth, *Punitive Damages in Arbitration* (1991) p.4, Petsche (2013) p.98 and the literature therein.

394 Farnsworth, *Punitive Damages in Arbitration* (1991) p.6, Petsche (2013) p.95.

395 The considerations of this section in the domestic arbitration context are even more applicable. One cannot stress enough how important the *clear and unambiguous* limitation to grant punitive damages is. Especially taking into account that the AAA Rules do not entail any ban to the tribunal's powers as compared to the provisions of the ICDR Rules or the JAMS Rules (see fn.397).

396 See section 7.3.1.

397 See, *e.g.*, Art. 31.5 of the 2014 ICDR Rules ("*Unless the parties agree otherwise, the parties expressly waive and forego any right to punitive, exemplary, or similar damages unless any applicable law(s) requires that compensatory damages be increased in a specified manner. This provision shall not apply to an award of arbitration costs to a party to compensate for misconduct in the arbitration.*"); Art. 31.2 of the 2015 JAMS Rules ("*Unless the parties agree otherwise, the parties expressly waive and forgo any right to punitive, exemplary or similar damages, unless a statute requires that compensatory damages be increased in a specified manner. This provision will not limit the Tribunal's authority to take into account a party's dilatory or bad faith conduct in the arbitration in apportioning arbitration costs between or among the parties.*").

> damages. The drafter who uses plain English, however, can eliminate the risk of an award of punitive damages.[398]

Therefore, parties wishing to narrow the tribunal's powers and exclude the possibility of facing the award of punitive damages should do so explicitly.[399]

In addition, of particular relevance with regard to the contractual limits to the tribunal's powers, is a part of the Restatement where it is reported that

> [a] particularly difficult issue is whether a provision that precludes the award of a form of damages (such as consequential damages or punitive damages) is a remedy limitation or a restriction on the arbitrators' authority. If the provision is a remedy limitation, a broad arbitration clause would give the tribunal the authority to rule on its validity with only very limited court review. If the provision is a restriction on the arbitrators' authority, a court could vacate the award under § 10(a)(4) if the tribunal violates the restriction by awarding such damages.[400]

The point made by the Restatement further strengthens the position that (any) limitation on the tribunal's authority (and especially the one to grant punitive damages) has to be made clearly and unambiguously. Moreover, it should be preferred that such a limitation is made within the scope of the agreement to arbitrate.[401]

It goes without saying and does not require more elaborate analysis that it is still necessary for the parties to request the tribunal to grant punitive damages. The tribunal would exceed its powers if it awards punitive relief on its own motion.[402]

Finally, it should be mentioned, that an award on punitive damages would likely survive a public policy challenge in the U.S. In any event, the tribunal should be concerned not

398 Farnsworth, *Punitive Damages in Arbitration* (1991) p.14.

399 It is reasonable to suggest that parties wishing to exclude the power to grant punitive damages should do so on the face of their agreement; it would be true even when they include arbitration rules that limit the tribunal's powers. Narrowing the scope of the arbitral tribunal's powers within the content of the agreement to arbitrate, might arguably affect whether the vacating court exercises a *de novo* or deferential review of the award.

400 The Restatement (second tentative draft) p.289.

401 Arguably, the standard of review may vary. It will depend on whether the court is convinced that remedial constraints are limitations to the tribunal's powers or "mere" remedy limitations. In the former case (particularly if limitations are included in the scope of the agreement to arbitrate) they might be considered as jurisdictional/threshold issues. See also section 7.1.2 and the Restatement (second tentative draft) pp.195-196 and pp.200-201.

402 It should be pointed out, however, that, for example, both the ICDR Rules and the JAMS Rules provide the tribunal with an authority to punish the parties for dilatory or bad faith conduct while deciding on the cost of the proceedings. See fn.397.

only with the fate of the award in the country of the seat, but also in the country of the possible enforcement. Since an award on punitive damages in most of the countries (but for the U.S.) may violate the public policy, arbitral tribunals would be rather reluctant to grant punitive damages. Even if they do so, it would be prudent and "*vital for arbitral tribunals clearly to distinguish between the amounts of compensatory and punitive damages awarded.*"[403]

7.4.3 Decision on specific performance

Specific performance as a remedy in the common law tradition is sometimes difficult to reconcile with the powers of arbitral tribunals to fashion relief. It has been noted that "*[...] the traditional common law rule is that specific performance is available only when damages are inadequate. The rule is an instance of the more general principle that equitable relief – specific performance being an equitable remedy – is awarded only when the legal remedy is inadequate.*"[404] The discussion here, however, should not focus on the position of a specific remedy as compared to damages, but rather on the power of the tribunal to grant this type of relief and the potential challenge against the award if specific performance is granted.

The answer herein should be fairly straightforward: in principle, the tribunal will have the power to award specific performance.[405] A standard, broad agreement to arbitrate should entail that specific performance is within the range of remedies at the tribunal's disposal. If not, however, a closer look at the institutional rules also clarifies that the tribunal should be equipped with such a power.[406] Similarly, the court in *Grayson-Robinson Stores v. Iris Construction Co.* held that "*[i]t would be quite remarkable if, after these parties had agreed that arbitrators might award specific performance and after the arbitrators had so ordered, the courts would, [...] frustrate the whole arbitration process by refusing to confirm the award.*"[407] Therefore, should the parties wish to limit the scope of relief at a tribunal's disposal, they should do so explicitly.

403 Petsche (2013) p.103; in this way, the tribunal could facilitate the possibility of a partial enforcement of the award.

404 Eisenberg & Miller (2013) p.6.

405 *Brandon, Jones, Sandall, Zeide, Kohn, Chalal & Musso, P.A. v. MedPartners, Inc.*, 203 F.R.D. 677, 686 (S.D. Fla. 2001) aff'd in part, appeal dismissed in part, 312 F.3d 1349 (11th Cir. 2002) ("*Arbitrators have the authority to remedy a breach (anticipatory or otherwise) of contract in any way reasonably related to the contract terms, including money damages or even specific performance.*"). See also Blackaby et al. (2015) p.519.

406 See, *e.g.*, Art. 31.1 of the 2016 JAMS Rules ("*The Tribunal may grant any remedy or relief, including, but not limited to, specific performance of a contract, which is within the scope of the agreement of the parties and permissible under the law(s) or rules of law applicable to the dispute[...].*"); R-47(a) of the 2013 AAA Rules ("*The arbitrator may grant any remedy or relief that the arbitrator deems just and equitable and within the scope of the agreement of the parties, including, but not limited to, specific performance of a contract.*"); notably, the ICDR Rules do not provide for such a clear-cut proviso regarding specific performance. See Art. 31 of the 2014 ICDR Rules.

407 *Grayson-Robinson Stores v. Iris Construction Co.*, 8 N.Y.2d 133, 137, 168 N.E.2d 377, 378-79 (1960).

It goes without saying that a tribunal would be powerless with regard to specific performance if parties do not plead in favor of it (either as a main, alternative or auxiliary claim). Therefore, in most cases, the decision granting a specific performance will not be susceptible to the "excess of powers" challenge.

7.4.4 Decision on contract adaptation and filling of gaps in the contract

On occasion, an arbitral tribunal is faced with a variation of a task that it is usually entrusted with, namely the contract adaptation and/or filling of gaps in the contract. Typically, such a request (especially contract adaptation) is brought before the tribunal if a dispute arises out of long-term, complex contracts. In addition, the power to fill gaps or revise contractual terms is usually perceived as a "creative competence" of an arbitral tribunal and put in direct opposition to its traditional adjudicatory function.[408] As such, arguably, it requires a direct authorization of parties in order to fulfill the task of contract revision.[409] In the context of American arbitration, however, another view has also been advanced. This reflection, in a nutshell, posits that the contract revision or filling of the gaps in a contract is nothing more than contract interpretation, and as such is presumptively for the arbitrators to deal with.[410] At the same time, however, arbitrators may not be willing to take up the task of contract revision.[411]

It is necessary to begin with the recommendation for parties drafting an agreement to arbitrate: it is better for the parties to frame the powers of an arbitral tribunal unequivocally so that there is no doubt as to their underlying intent. It is simply because an agreement to arbitrate would be always the point of departure for the analysis of whether parties conferred a specific power upon an arbitral panel. It has been suggested that

> [w]hen an arbitral panel is asked to take that step [i.e. to fill gaps in or to adapt contracts], the panel's first act should be to examine both the arbitration agreement and the law applicable at the seat of the arbitration (lex arbitri) for authority to fill gaps in or to adapt the contract.[412]

---

408 See, *e.g.*, Bernardini, *Stabilization and adaptation in oil and gas investments* (2008) p.107.

409 Bernardini, *Stabilization and adaptation in oil and gas investments* (2008) p.107 ("*The arbitration clause should therefore expressly confer the power to adapt the agreement and determine the manner for its exercise as well as the limits of the arbitrator's authority in that regard*"); Kolkey et al., (2012) p.242 ("*In order to be effective, an arbitration agreement would have to be explicit in conferring on an arbitral tribunal the power to fill gaps or adapt a contract*").

410 Rau, *"Gap Filling" by Arbitrators* (2015).

411 Argued in the broader context of international arbitration in general: see, *i.a.*, Blackaby et al. (2015) pp.524-527; Gaillard & Savage, *Fouchard Gaillard Goldman on International Commercial Arbitration* (1999) p.25.

412 Kolkey et al., (2012) p.241. Other authors underline that not only the law of the seat, but also the law applicable to the merits might be relevant in order to determine whether the tribunal may alter the contract. See Berger, *Power of Arbitrators to Fill Gaps and Revise Contracts to Make Sense* (2001) pp.10-11.

Although this observation is of a more general nature (thus not limited to the American reality *per se*), it puts forward a reasonable argument that should be equally valid in the context of American arbitration.

Holtzmann and Donovan on a similar note reflected that

> [b]ecause arbitration in the United States is a matter of contract under generally applicable principles of contract law, arbitrators have the authority to fill gaps in the contract or adapt the contract to fundamentally changed circumstances if the contract, the applicable law, or the arbitration agreement confers the authority to do so.[413]

That being said, it should be highlighted that even if an agreement to arbitrate does not offer the comfort of an arbitral tribunal's direct authorization, a tribunal's decision on contract adaptation or gap-filling is still well suited to survive a challenge at the post-award stage. As mentioned above, it is suggested that a gap-filling exercise is nothing more and nothing less than contract application in the event that an agreement to arbitrate has been drafted broadly.[414] Additionally, if the power to adapt a contract (*e.g.* price revision provisions) is included in the contract (but outside the agreement to arbitrate), it might be considered within the scope of the tribunal's (and the court's) authority to apply.[415] As a consequence of the Supreme Court decisions in *Bazzle, Stolt-Nielsen* and *Oxford Health*, certain gaps, depicted as a silence in the agreement, are for the tribunal to decide as long as it bases its decision on contractual application[416] and not on its own notion of public policy.[417]

7.5 *Decisions accessory to the parties' main submissions and the merits of the case*

Usually, in the framework of an arbitral award, the tribunal would need to not only present its determination on the main claims but also to award interest (section 7.5.1) and to allocate the costs of the proceedings (section 6.4.2). These topics will be analyzed below with some additional reflections on decisions on procedure (section 7.5.3).

---

413 Holtzmann et al., (2013) Chapter II(3)(b).

414 See, however, Berger, *Power of Arbitrators to Fill Gaps and Revise Contracts to Make Sense* (2001) p.8.

415 See, *e.g.*, *Gas Nat. Aprovisionamientos, SDG, S.A. v. Atl. LNG Co. of Trinidad & Tobago*, No. 08 CIV. 1109 (DLC), 2008 WL 4344525, at *1 (S.D.N.Y. Sept. 16, 2008).

416 *Oxford Health Plans LLC v. Sutter*, 569 U.S. 564, 571–72, 133 S. Ct. 2064, 2069–70, 186 L. Ed. 2d 113 (2013).

417 *Stolt-Nielsen*, 559 U.S. 662, 670-72, 130 S. Ct. 1758, 1767-68, 176 L. Ed. 2d 605 (2010).

7.5.1 Decision on interest

Since the value of an arbitral tribunal's decision on interest may be high or, on occasion, exceed the value of the main claim,[418] it is not surprising that parties may wish to challenge it on the excess of powers ground. It is tempting to argue that no authority to award interest has been granted since the FAA is silent on this point and that an agreement to arbitrate often does not give express powers for the tribunal to award interest. Generally, however, such an argument will be ill-founded and unsuccessful.

Traditionally, a broadly worded agreement to arbitrate would only *imply* that the tribunal has the power to award interest.[419] Conceivably, such an implication should suffice, because the decision on interest will generally follow the tribunal's decision on the main claim.[420] Therefore, if the main claim will not be awarded, there will be no decision on interest. If, however, parties wish to limit the tribunal's power to award interest, they should do so explicitly. As argued by Born, "*[t]he authority to award interest is an inherent element of a tribunal's adjudicatory authority and is implicitly contained within the terms of agreements to arbitrate, at least absent contrary indication by the parties.*"[421] Similarly, it has been pointed out by Rutledge and others that "*US Courts have generally held that arbitrators have the authority to award interest on arbitral awards. The decision to award interest and the applicable rate of interest are within the discretion of the tribunal, unless the parties have provided otherwise.*"[422]

418 See Sénéchal & Gotanda (2009) p.492, with some illustrative examples of awards therein.

419 It is argued that upon the inclusion of the ICDR or the JAMS Rules, these rules will constitute a source of the arbitral powers. See Art. 31.4 of the 2014 ICDR Rules ("*[...], and the tribunal may award such pre-award and post-award interest, simple or compound, as it considers appropriate, taking into account the contract and applicable law(s).*") and Art. 35.7 of the 2016 JAMS Rules ("*[...] the Tribunal may award such pre-award and post-award interest, simple or compound, as it considers appropriate, at such rate and from such date(s) as the arbitrator(s) may deem appropriate, taking into consideration the contract and applicable law*"); *cf* Art. 32.7 of the 2011 JAMS Rules ("*[...] and the Tribunal may award such pre-award and post-award interest, simple or compound, as it considers appropriate, taking into consideration the contract and applicable law.*"). For the tribunal's authority to award interest on an award until the "date of payment", see also Reisberg & Pauley (2013).

420 Even if a party seeks interest in a separate claim and not together with the main claim, a refusal to grant the latter will inevitably affect the former. See, *e.g.*, *Faison & Gillespie v. Lorant*, 187 N.C. App. 567, 579, 654 S.E.2d 47, 55 (2007) ("*In the alternative, defendants argue the interest awarded by the arbitrator was not a remedy, but a separate claim not before him under the Agreement. However, we conclude the interest awarded in the Arbitration Decision was an element of the remedies sought, rather than a separate claim. [...] the arbitrator identified the pled claims and the corresponding values upon which the interest would apply. Further, the interest calculations appeared in the section of the Arbitration Decision in which the damage awards were listed, which also came after the sections addressing plaintiff's claims and defendants' counterclaims. Therefore, the interest awarded in this case was not a separate claim, but an element of the remedies sought, assessed on values awarded on claims properly before the arbitrator.*").

421 Born, *International Commercial Arbitration* (2014) p.3103.

422 Rutledge et al. (2009) p.921.

If a tribunal is authorized to award interest, it entails that the tribunal is vested with a broad spectrum of powers.[423] Therefore, for example, a refusal to award interest has been considered within the tribunal's authority.[424] Moreover, it has been pointed out that "*[c]ourts usually uphold an arbitrator's award of pre-award interest (interest from the time of the breach or wrongful action up to the final arbitration award) and will not disturb the rate applied by the tribunal.*"[425] A closer look at institutional rules shows that an arbitral tribunal may even consider that not only pre-award, but also post-award interest is due.[426] The decisions on an interest rate, its accrual and the like should not be reviewed by the vacating court because it may not test the merits of the case.[427] Also, the way the tribunal frames the interest (*i.e.* as a separate claim or not) might affect the fate of the prospective award.[428]

As usual, parties should request the tribunal to calculate the interest. Nonetheless, Born observes that "*[...] courts have also upheld awards of interest even where the parties' contract and submissions did not specifically request it.*"[429] Arguably, the institutional rules that

423 Notably, in international arbitration, it might be relevant to determine what law applies to the issue of interest. For an overview see Born, *International Commercial Arbitration* (2014) pp.3105-3106. Born explains on p.3106 that "*[i]n [...] jurisdictions, including the United States, rules governing interest may be deemed 'procedural' or are governed by the law of the arbitral seat.*" See, however, Reisberg & Pauley (2013) p.26 ("*It is also generally well-accepted that arbitrators should look to the substantive law governing the claims when deciding whether interest should be awarded, for what period of time, and at what rate. This is because in most jurisdictions interest for the pre-judgment period is regarded as a matter of substantive law.*"), with a reference to the U.S. cases: *In re Exxon Valdez v. Exxon Corp.*, 484 F.3d 1098, 1101 (9th Cir. 2007) ("*It is well settled that prejudgment interest is a substantive aspect of a plaintiff's claim, rather than a merely procedural mechanism.*") and *Emmenegger v. Bull Moose Tube Co.*, 324 F.3d 616, 624 (8th Cir. 2003) ("*the question of prejudgment interest is a substantive one*"). The authors also admit that "*there remains substantial debate over the methods used by arbitrators in awarding interest, particularly regarding the use of simple or compound interest and how the rate of interest should be determined.*"

424 Born, *International Commercial Arbitration* (2014) p.3110 and the case law therein.

425 Rutledge et al. (2009) p.921 and case law therein (fn.218). See also *Foulger-Pratt Residential Contracting, LLC v. Madrigal Condominiums, LLC*, 779 F. Supp. 2d 100 (D.D.C. 2011).

426 See the rules mentioned in fn.419.

427 See section 3.2. Also in *J.A. Jones Const. Co. v. Flakt, Inc.*, 731 F. Supp. 1061, 1064 (N.D. Ga. 1990) the court rejected arguments that the tribunal exceeded its powers because: (i) it awarded pre-award interest, (ii) New Jersey law does not allow arbitrators to impose interest for any period prior to the making of the award itself, and (iii) it (the tribunal) calculated interest at a 10% rate which is higher than the lower rate prescribed by New Jersey Court Rules. The court held that "*[...] arbitrators do not "exceed their powers" unless they rule on matters outside of their proper consideration. [...] Thus, a court's ability to vacate an award under section 10(d) depends not on the outcome of a particular legal decision but rather on whether the arbitrators were requested to make the decision at all. [The challenging party] does not argue that the arbitrators lacked the power to consider the issue of interest as an assessment on compensatory damages. It argues only that the arbitrators calculated that interest in an improper manner and at an unlawful rate. The court therefore DENIES [The challenging party]'s motion to vacate the interest award [...]*".

428 If it is considered as an independent claim and the court is satisfied that the decision on interest should be vacated, it might be easier to separate it for the partial vacatur.

429 Born, *International Commercial Arbitration* (2014) p.3110, with a reference (footnote 600) to *Gordon Sel-Way, Inc. v. Spence Bros., Inc.*, 475 N.W.2d 704, 711 (Mich. 1991) ("*arbitrators committed no substantial or material error in including pre-award interest in their award, even though parties' contract was silent concerning right to interest*"); *Westminster Constr. Corp. v. PPG Indus., Inc.*, 376 A.2d 708, 711 (R.I. 1977)

provide that "*the tribunal may award such pre-award and post-award interest, simple or compound, as it considers appropriate, taking into consideration the contract and applicable law(s)*",[430] also give *carte blanche* to the tribunal to award interest as it wishes and not necessarily subject to the parties' submissions. The better view is, however, that the tribunal should refrain from granting interest unless requested. As long as the power to award interest might be implied or even inherent[431] and for this reason an agreement to arbitrate might be silent on that point, it does not change the fact that it is the parties' (and not the tribunal's) responsibility to seek relief. Therefore, the tribunal simply cannot award interests on its own volition.[432]

Finally, it should be mentioned that awards on interest may still be tested against public policy.[433] The window for the success in that regard is, however, extremely narrow.[434] Again, considering the Restatement's take on Section 10(a)(4) of the FAA, the public policy challenge will be included therein.[435] In sum, the tribunal's decision on interest would likely survive the "excess of powers" challenge.

7.5.2 Decision on costs

The monetary value of decisions on cost has become increasingly important in current arbitration practice.[436] Additionally, "*[c]ost awards, commentators have observed, are [...] by and large entrusted to the broad discretion of the arbitral tribunal appointed in each particular case – as a result of which cost awards vary wildly from case to case and 'sometimes fundamentally without any apparent reason.'*"[437] Finally, one should also be reminded that, in the FAA, no statutory provision regulating allocation of costs in arbitration exists.[438] For all these reasons, it is not surprising that parties (usually an award-debtor) are so eager to challenge cost awards. Though it does not change the fact that these parties are rarely successful.

("*arbitrators may award interest, even if not claimed, unless otherwise specifically provided by the parties in the agreement*").

430 Art. 31.4 of the 2014 ICDR Rules. See also Art. 32.7 of the 2011 JAMS Rules.

431 ILA, *ILA Report on Inherent Powers of Arbitral Tribunals* (2014) p.10 ("*With respect to damages, the Iran-US Claims Tribunal noted nearly thirty years ago that it was already 'customary for arbitral tribunals to award interest as part of an award for damages.' It found the power to award interest 'inherent in the Tribunal's authority to decide claims,' such that 'the exclusion of such power could only be established by express provision.' The tribunal in Vivendi v. Argentina confirmed that liability for interest remains 'an accepted legal principle.'*").

432 Unless, arguably, it is customary in the specific field and it is a party's "inherent expectation" to have interests award without asking for them.

433 Born, *International Commercial Arbitration* (2014) pp.3109-3110.

434 For further reading on public policy, see section 6.1.2.

435 See section 5.3.

436 Born, *International Commercial Arbitration* (2014) p.3099.

437 Smit & Robinson (2009) p.267.

438 Rutledge et al. (2009) p.924.

The discussion on costs in the context of American arbitration law has yet an additional twist, because of the so-called "American Rule" according to which parties to the arbitration should bear their own litigation costs[439] and U.S. law's incompatibility with other systems according to which all costs are to be allocated on the account of an award-debtor (*i.e.* "loser pays").[440] Although these two irreconcilable positions need to be duly acknowledged in the analysis, it is argued that they should not influence the vacating court in its deliberation process.

As always, the vacating court will first look at the scope of the agreement to arbitrate. Alas, parties do not very often express their views on the costs allocation in their initial agreement.[441] This will consequently lead to the review of the applicable international arbitration rules; these rules usually entail the provision allowing the tribunal to proceed with the allocation of costs.[442]

In the absence of an express agreement of the parties to let the tribunal decide on the allocation of costs, it has been reported that some courts found that the tribunal lacked authority to award legal fees.[443]

Rutledge and others explain, however, that

> [t]his approach is misguided, particularly in the context of international arbitration proceedings, where it is undisputed that tribunals and courts are not bound by rules of US civil procedure. The better view – which has been adopted by a number of US courts – is that arbitrators have inherent authority

439 Carter (2012) p.478.

440 For different approaches, see, *i.a.*, Kreindler, *Final Rulings on Costs: Loser pays all?* (2006) p.42.

441 In any event, a broad agreement to arbitrate might suffice to authorize the tribunal to award fees. See, *e.g.*, *In re Arbitration Between Gen. Sec. Nat. Ins. Co. & AequiCap Program Administrators*, 785 F. Supp. 2d 411, 419 (S.D.N.Y. 2011) ("*Here, we conclude that the Arbitration Clause was indeed a broad provision. The parties used expansive language to define the types of disputes to be submitted to arbitration and they declined to carve out or limit the types of relief that the Panel was entitled to award. Notably, in drafting the Arbitration Clause, the parties failed to signal that they intended to limit the authority conferred upon the Panel by restricting the types of relief that the Panel could award. In light of the breadth of the contractual language, and in the absence of any contracted-for limitations, we conclude that the Panel had the inherent authority to award attorney's fees.*"). If the parties expressly exclude the possibility of an award on costs, the court will give effect to such an agreement. Therefore, in the event costs were granted (notwithstanding an express exclusion), the court should vacate the award. See Born, *International Commercial Arbitration* (2014) p.3087.

442 See, *i.a.*, Art. 34 of the 2014 ICDR Rules ("*The arbitral tribunal shall fix the costs of arbitration in its award(s). The tribunal may allocate such costs among the parties if it determines that allocation is reasonable, taking into account the circumstances of the case.*"), and Art. 37.4 of the 2016 JAMS Rules ("*The Tribunal will fix the arbitration costs in its award. The Tribunal may apportion such costs among the parties if it determines that such apportionment is reasonable, taking into account the circumstances of the case.*").

443 Rutledge et al. (2009) pp.924-925 and p.926.

> to award attorneys' fees in international arbitration proceedings unless the parties have agreed otherwise.[444]

Also Born argues that "*[r]ather the presumptive rule in international arbitrations seated in the United States should be that, absent contrary agreement, the tribunal will have the authority to award the costs of legal representation.*"[445]

It should be added that allowing the authority to award costs means that the tribunal will have powers to decide on costs even if claimant withdrew its claim,[446] or in case of a negative jurisdictional award (*i.e.* the award where the tribunal finds that it is not competent to decide the case on merits).[447]

The cost award can also be used as a sanction for the party's bad faith conduct during the proceedings.[448] In fact, the court in *ReliaStar Life Ins. Co. v. EMC Nat'l Life Co.* held that a

> [p]rovision of arbitration agreement between insurers, stating that each party should bear expense of its own arbitrator and related outside attorney fees, and should jointly and equally bear with other party expenses of third arbitrator, did not limit arbitrators' authority to award attorney and arbitrator fees as sanction for bad faith conduct.[449]

It is reasonable to expect the parties to request an award on costs.[450] Arguably, however, based on the wording of the relevant provisions of the institutional rules, the tribunal's

444 Rutledge et al. (2009) pp.926-927.

445 Born, *International Commercial Arbitration* (2014) p.3091.

446 Rutledge et al. (2009) p.904 ("*[i]t is also within the tribunal's discretion to award costs in connection with the claimant's withdrawal of the action*"), referring to *Howard, Weil, Labouisse, Friedrichs Inc. v. Tower Hill Trading Co Ltd*, no 94 Civ 4709, 1995 WL 548846 (SDNY 1995).

447 Born, *International Commercial Arbitration* (2014) pp.3101-3102.

448 Art. 31.5 of the 2014 ICDR ("*Unless the parties agree otherwise, the parties expressly waive and forego any right to punitive, exemplary, or similar damages unless any applicable law(s) requires that compensatory damages be increased in a specified manner. This provision shall not apply to an award of arbitration costs to a party to compensate for misconduct in the arbitration.*"); Art. 31.2 of the 2016 JAMS Rules, Art. 30.2 of the 2011 JAMS Rules ("*Unless the parties agree otherwise, the parties expressly waive and forgo any right to punitive, exemplary or similar damages unless a statute requires that compensatory damages be increased in a specified manner. This provision will not limit the Tribunal's authority to take into account a party's dilatory or bad faith conduct in the arbitration in apportioning arbitration costs between or among the parties.*"). Importantly, see also the power to sanction as provided in Art. 33 of the 2016 JAMS Rules.

449 *ReliaStar Life Ins. Co. v. EMC Nat'l Life Co.*, 564 F.3d 81 (2d Cir. 2009). See also Art. 33 of the 2016 JAMS Rules.

450 See also *GPR, Inc. v. Phoenix Petroleum Co.* (1995, SDNY) 1995 US Dist LEXIS 7015, where the court rejected the argument that the tribunal exceeded its powers by awarding attorney's fees to petitioners. It concluded that since all parties sought costs and attorney's fees the tribunal has the authority to award them.

broad discretion to award costs will authorize the tribunal not to follow the parties' submissions on cost.[451] Therefore, as long as a tribunal acts within the limits of an agreement to arbitrate,[452] in case of awarding costs, it does not necessarily have to give deference to the parties' submissions.[453]

With respect to public policy it has been concluded that "*[t]he "American Rule" regarding costs of legal representation does not rise to the level of U.S. public policy, so as to forbid a tribunal's exercise of its authority under the parties' arbitration agreement or applicable institutional rules to award legal costs.*"[454]

Finally, one should be reminded that although the court should, under no circumstances, review the merits of the case, a remand[455] or modification[456] of the award may be in certain circumstances regarded as an appropriate measure to cure alleged deficiencies of the award.

7.5.3 Decisions on procedure

At first glance, it seems possible to argue that most of the procedural decisions that are not in line with a contractually agreed framework fits in comfortably with the "excess of powers" challenge. "*[S]trictly speaking, this is inappropriate.*"[457] The better view is, as explained earlier in this chapter, (i) to limit the application of the "excess of powers" ground to the tribunal's violations of its adjudicative function.[458] Even if one allows (ii) the alternative view and to accept the application of the "excess of powers" objection with regard to the violations of the parties' agreements on the procedure, the burden of proof

---

451 See the cited rules in fn.442.

452 See, however, *ReliaStar Life Ins. Co. v. EMC Nat'l Life Co.*, 564 F.3d 81 (2d Cir. 2009).

453 Especially when used as a sanction against a party. *ReliaStar Life Ins. Co. v. EMC Nat'l Life Co.*, 564 F.3d 81 (2d Cir. 2009). Arguably, in case of using costs as a sanctioning mechanism, even the reasonable costs which were not requested (by the adversary of the sanctioned party) might be awarded in exceptional circumstances. See also, extensive sanctioning powers under Art. 33 of the 2016 JAMS Rules.

454 Born, *International Commercial Arbitration* (2014) p.3091.

455 Domke et al., *Domke on Commercial Arbitration* (2015) § 40:11 ("*It is not necessary to remand to the arbitrator when the court can resolve any alleged ambiguities in the award as to form by means of modification, particularly "where the true intent of the arbitrator is apparent." However, it has been held that a court cannot modify an award in a manner which is completely contrary to the arbitrator's intent. Thus, a court should not award interest and costs where the arbitrator's specific intent was to deny such interest and costs based on his interpretation of the terms of the agreement. Similarly, the court should not order the matter remanded to the arbitrator for an additional hearing to determine the costs and interest where a party who had the opportunity to present evidence of prejudgment interests and costs to the arbitrator during the proceeding failed to do so.*").

456 Domke et al., *Domke on Commercial Arbitration* (2015) § 40:9 ("*Where the arbitrator committed an error in deciding that the allocation of costs of the arbitration had been submitted to arbitration, the proper remedy was the modification of the award.*"), referring to *Bernard v. Kuhn*, 65 Md. App. 557, 501 A.2d 480 (1985).

457 Born, *International Commercial Arbitration* (2014) p.3306 ("*In principle, an excess of authority should be limited to instances where an arbitral tribunal exceeds the substantive scope of the arbitration agreement (or parties' submissions in the arbitration), and not be extended to procedural irregularities (or noncompliance with the parties' agreement). Nonetheless, local law may adopt a different approach in particular jurisdictions.*").

458 See section 5.1.

needs to be material and thus challenges should be accepted only in very limited instances.[459] In principle, the reign over the procedure should be the tribunal's (managerial) prerogative once it is constituted and should not be allowed a second look at the post-award stage. This is particularly true, (iii) because decisions on procedure are used to enhance the efficiency of the process and eventually sanction bad faith conduct.

The reason why the concept of excess of powers prescribed by the FAA should be limited to the adjudicative powers of the tribunal is because it comprises two notions, namely "excess of powers" and "imperfect execution of [powers]". Conceptually, if the term "powers" has been used accordingly with references to "the excess" and "imperfect execution", it can be reasonably concluded that the meaning of the term "power" in both instances is the same. Importantly, Section 10(a)(4) of the FAA refers only to the use of the tribunal's powers that ultimately cause that the *mutual, final, and definite* award is *made*. It shows that the use of the tribunal's powers needs to have a well-defined causal link with the production of an arbitral award. Consequently, it should mean that the reference is made to the tribunal's adjudicatory powers and not so much to its powers over the procedure, which are often viewed as "incidental" to the adjudicatory powers.[460] Arguably, the procedural misconducts should then (to the extent possible) be subsumed by Section 10(a)(3) of the FAA[461] or the evergreen public policy exception.[462]

The alternative view, allowing the extension of the interpretation of the excess of powers ground for the procedural decisions that are not in accordance with the parties' agreement, would be the prevailing one, however. One of the reasons is the lack of other grounds to address these issues.[463] This is also aligned with the broad reading of the "excess of powers" ground adopted by the Restatement. In any event, the procedural irregularities have to be serious to trigger a successful challenge. Consequently, the Restatement reads that "*[t]he tribunal also exceeds its powers if the arbitral procedure is contrary in material respect to the agreement of the parties, including gap-fillers added by the arbitral rules the parties may*

459 See section 5.3.

460 ILA, *ILA Report on Inherent Powers of Arbitral Tribunals* (2014) p.7, referring to the tribunal's powers to shape the conduct of the proceedings ("*Depending on the circumstances, arbitrators may have the inherent or implied authority to establish rules for the conduct of hearings and to fix the forms of argument permitted (i.e., written or oral). Such exercises of authority, readily viewed as incidental to the adjudicatory function of tribunals, are often exercised without debate or serious question.*"). See also section 5.1.

461 Pursuant to Section 10(a)(3) of the FAA, the award may be vacated "*where the arbitrators were guilty of misconduct in refusing to postpone the hearing, upon sufficient cause shown, or in refusing to hear evidence pertinent and material to the controversy; or of any other misbehavior by which the rights of any party have been prejudiced.*" Although on its face value it does not address, for example, violation of the party-agreed procedure, but it makes a reference to the right to be heard which can potentially be violated if the party-agreed procedure is not followed.

462 See section 6.1.2.

463 Born, *International Commercial Arbitration* (2014) p.3306 ("*In jurisdictions with no statutory equivalent to Article 34(2)(a)(iv) [i.a. the United States], serious procedural irregularities are sometimes considered as an excess of authority (although, strictly speaking, this is inappropriate).*").

have incorporated into their agreement or by the applicable law."[464] Therefore, if the procedure selected by the tribunal is *materially* different from the one designed by the parties, the award granted by said tribunal may be vacated on the excess of powers ground.[465]

The Restatement also follows Hayford's argument that "*[i]f an arbitrator fails to comply with an express requirement set forth in the arbitration agreement as to the form, nature, or content of the arbitration award, the award will be vacated.*"[466]

Some authors point out that

> arbitrators also exceed their authority when they contravene express provisions in an arbitration clause governing how their award should be issued, such as a requirement that the award be accompanied by finding of fact and conclusions of law, or that arbitration be mandatory but the award non-binding, where arbitrators then purported to issue a binding award.[467]

In one reported case, it was held that "*it is clear that the provisions of the Agreement required the arbitrator to render a reasoned award, and if he failed to do so he thus exceeded his power and therefore vacatur is proper.*"[468]

In a nutshell, taking into account the arguments raised above, two conditions have to be met in order to successfully challenge an award based on the excess of powers ground and in connection with some procedural decisions of the tribunal: (i) parties need to *expressly, clearly and unambiguously* shape the procedure (preferably) in their agreement to arbitrate,[469] and (ii) the tribunal's procedural actions need to be *materially* different from the ones provided by the parties.[470] Importantly,

464 The Restatement (second tentative draft) p.290.

465 The Restatement (second tentative draft) p.290 makes a reference to *Cargill Rice, Inc. v. Empresa Nicaraguense de Alimentos Basicos*, 25 F.3d 223, 226 (4th Cir. 1994) ("*Arbitration awards made by arbitrators not appointed under the method provided in the parties' contract must be vacated.*"). Also, *Szuts v. Dean Witter Reynolds, Inc.*, 931 F.2d 830, 832 22 (11th Cir. 1991) ("*Because the arbitrators violated the provisions of the arbitration agreement requiring arbitration before at least three arbitrators, they exceeded their authority under the arbitration agreement.*").

466 Hayford, *Law in Disarray: Judicial Standards for Vacatur of Commercial Arbitration Awards* (1995-1996) pp.753-754.

467 Holtzmann et al., (2013) Chapter VII(2)(a)(6).

468 *Rain CII Carbon LLC v. ConocoPhillips Co.*, 2011 U.S. Dist. LEXIS 68994, at *15 (E.D. La. June 27, 2011), as reported in the Restatement (second tentative draft) p.290.

469 In principle, there is the possibility that parties came to some procedural arrangements after the tribunal is constituted.

470 If parties do not deviate from the procedure envisaged by the institutional rules, or their agreement is moot on the procedural aspects of the case, the tribunal, by and large, will be given wide authority to shape the procedure as it deems fit (save for the general notion of due process) thanks to the tribunal's *inherent* powers over the procedure. See, *i.a.*, ILA, *ILA Report on Inherent Powers of Arbitral Tribunals* (2014) p.7, referring to the tribunal's powers to shape the conduct of the proceedings ("*Depending on the circumstances, arbitrators may have the inherent or implied authority to establish rules for the conduct of hearings and to*

> an intentional deviation from the parties' agreed-upon procedures to protect the safety of the parties, to ensure the enforceability of the award, or to comply with the mandatory law of the seat (a violation of which might trigger [the setting] aside of the award) would not ordinarily be considered a material violation of the parties['] agreement. Although such deviation may violate certain provisions of the parties' agreement, it arguably is intended to serve the parties' larger purposes in submitting their dispute to arbitration and within the arbitrators' discretion and duty to render an enforceable award.[471]

Finally, it is necessary to respect the tribunal's autonomy in leading the arbitral process, which means that its procedural decisions should greatly escape the court's scrutiny. It is ultimately in the tribunal's hand to ensure that the dispute resolution process is efficient. It is also the tribunal's task to discipline parties for their misbehavior. Arguably, this power is inherent to the tribunal's task to administer the proceedings. Nonetheless, it is also provided in institutional rules.

Possibly the broadest authority is given under the new JAMS Rules which provide that

> [t]he Tribunal may order appropriate sanctions for failure of a party to comply with its obligations under any of these Rules or with an order of the Tribunal. These sanctions may include, but are not limited to, assessment of Arbitration Fees and Arbitrator compensation and expenses; assessment of any other costs occasioned by the actionable conduct, including reasonable attorneys' fees; exclusion of certain evidence; drawing adverse inferences; or, in extreme cases, determining an issue or issues submitted to Arbitration adversely to the party that has failed to comply.[472]

All in all, it is preferred to read the "excess of powers" ground only as the recourse against the tribunal's adjudicative function. Even if this is not the case and the interpretation is broadened due to some deficiencies in the FAA framework, the tribunal's procedural rulings should greatly survive the "excess of powers" challenge considering the broad managerial authority of the tribunal. In certain circumstances, decisions may also survive

---

fix the forms of argument permitted (i.e., written or oral). Such exercises of authority, readily viewed as incidental to the adjudicatory function of tribunals, are often exercised without debate or serious question.").

471 The Restatement (second tentative draft) p.218. See also ILA, *ILA Report on Inherent Powers of Arbitral Tribunals* (2014) p.19 ("*In deciding to arbitrate, parties consent to a legal process involving certain minimum standards of due process and fairness upon which they should not be able, consistent with that agreement, to renege. Arbitrators should be seen as having the authority to enforce these standards.*").

472 See Art. 33 of the 2016 JAMS Rules.

even when they contrast with the parties' procedural agreements, provided that they are in accordance with the due process requirement and public policy.

8 CONCLUDING REMARKS

The Federal Arbitration Act will soon celebrate its centennial. It still remains, however, a vital piece of legislation, that offers a fairly effective framework for the present arbitration system in the U.S., irrespective of its age. Throughout its long life, and following the Supreme Court's interpretation, the pro-arbitration, pro-enforcement standing of the FAA is regularly reaffirmed. The Court interpretations are not always free from controversy, however. For example, although the Supreme Court managed to highlight and enhance the supremacy of the FAA over the states' arbitration statutes, it is not necessarily clear whether the intention of the Congress at the beginning of the twentieth century was to create a body of substantive law on arbitration that would prevail over the competing provisions of state law. As highlighted by numbers of authorities, it is more plausible that the FAA was created as a procedural vehicle to be used in the federal courts and is nowadays reinvented by the Supreme Court.

In any event, federal arbitration law, restructured by the Supreme Court and applied nowadays has characteristics of a modern arbitration statute, which includes (among others): the general (federal) policy favoring arbitration, very limited (and arguably exclusive) grounds to challenge the award upon vacatur, a narrow (deferential) standard of review of the arbitral award and the possibility to cure the award if only partially flawed (by correcting it, remanding or confirming it in part).

The court deciding upon the challenge that the tribunal exceeded its "powers" will need to determine the applicable restrictions on the tribunal's powers. At first it will focus on the contractual underpinnings for arbitration, namely it will review the agreement to arbitrate and the parties' intention therein. Since agreements to arbitrate are, usually, drafted broadly, the vacating court may seek further guidance in the applicable arbitral rules and in the parties' subsequent requests, which also frame the arbitrators' powers. Finally, it is necessary to point out that tribunal's powers cannot violate the mandatory rules of public policy.

The concept of "excess of powers" that is based on the three pillars mentioned above (an agreement to arbitrate, the parties' requests and public policy) effectively shapes the analysis as to the limits to an arbitral tribunal's undertakings. The second prong of Section 10(a)(4) of the FAA, thus "imperfect execution of powers", addresses a failure to render a final and binding award.

It is important to note, however, that the alternative view for the post-award relief has been projected by the Restatement that concludes that the foreign awards that are rendered in the U.S. should be challenged under the grounds introduced in the New York Convention. It is yet to be seen, if the courts follow such an interpretation.

Additionally, over the years, the understanding of the notion of "excess of powers" has been expanded by the judiciary. The courts provided *i.a.* that confirmation of the award can be refused when it manifestly disregards the law or violates public policy. As discussed in detail in this chapter, however, only the public policy challenge should survive the *Hall Street* aftermath, that restricted the grounds for vacatur on the federal level to the statutory grounds prescribed by the FAA. Consequently, it means that any non-statutory grounds (but for public policy) should cease to exist or at the very most should be reconciled with the grounds pursuant to the FAA. As also reflected, the reconciliation should not be followed with an unnecessary expansion of the current understanding of the statutory grounds.

Some of the reflections that follow the analysis of the application of the excess of powers challenge to selected issues that might fall outside the arbitral tribunal's authority should be repeated. Firstly, the tribunal's ultimate undertaking is contract interpretation. In any case when the vacating court is satisfied that the tribunal's decision follows the arbitral panel's understanding of the contract, it will defer to the tribunal's findings and will likely confirm the award. It leads to the second conclusion that it is preferable for the parties to *clearly* and *unambiguously* restrict the tribunal's powers over contract interpretation or other aspects of arbitration that will fall outside the scope of the tribunal's authority. Thirdly, the exception to this basic rule occurs when the very existence of an agreement to arbitrate and, thus, of the tribunal's powers is at stake. In cases of jurisdictional/threshold issues, the mechanism reverses. It means that parties need to *clearly* and *unambiguously* vest the tribunal with power over the interpretation of the jurisdictional/threshold issues. If the transfer of powers over these gateway questions is not evident, the vacating court will exercise a full and independent review of the challenge (therefore, without any deference to the tribunal's decision on the issue). Finally, it is necessary to point out that some of the tribunal's procedural decisions will effectively fit within the excess of powers grounds. Although, the "excess of powers" challenge is better viewed as accommodating only the excess of adjudicatory powers of the arbitral tribunal, it is also acknowledged that in accordance with the current interpretation of the excess of powers challenge, the tribunal's departure from the contractually agreed (explicit) rules shaping the procedure may be successfully vacated pursuant to Section 10(a)(4) of the FAA.

VI The New York Convention of 1958 on the Recognition and Enforcement of Foreign Arbitral Awards

1 Introduction

The preceding analysis focused on the national frameworks designed to challenge the arbitral tribunals' awards at the seat of arbitration. Yet, the scrutiny of the award made in the country of enforcement might be equally perilous for the fate of the award. At the enforcement stage, the New York Convention of 1958 on the Recognition and Enforcement of Foreign Arbitral Awards (hereafter "the New York Convention" or "the Convention") is the most influential international instrument that should be taken into account.

Although the Convention does not refer to the concept of the arbitral tribunal's mandate, it is important to have a closer look at Article V(1)(c) of the Convention that inspired a similar provision which has been included in the Model Law on International Commercial Arbitration.[1] Pursuant to Article V(1)(c) of the Convention, an award may be refused recognition and enforcement if

> [t]he award deals with a difference not contemplated by or not falling within the terms of the submission to arbitration, or it contains decisions on matters beyond the scope of the submission to arbitration, provided that, if the decisions on matters submitted to arbitration can be separated from those not so submitted, that part of the award which contains decisions on matters submitted to arbitration may be recognized and enforced [...].

This provision is descriptive in nature, which makes it vulnerable to different ways of interpretation and (potentially) invites the actors to transplant their national concepts for challenging the award (on the basis of "excess of mandate" in particular) on the international level at the enforcement stage. Consequently further analysis is required with respect to the application of Article V(1)(c) of the New York Convention, which, for the purpose of this chapter would also be considered as the "excess of mandate" type of challenge.

1 For further reading on the Model Law, see Chapter II.

This introduction is followed by four sections. The first two sections give a brief overview of the system of enforcement and the (primarily) consensual nature of the "tribunal's mandate". The last two sections are essential for the discussion at hand.

The first section will deal with the general approach in which the courts undertake the review at the enforcement stage. The second one focuses on the recognized limits to the tribunal's mandate. The third section explains the New York Convention's approach to the "excess of mandate" type of challenge and the evolution of the international system of enforcement will be explained, starting with the preceding system of the Geneva Convention of 1927 on the Execution of Foreign Arbitral Awards (hereafter "the Geneva Convention").[2] It will be followed by the analysis of the preparatory work of the New York Convention and concluded with an overview of the hypothetical draft convention introduced by van den Berg in 2008 ("hereafter the Miami Draft").[3] What follows is a brief take on the tension between the different linguistic (authentic) versions of the text of the New York Convention and an analysis of the language used in Article V(1)(c) of the New York Convention. The last subsection is devoted to the issue of the interplay between different grounds to resist enforcement. The final section gives an overview of the application of the "excess of mandate" type of challenge to selected types of arbitral tribunal's decisions and uses the same division as in the previous chapters. It means that, initially, it is tested whether the tribunal's decision on selected types of parties' claims fits within the scope of the "tribunal's mandate". It is then followed by a "mandate" discussion on the process of the application of law by the arbitral tribunal, a discussion regarding different types of remedial authority and, finally, reflections on authority over different issues auxiliary to the parties' main claims.

2 Court standard of review at the enforcement stage

The enforcement courts generally endorse the pro-enforcement philosophy of the New York Convention (section 2.1). They will do so by limiting the scope of the review (section 2.2) and by using available remedies in favor of enforcement (section 2.3). Consequently, the award-debtors must defeat the heavy presumption that the award is final and binding.

2 For the text, see, *e.g.*, http://www.newyorkconvention.org/11165/web/files/document/1/5/15939.pdf [last accessed 14 August 2020].

3 For the text of the Miami Draft, see http://www.newyorkconvention.org/11165/web/files/document/1/6/16017.pdf [last accessed 14 August 2020].

2.1 Approach favoring enforcement of arbitral awards

The so-called "pro-enforcement bias" was described as a key to the appropriate reading of the New York Convention.[4] According to the opening part of Article V of the New York Convention, "*[r]ecognition and enforcement of the award may be refused, at the request of the party against whom it is invoked, only if that party furnishes to the competent authority where the recognition and enforcement is sought, proof that [...].*" Two words used in the provision deserve a closer look. Firstly, the term "only" (as in "*only if [...] party [...] furnishes proof that*") suggests that an arbitral award should be recognized and enforced but for the situations (and only in those situations) where the award-debtor is able to prove that the conditions of one of the listed Article V grounds are met.[5] Secondly, the use of the verb "may" (as in "*may be refused*") may imply that the enforcement court has a discretion to enforce the award notwithstanding the existence of the Article V grounds.[6] Consequently, in the light of its purpose, it is the finality of the award that needs to be cultivated. It means that the challenges against the award (i) can only be based on the exhaustive list of the Article V grounds, and (ii) even if the challenge fits within the scope of the enumerated grounds, it should only be accepted if it is grievous.

As mentioned above, the pro-enforcement philosophy of the New York Convention requires one to construe the list of Article V exhaustively.[7] It means that national systems

---

4 ICCA, *ICCA's Guide to the Interpretation of the 1958 New York Convention* (2011) p.14. Born, *International Commercial Arbitration* (2014) p.3412 ("*[n]ational courts and other authorities have uniformly recognized the foregoing purposes, often referring to the Convention's "pro-enforcement" objectives or purpose.*"). See, for example, *Int'l Standard Elec. Corp. v. Bridas Sociedad Anonima Petrolera, Indus. Y Comercial*, 745 F. Supp. 172, 176 (S.D.N.Y. 1990) ("*the basic thrust of the convention was to limit the broad attacks on foreign arbitral awards that had been authorized by the predecessor Geneva Convention of 1927*").

5 The reversal of the burden of proof from the party who seeks enforcement to the party resisting an arbitral award was an additional positively appraised amendment to the Geneva Convention framework of enforcement. It means that an arbitral award is enforceable *prima facie* unless proven otherwise. It has been argued that the standard of proof is rather high and that the alleged violation has to be substantive in order for the court not to reject it. See also Van den Berg, *The New York Convention of 1958: Towards Uniform Judicial Interpretation* (1981) p.9 an also p.264, ICCA, *ICCA's Guide to the Interpretation of the 1958 New York Convention* (2011) p.79, also Nacimiento (2010) p.210.

6 The interpretation of the verb "may" generated a heated debate amongst scholars. See, *i.a.*, Paulsson J., *May or Must Under the New York Convention: An Exercise in Syntax and Linguistics* (1998), Paulsson J., *Enforcing arbitral awards notwithstanding a local standard annulment (LSA)* (1998), Van den Berg, *Enforcement of Annuled Awards?* (1998). See also section 2.3.

7 See, *e.g.*, Van den Berg, *The New York Convention of 1958: Towards Uniform Judicial Interpretation* (1981) p.265, Van den Berg, *The New York Convention of 1958: An Overview* (2008) p.56, Lew et al., *Comparative International Commercial Arbitration* (2003) p.706 and Nacimiento (2010) p.209 ("*the objections to recognition and enforcement listed in Article V are meant to be exhaustive and national law cannot be the basis for any additional defense.*"), Kronke (2010) p.5, ICCA, *ICCA's Guide to the Interpretation of the 1958 New York Convention* (2011) p.80.

cannot supplement the system with any additional grounds.[8] The UNCITRAL Secretariat Guide concludes that "*[t]he conditions for recognition and enforcement in the Convention establish a 'ceiling', or maximum level of control, which Contracting States may exert over arbitral awards and arbitration agreements.*"[9] It is an important feature of the New York Convention, especially in the context of the "excess of mandate" type of challenge which is interpreted differently in various jurisdictions.[10]

It is significant to add that even though the list of Article v. grounds is rather short, not every violation would result in a successful challenge of the award.

The UNCITRAL Secretariat Guide is adamant in saying that:

> [t]he objective of the New York Convention is to facilitate the recognition and enforcement of arbitral awards to the greatest extent possible and to provide a maximum level of control which Contracting States may exert over arbitral awards. In accordance with this objective, the Convention grants courts of the Contracting States the discretion to refuse to recognize and enforce an award on the grounds listed in article V, without obligating them to do so.[11]

The question whether the court has a discretion or an obligation to refuse recognition and enforcement of the award has been the subject of a debate between scholars. In light of the abovementioned UNCITRAL recommendation, the better view is to accept the discretionary power of the enforcement courts. In any event, however, Nacimento aptly concluded that "*[...] in practice, the results in jurisdictions permitting judicial discretion hardly differ from those in jurisdictions precluding discretion.*"[12] The discretion should be therefore used as a way to accept only material violations that affect the award.[13]

8 This design has been maintained and reinforced in the Miami Draft. See article 5(1) of the Miami Draft ("*[e]nforcement of an arbitral award shall not be refused on any other ground that the grounds expressly set forth in this article*").

9 UNCITRAL, *UNCITRAL Secretariat Guide on the Convention on the Recognition and Enforcement of Foreign Arbitral Awards* (2016) p.2.

10 See Chapter II-Chapter V.

11 UNCITRAL, *UNCITRAL Secretariat Guide on the Convention on the Recognition and Enforcement of Foreign Arbitral Awards* (2016) p.125.

12 Nacimiento (2010) p.209.

13 Reisman & Richardson (2012) p. 28: "*In keeping with our understanding of the architecture of the [New York] Convention, we suggest that the discretionary part of Article V ought to be understood as a policy decision by the drafters to adopt what has been called elsewhere a "material violation" rather than 'technical discrepancy' approach.*" See also article 5(2) of the Miami Draft ("*[e]nforcement shall be refused on the grounds set forth in this article in manifest cases only*").

2.2 *The scope of the court's review*

As highlighted by Nacimiento, "*[t]he control of the enforcing court is limited to verifying whether a ground under Article V exists.*"[14] Consequently, one will find that "*[t]he grounds for refusal under article V do not include an erroneous decision in law or in fact by the arbitral tribunal.*"[15] It means that the merits of the arbitral decision are beyond the courts' control.

The enforcement courts follow this principle and accept the limited scope of their control over arbitration. For example, as persuasively concluded by a U.S. court:

> [w]e cannot understand how the Convention, created to assure consistency in the enforcement of foreign arbitral awards, would not be gravely undermined, if judges sitting in each of the many jurisdictions where enforcement may be obtained, were authorized by the Convention to undertake a de novo inquiry into whether the law the arbitrators said they were using was or was not properly applied by them. The plain answer is that the Convention does not, and could not, contemplate such a chaos.[16]

Courts in other jurisdictions share the vision that the merits of the case are delegated to the tribunal and that its conclusions should be final.[17]

As long as this principle seems rather clear, its application in the case of the "excess of mandate" type of challenge as envisaged in Article V(1)(c) of the New York Convention may create some difficulties, because the scope of the tribunal's mandate is closely intertwined with the decision rendered by the tribunal. As observed by van den Berg: "*[t]he principle that a court may not subject an arbitral award to a review on the merits is not*

14 Nacimiento (2010) p.210.

15 UNCITRAL, *UNCITRAL Secretariat Guide on the Convention on the Recognition and Enforcement of Foreign Arbitral Awards* (2016) p.126.

16 *Int'l Standard Elec. Corp. v. Bridas Sociedad Anonima Petrolera, Indus. Y Comercial*, 745 F. Supp. 172, 182 (S.D.N.Y. 1990).

17 See, *e.g.*, *Ukrainian dealer v. German manufacturer*, Oberlandesgericht, Munich, 30 July 2012 and Bundesgerichtshof, 23 April 2013, XXXIX Y.B. Comm. Arb. 394 (2014), *Joint Stock Company A v. Joint Stock Company B*, Higher Regional Court of Munich, 34 Sch 10/11, 14 November 2011, XXXVII Y.B. Comm. Arb. 231 (2012), *Sovereign Participations International S.A. v. Chadmore Developments Ltd.*, Cour d'Appel [Court of Appeal], 28 January 1999, XXIVa Y.B. Comm. Arb. 714, 721 (1999) ("*Even if the arbitral tribunal makes a gross mistake of fact or law, this is not a ground for refusing enforcement of the award.*"), *AB Götaverken v. General National Maritime Transport Company (GMTC), Libya and others*, Svea Court of Appeal (5th Dept.) Stockholm; Swedish Supreme Court, SO 1462, 13 December 1978; 13 August 1979, VI Y.B. Comm. Arb. 237, 240 (1981) ("*[...] when a request for enforcement of a foreign arbitral award is considered, there should, in principle, not be a review of the substance of the award*"). See also UNCITRAL, *UNCITRAL Secretariat Guide on the Convention on the Recognition and Enforcement of Foreign Arbitral Awards* (2016) p.126 and the case law therein.

unfettered, in the sense that the court may examine the award for the purposes of verifying the grounds for refusal of enforcement, e.g., excess by the arbitral tribunal of its authority."[18] This is also the reason why the award-debtor will likely be tempted to disguise its merits review as an "excess of mandate" type of challenge. Consequently, the mechanism that allows the court to look at the tribunal's decision comes with the obligation of judicial self-control.

2.3 *Remedies at the court's disposal*

In principle, since the enforcement court does not supervise and oversee the arbitral process, it is not required to have extensive remedial mechanisms at its disposal. Consequently, the New York Convention does not include an elaborate catalogue of remedial powers. It gives, however, sufficient tools to the enforcement courts to prevent the use of the Article V defenses as a challenge against technical and immaterial violations. It is particularly the case in the context of the "excess of mandate" type of challenge, because Article V(1)(c) of the New York Convention allows the partial recognition and enforcement of an award. This mechanism will work in addition to the discretionary power of the court to refuse recognition and enforcement only in cases of serious violations.[19]

The possibility to save a healthy part of the arbitral award has been expressly given to the courts in the New York Convention. Pursuant to the last part of Article V(1)(c) of the New York Convention, "*[...] if the decisions on matters submitted to arbitration can be separated from those not so submitted, that part of the award which contains decisions on matters submitted to arbitration may be recognized and enforced.*"[20] Van den Berg, based on the analysis of the *travaux préparatoires*, explained that "*[...] partial enforcement may be granted if the matter in excess of the arbitrator's authority is of very incidental nature and the refusal of enforcement would lead to unjustified hardship for the party seeking*

---

18 Van den Berg, *The New York Convention of 1958: An Overview* (2008) p.56 also Van den Berg, *The New York Convention of 1958: Towards Uniform Judicial Interpretation* (1981) p.270.

19 See also section 2.1.

20 The discussion on whether the partial enforcement also applies to the other grounds for refusal falls outside the scope of this book. For more on this topic see, e.g., Borris & Hannecke, *Article V: Grounds for Refusal of Recognition and Enforcement of Arbitral Awards. General* (2012) pp.266-267, and Born, *International Commercial Arbitration* (2014) p.3558.

enforcement".[21] The most recent UNCITRAL Secretariat Guide, however, confirms that the "*[...] application is much broader.*"[22]

The possibility of splitting the award into an enforceable and non-enforceable (defective) part is a powerful one, especially considering the great endorsement it receives.[23] In addition, it is consistent with the pro-enforcement spirit of the New York Convention. Some authors even argue that the "*partial recognition and enforcement of an award is mandatory where a clear separation is possible between the parts of the award that are covered by the arbitration agreement from those which are not.*"[24] This argument is appealing indeed if it is clear which parts of the award falls outside of the scope of the underlying agreement to arbitrate. This is not often the case, however. Perhaps, imposing an obligation on the courts is not the most sensible solution. Firstly, nothing in the text of Article V would suggest that the partial enforcement is a court's duty (and there is no sanction to enforce such a duty on the courts). Secondly, imposing a duty to partially enforce might create conditions where the courts would be more prone to (partially) refuse recognition and enforcement, which would be against the underlying goals of the Convention. It further means that the duty of partial enforcement would be counterproductive, because it would encourage the (enforcement) courts to (fully) review the scope of the agreement to arbitrate and eventually be more critical about it, whereas, arguably, full discretion gives more flexibility to the courts to enforce the whole award.[25]

3 LIMITS TO THE ARBITRAL TRIBUNAL'S "MANDATE" AT THE ENFORCEMENT STAGE

As has already been explained in the national chapters, there are, in principle, three relevant sources for a tribunal's "mandate".[26] The agreement to arbitrate is always a starting point

21 Van den Berg, *The New York Convention of 1958: Towards Uniform Judicial Interpretation* (1981) p.319. See also Born, *International Commercial Arbitration* (2014) p.3558 ("*The drafting history of Article V(1)(c) indicates that the provision was meant, in particular, to ensure that recognition of valid portions of an award would not be denied 'merely because a small detail fell outside the scope of the arbitral agreement.'*").

22 UNCITRAL, *UNCITRAL Secretariat Guide on the Convention on the Recognition and Enforcement of Foreign Arbitral Awards* (2016) p.181.

23 Born, *International Commercial Arbitration* (2014) p.3558 ("*Consistent with this provision, courts have granted partial recognition to awards, or made clear that they would be prepared to do so in appropriate cases.*").

24 Borris & Hannecke, *Excess of Competence or Jurisdiction, Article V(1)(c)* (2012) p.329. See also Born, *International Commercial Arbitration* (2014) p.3434 ("*Indeed, there is a substantial argument that the Convention not only permits, but also requires, recognition and enforcement of separable, valid portions of an award.*").

25 See also section 2.1.

26 Jarvin, *The sources and limits of the arbitrator's powers* (1996) p.140 ("*The arbitrator's authority is no broader than that defined by the parties and some of his duties are defined by law*").

(section 3.1). It is supplemented, however, by the parties' subsequent submissions (section 3.2). Finally, at the enforcement stage, rules of public policy at the place of enforcement may also play a role in determining whether the tribunal was well within the boundaries of its powers (section 3.3). These three concepts, in general, form the three keyholes test (section 3.4).

3.1 Agreement to arbitrate

It does not come as a surprise that the most important foundation of an arbitral tribunal's "mandate" is an agreement to arbitrate. It is not only the source, but also the restraint to the arbitral tribunal's powers.[27] Therefore, as long as the New York Convention sets out the internationally recognized standards with regard to the validity of the agreement to arbitrate,[28] in the context of the mandate it is the wording of the agreement that is essential.[29]

Parties, when drafting the contract, are free to choose the style in which they draft their arbitration clause. It can be broad and flexible or narrow and restrictive, depending on the scope that the parties are willing to submit to arbitration. Parties need to be aware, however, that the courts – following the underlying principle of the Convention[30] – will likely favor a broad interpretation of the agreements to arbitrate.[31]

Additionally, parties need to observe what the impact is of the applicable law and institutional rules on the scope of the tribunal's mandate. For example, Jarvin argues that

27 Haas (2002) p.499. Also Jarvin, *The sources and limits of the arbitrator's powers* (1996) p.142.

28 See Art. II(1) of the New York Convention ("*Each Contracting State shall recognize an agreement in writing under which the parties undertake to submit to arbitration all or any differences which have arisen or which may arise between them in respect of a defined legal relationship, whether contractual or not, concerning a subject matter capable of settlement by arbitration.*").

29 ICCA, *ICCA's Guide to the Interpretation of the 1958 New York Convention* (2011) pp.93-94 ("*[t]he language of the arbitration agreement that sets out what the parties have agreed to submit to the arbitral tribunal for determination is critically important; issues must remain within that scope.*"). Irrespectively of whether it is an arbitration clause to resolve future disputes or a submission agreement concluded after the dispute has arisen, both will be recognized under the Convention. See Art. II(1) of the Convention.

30 See section 2.1.

31 See, *e.g.*, *Mgmt. & Tech. Consultants S.A. v. Parsons-Jurden Int'l Corp.*, 820 F.2d 1531, 1534–35 (9th Cir. 1987) ("*Here, the parties agree the arbiters had authority to determine whether the gross billings exceeded $350 million. They disagree on whether the arbiters had the further authority to determine the amount of additional compensation due. The letter agreement indicates that '[a]ny dispute' which could not be 'settled amicably' would be resolved by arbitration. We construe the word 'any' broadly. Cf. Mediterranean Enterprises,* 708 F.2d at 1463 *('any dispute' read narrowly where limiting language of 'arising hereunder' immediately followed). An agreement to arbitrate 'any dispute' without strong limiting or excepting language immediately following it logically includes not only the dispute, but the consequences naturally flowing from it – here, the amount of additional compensation.*").

> [p]arties are not totally unrestricted in drawing up clauses submitting disputes to arbitration (or rather they may be unrestricted in what they agree but the effects of their agreement may be limited). First arbitration rules applicable may restrict the kind of disputes for which the rules have been envisaged and by referring to the rules of an institution the parties' agreement will include the limitations contained in the rules proper.[32]

It is also possible, however, that these supplementary sources of powers will provide for a more elaborate structure of the arbitral mandate,[33] especially in the context of its procedural authority. Consequently, it might affect the chances of success of the "excess of mandate" type of challenge.

3.2 *Parties' (subsequent) submissions*

At the enforcement stage, similar to the setting-aside review, the arbitral tribunal's "mandate" should be evaluated not only with reference to an abstract agreement to arbitrate,[34] but also with reference to the actual dispute that it needs to resolve. It means that the parties' claims and submissions will play a role in shaping the arbitral tribunal's "mandate". In this context, arguably, it is necessary to reflect (i) on the potential effect that the parties' submissions have on the mandate,[35] and (ii) on the exceptional character of the ICC Terms of Reference.

The parties' claims as formulated in their submissions are essential in the context of the Article V(1)(c) challenge. Consequently, one should not be satisfied only with the limits as set out by the arbitration agreement, but rather (also) consider subsequent submissions of the parties as the standard that shapes the arbitral tribunal's mandate.[36] It

32 Jarvin, *The sources and limits of the arbitrator's powers* (1996) p.142.

33 One more elaborate than the agreement to arbitrate itself.

34 See section 3.1.

35 One should know that there are different interpretations of Art. V(1)(c) of the Convention. In some jurisdictions this ground is considered only in the context of the scope of the underlying agreement to arbitrate without consideration of the parties' subsequent submissions. In these cases, however, *ultra petita* will be likely subsumed by other grounds for challenge, which will make the parties' submissions relevant in any event. For further reading, see section 4.2 and section 4.3.

36 Van den Berg, *The New York Convention of 1958: An Overview* (2008), p.59 ("*[i]n certain cases, the matters submitted by the parties to the arbitral tribunal's decision (i.e., its mandate) may be narrower than the scope of the arbitration clause. The distinction is, at least theoretically, important as ground c of Article V(1) is in the final analysis to be determined on the basis of the tribunal's mandate. However, the tribunal's mandate may be broadened by the parties' submissions beyond the scope of the arbitration clause if during the arbitration both parties explicitly or tacitly agreed to such an extension*"). See also Bernet & Meier (2013) p.214 ("*The enforcement of an arbitral award may be refused if it determines legal or factual issues which do not fall within the scope of the arbitration agreement. The parties may, however, expand the arbitral tribunal's competence*

is important to note that not only the initial exchange of submissions might be relevant in the context of the "excess of mandate" type of challenge. In cases where a modification of the claims is allowed during the proceedings, the "mandate" becomes a dynamic concept and a moving target whenever its excess is being alleged.

The ICC Terms of Reference might be considered as yet another source of the arbitral tribunal's mandate. On the one hand, it makes the concept of the mandate more static, because the parties will not be able to modify the scope of the issues submitted without the tribunal's approval.[37] On the other hand, the Terms of Reference might be an important source when the issues introduced therein go beyond the initial agreement to arbitrate and, yet, all parties agree.[38]

All in all, it is not only the agreement to arbitrate that needs to be consulted in case of the Article V(1)(c) challenge. It should always be kept in mind that the initial agreement to arbitrate, together with the parties' subsequent submissions, work in tandem.

3.3 *Mandatory rules of public policy character*

Due to the fact that the enforcement court may raise (*ex officio*) the argument of public policy,[39] public policy is also (potentially) relevant for the "excess of mandate" type of challenge. This would particularly be the case when the tribunal exercises certain powers that are unknown at the place of enforcement (*e.g.* granting punitive damages). Consequently, even if an award is well within the limits of the tribunal's "mandate" at the seat of arbitration, it may offend the public policy of the country where enforcement is sought.[40]

The definition of public policy will differ from jurisdiction to jurisdiction which means that apart from flagging the issue, no general conclusion can be given at this point. At the same time, however, the narrow interpretation of the public policy rules as a bar for enforcement should be endorsed. It means that Article V(2)(b) of the Convention should be understood as referring to international public policy.[41]

---

upon mutual agreement and a resulting award will be enforced despite the narrower initial scope of the arbitration agreement.").

37 See Art. 23(4) of the (draft) 2021 ICC Rules, Art. 23(4) of the 2017 ICC Rules, and Art. 23(4) of the 2012 ICC Rules. The tribunal's approval is arguably important if one considers that the mandate creates a legal tie between three equal entities (*i.e.* parties and the tribunal).

38 For a discussion relating to the modification of claims submitted *after* the Terms of Reference are signed, see section 5.1.5.

39 See Art. V(2)(b) of the Convention.

40 For example, in cases of punitive damages. See, *e.g.*, Borris & Hannecke, *Excess of Competence or Jurisdiction, Article V(1)(c)* (2012) p.325.

41 See ILA, *ILA Report on Public Policy as a Bar to Enforcement of International Arbitral Awards* (2002) pp.2-5.

In the same vein, the UNCITRAL Secretariat Guide concludes that

> [a]lthough different jurisdictions define public policy differently, case law tends to refer to a public policy basis for refusing recognition and enforcement of an award under article V (2)(b) of the New York Convention when the core values of a legal system have been deviated from. Invoking the public policy exception is a safety valve to be used in those exceptional circumstances when it would be impossible for a legal system to recognize an award and enforce it without abandoning the very fundaments on which it is based.[42]

It is sensible to consider that the Article V(2)(b) standard is one of international public policy, because it allows the tribunal to self-reflect on its mandate. Consequently, it would entail that in order to render an enforceable award the tribunal needs to comply with one considerably consistent standard of public policy without focusing on the peculiarities of each potential country of enforcement.

3.4 *The relevance of the parties' consent, their requests and the law: the three keyholes test*

Since the "mandate" is not defined in the Convention it is necessary to independently identify the sources of the arbitrators' powers. Unsurprisingly it is primarily based on the parties' consent and their request(s). For example, pursuant to the ICCA Guide, "*[i]n determining what the parties have submitted to the arbitral tribunal, regard must be had to the arbitration agreement and the claims for relief submitted to the arbitral tribunal by the parties.*"[43] All in all, one should not forget, however, that the parties' own design[44] should not conflict with the basic values of the legal system at the place of enforcement.[45]

---

42 UNCITRAL, *UNCITRAL Secretariat Guide on the Convention on the Recognition and Enforcement of Foreign Arbitral Awards* (2016) p.240. See also ICCA, *ICCA's Guide to the Interpretation of the 1958 New York Convention* (2011) p.71 ("*[t]he general rule to be followed by the courts is that the grounds for refusal defined in Article V are to be construed narrowly, which means that their existence is accepted in serious cases only. This is especially true with respect to claims of violation of public policy, which are often raised by disappointed parties but very seldom accepted by the courts.*").

43 ICCA, *ICCA's Guide to the Interpretation of the 1958 New York Convention* (2011) p.93.

44 See section 3.1 and section 3.2.

45 See section 3.3.

4 The New York Convention approach to the "excess of mandate" type of challenge

As already highlighted at the beginning, the Convention does not operate with the notion of the mandate. At the same time, Article V(1)(c) of the Convention, arguably, constitutes a type of post-award challenge towards the alleged "excess of mandate". Pursuant to this provision, the award may be refused recognition and enforcement if "*the award deals with a difference not contemplated by or not falling within the terms of the submission to arbitration, or it contains decisions on matters beyond the scope of the submission to arbitration [...].*"

Before applying the challenge to selected decisions of an arbitral tribunal, it is necessary to reflect briefly on the historical development of the enforcement system (section 4.1). Furthermore, one should analyze the (elusive) text of Article V(1)(c) of the Convention (section 4.3), including its different (equally authentic) linguistic versions (section 4.2) and finally analyze the potential tensions between competing defenses available under the architecture of Article V of the New York Convention (section 4.4).

4.1 Historical overview

To understand the meaning of the "excess of mandate" type of challenge under the New York Convention system it is useful to put the New York Convention enforcement regime in context. It entails that one should take into account (i) the shape of the same challenge under the Geneva Convention, (ii) the *travaux préparatoires* of the New York Convention, and (iii) the design of the challenge in the Miami Draft.[46]

Article 2(c) of the Geneva Convention provides that the recognition and enforcement of the award *shall* be refused if the national court is satisfied the "*the award does not deal with the differences contemplated by or falling within the terms of the submission to arbitration or that it contains decisions on matters beyond the scope of the submission to arbitration.*"[47] What can be thus easily observed is that, at the enforcement stage, the wording of the "excess of mandate" type of challenge remains in principle unchanged for almost a century now. Since it generates certain interpretative difficulties, the text will be closely reviewed below.[48]

46 For the sake of convenience, of the reader all texts of the relevant provisions have been set together in Table 3 at the end of this section.

47 For the text of the Convention, see http://www.newyorkconvention.org/11165/web/files/document/1/6/16020.pdf [last accessed 27 April 2020].

48 See section 4.3.

Although the final version of the New York Convention is very similar to the text of the Geneva Convention, the *travaux préparatoires* show that other concepts have also been taken into consideration. For example, the ICC Draft Convention[49] provided simpler wording by stating that the award will not be recognized and enforced if: "*[...] the award deals with a difference not contemplated by the agreement of the parties or that it contains decisions on matters not submitted to the arbitrators.*"[50] Notably, according to the ICC Draft, two concepts would be covered by the "excess of mandate" type of challenge. The first one requires a court to check if a dispute submitted was covered by the agreement to arbitrate, the second one was designed to see if the award conforms with the parties' requests.

The ICC's proposal did not survive, however, and was amended by the UN Draft.[51] The UN Draft reflected the rule expressed in the Geneva Convention.[52] Article IV(d) of the UN Draft reads that the court may refuse recognition and enforcement if satisfied "*that the award deals with a difference not contemplated by or not falling within the terms of the submission to arbitration or that it contains decisions on matters beyond the scope of the submission to arbitration [...].*"[53] The cryptic wording of the UN Draft made its way into the final version of the New York Convention and requires further analysis below.[54]

Before concluding, it is also necessary to explain van den Berg's proposal to the prospective changes in the New York Convention regime. For the fiftieth birthday of the New York Convention, a lively debate was provoked by van den Berg and his proposal for the revision of the New York Convention (*i.e.* "the Miami Draft"). In his critique, van den

49 The ICC issued its draft Convention aimed at facilitating the enforcement of awards related to international commercial disputes in 1953 and was a basis for the further work on the New York Convention. For the text of the ICC Draft Convention see http://www.newyorkconvention.org/11165/web/files/document/1/5/15940.pdf [last accessed 14 August 2020].

50 Art. IV(d) of the ICC Draft.

51 U.N. Doc. E/AC.42/4/Rev. 1 Annex p.2. See http://www.newyorkconvention.org/11165/web/files/document/1/5/15953.pdf [last accessed 14 August 2020]. The main differences between the ICC and UN Drafts related – among other things – to the concerns regarding the character of arbitral awards ('international' arbitral awards in the ICC Draft and 'foreign' arbitral awards in the UN Draft) or to the principle of reciprocity (enforcement of the award regardless of where it has been made in the ICC Draft, and an 'opt-in' system for applying the Convention only to the awards made in another Contracting State in the UN Draft. For more, see Van den Berg, *The New York Convention of 1958: Towards Uniform Judicial Interpretation* (1981) pp.6-10 and Briner & Hamilton (2008) pp.9-14.

52 It was explained by the ad hoc Committee on the Enforcement of International Arbitral Awards that: "*the first half of this clause reproduces Article 2(c) of the Geneva Convention, and is similar to Article IV(d) of the ICC draft*". No reason was given why the ICC proposal could not survive. For more, see U.N. Doc. E/AC.42/4/Rev.1 28 March 1955, p.10.

53 Art. IV(d) of the UN Draft.

54 See section 4.3.

Berg considered that the Convention should be modernized in order to remedy shortcomings that had become evident during years of interpreting the Convention.[55]

Among other inadequacies, he mentioned that a number of provisions are of an unclear character which raises difficulties with understanding their meaning. In this regard reference to Article V(1)(c) has also been made.[56] Consequently, the Miami Draft proposes the new, simplified wording of the "excess of mandate" type of challenge that obliges the court to refuse parties an enforcement request if "*[...] the relief granted in the award is more than or different from, the relief sought in the arbitration and such relief cannot be severed from the relief sought and granted.*"[57] This shape of the provision would, in turn, narrow the scope of application of the "excess of mandate" type of challenge to the *ultra* and *extra petita* scenarios.

Marike Paulsson suggested that "*the Miami draft seeks to contribute to validate the Drafter's intent and the meaning of little words like 'only' or 'may'. It is a pair of spectacles, a 'how to read this text' instrument*".[58] If one accepts her argument, it would mean that the "excess of mandate" type of challenge should not be interpreted excessively broad. It is yet to be determined, however, if enforcement courts indeed limit the application of the "excess of mandate" type of challenge to the *ultra* and *extra petita* scenarios.[59]

Table 3 The evolution of Article V(1)(c) of the New York Convention

The Geneva Convention	The ICC Draft	The UN Draft	The New York Convention	The Miami Draft
Art. 2(c)	Art. IV(d)	Art. IV(d)	Art. V(1)(c)	Art. 5(3)(c)
"*the award does not deal with the differences contemplated by or falling within the terms of the submission to arbitration or that it contains decisions on matters beyond the scope of the submission to arbitration.*"	"*that the award deals with a difference not contemplated by the agreement of the parties or that it contains decisions on matters not submitted to the arbitrators*"	"*that the award deals with a difference not contemplated by or not falling within the terms of the submission to arbitration or that it contains decisions on matters beyond the scope of the submission to arbitration [...].*"	"*the award deals with a difference not contemplated by or not falling within the terms of the submission to arbitration, or it contains decisions on matters beyond the scope of the submission to arbitration, [...].*"	*the relief granted in the award is more than or different from, the relief sought in the arbitration [...].*"

55 Van den Berg, *Hypothetical Draft Convention on the International Enforcement of Arbitration Agreements and Awards. Explanatory Note* (2009) pp.649-650 and also p.661.

56 Van den Berg, *Hypothetical Draft Convention on the International Enforcement of Arbitration Agreements and Awards. Explanatory Note* (2009) p.650: "*a number of provisions are unclear [...] [for instance] the words "terms of submission" and "scope of submission" to arbitration in art. V(1)(c) [...]*".

57 Art. 5(3)(c) of the Miami Draft.

58 Paulsson M. R. (2012) p.12.

59 See section 5.

4.2 Differences in the authentic versions of the text of the New York Convention

Since the Convention has been drafted in five equally authentic texts[60] it might be sensible to have a closer look at whether the language of Article V(1)(c) of the Convention is the same in its different language versions. Alas, due to the language capacities of the author the two remaining (authentic) versions of the Convention are not included in the comparison (Chinese and Russian). At the same time, however, the analysis of the three shows that certain distinctive elements exist in the text of the provision. For the sake of convenience, the three language versions have been reproduced below and divided into two separate hypotheses envisaged by Article V(1)(c) of the Convention.[61]

Table 4 Different authentic versions of Article V(1)(c) of the New York Convention

	The English version	The French version	The Spanish version
1.	*the award deals with a difference not contemplated by or not falling within the terms of the submission to arbitration,*	*Que la sentence porte sur un différend non visé dans le compromis ou n'entrant pas dans les prévisions de la clause compromissoire,*	*Que la sentencia se refiere a una diferencia no prevista en el compromiso o no comprendida en las disposiciones de la cláusula compromisoria,*
2.	*or it contains decisions on matters beyond the scope of the submission to arbitration*	*qu'elle contient des décisions qui dépassent les termes du compromis ou de la clause compromissoire*	*contiene decisiones que exceden de los términos del compromiso o de la cláusula compromisoria*

There are, in principle, two noticeable differences between the authentic versions of the "excess of mandate" provision. The first one relates to the fact that the French and Spanish versions of the Convention explicitly refer to two forms of the agreement to arbitrate,[62] whereas the English version does not. The second difference refers to a puzzle included in the English text, where the reference is made to "terms of the submission to arbitration" under the first hypothesis and to the "scope of the submission to arbitration" under the second hypothesis. This distinction will be discussed further below.[63] The French and the Spanish versions are somewhat different in this regard.[64] In the first hypothesis, the reference

60 See Art. XVI(1) of the Convention.

61 A similar exercise has been undertaken in the chapter on the Model Law. The texts of both instruments slightly differ, however.

62 See also fn.29.

63 See also section 4.3.2.

64 See the Table 4.

to *prévisions* (in the French version) or to *disposiciones* (in the Spanish version) is made only with regard to the arbitration clause.[65]

This comparative exercise of the different authentic versions of the Convention might suggest that the "excess of mandate" type of challenge under the New York Convention regime is in fact the challenge against the scope of the tribunal's jurisdiction rather than against the mandate, because the term "submission to arbitration" used in the English version is substituted with the explicit reference to two forms of the agreement to arbitrate (*i.e.* submission agreement and arbitration clause) in its French and Spanish versions.[66] Such a reading of the text, however, will exclude the possibility of reviewing the parties' *petita* under Article V(1)(c) of the Convention, whereas, arguably it has been drafted to tackle precisely these violations.

4.3 *Textual interpretation of Article V(1)(c) of the New York Convention*

As highlighted above, the text of Article V(1)(c) of the Convention is rather descriptive.[67] Ambiguity of the terms used therein might hinder the understanding and conceptualizing of the "excess of mandate type of challenge".[68] Therefore, it is necessary to focus on each term separately. The analysis will be therefore divided into sections. The first section will focus on the term "submission to arbitration" (section 4.3.1), then one will discuss the potential difference between "terms of the submission to arbitration" and the "scope of

65 It is true that the French and Spanish versions of the Convention also use different terms in the first and the second hypotheses. Arguably, however, the difference is less confusing. The first hypothesis refers to *le compromis (el compromiso)* and *la clause compromissoire (la cláusula compromisoria)* and the second hypothesis refers to *les termes du compromis (los términos del compromiso)* and *les termes de la clause compromissoire (los términos de la cláusula compromisoria)*.

66 As argued by Van den Berg on several occasions, there is no explanation in the literature why the difference between the English and French text of the New York Convention (as well as the Geneva Convention) even occurred. See Van den Berg, *The New York Convention of 1958: Towards Uniform Judicial Interpretation* (1981) p.315, and Van den Berg, *Failure by Arbitrators to Apply Contract Terms from the Perspective of the New York Convention* (2005) p.68.

67 For the sake of convenience, it might be useful to repeat the text of the provision. According to Art. V(1)(c) of the Convention the award may be refused recognition and enforcement if "*the award deals with a difference not contemplated by or not falling within the terms of the submission to arbitration, or it contains decisions on matters beyond the scope of the submission to arbitration.*"

68 It should be also noted that defining the meaning of the "excess of mandate" type of challenge might be difficult because different authors introduce different concepts explaining the meaning of Art. V(1)(c) of the New York Convention. See, for example, Borris & Hannecke, *Excess of Competence or Jurisdiction, Article V(1)(c)* (2012) p.311 (excess of jurisdiction and excess of competence), Azeredo da Silveira & Lévy (2008) (excess of jurisdiction and excess of mandate), Born, *International Commercial Arbitration* (2014) pp.3541-3559 (excess of authority), (Lew, Mistelis i Kröll, Comparative International Commercial Arbitration, 2003) p.714 (decisions *extra/ultra petita*), and Blackaby et al. (2015) pp.629-631 (excess of authority, *i.e. ultra petita* and excess of jurisdiction).

the submission to arbitration" (section 4.3.2). Finally, it would be useful to explore the notions of "a difference" (section 4.3.3) and "matters" (section 4.3.4).

4.3.1 The meaning of the "submission to arbitration"

The term "submission to arbitration" is the core element of Article V(1)(c) of the Convention, especially because it is included under both hypotheses of said provision.[69] Additionally, it is occasionally discussed with a reference to the arbitral tribunal's mandate,[70] which may create confusion. On the one hand, as already suggested above, it should be given a broad interpretation of covering both forms of the agreement to arbitrate. On the other hand, one should reflect whether the terms submission to arbitration go beyond the notion of agreement to arbitrate and therefore beyond the issue of excess of jurisdiction. These will be discussed further below.

The notion "submission to arbitration" should be deemed to cover not only a (formal) arbitration clause concluded prior to any dispute arising between the parties, but also subsequent agreements referring to arbitration in an already existing dispute (*i.e.* submission agreements).[71] At least three arguments have been advanced to support such a claim. First, one should reflect that the broad term (*i.e.* "submission to arbitration" instead of "arbitration agreement" or "arbitration clause") has been introduced intentionally by the drafters of the New York Convention.[72] Second, the wording of Article V(1)(c) differs from the expression used in the provisions V(1)(a) ("*agreement referred to in article II*") and V(1)(d) ("*agreement of the parties*").[73] Third, the simultaneous reading of the English, the French and the Spanish texts implies that the "submission to arbitration" should cover both the arbitration clause and the submission agreement.[74]

The simultaneous analysis of the authentic texts of the New York Convention might, however, unnecessarily narrow the interpretation of "submission to arbitration". As suggested above, since the French and the Spanish texts make direct reference to submission

69 See also section 4.3.2, which discusses the notions of the "terms" and the "scope" of the submission to arbitration.

70 Port et al. (2010) p.259 ("*[a]rticle V(1)(c) refers to the "submission to arbitration," which is synonymous with the arbitrator's mandate. This phrasing implies that V(1)(c) is applicable whenever the tribunal issues an award that goes beyond what the parties formally requested the tribunal to decide.*").

71 Haas (2002) p.499, and Port et al. (2010) p.265.

72 See the historical overview in section 4.1. See also Port et al. (2010) p.265.

73 Van den Berg, *The New York Convention of 1958: Towards Uniform Judicial Interpretation* (1981) p.315, Haas (2002) p.499, and Borris & Hannecke, *Article V: Grounds for Refusal of Recognition and Enforcement of Arbitral Awards. General* (2012) p.311.

74 Van den Berg, *The New York Convention of 1958: Towards Uniform Judicial Interpretation* (1981) pp.314-316, Azeredo da Silveira & Lévy (2008) pp.645-646, Port et al. (2010) p.265. See also fn.66.

agreement and arbitration clause, it might suggest that Article V(1)(c) of the Convention reflects only issues related to the scope of the tribunal's jurisdiction.[75]

Similarly, the UNCITRAL Secretariat Guide highlights that:

> [t]hough some authors have argued that article V (1)(c) provides a second, separate ground for refusal to enforce an award rendered ultra petita, courts have rejected challenges to recognition or enforcement under article V (1)(c) based on the fact that the arbitrators had exceeded their authority by deciding on issues or granting forms of relief beyond those pleaded by the parties.[76]

The limited case law supporting the UNCITRAL Secretariat's argument might not be sufficient and might not constitute the best approach.[77]

In discussing Article V(1)(c) of the Convention, it is sensible to take into account not only the scope of the agreement to arbitrate, but also the subsequent parties' submissions. Arguably, the provision of the Geneva Convention that mirrors the text of Article V(1)(c) of the New York Convention was designed to tackle the *petita* related issues.[78] Additionally, the ICC Draft recognized that there are two hypotheses that might be tackled under the third ground for recourse.[79]

In a similar vein, according to the ICCA Guide: "*[i]n determining what the parties have submitted to the arbitral tribunal, regard must be had to the arbitration agreement and the claims for relief submitted to the arbitral tribunal by the parties.*"[80] It is therefore aligned

---

75 See section 4.1. See also Azeredo da Silveira & Lévy (2008) p.649 ("*[n]either the English nor the French text of the Convention explicitly mentions that the limits of the arbitrators' authority are also to be set by the reference to the parties' claims. As a result, one can conclude, a priori, that Article V(1)(c) only pertains to the issue of the transgression, by the arbitrators, of the limits of the scope of their jurisdiction.*") It should be noted, that although the authors mentioned this line of argument, they also criticized it at the same time.

76 UNCITRAL, *UNCITRAL Secretariat Guide on the Convention on the Recognition and Enforcement of Foreign Arbitral Awards* (2016) p.175 *cf, e.g.*, Haas (2002) p.499 ("*whether the arbitrator has stayed within the limits of his mandate or not depends, according to the language in Art. V(1)(c), on the congruence between the 'terms of submission to arbitration' and the award, rather than congruity between the arbitration agreement and award.*").

77 Reference is made, assumingly for illustrative purposes, to the two U.S. cases.

78 See Art. 2 of the Geneva Convention that refers also to the *infra petita* decisions ("*If the award has not covered all the questions submitted to the arbitral tribunal, the competent authority of the country where recognition or enforcement of the award is sought can, if it think fit, postpone such recognition or enforcement or grant it subject to such guarantee as that authority may decide.*"). If in this second part of the article the hypothesis refers to the *infra petita*, it is reasonable to assume that the first part of this article (*i.e.* "*[...] the award does not deal with the differences contemplated by or falling within the terms of the submission to arbitration or that it contains decisions on matters beyond the scope of the submission to arbitration.*") refers to the *ultra* and *extra petita* scenarios.

79 See Art. IV(d) of the ICC Draft ("*that the award deals with a difference not contemplated by the agreement of the parties or that it contains decisions on matters not submitted to the arbitrators*").

80 ICCA, *ICCA's Guide to the Interpretation of the 1958 New York Convention* (2011) p.93.

with the two stages of the three keyholes test.[81] It means that the text of Article V(1)(c) of the Convention covers excess of the initial consent to arbitrate as well as the reference to the relief sought by the parties.

If one looks at the Convention through the lens of the Miami Draft, one would observe that the simplified language of the corresponding provision changes the term "submission to arbitration" into "relief sought in arbitration".[82] In his explanatory notes van den Berg suggests that "*[t]he matter of the relief granted outside the relief sought (extra petita) must be distinguished from the relief granted outside the scope of arbitration agreement but within the relief sought. In such a case, ground (a) of Art. 5(3) (invalid arbitration agreement) applies, and not ground (c).*"[83]

All in all, users of international arbitration should be well aware of these two competing definitions of "submission to arbitration" and their potential consequences. If they are to be understood only as the reference to the agreement to arbitrate, the *ultra* or *extra petita* challenges will need to be subsumed by the other grounds.[84] The alternative may entail that two different hypotheses will be subsumed under the same provision which would, in turn, mean that the standard for the court's review of challenges under the same provision might differ. Neither option is desirable which explains why the revision suggested by van den Berg should be welcomed.

4.3.2 The difference between the "terms" and the "scope" of the submission to arbitration

One of the arguments advanced by van den Berg when explaining the necessity of modernizing of the New York Convention is its unclear language.[85] Examples of the ambiguous wording presented by the author included the "terms of the submission to arbitration" as well as the "scope of the submission to arbitration".[86] The outstanding question therefore is, if it is possible to make sense of this difference and, if so, how?

---

81 See section 3.4.

82 Art. 5(3)(c) of the Miami Draft.

83 Van den Berg, *Hypothetical Draft Convention on the International Enforcement of Arbitration Agreements and Awards. Explanatory Note* (2009) p.661. However, following Van den Berg's previous writings, it seems acceptable for the parties' submissions to extend the arbitrators' mandate beyond the scope of the arbitration clause if both parties agreed to such an extension. For further reading, see Van den Berg, *The New York Convention of 1958: An Overview* (2008) p.59; similarly Rubino-Sammartano, *International Arbitration Law and Practice* (2001) p.957, where he notes that the arbitrators have exceeded their 'contractual' jurisdiction when the award contains a decision outside the ambit of the arbitration clause, even if the decision has not gone beyond the claims, counterclaims or defenses of a party to the proceedings.

84 Most likely under the public policy challenge (Art. V(2)(b) of the Convention). This creates, however, additional uncertainties, because amongst other things public policy can be raised by the court *ex officio*.

85 Van den Berg, *Hypothetical Draft Convention on the International Enforcement of Arbitration Agreements and Awards. Explanatory Note* (2009) p.650.

86 Van den Berg, *Hypothetical Draft Convention on the International Enforcement of Arbitration Agreements and Awards. Explanatory Note* (2009) p.650.

There are, in principle, two extremes, neither of which is a truly comforting solution. On the one hand, one could argue that the difference between these terms is relevant to identify two distinct concepts that are included in Article V(1)(c) of the Convention. On the other hand, it is possible to treat both terms (*i.e.* "the terms" and "the scope") as synonyms.

If one accepts that Article V(1)(c) makes a reference to two distinct concepts, one would need to tie the "terms of the submission to arbitration" to the reference to "dispute" and "the scope of the submission to arbitration" to the "matters".[87] When illustrated in the table, it would have the following design:

Table 5

1.	the award deals with *a difference*	not contemplated by or not falling within	*the terms* of the submission to arbitration
2.	[or] it contains decisions on *matters*	beyond	*the scope* of the submission to arbitration

The general understanding of this division is explained as relating to both the excess of jurisdiction (under the first hypothesis) and the excess of reference (under the second hypothesis).[88] Such an interpretation is, however, dangerous because it may create discrepancy in approaches to the challenges brought under Article V (1)(c) of the Convention. In other words, the matter related to the tribunal's jurisdiction, arguably, might invite a closer court scrutiny than the ones related to the mandate. The enforcement courts should, however, shy away from this differentiation and apply the deferential test only.[89] Arguably, they ought to remember that, contrary to the courts at the seat, their supervisory role is more limited in that they are not the appropriate forum for lengthy discussions about the scope issues (be it as it may the scope of jurisdiction or reference).[90] Importantly, the Miami Draft eliminates difficulties and reduces the necessary interpretation to the minimum.[91]

87 If one looks, for example, at the ICC Draft, this distinction would be more compelling. See Art. IV(d) of the ICC Draft ("*that the award deals with a difference not contemplated by the agreement of the parties or that it contains decisions on matters not submitted to the arbitrators*"). At the same time, however, it will prove that this provision was not designed to tackle only the scope of jurisdiction issues. Instead it had a two-layered design in mind. See also section 3.4.

88 See also fn.87.

89 See section 2.2.

90 Especially taking into account that it might be necessary to determine the law applicable to the scope (of jurisdiction) issues.

91 See Art. 5(3)(c) of the Miami Draft ("*the relief granted in the award is more than or different from, the relief sought in the arbitration [...].*").

The alternative is to treat these terms (*i.e.* "*terms*" and "*scope*" of the submission to arbitration) as synonyms. Generally, treating the terms as synonyms will not affect the two layers of the Article V(1)(c) test[92] because it is rooted in the interpretation of the "submission to arbitration" itself. In other words, even if "terms" and "scope" of the submission to arbitration are given the same meaning, it will require the review of both (i) the agreement to arbitrate[93] and (ii) the subsequent submissions.[94] At the same time it would facilitate the shift of a discussion towards the meaning (and differences) of the terms "a difference" and "matters".[95] These terms will be explained immediately below.

4.3.3 The meaning of "a difference"

In comparison to the interpretation of the "submission to arbitration" and other words used in Article V(1)(c) of the Convention, the words of "a difference" seems to draw relatively little attention. Nonetheless, linguistic choices when interpreting this term can predetermine what constitutes "a difference" that is covered by the submission to arbitration, as every option will have a different operating range.

Most commonly, "a difference" is equated with a "dispute" or a "claim".[96] For example, van den Berg suggests that "*the first type of allegation is that the arbitrator has dealt with a dispute which does not fall within the scope of the arbitral clause*".[97] Also if one looks at the corresponding provision of the Model Law, one will also see the reference to a "dispute".[98]

In the alternative, Di Pietro and Platte, while referring to the first part of Article V(1)(c) of the Convention, note that "*[it] deals with cases where the arbitrators are [...] alleged to have entertained a claim which parties did not want to refer to arbitration.*"[99]

Similarly, Azeredo da Silveira and Lévy contemplate that

> [r]ecognition and enforcement may be refused under Article V(1)(c) of the New York Convention only if the award deals with a 'difference' (in the French text 'differénd') not contemplated by or not falling within the terms of the submission to arbitration: with respect to the arbitrators' mandate, the

92 See section 3.4.

93 See section 3.1.

94 See section 3.2.

95 See section 4.3.3 and section 4.3.4.

96 Interestingly enough, on occasion, it is also explained as a "matter". See, *e.g.*, Rubino-Sammartano, *International Arbitration Law and Practice* (2001) p.957 ("*[t]his ground for refusal covers awards which have decided matters which are outside the ambit of the arbitration clause*").

97 Van den Berg, *The New York Convention of 1958: Towards Uniform Judicial Interpretation* (1981) p.314.

98 See Art. 34(2)(a)(iii) and Art. 36(1)(a)(iii) of the Model Law. For further reading, see also Chapter II.

99 Di Pietro & Platte (2001) p.158.

'difference' is determined by reference to the parties' opposing claims (or prayers for relief), not by reference to the issues.[100]

These terms demarcate the meaning of a "difference" well by referring to a contentious element existing between parties. At the same time, however, they bring around the interpretative difficulties as to the question whether Article V(1)(c) deals with jurisdictional challenges (*i.e.* scope of the agreement to arbitrate) alone or rather with the jurisdictional challenges as well as with a different creature, namely the "excess of mandate" type of challenge.[101]

As a consequence of the vague and unclear language[102] a provision corresponding to Article V(1)(c) of the Convention has been redrafted in the Miami Draft. Therefore, Article 5(3)(c) reads (in the relevant part) that the enforcement shall be refused if "*the relief granted in the award is more than, or different from, the relief sought in the arbitration.*" The provision is clear-cut as it requires a comparison between the relief sought by the parties (thus its competing requests for relief) and the relief granted by the tribunal.[103] Arguably, it reintroduces the application intended by the Geneva Convention.

4.3.4 The meaning of "matters"

It is necessary to point out at the outset that the analysis below is based on the supposition that the "terms" and the "scope" of the submission to arbitration have the same meaning under Article V(1)(c) of the Convention.[104] If this argument is accepted, one should further investigate the meaning of the term "matters" (or "decisions on matters" to be precise) and its potential distinction from the term "difference" which is also used in the context of the "submission to arbitration".[105]

The UNCITRAL Secretariat Guide suggests that the "matters" referred to in Article V(1)(c) of the Convention should be broadly defined and cover "subject matter

100 Azeredo da Silveira & Lévy (2008) p.660.

101 See also section 4.3.1 and section 4.4.

102 Apart from the phrases discussed in this section, also the expression "not contemplated by or not falling within" might cause certain interpretative difficulties, considering it being unnecessarily repetitive. One could argue that the wording of the English text comes from oversimplification of the French text of the Convention, which distinguishes that a difference can be either (i) "not contemplated by the submission agreement" or (ii) "not falling within the terms of arbitral clause" ("*un différend non visé dans le compromis ou n'entrant pas dans les prévisions de la clause compromissoire*"). Translation after Van den Berg, *The New York Convention of 1958: Towards Uniform Judicial Interpretation* (1981) p.315.

103 For the author's explanation, see Van den Berg, *Hypothetical Draft Convention on the International Enforcement of Arbitration Agreements and Awards. Explanatory Note* (2009) p.661.

104 See section 4.3.2.

105 Considering that the synonymous terms "terms of the submission to arbitration" and "the scope of the submission to arbitration" are tied, either with the reference to a "dispute" (the former) or with the "matters" (the latter).

jurisdiction" and "personal jurisdiction".[106] This argumentation, however, presupposes that the whole of Article V(1)(c) of the Convention (thus even its second hypothesis) deals with the jurisdictional challenges as opposed to the views presented herein.[107] The best fit for jurisdictional challenges (other than the scope of the agreement to arbitrate) is Article V(1)(a) of the Convention.[108]

An alternative to the UNCITRAL Secretariat's views to interpret the distinction between a "difference" and "decisions on matters" goes back to the suggested division included in the three keyholes test.[109] In principle, "a difference" is then given an interpretation of an abstract dispute that may occur between the parties, whereas "decisions on matters" relate to specifically submitted claims.[110]

As reflected by Kurkela:

> '[m]atters' beyond the scope of submission may include the difference although a difference as a word is perhaps closer to a disagreement or a larger subject matter. A 'matter' is closer to an issue. For instance the difference may be a distributorship agreement and 'the matter' failure to deliver on time or damages relating to unjust termination of the agreement. Further, 'the matter' may relate to a remedy sought by a party, e.g. declaratory relief, specific performance, injunction or damages. Within 'the difference' there may be various issues or matters, some of which are closely related to the difference itself but, which despite the closeness are not necessarily always directly within the scope of submission.[111]

It is rather undisputed that "decisions on matters" have to be something different than dealing with the "difference" submitted by the parties. Consequently, one may treat the "decisions on matters" as the tribunal's decisions on issues brought for determination which, however, lack the contentious component, for example, undisputed claims. Similarly, "decision on matters" might then include the tribunal's decisions on contract adaptation

106 For further reading, see UNCITRAL, *UNCITRAL Secretariat Guide on the Convention on the Recognition and Enforcement of Foreign Arbitral Awards* (2016) pp.177-180.

107 See section 4.3.1.

108 Even the UNCITRAL Secretariat Guide admits that the issues of "personal jurisdiction" are subsumed by the first ground for challenge. See UNCITRAL, *UNCITRAL Secretariat Guide on the Convention on the Recognition and Enforcement of Foreign Arbitral Awards* (2016) p.177 ("*In relation to the latter interpretation, it is notable that in any event, article V (1)(a) directly addresses consent of the parties.*").

109 See section 3 and section 3.4 in particular.

110 For a discussion on the meaning of the "submission to arbitration", see also Van den Berg, *The New York Convention of 1958: Towards Uniform Judicial Interpretation* (1981) pp.314-316.

111 Kurkela, *Due Process in International Commercial Arbitration* (2007) p.28.

or on filling the gaps.[112] In turn, it means that these types of decisions will also be susceptible to the "excess of mandate" type of challenge.

The last interpretation, arguably, explains that different types of tribunal's decisions will be subsumed by the "excess of mandate" type of challenge. The tribunal's mandate, in any event, finds its limits in the parties' agreement to arbitrate, which is further limited by their subsequent submissions.[113] The text of Article V(1)(c) does entertain two separate hypotheses for challenge (excess of jurisdiction and excess of mandate), even though it would be better to narrow the challenge to the assessment of the award against the submitted parties' *petita.*[114]

4.4 *Competing defenses: the interplay between the grounds for resisting recognition and enforcement under Article V(1) of the Convention*

The mechanism introduced in Article V(1)(c) is not independent from the other grounds of Article V(1) of the Convention. It can be generally stated that the defenses mentioned in Article V(1) complement each other. The interaction between Article V(1)(c) of the Convention and other grounds can, in principle, be structured on two levels: the first level refers to the basis of the authority of the arbitral tribunal, thus to the arbitration agreement and the second level refers to the general principles of the procedural fairness. One should note, however, that as a consequence of the interplay, it is not always easy to delineate which defense(s) should apply in order to effectively challenge an arbitral award. Accordingly, parties resisting enforcement usually decide to test an arbitral award against all (or almost all) the grounds listed in Article V of the Convention.

The first instance where the challenges are intertwined relates to the arbitral tribunal's jurisdiction. As observed above, Article V(1)(c) of the Convention requires the assessment of the scope of the agreement to arbitrate which means that it focuses on the tribunal's jurisdiction. For this reason, it competes with Article V(1)(a) of the Convention which squarely deals with (and is better fitted to tackle) jurisdictional objections.[115]

It is generally argued that the New York Convention separates situations where the challenge is directed towards the validity of the agreement to arbitrate[116] and those directed

---

112 See section 5.3.3.

113 See section 3 (and section 3.4 in particular).

114 See also section 4.3.1 and section 4.3.2.

115 Art. V(1)(a) of the Convention reads that an arbitral award may be refused recognition and enforcement if "*the parties to the agreement referred to in Article II were, under law applicable to them, under some incapacity, or the said agreement is not valid under the law to which the parties have subjected it or failing any indication thereon, under the law of the country where the award was made.*"

116 Art. V(1)(a) of the Convention.

towards the scope of the agreement to arbitrate.[117] "*Thus, Article V(1)(c) complements Article V(1)(a).*"[118] Both of these challenges will be jurisdictional in nature.[119] Perhaps the biggest struggle in identifying the appropriate ground of the Convention lies in the question whether a party was bound by the agreement to arbitrate. As observed by the UNCITRAL Secretariat Guide, "*[s]everal courts have therefore considered that ratione personae is also a "matter" within the meaning of article V (1)(c) and can therefore constitute a valid basis for an article V (1)(c) challenge to recognition or enforcement of an award.*"[120] The better view is, however, to address these objections under Article V(1)(a) of the Convention.[121]

The second instance where Article V(1)(c) of the Convention competes with other grounds of Article V of the Convention reflects the tension between the concept of the "excess of mandate" and due process. In principle, the second and the fourth defense of Article V(1) of the Convention refer to the fundamental fairness of the arbitral process. Whereas Article V(1)(b) of the Convention reads that the recognition and enforcement may be refused if "*the party against whom the award is invoked was not given proper notice of the appointment of the arbitrator or of the arbitration proceedings or was otherwise unable to present his case*". Article V(1)(d) of the Convention provides that recognition and enforcement of the award may be refused if "*the composition of the arbitral authority or the arbitral procedure was not in accordance with the agreement of the parties, or failing such agreement, was not in accordance with the law of the country where the arbitration took place.*" Some illustrations will be given below, which show the tension between both of these grounds.

For example (in the context of the competition with Article V(1)(b) of the Convention), since the right to be heard plays a fundamental role in any dispute resolution process, it cannot be disregarded by arbitrators. An arbitral tribunal's decision which comes to the parties unexpectedly might infringe the parties' right to present their case. Therefore, as rightly pointed out:

---

117 Art. V(1)(c) of the Convention.

118 Azeredo da Silveira & Lévy (2008) p.640.

119 The severance of the validity and the scope questions raises a number of difficulties, one of them being the question of applicable law. As long as Art. V(1)(a) of the Convention clarifies what law applies to the question of the validity of the agreement to arbitrate, Art. V(1)(c) of the Convention is silent on the issue. See also Born, *International Commercial Arbitration* (2014) pp.3550-3552.

120 UNCITRAL, *UNCITRAL Secretariat Guide on the Convention on the Recognition and Enforcement of Foreign Arbitral Awards* (2016) p.178. For the case law, see pp.178-180 therein. See also *Fiat S.p.A. v. Ministry of Fin. & Planning of Republic of Suriname*, No. 88 CIV. 6639 (SWK), 1989 WL 122891, at *5 (S.D.N.Y. Oct. 12, 1989). For further reading, *i.a.*, Port et al. (2010) pp.277-279.

121 See, *i.a.*, UNCITRAL, *UNCITRAL Secretariat Guide on the Convention on the Recognition and Enforcement of Foreign Arbitral Awards* (2016) p.183 ("*[...] addressing whether a party has consented to arbitrate under article V (1)(a) is ultimately consistent with the distinct purposes [that] articles V (1)(a) and V (1)(c) [...] were given by the drafters of the Convention.*").

> [...] if a tribunal bases its award on considerations that are capable of surprising the parties, the arbitral tribunal exceeds its competence it if does not give the parties the opportunity to respond to these considerations. In this case, the defense under Article V(1)(c) with respect to the agreement of the parties overlaps with the scope of Article V(1)(b) concerning the parties' right to be heard.[122]

In addition, Borris and Hannecke, point out the usefulness of invoking Article V(1)(b) of the Convention in cases where the award is made *infra petita*.[123] The authors advance the opinion that "*[i]n any case, where the failure of an arbitral tribunal to deal with questions submitted by the parties constitutes a violation of due process, refusal of recognition and enforcement may be justified under Article V(1)(b).*"[124]

In a similar vein, in some instances it might be potentially difficult to choose whether Article V(1)(c) or Article V(1)(d) of the Convention is the appropriate ground for a challenge. Reference to the irregularity of the arbitral procedure might be particularly tempting when testing the arbitral tribunal's decisions on applicable law which might be somewhat different from the parties' expectations.[125] It has been concluded, however, that: "*[t]he procedural-irregularity defence is seldom applied in the context of choice of law. A tribunal's disregard of the parties' instructions pertaining to the governing law does not, as a rule, fall within the scope of procedural irregularity; it is an excess-of-power defence.*"[126]

Moreover, one might question under which ground the power of acting as *amiable compositeur* should be subsumed. In the view of most scholars, acting as *amiable compositeur* without the parties' authorization might simultaneously trigger defenses pursuant to Article V(1)(c) and Article V(1)(d) of the Convention as it violates approved procedural rules and constitutes a transgression of the mandate.[127] Haas argues that "*[w]hether and under which conditions the arbitral tribunal is authorized to grant an award based on equity is a question of the applicable procedural rules determined pursuant to Art. V(1)(d).*"[128]

122 Borris & Hannecke, *Excess of Competence or Jurisdiction, Article V(1)(c)* (2012) p.327, also Azeredo da Silveira & Lévy (2008) p.655 (the authors, however, seem to suggest Art. V(1)(d) of the New York Convention as the basis for violation of due process and proper defense in the face of a "surprise decision"). See also Scherer, *Violation of Due Process* (2012) pp.307-308, and Born, *International Commercial Arbitration* (2014) p.3518.

123 See also section 5.1.6.

124 Borris & Hannecke, *Excess of Competence or Jurisdiction, Article V(1)(c)* (2012) p.326.

125 See also section 5.2.

126 Moss, *Can an arbitral tribunal disregard the choice of law made by the parties?* (2005) p.15. As reported by Jarvin not all countries take such an approach. See Jarvin, *Irregularity in the Composition of the Arbitral Tribunal and the Procedure* (2008) p.730.

127 Haas (2002) p.502, Borris & Hannecke, *Improper Tribunal Composition and Flawed Proceedings, Article V(1)(d)* (2012) pp.351-353. See also section 5.2.5.

128 Haas (2002) p.502.

Conversely, Di Pietro and Platte consider that

> only application of procedure that was not in accordance with the parties' agreement may be remedied under Article V(1)(d). Thus, if the parties' agreement to vest the arbitrator with the power to act as amiable compositeur had no impact on procedure, it seems that Article V(1)(d) is not the proper remedy.[129]

All in all, the better view is to include the challenges against the non-authorized use of *ex aequo et bono* under Article V(1)(d) of the Convention, because it relates to the method of the tribunal's reasoning and not to the question related directly to the compliance with the submission to arbitration. Notably, it has also been suggested that the violation of the principle *ne ultra petita* might constitute a defective arbitral procedure and as such be open for a challenge under Article V(1)(d) instead of Article V(1)(c) of the Convention.[130] This is perhaps not the most sensible solution. If the tribunal awards more than has been requested, it will violate the disposition given to it by the parties and not the procedure to be followed (this hypothesis would fit squarely with the Article V(1)(c) defense). Even in cases where Article V(1)(c) of the Convention is considered a jurisdictional (and not a mandate) challenge, one should argue that *ne ultra petita* would fit better under the hypothesis of Article V(2)(b) of the Convention (*i.e.* public policy) rather than be subsumed under Article V(1)(d). All these examples show that it is not always easy to pinpoint what ground is suitable for the "excess of mandate" type of challenges.

5 Application of the "excess of mandate" type of challenge to selected decisions of the arbitral tribunal

Having explained the limits of the arbitral tribunal's authority[131] and the general New York Convention take on the "excess of mandate" type of challenge,[132] it is necessary to evaluate this challenge accordingly by applying the test to the selected types of decisions that the tribunal will inevitably take during the arbitral process. The division is made thematically and will start with decisions on parties' claims (section 5.1). What follows is the review of the tribunal's application of law (5.2). Subsequently, the tribunal's decision on remedies will be discussed (section 5.3) with some additional reflections on the tribunal's decisions on issues that are accessory to the main claims made by the parties (section 5.4).

129 Di Pietro & Platte (2001) p.164.

130 Borris & Hannecke, *Improper Tribunal Composition and Flawed Proceedings, Article V(1)(d)* (2012) p.351.

131 See section 3.

132 See section 4.

5.1 Decisions on parties' claims

The first category of the tribunal's decisions that are being analyzed focuses on the nature of the claim, namely on its origin. Therefore, the following sections will concentrate on contractual claims and counterclaims (section 5.1.1 and section 5.1.2), tribunal's decisions dealing with set-off (section 5.1.3) and claims based on torts (section 5.1.4). Finally, the decision on the modification of the initially submitted claims (section 5.1.5) as well as decisions *infra petita* (section 5.1.6) will be reviewed.

5.1.1 Decision on contractual claims

In principle, claims arising out of contractual relationships are the most typical of all claims that could be brought by the parties in arbitration. After all, agreements to arbitrate are inserted in the contracts precisely because the mechanism for dealing with the potential (contractual) disputes is needed. In turn, the "excess of mandate" type of challenge requires the enforcing court to see whether the (contractual) claims submitted fit within the scope of the initial agreement to arbitrate. It means that an enforcement court needs to determine (i) whether the contractual claims comply with the limits imposed by the agreement to arbitrate and (ii) whether the claims awarded are the same that have been requested by the parties.[133] Of course, the contractual claims granted should not violate public policy in the country of enforcement.[134]

It is rather unlikely that the contractual claims will fall outside the scope of the agreement to arbitrate, especially if the parties use the available framework of the institutional model clauses. These are generally designed to cover a broad spectrum of disputes, having contractual disputes at their core.[135] Consequently, "*[...] parties seeking to limit the tribunal's decision to a narrow matter should do so with precision in the formal submission.*"[136] Additionally, the enforcement courts should give a great deference to the tribunal's findings

133 See also Port et al. (2010) p.260.

134 See section 3.3.

135 See, *e.g.*, the UNCITRAL Model Arbitration Clause for contracts ("*Any dispute, controversy or claim arising out of or relating to this contract, or the breach, termination or invalidity thereof, shall be settled by arbitration in accordance with the UNCITRAL Arbitration Rules.*"), the Standard 2017 ICC Arbitration Clause ("*All disputes arising out of or in connection with the present contract shall be finally settled under the Rules of Arbitration of the International Chamber of Commerce by one or more arbitrators appointed in accordance with the said Rules.*"), the 2014 LCIA Model Clause ("*Any dispute arising out of or in connection with this contract, including any question regarding its existence, validity or termination, shall be referred to and finally resolved by arbitration under the LCIA Rules, which Rules are deemed to be incorporated by reference into this clause.*").

136 Port et al. (2010) p.266.

as to the scope of the agreement to arbitrate,[137] especially taking into account that their supervisory role over the arbitration process is limited.[138]

The second hypothesis of Article V(1)(c) of the New York Convention requires an enforcing court to assess if the award responds to the claims submitted.[139] For this reason, however, the prayers for relief should be drafted in a clear and tangible manner in order to condition the limits of the arbitral tribunal's authority.[140] Conversely, ambiguous prayers for relief will burden the determination of the arbitral tribunal's authority instead of providing guidance.[141] Consequently, in cases of vague contractual claims, the tribunal should benefit from the exclusive power to interpret the claim.[142]

Additionally, Haas observes that:

> [i]f parties did not stipulate what issues may be submitted to arbitration, then the powers to adjudicate are not exceeded if the arbitration panel awards the parties more, less, or something other than that which the parties petitioned or argued for as long as the award is covered by the scope of the arbitration agreement.[143]

The parties' conduct during the arbitral process is essential in this regard. In case of contractual claims, if respondent fails to address that the tribunal goes beyond the scope of the initial agreement to arbitrate or that the claims submitted are vague, it might lose its right to invoke the Article V(1)(c) defense at the enforcement stage.

Finally, it should be noted that contractual claims, even within the scope of the agreement to arbitrate and properly submitted for the tribunal's consideration might be beyond the scope of what the parties may delegate for the arbitral adjudication. The

---

137 Port et al. (2010) p.261 ("*In addition to narrow construction, many jurisdictions apply a presumption that an arbitral award was issued within the scope of the arbitrator's authority.*").

138 This would be one of the roles of the court at the seat of arbitration.

139 Haas (2002) p.500 ("*The arbitrator exceeds the limits of his competence if he adjudicates on points of dispute which the parties have not agreed to assign to him (ultra petita).*").

140 See, *e.g.*, Karrer, *Must an Arbitral Tribunal Really Ensure that its Award is Enforceable?* (2005) p.431 ("*[m]any parties find it difficult to state their prayers for relief in an intelligible way. For instance, they will use the word, 'alternatively' when they mean 'subsidiarily'. One also sees far too many requests for declaratory awards, legal grounds for particular types of relief that may limit the relief requested to those grounds alone, and other such mistakes. The arbitral tribunal can help here.*").

141 In that case, arguably, the arbitral tribunal or the enforcement court that examines the Art. V(1)(c) application ambit of the arbitral tribunal's authority based on the two-level test should take a step back from the second level and satisfy itself with the first level conclusions. See also section 4.3.1.

142 Karrer, *Must an Arbitral Tribunal Really Ensure that its Award is Enforceable?* (2005) p.431 ("*claims that the arbitral tribunal has ruled ultra petita come mostly from parties incapable of defining their petita in the first place. If the award states first what the arbitral tribunal understands the petita to be, and then proceeds to deal with all of them and only them, claims of ultra petita will fail.*").

143 Haas (2002) p.501.

enforcement court will be able to control the (contractual) claims against its own public policy.[144]

5.1.2 Decision on contractual counterclaims

Counterclaims are a distinct category of claims that are brought by respondent. It means that they are independent from the claims brought by claimant. Generally, out of the three keyholes questions, the issue of (contractual) counterclaims triggers particularly the first question relating to the scope of the agreement to arbitrate.[145] The answers to the remaining two, although equally relevant, will not differ from the ones already submitted above.[146]

In principle, counterclaims will need to satisfy the same requirements as the claims brought by the claimant.[147] It means that contractual counterclaims should fit comfortably in the scope of the broad agreements to arbitrate, for example, when the institutional model clauses are used. The additional controversy arises, however, in cases where the counterclaims have their legal basis under a different contract.

Where the counterclaims are brought based on the other contractual relationship, the outstanding question therefore would be whether it will be within the scope of the agreement to arbitrate. Borris and Hannecke conclude that "*[a] counterclaim can be considered as encompassed by the arbitration agreement if the contract from which the counterclaim arises is closely connected to the contract containing the arbitration agreement [...].*"[148] It would be especially the case when the agreement to arbitrate is sufficiently broad (particularly if one uses the "*in connection with*" formula). It is important to note, however, that the parties' choices of arbitration rules[149] and their conduct in arbitration might be contributing factors in assessing whether counterclaims can be entertained by the tribunal.[150]

Additionally, Borris and Hannecke argue that:

144 See section 3.3.

145 Borris & Hannecke, *Excess of Competence or Jurisdiction, Article V(1)(c)* (2012) p.315.

146 See section 5.1.1.

147 See also section 5.1.1.

148 Borris & Hannecke, *Excess of Competence or Jurisdiction, Article V(1)(c)* (2012) p.315.

149 See, *e.g.*, Art. 19(3) of the 1976 UNCITRAL Rules with a strict requirement ("*In his statement of defence, or at a later stage in the arbitral proceedings if the arbitral tribunal decides that the delay was justified under the circumstances, the respondent may make a counter-claim arising out of the same contract or rely on a claim arising out of the same contract for the purpose of a set-off*"). See, however, Art. 21(3) of the 2010 UNCITRAL Rules which (in the relevant part) reads that "*[...] the respondent may make a counterclaim or rely on a claim for the purpose of a set-off provided that the arbitral tribunal has jurisdiction over it.*"

150 Borris & Hannecke, *Excess of Competence or Jurisdiction, Article V(1)(c)* (2012) p.315 ("*[u]nless the applicable arbitration rules explicitly provide for the admissibility of (particular) counterclaims, or the claimant agrees on the admissibility of the counterclaim(s) raised by the respondent, any counterclaim has to be covered by the existing arbitration agreement between the parties.*").

> [f]or reasons of procedural economy, it has been argued that in addition to the requirement of a close connection between the relevant contracts, counterclaims should only be admitted if the counterclaims themselves are closely connected to the main claim. By imposing the additional requirement of a close connection between claim and counterclaim, the respondent is supposed to be prevented from raising only vaguely related counterclaims in an attempt to delay the arbitral proceedings. However, unless the parties agree on procedural rules imposing such an additional requirement, the better reasons speak for admitting counterclaims – insofar as they are covered by the arbitration agreement.[151]

This is a reasonable approach. It is rather an argument addressed to the arbitral tribunal, however, and not to the enforcement court. The latter is not (or should not) be occupied with the assessment of the efficiency of the arbitral process.

As mentioned above, and similar to the contractual claims, the parties' request will be *condition sine qua non* for the tribunal's authority to award the claim.[152] This will also be reviewed by the enforcement court under the Article V(1)(c) mechanism. Finally, it is also necessary that contractual counterclaims do not violate public policy at the enforcement stage.[153]

5.1.3 Decisions on set-off

Claims for the purpose of set-off can be distinguished from other (counter)claims brought by respondent.[154] Generally, set-off is a defensive mechanism against the claim. For the research at hand, it is considered a substantive law device that allows for reduction in the value of the monetary claim by extinguishing the initial claim with a mutual, liquid monetary claim.[155] Importantly, considering the defensive character of set-off claims, they cannot exceed the value of the initial claim.

In the context of the "excess of mandate" type of challenge, set-off claims will be mostly reviewed by considering them in the context of the scope of the agreement to arbitrate. It means that one must observe if the Article V(1)(c) challenge might be successful if (i) the set-off is governed by the same agreement to arbitrate, (ii) in a multi-contract reality, the

151 Borris & Hannecke, *Excess of Competence or Jurisdiction, Article V(1)(c)* (2012) p.316.

152 See also section 3.2 and section 5.1.1.

153 See section 3.3.

154 Of course, set-off claims are not exclusively for the respondent to raise, they can also be brought by claimant.

155 Set-off claims have been the subject of many major studies. For further reading, see in particular Fountoulakis (2011) and Pichonnaz & Gullifer (2014). For articles, see also, *i.a.*, Craig, *The arbitrator's mission and the application of law in international commercial arbitration* (2010), Karrer, *Jurisdiction on set-off defences and counterclaims* (2001), Pavić (2006), Schöll (2006), Poudret & Besson (2007) pp.274-280, Mourre, *The Set-off Paradox in International Arbitration* (2008), Fortún (2010), Carducci (2013) and Scherer, *The Award and the Courts, Set-Off in International Arbitration* (2015).

set-off claim is brought based on a different contract not covered by the underlying agreement to arbitrate, and finally (iii) the tribunal decides to set-off the initial claim *ex officio*. All of the above is built under the assumption that set-offs are properly objected to (by the opposing party).

The first scenario does not trigger any controversies considering that a set-off has been requested by a party. It would be equally true in case of a multi-contract reality where multiple contracts are governed by a single agreement to arbitrate (for example when the "in connection with" formula is used).[156] It would be a flaw to accept the challenge over the decision granting set-off in cases where the (set-off) claim itself is covered by the underlying agreement to arbitrate.

The second scenario is somewhat different. It entails that the initial agreement to arbitrate does not cover claims brought for the purpose of set-off. Consequently, it would go squarely to the issue of the scope of the parties' consent and would disallow the tribunal to entertain the set-off claim.[157] At the same time, however, one should not forget the defensive character of set-offs and the procedural efficiency of dealing with all claims (the concept of the "one-stop arbitration"). After all the parties' consent is to contract out the resolution of their disputes and have them resolved promptly. Assuming that the set-off claim is already liquid and respondent itself is willing to use the proceedings already in place (instead of commencing new ones), there is a good reason to allow the resolution of disputes at once.[158] One should also keep in mind that the enforcement court does not supervise the arbitral process. Therefore, it should be for the court at the seat of arbitration to assess if the set-off claim should be allowed or not.

---

156 Additionally, Port, Bowers and Noll analyze the temporal aspect of related contracts and the extension effect if no conflicting provisions occur. See Port et al. (2010) p.279 ("*Although analyses in this area tend to be highly fact-specific, a broad arbitration clause in an agreement may apply to a later, related agreement between the same parties, if the later agreement does not contain an arbitration clause and does not repudiate that of the first. Courts thus have rejected V(1)(c) defenses brought on the grounds that the tribunal exceeded its authority by applying an arbitration clause from an earlier agreement to disputes concerning a later agreement.*").

157 Borris & Hannecke, *Excess of Competence or Jurisdiction, Article V(1)(c)* (2012) p.315 ("*Generally, a crossclaim asserted by way of set-off does not fall within the scope of the arbitration agreement where no close connection to the contract containing the arbitration agreement can be assumed. Since the arbitral process rests entirely on the parties' agreement to arbitrate, the scope of the arbitration cannot be extended beyond the parties' shared intention. In case of a contravening intention of the parties, considerations of procedural economy cannot provide a sufficient basis for assuming the competence of the arbitral tribunal to consider the claim for set-off.*").

158 Borris & Hannecke, *Excess of Competence or Jurisdiction, Article V(1)(c)* (2012) p.315 ("*However, it has been argued that the arbitral tribunal is also justified in assuming its jurisdiction in cases in which the amount of the counterclaim raised as a set-off defense is not disputed or in which the counterclaim is already liquid (e.g. because it has been conceded or has already been finally decided by a court or arbitral tribunal). Under such (rare) circumstances, there is no reason why the arbitral tribunal should not consider the set-off defense.*").

Under the third scenario the tribunal independently decides to extinguish the claim with the mutual liquid debt. As always, however, the "*[...] ultra petita claim became the activity of the arbitral tribunal, though starting within the limits imposed by the mandate given by the parties, [it] has gone beyond what was originally allowed.*"[159] Consequently, setting-off claims independently (*ex officio*) might potentially lead to the non-enforcement of the award. It will be equally true in cases where the tribunal finds that there is a set-off claim and invites parties to comment on it,[160] as well as in cases where the tribunal surprises parties with the non-invoked *ipso iure* set-offs.[161] These cases, however, are better suited to be discussed under other (due process oriented) grounds for recourse.[162]

5.1.4 Decision on claims/counterclaims based on torts or pre-contractual liability

Another issue worth discussing in the context of the legal basis for the claim is the fate of the award granting relief not based on the contract itself, but rather on torts or pre-contractual liability. Unsurprisingly, this mostly touches upon the issue of the scope of the agreement to arbitrate. At the same time, an additional problem arises. In essence it relates to the possibility for the tribunal to requalify the legal basis for the claim (from a contractual one to torts).

In principle, the first issue has already been discussed in detail above.[163] Ultimately, the question whether the tort claims are within the scope of the submission to arbitration will depend primarily on the wording of the agreement to arbitrate. Generally, however, the broadly drafted agreements to arbitrate (such as model institutional clauses)[164] will cover claims of non-contractual nature provided that they are "in connection with" or "related to" the underlying contract. In these cases, the enforcement court should be guided by the pro-enforcement philosophy and should not accept the challenge against the award.[165]

The second issue relates to the freedom of the tribunal in finding the legal basis for the relief granted. It entails that the tribunal considers that the claim requested should be granted. At the same time, however, it disagrees with the way the claim is brought. In other words, the tribunal awards the party with its request, but it justifies the award differently (for example by relying on its own legal expertise).[166] This should be avoided. Similar to

159 Di Pietro & Platte (2001) p.160.
160 In this case the tribunal risks a challenge of pleading for the party.
161 In this case the tribunal may face another challenge focused on a due process violation. See section 4.4.
162 See, *e.g.*, Art. V(1)(b) or Art. V(2)(b) of the Convention. See also section 4.4.
163 See sections 5.1.1-5.1.3.
164 See fn.135.
165 Arguably, even in the absence of the "in connection with" formula, the award might still survive the post-award challenge, considering that (in the absence of the contrary intention) parties are likely to bring all disputes to be resolved to the same forum.
166 See also section 5.2.

what has been discussed in the context of set-off claims,[167] irrespective of whether the tribunal invites the parties to comment on the issue or "surprises" them with its "requalification", it will violate due process. These arguments do not fit the hypothesis of "excess of mandate" type of challenge, however.

5.1.5 Decision on new claims/counterclaims and change of claims/counterclaims

Since the arbitral tribunal's mandate is structured by the claims submitted,[168] any addition or alteration to the parties' submissions effectively modifies the scope of the tribunal's power to adjudicate. In the context of the "excess of mandate" type of challenge, in turn, it might have an impact on the fate of the award at the post-award stage. In particular, it is necessary to reflect on the impact of (i) the parties' conduct and (ii) the (ICC) Terms of Reference (if applicable).

As discussed above,[169] although the Convention does not operate with the concept of the arbitral tribunal's mandate, it does allow the enforcement court to assess what claims have been introduced for the tribunal to decide. The tribunal's decision is reviewed on the second level of the "excess of mandate" type of challenge.[170] It needs to be observed that the amendment of the initially submitted claims affects this level of review. Consequently, if there is not sufficient reaction to the change of claim, one might consider that the modification is (impliedly) accepted.[171] This is why the parties' conduct in the proceedings is essential and will affect the chances for successful challenge at the post-award stage.

Yet another issue relates to the tribunal's power over the amendment of the claim. Put differently, the question arises if the tribunal is able to reject the submitted change of claims. On the one hand, it should have a say, because it affects the scope of its duties (and the mandate). On the other hand, however, there is a risk of the violation of the parties' right to present its case if the tribunal rejects amendment or the addition of a new claim, especially if the modification is accepted by all disputants. In any event, the better view is to allow the tribunal to decide on the modifications to the claims submitted. Ideally, the tribunal designates a cut-off date for any possible alterations at the outset of the proceedings. Even without it having the efficiency of the arbitral process in mind, the tribunal should be able to impose limitations to the parties' actions that affect the structure of their (initially submitted) claims. Without such a power, the tribunal may risk an ever-increasing flow of new claims. All in all, violation of the right to be heard will be subsumed by another

167 See section 5.1.3.
168 See section 3.2.
169 See section 3.4.
170 See section 3.2.
171 Although, generally, the modification of the claims should fit within the scope of the underlying agreement to arbitrate, at times one may find that lack of opposition to the amendment amounts to a tacit acceptance of the extension of the scope of the initial agreement to arbitrate.

ground for resisting recognition and enforcement, and thus will not be considered as the "excess of mandate" violation.[172]

Additionally it is necessary to briefly discuss the (ICC) Terms of Reference. As explained above,[173] the Terms of Reference are a source of the tribunal's adjudicative authority and they may add a layer of complexity in the context of the "excess of mandate" type of challenge. Azeredo da Silveira and Lévy have concluded that, in principle, the Terms of Reference will not be considered to be a fresh agreement to arbitrate for the purposes of the Article V(1)(c) defense,[174] unless the enforcement court is satisfied that both parties have intended to modify their initial agreement to arbitrate.

At the same time, however, the Terms of Reference cause some complications in cases where the claims are modified after the Terms of Reference have been signed and approved.[175] Taking the ICC Terms of Reference as an example, one should observe that the tribunal has been given a stronger mandate to control the scope of changes to the claims initially submitted and evidenced by the Terms of Reference.[176] It means that on the one hand, the parties' conduct is essential, on the other hand, however, the tribunal has a procedural tool to restrict the expansion of the initially submitted *petita*.

5.1.6 Decisions not covering all claims

If the tribunal fails to address all of the issues submitted by the parties, it renders its award *infra petita*. This creates an inconvenience for the parties, as it fails to provide them with all the answers they were seeking. Consequently, one may argue that the tribunal neglects its adjudicative role and, thus, the "excess of mandate" type of challenge should be available for the parties. Article V(1)(c) of the Convention, however, is not fit to entertain such an objection.[177]

The first argument against an application of the Article V(1)(c) defense to *infra petita* decisions is a historical one. Arguably, the historical context is important in the interpretation of Article V(1)(c) of the Convention considering how much the language of the provision resembles the corresponding text of the Geneva Convention.[178]

Further, although the two provisions are very similar, Article V(1)(c) *does not* include the part of Article 2 of the Geneva Convention that reads that

172 See Art. V(1)(b) of the Convention.

173 See section 3.2.

174 See section 3.1 and section 3.2.

175 In the case of the ICC Proceedings approved by the ICC Court. See Art. 23(4) of the (draft) 2021 ICC Rules, Art. 23(4) of the 2017 ICC Rules, and Art. 23(4) of the 2012 ICC Rules.

176 See Art. 23(4) of the (draft) 2021 ICC Rules, Art. 23(4) of the 2017 ICC Rules, and Art. 23(4) of the 2012 ICC Rules.

177 See, *e.g.*, Van den Berg, *The New York Convention of 1958: Towards Uniform Judicial Interpretation* (1981) p.321, Haas (2002) p.501, and Port et al. (2010) p.277.

178 See also section 4.1.

> [i]f the award has not covered all the questions submitted to the arbitral tribunal, the competent authority of the country where recognition or enforcement of the award is sought can, if it think[s] fit, postpone such recognition or enforcement or grant it subject to such guarantee as that authority may decide.

Consequently,

> [a]s recorded in the travaux préparatoires of the New York Convention, the omission of language in the 1927 Geneva Convention allowing postponement of recognition or enforcement, or granting enforcement subject to a guarantee, of any award that 'has not covered all the questions submitted to the arbitral tribunal', was a 'significant change' from the wording of the 1927 Geneva Convention.[179]

The second argument follows the first one and stems from the textual interpretation of Article V(1)(c) of the Convention.[180] Put differently, the wording of Article V(1)(c) does not include any reference to the *infra petita* decisions, which is a departure from its predecessor. In turn, considering the underlying pro-enforcement philosophy behind the Convention and the exhaustive character of the list of challenges,[181] nothing in the text of Article V supports the notion that recourse against the *infra petita* award is still possible.[182] Two reported Luxembourg cases are to the same effect.[183]

Another reason that is usually advanced against the inclusion of *infra petita* is a remedial power of partial enforcement given to the enforcement courts.[184] As argued by van den

179 UNCITRAL, *UNCITRAL Secretariat Guide on the Convention on the Recognition and Enforcement of Foreign Arbitral Awards* (2016) p.177, with a reference to U.N. Doc. E/2822/Add. 4, p.6.

180 Or even, arguably, of the Art. V in general.

181 See also section 2.1.

182 See also UNCITRAL, *UNCITRAL Secretariat Guide on the Convention on the Recognition and Enforcement of Foreign Arbitral Awards* (2016) p.177 ("*Nothing in the language of article V (1)(c) grants enforcing authorities the discretion to refuse or otherwise limit the recognition or enforcement of an award which has failed to address all issues submitted by the parties, but which is otherwise enforceable as to the issues addressed*"), and Port et al. (2010) p.277.

183 *Kersa Holding Company Luxembourg v. Infacourtage, Famajuk Investment and Isny*, Cour Superieure de Justice, not indicated, 24 November 1993, XXI Y.B. Comm. Arb. 617, 625 (1996) ("*As to the reproach that the arbitral tribunal did not decide on all the points of the dispute ..., this ground, even if established, could not hinder the recognition of the awards, as an infra petita decision is not sanctioned by the New York Convention.*"), *Sovereign Participations International S.A. v. Chadmore Developments Ltd.*, Cour d'Appel [Court of Appeal], 28 January 1999, XXIVa Y.B. Comm. Arb. 714, 721 (1999) ("*In so far as this ground for appeal reproaches the arbitrators for not deciding on all issues of the dispute, this ground, even if proven, could not prevent the recognition of the award, as the case of 'infra petita', which is, on the contrary, a ground for setting aside under Art. 1023 CCP, is not provided for in the Convention.*").

184 See section 2.3.

Berg, "*the "replacement" of Article 2(2) of the Geneva Convention resulted in a different proviso in Article V(1)(c) which concerns the partial enforcement of an award ultra or extra petita*".[185] Similarly, other authors observe that "*[t]he Article V grounds for refusal of enforcement are considered exhaustive, and none mention awards infra petita. Indeed, the fact that partial enforcement of awards is permissible under V(1)(c) lends credence to the enforceability of infra petita awards.*"[186] Importantly, one should not forget that the enforcement court is the court of a secondary jurisdiction. For this reason, the remedial power of partial enforcement should suffice to address the *infra petita* decisions.[187]

The argument that *infra petita* decisions should be challengeable at the enforcement stage is not voiced by many authors. It does exist, however.[188] Perhaps most evocatively Born suggests that

> [...] at least some infra petita arguments should be permitted under Article V(1)(c). In at least some instances, an arbitral tribunal's failure to address an issue (or issues) can affect the decisions on those claims which the award does address. By failing to consider particular claims or issues, the arbitral tribunal's award on other issues may be fundamentally flawed or unjust, warranting non-recognition under Article V(1)(c).[189]

It is true that the inconvenience of the *infra petita* award should not pass unnoticed.[190] The better view, however, is to tackle it at the place of arbitration in the setting-aside

185 Van den Berg, *The New York Convention of 1958: Towards Uniform Judicial Interpretation* (1981) p.320.

186 Port et al. (2010) p.277.

187 See also the Restatement (second tentative draft) p.201 ("*The text of Article V(1)(c), however, does not support extending the Section to an incomplete award. Indeed, an 'incomplete' award might be characterized as a partial award – an award that resolves some but not all issues in dispute – and be enforceable as such.*").

188 See, *e.g.*, Born, *International Commercial Arbitration* (2014) p.3557, and Kreidi (2013) pp.51-52.

189 Born, *International Commercial Arbitration* (2014) p.3557. See also Haas (2002) pp.500-501 ("*Some hold the view that the arbitration powers are exceeded (in the form of abstention) in cases where the tribunal's task can only be properly accomplished by handing down a single award covering the entire dispute and an award cannot be made concerning the remaining issue still pending arbitration.*"), and Borris & Hannecke, *Excess of Competence or Jurisdiction, Article V(1)(c)* (2012) p.326 ("*[...] a different view may be justified in (exceptional) circumstances, namely in cases in which only comprehensive decision on all submitted issues can be regarded as a sensible compliance with the arbitrators' duties under the arbitration agreement.*").

190 See Blackaby et al. (2015) p.585 ("*Where an arbitral tribunal fails to deal with all of the issues referred to it for determination, it is usually said that the award should at least be held valid in respect of the issues with which it does deal. However, this is perhaps too simplistic. The significance of the issues that were not dealt with must be considered in relation to the award as a whole. For example, it is not difficult to envisage a situation in which the issues that were overlooked were of such importance that, had they been dealt with, the whole balance of the award would have been altered and its effect would have been different.*").

proceedings[191] and not at the enforcement stage.[192] The same conclusions can be reached, considering that the Miami Draft does not reintroduce the possibility to refuse recognition and enforcement of the arbitral award *infra petita*.

5.2 *Process of application of law by the arbitral tribunal*

The following sections focus on the different legal rules the tribunal is required to apply. One should therefore initially reflect on the tribunal's methodology in finding the applicable law (section 5.2.1) and on the tribunal's decision regarding which law applies (section 5.2.2). Consequently, it is necessary to analyze the process of application of the substantive law including application of its mandatory provisions by the arbitral tribunal (section 5.2.3 and section 5.2.4). Finally, it is necessary to briefly contemplate the issue of decisions reached *ex aequo et bono* (section 5.2.5). All of the above is discussed in the context of the "excess of mandate" type of challenge at the enforcement stage.

5.2.1 Decision on the method of determining applicable law

Deciding the method of selecting the applicable law may have been the first action the arbitral tribunal will undertake. This is a relevant step whenever the parties fail to expressly designate the law applicable to the substance of the case.[193] It leaves two hypotheticals. Under the first one, parties themselves choose an applicable method of selecting the governing law. Under the second one, the tribunal needs to find the method of selection itself, based on its expertise and opposing submissions of the parties. The outstanding question is whether the tribunal's decision may be challenged under the "excess of mandate" type of challenge.

In the first hypothetical one would assume that the parties did not make a choice of applicable law and instead they "only" agreed on the specific conflict of laws rules to be used as a tool for finding the applicable law. If the tribunal follows the parties' choice, yet makes a mistake, its decision should escape the review under Article V(1)(c) of the Convention, because the merits of the award should not be reopened by the enforcement court.[194] Even when the tribunal disregards the express choice of the conflict of laws rules, its decision should survive the Article V(1)(c) challenge. Instead, it might trigger the Article

191 See, *i.a.*, Chapter II-Chapter V.

192 Even if the *infra petita* challenge is accepted at the enforcement stage, it might very well trigger other Art. V defenses. For example, the violation of the right to be heard and Art. V(1)(b). See also section 4.4. The alternative introduced by Born is to apply Art. V(1)(d) of the Convention, see Born, *International Commercial Arbitration* (2014) p.3557.

193 In case parties choose the law that will apply to their dispute, the step discussed under this section will be omitted. This situation will be further discussed under the following section. See section 5.2.2.

194 See also section 2.2.

V(1)(d) mechanism, considering that the tribunal failed to follow the procedure agreed by the parties.

The second hypothetical presupposes that the parties are not in agreement on what law applies to the substance of the dispute, nor are they in agreement as to the approach the tribunal should undertake to find the governing law. In this case it is likely that the parties will submit opposing views on the issue of applicable law. At the same time, the arbitration law of the seat often offers a fallback rule that gives the tribunal authority (and discretion) to determine what law shall apply to the merits of the dispute.[195] Sometimes it will require to follow the conflict of laws analysis, on other occasions it will allow for a direct choice of applicable law.[196] Importantly, such an authority is tied to the place where the arbitration takes place and not where the award is being enforced. Under the second scenario, finding the appropriate conflict of laws rules will be well within the tribunal's adjudicative powers and will be exempted from the court's review on the merits.[197] This is particularly true with the enforcement court's review. All in all, the tribunal's decision on selecting the method of determining the applicable law should escape the challenge of Article V(1)(c) of the Convention.

5.2.2 Decision on applicable law

The question whether Article V(1)(c) of the Convention applies as well to the tribunal's decision on applicable law is not a new one. Already more than twenty years ago, De Ly reflected that "*[i]t has hardly been analyzed whether this provision [Article V(1)(c) of the Convention] is purely procedural or whether it may also be interpreted in a substantive sense allowing the refusal of recognition or enforcement if the arbitrators have failed to apply the proper conflict or substantive rules.*"[198] This requires the analysis of three hypotheticals, namely (i) the parties agreed upon the choice of law provision in their contract, (ii) there is no choice of law clause, but parties submit their views on what law should apply, or (iii) the parties have not included a choice of law clause, nor do they indicate what law governs. In principle, the reflections discussed under this section are closely connected to (sometimes inseparable from) the tribunal's choice for a method of selection of applicable law.[199] For these reasons, these two sections should be read together.

195 See, for example, Art. 28(2) of the Model Law.

196 See, *e.g.*, Art. 28(2) of the Model Law (for the conflict of laws route) and Art. 1511 of the French CCP (for the direct approach). See also Chapter II, Chapter III, and Chapter VII.

197 See section 2.2.

198 De Ly, *Judicial Review of the Substance of Arbitral Awards* (1994) p.355.

199 See section 5.2.1.

If the parties introduce in their contract what law will govern it, this choice should be, in principle, conclusive for the arbitral tribunal.[200] At the same time, however, deciding against the parties' choice might not be easily exposed to the "excess of mandate" type of challenge at the enforcement stage. In order to determine the availability of the recourse, one might distinguish a situation where the tribunal fails to apply the express choice by mistake and deliberately.

With regard to the former, as long as the authorities seem to agree that the tribunal's decision will escape the court's scrutiny due to the fact that the award is not susceptible to the merits review,[201] there is less compromise with regard to the question what happens if the tribunal disregards a controlling choice of the parties.

On the one hand, as explained above, the parties' instructions should be decisive to the tribunal,[202] on the other hand, Born argues that

> [...] an erroneous choice-of-law decision, including disregarding a choice-of-law agreement, is an error of substance, not an excess of authority. Some authorities have adopted contrary views, but this is clearly in error: a mistake as to the choice of applicable law, including a failure to apply the parties' choice-of-law clause, is only a mistake concerning the merits of the parties' dispute. Even where an arbitral tribunal wrongly concludes that a choice-of-law clause does not apply, or is unenforceable, or should not be given effect for other reasons, its decision is not an excess of jurisdiction, but a mistake of substance on matters within the tribunal's jurisdiction.[203]

200 Borris & Hannecke, *Excess of Competence or Jurisdiction, Article V(1)(c)* (2012) p.321 ("*In particular, where the parties have agreed on a specific substantive law to be applied to the substance of the dispute and the arbitral tribunal applies a different set of rules, the arbitral tribunal acts in excess of its competence within the meaning of Article V(1)(c).*"). See also Haas (2002) p.503 ("*If the parties instruct the arbitral tribunal to decide the dispute under a particular national law, the award will not be enforceable if the arbitral tribunal clearly and arbitrarily applies another municipal law to the substance of the dispute or to the arbitration proceedings.*").

201 See, *i.a.*, Borris & Hannecke, *Excess of Competence or Jurisdiction, Article V(1)(c)* (2012) p.321 ("*[...] if the arbitral tribunal interprets the choice of law incorrectly and thus erroneously applies incorrect rules, this does not constitute a ground for refusal under Article V(1)(c). In [this] case a review of the arbitral tribunal's interpretation of the parties' choice of law would lead to a prohibited review of the reasoning in substance (révision au fond).*"), Haas (2002) p.503 and Born, *International Commercial Arbitration* (2014) p.3554. See also *Int'l Standard Elec. Corp. v. Bridas Sociedad Anonima Petrolera, Indus. Y Comercial*, 745 F. Supp. 172, 182 (S.D.N.Y. 1990) ("*We cannot understand how the Convention, created to assure consistency in the enforcement of foreign arbitral awards, would not be gravely undermined, if judges sitting in each of the many jurisdictions where enforcement may be obtained, were authorized by the Convention to undertake a de novo inquiry into whether the law the arbitrators said they were using was or was not properly applied by them. The plain answer is that the Convention does not, and could not, contemplate such a chaos.*").

202 See fn.200.

203 Born, *International Commercial Arbitration* (2014) p.3554.

Even Born, however, acknowledges that "*[c]ases where an arbitral tribunal refused to give effect to an applicable, enforceable choice-of-law clause, manifestly refusing to uphold the parties' agreement in favor of its own notions of equity, could give rise to excess of authority or public policy objections.*"[204] Therefore, the parties' explicit (and undisputed) choice of law should be controlling. Otherwise, the award might be challenged under Article V(1)(d) of the Convention (failure to follow the agreed procedure)[205] or Article V(2)(b) of the Convention (violation of public policy) in cases where the tribunal fails to follow the parties' choice of applicable law.

The second hypothetical presupposes that the parties do not include the choice of law provision in their contract, but they introduced arguments in support of their view of what law applies. Usually, the parties would not be in agreement on what law applies. In this instance, it would be the tribunal's prerogative to decide on the issue of governing law. Consequently, even in cases of error, the tribunal's decision would not be reviewable.[206]

In the third, highly rare scenario, where no instructions or guidance is given by the parties as to the law governing the merits of the case,[207] the tribunal will need to determine the applicable law on its own. The tribunal's decision should not be reviewable under Article V(1)(c) of the Convention. As long as the arbitral panel consults its findings with the parties it should survive also other prospective challenge avenues at the enforcement stage.[208]

5.2.3 Ascertaining the content of applicable law by the arbitral tribunal

The adjudicative aspect of the tribunal's activity in the majority of cases requires the tribunal to apply the law. In contrast with the traditional court's proceedings, however, the tribunal's legal conclusions should, in principle, escape the court's merits review.[209] It entails that *by no means* should the Article V(1)(c) challenge be invoked to test the tribunal's legal conclusions properly brought by the parties in arbitration. A few reflections need to be

---

204 Born, *International Commercial Arbitration* (2014) p.3554.

205 This is, however, a minority view. See Kreindler et al., *Commercial Arbitration in Germany* (2016) p.345.

206 It is likely that the tribunal will follow one of the views presented. In all cases, it should avoid surprising the parties as to their decision on applicable law, since it might violate the parties' right to be heard. This would be arguably reviewable under Art. V(1)(b) of the Convention and not under Art. V(1)(c). See also section 4.4.

207 Therefore, no choice of law clause is included in the contract nor do the parties submit their views as to what law applies.

208 See also section 4.4. For further reading, see also ILA, *ILA Report on Ascertaining the Contents of the Applicable Law in International Commercial Arbitration* (2008), p.16.

209 See section 2.2. Kaufmann-Kohler, *The Arbitrator and the Law: Does He/She Know It? How? And a Few More Questions* (2005) p.635 ("*[i]ndeed, matters involving the application of substantive law by the arbitrators largely escape any control by the courts, be it at the annulment or the enforcement stage, except perhaps under the US standard of manifest disregard of the law [...].*").

given on (i) the tribunal's independent investigations (and the parties' duty to educate the tribunal) and on (ii) surprising the parties with the legal findings.

The well-known adage *iura novit curia* (the court knows the law) that is applicable in many court proceedings, illustrates the phenomenon of the ascertaining of the law by a judge. According to this principle a judge is free to determine applicable law *ex officio*, thus independent from the parties' submissions.[210] The application of *iura novit curia*, or, as some suggest, *iura novit arbiter* in international commercial arbitration remains the subject of a lively debate.[211] For the purpose of the analysis at hand, one should advocate that leaving the arbitral tribunal with the discretion to make its own findings on applicable law is a sensible solution.[212] At the same time, it should not go as far as imposing the obligation of finding the law upon the arbitral tribunal, since such a duty might be misplaced and excessively burdensome.[213] It should be noted, however, that an arbitral panel should exercise its discretion to make independent findings only if necessary in order to verify or supplement what the parties in their submissions may have left open or unclear.[214]

At the same time, the parties – in their own interest – should educate the arbitral panel and acquaint it with the relevant legal provisions in order to avoid – as suggested by Kurkela – the risk of the misapplication of (foreign) law or errors in its interpretation by the arbitral panel.[215] Generally, such a burden of education can be aligned with the burden of proof.[216] It does not mean, however, that the law should be treated as a fact and applicable only when proven. It only means that the parties shall assist the tribunal with understanding the foreign legal system. Conversely, if the parties fail to establish the contents of the

---

210 Kurkela, *'Jura Novit Curia' and the Burden of Education in International Arbitration – A Nordic Perspective* (2003) p.489 ("*The jura novit curia principle empowers the courts to qualify the issues in a manner departing from that proposed by the parties. The courts also have the freedom to identify and apply such rules of substantive law as are deemed applicable by the court even in the absence of any reference to those rules or claims as to their application by the parties.*").

211 See, *e.g.*, Kurkela, *'Jura Novit Curia' and the Burden of Education in International Arbitration – A Nordic Perspective* (2003), Kaufmann-Kohler, *"Iura Novit Arbiter" – est-ce bien raisonnable? Réflexions sur le statut du droit de fond devant l'arbitre international* (2004), and Lew, *Iura Novit Curia and Due Process* (2011).

212 Kaufmann-Kohler, *The Arbitrator and the Law: Does He/She Know It? How? And a Few More Questions* (2005) p.636 ("*The Parties shall establish the contents of the law applicable to the merits. The Arbitral Tribunal shall have the power, but not the obligation, to make its own inquiries to establish such contents. If the contents of the applicable law are not established, the Arbitral Tribunal is empowered to apply any rules of law which it deems appropriate.*").

213 Kaufmann-Kohler, *The Arbitrator and the Law: Does He/She Know It? How? And a Few More Questions* (2005) p.636, also Lew, *Iura Novit Curia and Due Process* (2011) p.411.

214 Kurkela, *'Jura Novit Curia' and the Burden of Education in International Arbitration – A Nordic Perspective* (2003) p.496.

215 Kurkela, *'Jura Novit Curia' and the Burden of Education in International Arbitration – A Nordic Perspective* (2003) p.494.

216 Kurkela, *'Jura Novit Curia' and the Burden of Education in International Arbitration – A Nordic Perspective* (2003) p.494 ("*The division of this duty [burden of education] may be allocated by the Tribunal between the parties and the arbitrators applying mutati mutandis the rules of the burden of proof perhaps slightly tilted towards the arbitral tribunal*").

applicable law themselves, it is reasonable for the arbitral tribunal to take over and use its discretion in order to ascertain and apply the law.[217] It can be argued that the arbitral tribunal's discretion can go as far as to the application of *lex mercatoria* in the absence of a clear choice of law provision.[218]

As a general rule, it is therefore concluded that the decision by an arbitral tribunal based on the legal arguments different from the parties' submissions will not amount to the violation challengeable under Article V(1)(c) Convention.[219] For example, the U.S. District Court for the Southern District of California rejected as misguided the party's assertions that the tribunal issued a ruling based upon legal theories not contemplated by and/or asserted by the parties. It held that "*[t]his Court cannot refuse to confirm the Award simply because the legal theories and conclusions presented in the Award differ from those contemplated by the Parties in their pleadings. Legal theories used by adjudicators to resolve contract disputes are not considered oral amendments to the contract or the arbitration agreement.*"[220]

The abovementioned general rule will not apply, however, according to Azeredo da Silveira and Lévy in two instances, namely (i) when the parties expressly prohibit the arbitral tribunal to reach its decision on grounds different than those raised by the parties and (ii) when "*the arbitrators' legal findings are entirely unrelated to the parties' submissions, and if it appears, as a consequence, that such findings would 'take the parties by surprise' [...].*"[221] Arguably, however, "surprise" decisions will violate the right to be heard, and will thus trigger Article V(1)(b) of the Convention[222] and not the "excess of mandate" type of challenge.

5.2.4 Application of mandatory rules of law by the arbitral tribunal

From the arbitrators' perspective, it should be clear that it is within their mandate to apply mandatory laws.[223] Additionally, in the light of professional scrutiny, such an application

---

217 Azeredo da Silveira & Lévy (2008) p.653, and Port et al. (2010) p.273.

218 *Bank A. v. Bank B*, Landesgericht [Court of First Instance], Hamburg 18 September 1997, XXV Y.B. Comm. Arb. 714 (2000).

219 Port et al. (2010) p.272 ("*Arbitral tribunals are not limited to rendering an award based on the legal theories brought forward by the parties. An award rendered on the basis of a legal theory other than the theories argued by the parties will not, on that basis alone, run afoul of [Article] V(1)(c). A tribunal may apply law not referenced in the pleadings, as long as in so doing, the tribunal does not exceed the scope of the arbitration agreement.*"), and Borris & Hannecke, *Excess of Competence or Jurisdiction, Article V(1)(c)* (2012) pp.326-327.

220 *Ministry of Def. & Support for Armed Forces of Islamic Republic of Iran v. Cubic Def. Sys., Inc.*, 29 F. Supp. 2d 1168, 1173–74 (S.D. Cal. 1998), aff'd in part, vacated in part, remanded sub nom. *Ministry of Def. & Support for the Armed Forces of the Islamic Republic of Iran v. Cubic Def. Sys., Inc.*, 665 F.3d 1091 (9th Cir. 2011). One should note, however, that the argument was raised under Art. V(1)(a) of the Convention.

221 Azeredo da Silveira & Lévy (2008) p.655.

222 See section 4.4.

223 (Code of Civil Procedure, Book IV, Arbitration, 2011) pp.477-479. It is particularly true if one considers that "*[s]tate courts have a tendency to focus on the law. It should therefore be made easy for State judges to*

may be even indispensable. Paulsson convincingly argues that "*the mandate of arbitration agreements – unless they are couched in unusually narrow terms – is the fair resolution of disputes, not the vindication of contracts.*"[224] Therefore, the arbitral tribunal should revise the implication and the relevance of the applicable mandatory legal provisions when issuing the award to circumvent the likelihood of the award being challenged at the post-award stage.[225] That being said, one should further (briefly) address two hypotheticals: (i) the tribunal raises a mandatory law issue *ex officio* or (ii) the tribunal wrongly applies rules of mandatory nature.

In principle, the arbitral award should survive the Article V(1)(c) challenge, even if the tribunal does apply mandatory legal provisions on its own initiative. Such an undertaking should not be considered to go beyond the tribunal's submissions to arbitration. At the same time the tribunal should provide the parties with an opportunity to comment on its findings.[226]

Also, misapplication of the law should escape the court's scrutiny, because of the deferential status of the enforcement court's review.[227] Arguably, it would equally apply to both the "excess of mandate" type of challenge and the challenge against public policy violation at the enforcement stage.[228]

In the context of the violation of public policy at the enforcement stage, one should not forget that

> [...] Contracting States are permitted to invoke Article V(2)(b)'s public policy defense only exceptionally, as a narrow and specific departure from the Convention's generally-applicable requirement of recognition. Moreover, Article V(2)(b) should be invoked only in order to safeguard fundamental, mandatory policies of a Contracting State, which are clearly articulated in constitutional, legislative, or judicial instruments, and which are not contrary to the Convention's basic purposes or to state practice under the Convention.[229]

---

see that 'their' law has been complied with." See Karrer, *Must an Arbitral Tribunal Really Ensure that its Award is Enforceable?* (2005) p.430.

224 (Code of Civil Procedure, Book IV, Arbitration, 2011) p.477.

225 It would be particularly important in the context of a potential challenge at the seat of arbitration. At the same time, however, arguments might be equally raised at the enforcement proceedings.

226 It would otherwise face the challenge under Art. V(1)(b) of the Convention.

227 See section 2.2 and section 5.2.3.

228 See, however, Hwang & Lai (2005) p.24 ("*A supervisory or enforcing court should not second-guess a tribunal, and the risk of arbitral error is inherent in the acceptance of the process. However, parties do not bargain for a perverse and manifest error that calls out for correction. To ignore such errors would be to accept that the arbitral process can condone miscarriages of justice.*").

229 Born, *International Commercial Arbitration* (2014) p.3663.

Generally speaking, the wrongful application of mandatory (applicable) law might have nothing to do with the law and policies of the enforcement country which should, in turn, exclude the possibility of the enforcement court to reassess the tribunal's conclusions.

5.2.5 Decision reached *ex aequo et bono* or as *amiable compositeur*

When looking back in time, one could distinguish the different roles played by judges and arbitrators. Whereas the role of the former was the one of applying the law, the role of the latter was the one of achieving equity.[230] In the context of modern international arbitration, the role of the arbitrator greatly evolved.[231] Indeed,

> [a] new kind of arbitration, based on law, has emerged, as part of which the arbitrator is supposed to apply the rules of law laid down by the legislator. 'Amiable composition' (i.e. arbitration based on equity) has become the exception and arbitration statutes treat it as such, sometimes even ignoring it.[232]

Importantly, although addressed by the national arbitration acts, the notion of the decision reached *ex aequo et bono* or as *amiable compositeur*[233] is not included in the framework of the Convention. This, in turn, triggers the question if and how the tribunal's decision reached *ex aequo et bono* can be challenged at the enforcement stage.

In principle, (i) the tribunal's *ex aequo et bono* decision can be challenged at the enforcement stage if it is reached without the parties' authorization. One should accept, however, (ii) that holding the authority to decide in equity does not prevent the tribunal from applying the law. Finally, as already highlighted elsewhere,[234] a decision reached *ex*

230 Mayer, *Reflections on the International Arbitrator's Duty to Apply the Law – The Freshfields Lecture 2000* (2001) p.235.

231 See, in general, (Stone Sweet & Grisel, 2017).

232 Mayer, *Reflections on the International Arbitrator's Duty to Apply the Law – The Freshfields Lecture 2000* (2001) p.235.

233 Although some authors acknowledge that there is a difference between the notion of *amiable compositeur* and the notion of *ex aequo et bono*, the in-depth analysis of such a difference for the purpose of the current research would be misplaced (especially taking into account that the definitions of both terms vary). As mentioned by Born in Born, *International Commercial Arbitration* (2014) p.2772, "*[t]he essential principle of each term is that arbitrators are not obliged to decide the parties' dispute in accordance with a strict application of legal rules; rather, the arbitrators are expected to decide in light of general notions of fairness, equity and justice.*" Therefore, the general concept of achieving equity (which is common for both principles) will be considered jointly under the term of *ex aequo et bono*. For further reading, see, *e.g.*, Rubino-Sammartano, *Amiable Compositeur (Joint Mandate to Settle) and Ex Bono et Aecquo (Discretional Authority to Mitigate Strict Law): Apparent Synonyms Revisited* (1992), Maniruzzaman, *The Arbitrator's Prudence in Lex Mercatoria: Amiable Composition and Ex Aecquo Et Bono in Decision Making* (2003), and Suchoža & Hučková Palková (2012) pp.268-273.

234 See section 4.4.

aequo et bono might simultaneously trigger different challenges. These points will be analyzed below.

The underlying condition for the arbitral tribunal to decide *ex aequo et bono* or to reach its conclusion as *amiable compositeur* is the unequivocal agreement of the parties.[235] It is so required because of the exceptional character of the *ex aequo et bono* power. For example it has been explained that an express consent of the parties to act as *amiable* compositeur will give the arbitrators the power to "*soften the mechanistic application of statutory or other provisions of national law; they could not, however, be used to vary a term or condition of the contract.*"[236] Although, as demonstrated above, the power to decide *ex aequo et bono* is not addressed in the Convention itself, the parties' explicit authorization to decide *ex aequo et bono* is usually required by national laws[237] and arbitration rules.[238]

A separate question relates to the instances where the arbitral tribunal is vested with the power to act as *amiable compositeur* but reaches its conclusions by applying the law. Generally, if the award can be produced in accordance with law (which should, as a rule, represent principles of equity, justice and fairness) it would be unreasonable to force the arbitral tribunal to find equity outside the law. It has been argued that "*[a]miable composition does not mean that an arbitrator cannot apply rules of substantive law, it simply removes the imperative or obligatory character of such law and allows the arbitrator to choose that which he wishes to apply.*"[239] In turn, "*if the parties grant the arbitral tribunal the authority to render an award based on equity, in most cases this authorizes but does not require the arbitral authority to base his award on principles of equity.*"[240]

Although it is uncontroversial to say that the decision *ex aequo et bono* will be at risk at the enforcement stage when granted without the parties' express authorization, the outstanding question is which defense will apply. In these cases, generally, the choice exists

235 Born, *International Commercial Arbitration* (2014) pp.3554-3555 ("*As discussed above, most national arbitration legislation and institutional rules permit arbitration ex aequo et bono and amiable composition, where arbitrators are not constrained by applicable rules of substantive law, but require an express agreement to this effect.*").

236 Craig, *The arbitrator's mission and the application of law in international commercial arbitration* (2010) p.268.

237 See, *e.g.*, Art. 28(3) of the Model Law, Art. 1512 of the French Code of Civil Procedure or Section 46(1)(b) of the English Arbitration Act.

238 See, *e.g.*, Art. 35(2) of the 2010 UNCITRAL Rules, Art. 33(2) of the 1976 UNCITRAL Rules, Rule 31.2 of the 2016 SIAC Rules, Section 23.3 of the 1998 DIS Rules (different formulation under Art.24.4 of the 2018 DIS Rules, effectively leading to the same result), Art. 21(3) of the (draft) 2021 ICC Rules, Art. 21(3) of the 2017 ICC Rules, Art. 21(3) of the 2012 ICC Rules, Art. 22(4) of the 2014 LCIA Rules, Art. 22.4 of the 2020 LCIA Rules, Art. 31(3) of the 2014 ICDR Rules, Art. 31.1 of the 2016 JAMS Rules.

239 Poznanski (1987) p.79.

240 Haas (2002) p.502, also Borris & Hannecke, *Excess of Competence or Jurisdiction, Article V(1)(c)* (2012) p.322.

between Article V(1)(c) (the "excess of mandate" type of challenge) and Article V(1)(d) of the Convention (procedure incompliant with the parties' agreement).[241]

If one considers that the decision *ex aequo et bono* is a separate form of the tribunal's mandate, then one might be tempted to apply for the Article V(1)(c) defense.[242] At the same time, however, an *ex aequo et bono* decision affects the tribunal's reasoning, an explanation of the tribunal's conclusions. Consequently, it can be argued that this is the issue which is unrelated to question the scope of the parties' submission.[243]

If this argument is accepted, Article V(1)(d) of the Convention might be of relevance in the context of the tribunal's *ex aequo et bono* decision.[244] Arguably, the latter solution (*i.e.* Article V(1)(d) of the Convention) fits the structure of Article V of the Convention better. Indeed, it is more compelling to consider that under Article V(1)(c) of the Convention the reviewing court should check only what "differences" and "matters" have been submitted to arbitration.

In any event, convincing that the national court whether the arbitral tribunal acted as *amiable compositeur* can be difficult. For example, in a case before the U.S. enforcement court, the court held that taking into account that the arbitral panel "*relied upon a distinguished legal expert on the matter in issue*", it did not act as *amiable compositeur.*[245] Further, the court observed that the "*[...] amiable compositeur argument is a not especially elegant masque that seeks to conceal the fatal weakness of ISEC's defense: we are forbidden*

241 See also section 4.4.

242 Born, *International Commercial Arbitration* (2014) p.3555 ("*Where arbitrators act ex aequo et bono or as amiable compositeurs, without such an agreement by the parties, they exceed their authority, rather than merely making errors in the exercise of their authority. Put simply, as national legislation establishing safeguards regarding such arbitral proceedings makes clear, an arbitration ex aequo et bono and amiable composition is a different form of proceeding, involving a different type of authority, than other types of arbitration; it is not merely an error in application of relevant substantive legal rules or interpretation of the parties' contract or choice-of-law clause. An arbitral tribunal's exercise of such authority, without the parties' agreement, is an excess of authority under Article V(1)(c).*"). See also Haas (2002) p.502, Craig, *The arbitrator's mission and the application of law in international commercial arbitration* (2010) pp.269-270, and Borris & Hannecke, *Excess of Competence or Jurisdiction, Article V(1)(c)* (2012) p.321.

243 Azeredo da Silveira & Lévy (2008) p.665 ("*that the arbitrators have acted as amiable compositeurs despite the absence of agreement thereon between the parties is a substantive issue which does not constitute a ground, in the sense of Article V(1)(c) of the New York Convention, for refusing to enforce an award. Indeed, if they decide ex aequo et bono without authorisation, the arbitrators exceed neither their jurisdiction (which pertains to the subject matter of the dispute) nor their mandate (which pertains to the parties' respective claims). Deciding ex aequo et bono neither relates to the arbitration agreement, nor concerns the operative of the award. It rather concerns the reasoning of the arbitrators, which is not a matter to be reviewed under Article V(1)(c) of the Convention. This view is however not unanimously accepted.*"). See also Haas (2002) p.502, Kreindler et al., *Commercial Arbitration in Germany* (2016) p.345 (in the context of the German Arbitration proceedings, equally applicable to the enforcement proceedings, see therein p.370) ("*[...] a decision ex aequo et bono without express authorization is considered a violation of procedure.*"). See also section 4.4.

244 See also fn.242.

245 *Int'l Standard Elec. Corp. v. Bridas Sociedad Anonima Petrolera, Indus. Y Comercial,* 745 F. Supp. 172 (S.D.N.Y. 1990).

under the Convention to reconsider factual findings of the arbitral panel."[246] In another case of the U.S. enforcement proceedings, the defendant contested the arbitral award arguing that the arbitral tribunal "*did not base its damage award on the evidence presented and instead acted as an amiable compositeur, which tries to reach merely an equitable, and not necessarily legal, result.*"[247] The enforcement court, in turn, found that "*[i]n fashioning its damages award, the Tribunal carefully considered both the EPSA and Libyan law, as well as the submissions and arguments of the parties. The Court finds that there is nothing 'completely irrational' about the Tribunal's award or its reading of the parties' contract.*"[248] The court also concluded that determining if the tribunal "exceeded its powers" cannot lead to the reexamination of the merits.[249] Indeed, as explained above, considering the architecture of the Convention, the better view is to subsume the challenge against the *ex aequo et bono* decision under Article V(1)(d) of the Convention.

5.3 *Decisions on remedies*

The penultimate category of decisions investigates if the "excess of mandate" type of challenge can be potentially applicable to tribunals' decisions on remedies. In this context, three types of remedies have been distinguished: damages (section 5.3.1), specific performance (section 5.3.2), and contract adaptation and filling the gaps (section 5.3.3).

5.3.1 Decision on damages

Damages claims are perhaps the most commonly sought remedies. In general, they are the basic remedy available under any legal system for a breach of contract and should be, in principle, easily available for the arbitral tribunal. In the context of the "excess of mandate" type of challenge, one should reflect, however, whether the tribunal's decision can be challenged (under the Article V(1)(c) ground) if the tribunal awards (i) more damages than claimed or (ii) something different than claimed. Additionally, the question arises if the decision is subject to a challenge in cases where the tribunal grants damages (iii) excluded by the parties' agreement or (iv) unknown at the place where the enforcement should take place.

The first hypothetical touches upon the *ne ultra petita* (not beyond request) principle. Obviously, the situation where the relief granted is higher than sought should be remedied

246 *Int'l Standard Elec. Corp. v. Bridas Sociedad Anonima Petrolera, Indus. Y Comercial*, 745 F. Supp. 172, 181 (S.D.N.Y. 1990).

247 *Nat'l Oil Corp. v. Libyan Sun Oil Co.*, 733 F. Supp. 800, 816 (D. Del. 1990).

248 *Nat'l Oil Corp. v. Libyan Sun Oil Co.*, 733 F. Supp. 800, 818-19 (D. Del. 1990).

249 See *Nat'l Oil Corp. v. Libyan Sun Oil Co.*, 733 F. Supp. 800, 819 (D. Del. 1990) ("*[i]t is not this Court's role ... to sit as the panel did and reexamine the evidence under the guise of determining whether the arbitrators exceeded their powers [...] the Court will not inquire any further.*").

at the post-award stage. This requires an assessment of what disputes and matters have been submitted to the arbitrators and if their conclusions go beyond what has been requested. As such, arguably, it fits within the scope of the "excess of mandate" type of challenge.[250] For example, one German enforcement court while admitting that the *ultra petita* award would be susceptible under Article V(1)(c) of the Convention, ultimately rejected the argument that the claimant had been awarded more damages.[251] Importantly, the broader relief than the party had expected might be provided by the statutory provision of the law governing the arbitration. In this regard decisions granting more damages, even if not requested, can still be enforced.[252]

In the case of the second scenario, conclusions similar to the first one would apply. In principle, a situation where the tribunal granted a remedy different than requested (provided that the parties did not submit alternative claims) should fit within the scope of Article V(1)(c) of the Convention, because in this case the tribunal's undertaking will be incompliant with the parties' request.[253]

---

250 See Haas (2002) p.500 ("*The arbitrator exceeds the limits of his competence if he adjudicates on points of dispute which the parties have not agreed to assign to him (ultra petita).*"). See, however, UNCITRAL, *UNCITRAL Secretariat Guide on the Convention on the Recognition and Enforcement of Foreign Arbitral Awards* (2016) p.175.

251 *Seller v. Buyer*, Oberlandesgericht [Court of Appeal], Stuttgart, 1 Sch 12/01, 6 December 2001, XXIX Y.B. Comm. Arb. 742, 746 (2004) ("*Enforcement of the arbitral award must not be denied because the award granted the claimant more than it claimed. The claimant did indeed seek payment of DM 119,621, according to the defendant's statement of the facts, [whereas] the defendant was directed to pay DM 129,621. The [award in] excess of the claim falls under the [objection of] excess of the arbitration agreement in Art. V(1)(c) [of the] Convention [...]. However, the arbitral award does not exceed the claim. The amount of the claim is not determined by the wording of the request; rather, the dispositive part of the decision must objectively correspond to the relevant presentation of the facts. According to the arbitral award, the sum of DM 129,621 results from adding up the invoices claimed, so that the arbitral tribunal correctly assumed that the request for DM 119,621 was a writing error that could easily be corrected.*").

252 *M & C Corp. v. Erwin Behr GmbH & Co., KG*, 87 F.3d 844, 850 (6th Cir. 1996) ("*Because the damages are considered compensatory, the arbitrator correctly concluded that payment of such compensation pursuant to M.C.L. § § 600.2961(5)(b) was envisioned by the terms of reference. Those terms broadly state that Connelly 'has suffered monetary damages as a result of [Behr's] failures [to pay the full amount of commissions due].' Terms of Reference, Article III(A)(c). Although Connelly does then seek monetary damages estimated to be $750,000, that request specifies that the damage amount represents only the actual amount of the 'unpaid commissions to Plaintiff, without deduction or offset.' The terms of reference also explicitly provide that Connelly seeks 'other relief that is available under the applicable law to compensate it for losses 'as a result of [Behr's] failures [to pay the full amount of commissions due].' We conclude that the M.C.L. § § 600.2961 damage award thus was within the scope of the arbitrator's terms of reference, that it did not raise a new theory of liability, and that it did not impose a new evidentiary requirement upon Behr.*"). See also Port et al. (2010) pp.268-269, also Azeredo da Silveira & Lévy (2008) pp.655-656, similarly Borris & Hannecke, *Excess of Competence or Jurisdiction, Article V(1)(c)* (2012) p.325 ("*In spite of the principle of ne ultra petita, an arbitral tribunal may be justified, depending on the applicable (substantive) law, in granting higher damages than the nominal amount claimed.*").

253 See, *e.g.*, *AB Götaverken v. General National Maritime Transport Company (GMTC), Libya and others*, Svea Court of Appeal (5th Dept.) Stockholm; Swedish Supreme Court, SO 1462, 13 December 1978; 13 August 1979, VI Y.B. Comm. Arb. 237 (1981). In this case, the court was faced with the assertion that the arbitrators

For example, in one case, a Canadian court concluded that:

> [i]n addition to rendering an unreasoned award – against the express wishes of the parties – the arbitrators cancelled ab initio the distribution contract when this was not required of them. In addition, they appear to have ordered the respondent to pay punitive damages, which exceeded their jurisdiction. [...] Therefore, even if the recognition of the award is not against public order, it seems clear that homologation of the award could be refused on the basis of art. 950(4) [...] C.C.P.[254]

The thirds scenario reflects instances where the argument is raised that certain remedies have been excluded by the parties' agreement in the underlying contract. Often, however these challenges are based on objections to the arbitrators' substantive contract interpretations or legal conclusions and as such do not present the true Article V(1)(c) defense. As explained by Azeredo da Silveira and Lévy "*the argument that the arbitrators have awarded remedies that were not foreseen by the contract or that were specifically excluded by it only relates to the arbitral tribunal's substantive findings and cannot justify a refusal to enforce the award under Article V(1)(c).*"[255] Consequently, when the award-debtor seeks to improperly characterize a substantive objection to the merits of the arbitral tribunal's decision, its defense should fail under Article V(1)(c) of the Convention.[256]

As one of the leading examples one could mention *Parsons & Whittemore Overseas Co., Inc. v. Société Générale de L'Industrie Du Papier (RAKTA)*, where the U.S. enforcement court concluded that

> [a]lthough the Convention recognizes that an award may not be enforced where predicated on a subject matter outside the arbitrator's jurisdiction, it does not sanction second-guessing the arbitrator's construction of the parties' agreement. The appellant's attempt to invoke this defense, however, calls upon the court to ignore this limitation on its decision-making powers and usurp the

exceeded their authority as they decided to reduce the price although they had never been asked to determine whether there should be a price reduction. The court concluded that the arbitrators' authority included power to adjust the price, as "*[...] the reduction was not an unsolicited award of damages to GMTC but rather a price adjustment connected with the general determination that GMTC owed the last instalment.*".

254 *Smart Systems Technologies Inc. c. Domotique Secant inc.*, 2008 QCCA 444 (CanLII), par. 31, http://canlii.ca/t/284nq#par31, [last accessed 14 August 2020].

255 Azeredo da Silveira & Lévy (2008) p.665.

256 See section 2.2.

> arbitrator's role. The district court took a proper view of its own jurisdiction in refusing to grant relief on this ground.[257]

The challenge was brought in the situation where the contract stipulated '*neither party shall have any liability for loss of production*' and $185,000 was awarded for loss of production. The court held that "*[t]he tribunal cannot properly be charged, however, with simply ignoring this alleged limitation on the subject matter over which its decision-making powers extended. Rather, the arbitration court interpreted the provision not to preclude jurisdiction on this matter.*"[258]

Similarly, in another case the enforcement court concluded that "*[i]n ignoring the limitation of damages clause the arbitrators were clearly attempting to give effect to the essential terms of the contract and the intent of the parties. Accordingly, the Court is satisfied that their disregard of the limitation of damages provision drew its essence from the contract.*"[259] Other court decisions are to the same effect.[260]

At the same time, however, van den Berg is of the position that

> with respect to the first part of ground (c) an award that 'deals with a difference not contemplated by or not falling within the terms of the submission to arbitration' is not confined to consideration of the claims asserted by the parties, but may also include the circumstance that the arbitrators have seriously ignored, in their analysis, the application of the terms of the contract, as pleaded by the parties. Thus, if an arbitrator ignores express provisions in a contract, it can be argued that he fails to deal with the difference between the parties[261]

In rebuttal to his arguments Azeredo da Silveira and Lévy observed that:

257 *Parsons & Whittemore Overseas Co., Inc. v. Societe Generale De L'Industrie Du Papier (RAKTA)*, 508 F.2d 969, 977 (C.A.N.Y. 1974).

258 *Parsons & Whittemore Overseas Co., Inc. v. Societe Generale De L'Industrie Du Papier (RAKTA)*, 508 F.2d 969, 976 (C.A.N.Y. 1974).

259 *Jacada (Europe), Ltd. v. Int'l Mktg. Strategies, Inc.*, No. 1:02-CV-479, 2003 WL 24267645, at *4 (W.D. Mich. Oct. 22, 2003), aff'd, 401 F.3d 701 (6th Cir. 2005).

260 See, *e.g.*, *Fertilizer Corp. of India v. IDI Management, Inc.*, 517 F.Supp. 948 (D.C.Ohio, 1981) ("*Under the Convention on the Recognition and Enforcement of Foreign Arbitral Awards, arbitrators did not exceed their authority in granting consequential damages in [the] arbitral award, even though an express c[l]ause in the contract of which the arbitration arose excluded such damages.*"). Also *In re Arbitration Between Millicom International v. N.V. and Motorola, Inc., Proempres Panama, S.A.*, 2002 WL 472042, at *6 (S.D.N.Y.,2002). (The award was confirmed in the case where the arbitral tribunal granted a remedy not specified in the contract despite the objection of one party).

261 Van den Berg, *Failure by Arbitrators to Apply Contract Terms from the Perspective of the New York Convention* (2005) p.69.

> Van den Berg's suggestion is that, faced with an exceptionally untenable award, the judge may find in Article V(1)(c) of the New York Convention a basis to refuse enforcement. His view is that, in rendering such an award, the arbitrators did exceed their mandate, given that the parties had not commissioned them to disregard logic (of facts and law). This motive is praiseworthy but would defeat the spirit of Article V(1)(c).[262]

Indeed, if the enforcement court is allowed to scrutinize the contract interpretation undertaken by the arbitral tribunal, the court's review will be far from deferential.[263]

The fourth scenario where the tribunal applies the type of damages that are unknown in the country of enforcement needs to be addressed only briefly. In principle, the focus therein would not be directed at the comparison between the relief sought and that granted. Rather, the court will inquire if the type of damages that is to be enforced is in accordance with the public policy of the country of enforcement.[264] This would be particularly the case with punitive damages.

5.3.2 Decision on specific performance

The second, common type of remedy is specific performance. Although it is a different remedy, and its relevance and scope of application might vary in different jurisdictions, for the purpose of the Article V(1)(c) challenge the analysis will not differ much from the one above. Therefore, the conclusions presented in the previous section would apply to decisions on specific performance.[265] In principle, it means that the award might not be enforced if specific performance is granted (i) without the parties' request or (ii) against the explicit limitation prescribed in the agreement to arbitrate. As explained above, even in those instances refusal of recognition and enforcement will not be automatic however.[266]

5.3.3 Decision on contract adaptation and filling of gaps

The last type of remedy discussed is perhaps the most controversial one. The outstanding question related to the tribunal's power to adapt the contract or to fill the contractual gaps is whether it is "simply" a dimension of contract interpretation or, rather, it extends beyond the adjudicative function of the tribunal giving the arbitral panel the power to shape the parties' legal relationship. All in all, such a power will be highly dependent on the law of the arbitral seat as well as the law applicable to the merits of the case.[267] In principle, as

262 Azeredo da Silveira & Lévy (2008) p.662.
263 See section 2.2.
264 See section 3.3.
265 See section 5.3.1.
266 See analogous hypothetical in section 5.3.1.
267 See also Chapter II-Chapter V.

always when assessing the challenge under Article V(1)(c) of the Convention, the court will have a look at the limits to the tribunal's "mandate" expressed in (i) the parties' agreement to arbitrate and (ii) the parties' subsequent submissions,[268] and finally, (iii) the public policy of the enforcement state may also play a role.[269]

The scope of the initial agreement to arbitrate will be, arguably, the most relevant one in the context of the tribunal's power to adapt the contract or fill the contractual gaps. Yet, the parties rarely define the tribunal's powers to adapt the contract in their agreement to arbitrate. The contract adaptation clauses, however, may be found in the contract itself (thus outside the agreement to arbitrate). Because of the exceptional character of this power, the tribunal should refrain from exercising this power even if the agreement to arbitrate is drafted broadly. Arguably, if the limitation of the tribunal's power, however, is located outside the agreement to arbitrate, it might be considered part of the contract, and as such, left for the arbitrators and the court to interpret.[270]

As always, the tribunal's decision should be based on the parties' request. The enforcement court needs to be satisfied that the tribunal does not act on its own volition when it comes to the contract adaptation. If the tribunal goes beyond what is requested and adapts the contract on its own initiative, it might indeed be considered as shaping the legal relationship between the parties without their consent. Such an award will be open for challenge under Article V(1)(c) of the Convention.

Since different legal systems view the contract adaptation powers differently, in the context of the Convention no universal answer can be given. In principle, not all jurisdiction may even allow the parties to delegate such a power to the arbitral tribunal. Therefore, tinkering with the contract beyond the mere contract adaptation might be challenged against public policy at the country of enforcement.[271]

5.4 *Decisions accessory to the parties' main submissions*

The last categories of decisions are inherent to the adjudicative process at large, but are at the same time, separate from the tribunal's decision on the main parties' claims. These include the tribunal's decision on interest (section 5.4.1), costs (section 5.4.2) and procedural decisions (section 5.4.3).

268 See section 3.

269 See section 3.3.

270 See also section 5.3.1.

271 Additionally, the tribunal should, when exercising its contract adaption powers, keep the applicable mandatory rules in mind.

5.4.1 Decision on interest

Awarding interest might constitute a substantial monetary value and, at the same time, might require a complex legal analysis independent from the one on the main claim. The issues that might be relevant when the enforcing court is faced with the challenge against the tribunal's decision on interest, will include, amongst other things, the determination of the applicable law (to the issue of interest), the starting date for accrual, the rate and the type of the interest. The analysis herein, however, should be limited to the question when would the enforcement court accept the challenge against the decision on interest under Article V(1)(c) of the Convention.

In general, the approach to the decision on interest would be similar to the tribunal's decisions on remedies that were discussed above.[272] It means that, in principle, if the parties agree to limit the tribunal's authority to award interest, or the tribunal granted more interest than claimed, or when the interest itself violates the public policy of the country of enforcement, the tribunal's award should be susceptible to challenge.

It is necessary to highlight, however, that the decision on interest have a special status that distinguishes it from the abovementioned analysis. A power to award interest is rarely addressed in national arbitration acts or even in institutional arbitration rules.[273] The New York Convention is also silent on the issue of interest. Often it is concluded, however, that awarding interest is an inherent power[274] closely associated with the adjudicative function of the arbitral tribunal.

For example, a German court enforced the tribunal's decision awarding more interest than claimed. The court concluded that

> [...] the arbitral tribunal can in its discretion and on its own initiative award interest and compound interest for the time until the rendition of the award and for the time after the rendition of the award. The fact that more interest was awarded than it was claimed is not at odds with the [shipowner's] claim, since this claim clearly cannot be read to limit the power of the arbitral tribunal to award more interest. Hence, the arbitrators did not exceed their authority in the sense of Art. V(1)(c).[275]

Even though the tribunal's award on interest might have higher chances of surviving challenges even if the interest is more than requested, the tribunal should, as always, make

272 See section 5.3.1.
273 See further Chapter VII.
274 See, *e.g.*, ILA, *ILA Report on Inherent Powers of Arbitral Tribunals* (2014) p.10.
275 *Shipowner v. Time charterer*, Oberlandesgericht [Court of Appeal], Hamburg, 30 July 1998, XXV Y.B. Comm. Arb. 714, 716 (2000).

sure that the parties are heard. At the enforcement stage, public policy might also be of relevance, especially in countries that do not recognize awards on interest.[276]

5.4.2 Decision on costs

Decisions on costs might be financially significant. Additionally, the rules on cost allocation varies between jurisdictions. It is important to note, however, that decisions on costs, in the same way as decisions on interest, might be (inherently) left out for the tribunal to decide, especially considering that it could be the ultimate tool for the tribunal to discipline parties for their behavior during the proceedings.

When faced with the Article V(1)(c) challenge against the decision on costs, the enforcement court would inevitably review the scope of (i) parties' underlying agreement to arbitrate[277] as well as (ii) parties' submissions.[278] It will also take into account public policy of country of enforcement. This analysis will be similar to the one already explained above.[279] Therefore, generally speaking, the tribunal will award costs in accordance with the tribunal's agreement to arbitrate, when asked and if it does not violate public policy.

Consequently, the award on costs was enforced in a case when

> [...] petitioners agreed to the award of such fees by placing a request for "reasonable attorney's fees" in their demand for arbitration. [...] Petitioners also acquiesced in the award of such fees by requesting attorney's fees in their post-hearing briefs [...] as well as by failing to object to such fees during the final arguments on April 15, 1993. [...] [P]etitioners objected to the award of attorney's fees only after the arbitrators had rendered the May Award, at which point it was clear that any attorney's fees to be awarded would be awarded to respondents.[280]

In another case it was held that "*[s]ince we find the arbiters' authority to reach the main decision was within the scope of the letter agreement, it follows [that] the arbiters also had the authority to award costs and fees for obtaining the arbitral decision.*"[281]

Importantly, the tribunal's decision on costs may take into account the parties' conduct during the proceedings. A decision on costs will be therefore a managerial decision of the arbitral tribunal, who should be able to sanction delaying tactics of the parties.

276 Blackaby et al. (2015) pp.527-528. See also section 4.4.
277 See section 3.1.
278 See section 3.2.
279 See section 5.3.1 and section 5.4.1.
280 *Spector v. Torenberg*, 852 F. Supp. 201, 210 (S.D.N.Y. 1994).
281 *Mgmt. & Tech. Consultants S.A. v. Parsons-Jurden Int'l Corp.*, 820 F.2d 1531, 1534–35 (9th Cir. 1987).

Consequently, the tribunal's decision on costs may survive the challenge at the enforcement stage even if it is not in line with the parties' request.[282]

5.4.3 Decision on procedure

The procedural decisions of an arbitral tribunal serve a significant role in the arbitral process. They are, generally, of managerial nature. By no means shall Article V(1)(c) of the Convention be considered as a backdoor for the review of the merits of the award or the arbitral tribunal's procedural rulings.[283] The procedural rulings do not fit within the scope of the "excess of mandate" type of challenge.[284] In the context of the challenge at the enforcement stage, one should consider Article V(1)(d) of the Convention instead.[285] In the relevant part, Article V(1)(d) of the Convention reads that the award may be refused recognition and enforcement when "*[...] the arbitral procedure was not in accordance with the agreement of the parties, or, failing such agreement, was not in accordance with the law of the country where the arbitration took place [...].*"[286]

A similar conclusion was reached by an English enforcement court. In *Minmetals Germany GmbH v. Ferco Steel Ltd*, the court held that:

> The function of this exception [i.e. Art. V(1)(c) of the Convention] is to exclude from enforcement awards made on issues falling outside those which were referred for decision to the arbitrators. The vice of the awards upon which Ferco rely is the arbitrators' reliance on evidence derived from their own investigations and not previously provided to Ferco. That evidence, however, went to a central issue within the overall dispute referred to arbitration, namely what loss had been caused to Minmetals by Ferco's breaches of contract. Whether in relying upon that evidence or in omitting to disclose it to Ferco

282 More and more, the tribunal will find the power to sanction the parties' conduct in the applicable arbitration rules. See, *e.g.*, Art. 38(5) of the (draft) 2021 ICC Rules, Art. 38(5) of the 2017 ICC Rules, and Art. 37(5) of the ICC 2012 Rules. See also Chapter VII below.

283 Born, *International Commercial Arbitration* (2009) p.2801 ("*Challenges to awards under Article V(1)(c) are sometimes (but mistakenly) based on objections to the arbitrators' substantive contract interpretations or legal conclusions, or to the arbitrators' procedural rulings. In neither instance is a true Article V(1)(c) defense present. Rather, the defendant seeks to characterize a substantive objection to the tribunal's decision (which is not permitted by Article V) or a complaint about the fairness of the arbitral procedures (which is dealt with by Articles V(1)(b) or V(1)(d)) as a jurisdictional claim. In particular, arbitral awards are not infrequently challenged on the grounds that the arbitrators exceeded their authority in awarding particular damages or other relief.*"). See also section 4.4.

284 Born, *International Commercial Arbitration* (2014) p.3555 ("*The same basic analysis applies to claims that recognition should be denied under Article V(1)(c) because of the arbitrators' procedural rulings. This is in fact a complaint about the fairness of the arbitral procedures or the arbitrators' compliance with the parties' agreed arbitral procedures, which is properly dealt with under Articles V(1)(b) or V(1)(d).*").

285 Or else, Art. V(1)(b) of the Convention. See also section 4.4.

286 See Art. V(1)(d) of the Convention.

> the tribunal acted in accordance with the CIETAC rules or with any other procedural requirements of Chinese law is entirely irrelevant to the question whether the tribunal's decision was inside or outside 'the scope of the submission'. That scope falls to be defined by reference to the issues to be resolved by the arbitrators and not by reference to the procedure to be adopted for that purpose. This is clear beyond doubt from the wording of s. 103(2)(c) which expressly covers deviation of the actual procedure from the agreed procedure.[287]

All in all, parties resisting recognition and enforcement should be cautious what grounds they employ for challenge; in the case of the tribunal's procedural decisions, Article V(1)(d) of the Convention is a more sensible solution.

6 Conclusions

Article V of the New York Convention is often perceived as the heart of the Convention. It protects parties from grievous mischief of the arbitral tribunal. It is only logical that the mechanism against the "excess of mandate" type of violation is also introduced within the ambit of said provision.

It is noteworthy, however, that the enforcement courts respect the underlying principles of the New York Convention and apply Article V narrowly, giving a great deference to the tribunal's legal findings. Additionally, the starting point for the enforcement courts' analysis is the presumption that the arbitral tribunal had acted within its authority. Taking into account the limited review of the content of the award, the low success rate of the Article V(1)(c) challenge is not surprising. It can be therefore argued that defeating the arbitral tribunal's conclusions upon the alleged "excess of mandate" type of challenge is rather theoretical.

Article V(1)(c) of the Convention does not have a uniform interpretation. It is because the language remains unclear, repetitive and vexatious, which unnecessarily burdens the process of interpretation. On the one hand, it has been suggested that Article V(1)(c) of the Convention focuses on the issue of the scope of jurisdiction only, on the other hand, arguably, the broad notion of "submission to arbitration" may cover not only the notion of the agreement to arbitrate but also the parties' subsequent submissions. The better view is to follow the second interpretation allowing the Article V(1)(c) challenge to be employed in *ultra* or *extra petita* context.

287 *Minmetals Germany GmbH v. Ferco Steel Ltd* [1999] C.L.C. 647 at [656].

Not least important is the fact that the "excess of mandate" type of defense can be successfully invoked *only* against substantial findings of the arbitral tribunal which are different or higher than the parties' claims. Therefore, the court's review should be restricted to the mere comparison of what the parties claimed and what they have been awarded. It has been recapped by the clear-cut provision in the Miami Draft which reads that the award shall be refused recognition if "*the relief granted in the award is more than, or different from, the relief sought in the arbitration.*" By no means should the Article V(1)(c) challenge amount to appeal against the arbitration award, nor should it be allowed against procedural findings of the arbitral tribunal.

Additionally, the analysis of the case law indicates that even when the allegations of the party resisting enforcement are sound (for example when the tribunal awarded damages which were explicitly excluded from the contract), the courts are rather unwilling to refuse enforcement of the arbitral award.

As tempting as it may be, the arbitral tribunal's decisions regarding applicable law as a part of the arbitral tribunal's substantive findings should not be tested by the enforcement courts. Having in mind that modern arbitration is a legal process (based on law), it is within the arbitral tribunal's discretion to choose the applicable law. Arguably, although it is a discretion in a legal sense, finding the applicable law is the professional duty of the arbitral panel. For this reason, the arbitral tribunal willing to produce an enforceable award should carefully motivate and explain the legal underpinning of the decision. This professional duty will remain intact even when the arbitral tribunal is allowed to decide in equity (therefore acting as *amiable compositeur* or deciding *ex aequo et bono*).

Reaching decisions based on the general notion of equity or fairness without express consent from the parties will generally be open for a challenge at the enforcement stage. The better view, however, is to challenge such a tribunal's excessive undertaking under the Article V(1)(d) challenge rather than under the "excess of mandate" type of challenge. One should note, however, that even when the tribunal is duly authorized by the parties, it will be appropriate for the arbitrators, before accepting the mandate of *amiable composition*, to examine whether the parties are actually able to vest the arbitral tribunal with the power to decide in equity.

From time to time the defense introduced in Article V(1)(c) of the Convention competes with the other defenses mentioned in Article V(1) of the Convention. Determining which defense should apply might be decisive for a successful challenge. Again, taking into account the narrow interpretation of Article V(1)(c) of the Convention, a party resisting enforcement might consider invoking the isolated "excess of mandate" defense only when the relief granted is different or somewhat higher than the relief sought.

Last, but not least, the importance of public policy should be highlighted. Due to the fact that the notion of public policy is dynamic and elusive, it is very appealing to the parties that apply public policy defense as their last line of defense. It can be argued that the impact of public policy on the "arbitral tribunal's mandate" is limited to instances where the relief granted violates the very basic notion of justice in the country of enforcement. In rare circumstances, it might be the case when the award infringes mandatory laws (however not all of them) or is based on legal instruments unknown to the legal system of the country of enforcement (for example granting punitive damages).

Considering the rather unclear scope of application and the pro-arbitration philosophy that underlies the Convention, one should conclude that Article V(1)(c) of the Convention will be successful only in exceptional circumstances.

Part II

VII The Comparative Law Analysis

1 Preliminary remarks

1.1 Setting the scene

The previous chapters were dedicated to explaining how different national courts approach allegations that the tribunal exceeded the mandate given to it. As already explained in the introductory chapter the (non)compliance with the mandate can be tested at two stages of the post-award process: during the setting-aside proceedings at the seat of the arbitral tribunal and during the enforcement phase in the country where the award is brought for enforcement.[1] This, in turn, makes both the national arbitration acts and the New York Convention relevant for the research at hand: the national legislation becomes primarily relevant when the award is being challenged at the setting-aside phase, with the New York Convention being the ultimate tool for resisting enforcement at the enforcement stage.[2] Taking into account that the challenge against an arbitral award can be brought at two different post-award stages, the comparison should correspond to such a two-level division.

In principle, the analysis will not follow the classical comparative law divide between common law and civil law systems, because it is not as useful as in other areas of law. Instead, arguably, a line should be drawn between the Model Law jurisdictions (that includes both civil and common law countries *i.a.* Canada, Germany, Poland, Singapore etc.) and jurisdictions that do not follow the Model Law structure (*i.a.* France, England, the U.S., the Netherlands, Switzerland and Sweden etc.). One may observe that the states that do not follow the Model Law scheme are the major arbitration centers with established arbitration practice.[3] The rationale for *not* following the Model Law might be explained with the goal of preserving their competitive edge, providing for a unique set of tools

1 See Chapter I.

2 Generally, an arbitral award can be enforced, even if it does not adhere to all requirements envisaged by the New York Convention, when a party is able to rely on other enforcement mechanism, for example, on national legislation. See Art. VII of the New York Convention, with a comment *i.a.* by Van den Berg, *The New York Convention of 1958: Towards Uniform Judicial Interpretation* (1981) pp.81-90. In cases of the "excess of mandate" challenge this solution will be rather moot and for that reason will not be discussed further.

3 De Ly, *Paradigmatic Changes – Uniformity, Diversity, Due Process and Good Administration of Justice: The Next Thirty Years* (2016) p.23 ("*Notwithstanding the major breakthrough brought about by the Model Law, the picture remains one of divergence in the western world with major arbitration centres in London, Paris, New York, Zurich or Geneva having arbitration laws based on different traditions, assumptions, approaches and rules.*").

sought by the users of international arbitration.[4] Selected representatives of these countries constitute a sample for the comparison at hand.

As explained above, the comparison should be made at two levels. At the first level, the comparison between different mechanisms to challenge the alleged excess needs to be carried out on the national level. It means that, one should examine the Model Law, which, as explained, constitutes the framework that national legislators (from both civil and common law countries) may rely upon while drafting their arbitration acts. The Model Law approach, in turn, needs to be contrasted with the rules applicable to the setting-aside procedure in France,[5] England[6] and the U.S.[7] These four legal systems may be evaluated horizontally at the same level.

The second level, which is the enforcement stage, requires an analysis of the application of the New York Convention. Mostly, national courts, while interpreting the Convention, do that in a uniform and consistent manner.[8] In principle, they also resist the temptation of transplanting the national concepts at the international level. It does not change the fact, however, that the challenging parties often keep insisting on relying on those alluring (national) notions. Therefore, the vertical comparison might also be relevant.

The comparison, to a large extent, will follow the structure used in the previous chapters. It will start with a brief summary of the prerequisites for filing the motion to challenge the arbitral award and the reflections on the national courts' standards of review of said awards. Further, it is necessary to describe the different sources for the tribunal's mandate. Consequently, one should identify and contrast different mechanisms available for challenging the arbitral tribunal's excess of mandate. Finally, the application of these tools should be tested against different decisions undertaken by the arbitral tribunal during the arbitral process.

Before going further into details, it is reasonable to put the comparison in context, which may explain how the different systems evolved (section 1.2) and operate (sections 1.3 and section 1.4).

1.2 *"If it ain't broke don't fix it" and the legislative timeline*

Chronologically, the Federal Arbitration Act is the oldest arbitration act analyzed herein that is still in force. It was enacted in 1925, based on the similar (New York) state statute, which was tailored specifically to address the need of merchants. At the time, England

4 See also section 1.3.
5 See Chapter III.
6 See Chapter IV.
7 See Chapter V.
8 See Chapter VI.

already had its arbitration act but the courts in England were known for the "*judicial hostility*" which Americans wanted to minimize.[9] The FAA applies ever since and includes annulment mechanisms against an arbitral award that was made with the excess of the tribunal's powers or the imperfect execution of their powers.

The second mature instrument that is being compared here is the 1958 New York Convention. It superseded the 1927 Geneva Convention and it intrinsically contributed to the development of international arbitration by limiting the burden that is imposed on the enforcement of the arbitral bargain and by harmonizing the interpretation of issues surrounding arbitration.[10] Notably, however, the challenge mechanism regarding the excess of the terms and the scope of the submission to arbitration has not been clarified in the New York Convention, which means that it did not improve the vagueness of the proviso in national law which has remained unchanged for almost a century now.

The success of the New York Convention led the UNCITRAL to introduce in 1985 the framework legislation known as the UNCITRAL Model Law. The Model Law has been further revised in 2006, but those changes, in principle, do not affect the research at hand, because they did not relate to the challenge mechanism at the post-award stage. Importantly, however, the Model Law setting-aside mechanism has been structured on the text of the New York Convention which guaranteed (or at least aimed to guarantee) the convergence in application of both instruments.

Following the chronology of enactment, the English Arbitration Act of 1996 is another legal system reflected upon. The historical context is, however, of particular importance here. Before the enactment of the 1996 Act, the English arbitration system and its judicial review mechanism were criticized as being incomprehensible and inaccessible to international users.[11] In particular, it allowed the courts to hear the challenge not only on the elusive statutory grounds (*i.e.* where the tribunal had misconducted itself or the proceedings)[12] but also under the courts' inherent jurisdiction. The English arbitration regime dramatically changed with the introduction of the 1996 Act. The Act includes an exhaustive catalogue of grounds upon which the award can be challenged including, among others, the "excess of powers" ground.

The most recent arbitration statute that is being compared is the French Arbitration Act, a part of the French Code of Civil Procedure. It was amended in 2011 in order to reflect modern arbitration practice and it does so successfully. Yet, in the context of a challenge against the tribunal's failure to comply with its mandate, not much has

9 The evolution of the English setting-aside procedure has been discussed in Chapter IV.

10 For further reading, see Van den Berg, *The New York Convention of 1958: Towards Uniform Judicial Interpretation* (1981).

11 For further reading, see Chapter IV.

12 See Chapter IV.

changed.[13] The elusive and potentially capacious concept of "the excess of mandate" introduced at the beginning of the 1980s[14] has survived the changes in the system.

The first preliminary observation is that the "excess of mandate" challenges remain unchanged notwithstanding other alterations made in the legal instruments analyzed. Possibly this is because courts in respective jurisdictions are reluctant to accept the arguments that are brought by dissatisfied parties to arbitration and do not allow a broad interpretation of the relevant provisions. At the same time, the need for change is recognized by some scholars and in some jurisdictions.[15]

1.3 *Harmony and divergence: the impact of the Model Law*

As highlighted above in the first section,[16] international arbitration regimes can be divided into those that follow (even in *verbatim*) the text of the Model Law and those that prefer to maintain their own distinctive shape and status. The latter mostly applies to the developed arbitration systems (such as the U.S., France and England) with a longer historical standing than that of the Model Law.

At the same time, the impact of the Model Law remained unprecedented, even with regard to countries that did not decide to adopt it. It is important to note, for example, that the drafters of the English Arbitration Act took into careful consideration the work of the UNCITRAL and the solutions introduced in its Model Law. Consequently, many of the principles that underlie the Model Law have also been included in the English Arbitration Act. Accordingly, the English Arbitration Act envisages that the setting-aside mechanism consists of a closed catalogue of grounds to challenge. As will be shown however, it nonetheless maintained its distinctive features from the Model Law challenge mechanism. Additionally, if one looks at the (draft) Restatement on International Commercial Arbitration prepared by the American Law Institute, one may conclude that the

13 At least to the jurisprudence and leading scholars. See, however, Chapter III where it is argued that the cosmetic changes made to the provision may give rise to the new legal arguments and more excessive use of the "excess of mandate" provision.

14 For the analysis of the 1980s reform including a comparison with the prior legislation, see, *i.a.*, Carbonneau, *The Reform of the French Procedural Law on Arbitration: An Analytical Commentary on the Decree of May 14, 1980* (1981) pp.273-339.

15 Briefly speaking, see for example, Albert Jan Van den Berg proposal for the new New York Convention (available at http://www.newyorkconvention.org/draft+convention [last accessed 28 April 2018]. In the context of the "excess of mandate" challenge see also changes implemented in the (new) Dutch Arbitration Act (see Art. 1065(1)(c) and Art. 1065(4) of the Dutch CCP) requiring the "violation" of the mandate to be serious in nature and the changes proposed in the Swedish Arbitration Act (see, *e.g.*, http://kluwerarbitrationblog.com/2015/10/17/time-to-upgrade-review-of-the-swedish-arbitration-act/ [last accessed 29 April 2018] and http://arbitrationblog.kluwerarbitration.com/2018/04/09/the-swedish-government-revives-efforts-to-modernise-the-arbitration-act/ [last accessed 29 April 2018].

16 See section Chapter VII.

recommendations therein would effectively lead to the alteration of the existing system of the post-award relief into the mechanism that follows the Model Law structure.

Similarly, in the U.S., the (draft) Restatement advocates the use of the New York Convention's grounds for resisting enforcement as grounds for setting aside in international arbitration cases with the seat in the U.S. Such a recommendation leads to the modification of the existing system of post-award relief in a way that effectively transforms the U.S. annulment system into a Model Law one.

This leads to the second opening reflection, *i.e.*, the importance and the harmonizing effect of the apparatus prepared by the UNCITRAL (and drafters of the New York Convention beforehand) as well as the appreciation for the principles contained in these uniform instruments.

1.4 Apples and oranges: distinctive features of analyzed systems

Notwithstanding the effect that the Model Law has had globally, it is necessary to explain a few particularities of the non-Model Law arbitration systems in order to understand how these regimes operate.[17]

At the outset, one should look at the U.S. arbitration system. First, it is organized judicially on two levels: state and federal.[18] Secondly, arbitration legislation is also organized on state and federal level.[19] Thirdly, due to so-called "*Arbitration Trilogies*" introduced by the U.S. Supreme Court since the 1980s, the arbitral system in the U.S. has changed significantly and, nowadays, the FAA does not resemble the same instrument that was introduced at the beginning of the twentieth century. Instead, following the meaning that was given to the FAA by the U.S. Supreme Court's Justices it rather preempts the use of state legislation on arbitration.[20]

Importantly, the U.S. arbitration regime nowadays covers not only commercial but also (*i.a.*) consumer and employment disputes which constitutes a relevant factor in the way the system operates. For some time now, attempts are being made to limit the availability of predispute agreements to arbitrate *i.a.* consumer or employment disputes.[21] Yet, the Arbitration Fairness Act has not been enacted by Congress despite the fact that it was introduced several times for a discussion and it is unlikely that it will catch its momentum any time soon.

---

17 In this section the systems will be considered in the order of their enactment.

18 See Chapter V.

19 See, for example, the Federal Arbitration Act and the California (state) legislation based on the Model Law (http://www.uncitral.org/uncitral/en/uncitral_texts/arbitration/1985Model_arbitration_status.html [last accessed 14 August 2020].

20 See Chapter V.

21 See Chapter V.

As pointed out above, the Restatement on International Commercial Arbitration, when completed, will be a strong persuasive authority. In turn, it may influence the way American courts will apply the FAA. If the ALI's postulates are accepted, the arbitration system will effectively become a dualistic one with a separate set of rules applicable to domestic and international arbitration.

A similar dualistic approach is a distinctive feature of the French system.[22] The division is made in order to attract the users of international arbitration. The French international arbitration regime is broadly praised for its liberal stand allowing a great freedom for parties to shape their arbitrations as they see fit. It may be contrasted with the domestic system which has a more traditional undertone.[23] Importantly, the international system, however, is not completely independent from the domestic one.[24]

Finally, the English system is known, for example, for its (opt-in) mechanism allowing the parties to appeal on point of law. This solution, albeit nowadays limited in scope, can be traced to the former arbitration regime where national judges had much greater powers over the conduct of arbitration and the way arbitrators were fulfilling their mandate. It also leads to the conclusion that history plays a great role in understanding the interaction between courts and arbitral tribunals in England.

The final preliminary observation is that non-Model Law systems are structured based on their own ideas and values that also need to be taken into account during the comparison, despite the relevance of the Model Law and its approach.

2 Court standard of review of arbitral awards

One of the key features of the international arbitration system is the deference given by the national courts' judges to the arbitral tribunals' conclusions (section 2.1). In consequence of the pro-arbitration bias, courts refrain from reviewing the merits of the award (section 2.2) and, to the extent possible, make efforts to remedy deficiencies in the arbitral awards (section 2.3). These points will be briefly addressed below.

22 Also see, *e.g.*, the Singaporean arbitration regime.

23 The question that follows is whether it may influence the perception of the mandate. In other words, whether there is a difference in the tribunal's mandate in domestic and international arbitration.

24 See Chapter III.

2.1 *The pro-arbitration approach of national courts in the context of the challenge*

All analyzed systems are renowned for their pro-arbitration standing. This pro-arbitration standing is not included under a single proviso, however. Instead, it is an underlying spirit of the international arbitration regime that persuades the courts to limit their intervention in the arbitral process. At the post-award stage, it means that the possibility of challenge is limited in time, with only an exhaustive list of grounds that can be invoked for a challenge. Additionally, the listed grounds are to be interpreted narrowly. Importantly, courts accept the exceptional character of the post-award revision and they respect the finality of the award as well.

In the Model Law jurisdictions, the exhaustive character of the grounds to set the award aside is confirmed, for example, by the *travaux préparatoires* of the German Arbitration Act. As explained by scholars, "*[t]he grounds for setting aside are exhaustively listed in s.1059 para 2 ZPO as the wording ('only') demonstrates.*"[25] Also national courts from the Model Law jurisdictions adhere to the narrow standards of judicial control at the post-award stage.[26]

Similarly, Article 1518 of the FCCP reads that an action to set aside is the only available recourse against an award. It is also confirmed that the list under Article 1520 of the FCCP is exhaustive[27] and the merits of the award should not be reviewed.[28] The leading principle of the English Arbitration Act is the "non-interventionist" approach of the courts in arbitral matters.[29] The drafters of the EAA ensured therefore that the list of irregularities against which the award can be challenged is limited,[30] with the irregularity having a high standard of being "serious" and causing "substantial injustice".[31] In one case, even before the 1996 reform, the court held that "*[...] as a matter of general approach, the courts strive to uphold*

---

25 Kreindler et al., *Commercial Arbitration in Germany* (2016) p.335. The authors refer the *travaux préparatoires* of the German Arbitration Act, namely to the Government bill, BT-Drucks 13/5274 p.58.

26 See, *e.g.*, *Quintette Coal Ltd. v. Nippon Steel Corporation*, 1991 CanLII 5708 (BC CA), par. 32, http://canlii.ca/t/231lq#par32, [last accessed 14 August 2020], *Bayview Irrigation District #11 v. United Mexican States*, 2008 CanLII 22120 (ON SC), par. 63, http://canlii.ca/t/1wwtf#par63 [last accessed 14 August 2020], *CRW Joint Operation v. PT Perusahaan Gas Negara (Persero) TBK* [2011] SGCA 33, [2011] 4 SLR 305 at [25].

27 See, *e.g.*, (albeit under the previous setting-aside mechanism) CA Paris, 10 January 2012, Rev. Arb. 2012, p.203 that reads that "*the action to set aside in international matters is available only under grounds exhaustively listed in Article 1502 of the Code of Civil Procedure.*" ("*Le recours en annulation d'une sentence arbitrale rendue en matière internationale n'est ouvert que dans les cas limitativement énumérés par l'article 1502 du Code de procédure civile.*"). For further reading, see Bensaude (2015) p.1176, and Loquin (2015) p.420.

28 See also Chapter III. See also section 2.2 below.

29 See Section 1(c) of the EAA.

30 DAC, *Report on the Arbitration Bill* (1996) para 282. For the summary, see also *Petroships Pte Ltd v. Petec Trading and Investment Corporation and Ors* [2001] 2 Lloyd's Rep. 348.

31 For further reading, see Chapter IV and section 3 below.

arbitration awards. They do not approach them with a meticulous legal eye endeavoring to pick holes, inconsistencies and faults in awards and with the objective of upsetting or frustrating the process of arbitration."[32] Similarly, the U.S. Supreme Court held that "*courts may vacate an arbitrator's decision 'only in very unusual circumstances'.*"[33] Such a strong federal policy favoring arbitration guides lower courts in their decisions on the vacatur of arbitral awards.[34]

Unsurprisingly, the ultimate goal of the New York Convention is to ensure that foreign arbitral awards are recognized and enforced in the territory of the Contracting States. Accordingly, "*[c]ourts approach enforcement under the New York Convention with strong pro-enforcement bias and a pragmatic, flexible and non-formalistic approach. This commendable liberal attitude fully exploits the potential of this most successful treaty [...].*"[35]

For example, a U.S. court persuasively held that:

> The 1958 Convention's basic thrust was to liberalize procedures for enforcing foreign arbitral awards[.] While the Geneva Convention placed the burden of proof on the party seeking enforcement of a foreign arbitral award and did not circumscribe the range of available defenses to those enumerated in the convention, the 1958 Convention clearly shifted the burden of proof to the party defending against enforcement and limited his defenses to seven set forth in Article V.[36]

It has been also established that the recognition and enforcement can only be refused under the limited grounds listed in the Convention, with no availability of review of the merits.[37]

The general pro-arbitration thrust of the analyzed legal systems leads many of the challenges against the tribunal's actions to inevitable failure. At the same time, the exceptional recourse against the award gives the courts a possibility to remedy the grievous wrongdoings of the arbitral tribunals.

---

32 *Zermalt Holdings v. Nu-Life Upholstery Repairs* [1985] 2 EGLR 14, as referred to in *ABB AG v. Hochtief Airport GMBH, Athens International Airport S.A.* [2006] EWHC 388 (Comm), 2006 WL 755473 at [64].

33 *Oxford Health Plans LLC v. Sutter*, 133 S. Ct. 2064, 186 L. Ed. 2d 113 (2013).

34 For further reading, see Chapter V.

35 ICCA, *ICCA's Guide to the Interpretation of the 1958 New York Convention* (2011) p.71.

36 *Parsons & Whittemore Overseas Co., Inc. v. Societe Generale De L'Industrie Du Papier (RAKTA)*, 508 F.2d 969, 973 (2d Cir. 1974).

37 See also Chapter VI.

2.2 The scope of the court's review

The principle that the courts should not review the merits of the tribunal's decisions is closely aligned with the pro-arbitration policy discussed above.[38] As noted, the courts usually accept their limited role in the arbitral process and acknowledge that reassessment of the merits should not be made. Generally, such a narrow scope of the review can be implied from the exhaustive list of irregularities that may give rise to the parties' challenge at the post-award stage.[39] The problem at hand, however, is how "the excess of mandate" type of challenge is reviewed by the court.

The considerable amount of friction arises from the fact that the grounds for challenge are generally non-exclusive in the sense that the same factual underpinning may give rise to different venues for the post-award challenge. In particular, the challenge against the mandate might not be immediately distinguishable from the challenge of the tribunal's jurisdiction. Yet, the way it is tested, *i.e.* the scope of the court's review, might be (and should be) different. In instances where there are legitimate concerns as to the tribunal's jurisdiction (namely, no valid or existing agreement to arbitrate) the court's scrutiny may be exceptionally enhanced. If, however, the objections relate to the tribunal's mandate, the heightened level of a court's review may effectively result in a review of the merits of the award.

Difficulties in balancing the scope of the review as to the "excess of mandate" type of challenge exist in the Model Law jurisdictions. The reason is that the rule of Article 34(2)(a)(iii) of the Model Law is usually implemented without any changes despite the fact that it is not easy to comprehend.[40] The question therein is whether this proviso deals with the scope of the tribunal's jurisdiction or the tribunal's mandate.[41] As explained elsewhere, the better view is to restrict the interpretation of this provision to the "excess of mandate" type of challenge and to deal with all jurisdictional concerns under Article 34(2)(a)(i) of the Model Law. This way, the sensible solution for the courts when faced with the Article 34(2)(a)(iii) challenge would be to apply the general rule and to give deference to the tribunal's findings (and refrain from reevaluating the tribunal's decision).

Under the French international arbitration regime, "*le principe de non-révision au fond*" is also a leading principle. Accordingly, the courts' control going beyond the scope of Article 1520 of the CCP is prohibited.[42] Importantly, the French setting-aside court will be able to analyze all the legal and factual elements having implications on the mandate

---

38 See section 2.1.

39 See section 2.1 above.

40 See, *e.g.*, Art. 1059(2)(1)(c) of the GCCP, also Section 3(1) and Section 24 of the SIAA. Occasionally it is modified, however, see *e.g.* Art. 1206(1)(3) of the Polish CCP.

41 For further reading, see Chapter II.

42 For further reading, see Chapter III.

of the arbitral tribunal.[43] Usually, however, the tribunal's findings remain respected. The English system proves to be, again, the most detailed one. Section 67 of the EAA deals with the tribunal's jurisdiction and, according to authorities, many courts consider that they owe no deference to the tribunal's jurisdictional findings (including the question of the scope of the substantive jurisdiction)[44] and prefer to rely on their own independent findings on facts and law.[45] Conversely, Section 68 of the EAA which includes an exhaustive catalogue of serious irregularities,[46] including the "excess of powers" ground for challenge, was introduced to limit judicial interference with the award. In addition, it imposes two conditions (the irregularity has to be serious and cause substantial injustice) that have to be satisfied in order for the court to accept the challenge. In the U.S., the standard of review under Section 10 of the FAA is extremely narrow as well. What naturally follows, is that the courts may not review and correct the tribunal's conclusions.[47] They will be allowed, however, to independently determine if the grounds for vacatur exist. It is necessary to add, however, that the excess of powers ground has a rather broad scope, including jurisdictional/threshold issues,[48] which means that, similar to the Model Law system, certain difficulties may occur with regard to the level of scrutiny exercised by the courts.[49] Arguably, possible complications may also arise in the context of judicially created grounds for vacatur (assuming they are still available to the parties)[50] that have a potential to interfere with the tribunal's conclusions on the merits.[51]

Finally, national courts[52] at the enforcement stage routinely refuse to review the merits of the case.[53] In the words of one court: "*[...] the animating principle of the [New York]*

---

43 See, *e.g.*, Cour de Cassation Civ 1ère, 6 October 2010, *Fondation Albert Abela Family v. Fondation Joseph Abela Family*, Rev. Arb. 2010, p.969.

44 Notably, the question of the scope of the substantive jurisdiction includes the determination of "*what matters have been submitted to arbitration in accordance with the agreement to arbitrate*". See Section 30(1) of the EAA. For further reading, see also Chapter IV.

45 See Chapter IV.

46 Therefore, it is prohibited for the court to add more irregularities to the list.

47 See, *e.g.*, *United Paperworkers Int'l Union, AFL-CIO v. Misco, Inc.*, 484 U.S. 29, 36, 108 S. Ct. 364, 370, 98 L. Ed. 2d 286 (1987) ("*the courts play only a limited role when asked to review the decision of an arbitrator. The courts are not authorized to reconsider the merits of an award even though the parties may allege that the award rests on errors of fact or on misinterpretation of the contract.*"). For further reading, see Chapter V.

48 See Chapter V.

49 One has to assess if the objections raised under the excess of powers challenge are of jurisdictional or non-jurisdictional nature. The latter resembles the "excess of mandate" type of challenge. See also reflections regarding Art. 34(2)(a)(iii) of the ML under this section.

50 See *Hall Street Assocs, LLC v. Mattel, Inc.* 552 U.S. 576, 128 S. Ct. 1396, 170 L. Ed. 2d 254 (2008).

51 For example, testing whether the arbitral award "manifestly disregarded the law", "drew its essence from the agreement of the parties". For further reading, see Chapter V.

52 Especially courts from the jurisdictions analyzed herein.

53 See, for example, *Ukrainian dealer v. German manufacturer*, Oberlandesgericht, Munich, 30 July 2012 and Bundesgerichtshof, 23 April 2013, XXXIX Y.B. Comm. Arb. 394 (2014), *Joint Stock Company A v. Joint Stock Company B*, Higher Regional Court of Munich, 34 Sch 10/11, 14 November 2011, XXXVII Y.B. Comm.

Convention, that the Courts should review arbitrations for procedural regularity but resist inquiry into the substantive merits of awards, is clear from the notes on this subject by the Secretary-General of the United Nations."[54] Another court added that "*[e]xtensive judicial review frustrates the basic purpose of arbitration, which is to dispose of disputes quickly and avoid the expense and delay of extended court proceedings.*"[55] Since Article V(1)(c) of the New York Convention has almost the same wording as Article 34(2)(a)(iii) of the Model Law, the risks related to the scope of the review are, arguably, similar.[56] Potentially, however, the tension may even be bigger, because the enforcement proceedings of the same award might be brought to a number of enforcement courts. If different courts adopt different standard of review, it will keep up with expectations of the spirit behind the New York Convention. Consequently, a high degree of deference should be welcomed with regard to court's control under Article V(1)(c) of the New York Convention.

Similar to the previous section, it is concluded that court should be able to control and remedy serious deficiencies of arbitral decision-making process. It does not change the fact, however, that such a control should not trigger deciding the case anew by the court.

2.3 *Remedies at the national courts' disposal*

In the analyzed jurisdictions, the courts are given similar set of remedial tools, which essential aim is to save the award if only possible. The more detailed analysis has been provided under chapters discussing each legal system separately.[57] In principle, the courts may (i) save a "healthy" part of the award if it is severable from the part affected by default. Depending on the jurisdiction the courts may also be authorized, for example, (ii) to remit the award back to the tribunal to eliminate the defect, or even (iii) to correct the award in limited and exceptional circumstances.

The Model Law system, based on the idea already developed under the New York Convention regime is representative for the scope of remedial powers given to the courts. According to Article 34(2)(a)(iii) of the Model Law,[58] if it is possible to separate the decisions on matters submitted to arbitration from decisions on matters not so submitted, "*only that part of the award which contains decisions on matters not submitted to arbitration may*

Arb. 231 (2012), *Int'l Standard Elec. Corp. v. Bridas Sociedad Anonima Petrolera, Indus. Y Comercial*, 745 F. Supp. 172, 182 (S.D.N.Y. 1990).

54 *Int'l Standard Elec. Corp. v. Bridas Sociedad Anonima Petrolera, Indus. Y Comercial*, 745 F. Supp. 172, 178 (S.D.N.Y. 1990).

55 *Parsons & Whittemore Overseas Co., Inc. v. Societe Generale De L'Industrie Du Papier (RAKTA)*, 508 F.2d 969, 977 (2d Cir. 1974).

56 See reflections as to the Model Law above.

57 See chapters Chapter II-Chapter V.

58 The question, whether this standard should apply also to other grounds for setting aside falls outside the scope of this research.

be set aside […]." Additionally, the power to remit the case to the arbitral tribunal is also made available, but only upon the parties' request.[59]

In France, partial setting aside is also available. According to Article 1527(2) of the FCCP the part of the award not overturned by the court shall be deemed enforced. This would be a principal remedy for the courts. Conversely to the Model Law courts, the French courts will not, in principle, have a power to remit the case back to the tribunal (under the French international arbitration regime).[60] Notably, however, the French courts do not hesitate to sanction the abusive use of the right to set aside.[61] The English catalogue of remedies is the broadest one (of all reviewed jurisdictions) and it varies depending on whether the challenge is brought under Section 67 of the EAA (substantive jurisdiction), Section 68 of the EAA (serious irregularity) or Section 69 of the EAA (appeal on point of law). The whole catalogue has been introduced elsewhere.[62] In principle, however, one should note (i) that saving the healthy part of the award is always possible under the English regime,[63] irrespective of which challenge is used and (ii) that the court may remit the award back to the tribunal following the objections under Sections 68 and 69.[64] Finally, in the U.S., the Federal Arbitration Act, under Section 11, allows the courts to (*i.a.*) "*make an order modifying or correcting the award*".[65] Effectively, however, it leads to the same results as a partial vacatur.[66] According to Section 10(b) of the FAA, the remand[67] is available but only when "*an award is vacated and the time within which the agreement required the award to be made has not expired*". Following arguments of the the Restatement, in exceptional circumstances, the courts will be able to use the power to remand even without

59 See Art. 34(4) of the ML. Singapore did not alter this provision. Germany included the provision, albeit with a modification (Art. 1059(4) of the GCCP). Essentially, it allows the court to remit the case back to the tribunal after the setting aside of the award and not pending setting-aside proceedings as suggested in the Model Law. Not all jurisdictions adopted this provision, however. See as reported by Born, *International Commercial Arbitration* (2014) p.3153.

60 See Chapter III. That being said, one should observe that, in exceptional cases, application for revision ("*recourse en révision*") will be given to the parties. Then the tribunal should be addressed directly (Art. 1502(2) of the FCCP).

61 CA Paris, 21 January 1997, *Société Nu Swift PLC v. Société White Knight et autres*, Rev. Arb. 1997, p.429, CA Paris, 6 May 2004, *Carthago Films v. Babel Productions*, Rev. Arb. 2006, p.661.

62 See Chapter IV.

63 Either by setting aside only a part of the award or declaring only a part of the award to be of no effect. For further reading, see Chapter IV.

64 See Section 68(3)(a) and Section 69(7)(c) of the EAA. These provisions differ slightly in their wording.

65 See Chapter V.

66 For further reading, see Chapter V.

67 Which is the term used in the U.S. contemplating the court's reference back to the tribunal with the aim of eliminating the deficiencies in the award in order to salvage it.

vacating the award first.[68] Importantly, according to authorities, the courts in the U.S. can exercise such a power on their own motion.[69]

The enforcement courts, applying the New York Convention will also be allowed to sever and enforce the healthy part of the award even if some objections resulting from the "excess of mandate" type of the challenge were accepted. This can be found under Article V(1)(c) of the New York Convention.[70] Since the enforcement court does not exercise a supervisory role over the arbitration, other powers become redundant.

In conclusion, although some differences exist (*e.g.* whether powers can be exercised by the courts on its own motion or only following the parties' motion), the overarching aim of salvaging the award to the utmost is achieved in all jurisdictions.

3 Different standards for the "arbitral tribunal's mandate" and variations of recourse against its excess

In order to determine when (and whether) the "tribunal's mandate" is exceeded it is first necessary to identify its sources and limits (section 3.1). An initial observation worth noting is that in all reviewed jurisdictions said sources and limits remain the same. Only by having them defined is it possible to assess when the excess takes place. Secondly, it is sensible to discuss the use of different concepts within the analyzed legal regimes (section 3.2). Notably, although the structure of the mandate (*i.e.* what it is based on) is in principle the same, the concepts for challenging the excessive use of the mandate by the tribunal may vary (section 3.3). In addition, it is important to analyze how these grounds for challenge fit in the overall framework for testing the award for alleged deficiencies before the annulment or enforcement courts (section 3.4).

3.1 Limits to the arbitral tribunal's "mandate"

As highlighted in the introductory chapter of this study, the tribunal's mandate can be considered in two dimensions.[71] In the first one, the focus is on the contractual delegation of the parties to have their disputes resolved by (private) arbitral tribunals and not by national courts. The parties, however, would have lacked the authority to assign dispute resolution powers to the tribunal if the states had not accepted that arbitral tribunals are

68 Even though the FAA itself does not expressly authorize them to do so. See the Restatement (third tentative draft) pp.80-85. See also Chapter V.

69 See the Restatement (third tentative draft) p.82 and p.85.

70 As mentioned above, it has been a basis for the text of Art. 34(2)(a)(iii) of the ML.

71 See Chapter I.

capable of exercising the role of the judiciary. Sharing the state monopoly (of finally resolving the disputes between the parties) with the arbitral tribunals is the second dimension of the arbitral tribunal's mandate. Consequently, one can list the agreement to arbitrate (section 3.1.1), the parties' submissions (section 3.1.2) and mandatory rules of public policy character (section 3.1.3) as the sources structuring the tribunal's mandate.

3.1.1 Agreement to arbitrate

It is rather uncontroversial that the inquiry determining the confines of the arbitral tribunal's mandate should start with an investigation of the underlying agreement to arbitrate. On the one hand, the parties' initial consent to arbitrate mostly defines the limits to the actions the parties themselves may undertake or claims they themselves may bring before the arbitral tribunal at the later stage rather than explicitly define the scope of the tribunal's mandate. On the other hand, reference to the institutional rules in the agreement to arbitrate may shed some light on the parties' expectations as to the actions the tribunal may undertake.

As a brief summary, both the Model Law systems and non-Model Law ones recognize that the agreement to arbitrate may be concluded both before and after the disputes arises. If it is the former it will (usually) take the form of an arbitration clause,[72] if it is the latter it will take the form of a separate submission agreement.[73] Notably, if the agreement to arbitrate is introduced after the dispute arises, it may provide a more elaborate structure of the arbitral tribunal's mandate.

Additionally, it is necessary to point out that broadly drafted agreements to arbitrate will be given a generous interpretation by the reviewing courts in all analyzed legal systems. In the absence of a clear statement to the contrary (*i.e.* unless the agreement to arbitrate is drafted narrowly), the tribunal's discretion would often include all the disputes that have been brought by the parties.[74] Furthermore, as hinted above, it is generally accepted that the reference to the institutional rules in the agreement to arbitrate extends the framework on which the parties structure their intent and may further clarify the envisaged scope of the tribunal's mandate.[75]

Overall, the agreement to arbitrate is an essential element to determine the scope of the intended mandate. Yet, since it is usually drafted in a rather expansive manner, it

72 A separate agreement to arbitrate before the dispute arises is of course possible as well.

73 See for the Model Law: Art. 7(1) of the 1985 ML, Art. 7(1) of the 2006 ML (option I) or Art. 7 of the 2006 ML (option II). For the Germany Arbitration Act, see Art. 1029 of the GCCP (Art. 1029(2) in particular). For Singapore, see Section 2A(2) of the SIAA. For non-Model Law jurisdictions see Art. 1507 of the FCCP in France (albeit implicitly), Section 6(1) of the EAA in England and Section 2 of the FAA in the U.S. For further reading, see also Chapter II-Chapter V. At the enforcement stage, courts are also obliged to recognize agreements to arbitrate of existing or future disputes (Art. II(1) of the NYC).

74 See also sections 3.1.2 and 3.1.3. For further reading, see Chapter II-Chapter V.

75 For further reading, see also Chapter II-Chapter V.

requires additional inquiry into the parties' subsequent submissions in order to fully grasp what the tribunal is allowed.

3.1.2 Parties' (subsequent) submissions

Having in mind that the agreement to arbitrate provides only a scaffold for the arbitral tribunal's mandate, it is truly the parties' submissions that set the boundaries to the scope of the tribunal's mandate. Notably, however, these submissions may affect the mandate in two ways: either by limiting the scope of the initial (usually broad) agreement to arbitrate or potentially expand it.

All reviewed jurisdictions recognize the importance of the parties' submissions for defining the tribunal's adjudicative powers.[76] Furthermore, it is a general understanding that all the matters in dispute (thus claims over which the tribunal has a power) should be submitted (therefore defined) at the initial stage of proceedings, because it gives a clear indication of the constraints of the tribunal's mandate at the outset of the arbitration. Additionally, the parties' claims should fit within the scope of the agreement to arbitrate. If they do not, all the parties involved should unambiguously consent to such a modification.

Importantly, expressing a consent to the alteration of the agreement to arbitrate should be approached cautiously. If a party does not wish to extend the adjudicative powers of the tribunal, it should expressly voice its objections. Otherwise, its silence may be considered as a tacit acceptance and disqualify any challenge to such an extension at the post-award stage. This conclusion will equally be valid in cases where the new submissions do not go beyond the scope of the initial agreement to arbitrate, but expand claims originally submitted.[77] In this case, the opposing party should also react immediately or else risk that its challenge at the post-award stage will not succeed.

All jurisdictions recognize also the exceptional character of the ICC Terms of Reference. In principle, it is considered as an additional instrument that structures the agreed scope of the parties' submissions and, in turn, the tribunal's adjudicative mandate in a more definite manner. Even with the ICC Terms of Reference, however, modifications of the claim may occur.

One should therefore conclude that all of the parties' submissions are relevant in determining the ultimate framework on which the tribunal may rely in its decisions. It will hold true both at the setting-aside stage and enforcement stage.[78]

---

76 The outstanding question is whether it limits the tribunal's jurisdiction or mandate or a yet entirely different concept. This will be discussed in section 3.2.

77 The issues surrounding changes of claim will be discussed further in section 4.2.5.

78 Under the New York Convention regime.

3.1.3 Mandatory rules of public policy character

As highlighted above, the tribunal's mandate is based primarily on the parties' consensus. Yet, it should not be forgotten that the party autonomy finds its limits in the underlying principles of each legal system. In other words, the essential concepts of each system, which take the form of public policy rules, cannot be overridden by the parties' agreement.[79]

The notion that public policy rules have to be respected is recognized both in Model Law and non-Model Law jurisdictions. All jurisdictions have a similar understanding that public policy may be violated only in exceptional circumstances. Nonetheless, similar does not mean the same, which may lead to differences in interpretation of public policy rules.[80] At this point, it suffices to say that the most basic values of the legal system (for example the right to be heard or prohibition of bribery) have to be infringed in order to trigger a public policy violation.[81]

In addition, one should observe *who* can raise an argument that the excess of the tribunal's mandate violates public policy. In the Model Law jurisdictions, public policy can be raised *ex officio*.[82] Arguably, the consequences of the setting-aside procedure in France are the same, because the court will take the task of applying the law to the facts presented by the parties.[83] Conversely and arguably, in England the public policy violation should be raised by the parties.[84] In the U.S., the public policy challenge is a judicially created ground for vacatur. It should be noted, however, that its future after *Hall Street* remains uncertain.[85] If it does survive in the post-*Hall Street* reality, following the Restatement's view, the court on its own motion will be able to check if the award complies with public policy.[86]

---

79 Additionally, the provisions of the applicable arbitration laws even, if not mandatory, may provide a certain structure for the tribunal's mandate, because they will include fallback mechanisms on which the tribunal may rely (for example, power to grant interim measures, power to award costs etc.).

80 For further reading, see Chapter II-Chapter V. Since it is not always applicable (or of immediate relevance), public policy (conversely to the agreement to arbitrate and parties' submissions, *i.e.* the first two sources of the tribunal's mandate) will only be mentioned in selected subsections of section 4.

81 An elaborate analysis, however, escapes the scope of the research at hand.

82 See Chapter II.

83 See Chapter III.

84 Public policy is mentioned in the list of "serious irregularities" under Section 68(g) of the EAA and as such may be pleaded by the parties. Under the Section 67 challenge, one may also, arguably, look at the general clause subjecting party autonomy to limits safeguarding "public interest" (see Section 1(b) of the EAA). There are, however, different views on the meaning of Section 1(b) of the EAA. For further reading, see Chapter IV.

85 See Chapter V.

86 See the Restatement (second tentative draft) p.313. It is based, however, on the philosophy advocated by the Restatement where the New York Convention system is used for vacatur purposes in the U.S (in the context of international arbitral awards). Arguably, the courts should be able to review if the award violates public policy even if vacatur is governed by Section 10 of the FAA. For further reading, see Chapter V.

The mandate of the tribunal to resolve the disputes between the parties is given by the parties. Yet it should never be forgotten that the power of the parties to delegate the dispute resolution has ultimately been granted by the states themselves. That is why they should be able to test if the values they find important have been respected.

3.2 *The analysis of different concepts of "mandate", "mission", "powers", "authority"*

As highlighted above, the different national concepts reviewed herein are structured on the same sources: the agreement to arbitrate, the parties' submissions and the public policy rules stemming from the applicable law. Since the framework on which they are built upon is the same, they are often discussed together under the heading "excess of powers",[87] "excess of authority",[88] "excess of mandate"[89] or the like. Nevertheless, one should not readily infer that the scope of application of these concepts is identical. Therefore, it is necessary to identify (i) what type(s) of *formulae* different legal regimes employ and (ii) what exactly they entail. Consequently, (iii) one should seek to establish how the excess of such formulae is sanctioned. These will be discussed below under sections 3.2.1-3.2.3.[90]

3.2.1 The notion of "mandate" and "mission"

The first relevant notion is the "mandate". It finds its way into two of the studied legal regimes: in the Model Law and in French international arbitration law.[91]

In the Model Law, it is mostly relevant to determine the temporal aspect of the adjudicative powers that the tribunal has over the parties' dispute, because the term is only used while the termination of the mandate is being discussed. Importantly, "termination" is the term used to discuss a situation where an arbitrator withdraws from the office or parties agree to the termination of the mandate[92] or to explain that the arbitral tribunal's role is over when the arbitral proceedings are terminated.[93] In other words, it means that

87 See, for example, Blackaby et al. (2015) pp.584-585.

88 See, *e.g.*, Born, *International Commercial Arbitration* (2014) pp.3287-3309.

89 See, *e.g.*, Blackaby et al. (2015) p.92 ("*An arbitration agreement confers a mandate upon an arbitral tribunal to decide any and all of the disputes that come within the ambit of that agreement. It is important that an arbitrator should not go beyond this mandate. If he or she does so, there is a risk that his or her award will be refused recognition and enforcement under the provisions of the New York Convention.*"). The authors refer to Art. V(1)(c) of the NYC as well as Art. 34(2)(a)(iii) and Art. 36(1)(a)(iii) of the ML.

90 The comparison of all these standards will be undertaken in section 3.3. The placement of the "excess of mandate" type of challenge within the architecture of the post-award review is also relevant and will be discussed in section 3.4.

91 Considering that the French term "*mission*" will be translated as "mandate" as it is usually the case. The better view would be, however, to leave the term mission.

92 See in particular Art. 14 of the ML. Also Art.15 of the ML. For further reading, see Chapter II.

93 See Art. 32(3) of the ML.

the "termination" has nothing to do with any type of post-award recourse against the tribunal's wrongdoing.[94]

Under the French international arbitration regime (in its French version), the term "*mission*" is used. It is regularly translated into English as "mandate"; hence, it is discussed together with the Model Law.[95] On the one hand, it also reflects the temporal characteristic of the tribunal's adjudicative powers by delineating when it begins and ends and in this sense does not have anything to do with the annulment of the arbitral award.[96] On the other hand, it also explicitly allows for the post-award recourse in cases when "*the tribunal ruled without complying with the mandate conferred upon it.*"[97] The mandate, therefore, can be tested against its envisaged limits[98] after the award is rendered. Additionally, one should argue that acting in *amiable composition* should be considered as a separate type of tribunal's mandate (that can be also tested at the setting-aside stage).[99]

3.2.2 The notion of "powers"

The second relevant notion is the notion of the tribunal's "power" or "powers". It is used in the Model Law,[100] in the French (international) arbitration statute,[101] in the English Arbitration Act[102] and in the Federal Arbitration Act[103] in the U.S. If put in context, the term very often refers directly to the tribunal's procedural powers,[104] amongst others, to grant interim reliefs,[105] to rule on the request for verification of handwriting[106] or to order

94 The Model Law approach to the "excess of mandate" type of challenge will be discussed further below, in section 3.3.

95 For further reflections on the use of "mandate" and "mission", see Chapter III.

96 See Art. 1456(1) and Art. 1457(1) of the FCCP. Yet, and importantly, the award will be annulled if it is rendered after the allocated time. See also Chapter III.

97 See Art. 1520(3) of the FCCP. Notably, in the draft version prepared by the *Comité Français de l'Arbitrage*, it has been suggested to also include the recourse in cases when the tribunal "*ruled after its mandate has expired.*"

98 See section 3.1.

99 See Art. 1512 of the FCCP ("*Le tribunal arbitral statue en amiable composition si les parties lui ont confié cette mission.*"). Notably, the translation used herein reads that: "*[t]he arbitral tribunal shall rule as amiable compositeur if the parties have empowered it to do so.*" Consequently, it loses the direct reference to the arbitral tribunal's mandate. In this case, perhaps it is better to follow the one offered by Bensaude in Bensaude (2015) p.1157, who suggested that "*[t]he arbitral tribunal shall decide as amiable compositeur if the parties have entrusted the tribunal with such mission.*"

100 See Art. 17 and Art. 19 of the ML.

101 As "*pouvoir*"; see Art. 1470 of the FCCP. "*Pouvoir juridictionnel*" is also used in the context of the tribunal's competence-competence, see Art. 1465 of the FCCP.

102 See, *i.a.*, Sections 33(2), 37, 38, 39, 41, 56, 65 of the EAA. Section 31(4) of the EAA uses "power to rule on its own jurisdiction".

103 Section 10(a)(4) of the FAA.

104 See in general Art. 19 of the ML.

105 See, *e.g.*, Art. 17 of the ML, Section 39 of the EAA. In France, see Art. 1468 of the FCCP (the term "power" is not used in this context, the meaning of the provision is the same, however).

106 See Art. 1470 of the FCCP.

a party or witness to be examined on oath or affirmation.[107] In the U.S., importantly, the term "powers" is used only in the context of "excess".

Notably, however, only in the last two jurisdictions (in England and in the U.S), *excess* of powers is sanctioned. The scope of application of those standards differs greatly between these two common law countries. For example, the English Arbitration Act defines quite a few of the tribunal's "powers",[108] whereas as pointed out above, the FAA itself does not refer to any powers that are given to the arbitral tribunal and it only provides for the challenge if "powers" of the tribunal are exceeded. In turn, it makes this ground potentially broad in the scope of application.

In England, the "excess of powers" challenge is introduced in the exhaustive list of "*serious irregularities affecting the tribunal, the proceedings or the award.*"[109] Additionally, it is explicitly mentioned that "excess of powers" is different from "excess of jurisdiction". Therefore, it is closely connected with procedural aspects of the fulfillment of the tribunal's adjudicative duty.[110]

In the U.S., conversely, the "excess of powers" challenge corresponds to the vast array of objections and not only to the procedural powers of the arbitral tribunal. It is necessary to point out, that as long as the challenges under this ground are accepted only exceptionally, it is invoked in many circumstances. It so happens, because, as mentioned above, "powers" are not defined in the FAA, which creates a potential risk of the applicant expanding the definition of the "powers" and its alleged "excess".[111] An additional problem arises from the fact that the FAA does not include a separate ground for the tribunal's excess of jurisdiction, making the "excess of powers" ground appropriate to address "jurisdictional/threshold"[112] and non-jurisdictional objections under the same ground for vacatur.[113] It leads to the conclusion that excess of jurisdiction, adjudicative and procedural powers will be tested under the same "excess of powers" ground in the U.S., which makes this ground more significant than in the English context.

---

107 See Section 38(5) of the EAA.

108 See fn.102.

109 See Section 68(1) of the EAA.

110 For further reading, see Chapter IV.

111 See Chapter V.

112 See Chapter V.

113 See the Restatement (second tentative draft) pp.283-297 and Bermann, *'Domesticating' the New York Convention: the Impact of the Federal Arbitration Act* (2011) pp.317-332. In a nutshell, the Restatement's philosophy is to make use of the New York Convention grounds at the vacatur stage (in the context of international arbitration awards rendered in the U.S.). It will effectively bring the FAA vacatur mechanism closer to the Model Law approach. For further reading, see Chapter V.

3.2.3 The notion of "authority"

The "authority" of the arbitral tribunal is mentioned only in two acts discussed: in the Model Law and in the English Arbitration Act. In the Model Law, the tribunal's "authority" is used in the context of Article 16(2) which deals with the tribunal's jurisdiction and the moment the party raises objections; in the relevant part it reads that "*[a] plea that the arbitral tribunal is exceeding the scope of its authority shall be raised as soon as the matter alleged to be beyond the scope of its authority is raised during the arbitral proceedings.*"[114] In the English Arbitration Act, the term "authority" is used when "revocation of authority"[115] and "death of arbitrator"[116] is discussed.

Arguably the use of this notion in the Model Law context is more (albeit indirectly) useful for the research at hand, because it deals with the parties' right to object to the tribunal's actions exceeding the scope of authority.[117] Acknowledging that "authority" should be interpreted as "jurisdiction",[118] this proviso may prove to be relevant while exercising the right to challenge under Article 34 of the Model Law.[119]

3.3 *Different approaches to the "excess of mandate" type of challenge*

The initial conclusion arising from the previous section[120] is that all of the terms are used in more than one system, even if they do not operate in the context of challenging the award. The table below shows which terms are implemented in the specific legal act(s).

Table 6

	"mandate"[121]	**"power(s)"**	**"authority"**
The Model Law	x	x	x
The French International Arbitration Law	x	x	-
The English Arbitration Act	-	x	x
The Federal Arbitration Act	-	x	-
The New York Convention	-	-	-

114 Art. 16(2) of the ML.
115 Section 23 of the EAA.
116 Section 26 of the EAA.
117 The way the term "authority" is used in the EAA resembles the way the term "mandate" is used in the Model Law. In fact, Section 23 of the EAA is based on Art. 14 of the ML. See also section 3.2.1.
118 Art. 16 of the ML is the only element of Chapter IV of the ML entitled: "Jurisdiction of Arbitral Tribunal".
119 See further section 3.3 and section 3.4.
120 See section 3.2.
121 This is the term used in the English versions or translations. For further reading, see in particular Chapter II and Chapter III.

Notably, one may observe that all of these elusive notions are introduced in the Model Law. Yet, in the Model Law (and the New York Convention) context, none of them applies to the tribunal's violations that could be qualified as a type of "excess of mandate".[122] In the French International Arbitration Law, the notions of "mandate" and "powers" are used but only the former is sanctioned under one of the grounds for setting aside, namely, when the tribunal fails to comply with its mandate.[123] The English Arbitration Act refers to the tribunal's powers and its authority. The challenge, however, can be filed only against the "excess of powers".[124] Under the U.S. arbitration system, only the reference to the "tribunal's powers" is made and, importantly, only when the challenge against "the excess of powers" is introduced. It means that the Federal Arbitration Act itself does not define what the term "powers" entails, leaving it for the courts to decipher its meaning. Finally, it is necessary to stress that the New York Convention avoids using any of these concepts.

The Model Law as well as the New York Convention approach the "excess of mandate" type of challenge by confronting the tribunal's award with the parties' "submission to arbitration".[125] On the one hand, the whole proviso is rather long and opaque, on the other hand it eliminates the need of using the elusive concepts (such as the mandate).[126] Additionally, however, it ensures a certain degree of coherence between setting aside system in the Model Law jurisdictions and enforcement under the New York Convention.[127] In principle, therefore, the "excess of mandate" type of challenge may be successfully invoked only in cases where the relief granted is higher or different than sought. If applied in such a narrow fashion, it makes the chances of a successful challenge very limited.[128]

The French international arbitration regime is the only system where an award-debtor may challenge the tribunal's failure to comply with its mandate. It covers not only instances where the tribunal awards more or something different than it was asked to. It also applies, *i.a.*, when the tribunal fails to comply with the contractually agreed procedural rules or with the parties' choice of rules applicable to the merits of the case.[129] The French courts regularly prevent the parties from broadening the interpretation of this ground of recourse.

---

122 See Art. 34(2)(a)(iii) of the ML.

123 See Art. 1520(3) of the FCCP.

124 See Section 68(2)(b) of the EAA.

125 See Art. 34(2)(a)(iii) of the ML and Art. V(1)(c) of the NYC.

126 If the concept of "excess of mandate" or "excess of powers" were to be used in the ML or the NYC, it may increase the risk of a divergent application in different jurisdictions.

127 See further Chapter II and Chapter VI.

128 For a more detailed analysis, see also Chapter II and Chapter VI.

129 See Chapter III. Parenthetically it is noted that Poudret and Besson in their seminal work, classified the "excess of mandate" ground (present in the French, Dutch and Swedish legal systems) under the bigger heading of recourse against of *procedural* issues. See Poudret & Besson (2007) pp.741-747 (under the sub-heading 9.5.5.3 which is nested under the heading 9.5.5 "Procedural grounds for challenge").

The English and the U.S. arbitration regimes operate with a recourse against "excess of powers". The scope of the application differs greatly, however. As pointed out above,[130] in England, the excess of powers is contrasted with the excess of substantive jurisdiction to make sure that these terms are not treated as synonyms. In turn, and in contrast with the abovementioned systems (*i.e.* the Model Law and French international arbitration regime), if the tribunal grants a relief higher or different than sought, it will exceed its jurisdiction rather than its powers.[131] Moreover, the "excess of powers" challenge can be successfully invoked against the tribunal's use of powers that it never possessed. In other words, wrongful use of powers does not constitute its "excess".[132] It makes the scope of application of this ground extremely narrow. However, it is important to observe the whole list of serious irregularities when seeking the recourse for the tribunal's failures.[133] In the U.S., conversely, the "excess of powers" challenge accommodates not only instances where the tribunal awards more than sought, but also when it exceeds its jurisdiction (jurisdictional/threshold issues),[134] decides on matters that are inarbitrable or violates agreed procedure or public policy. It means that it covers a plethora of cases. It does not change the fact that the courts accept only most grievous, exceptional challenges.

National courts approach the challenge in a robust, pro-arbitration fashion which is praiseworthy, because the "excess of mandate" type of challenge has the potential of accommodating many of the objections that a dissatisfied party may have (including the review of the merits). Consequently, although the scope of application of the "excess of mandate" type of challenge may vary between jurisdictions, it is in any event seldom accepted by the judiciary.

3.4 The place of the "excess of mandate" type of challenge in the post-award architecture of selected systems

The "excess of mandate" type of challenge should always be considered in the matrix of the post-award recourse that is at the parties' disposal. It means that one should observe where the "excess of mandate" type of challenge is placed.[135] Additionally, a party wishing to challenge the award should always consider all available avenues in order to determine which is the most suitable. That being said, some factual underpinnings may give rise to more than one challenge at a time. Consequently, for practical reasons parties challenging

---

130 See section 3.2.2.

131 For further reading, see Chapter IV.

132 For further reading, see Chapter IV.

133 See section 3.4.

134 See Chapter V and section 4.1 below.

135 For example, in the Model Law, this type of challenge is placed amongst grounds that need to be brought by the parties themselves. In England, the "excess of powers" is situated in the list of "serious irregularities" and made explicitly distinct from the excess of jurisdiction.

the arbitral award often argue that the same tribunal's actions trigger different grounds for setting aside. As long as it may hold true, parties should carefully pick the weapon of their choice since it may influence their chances for a successful challenge.

There are two main areas of tension between the "excess of mandate" type of challenge and other different grounds for setting aside. The first one has already been briefly discussed above and deals with the distinction between the excess of mandate and of jurisdiction.[136] The second one relates to the conflict with the grounds applicable to the procedural wrongdoings of the arbitral tribunal.

As to the first point, once again, one should note that the limits to the arbitral tribunal's mandate are the same as the limits to the tribunal's jurisdiction. In the context of the research at hand, therefore, it is sometimes difficult to recognize which issues should be treated as jurisdictional ones and which should be distinguished as issues of the mandate. It is particularly the case with the question as to the scope of jurisdiction and the scope of the mandate.[137] The distinction is important, because it changes (or at least it may change) the way setting-aside courts approach the arbitral award at the post-award review.[138]

The problem arises in many jurisdictions, albeit in different forms. For example, it remains debated to date whether the third ground for setting aside listed in the Model Law deals with the scope of jurisdiction or the scope of the "mandate" (or both).[139] The prevailing view is to deal with the jurisdictional objections under the first head of the setting-aside proviso (Article 34(2)(a)(i) of the ML) and with excess of the scope of submission under the third head (Article 34(2)(a)(iii) of the ML) but not all agree.[140] Under the French International Arbitration Law the issue does not raise many questions, since, as explained by Bensaude: "*Art. 1520(1) provides that a party may obtain the setting aside of an award, or the annulment of the enforcement order, where the arbitral tribunal has wrongly retained or denied jurisdiction.*"[141] Since the English Arbitration Act introduces a separate mechanism for the review of substantive jurisdiction (including "*what matters have been submitted to arbitration in accordance with the arbitration agreement*"[142]) and for "excess of powers",

136 See also section 2.2 of this chapter (on the scope of the court's review).

137 Arguably, the problem with the distinction between the tribunal's jurisdiction and its mandate in the context of the agreement to arbitrate goes closely in line with Paulsson's observations on jurisdiction and admissibility. See Paulsson J., *Jurisdiction and Admissibility* (2005); also Paulsson J., *The Idea of Arbitration* (2013) pp.82-90.

138 For further reading, see the Chapter II-Chapter V.

139 See Art. 34(2)(a)(iii) of the ML. See further Chapter II.

140 Kreindler et al., *Commercial Arbitration in Germany* (2016) pp.338-340. See further Chapter II.

141 Bensaude (2015) p.1179. See, however, (in the context of the old FCCP) Poudret & Besson (2007) p.730 ("*French case law has filled this gap by considering that the arbitrator who wrongly declines his jurisdiction violates his mission so that the ground of NCPC, Art.1502(3) is admissible*"). At the same time, Art. 1520(1) of the new FCCP is better suited for this purpose.).

142 See Section 30(1)(c) of the EAA.

these concerns should not arise.[143] In the U.S. the problem is evident because the "excess of powers" ground for vacatur can be invoked in various instances, also in cases of so-called "jurisdictional/threshold issues".[144] These types of questions (and only them) allow the court to exercise an enhanced level of scrutiny while reviewing the arbitral award. The issue as to the scope of the submission to arbitration is amongst "jurisdictional/threshold" issues; whether it should allow the courts to independently (from the tribunal's conclusions) asses the scope of the submission to arbitration remains debatable.[145] The New York Convention system brings about the same difficulties as the Model Law, therefore the analysis above applies to it as well. The second area where tension may occur is arguably less frequent. On occasion, however, it might be difficult, for example, to qualify the challenge against the tribunal's *ex aequo et bono* decision without the parties' explicit authorization or the tribunal's decision that "surprises" parties. In the Model Law (and the New York Convention) system such decision might be placed either under Article 34(2)(a)(iii) or (iv) of the Model Law (Article V(1)(c) or (d) in the context of the New York Convention).[146] In France, those challenges will likely be subsumed under the "excess of mandate" challenge[147] or under violation of "due process".[148] In England, it may trigger different types of irregularities (other than the "excess of powers") listed under Section 68 of the Act.[149] In the U.S., yet again, the excess of powers will come into play. It may be supplemented, however, by the judicially created *manifest disregard of the law*, albeit its uncertain fate after *Hall Street*.[150] These issues, and more, will be comprehensively discussed in the section that follows.[151] In a nutshell, however, while challenging the award, parties should not forget about the systemic context of the "excess of mandate" type of challenge.

143 See also Chapter IV.
144 See further Chapter V.
145 See Chapter V.
146 See Chapter II and Chapter VI.
147 When usurping the *ex aequo et bono* powers. See also Chapter III.
148 In the context of "surprising" parties. Art. 1520(4) of the FCCP. See also Chapter III.
149 For example, for the surprising of parties, the challenge under Section 68(2)(a) of the EAA might be more appropriate. See Chapter IV.
150 *Hall Street*, 552 U.S. 576, 585, 128 S. Ct. 1396, 170 L. Ed. 2d 254, 2008, A.M.C. 1058 (2008). For further reading, see Chapter V.
151 See section 4.

4 The application of different standards of the "excess of mandate" type of challenge to selected issues that might fall outside the arbitral tribunal's adjudicative authority

The "excess of mandate" type of challenge has the potential of being useful against different categories of tribunal's decisions. These decisions can be grouped depending on whether they reflect the tribunal's conclusions on the parties' claims (section 4.2) and requested remedies (section 4.4). Additionally, it is necessary to reflect the way the tribunal applies the law (section 4.3) and how it deals with the parties' requests accessory to the main relief sought (section 4.5). Before deciding on the merits of the case, however, the tribunal needs to establish its own jurisdiction. As much as decisions on jurisdiction escape the scope of the research at hand, it is necessary to highlight few difficulties that they may cause (particularly in the U.S. setting) (section 4.1).

4.1 Decisions on jurisdiction

As already suggested above,[152] the challenge of the tribunal's jurisdiction should be distinguished from the challenge of the tribunal's mandate. This is important, because it may alter the level of the court's scrutiny over the award. This is also why, in principle, the challenge against the tribunal's jurisdiction and "the mandate" should be dealt with separately and not under the same setting-aside ground.

One should observe, however, that the U.S. arbitration regime qualifies jurisdictional objections under the "excess of powers" ground for vacatur. It is a way to overcome the deficiency of the system, namely the absence of the positive competence-competence rule. There is a risk involved with such a development. Namely, on a case-by-case basis, it is necessary to establish which challenge falls into the category of a jurisdictional "excess of powers" challenge and which is an ordinary "excess of powers" challenge. The issues involved are: matters of existence, validity or scope of the agreement to arbitrate, availability of class arbitration or subject matter arbitrability. In this sense, the so-called jurisdictional/threshold issues (or "gateway issues") are a unique feature of the U.S. arbitration system.[153]

Generally, in other systems, the main difficulty arises in connection with the questions as to the scope of the agreement to arbitrate and the scope of the parties' submissions and delineating whether they fit in with the category of jurisdictional questions or not. As such,

152 See section 2.2 and section 3.4.

153 For further reading, see Chapter V.

it has been discussed briefly above and will be discussed, if necessary, below.[154] Other than that, decisions on the tribunal's jurisdiction fall outside the scope of the research at hand.

4.2 *Decisions on parties' claims*

The analysis will follow the division already used in the previous chapters. Therefore, the connecting factors under this section will be the legal nature of the claim and who brought it. Consequently, the separate sections will be devoted to reflect on decisions on contractual claims and counterclaims (section 4.2.1 and section 4.2.2), set-off claims (section 4.2.3), and tortious claims (section 4.2.4). In addition, it is necessary to analyze the tribunal's decisional powers over new and modified claims (section 4.2.5), as well as the fate of decisions not covering all claims/counterclaims (section 4.2.6).

4.2.1 Decision on contractual claims

Contractual claims are perhaps the most natural relief sought. Consequently, deciding on contractual claims is arguably the arbitral tribunal's *raison d'être*. As such, it will be at the core of the tribunal's mandate to resolve those claims and the tribunal's conclusions should generally survive post-award challenges.

That being said, if the limits to the tribunal's mandate are trespassed, the tribunal's decision is susceptible to a setting-aside procedure. This may happen (i) when the tribunal grants a contractual claim that, allegedly, has not been requested or (ii) when contractual claims of a party go beyond the envisaged scope of the agreement to arbitrate. All of the reviewed legal systems provide a recourse for these types of violations. Notably, however, they are sometimes classified as issues of jurisdiction rather than of mandate.

The first scenario envisages that the contractual claim has not been requested, yet was granted by the tribunal. Under the Model Law (and the New York Convention), it will be dealt with under the "excess of mandate" type of challenge.[155] Similarly, in France, Article 1520(3) of the FCCP will be invoked.[156] In England, however, the approach would be different. According to the English Arbitration Act, the question as to what matters have been submitted to arbitration would involve the review of the tribunal's substantive jurisdiction rather than any other challenge mechanism.[157] In the U.S., the concept of "excess of powers" in its traditional meaning will be used.[158]

154 See section 2.2 and section 3.4.

155 Art. 34(2)(a)(iii) of the ML and Art. V(1)(c) of the NYC. See also Chapter II and Chapter VI.

156 See Chapter III.

157 See Section 67 of the EAA in connection with Section 30(1)(c) of the EAA. For further reading, see Chapter IV.

158 Section 10(a)(4) of the FAA. See Chapter V.

Under the first scenario one should observe two variations, namely whether the "excess of mandate" type of challenge would be available (i) if a party alleges that the tribunal granted a claim that has not been requested and where in fact the tribunal has "just" interpreted a vague claim or (ii) if the tribunal granted a claim that has been requested but based on a modified legal basis.

The first variation would get the same treatment as any other objections dealing with the excess of the relief granted. It means that the same mechanism as mentioned above may be invoked. In any event, however, it is necessary to stress that the tribunal should be given autonomy in interpreting the claim without the setting-aside court reassessing what the vague claim meant.[159] In other words, the tribunal's decision on the vague claim should survive the challenge.

The second variation (of the first scenario) relates to the requalification of the relief sought. Put differently, it concerns the situation where the claimant seeks a relief but substantiates it with, for example, tortious liability. In turn, the tribunal grants it, but on the basis of the contract infringement (rather than on tortious liability as pleaded). Such a tribunal's undertaking might not fit into the "excess of mandate" type of challenge. Under the Model Law (as well as the New York Convention), it may very well trigger the procedural grounds for recourse (violation of due process).[160] The same goes for France[161] and England.[162] In the U.S., due to the wide range of the "excess of powers" challenge, it will remain under the scope of Section 10(a)(4) of the FAA.[163]

The second scenario envisages that the relief has been requested, but goes beyond the initial agreement to arbitrate and that the tribunal violates the scope of its mandate. In principle, in the context of the contractual claims, such a hypothetical is unlikely to occur if one assumes that arbitration is a way to resolve (at least) contractual disputes. Logically, what follows is that all contractual disputes should be subjected to the tribunal's determination. It might happen however, that the agreement to arbitrate is evidently narrow and consequently, the tribunal should comply with the limits imposed. This type of objection is likely to be classified as a jurisdictional challenge relating to the scope of the agreement to arbitrate.[164] This way, not only the "excess of mandate" type of challenge but also different grounds in the Model Law (as well as the New York Convention)[165] and in France[166] may be relevant. In England, the substantial jurisdiction challenge will remain

159 See also section 4.2.4.

160 See Art. 34(2)(a)(ii) and Art. 34(2)(a)(iv) of the ML and Art. V(1)(b) and Art. V(1)(d) of the NYC. See also Chapter II and Chapter VI.

161 Art. 1520(4) of the FCCP. See also Chapter III.

162 Section 68(2)(a) or Section 68(2)(b) of the EAA. See Chapter IV.

163 See Chapter V.

164 See section 2.2, section 3.4, and section 4.1.

165 See Art. 34(2)(a)(i) of the ML and Art. V(1)(a) of the NYC. See also Chapter II and Chapter VI.

166 Art. 1520(1) of the FCCP. See also Chapter III.

applicable.[167] In the U.S., yet again, the violation may constitute "excess of powers", but be considered as a jurisdictional/threshold issue.[168]

4.2.2 Decision on contractual counterclaims

Contractual counterclaims – as contractual claims – also have their legal basis in contract. They deserve separate attention, however, because they are brought in response to the initial claims. At the same time, they are independent from them. Consequently, for example, their value may be higher than the claim to which they respond.

The tribunal's decision on contractual counterclaims might be approached from two angles. On the one hand, it is necessary to reflect on counterclaims as parties' submissions limiting the role of the arbitral tribunal. On the other hand, counterclaims should be considered in the context of the respondent's ability to present its case, especially if rejecting the counterclaim would influence the party's right to be heard.

If counterclaims are approached as a submission that shapes the role of the arbitral tribunal,[169] then, in turn, the tribunal's decision on contractual counterclaims can be challenged in the same way as its decisions on contractual claims. Therefore, the reflections from the previous section apply in this context in full.[170] Essentially, it would be rare to find an instance where the tribunal exceeds its mandate by deciding on a counterclaim. It is so, because of the character of the counterclaim, which would make it more of a jurisdictional rather than a mandate question.

As hinted above, the decision on counterclaims may also trigger different grounds for recourse however. This might be particularly the case in a multi-contract reality. When a counterclaim arises from a contract that is different from the one used by claimant, one must reflect, on the one hand, whether the tribunal is competent to decide on issues arising from a different contract (as requested by respondent) and, on the other hand, whether rejecting the counterclaim will influence the party's right to present its case. In these instances, the general notions of excess of jurisdiction[171] or violation of due process[172] would be the more appropriate recourse against the award.

---

167 See Section 67 of the EAA. See also Chapter IV.

168 See section 4.1 above and Chapter V.

169 See section 3.1.2.

170 See section 4.2.1.

171 Art. 34(2)(a)(i) of the ML, Art. 1520(1) of the FCCP, Section 67 of the EAA, Section 10(a)(4) of the FAA (as a jurisdictional/threshold issue). See also Art. V(1)(a) of the NYC.

172 Art. 34(2)(a)(ii) of the ML, Art. 1520(4) of the FCCP, Section 68(2)(a) of the EAA, Section 10(a)(3) and Section 10(a)(4) of the FAA. See also Art. V(1)(b) of the NYC.

4.2.3 Decision on set-off

The initial problem with the analysis on set-off arises from the fact that it can operate as a procedural or substantive device. As can be seen in the previous chapters, the analysis has been primarily directed at set-off considered as a substantive tool.[173] It consequently means that set-off has been treated as a defensive mechanism available to extinguish mutual, payable claims between the parties. Additionally, (substantive) set-off shares the fate of the initial claims and cannot exceed its value. These features distinguish set-off from the counterclaim.[174] Leaving aside the "simple" scenarios, where set-off is based on or related to the same contract,[175] one should reflect whether the tribunal's decision allowing (or rejecting) set-off may be found in excess of the tribunal's mandate in (i) a multi-contract reality and (ii) when the tribunal deals with set-off issues *ex officio*.

At the outset, there are three important preliminary observations that need to be properly introduced to narrow the range of the issues discussed below. First, yet again, the difficulty may arise to determine whether a challenge to a set-off decision is aimed at the tribunal's jurisdiction or mandate.[176] In principle, the conclusions offered in the previous sections[177] would apply to set-off claims as well. In a multi-contract reality, however, there might be additional arguments in favor of the tribunal accepting set-offs even when based on a different contract.[178] Second, invoking set-offs may trigger complex applicable law questions that the tribunal will be required to answer.[179] These will not be dealt with at this point.[180] Third and interrelated to the second point raised, if set-off is to be considered as of a procedural nature (instead of being a substantive defense) then the power of the tribunal to grant it is based on a different source and consequently the challenge against

173 See Chapter II-Chapter V. Arguably, if the tribunal relies on the powers of setting-off treated as a judicial remedy that is available under the law of the seat (see, *e.g.*, statutory set-off or *compensation légale*), the potential challenge against its decision may be different than the challenge in cases where the decision is based on substantive set-off.

174 For further reading on counterclaims, see section 4.2.2.

175 Either on a contractual or non-contractual basis. In these instances, conclusions from other sections will apply. In principle, this will again trigger mostly jurisdictional considerations. Therefore, if the set-off claim is based on (or related to) the same contract, it is likely that the tribunal will be able to accept jurisdiction over this claim. The tribunal's decision could be subsequently challenged under Art. 34(2)(a)(i) of the ML, Art. 1520(1) of the FCCP, Section 67 of the EAA, Section 10(a)(4) of the FAA (as a jurisdictional/threshold issue). Also Art. V(1)(a) of the NYC. See further section 4.2.1, section 4.2.2 and section 4.2.4. Importantly, in the Model Law (and the New York Convention) context also Art. 34(2)(a)(iii) of the ML and Art. V(1)(c) of the NYC might be potentially applicable. See Chapter II and Chapter VI.

176 See, *e.g.*, section 3.4.

177 See other sections under section 4.2. See also *e.g.* fn.175.

178 The issue will be discussed immediately below.

179 The tribunal faced with a dilemma on what law applies to the set-off will inevitably determine the legal character of set-off (if it is indeed a substantive defense or rather if it should be treated "only" as a procedural tool) and how set-off operates. For further reading, see also Pichonnaz & Gullifer (2014) pp.69-105.

180 If a tribunal finds that the set-off is of substantive law character, its decision should resist any subsequent challenge following the "no review on the merits" principle. See further section 2.2 and section 4.3.3.

such a power should also be formulated differently.[181] The issues concerning procedural set-off will be briefly addressed at the end of this section.

In a multi-contract context, set-off may be based on a different contract than the one including the agreement to arbitrate. It can even be more complicated if contracts have competing dispute resolution clauses. In these instances, there are strong arguments to consider that the tribunal lacks jurisdiction to entertain set-off claims.[182] At the same time, however, it is reasonable to conclude that the tribunal should allow all substantive defenses that it is presented with. Arguably, the onus of successfully pleading set-off is rather high, which means that the tribunal would only accept it in profoundly clear circumstances.

Finally, (the tribunal's) acknowledging (substantive) set-off leads to the final resolution of the dispute which is the ultimate mission of the arbitral tribunal.

Pichonnaz and Gullifer have aptly suggested that:

> [...] the best practice is for an arbitral tribunal also to adjudicate the cross-claim, despite the absence of original jurisdiction. One reason is linked to the efficiency of arbitral proceedings but, moreover, it takes into account the fact that refusing to take account of a set-off of a substantive nature, which has possibly already been triggered outside of court proceedings, places too much weight on the right of the cross-debtor to have his arguments heard by the judge who would have had jurisdiction. By relying on set-off, the cross-creditor has, at least de facto, renounced the original jurisdiction. Finally, an arbitral tribunal avoids the schizophrenic situation of rendering an award which is already inadequate as a matter of substantive law, since the main claim may have already been reduced by the effect of (extrajudicial) set-off.[183]

Leaving aside a discussion regarding excess of jurisdiction,[184] the better view is to conclude that the discretion on set-offs should be within the scope of the tribunal's adjudicative authority, making a decision on set-off resistant to the "excess of mandate" type of challenge.

---

181 It means, that a different ground for challenge might be then relevant, for example the one related to the agreed procedure or due process.

182 For further reading, see section 4.2.1 and section 4.2.2. In cases of lack of jurisdiction claims the award might be challenged under Art. 34(2)(a)(i) of the ML, Art. 1520(1) of the FCCP, Section 67 of the EAA, Section 10(a)(4) of the FAA (as a jurisdictional/threshold issue). Also Art. V(1)(a) of the NYC. Art. 34(2)(a)(iii) of the ML and Art. V(1)(c) of the NYC might be potentially applicable as grounds for testing the "scope" question. See further Chapter II and Chapter VI.

183 Pichonnaz & Gullifer (2014) p.59.

184 In principle, although the award should survive a potential attack on the basis of "excess of mandate", it might still be susceptible to the "excess of jurisdiction" challenge.

The tribunal's adjudicative authority, however, does not give it the power to grant set-off without a party's request. That would likely violate the principle of equal treatment of the parties and trigger the relevant due process ground for challenge.[185]

4.2.4 Decision on claims/counterclaims based on torts and pre-contractual liability

Not all claims[186] brought in arbitration arise out of contract. Occasionally, an aggrieved party argues that the tribunal is not authorized to adjudicate non-contractual issues even if brought to the attention of the tribunal by its adversary. In principle, most of the abovementioned analysis will apply here equally.[187] Yet, in the context of decisions on torts, it might be useful to briefly readdress the questions: (i) if the non-contractual claims fit within the scope of the agreement to arbitrate and (ii) whether the tribunal is able to modify the legal basis of the claim from a tortious to a contractual one.

The answer to the first question, primarily and inevitably, depends on the parties' drafting abilities. In other words, if the agreement to arbitrate is sufficiently narrow, there should be no problem in determining that the parties' intention was to limit the availability of an arbitral recourse only to certain category of disputes.[188] Conversely, model (institutional) arbitration clauses are designed to cover all disputes including those that are non-contractual in nature.[189] In addition, and importantly, parties must be reminded of the general pro-enforcement position of the national courts in the studied legal systems.[190] It entails that in case of doubts, it is likely that the agreements to arbitrate will be interpreted broadly, because it will be presumed that parties intended to resolve all disputes related to the transaction in dispute by the same arbitral panel.

For example, in one of the Model Law countries it was decided that the language *"any disputes between [the parties] shall be "settled by" or "determined by" arbitration"* was broad

185 See Art. 34(2)(a)(ii) and Art. 34(2)(a)(iv) of the ML and Art. V(1)(b) and Art. V(1)(d) of the NYC; Art. 1520(4) of the FCCP, Section 68(2)(a) or Section 68(2)(b) of the EAA. See also Chapter II, Chapter III, Chapter IV, and Chapter VI. Under the FAA, it is likely that Section 10(a)(4) will be applicable as much as Section 10(a)(3) seems to be of relevance. For further reading, see Chapter V.

186 For the purpose of this section "claims" will entail both "claims" and "counterclaims".

187 See section 4.2.1 in particular.

188 For example, contractual disputes or disputes relating only to the quality of goods etc.

189 See, *e.g.*, the UNCITRAL Model Clause (*"Any dispute, controversy or claim arising out of or relating to this contract, or the breach, termination or invalidity thereof, shall be settled by arbitration [...]."*), the SIAC Model Clause (*"Any dispute arising out of or in connection with this contract, including any question regarding its existence, validity or termination, shall be referred to and finally resolved by arbitration [...]."*), the ICC Standard Clause (*"All disputes arising out of or in connection with the present contract shall be finally settled [...]."*), the LCIA Recommended Clause (*"Any dispute arising out of or in connection with this contract, including any question regarding its existence, validity or termination, shall be referred to and finally resolved by arbitration [...]."*), the ICDR Short Form Standard Clause (*"Any controversy or claim arising out of or relating to this contract, or the breach thereof, shall be determined by arbitration [...]."*).

190 See section 2.1.

enough to include tort claims.[191] Similarly, it has been argued that under French law "*[a] broadly worded clause will generally be found to cover both contract and tort claims arising out of or in connection with the contract at issue.*"[192] Under the English arbitration regime, following the House of Lords decision in *Premium Nafta Products Ltd v. Fili Shipping Ltd*,[193] the parties will be presumed to opt for a "one-stop method of adjudication", and therefore have intended to have all disputes resolved by the same (arbitral) forum.[194] U.S. courts regularly accepted that an arbitral tribunal had power to decide on tort claims.[195] At the enforcement stage (under the New York Convention), an award-debtor would have to defeat the presumption that the tribunal had acted within its authority which is aligned with the pro-enforcement sentiment of the New York Convention.[196]

In response to the second question, the tribunal may be able to requalify the legal basis for the claim either when (i) alternative bases of claims have been submitted, or (ii) if the requalification is a result of the interpretative exercise undertaken by the tribunal when faced with vague or ambiguous claims (which were not properly contested by the adversary). In those instances, an "excess of mandate" type of challenge might be invoked (albeit rather unsuccessfully). The situation slightly differs when a party did not submit an alternative legal argumentation supporting a claim, yet the tribunal decides to grant this claim on a different legal basis as pleaded, without hearing the parties. This may be considered as a violation of due process.[197] All in all, any mechanisms triggered are the same as in the context of contractual claims presented above.[198]

4.2.5 Decision on new claims/counterclaims and change of claims/counterclaims

The parties' claims delineate an arbitral tribunal's mandate at the outset of the arbitral process. If the tribunal is already constituted, any change in the parties' submissions (including submitting new claims or the modification of claims submitted) would inevitably affect the parties' expectations and, in turn, the tribunal's obligations (as a part of its mandate). This unfolds into three questions: what if new submissions go beyond (i) the agreement to arbitrate or (ii) the parties' initial submissions, and finally (iii) whether acting on the new claims may be considered in excess of the mandate.

191 *Dunhill Personnel System Inc. v. Dunhill Temps Edmonton Ltd.*, 1993 CanLII 7171 (AB QB), par.6 http://canlii.ca/t/28p21#par6 [last accessed 14 August 2020]. See Chapter II.

192 Bensaude (2015) p.1181. See Chapter III.

193 *Premium Nafta Products Ltd v. Fili Shipping Ltd* [2007] UKHL 40.

194 See Chapter IV.

195 See Chapter V. In particular the case law under fn.327.

196 See Chapter VI.

197 See also section 4.2.1. If, however, due process is respected, it is likely that the tribunal's decision will stand, unless contrary to (international) public policy.

198 See section 4.2.1.

The first question has been discussed in detail above.[199] Therefore, it is sufficient to say that the (new) claims should fit within the scope of the agreement to arbitrate. Even if they go beyond the scope of the agreement to arbitrate, however, the parties' conduct is important. The absence of an objection might be considered as an implied acceptance of the expansion of the tribunal's jurisdiction and its mandate.[200]

In response to the second question, one should conclude affirmatively that new claims may go beyond the parties' initial submissions. One should not forget, however, that from the moment when the tribunal accepts its mandate, it is not only the parties but also the arbitral panel that should have a say in the shape of its mandate. In other words, the change in request sought should be conditioned upon the tribunal's consent. This, in turn, leads to the third point of inquiry.

Acting on the newly submitted claims should fit well within the tribunal's adjudicative function. At the same time, one should observe that all reviewed legal systems (save one) are silent on the issue. Only the Model Law, under Article 23(2), provides that "*[u]nless otherwise agreed by the parties, either party may amend or supplement his claim or defence during the course of the arbitral proceedings, unless the arbitral tribunal considers it inappropriate to allow such amendment having regard to the delay in making it.*"[201] Arguably, however, under this rule the tribunal may refuse to accept amendments only if there is a risk of delays in the proceedings (and if the provision is not contracted out by the parties).[202]

Although the reviewed legal systems (but for the Model Law) are silent on the matter of admission of new claims, the institutional rules are not. In principle, all modern arbitration rules contemplate the tribunal's power to act on the amendments of the claims.[203] At the same time, they do differ on the way the tribunal is allowed to execute its power.[204]

199 As discussed above in section 3.1.1 and sections 4.2.1-4.2.4.

200 Importantly, the issue of amended claims is addressed in the arbitration rules. When it happens, it is sometimes stated that the amendments should fit within the limits of the agreement to arbitrate. See, *e.g.*, Art. 20 of the 1976 UNCITRAL Rules ("*However, a claim may not be amended in such a manner that the amended claim falls outside the scope of the arbitration clause or separate arbitration agreement.*"), Rule 20.5 of the 2016 SIAC Rules, Art. 9 of the 2014 ICDR Rules, Art. 6.1 of the 2016 JAMS Rules. Sometimes the reference is made directly to the tribunal's jurisdiction and not to the agreement to arbitrate. See for example Art. 22 of the 2010 UNCITRAL Rules ("*[...] However, a claim or defence, including a counterclaim or a claim for the purpose of a set-off, may not be amended or supplemented in such a manner that the amended or supplemented claim or defence falls outside the jurisdiction of the arbitral tribunal.*").

201 For further reading, see Chapter II.

202 See A/CN.9/WG.II/WP.42, Art. 41, note 27(a) and A/CN.9/233, para 187. For further reading, see also Chapter II.

203 See Art. 20 of the 1976 UNCITRAL Rules, Art. 22 of the 2010 UNCITRAL Rules, Rule 20.5 of the 2016 SIAC Rules, Art. 23(4) of the 2017 ICC Rules, Art. 23(4) of the 2012 ICC Rules, Art. 22.1(a) of the 1998 LCIA Rules, Art. 22.1(i) of the 2014 LCIA Rules, Art. 22.1(i) of the 2020 LCIA Rules, Art. 9 of the 2014 ICDR Rules, and Art. 6.1 of the 2016 JAMS Rules.

204 *Cf* the broadest powers are under the LCIA Rules along with the ICC Rules and the UNCITRAL Rules.

In any event, the decision on new claims will likely resist the "excess of mandate" type of challenge.[205]

4.2.6 Decision not covering all claims/counterclaims

The core function of the arbitral tribunal is to resolve the disputes between parties. In other words, the adjudicative function is to decide *all* claims that have been brought to the tribunal's attention. That is why it is occasionally argued that the failure to render a decision on all claims amounts to the rewriting of the tribunal's mandate. The question that follows this argumentation is whether an *infra petita* situation should lead to the annulment of the arbitral award at the post-award stage.

At the outset one should consider that an *infra petita* decision will be tested mainly against the parties' submissions.[206] Moreover, deciding upon the parties' dispute does not mean that all arguments brought by the parties have to be addressed in the award. Further, it will generally be presumed that the tribunals fulfill their adjudicative function in full. Arguments to the contrary would be particularly difficult to plead in cases where the tribunal concludes its award with a phrase "*reject any and all other claims*" or the like. Even if such a closing statement is not used, it might be difficult to attribute the intention of reformulating the scope of the mandate to the tribunal.[207] Finally, if the abovementioned presumption is not rebutted, the tribunal's decision will have a *res iudicata* effect and will be enforceable. Generally, those conclusions will apply equally under each system reviewed. That being said, one should review how the issue of *infra petita* is addressed.

The reflections are divided as follows: (i) whether *infra petita* is an independent ground for annulment, (ii) if not, whether the *infra petita* arguments may be subsumed by any of the grounds available, and finally (iii) what are the available remedies for combating the inconvenience of an award that is *infra petita*.

Apart from England, none of the reviewed systems provides for the *infra petita* ground as a reason for annulment of the award. While drafting the Model Law, it was suggested to include *infra petita* within the list of grounds for recourse against the award, but the proposal was eventually rejected.[208] In France, while it may be argued that a failure to decide on all issues is a failure to comply with the mission, the argument will not be easily convincing for the courts, because the standard mechanism would be to apply to the tribunal for an additional award.[209] As explained, only in England "*failure by the tribunal to deal with all the issues that were put to it*" may amount to a serious irregularity that causes substantial injustice which may, in turn, lead to the successful challenge against the

205 The outstanding question would be if it will survive due process challenges.

206 It means that the scope of the agreement to arbitrate and public policy are of secondary importance.

207 Arguably, it should show that the tribunal knew about the issue and intentionally left it undecided.

208 See Chapter II.

209 See Art. 1485(2) of the FCCP. See also Chapter III.

award.[210] In the U.S., there is no *infra petita* ground for recourse.[211] Similarly, the New York Convention does not envisage *infra petita* in its exhaustive list of grounds for refusal which was a departure from the text of the Geneva Convention, which did consider what the enforcement court ought to do when faced with an *infra petita* decision.[212]

One should always bear in mind that the setting-aside procedure is only allowed in limited instances.[213] This means that grounds for recourse that are not listed are not available. Arguably, this is particularly true when a ground has been contemplated by the drafters but eventually excluded in the final text, as in the case of the Model Law. Yet, occasionally it has been held that the *infra petita* may resurface in the context of an "excess of mandate" type of challenge.[214] The better view is to reject the possibility to invoke this line of arguments unless it amounts to the violation of (international) public policy[215] and rely on other remedial mechanisms such as an additional award.

Although the setting-aside avenue is (in principle) foreclosed for parties faced with an arbitral decision that does not address all relevant prayers for relief, parties have other tools available at the arbitral seat to mitigate this failure.[216] In three systems, the Model Law, France and England it is possible to request the tribunal to render an additional award on the issues omitted.[217] Conversely to other systems, however, the FAA does not provide any mechanism of direct application to the tribunal with regard to an additional award. Instead, it seems that parties should make use of the corrective powers of the court and ask that the award be remanded back to the tribunal.[218] The power to remit will also be available to the courts in the Model Law[219] countries and in England.[220] In France, the power to remit would be generally unavailable.

210 See Section 68(2)(d) of the EAA.

211 See Chapter V.

212 See Art. 2(2) of the 1927 Geneva Convention. Also Chapter VI.

213 See section 2.1.

214 *BLB and another v. BLC and others* [2013] SGHC 196 at [94-99]. See Chapter II.

215 Or other grounds if available. For example, "breach of natural justice" under Section 24(b) of the SIAA.

216 It means that the New York Convention relies on the powers available in the national arbitration systems. See Chapter VI.

217 See Art. 33(3) of the ML, Art. 1485(2) of the FCCP and Section 57(3)(b) of the EAA. Importantly, the EAA includes other remedial instruments, for example the request for clarification under Section 57(3)(a); exhausting the corrective measures available under Section 57 of the EAA (*e.g.* correction of award or additional award) is a prerequisite to challenge the award in England, where the recourse against *infra petita* is allowed. Arguably, courts in other systems will also take into account whether parties attempted to cure the award albeit not as a formal step for the post-award challenge procedure.

218 See Chapter V.

219 Art. 34(4) of the ML.

220 See Section 68(3) of the EAA. Notably, it should be the first remedial mechanism used by the court. See *The Secretary of State for the Home Department v. Raytheon Systems Limited* [2015] EWHC 311 (TCC) at [3] (*"It is clear that remission is the 'default' option and the Court cannot set aside unless it would be 'inappropriate' to remit."*). See also Chapter IV.

4.3 *Process of application of law by the arbitral tribunal*

As will be observed in the sections that follow, the process of application of law is inherent to the tribunal's adjudicative function. Having in mind that no appeal on the merits is available, the tribunal's decision will not be easily susceptible to challenge.

The process of application of law by the arbitral tribunal in principle can be divided into the following steps: initially, the tribunal may need to choose the method it will use to ascertain which law is applicable (section 4.3.1); consequently the tribunal will need to decide on applicable law (section 4.3.2) and decipher its content (section 4.3.3). While interpreting the rules of the applicable substantive law, the tribunal may need to carefully weigh in rules of public policy nature (section 4.3.4). The last section will reflect on the tribunal's powers to bypass the application of rules of law (section 4.3.5).

4.3.1 Determining the method of selection of applicable law

Determining what law applies to the dispute has a substantial impact on the outcome of the case.[221] This is why the most desirable solution is for the parties to designate the applicable law in their contract. However, if the parties fail to choose the applicable law, the tribunal needs to make a choice between one of two selection methods: either conflict of laws rules or direct choice of law ("*voie directe*").

Three of the reviewed systems, the Model Law, England and France, provide a fallback mechanism on which the tribunal may rely: in the Model Law and in England, the tribunal should follow the conflict of laws analysis in order to determine the applicable law,[222] whereas in France the tribunal would be allowed to decide directly which rules of law apply.[223] In the U.S., there is no default method. Arguably, this leaves room for the tribunals to opt for the freedom of *voie directe*.[224]

The New York Convention has not been designed to resolve issues on how the tribunal should determine applicable law.

Arguably, if parties (jointly) designate certain conflict of laws rules for the purpose of determining the applicable law,[225] the tribunal should follow their wish. If the tribunal

221 As it has been observed in the previous chapters the tribunal may be forced to determine what law applies (i) to the substantive validity of the agreement to arbitrate and (ii) to the merits of the case. This distinction will not be immediately useful for the purpose of the research at hand and will not be discussed further.

222 See Art. 28(2) of the ML and Section 46(3) of the EAA. See Chapter II and Chapter IV.

223 Art. 1511 of the FCCP. See also Chapter III.

224 Especially taking into account that institutional rules fill the gap and do not require any recourse to private international law rules. See, *e.g.*, Art. 31.1 of the 2014 ICDR Rules and Art.19.1 of the 2016 JAMS Rules. See also Chapter V.

225 It would be an extremely rare occurrence. If parties already make an effort to determine governing rules, it would be much more efficient to include a choice of law clause rather than a choice of private international law rules.

ignores the parties' choice, the subsequent award might be at (limited) risk. Under the Model Law (and the New York Convention), the most sensible solution would be to classify the tribunal's decision as a procedural wrongdoing.[226] In France, the issue would remain under the excess of mandate challenge.[227] Under the English and the U.S. regimes the excess of powers ground would be vital.[228]

Similarly, in a highly unlikely scenario, the tribunal's decision might be annulled,[229] if the tribunal seated in the Model Law jurisdictions or England uses a direct approach without the parties' authorization. Those failures, however, would fit more convincingly under other grounds for challenge, different from the "excess of mandate" type of challenge.[230] In the English context one should also keep in mind the appeal on point of law.[231] The requirements (for a successful appeal on point of law) are, however, extremely high.

4.3.2 Decision on applicable law

In principle, the reflections presented above[232] will equally apply to the tribunal's decision on applicable law. The focus is slightly shifted, however, from the *methods* of finding the applicable law to the decision on the applicable law itself. As has been observed in the previous section, determining what law applies might greatly influence the final decision on the merits. As always, the parties' choice is decisive. Otherwise the tribunal has a wide discretion to decide what law applies.[233]

The tribunal's independence is based on the fallback mechanisms available in the reviewed legal systems. As already explained, the tribunal should follow the conflict of laws analysis under the Model Law and the English arbitration regime,[234] and may directly select governing *rules of law* under the French system. The FAA is silent on the issue. The

226 See Art. 34(2)(a)(ii) and Art. 34(2)(a)(iv) of the ML and Art. V(1)(b) and Art. V(1)(d) of the NYC. See also Chapter II and Chapter VI.

227 Section 1520(3) of the FCCP. See also Chapter III.

228 Section 68(2)(b) of the EAA and Section 10(a)(4) of the FAA. See further Chapter IV and Chapter V.

229 Or eventually refused recognition and enforcement under the New York Convention. See fn.230.

230 See Art. 34(2)(a)(ii) and 34(2)(a)(iv) of the ML and Section 68(2)(a) or Section 68(2)(b) of the EAA. See Chapter II and Chapter IV. For the recognition stage, see Art. V(1)(b) and Art. V(1)(d) of the NYC and Chapter VI.

231 See further Chapter IV.

232 See section 4.2.1.

233 In case parties have designated the applicable law and their choice has been subsequently ignored it might trigger the "excess of mandate" type of challenge in the non-Model Law jurisdictions (*i.e.* Art. 1520(3) of the FCCP, Section 68(2)(b) of the EAA, Section 10(a)(4) of the FAA) and a procedural violation under the Model Law and the New York Convention systems (Art. 34(2)(a)(iv) of the ML and Art. V(1)(d) of the NYC).

234 See Art. 28(2) of the ML and Section 46(3) of the EAA. See Chapter II and Chapter IV.

international arbitration rules of the U.S. arbitral institutes fill this gap by giving the tribunal similar powers as in France.[235]

It is important to notice that under the French and (arguably) the U.S. systems, the tribunal is free to opt for both the law and the *rules of law* it considers appropriate. Conversely, the Model Law and the English Arbitration Act only make reference to the law. It means that under the Model Law and the English system the tribunal's decision to apply rules of law on its own motion could be challenged. Arguably, it should be considered as a procedural violation in the Model Law jurisdictions (and at the New York Convention enforcement stage).[236] In England, the challenge might fall under the "excess of powers" ground.[237] The parties' conduct, when addressed with the suggestion of the application of the rules of law will be essential.[238]

Ultimately, the tribunal misuses its discretion if the parties are surprised by the law chosen by the tribunal. It may happen when the tribunal, after having heard the parties' pleadings on applicable law, decides to opt for law not presented by any of the parties. This, again, would most likely be a due process violation. Therefore, it will likely trigger other procedural grounds for a challenge,[239] including public policy.[240] Perhaps the only exception is the U.S. system, where Section 10(a)(4) of the FAA (the excess of powers ground) might be vital.

4.3.3 Ascertaining the content of applicable substantive law by the arbitral tribunal

The function of the tribunal, *i.e.* its mandate, is to resolve the dispute between the parties, which inherently involves applying the (substantive) law to the facts of the case. Taking into account that courts in a post-award stage are not allowed to review the merits of the case,[241] the tribunal's interpretation of the applicable legal rules should, in principle, escape the scrutiny of the courts' review under all systems. Consequently, the erroneous application of legal rules by the tribunal should not be accepted by national courts.[242]

---

235 See, *e.g.*, Art. 31.1 of the 2014 ICDR Rules and Art. 19.1 of the 2016 JAMS Rules.

236 See Art. 34(2)(a)(ii) and Art. 34(2)(a)(iv) of the ML. For the recognition stage, see Art. V(1)(b) and Art. V(1)(d) of the NYC. See further Chapter II and Chapter VI.

237 Section 68(2)(b) of the EAA. Considerably, Section 68(2)(a) of the EAA might also be of relevance. See also Chapter IV.

238 Arguably, if asked (by the tribunal) for comments, and the parties do not advance any arguments, they may broaden the scope of the tribunal's powers.

239 Art. 34(2)(a)(ii) and Art. 34(2)(a)(iv) of the ML. Art. 1520(4) of the FCCP, Section 68(2)(a) of the EAA. For the recognition stage, see Art. V(1)(b) and Art. V(1)(d) of the NYC. See further Chapter II, Chapter III, Chapter IV and Chapter VI.

240 Art. 34(2)(b)(ii) of the ML, Art. 1520(5) of the FCCP and at the recognition stage, Art. V(2)(b) of the NYC.

241 See section 2.2.

242 The limited exception is an appeal on point of law (Section 69 of the EAA) under the English system. See further Chapter IV. Additionally, one should remember the uncertainty created by the "manifest disregard

Yet, since the process of the interpretation of the law is in the functional core of the tribunal's mandate, it is necessary to reflect if and to what extent the tribunal may rely on its own legal knowledge.

All systems acknowledge that the tribunal may and should rely on its own legal knowledge when the dispute is to be decided in accordance with legal rules. It is always important, however, that the tribunal gives the parties an opportunity to respond to its own legal findings. In other words, surprising the parties with its own legal findings may give rise to a challenge.

At the same time, to some extent this will be considered a procedural wrongdoing rather than the tribunal's excess of mandate. In the Model Law jurisdictions, surprising parties will likely trigger Article 34(2)(a)(ii) (inability to present one's case) or Article 34(2)(b)(ii) (public policy), whereas in France it will be reasonable to invoke Article 1520(4) of the FCCP (violation of the *principe de la contradiction*). In England, instead of the excess of powers, surprising parties will be subsumed by Section 68(2)(a) of the EAA (giving parties an opportunity to present their case). In the U.S., the excess of powers ground will still be the ground best suited for a challenge.[243] Under the New York Convention, Articles V(1)(b) and V(2)(b) will be vital.[244]

4.3.4 Application of mandatory rules of law (of public policy character) by the arbitral tribunal

Mandatory rules of law constitute important architectural elements of each legal system. Not all mandatory rules are alike, however. "Simple" and "overriding" mandatory rules can be distinguished.[245] The tribunal should ensure the compliance of its award with the former (that is simple mandatory rules, if they form part of the applicable law) and with the latter (*i.e.* the overriding mandatory rules) at all times.

As already explained above,[246] the process of application of the law will greatly escape the court's scrutiny. Yet, having in mind the special status of mandatory rules, one should reflect further, whether it is possible to successfully challenge the award when (i) the tribunal invokes mandatory rules on its own motion or (ii) when it wrongly applies mandatory rules.

---

of the law" as a vacatur ground in the U.S. As argued elsewhere, even if "manifest disregard of the law" survived the U.S. Supreme Court decision in *Hall Street*, it would eventually be available only when a "disregarded rule" is of public policy character (see section 4.3.4). For further reading, see Chapter V.

243 Section 10(a)(4) of the FAA. See Chapter V.

244 See Chapter VI.

245 For further reading, see, *i.a.*, ILA, *ILA Report on Ascertaining the Contents of the Applicable Law in International Commercial Arbitration* (2008) p.21, and Radicati di Brozolo (2012) p.50.

246 See section 4.3.3.

All systems recognize that the tribunal should identify and apply mandatory rules of a public policy character even if this means that the tribunal invokes them *ex officio* or even contrary to the parties' agreement[247] or their pleadings. Of course, the tribunal should communicate the decision to the parties or else it will not conform to its due process obligation.[248] The difference with the tribunal's decision on other legal rules is that the tribunal's decision that disregards or fails to identify and apply applicable public policy rules will be susceptible to the challenge on public policy grounds.[249] One should be careful, however, what standards of public policy the court in question applies.[250]

In principle, the wrong application of mandatory rules by the arbitral tribunal will not be reviewable under the "excess of mandate" type of challenge, because the courts in a post-award stage should not be involved in the review of the merits of the case.[251] In exceptional circumstances, however, one may argue that when the mistake made by the tribunal is serious, the award might be potentially exposed to the public policy challenge.[252] Additionally, and only in extremely limited circumstances, an appeal on point of law might be available in England. Finally, in the U.S. context one should not disregard "manifest disregard of the law", even if its viability post-*Hall Street* is doubtful.[253]

247 If parties choose law A in order to circumvent the application of otherwise applicable rules of public policy character of law B, then the tribunal should be able to address this and decide on the basis of the public policy rules of law B if it (the tribunal) considers that they might have an effect on the fate of the award.

248 As elaborated further under the previous section, see section 4.3.3.

249 See Art. 34(2)(b)(ii) of the ML and Art. 1520(5) of the FCCP. In England, public policy is listed in Section 68(2)(g) of the EAA among other serious irregularities that constitute substantial injustice. In the U.S. one may be tempted to invoke the "manifest disregard of the law" doctrine or (the non-statutory ground of) public policy. The better option is to follow the Restatement's interpretation of the FAA and to base one's challenge on Section 10(a)(4) of the FAA. At the enforcement stage Art. V(2)(b) of the NYC will be of relevance. It should be also pointed out that public policy might be raised *ex officio* by the court at the post-award stage.

250 See Chapter II-Chapter V.

251 See section 2.2.

252 As explained in fn.249. This argument, however, contradicts the underlying principle of no review on the merits and is generally rejected. See Born in Born, *International Commercial Arbitration* (2014) p.3707, arguing in the context of enforcement proceedings, that "*[i]t is an almost sacrosanct principle of international arbitration that courts will not review the substance of arbitrators' decisions contained in foreign or nondomestic arbitral awards in recognition proceedings. Virtually every authority acknowledges this rule and virtually nobody suggests that this principle should be abandoned.*" The room for a different view has been opened by Hwang and Lai in Hwang & Lai (2005) p.24, who concluded that "*[a] supervisory or enforcing court should not second-guess a tribunal, and the risk of arbitral error is inherent in the acceptance of the process. However, parties do not bargain for a perverse and manifest error that calls out for correction. To ignore such errors would be to accept that the arbitral process can condone miscarriages of justice.*".

253 By and large, the wrongful application of the "overriding" public policy rules (as a "public policy" violation) might be tested, albeit unlikely successful, against Section 10(a)(4) of the FAA. See Chapter V.

4.3.5 Decision based on equity or reached *ex aequo et bono*

The final point that needs to be addressed under this section is the possibility for the tribunal to render a decision without a reference to the legal rules themselves. In other words, the tribunal's mandate to resolve the dispute no longer relies on a legal framework, but rather on the tribunal's understanding of what solution is just and fair under the circumstances of the case. One should not forget that, in these rather unusual and rare instances, it is the parties themselves that grant the power to the tribunal to decide in this fashion, namely *ex aequo et bono* or acting as *amiable compositeur*.

This power is exceptional[254] and this is why parties need to express a clear intention that they entrust the tribunal with it. This rule is explicitly stated in three of the studied legal systems, namely in the Model Law, in the French legal system and in the English Arbitration Act.[255] In the U.S., the issue has not been dealt with within the FAA itself. Nor has it been at the enforcement stage based on the New York Convention regime. This *lacuna*, however, is filled by most (if not all) leading institutional rules.[256]

If the tribunal usurps the power to decide *ex aequo et bono* (*i.e.* without the parties' express authorization), its decision will likely be set aside. Under the Model Law (and the New York Convention) regime, there are two competing challenges. Deciding *ex aequo et bono* without express authorization may be qualified either under the "excess of mandate" type of challenge (*i.e.* Article 34(2)(a)(iii) of the Model Law and Article V(1)(c) of the New York Convention) or as a question of procedure and challenged under Article 34(2)(a)(iv) of the Model Law and Article V(1)(d) of the New York Convention. The better view is to qualify this wrongdoing as a procedural one. At the same time, however, excess of mission (in France) or excess of powers (in England and in the U.S.) would be used.[257]

254 Arguably, the power to decide *ex aequo et bono* is so exceptional that it forms a separate "genre" of the tribunal's mandate, which should not be reconciled with its traditional meaning. This should be particularly true with reference to the French system (see further section 3.2.1). If this argument is accepted, it would mean that the mandate to decide *ex aequo et bono* is there not "only" to mitigate the effects of strict application of the law, but rather to free the tribunal from any reference to the law. Consequently, only the strict application of the law would constitute non-compliance with the tribunal's mandate (unless the "strict" application leads to "just" results and has been reasoned as such). The tribunal will be therefore able to apply the law, but should be always mindful of its *ex aequo et bono* hat.

255 See Art. 28(3) of the ML, Art. 1512 of the FCCP and Section 46(1)(b) of the EAA.

256 See Art. 35(2) of the 2010 UNCITRAL Rules, Art. 33(2) of the 1976 UNCITRAL Rules, Rule 31.2 of the 2016 SIAC Rules, Section 23.3 of the 1998 DIS Rules (different formulation in the Art 24.4 of the 2018 DIS Rules, effectively leading to the same result), Art. 21(3) of the (draft) 2021 ICC Rules, Art. 21(3) of the 2017 ICC Rules, Art. 21(3) of the 2012 ICC Rules, Art. 22(4) of the 2014 LCIA Rules, Art. 22.4 of the 2020 LCIA Rules, Art. 31(3) of the 2014 ICDR Rules, Art. 31.1 of the 2016 JAMS Rules.

257 Art. 1520(3) of the FCCP, Section. 68(2)(b) of the EAA and Section 10(a)(4) of the FAA. In the U.S. context, one might also consider the doctrine of "manifest disregard of the law". For further reading, see the Chapter V.

Notably, however, considering the no-merits review principle at the post-award stage, it might be difficult to successfully challenge the tribunal's *ex aequo et bono* decision, especially when it is disguised with a reference to legal rules.

Finally, even if the tribunal is granted the power of *ex aequo et bono*, it should, at all times, adhere to the principles of due process and (international) public policy. The violation of these principles will be susceptible to a successful challenge at the post-award stage on grounds not related to the "excess of mandate".[258]

4.4 *Decisions on remedies*

Ultimately, in order to complete its adjudicative mandate, the tribunal needs to reach (in its award) a decision on remedies sought by the parties. In the context of the research at hand one should reflect, however, when the tribunal's decision might be attacked with the "excess of mandate" type of challenge. The study focuses mostly on three distinctive categories of remedies: damages (section 4.4.1), specific performance (section 4.4.2), and contract adaptation (section 4.4.3).[259]

4.4.1 Decision on damages

The first type of decision on remedies that requires further analysis is the tribunal's decision on damages sought. Arguably, damages are the primary relief available for the parties in international arbitration. Consequently, due to their universal character, it is somewhat expected that a tribunal will have the power to award them. Nonetheless, in certain circumstances, a tribunal's decision on damages might be potentially at risk at the post-award stage. These instances include situations where the tribunal grants damages (i) higher than sought, (ii) different than sought, (iii) specifically excluded by the parties, or (iv) unknown to the system where the post-award review takes place (for example, when punitive damages are granted).

The first scenario is a classic example of *ultra petita*. It means that if the amount of the awarded damages is higher than requested the award might be challenged, because the tribunal is allowed to use its adjudicative powers only within the limits of the parties' requests. In principle, all reviewed systems tackle this hypothetical under the "excess of

258 See therefore (for due process violations) Art. 34(2)(a)(ii) of the ML, Art. 1520(4) of the FCCP, Section 68(2)(a) of the EAA, Section 10(a)(3) and Section 10(a)(4) of the FAA and (for public policy violations) Art. 34(2)(b)(ii) of the ML and Art. 1520(5) of the FCCP. In England, public policy is listed in Section 68(2)(g) of the EAA, in the U.S. in Section 10(a)(4) of the FAA and Art. V(2)(b) of the NYC at the enforcement stage. See also fn.249.

259 Although many more remedial powers may be available in the different legal systems, arguably these additional powers might be subsequently analyzed under one of the three categories proposed.

mandate" type of challenge.[260] If the post-award court accepts the challenge, it is likely that it (the challenge) will affect only the part that has been requested above the *petita*.[261]

Under the second scenario, a party in arbitration anticipates being granted damages (as requested) and, instead, the tribunal awards the specific performance of the contract. Undoubtedly, unless the parties have submitted alternative claims, such a tribunal's decision will not be in conformity with the parties' *petita*[262] and consequently may be effectively challenged at the post-award stage based on the "excess of mandate" type of challenge.[263]

The third hypothetical envisages a situation where the parties limited the tribunal's remedial power in the underlying agreement to arbitrate, and the tribunal did not comply. Once again, these types of tribunal's actions might qualify as an "excess of mandate" and be subsequently challenged.[264]

Yet, it may also be the case that the contract includes a separate clause (independent from an agreement to arbitrate) that excludes certain types of damages from being sought. This type of clause imposes a restriction on the parties and not on the tribunal. Therefore, this slight modification will have a lesser effect on the tribunal's mandate, because it refers to the tribunal's remedial powers only indirectly. Consequently, since contract interpretation is an exclusive prerogative of the arbitral tribunal, the courts might be averse to accept the challenge over the tribunal's decision granting such a requested remedy.[265]

The final issue that needs to be discussed is the instance where the tribunal awards damages that are foreign to the system where the arbitration takes place or where the award is being enforced. This hypothetical is based on the assumption that the damages are being properly requested by the parties. In these circumstances, the national court at the post-award stage would most likely be required to answer the question if the award granting (for example) punitive damages does not violate the (international) public policy, rather than the question whether the tribunal exceeded its mandate by granting them.[266] In any event, as suggested elsewhere,[267] it would be sensible for the tribunal to distinguish

260 Art. 34(2)(a)(iii) of the ML, Art. 1520(3) of the FCCP, Section 10(a)(4) of the FAA and also at the enforcement stage Art. V(1)(c) of the NYC. In the Model Law context, not all authors agree that it should be subsumed under Art. 34(2)(a)(iii) of the ML. See, for example Kreindler et al., *Commercial Arbitration in Germany* (2016) p.340. For further reading, see Chapter II. In England, Section 68(2)(b) of the EAA should apply. See also Chapter IV.

261 Therefore the "healthy" part of the award will be severed and saved for enforcement. See section 2.3.

262 This would likely be qualified as an *extra petita* violation. Sometimes it might be difficult to define if the violation is more of an *ultra* or *extra petita* nature. Arguably, this distinction is not essential, because both violations will be successfully challenged.

263 See fn.260.

264 See fn.260. See, however, (in particular) Chapter IV where, potentially, also Section 67 of the EAA (challenge to the substantive jurisdiction) might be applicable.

265 See for example *Parsons & Whittemore Overseas Co., Inc. v. Societe Generale De L'Industrie Du Papier (RAKTA)*, 508 F.2d 969, 976 (2d Cir. 1974). For further reading, see Chapter VI.

266 For further reading, see Chapter II-Chapter V.

267 Blackaby et al. (2015) p.519.

the punitive portion of damages as a separate claim in order to make sure that it can be severed from the other part of the award at the enforcement stage.

4.4.2 Decision on specific performance

Specific performance has been the second category of remedies selected for this analysis. The initial hypothesis was that it may be necessary to distinguish specific performance as a separate category of remedy due to the fact that it is approached differently in the countries with a civil law and common law tradition. Yet, the research has shown that the arbitral tribunals will have ample discretion to grant specific performance both in civil law and common law countries.[268] Consequently, it will rarely happen that its decision on specific performance will be open to an "excess of mandate" type of challenge. The only instances that will be relevant have been already discussed in the previous section.[269] In principle, the tribunal will not be allowed to grant specific performance if not requested by the parties or if such a remedial power has been expressly excluded in the underlying agreement to arbitrate.

4.4.3 Decision on contract adaptation and filling of gaps in the contract

The last type of remedial power that needs to be discussed is the contract adaptation and the tribunal's gap-filling exercise. It is an important tool, because (if available) it allows the tribunal to modify the contract if changed circumstances undermine the initial spirit of the agreement or it allows the tribunal to eliminate ambiguities existing in the contract. It may be particularly relevant in long-term and complex contracts where it is not possible to agree on all aspects of the agreement.

On the one hand, it has been pointed out that, in cases of contractual gap-filling, the tribunal will step into the parties' shoes and create the legal relationship anew. Consequently, some argue that it goes beyond the tribunal's adjudicative function, because no dispute exists between the parties. On the other hand, it has been suggested that contract adaptation and gap-filling is no more than the mere exercise of traditional contract interpretation and even if it goes beyond that, the parties should be allowed to grant this extra power to the tribunal.

None of the reviewed systems include any express rule on the power to fill the gaps in the contract by the arbitral tribunal. It has been discussed during the drafting process of the Model Law, but was left outside the structure of the final text.[270] In France, *arbitrage juridictionnel* (being a dispute resolution mechanism) is distinguished from *arbitrage*

268 For further reading, see Chapter II-Chapter V.

269 See section 4.4.1.

270 See A/CN.9/WG.II/WP.41 para 11, A/CN.9/WG.II/WP.44 para 32. See also Chapter II.

contractuel (being more of a creative device).[271] Nevertheless, the French arbitration regime does not include any explicit provisions authorizing the tribunal (in *arbitrage juridictionnel*) to fill the gaps. Similarly, the English Arbitration Act and the Federal Arbitration Act are silent also on the issue.[272]

One should, therefore, conclude that if the parties wish to vest the tribunal with the power to adapt the contract or to fill the gaps in the contract, it is sensible for them to include express contractual provision to that effect. Otherwise, the tribunal's decision might be open to attacks under the "excess of mandate" type of challenge in all systems.[273] Even in the absence of the express contractual disposition granting the tribunal the power to fill gaps, its decision might still survive the challenge, because it might be considered that the tribunal "only" interprets the contract (by giving the meaning to the gaps in the contract) based on the parties' submissions. Similar to what has been discussed above,[274] the tribunal's decision might be successfully challenged if the tribunal's decision goes beyond what has been requested or if it defies an explicit contractual limitation to their gap-filling powers.[275]

4.5 *Decisions accessory to the parties' main submissions and merits of the case*

The last category that has been given importance relates to decisions that do not affect decisions on main claims *per se* but are inherent to the arbitral adjudicative process. Three main categories may be therefore identified: decisions on interest (section 4.5.1), decisions on costs (section 4.5.2), and procedural decisions undertaken during the process (section 4.5.3).

---

271 See Chapter III.

272 See Chapter IV and Chapter V. Yet, it is often argued that Section 46(1)(b) of the English Arbitration Act, that allows the parties to confer powers on the tribunal, recognizes that a gap-filling authority may be entrusted to the tribunal. The argument will be equally true in the U.S. context.

273 See Art. 34(2)(a)(iii) of the ML, Art. 1520(3) of the FCCP, Section. 68(2)(b) of the EAA, Section 10(a)(4) of the FAA and Art. V(1)(c) of the NYC.

274 See section 4.4.1.

275 Even then, however, it would very much depend on the circumstances of the case. It is possible that, for example, parties included in their contract a clause limiting the powers of the tribunal to modify the contract. In turn, the tribunal, while distilling the true intention of the parties, interpreted the contract in a way that it can be considered as its modification. In this case, arguably, the tribunal's decision might still survive the challenge. Otherwise, the parties will limit the tribunal's adjudicative powers to the extent of tying the tribunal's hands in contract interpretation and in the search of the underlying spirit of the parties' agreement.

4.5.1 Decision on interest

Interest remains a vital part of the compensation recoverable through arbitration. Similar to other elements, the tribunal's decision-making process regarding interest can be divided into several steps. The most important would include determining the applicable law (to the issue of interest),[276] deciding what should be the starting date for accruing interest and setting up an appropriate rate and type of interest. Although these elements often require elaborate analysis, the reflections presented herein should be limited to the extent that the tribunal's decision on interest might be susceptible to the "excess of mandate" type of challenge.[277]

At the outset, it is necessary to highlight that only one of the reviewed legal systems addresses the issue of interest: the English Arbitration Act in Section 49 provides a comprehensive explanation as to what powers the tribunal has with regard to awarding interest (in the absence of the contrary agreement of the parties). To the contrary, the Model Law itself,[278] the French Code of Civil Procedure, the Federal Arbitration Act and the New York Convention are silent on the issue. "*Even in the absence of the express statutory authority, there should be no doubt concerning the authority of an arbitral tribunal to award interest.*"[279]

Moreover, it is difficult to recognize consistency in the approach in the leading institutional rules (that have been reviewed): some of them do contain rules regarding the power to award interest[280] and others do not.[281] It has been suggested that

> [m]ost institutional rules of arbitration do not contain express provisions for the payment of interest, largely because their drafters assumed that an arbitral tribunal has the power to make an award in respect of interest in just the same way as it has the power to make an award in respect of any other claims submitted to it.[282]

---

276 And an additional question, whether they are of procedural or substantive character.

277 For further reading on awarding interest in international commercial arbitration, see, *i.a.*, Blackaby et al. (2015) pp.527-532, and Born, *International Commercial Arbitration* (2014) pp.3102-3112.

278 Notably, some of the Model Law countries decided to include a provision on interest in their statutory framework. See, *e.g.*, Art.12(5)(b) of the SIAA.

279 Born, *International Commercial Arbitration* (2014) p.3103.

280 Particularly from the arbitral institutions originating from the common law jurisdictions. See, *e.g.*, Art. 26.4 of the 2014 LCIA Rules, Art. 26.4 of the 2020 LCIA Rules, Art. 31.4 of the ICDR Rules and Art. 32.7 of the JAMS Rules. See also Rule 32.9 of the 2016 SIAC Rules.

281 The 1976 UNCITRAL Rules, the 2010 UNCITRAL Rules, the (draft) 2021 ICC Rules, 2017 ICC Rules, the 2012 ICC Rules and the 1998 DIS Rules are silent on the power of the tribunal to award interest.

282 Blackaby et al. (2015) p.528. The authors explain further that "*[t]he right to interest will therefore flow from the parties' underlying contract (that is, from a contractual provision for the levying of late payment interest), or by virtue of the applicable law.*"

In addition, the text of the ILA Report on Inherent and Implied Powers of Arbitral Tribunals may lead to the conclusion that awarding interest in international commercial arbitration belongs to a catalogue of arbitral tribunal's inherent powers.[283]

Even if the power to award interest is inherent or implied (and as such is not addressed neither in the agreement to arbitrate itself (including applicable arbitration rules), nor in the applicable arbitration act), a decision on interest, as always, needs to be tested against the agreement to arbitrate, the parties' submissions and public policy rules if it is being challenged under the "excess of mandate" type of challenge. Consequently, the tribunal's decision may be set aside if: (i) the interest issue is not in accordance with the parties' explicit agreement (*i.e.* when the parties decide to limit the powers to award interest and the tribunal does not comply), (ii) the tribunal awards interest higher or different than sought, or (iii) the (type of) interest violates the public policy rules of the seat (or the place of enforcement). It means that, in principle, a decision on interest would be challengeable in the same circumstances that have been already discussed above in the section on damages.[284]

Contrary to the tribunal's decision on damages, however, it is important to highlight, that the decision granting interest might still survive the challenge at the post-award stage even when it is made on the tribunal's own motion (thus without a party's request). It might be the case, for example, in cases where the applicable (substantive) law includes the rule allowing (or even requiring) the tribunal to grant statutory interest automatically when the main claim is granted. There are reported courts' decisions that upheld the tribunals' decisions on interest even in the absence of the parties' request.[285] In any event, it is sensible for the tribunal to follow the parties' *petita*.

4.5.2 Decision on costs

The decision on costs deserves separate attention for (at least) several reasons: first, its monetary value might be substantial; second, the standard for allocating costs differs greatly between jurisdictions;[286] third, very often tribunals enjoy a broad discretion with respect to awarding costs; and finally, the decision on costs is an important procedural tool available

283 ILA, *ILA Report on Inherent Powers of Arbitral Tribunals* (2014) p.10.

284 See section 4.4.1.

285 See a discussion on the issue (in particular) in Giraud (2017) pp.272-275. Also see Born, *International Commercial Arbitration* (2014) p.3110 with a reference (in fn.600) to *Gordon Sel-Way, Inc. v. Spence Bros., Inc.*, 475 N.W.2d 704, 711 (Mich. 1991) ("*arbitrators committed no substantial or material error in including pre-award interest in their award, even though parties' contract was silent concerning right to interest*"); *Westminster Constr. Corp. v. PPG Indus., Inc.*, 376 A.2d 708, 711 (R.I. 1977) ("*arbitrators may award interest, even if not claimed, unless otherwise specifically provided by the parties in the agreement*").

286 For example (i) "cost follow the event" or (ii) the so-called American Rule. See further Kreindler, *Final Rulings on Costs: Loser pays all?* (2006) p.42.

to the tribunal to discipline parties and to promote good faith in the conduct of the proceedings.

Once again, only one legal system, namely the English Arbitration Act, provides a set of default rules governing the tribunal's powers to deal with costs.[287] The Model Law itself[288] and the other reviewed legal systems are silent on the issue. This *lacuna* is usually filled by the arbitral institutions that address the tribunal's powers regarding the costs in their arbitration rules.[289] As observed in the first paragraph, the discretion given to the tribunal is rather broad and for this reason the post-award challenge would be rather futile.

When testing a decision on costs against the "excess of mandate" type of challenge,[290] one might reflect on three basic hypotheticals: (i) the tribunal's decision disregards express contractual provisions regarding costs (*e.g.* allocating costs, limiting the tribunal's powers to grant costs etc.), (ii) the tribunal awards costs not requested, or (iii) the costs granted violates public policy rules. These conclusions are similar to what has been discussed above. Consequently, the previous conclusions would apply to the tribunal's decision on costs as well.[291] A few additional remarks regarding the decision on costs should be given, however.

In principle, it is rather unusual to constrain the tribunal's authority in awarding costs. For this reason, and taking into account the broad powers given by the institutional rules, each modification intended by the parties (aimed at limiting a tribunal's powers to award costs) should be made clear. If such a variation is made, the tribunal should respect it.[292]

As suggested at the outset, the decision on costs will possibly be the tribunal's last remedy through which it can penalize parties for their behavior during the proceedings. This sanction is an essential procedural mechanism at the tribunal's disposal and deserves a special status, because it is directed against a party frustrating the proceedings and functions as a defense for the proper fulfillment of the tribunal's adjudicative mandate. Consequently, under certain circumstances, the tribunal should be allowed to deviate from the parties' submissions on costs and to award the costs differently than requested (or

287 See Sections 59-65 of the EAA. For further reading, see Chapter IV.

288 Although the Model Law itself is silent on the issue, countries adopting the Model Law may implement a provision on costs themselves. See, *e.g.*, Art. 1057 of the GCCP. Importantly, as explained in Kreindler et al., *Commercial Arbitration in Germany* (2016) p.295, the tribunal will be able to decide on costs even without the parties' request. See further Chapter II. Additionally, one should note that UNCITRAL considered including express provision on costs. For further reading, see A/CN.9/460 paras 107-114.

289 See, *i.a.*, Arts. 40-43 of the 2010 UNCITRAL Rules, Art. 38 of the (draft) 2021 ICC Rules, Art. 38 of the 2017 ICC Rules, Art. 37 of the 2012 ICC Rules, Arts.32-26 of the 2018 DIS Rules, Section 35 of the 1998 DIS Rules, Rule 35-37 of the 2016 SIAC Rules, Art. 28 of the 2014 LCIA Rules, Art. 28 of the 2020 LCIA Rules, Art. 34 of the 2014 ICDR Rules and Art. 37 of the 2016 JAMS Rules.

290 Art. 34(2)(a)(iii) of the ML, Art. 1520(3) of the FCCP, Section 68(2)(b) of the EAA, Section 10(a)(4) of the FAA and also at the enforcement stage Art. V(1)(c) of the NYC.

291 See section 4.4.1 and section 4.5.1.

292 The exception to this rule might be the parties' bad faith procedural conduct. See further, the next paragraph of this section and *ReliaStar Life Ins. Co. of N.Y. v. EMC Nat. Life Co.*, 564 F.3d 81 (2d Cir. 2009).

arguably even if not requested).[293] In exceptional circumstances, also a tribunal's decision disregarding the parties' contractual stipulation on allocating of costs may also survive the challenge at the post-award stage.[294]

Finally, one should observe that an express power to punish a bad faith conduct while awarding costs becomes one of the increasingly popular tools included in the recent round of amendments made to the institutional rules.[295] These changes have been introduced by the major institutions in France, England and the U.S. Arguably, however, also in the Model Law jurisdictions (and under the New York Convention regime) the authority to discipline the party with the costs' award will be given full effect.[296]

293 This is however unlikely, since in most cases the parties submit their costs. If the parties' costs are not submitted (thus not requested), the tribunal will face the problem of estimating the amount of the costs and for that it is not competent. This hypothetical would therefore include two assumptions: (i) party A misbehaves during the proceedings and the tribunal can only discipline it with the award on costs, and (ii) party B does not request any legal costs. One option is that party A will need to cover costs of arbitration, but for party B's legal costs. An alternative would be that it also covers the costs of legal representation of party B (still as a sanction for bad faith conduct). Yet, arguably, the tribunal would not be competent to estimate the costs of legal representation (even "reasonable" ones). It would then have to turn back to the parties or, again arguably, might award to party B the costs of legal representation up to the amounts of the statutory lawyer's fees under the regime in the seat of arbitration.

294 See *ReliaStar Life Ins. Co. of N.Y. v. EMC Nat. Life Co.*, 564 F.3d 81 (2d Cir. 2009). For further reading, see Chapter V.

295 See Art. 38(5) of the (draft) 2021 ICC Rules, Art. 38(5) of the 2017 ICC Rules. Also Art. 37.5 of the 2012 ICC Rules ("*In making decisions as to costs, the arbitral tribunal may take into account such circumstances as it considers relevant, including the extent to which each party has conducted the arbitration in an expeditious and cost-effective manner.*"), Art. 28.4 of the 2014 LCIA Rules ("*[...] The Arbitral Tribunal may also take into account the parties' conduct in the arbitration, including any co-operation in facilitating the proceedings as to time and cost and any non-co-operation resulting in undue delay and unnecessary expense. Any decision on costs by the Arbitral Tribunal shall be made with reasons in the award containing such decision.*"), Additionally, Art. 28.4 of the 2020 LCIA Rules includes a direct reference not only to parties but also to their "authorised representatives". The most recent 2016 JAMS Rules go even further by not limiting the disciplining power only to the award on costs; see Art. 33.1 of the 2016 JAMS Rules ("*The Tribunal may order appropriate sanctions for failure of a party to comply with its obligations under any of these Rules or with an order of the Tribunal. These sanctions may include, but are not limited to, assessment of Arbitration Fees and Arbitrator compensation and expenses; assessment of any other costs occasioned by the actionable conduct, including reasonable attorneys' fees; exclusion of certain evidence; drawing adverse inferences; or, in extreme cases, determining an issue or issues submitted to Arbitration adversely to the party that has failed to comply.*"); *cf* Section 35(2) of the 1998 DIS Rules, Art. 42(1) of the 2010 UNCITRAL Rules and Art. 34 of the 2014 ICDR Rules. These rules allow the tribunal to take "the circumstances of the case" into account when awarding costs. Arguably, such wording would also allow the tribunal to discipline parties, albeit impliedly. See also Art. 33(3) of the 2018 DIS Rules, where the reference is made as to whether parties have conducted arbitration efficiently.

296 See, *e.g.*, Kreindler et al., *Commercial Arbitration in Germany* (2016) p.297. It will be particularly true if the 2012 ICC Rules are applicable. Arguably, however, even in the case of the 1998 DIS Rules or the 2010 UNCITRAL Rules that only provide that the tribunal may take "the circumstances" of the case into account when awarding costs, should be sufficient. See fn.295.

4.5.3 Decisions on procedure

The tribunal's *raison d'être* is to resolve the dispute between the parties. This is observed by the adjudicative dimension of the tribunal's mandate.[297] Conversely to this main role,[298] its procedural decisions have a completely different function, namely managing the arbitral process. In other words, the procedural decisions are, therefore, the means for the tribunal to control the efficient fulfillment of its adjudicative mandate. As such they are (only) complimentary to the core, dispute resolution function of the arbitral tribunal and falls within the scope of the tribunal's autonomy.

If these arguments are accepted, the procedural decisions of the arbitral tribunal should not be easily susceptible to the "excess of mandate" type of challenge. Yet, in certain jurisdictions, it would be still possible to invoke this ground for challenge against the tribunal's procedural wrongdoings under the presumption that the tribunal failed to comply with the limits to its mandate, *i.e.* the agreement to arbitrate, the parties' submissions and public policy rules (of the seat).[299] Therefore, the issue deserves further analysis.

In principle, the Model Law as well as the New York Convention envisage a system where procedural decisions (that are not in accordance with the limits to the "arbitral tribunal's mandate") escape the courts' scrutiny under the "excess of mandate" type of challenge.[300] The reason for that is simply because the subsequent ground on the list (in both challenge procedures) gives the parties an opportunity to object to the award if the procedure was not in accordance with the agreement of the parties[301] or not in accordance with the law of the seat (if parties did not agree on the procedure).[302] Therefore, testing the tribunal's procedural decisions might be better suited under a different ground than the "excess of mandate" type of challenge.

In the remaining jurisdictions, however, the decisions on procedure might be very well suited for the challenge under the "excess of mandate" type of challenge. In France, if the parties explicitly agree that a certain procedure should be followed, the tribunal is obliged to comply. Otherwise its award might be set aside on the basis of a failure to comply with the mandate. Other grounds, however, might be also relevant and, importantly, the French courts might decide to requalify the challenge if needed.[303] In England, Section 68 of the EAA (serious irregularity) might be available for the same reasons. Although the EAA

297 See further section 1.3 of Chapter VIII (on the adjudicative dimension of the tribunal's mandate).

298 See section 3.1; also Chapter I.

299 Depending on the factual underpinning of the case it is likely, however, that the tribunal's procedural decision will be also susceptible to review under other, competing grounds for challenge such as violation of due process or violation of (international) public policy.

300 Which is prescribed under Art. 34(2)(a)(iii) of the ML and Art. V(1)(c) of the NYC.

301 Importantly, however, even if the parties had agreed on the procedure, their agreement cannot be in conflict with the mandatory provisions of the Model Law.

302 See Art. 34(a)(iv) of the ML and Art. V(1)(d) of the NYC.

303 In these cases, Art. 1520(4) and Art. 1520(5) of the FCCP might be particularly relevant.

offers an independent ground for the tribunal's failure to comply with the procedure selected by the parties,[304] as observed by scholars, "*[i]n practice, this head will be of little significance [...].*"[305] Therefore, it may leave some room for applying other grounds listed as serious irregularities, including the "excess of powers".[306] In the U.S., the prevailing view is that the "excess of powers" ground will be at the parties' disposal, particularly considering the broad interpretation given to this ground by the Restatement.[307] Even though these systems allow the challenge, the burden of proof is rather high, because the party bringing the challenge has to show that "*[...] the alleged deviation from prescribed procedures is material.*"[308]

One should reflect further, however, on the one specific hypothetical. In this scenario, parties agree to modify (or add) certain procedural rule(s) after the tribunal had accepted its mandate. By doing so, the parties, in principle, would expect the tribunal to comply with their procedural demands. The outstanding question would be, what if the tribunal does not follow their instructions? Is a tribunal's non-compliance in this case sufficient to trigger the "excess of mandate" type of challenge (or other applicable ground)?

Although many would answer the last question in the affirmative, having in mind the scope of grounds for recourse, such a conclusion should not be automatic nor immediately drawn. Instead one should balance two principles: party autonomy and tribunal's autonomy. The former is an underlying foundation of modern international arbitration and allows the parties to create a bespoke procedural vehicle for resolving their dispute. The latter is important for the tribunal to properly (and efficiently) fulfill its adjudicative mandate.

It is undisputable that party autonomy gives the parties the right to structure the arbitral process as they will. Nonetheless, arguably, this right should not be unlimited. Possibly the best cut-off point is the moment when the tribunal accepts its mandate, because the new legal relationship is created at that time between three entities – the tribunal and the two parties.

Consequently, from this point in time, the tribunal should have a right to its own vision and expectations regarding the endeavor based on the available legal framework (*i.e.* the

304 Section 68(2)(c) of the EAA.

305 See Merkin & Flannery, *Arbitration Act 1996* (2014) p.312.

306 Section 68(2)(b) of the EAA (excess of powers). See also Merkin & Flannery, *Arbitration Act 1996* (2014) p.312. Another possibility may include Section 68(2)(a) of the EAA (duty to act fairly).

307 Section 10(a)(4) of the FAA. See also section 3.2.2 above, discussing the meaning of "powers". In the U.S. Chapter it has been argued, contrary to the prevailing opinion, that Section 10(a)(4) of the FAA should be limited only to challenges against the tribunal's adjudicative powers or to powers that affect the shape of the *final* award. For further reading, see [the U.S. Chapter].

308 The Restatement (second tentative draft) p.206. The Restatement's description would be equally true in the context of the French and the English systems. Under the French regime, an aggrieved party needs to establish that the tribunal's procedural decision caused it harm. According to the English Arbitration Act, the basic requirements under the Section 68 challenge are that a party furnishes proof that the "irregularity" is serious and causes substantial injustice. For further reading, see Chapter III and Chapter IV.

agreement to arbitrate, the parties' submissions and the arbitration law of the seat). This is important, because it allows the tribunal to plan and structure (thus, to manage) the proceedings in the way it deems the most efficient in order to resolve the dispute between the parties, hence to fulfill its adjudicative mandate.[309] Consequently, the tribunal, faced with the parties' joint procedural request (made after acceptance of its mandate), should have an opportunity to reject it without risking its award being challenged for non-compliance with the mandate.

In any event, the tribunal's power to disregard the parties' (joint) request made after acceptance of the mandate should not be treated lightly. It is only reasonable to give such a power to the tribunal in cases where the joint request may frustrate the proceedings. In other words, having in mind that the priority for the tribunal is to carry out its adjudicative mission, the disregard should only be permitted if the tribunal finds that the proper fulfillment of its adjudicative function is threatened by the parties' (joint) procedural request (for example by delaying the process or by adding layers of complexity which one could have not foreseen at the outset of the process).

In most cases, however, the parties' (procedural) requests will not impose such a risk.[310] Indeed, in most cases, cooperation with the parties and a dialogue will be the most efficient methods for the tribunal to fulfill its adjudicative function uninterruptedly. These tools, mostly based on the tribunal's managerial skills, therefore, should be used by the tribunal at first. Only in exceptional circumstances, may it opt to disobey parties' (joint) procedural directives. If the power is exceedingly or unjustifiably used, both parties may decide to terminate the mandate.[311] If the argument allowing the tribunal to disregard the parties' joint procedural request is rejected, the tribunal's options are limited. The most evident (and extreme) one is for the tribunal to resign.[312] It is, however, highly unsatisfactory, because it will frustrate the procedure even more than the (potentially frustrating) party's joint request. In exceptional circumstances, it might also trigger an issue of civil liability of the tribunal. Another option is for the tribunal to use its persuasive authority and to convince the parties of the better way forward. All in all, it is the tribunal who manages the procedure and it should be one of its skills to reclaim the power over the procedure even if it is occasionally frustrated by the parties and their ideas.

---

309 See further section 1.3 of Chapter VIII (on the adjudicative dimension of the tribunal's mandate).

310 It is likely that the parties in dispute reach a procedural agreement in the midst of the proceedings (only) if they find that the tribunal's procedural or managerial guidance is insufficient. If their undertakings are indeed caused by the tribunal's weakness it might be considered as a warning. Consequently, the tribunal may humbly follow the parties' suggestions or discuss with the parties any alternative it has in mind. In the latter case, it will show its intention to reclaim the reign over the proceedings.

311 See Art. 14 of the ML, Art. 1458 of the FCCP and Section 23 of the EAA. Neither the FAA nor the NYC has any provision on the issue.

312 See Art. 14 of the ML, Art. 1457 of the FCCP and Section 25 of the EAA. Neither the FAA nor the NYC has any provision on the issue.

5 Comparative assessment

Having explained the approach of the different systems to the "excess of mandate" type of challenge it is necessary to outline the main similarities and differences observed (section 5.1) and to explain them (section 5.2 and 5.3).[313]

5.1 *Leading similarities and differences*

A comparative analysis of the "excess of mandate" type of challenge has shown that many features of the post-award review have proved to be similar. Nonetheless, this recourse does not enjoy a homogenous interpretation under all legal systems.

The first of the leading similarities is the pro-arbitration (or pro-enforcement) drive of all the analyzed legal systems. All these instruments recognize that the review on the post-award stage is the extraordinary means of recourse and that the challenge against the arbitral award can only be successful in exceptional circumstances, which are listed in the provisions dealing with post-award recourse. Virtually in all systems, these lists are considered to be exhaustive (arguably, even in the U.S. in the post-*Hall Street* reality).

Secondly, in all systems, it is a party (usually an award-debtor) that needs to bring the "excess of mandate" type of challenge before the court. In none of the reviewed jurisdictions will a court assess a tribunal's compliance with its mandate *ex officio*. Importantly, however, all courts will take into account the parties' conduct during the arbitration, which means that the challenging parties should react to the tribunal's alleged violation of the mandate the moment they find it happened. Otherwise, they might be estopped from raising the same arguments at the post-award stage.

Thirdly, it is also similar how the courts approach the award when faced with it at the post-award stage. In principle, they will be guided by the systemic pro-validity and pro-enforcement approach which manifests itself in several ways. For example, it has been confirmed that the "excess of mandate" type of challenge will not be accepted as a vehicle to review the merits of the case. Additionally, even if a challenge has some merits, national courts in all analyzed legal systems will likely use their remedial power to minimize the effects the challenge has on the arbitral award. Put differently, courts will, generally, try to sever the defective part of the award and enforce a healthy part whenever possible.

Fourthly, although with divergent approaches to the "excess of mandate" type of challenge (which will be explained below), all jurisdictions recognize the same constraints to the tribunal's mandate. Under each legal system (thus both at the setting-aside and

313 As explained at the outset (see section 1), generally, the comparison comprises the national legal systems and the Model Law that are being used as a basis for adopting arbitration laws. The New York Convention is analyzed only in the second stage of the comparison, since it requires a vertical comparison.

enforcement stage), the analysis will be based on three pillars: the agreement to arbitrate, the parties' (subsequent) submissions and the public policy rules (in the case of setting-aside proceedings – rules of the seat, in the case of enforcement proceedings – rules of the place of enforcement). It shows the importance of party autonomy and public policy rules which complement the shape of the mandate introduced by the parties.

Fifthly, one should note that the "excess of mandate" type of challenge is just a piece of a post-award review mechanism. It means that it might be occasionally difficult to identify whether a challenge should be subsumed under an "excess of mandate" or under a different basis. "The usual suspects" that would compete with an "excess of mandate" ground include the "excess of jurisdiction" and the "due process violation" type of grounds (which can be named differently in the different systems). This clash exists in all the reviewed systems, arguably, but for the U.S. if the FAA's "excess of powers" ground is interpreted according to the (draft) Restatement arguments (which advocates for the incorporation of all of the New York Convention grounds for challenge under the "excess of powers" head).

The final similarities can be observed on the level of the application of the "excess of mandate" type of challenge.

For example, and in principle, in all systems (but for the English regime), if the tribunal grants a claim that has not been requested (*ultra petita*), it will be identified as an "excess of mandate" violation (in England it would be an "excess of jurisdiction" violation under Section 67 of the EAA). There are variations on this hypothetical, however, which might induce the application of other grounds for recourse (as suggested in the preceding paragraph). Another example, *i.e.* when the tribunal failed to decide on all claims (*infra petita*), it will not have the potential to be successfully challenged at the post-award stage under any system except for the English Arbitration Act (see Section 68(2)(d) of the EAA).

Decisions regarding the application of law by the tribunal would generally escape a court's scrutiny under the "excess of mandate" type of challenge in all the reviewed systems. Possibly, the only exception is the U.S. system in its shape as offered by the (draft) Restatement. In this case, as explained above, all of the New York Convention grounds will be available under the FAA's "excess of power" ground, which makes its application rather broad. In other systems, possible wrongdoing in the process of application of law would likely be classified under other grounds of recourse.

Decisions on remedies are intertwined with the parties' claim which has been discussed above. It therefore means that they might be subjected to the "excess of mandate" type of challenge under the *ultra petita* scenario in all systems.

In principle, in the last category of decisions, decisions on interest and costs will have similar treatment in all systems. It means that they will be susceptible to the "excess of mandate" type of challenge in cases where they do not comply with the defined limits (the agreement to arbitrate, the parties' requests and the rules of public policy). At the same time, however, these decisions have a somewhat "special" status which increases their chances of surviving the "excess of mandate" type of challenge even when they go beyond the parties' *petita*. In the case of decisions on interest, the tribunal might, for example, rely on the statutory interest regulation allowing it to grant interest as a default option even if not explicitly demanded by the parties. In the case of decisions on costs, the enhanced powers of the tribunal (to award costs differently than agreed and/or requested) will be recognized by all systems when the tribunal needs to discipline the parties.

Having discussed the similarities, it is necessary to reflect on the characteristic features that distinguish the reviewed legal systems from each other.

The first noticeable difference relates to the diversity of the concepts used at the post-award stage to challenge the tribunal's mandate. The Model Law and the New York Convention, in principle, refer to the tribunal's decisions going beyond the submission to arbitration; the interpretation as to the scope of this proviso differs among states adopting the Model Law. Furthermore, the French regime is the only system (out of those selected for the comparison) that allows the challenge in cases where the tribunal fails to comply with the mandate given. Finally, the common law jurisdictions – the English Arbitration Act and the U.S. federal arbitration law – refer to the notion of "excess of powers". Notably, however, the understanding of the meaning of the "excess of powers" ground in England and in the U.S. is completely different.

Additionally, there are minor differences as to the structure of the post-award challenging mechanism. On the one hand, Article 34 of the Model Law (as well as Article V of the New York Convention) distinguishes two categories of grounds, one that has to be brought by the parties and the other one that can be raised by the court on its own motion. Other systems do not make such a distinction. The French courts on the other hand will be able to requalify the challenge if raised under an incorrect head of Article 1520 of the FCCP. The English Arbitration Act distinguishes three separate recourse mechanisms (the tribunal's substantive jurisdiction, serious irregularities and appeals on point of law). Each of those has its own character. In other systems, the grounds are listed within one set of grounds for recourse. In the U.S. one should still be careful with regard to the viability of judicially created grounds for recourse, notwithstanding their uncertain future post-*Hall Street*.

The second difference is the degree of deference granted by the judiciary to the tribunal's decision at the post-award stage (when the challenge is brought based on the "excess of mandate" argument). In Model Law jurisdictions, the scope of the court's review when faced with the "excess of mandate" type of challenge is not uniform. Arguably, however, the better view is to expect the court to give deference to the tribunal's findings. Conversely, in France (when the award is challenged for the tribunal's non-compliance with the entrusted mandate), the courts will be able to exercise a full and independent analysis. Similarly, in England (particularly in cases where the challenge is brought against the tribunal's substantive jurisdiction), the courts will have an opportunity to rehear the case. Although the power of full review is also available when "serious irregularities" are involved (thus *i.a.* "excess of powers"), the test is filtered by the standard of "seriousness" of the irregularity and the substantial injustice it causes. In the U.S. everything depends on whether the "excess of powers" challenge reflects the jurisdictional/threshold objections or any other objections. If the objections are not jurisdictional ones, then the standard of review is extremely limited and deferential. In cases where the challenge deals with the jurisdictional/threshold issues, the default rule is that courts will be able to undertake a full review unless the parties' clearly and unmistakably consent to delegate the powers to deal with jurisdictional/threshold issues to the tribunal. In those cases, the tribunal's decision will be given the same (deferential) treatment as other non-jurisdictional objections. On the enforcement level, the pro-enforcement drive of the New York Convention also promotes the high degree of deference to the tribunal's decision.

On the level of application of the "excess of mandate" type of challenge some discrepancies can also be observed.

The first difference has already been suggested earlier in this section: the English model encompasses that the *ultra petita* challenges are better suited under Section 67 of the EAA, which is designed to seek a recourse against the tribunal's substantive jurisdiction. Other models envisage the *ultra petita* scenario in the core of the "excess of mandate" type of challenge. Additionally, only the English regime provides for recourse against *infra petita* awards. Interestingly, however, the *infra petita* challenges will be brought under a different challenge procedure than the *ultra petita* ones (challenge against serious irregularity, thus the Section 68 challenge instead of the Section 67 challenge).

The second general difference relates to the next type of tribunal's decisions. This type deals with the process of application of law by the tribunal. It has been explained above that the exercise of application of law will largely escape the court's scrutiny (at least if brought under the excess of mandate type of challenge). Nonetheless, the situation will change the moment the tribunal relies on the power to decide *ex aequo et bono*. Under the Model Law (and the New York Convention) regime there are different views as to the ground that is appropriate to challenge the tribunal's decision *ex aequo et bono*; the "excess of mandate" type of challenge competes there with other more procedural grounds for recourse (violation of due process). In France, notably, the mandate to decide *ex aequo et bono* would be considered as a distinct type of mandate (see Article 1512 of the FCCP). Consequently, the recourse against the violation of the mandate will be immediately appropriate. In England, the "excess of powers" challenge will be available. Arguably, however, it does not entail that deciding *ex aequo et bono* will be considered as a separate type of mandate. In the U.S., apart from the "excess of powers" challenge, one should still consider the availability of the "manifest disregard of the law" challenge (notwithstanding its uncertain future), because in its traditional interpretation, it closely resembles the instances where the tribunal usurps the power to decide *ex aequo et bono*.

The final important difference concerns the tribunal's procedural decisions. They have a special status because they are expressions of the tribunal's managerial powers. If they violate the parties' freedom to shape the arbitral procedure, a party might be tempted to invoke the "excess of mandate" type of challenge against the tribunal's alleged wrongdoing. In the Model Law (and the New York Convention) context such an argument will, arguably, not survive, because non-compliance with the procedure designed by the parties is classified under a different ground for recourse. Conversely, under the French international arbitration regime, it might be considered as the tribunal's failure to comply with the mandate. The English Arbitration Act designates a specific ground that deals with the tribunal's failure to conduct the proceedings in accordance with the procedure agreed by the parties. Notwithstanding such a designation, the "excess of powers" ground and other grounds defined as serious irregularities will remain of relevance at the post-award stage. In the U.S. context, the "excess of powers" challenge proves to be, yet again, of practical relevance.

All in all, users of international arbitration might find comfort in the fact that the post-award review is guided by similar principles that favor arbitration. At the same time, however, the successful application of the post-award's regulation requires careful analysis which is not limited to the pro-arbitration standards, but rather focused on details and the intricacies of each system.

5.2 *Explaining the similarities*

Below, the basic rationale will be explained for the high level of convergence that is achieved on the post-award stage of arbitration. First, one may highlight the impact of the New York Convention and the Model Law (section 5.2.1). Additionally, as has been observed at the outset of this analysis,[314] a number of theories have been advanced in an attempt to define the nature of arbitration. Two "pure" theories (that compete with each other) emphasize either the contractual or jurisdictional character of arbitration. The priority given to one of these theories will have a direct impact on the scope of the tribunal's mandate and consequently on the test for its alleged excess. Therefore, the influence of the contractual theory of international arbitration (section 5.2.2) and the jurisdictional theory of international arbitration (section 5.2.3) need to be briefly analyzed.

314 See Chapter I.

5.2.1 The harmonizing effect of the New York Convention and the UNCITRAL's undertakings

The New York Convention has a strong position in the field of international commercial law. As many as 159 countries are a party to the Convention to date.[315] It is generally recognized that "*[t]he purpose of the New York Convention is to promote international commerce and the settlement of international disputes through arbitration.*"[316] The Convention's core aim therefore is to ascertain that international arbitral awards are enforced and that the judges are driven by the Convention's pro-enforcement sentiment. Much effort has been put into ensuring such an approach, including enhancing public availability of the information on the New York Convention (both on its interpretation and case law)[317] and educating actors (judges in particular) involved in international commercial arbitration.[318]

Arguably, the success of the 1958 New York Convention is one of the main reasons for the high level of convergence in the shape of the post-award recourse in the contemporary practice of international arbitration. The Convention is informative that the grounds for a successful challenge against an arbitral award are limited and exhaustive and that no review on the merits should be allowed. Additionally, it is straightforward in setting the maximum standards to the procedure of recognition and enforcement.[319]

The solutions introduced first in the New York Convention, intended to apply at the enforcement stage, were further developed by UNCITRAL in its subsequent undertaking – the Model Law. The Model Law includes, *i.a.*, the same limited list of grounds to challenge the award at the setting-aside proceedings and follows the same pro-arbitration principles as set out in the New York Convention. Consequently, the Model Law further enhances a harmonized application of the same principles as set out in the New York Convention.[320]

315 See http://www.uncitral.org/uncitral/en/uncitral_texts/arbitration/NYConvention_status.html [last accessed 29 April 2018].

316 See ICCA, *ICCA's Guide to the Interpretation of the 1958 New York Convention* (2011) pp.14-15.

317 See, for example, *UNCITRAL Secretariat Guide on the Convention on the Recognition and Enforcement of Foreign Arbitral Awards* available at http://www.uncitral.org/pdf/english/texts/arbitration/NY-conv/2016_Guide_on_the_Convention.pdf [last accessed 14 August 2020] or *ICCA's Guide to the Interpretation of the 1958 New York Convention* available at http://www.arbitration-icca.org/media/1/13890217974630/judges_guide_english_composite_final_jan2014.pdf [last accessed 14 August 2020]. See also http://www.newyorkconvention.org/ [last accessed 14 August 2020], and http://newyorkconvention1958.org/ [last accessed 14 August 2020], http://www.kluwerarbitration.com/CommonUI/NYC.aspx [last accessed 14 August 2020].

318 Apart from the guides enumerated above (fn.317), see also, *i.a.*, http://www.uncitral.org/uncitral/en/publications/online_resources.html [last accessed 14 August 2020]. Additionally, see also "the New York Convention Roadshow" – series of colloquia for judges on the New York Convention organized by the ICCA. For further reading, see http://www.arbitration-icca.org/NY_Convention_Roadshow.html [last accessed 14 August 2020].

319 See Art. III of the NYC.

320 See also Kröll, *Arbitration* (2012) pp.90-91.

Additionally, UNCITRAL makes every effort to inform and educate how the Model Law should be applied and how it is applied.[321] Importantly, the Model Law has a harmonizing effect not only on the states that have decided to adopt it, but also on the non-Model Law jurisdictions like England and the U.S.[322]

All in all, the states that are willing to adhere to the New York Convention's underlying policies (and/or those of the Model Law), are also likely to follow the same non-interventionist approach as a fundamental structure to their own international arbitration regimes.[323] Consequently, the basic rules and procedures governing the "excess of mandate" type of challenge are largely similar. It also explains why the same "excess of mandate" type of challenge can be invoked.

5.2.2 The importance of party autonomy in structuring the adjudicative mandate

Earlier in this chapter the limits to the "arbitral tribunal's mandate" have been explained.[324] As one may readily observe, the tribunal's adjudicative authority will be only as broad as parties would allow it to be. It is so, because modern arbitration statutes emphasize the role of party autonomy – instead of providing a "one size fits all" statutory mechanism, they give parties a great freedom to tailor the arbitral process in accordance to their needs.

As explained by Kröll:

> [f]rom a purely rule based legal perspective, the statutory (public) sources are of primary importance, since they determine how much room is left for party autonomy. In practice, however, the contractual sources are of greater importance, since modern arbitration laws now clearly embrace the principle of party autonomy. The role of party autonomy receives further protection from the international and regional conventions, where they apply.[325]

This holds true for all the analyzed systems, including the New York Convention at the enforcement stage. Consequently, it explains why the contractual component is essential for defining the structure of the adjudicative mandate.

It can be observed therefore that the starting point for ascertaining if the tribunal indeed exceeded its adjudicative mandate is an interpretation of the initial agreement to arbitrate and the parties' subsequent agreements. In principle, all reviewed systems recognize this

---

321 See http://www.uncitral.org/uncitral/en/uncitral_texts/arbitration/1985Model_arbitration.html [last accessed 14 August 2020]. In particular, see *UNCITRAL 2012 Digest of Case Law on the Model Law on International Commercial Arbitration* and the CLOUT database therein.

322 See further section 1.3.

323 See also Sanders, *Arbitration* (1996) pp.35-36.

324 See section 3.1.

325 Kröll, *Arbitration* (2012) p.92.

approach; what may differ, however, is the degree of deference that is given to the parties' choice when a court needs to balance in between the parties' and the tribunals' autonomy.

As explained already in the introduction,[326] the parties use their autonomy to contract out from the court system and to delegate dispute resolution functions to the tribunal. The mechanics of adjudication remain the same, however. Therefore, arbitration relies on the adversarial character of resolving disputes, where the parties' requests are essential. Consequently, all systems recognize that the tribunal's mandate to adjudicate is framed by the parties' dispositions (even though there is no consensus on whether this constitutes a mandate or a jurisdictional aspect of the tribunal's role).

Additionally, it is undisputed that party autonomy is also relevant when shaping the procedure. All systems are similar in the sense that they intentionally include only limited directives on how the procedure should be conducted and protect the parties' right to tailor the arbitral process by allowing recourse at the post-award stage in cases where the tribunal does not comply with the parties' joint (procedural) instructions.

Yet, it should be underlined that there is no convergence whether alleged non-compliance with the parties' joint (procedural) instructions should be considered under the "excess of mandate" type of challenge. Arguably, if one considers that the functional (thus adjudicative) aspect of the mandate is more important than the contractual element, then the failure to comply with the parties' procedural wishes may escape the scope of the "excess of mandate" type of challenge.

5.2.3 The tribunal's autonomy: the significance of the arbitral tribunal's managerial toolbox

The arbitral tribunal, similar to the parties, has its own autonomy. One may identify it, while observing the mandate from a functional (rather than a contractual) perspective. Consequently, one may argue that the tribunal's autonomy has its roots in the jurisdictional nature of arbitration, where the function (*i.e.* to adjudicate, to render a binding and enforceable award upon the parties) is the most important element of the mandate. Arguably, and in certain (procedural) aspects only, the tribunal's autonomy may even take over the parties' autonomy the moment the tribunal is constituted.

The tribunal's autonomy is relevant, because it allows the tribunal to properly fulfill its adjudicative mandate. Put differently, the tribunal requires a certain managerial flexibility in order to render an enforceable award. The arbitration regimes that have been analyzed recognize the necessity of allowing the tribunal adequate freedom in presiding over proceedings. The "special status" of the tribunal's decisions on costs, interest and procedure evidences that. Consequently, one may argue that the analyzed legal systems accept not

326 See Chapter I, p.7.

only the contractual underpinning of the tribunal's mandate, but also the jurisdictional nature of the mandate.

5.3 *Explaining the differences*

Notwithstanding the harmonizing efforts on the transnational level and a number of similarities between the systems, the "excess of mandate" type of challenge is still applied differently. This trend can be explained by the competition between "arbitration-friendly" systems (section 5.3.1) and the autonomous development of the system (section 5.3.2).

5.3.1 The ongoing competition between the leading arbitral centers

It is undisputed that at a macro level all reviewed systems share a similar pro-arbitration philosophy.[327] At the same time, however, each jurisdiction is active in regulatory competition between states in attempts to attract actors active in arbitration. Consequently, these centers are not interested in the full harmonization of the arbitration regulations. Instead, they are likely to cultivate the unique features they offer and the divergence in their approach to arbitration.[328] It will equally hold true to the Model Law and non-Model Law jurisdictions.[329] It is important to note, however, that this reasoning is applicable on the national level of the comparison (thus excluding the New York Convention's enforcement stage).

Arguably, this ongoing competition also explains the dissimilarities between the approaches to the "excess of mandate" type of challenge.[330] It has been explained that there is no uniformity in interpretation of the "excess of mandate" type of challenge throughout the jurisdictions that have adopted the Model Law. Likewise, the failure to comply with the mandate as used in France is not the same concept as the "excess of powers" used in England or in the U.S. Notably, the discrepancy exists also between the two latter common

327 See further section 5.2.1.

328 See also De Ly, *Paradigmatic Changes – Uniformity, Diversity, Due Process and Good Administration of Justice: The Next Thirty Years* (2016) pp.21-23 (p.23: "*Notwithstanding the major breakthrough brought about by the Model Law, the picture remains one of divergence in the western world with major arbitration centres in London, Paris, New York, Zurich or Geneva having arbitration laws based on different traditions, assumptions, approaches and rules. No substantial modification of the Model Law being contemplated and no major changes to be expected in non-Model Law countries, an alignment between these two families cannot be expected in the near future.*").

329 The Model Law does not have to be adopted in *verbatim* which makes room for introducing the unique features of an arbitration regime.

330 As well as the post-award architecture at large. For example, two separate lists of grounds that have to be raised by the parties and *ex officio* by the court itself under the Model Law and the New York Convention; three separate challenge mechanisms (substantive jurisdiction, serious irregularities and an appeal on point of law) under the English Arbitration Act etc.

law jurisdictions, notwithstanding the fact that the terminology ("excess of powers") is, in principle, the same.

Unsurprisingly, the scope of the "excess of mandate" type of challenge will depend on the meaning of "the mandate" itself. Consequently, yet again, one should reflect which aspect of "the mandate" (the contract or the function) is prioritized. Arguably, it leads to more theoretical reflections on the nature of arbitration (contractual or jurisdictional). Neither of the (analyzed) post-award systems, however, may be analyzed with the reference to one of those theories alone, albeit one of them might be more useful than the other in certain cases. In general, the review against the alleged excess of the tribunal's mandate should be always based on the balancing exercise between party autonomy and tribunal's autonomy.

5.3.2 Historical development and legal heritage

Another reason why the systems differ is rooted within their heritage and historical development. As highlighted immediately above,[331] each system is eager to preserve its competitive edge developed over the years or eventually reverse the trend, which is considered unattractive for international arbitration users. It means that the legal heritage and the development remain important factors explaining distinctive views on the "excess of mandate" type of challenge. With that in mind, one should reflect on the evolution of the Model Law and the English and the U.S. arbitration systems.

For example, the Model Law is a product of an extensive debate under the auspices of the United Nations. In turn, thanks to the contribution of representatives of different legal cultures, the application of the Model Law is, in principle, universal. Yet, since it is "only" a model legislation, it naturally evolves in different ways in each country where it is implemented. Consequently, it is possible, that depending on the legal culture of the adopting country, the "excess of mandate" type of challenge might be interpreted differently by the courts which, in turn, hinders the level of uniformity in the application of this mechanism of recourse.

Arguably it is the English regime that transformed the most by overcoming historical hostility towards arbitration. Notably, however, even after modifications, it remains the system with a rather unique structure of three separate challenge mechanisms, including an (opt-out) appeal on point of law. In any event, the pro-arbitration drive of the 1996 Arbitration Act does not leave room for doubt that the recourse against an arbitral award is exceptional.

Finally, it should be pointed out that the Federal Arbitration Act has been introduced in the U.S. at the beginning of the early twentieth century to defy infamous (judicial)

331 See section 5.3.1.

hostility towards arbitration. Nowadays, however, the value of this statutory framework is limited, because the U.S. Supreme Court, through its decisions, effectively creates the arbitration system anew. The degree of deviation from the statutory framework is unique; at the same time, the U.S. Supreme Court's modification of the system is used to (repeatedly) confirm the federal policy favoring arbitration and to evidence the great deference given to arbitrators' findings. Consequently, U.S. courts tend to hold parties to their arbitration bargain and rarely accept arguments that the tribunal exceeded its powers. Another layer of the evolution of the U.S. system may be added by the ALI Restatement on International Commercial Arbitration. It remains to be seen whether the Restatement triggers structural (statutory) changes of the system or by means of its persuasive force impacts the system.

All in all, the development of the arbitration system(s) inevitably has an impact on the interpretation of the individual elements of the post-award architecture, including on the "excess of mandate" type of challenge.

VIII Conclusions and recommendations

1 Conclusions

1.1 Preliminary observations

The purpose of this study was to identify the similarities and differences between different concepts of the "excess of mandate" type of challenge and to determine how the national courts review arbitral awards on the basis of "excess of mandate" (and, consequently, in what instances they accept that a tribunal violated its mandate). Following the introductory chapter, the book has been divided into two parts.

The first part included reflections on three national legal regimes (*i.e.* France, England, and the U.S.) as well as on the UNCITRAL Model Law and the New York Convention. The international instruments (the Model Law and the New York Convention) were introduced respectively in Chapters II and VI of Part I, whereas the national statutory frameworks of France, England and the U.S. were presented in Chapters III, IV and V.

The second part was comprised of the preliminary remarks together with a comparative law analysis, including an explanation for the (leading) similarities and differences of the studied systems in Chapter I and the general research conclusions, propositions and the directions for further research in Chapter II.

As a final preliminary observation, one should be reminded that the structure of the comparative law chapter (Chapter I of Part II) mirrored the structure of each of the chapters of Part I. It means that the first part of each chapter was dedicated to discussing the general rules governing the challenge at the post-award stage, whereas the second part dealt with the application of the "excess of mandate" type of challenge to different decisions made by arbitral tribunals. The division of the arbitral tribunal's decisions into several types was aimed at pinpointing a potential rationale for successful challenges against the "excess of mandate".[1]

1.2 Pro-arbitration standard eliminating the possibility of review on the merits

At the outset, it is necessary to recap that all systems are driven by a pro-arbitration (or pro-enforcement in the case of the New York Convention) thrust. It means, amongst other

1 See also below sections 1.6-1.10.

things, that all elements of the statutory architecture of arbitration regimes are set to enhance the finality of arbitral decisions. All systems recognize the exceptional character of the post-award recourse against the award. Moreover, the list of the setting-aside grounds is exhaustive and interpreted narrowly. Additionally, the national courts have ample tools to save at least a part of the award in case some deficiencies are found which, however, do not warrant a full set aside or full refusal to enforce.

Most importantly, however, the pro-arbitration policy reinforces the deference to the finality of the tribunal's award. Consequently, it is repeatedly confirmed that no review of the merits is possible. The courts may not, and should not, get involved in reassessing the tribunal's conclusion on the level of the substantive dispute between the parties. Deference intends to avoid that the tribunal's decision on the merits would be nothing else than the adjudication of the first instance subject to an ordinary appeal to a court of higher instance.

The "no review on the merits" principle is particularly relevant in the context of the "excess of mandate" type of challenge if one considers that this recourse gives a court an opportunity to evaluate how the tribunal exercised its adjudicative function. This may, in turn, attract a closer look at the "correctness" of the tribunal's decisions. In any event, the courts to date restrict the review undertaken and defer to the tribunal's findings.

1.3 *Two dimensions of the "tribunal's mandate" and limits that might be exceeded*

The analysis of Chapter I of Part II (the comparative law chapter) confirmed a hypothesis presented in the introduction that the arbitral tribunal's mandate has two dimensions and the alleged excess of the mandate is to be considered in each of these dimensions. The first dimension is a contractual one, whereas the second one focuses on the adjudicative function delegated to an arbitral tribunal. Consequently, all analyzed systems recognize the importance of three elements in defining the tribunal's mandate: an agreement to arbitrate, the parties' subsequent submissions and fundamental rules of public policy.

In the contractual dimension, the tribunal's mandate is shaped by the parties themselves. Therefore, it is an agreement to arbitrate that (initially) plays a key role in structuring the scope of the tribunal's mandate, because in an agreement to arbitrate parties convey their intention to resolve their disputes in arbitration. In other words, they consent to vest the adjudicative mandate in an arbitral tribunal (and not in a court). Additionally, they are able to express their expectations (usually by a reference to the arbitration rules) on how the arbitration is to be conducted.

The abstract scope of the mandate outlined in the agreement to arbitrate, however, needs to be supplemented by the parties' submissions when the dispute arises. It is only then that the tribunal is given the power to adjudicate *in concreto*. Importantly, the mandate in the first dimension might be a dynamic concept when introduced claims change or parties reach an agreement modifying the way the arbitration is conducted during the proceedings. The question that remains open is whether the tribunal that is unwilling to accept these dynamics may be found in excess of its mandate.

The second dimension focuses more on the tribunal's adjudicative function and as such it is perhaps better to refer to the tribunal's *mission* rather than the mandate. As explained above, it is the parties that agree to defer to the tribunal's (and not a court's) resolution of their disputes. It is only possible, however, because states themselves delegate their monopoly to adjudicate to arbitral tribunals. Parties are therefore just the agents through which states empower tribunals with their adjudicative function.

Arguably, the power to adjudicate is also *a duty* to resolve the dispute. Consequently, it requires that the tribunal should be granted access to certain (procedural) tools and powers that ensure that the obligation to resolve a dispute is fulfilled.[2] As a result, one might reason that there are few limits on the tribunal's adjudicative powers imposed by states. In principle, the constraints are limited to compliance with the rules of (international) public policy of the seat (or, in the case of the New York Convention, of the enforcement state). Consequently, these limitations are far more static and predictable than the limitations introduced by the parties.

Both dimensions are relevant in an assessment of the proper fulfillment of a tribunal's mandate. Consequently, both dimensions will be relevant when the mandate is reviewed at the post-award stage. The distribution of accents between them, however, might influence the way the "excess of mandate" type of challenge is applied. Put differently, depending on if the court is willing to accept that the "excess" refers more to one of the dimensions of the mandate than the other (contractual or functional), its choice will likely influence, in turn, the way it approaches the challenge itself.[3] This would be particularly true in the context of a tribunal's non-compliance with the parties' agreement to modify the scope of the dispute or with their procedural directives advanced after the constitution of the tribunal.

2 It is closely linked with the tribunal's managerial authority over the procedure. For further reading see section 4.5.3 of Chapter VII.

3 Arguably, if the court is prone to look at the "excess of mandate" type of challenge in the contractual dimension it would be close to what is being reviewed under the "excess of jurisdiction" challenge; if, however, it will analyze the "excess of mandate" type of challenge in the functional dimension, it will likely find similarities between the mandate violations and due process violations. Additionally, since the functional aspect refers to the decision-making process, the analysis runs the risk of a merits review.

1.4 *The use of the "mandate" in statutory frameworks in the analyzed legal systems*

The general conclusion is that there is no consistency in the use of the term "mandate" in the statutory texts. The Model Law makes use of the term only as a definition of a timeframe to the tribunal's adjudicative powers. Only the French system refers to the "mandate" at the post-award stage. Conversely, the common law jurisdictions prefer to apply "the excess of powers" test. A detailed analysis of the terminology used in the selected systems has been introduced above.[4] In general, the discrepancy is evident, which leads to the conclusion that one should be careful in assessing "excess of mandate" challenges under the assumption that the concept will be understood in an identical or similar fashion in the jurisdictions reviewed.

1.5 *Possible difficulties in selecting appropriate grounds to challenge awards on the basis of "excess of the tribunal's mandate"*

The difficulties in applying the "excess of mandate" types of challenge arise, because the same factual underpinning may trigger different avenues of recourse against the arbitral award. As a consequence, it is occasionally difficult to identify which ground for challenge is the most suitable one.

There are two areas in which the tension is visible: the first is between the "excess of mandate" type of challenge and the excess of jurisdiction challenge; the second clash is with due process violations. These have been discussed in detail in section 3.4 of the comparative chapter.[5] In principle, the application of an inappropriate ground might have a detrimental effect on the successfulness of the challenge.

These problems are related to the two dimensions of the tribunal's mandate mentioned above.[6] Essentially, the jurisdictional and the mandate issues have their cause in the same contractual bases for the tribunal's activities, whereas due process and the mission violations arise from the way the adjudicative function is fulfilled by the tribunal. In turn, one may wonder whether the "excess of mandate" type of challenge has added value, if the same wrongdoings are covered by other grounds for challenge such as the violation of the agreement to arbitrate or of due process.

4 See section 3.2 of Chapter VII.

5 See Chapter VII.

6 See section 1.3.

1.6 *Availability of the "excess of mandate" type of challenge against the tribunal's decisions on claims*

In the previous chapters, claims have been differentiated and assessed separately. The aim was to observe if the approach towards the relief granted differs depending, for example, on the legal basis of the claim (contractual or not) and on the sequencing of the claims (whether it is brought as a claim, counterclaim or a set-off etc.).

The analysis has shown that the "excess of mandate" type of challenge should be available, irrespective of the abovementioned division, in instances where the tribunal granted a claim that had not been requested, *i.e.* where the relief granted was higher or even different than the one sought. Notably, if the award does not respond to all claims, the annulment (on the basis of the "excess of mandate" type of challenge) will not be, in principle, allowed in any of the (analyzed) legal systems (apart from England).[7]

That being said, a number of difficulties has been observed, particularly in cases where: (i) the claims or counterclaims brought arise from different contracts, (ii) the set-off claims are based on a different contract than the initial claim and, finally, (iii) the tribunal decides to requalify the legal basis for the claim requested and granted the requested relief based on such a recharacterization.

These instances might potentially be considered under the "excess of mandate" type of challenge, because they relate to the relief granted by the tribunal and, more generally, to the tribunal's duty to adjudicate the dispute brought before it. It is likely, however, that they would be nonetheless subsumed under other grounds, namely excess of jurisdiction (in the case of multi-contract examples, where the jurisdiction of the tribunal to deal with the issues arising out of different contracts is in question) and due process or public policy violation (when the parties were not heard as to the requalification of claims and consequently "surprises" them).

One additional conclusion should be given in the context of set-offs arising out of different contracts. Although, on occasion, the jurisdiction (or the mandate) of the tribunal to decide on the set-off claim might be questioned, there are strong arguments that justify the tribunal taking upon its adjudicative mandate and including set-offs in calculations of the final award.[8] Considering, once again, that the ultimate goal of the arbitral tribunal is to resolve the dispute between the parties, it should allow them to use all available substantive defenses. Otherwise, instead of challenges of the "excess of mandate", it may, potentially, face the challenge of violation of a party's right to present its case.

---

7 They do, however, offer other tools to remedy such an alleged failure. See section 4.2.6 of Chapter VII.

8 See also section 4.2.3 of Chapter VII.

1.7 *Availability of the "excess of mandate" type of challenge to the process of application of law*

By and large, it has been observed that the process of application of law by the arbitral tribunal escapes a court's scrutiny under the "excess of mandate" type of challenge. Similar to the tribunal's decision on claims, the process of application of law has been also deconstructed into smaller pieces, starting from the method of selection of the applicable law through the choice of applicable law, with separate sections related to the application of substantive law and the mandatory rules of law. Final reflections dealt with a tribunal's decision based on standards such as *amiable composition* or *ex aequo et bono.*

As already suggested, in general, a tribunal's legal conclusions (even if deemed by the court as "erroneous") are largely safe, unless they violate the public policy of the seat (or of the place of enforcement in the case of the New York Convention). It is so, because of the fundamental principle of no review on the merits. It gives the much needed flexibility to the arbitral tribunal, whose adjudicative mandate is inherently connected to the process of application of law.

It is important to note, however, that in the context of the choice of method of selection of the applicable law (*e.g.* conflict of laws analysis or *voie directe*) or designation of applicable law, the "excess of mandate" type of challenge (in non-Model Law jurisdictions) might be available in cases where the parties' mutual choice is disregarded by the tribunal. As always, the parties' disposition (especially a joint one) is paramount. If the tribunal deliberately decides to ignore the parties' choice, it will fail to comply with its mandate. Even more so, if the parties were not heard on the tribunal's findings on the applicable law. Although the "excess of mandate" type of challenge might be available, it is likely to compete with other grounds, such as violation of due process or public policy.

In order to properly fulfill its mandate, the tribunal should be able to rely on its own legal expertise. It is also important that the tribunal addresses potential issues related to the applicable mandatory rules. This does not change the fact, however, that the tribunal needs to give parties a chance to comment on its legal analysis. It further means that the tribunal cannot "surprise" the parties with its legal conclusions. Although it relates greatly to the performance of the tribunal's mandate, this violation is, again, more suitably addressed under the due process or public policy grounds.

The last observation to be made deals with the tribunal's decision *ex aequo et bono.* In the Model Law systems (and under the New York Convention), deciding *ex aequo et bono* without express authorization might be qualified under the two competing grounds, namely the "excess of mandate" type of challenge and the violation of due process. At the same time in other jurisdictions, the "excess of mandate" type of challenge alone would be the most suitable. Especially in the French context, one could observe that, arguably, deciding *ex aequo et bono* constitutes an independent type of tribunal's mandate and can be challenged if not based on an authorization by the parties.[9]

1.8 Availability of the "excess of mandate" type of challenge to tribunal's decisions on remedies

Although separating "decisions on claims" from "decisions on remedies" (which usually are the same decision granting/rejecting *e.g.* "claim for damages") might be considered as artificial, it was important in order to identify whether any emphasis is put on a type of claim or on a type of remedy sought during the application of the "excess of mandate" type of challenge.

The broad scope of the tribunal's remedial powers is essential in the proper fulfillment of its adjudicative mission. The analysis focused on the three (arguably) most common categories of remedies sought in arbitration: damages, specific performance and contract adaptation and gap-filling.

In principle, the standard constraints will apply, which means that the tribunal is only allowed to use these remedial tools when parties request it to do so. Consequently, an award granting damages higher or different than sought will be an adequate basis to invoke the "excess of mandate" type of challenge.[10] Similarly, if any remedial power is expressly excluded by the parties in their agreement to arbitrate, the tribunal should respect such a limitation.

It has been observed, however, that the courts will accept that the tribunal may have a broader remedial discretion if it comes from the parties (either expressed in the contract or coming from applicable substantive law). It means that there is no controversy in the tribunal awarding specific performance (if asked) nor is there a controversy when the tribunal awards the type of damages that are foreign to the place of arbitration (such as punitive damages). In any event, it is sensible for the tribunal to sever them (*e.g.* punitive damages) and include them as an independent part of the award in the anticipation of a potential challenge.[11]

Finally, one should note that parties are well advised to be explicit in granting the tribunal gap-filling authority. As long as the award might survive the "excess of mandate" type of challenge, it will be more susceptible to a successful recourse without express contractual provisions allowing the tribunal to fill the gaps. It is especially so considering that none of the reviewed arbitration systems include a specific rule addressing the tribunal's power to fill the gaps.

---

9 See Art. 1512 of the FCCP.

10 It is likely that the annulment will affect only the amount that goes beyond the parties' request.

11 This way there will be no problem in enforcing the remainder of the award.

1.9 *Availability of the "excess of mandate" type of challenge to tribunal's decisions accessory to the parties' main submissions*

The adjudicative process involves not only decisions on the parties' main claims, but also on interest (to main claims seeking monetary relief) and on the costs of the arbitration. These decisions might be considered as inherent to the arbitral adjudicative process and as such deserve separate attention.

In principle, the decisions on interest should be tested against the "excess of mandate" type of challenge in the same fashion as any other decisions. It means that if parties agree to limit the tribunal's powers to award interest or the interest granted is higher or different from the one sought, parties may have a legitimate reason to seek a recourse. Importantly, however, on the occasion when the main claim is granted, the substantive law may authorize the tribunal to award interest. If such a default mechanism is available, the tribunal's decision might be upheld even in the absence of the parties' request. In any event, it is better for the tribunal to be guided by the parties' petitions.

Also a decision on costs has a special status, because of its important procedural function of disciplining the parties. Consequently, the review of the "excess of mandate" should be slightly modified. It does start with the traditional analysis, namely with a review whether the parties did limit the power to award costs and a comparison between the parties' requests on costs with the tribunal's findings. An extra layer of deference, however, should be given if the court finds that the tribunal had disregarded the parties' instructions regarding costs in order to penalize their conduct during the proceedings. In principle, such a disciplining mechanism should be well within the tribunal's adjudicative mandate even if it does not correspond to the parties' *petita* (thus, arguably, the mandate in its contractual dimension). Therefore, it should survive the "excess of mandate" type of challenge.

1.10 *Application of the "excess of mandate" type of challenge to the tribunal's procedural decisions*

One of the undisputed values of arbitration is that the parties are able to shape the proceedings in accordance with their preference instead of following the procedural structure of a certain legal system. When the tribunal is given its adjudicative mandate, it is expected to follow the parties' procedural demands. Consequently, if the tribunal does not comply with these procedural instructions, its decision might be challenged at the post-award stage.

At first, it is important to highlight that the tribunal's decisions on procedure do not have an adjudicative function. Instead, they are rather managerial tools at the disposition of the arbitral tribunal. If one considers the two dimensions of the mandate, one should conclude that these decisions should not fit comfortably with the scope of the "excess of mandate" type of challenge. This is not to say, however, that parties should be barred from raising objections at the post-award stage. The only concern regards too broad an interpretation of the "excess of mandate" type of challenge.

Consequently, the research has shown that all the systems recognize that the parties should be able to challenge such a tribunal's decision. Importantly, however, the Model Law and the New York Convention systems designate a separate ground for the tribunal's decisions that do not follow the procedure, whereas other jurisdictions (France, England and the U.S.) will consider such a violation under the "excess of mandate" type of challenge.[12] At the same time, it is recognized that not every deviation from the prescribed procedures will suffice to successfully challenge the award – it has to be material. Taking into account the functional dimension of the tribunal's mandate,[13] it has been argued that such a procedural deviation should also be connected with the adjudication of the parties' claims in order to be subsumed under the "excess of mandate" type of challenge.

As highlighted above,[14] the tribunal's mandate in a contractual dimension might be considered as a dynamic concept, *i.e.* exposed to potential alterations made by the parties. In the context of the adjudicative function of the tribunal, it relates to modifications of claims brought by the parties. The question is whether, and if so, to what extent, parties may modify the procedural conduct. Put differently, does the tribunal (that has accepted its mandate) put its award at risk if it refuses to comply with the joint procedural request (*e.g.* an additional round of submissions made by the parties during the arbitral process)?

Possibly, the answer to this question is the most controversial issue related to the tribunal's procedural decisions. It shows the tension between party autonomy (and its limits) and the tribunal's autonomy to properly fulfill its adjudicative function. It has been concluded that the tribunal should be able to refuse to follow the parties' procedural instructions that are given after the tribunal's acceptance of the mandate without putting its award at risk. That being said, the tribunal should not make use of such a power lightly. It should only be available at the tribunal's disposal if the parties' joint request imperils the fulfillment of the adjudicative function. In most instances, however, the performance of the adjudicative function will not be endangered. Additionally, the tribunal should be able to persuade the parties of its vision of the procedural conduct or at least to convince

12 Although in England a separate ground for the "failure by the tribunal to conduct the proceedings in accordance with the procedure agreed by the parties" exists (see Section 68(2)(c) of the EAA), due to its limited practical significance, it is possible that other heads from the list of serious irregularities will apply. See further Chapter VII.

13 See section 1.3.

14 See section 1.3.

them of a solution that is satisfactory to all. Consequently, disregard of a joint procedural agreement should be allowed, but only in exceptional circumstances.

1.11 *Looking at the concept of the tribunal's mandate through lenses of the post-award challenge against its excess*

A closer look at the "excess of mandate" type of challenge made it possible to identify several conclusions regarding the nature and the concept of the arbitral tribunal itself. It holds true, even though the "excess of mandate" type of challenge is not understood everywhere in the same fashion and that different accents may play a role.

At the same time, however, it remains undisputed that the tribunal's findings on the merits escape the court's control (no review on the merits). It is important because it shows that the dispute resolution function is truly delegated outside the court system. In turn, the courts have no intention of reclaiming their dispute resolution power and they are generally satisfied with their supervisory role over the arbitral process.

Additionally, it is concluded that both dimensions of the tribunal's mandate, namely its contractual nature and adjudicative function are relevant in addressing the tribunal's potential violation at the post-award stage. It further means that the definition of the tribunal's mandate should not only be limited to either of those dimensions. Moreover, because of these two dimensions, a number of tensions may occur. These are related to a competition between party and tribunal's autonomy.

Another finding deals with the "dynamics" of the concept of the mandate. In other words, the question is whether the mandate can be altered during the proceedings, and who has the power to modify it. Obviously, it is the parties that are able to change the scope of the mandate by modifying the scope of their submission. In principle, however, this should be allowed only with the permission of the tribunal. Notably, it is less clear, if the same principle would apply to the control over the procedure. Arguably, after the mandate is accepted, the tribunal should be able to reject the parties' procedural instructions if they threaten the fulfillment of the adjudicative function. In any event, in the context of the "excess of mandate" type of challenge, it might be relevant to identify if the concept of the mandate is dynamic or static.

1.12 *Potential changes in the shape of the arbitral tribunal's mandate*

Traditionally, international arbitration has been valued for its informal and confidential character, for the possibility of the proceedings to be tailor-made to the parties' needs and for the ease of enforcement of the arbitral award. In this matrix, the adjudicative mission affected only the parties involved and could be reasonably analyzed in its contractual dimension.[15]

It is yet to be seen, however, if the ongoing developments in international arbitration will not or should not affect the shape of the tribunal's mandate. If one considers the increased judicialization and formalization of the arbitral process, the phenomenon of a "due process paranoia" and the abuse of process, one may wonder if the parties' continuous influence on the shape of the tribunal's mandate should not be constrained and the power over the procedure not be given to the tribunal (after it is constituted). At the same time, one may reflect if the impact of the development of investor-state arbitration may have on international commercial arbitration (together with an increased number of stakeholders) will not result in a different understanding of the tribunal's mandate in its adjudicative dimension. It brings potential risks at the post-award stage, considering that new arguments against the "excess of mandate" will be brought and it will be up to the courts of each individual jurisdiction to decide as to the scope of the tribunal's autonomy. Consequently, instead of a common framework for this basic notion, the approaches might increasingly diverge.

2 Recommendations

Based on the abovementioned conclusions, the research offers a few propositions addressed to the parties in arbitration (section 2.1), for arbitrators and judges (section 2.2) and for legislators/UNCITRAL (section 2.3). These will be presented below.

2.1 *Recommendations for parties*

Since arbitration is contractual by nature, the best way to influence the mandate is to do so by the parties' consent, shaped and controlled. By means of the agreement, therefore, the parties may tailor the tribunal's mandate to its needs (section 2.1.1) or try to exclude the possibility of the "excess of mandate" recourse (section 2.1.2). Whatever they decide, it is preferable that they undertake a more conscious choice of what they expect from arbitrators.

2.1.1 Shaping the mandate

The first solution available for the parties is to be more attentive to the tribunal's rights and obligation at the outset of the proceedings or even at the stage of drafting their

15 See section 1.3.

agreement to arbitrate. This way, the parties' choices will be controlling to the tribunal, and, at the same time, it will give a clear(er) structure of what parties expect from the tribunal and the arbitral process itself. Arguably, it holds true particularly if parties wish to narrow the mandate of arbitral tribunal.

If arbitrators learn what "type" of mandate will be entrusted to them before they accept their function, it is less likely that they will "exceed" (in the eyes of the aggrieved party) the mandate at the later stage. Therefore, even in cases where the agreement to arbitrate is broad, parties may supplement it with additional provisions on the tribunal's rights and obligations. This may include (or expressly exclude) for example:

1. The tribunal's powers regarding set-off,
2. The tribunal's powers to perform independent legal research,
3. The scope of the tribunal's remedial powers (especially in the context of filling gaps),
4. The scope of the tribunal's sanctioning authority,
5. The tribunal's sovereignty over the proceedings.

Of course, such inclusions will become a "double-edged sword" that will limit the availability of the recourse at the post-award stage. This, however, is the goal of the "one-stop shop for arbitration", the notion that has the finality of the arbitral award at heart.

2.1.2 Exclusion agreements

In principle, parties wishing to ensure the finality of the arbitral award have yet another option, namely, they may try to contract out of the (part of) post-award review mechanism, by way of an exclusion agreement in their contract.

Unsurprisingly, the purpose of the exclusion agreement is to agree that the tribunal's decision is final and that the post-award recourse is excluded. It is also, at least theoretically, possible that parties instead of completely excluding the post-award recourse, narrow it. Limiting the scope of the post-award recourse might be a particularly useful tool especially in the context of the challenge against the alleged "excess of mandate". At the same time, however, it is necessary to note that the construction of the international arbitration regime at the arbitral seat might not allow the parties to contract out from the post-award judicial control.

In general, the setting-aside provisions in the reviewed systems constitute their integral part designed to tackle only a limited number of serious violations. Because of this exclusivity, the setting-aside provisions will likely be considered as a mandatory part of the arbitration law. Consequently, the parties' agreement to modify the structure of the post-award review might not be allowed or be allowed only in a specific form. For the research at hand, it is therefore relevant to reflect whether it is possible to eliminate the "excess of mandate" type of challenge.

No uniform answer can be given in the Model Law context. The problem arises, because "*[m]ost national arbitration statutes do not contain provisions expressly addressing the validity or enforceability of agreements excluding annulment rights. That is true, in particular, of the UNCITRAL Model Law, where neither Article 34 nor any other provision of the statute addresses the issue.*"[16] Additionally, the Model Law courts reach different conclusions as to the validity of the exclusion agreements.[17] Therefore, parties are required to investigate if the designated seat will enforce the exclusion agreement. For example, in Belgium according to Article 1718 of BJC the explicit exclusion agreement made in the agreement to arbitrate or later will be enforceable provided that none of the parties is connected to Belgium.[18] Moreover, in Germany it seems that opting-out of the "excess of mandate" type of challenge would be possible, but only *after* the award is rendered.[19] These conclusions may not apply, however, to other Model Law jurisdictions.[20]

As explained in the Chapter on the French system, after the 2011 reform, parties may contractually waive their rights to seek annulment of the arbitral award.[21] Importantly, however, the policy choice made by the French legislator entails that "*[e]ither the parties choose not to have any right to seek a set-aside in France, or they maintain the review by the French courts as provided for under French law.*"[22] It means that excluding Article 1520(3) of the FCCP alone will not be possible.

Similar difficulties will appear under the English system, because the "excess of powers" challenge is included in the list of serious irregularities of Section 68 of the EAA. Since Section 68 of the EAA is a mandatory provision,[23] the parties' agreement to narrow (Section 68) post-award recourse will not be enforceable. Also in the U.S. it will not be possible to enforce the agreements that narrow the scope of the post-award review.

The Restatement concluded that

> [p]arties may not by agreement reduce or eliminate the grounds for vacating or denying confirmation of a U.S. Convention award or for denying recognition or enforcement of a foreign Convention award, including by agreeing to subject their dispute to the arbitration law of a state within the United States that allows

16 Born, *International Commercial Arbitration* (2014) p.3368.

17 Born, *International Commercial Arbitration* (2014) pp.3368-3367.

18 See Art. 1718 of the BJC. For further reading, see also Verbruggen, *Commentary on Part VI of the Belgian Judicial Code, Chapter VII: Article 1718* (2016) pp.489-494.

19 Kreindler et al., *Commercial Arbitration in Germany* (2016) p.329. Scherer, *The fate of parties' agreements on judicial review of awards: a comparative and normative analysis of party-autonomy at the post-award stage* (2016) p.444.

20 For further reading, see also Born, *International Commercial Arbitration* (2014) pp.3364-3378.

21 Art. 1522 of the FCCP. For further reading, see Chapter III.

22 Scherer, *The fate of parties' agreements on judicial review of awards: a comparative and normative analysis of party-autonomy at the post-award stage* (2016) p.443.

23 See Schedule 1 of the EAA.

> reduced review or provides fewer grounds for such relief than those provided in the applicable Convention.[24]

This is also in line with the Supreme Court decision in *Hall Street Assocs, LLC v. Mattel, Inc.*[25] Although it might be difficult to enforce such an agreement under the current system, the use of party autonomy at the post-award stage is increasingly endorsed by scholars which may change the dominant approach.[26]

2.1.3 Inclusion of the appeal mechanism

Instead of limiting the scope of the post-award review, parties may also wish to broaden it. Similar to the narrowing of the post-award review, however, in many jurisdictions expanding the scope of the post-award judicial control might not be possible. That being said, parties may contemplate introducing an arbitral appeal mechanism instead. This way they will be able to control any potential mistakes the tribunal made and will not need to disguise its merits review with the "excess of mandate" type of challenge.

2.2 Recommendations for arbitrators and judges

Another groups of actors that are affected by the concept of the mandate are arbitrators during the proceedings and judges at the post-award stage. Recommendation for each of the group will be presented in the separate sections below (section 2.2.1 and section 2.2.2).

2.2.1 Active participation of the tribunal in structuring the mandate

As explained above, arbitrators should feel comfortable in fulfilling their mandate and have a right to expect that their adjudicative function comes with degree of autonomy which inherently includes managerial powers over procedure, thus also over the parties. This autonomy should be used with care, however.

Arbitrators can benefit from employing the two-dimension concept of their mandate in order to better understand their role as arbitrators. Additionally, defining dimensions would allow both the parties and the arbitrators to better communicate their expectations during the lifecycle of the arbitral proceedings. Arguably, it would in turn enhance efficiency of the proceedings and reduce the likelihood of the post-award challenge.

24 The Restatement (second tentative draft) p.304.

25 *Hall Street Assocs, LLC v. Mattel, Inc.* 552 U.S. 576, 128 S. Ct. 1396, 170 L. Ed. 2d 254 (2008).

26 See Born, *International Commercial Arbitration* (2014) pp.3364-3378, and Scherer, *The fate of parties' agreements on judicial review of awards: a comparative and normative analysis of party-autonomy at the post-award stage* (2016) pp.437-457.

Therefore, it is recommended that tribunals take an active role in defining (or clarifying) their mandates (in both dimensions) at the outset of the proceedings.

2.2.2 Following "no review on the merits" approach by judges

The undertaken analysis has shown that the reviewing courts are not easily persuaded by the arguments raised against the tribunals' decisions on the basis of the "excess of mandate" type of challenge. This position should be complimented. Consequently, the recommendation that can be given to the judges continue to apply the pro-arbitration design of arbitration laws.

Additionally, the study shows that looking at the mandate from the two-dimension perspective (by identifying the adjudicative and contractual aspect of the tribunal's mandate)[27] helps to conceptualize what authority is given to the tribunal. In turn, it facilitates explaining what aspects of the tribunal's decision should be actually controlled by the court at the post-award stage. Consequently, using the two-dimension of the tribunal's mandate can be a useful tool for the courts when deciding on the "excess of mandate" challenge.

In particular, the court is faced with "excess of mandate" type of challenge and required to review at the adjudicative dimension of the mandate, should always remember to refrain from acting as an appeal body for the arbitral tribunal's decision.[28]

It all leads to the conclusion that the courts should not allow the parties to use the "excess of mandate" type of challenge as a disguised vehicle for reviewing the merits of the arbitral tribunal's award.

2.3 Recommendations for legislators/the UNCITRAL

The study have shown that there is a room for improvement for each of the analysed systems in the context of the "excess of mandate" type of challenge. There are several ways the policy makers can address this post-award mechanism. One is to abolish (if existing) the reference to the mandate (section 2.3.1), the second is to follow the Swiss model (section 2.3.2). Thirdly, one should consider the formula created by van den Berg for the purpose of the amendment of the New York Convention (or its variation) (section 2.3.3). Finally, the UNCITRAL may address interpretative difficulties in the Recommendation (section 2.3.4).

27 See also section 1.3 of Chapter VIII (on the dimensions of the tribunal's mandate).

28 See also section 1.2 of this Chapter.

2.3.1 Abolishing the reference to the tribunal's mandate at the post-award stage

As explained above, the "excess of mandate" type of challenge may at times create difficulties in interpretation, because it refers to the tribunal's mandate in two dimensions: the first one relates to the contractual aspect of the mandate, whereas the second to the (adjudicative) function of the tribunal.[29]

As for now, the courts are willing to limit their inquiry and not review the merits of the case.[30] It means that the "excess of mandate" type of challenge is, in principle, limited to a review of the award against the *ne ultra petita* principle which prohibits the tribunal to grant a relief beyond what was requested. At the same time, however, this ground for recourse has the potential of accommodating many more prospective challenges: on the one hand challenge those of procedural nature, on the other hand attracting merits review. Moreover, it often competes with other grounds for recourse – the excess of jurisdiction and violation of due process. It means that it does create confusion in its application, and, arguably is not needed considering that other grounds may be invoked.

All in all, instead of referring to the tribunal's mandate, the post-award recourse should only address decisions that grant more than has been requested. In the alternative, the statutory frameworks should be more explicit on what the mandate entails (and, in turn, which dimension of the mandate is relevant).[31]

2.3.2 The Swiss model

As explained immediately above, one of the solutions preventing the interpretative difficulties regarding the "excess of mandate" type of challenge is (simply) to avoid making reference to the tribunal's mandate at the post-award stage.[32] This is precisely the solution enacted in the Swiss Private International Law Act ("PILA").[33]

Pursuant to Article 190(1)(2) of the Swiss PILA:

> The award may only be annulled:
> a) if the sole arbitrator was not properly appointed or if the arbitral tribunal was not properly constituted;
> b) if the arbitral tribunal wrongly accepted or declined jurisdiction;
> c) if the arbitral tribunal's decision went beyond the claims submitted to it, or failed to decide one of the items of the claim;

29 See section 1.3.

30 See section 2.2.

31 See also section 2.3.2.

32 See section 2.3.1.

33 Switzerland's Federal Code on Private International Law (1987), translation available at https://www.swissarbitration.org/files/34/Swiss%20International%20Arbitration%20Law/IPRG_english.pdf [last accessed 19 January 2019].

d) if the principle of equal treatment of the parties or the right of the parties to be heard was violated;
e) if the award is incompatible with public policy.

One should observe that instead of a reference to the elusive mandate, ground (c) operates with the notion of claims submitted (*petitum*). This way, it easily addresses only the instances where the tribunal decision exceeds the relief sought or when the decision fails to address all of the claims submitted. Additionally, it fits well with the remaining grounds for recourse under the Swiss PILA, and arguably, without overlap. Such a limited recourse is to be preferred and recommended to be followed as a model construction for the post-award relief.

2.3.3 The "van den Berg formula"

Almost ten years ago, at the ICCA Congress in Dublin that celebrated the fiftieth birthday of the New York Convention, van den Berg in his keynote speech proposed a hypothetical draft Convention focused on enforcement of arbitral awards, which was later echoed as the "Dublin draft".[34] It was intended to modernize and improve the functioning of the New York Convention. In his proposal, among other things, van den Berg had modified the wording of Article V(1)(c) of the New York Convention.

The draft text of said provision reads that the enforcement of the award shall be refused if "*the relief granted in the award is more than, or different from, the relief sought in the arbitration and such relief cannot be severed from the relief sought and granted [...].*"[35]

This research shows that, the formula used by van den Berg, as an alternative to the Swiss model, should be endorsed. It is clear and addresses only the instances where the tribunal goes beyond its adjudicative authority. Although van den Berg's proposal did not gain sufficient momentum to change the New York Convention, it remains a valuable piece of draft legislation.

Consequently, policy-makers should take benefit from its coherence. They can do so in a number of ways.

One is to consider the Miami draft (at least in the context of the "excess of mandate" type of challenge) as an interpretative tool for the New York Convention.[36] Since the mechanism of the New York Convention was later included in the UNCITRAL Model Law, the Miami Draft may serve in a similar capacity for Article 34(2)(a)(iii) of the Model Law as well.

34 See also Chapter VI. The "Dublin draft" was subsequently dubbed the "Miami draft".
35 See Art. 5(3)(c) of the Miami Draft.
36 Paulsson M. R. (2012) p.12. See also section 2.3.4.

Secondly, the UNCITRAL may take upon the draft as the basis for its future work. As explained above, even if it is concluded that the New York Convention is not ripe for a change, the van den Berg's proposal may easily be adopted for the purposes of the Model Law. This way, it might become a drive behind the change of the post-award mechanism offered in the Model Law itself and it might even trigger the "bottom-up" reform of the (New York Convention) enforcement system. Even if the consequences will not go as far, it will still provide an improvement for the modern model legislation.

If (the modified version of) van den Berg's proposal were to be included in the Model Law, it may look as follows:

> Article 34 – Application for setting-aside as exclusive recourse against arbitral award
> 1. An arbitral award shall only be set aside on the grounds expressly set forth in this article.
> 2. An arbitral award shall be set aside on the grounds set forth in this article in manifest cases only.
> 3. An arbitral award may be set aside if, at the request of the party against whom the award is invoked, that party asserts and proves that:
> a) there is no valid arbitration agreement under the law of the country to which the parties have subjected it or, failing indication thereon under the law of this State; or
> b) the party against whom the award is invoked was not treated with equality or was not given a reasonable opportunity of presenting its case; or
> c) the relief granted in the award is more than, or different from, the relief sought in the arbitration and such relief cannot be severed from the relief sought and granted; or
> d) the composition of the arbitral tribunal was not in accordance with the agreement of the parties, or in the absence of such an agreement, not in accordance with this Law; or
> e) the arbitral procedure was not in accordance with the agreement of the parties, or in the absence of such an agreement, not in accordance with this Law; or
> f) the award is subject to appeal on the merits before an arbitral appeal tribunal or a court in this State; or
> g) the award would violate international public policy.
> 4. The court may on its own motion set an arbitral award aside on ground (g) of paragraph 3.
> 5. The party against whom the award is invoked cannot rely on grounds (a) to (e) of paragraph 3 if that party has not raised them in the arbitration without

undue delay after the moment when the existence of the ground became known to that party.

6. (optional) By way of a specific agreement the parties may, at any time, expressly waive their right to bring an action to set aside on grounds (a) to (f) of paragraph 3.

The necessary changes have been made to fit in the context of the setting-aside and not the enforcement procedure. Additionally, the provision addressing the exclusion agreements has been added. For the sake of convenience, the comparison table is presented below.

Table 7

Article 5 of the Miami Draft	*The proposal for the new Article 34 of the Model Law*
Article 5 – Grounds for Refusal of Enforcement	*Application for setting-aside as exclusive recourse against arbitral award*
1. Enforcement of an arbitral award shall not be refused on any ground other than the grounds expressly set forth in this article.	*1. An arbitral award shall only be set aside on the grounds expressly set forth in this article.*
2. Enforcement shall be refused on the grounds set forth in this article in manifest cases only.	*2. An arbitral award shall be set aside on the grounds set forth in this article in manifest cases only.*
3. Enforcement of an arbitral award shall be refused if, at the request of the party against whom the award is invoked, that party asserts and proves that:	*3. An arbitral award may be set aside if, at the request of the party against whom the award is invoked, that party asserts and proves that:*
(a) there is no valid arbitration agreement under the law of the country where the award was made; or	*(a) there is no valid arbitration agreement under the law of the country to which the parties have subjected it or, failing indication thereon under the law of this State; or*
(b) the party against whom the award is invoked was not treated with equality or was not given a reasonable opportunity of presenting its case; or	*(b) the party against whom the award is invoked was not treated with equality or was not given a reasonable opportunity of presenting its case; or*
(c) the relief granted in the award is more than, or different from, the relief sought in the arbitration and such relief cannot be severed from the relief sought and granted; or	*(c) the relief granted in the award is more than, or different from, the relief sought in the arbitration and such relief cannot be severed from the relief sought and granted; or*
(d) the composition of the arbitral tribunal was not in accordance with the agreement of the parties, or in the absence of such an agreement, not in accordance with the law of the country where the award was made; or	*(d) the composition of the arbitral tribunal was not in accordance with the agreement of the parties, or in the absence of such an agreement, not in accordance with this Law; or*
(e) the arbitral procedure was not in accordance with the agreement of the parties, or in the absence of such an agreement, not in accordance with the law of the country where the award was made; or	*(e) the arbitral procedure was not in accordance with the agreement of the parties, or in the absence of such an agreement, not in accordance with this Law; or*

(f) the award is subject to appeal on the merits before an arbitral appeal tribunal or a court in the country where the award was made; or	*(f) the award is subject to appeal on the merits before an arbitral appeal tribunal or a court in this State; or*
(g) the award has been set aside by the court in the country where the award was made on grounds equivalent to grounds (a) to (e) of this paragraph; or	*(deleted)*
(h) enforcement of the award would violate international public policy as prevailing in the country where enforcement is sought.	*(g) the award would violate international public policy.*
4. The court may on its own motion refuse enforcement of an arbitral award on ground (h) of paragraph 3.	*4. The court may on its own motion set an arbitral award aside on ground (g) of paragraph 3.*
5. The party against whom the award is invoked cannot rely on grounds (a) to (e) of paragraph 3 if that party has not raised them in the arbitration without undue delay after the moment when the existence of the ground became known to that party.	*5. The party against whom the award is invoked cannot rely on grounds (a) to (e) of paragraph 3 if that party has not raised them in the arbitration without undue delay after the moment when the existence of the ground became known to that party.*
	(optional) 6. By way of a specific agreement the parties may, at any time, expressly waive their right to bring an action to set-aside on grounds (a) to (f) of paragraph 3.

Arguably, this mechanism will also fit comfortably with the architecture of both Model Law and non-Model Law jurisdictions and it will not conflict with the New York Convention.

2.3.4 The UNCITRAL Recommendation regarding the interpretation of its instruments

As an alternative for the modification of Article 34 of the Model Law, the UNCITRAL may also introduce a recommendation regarding the interpretation of Article 34(2)(a)(iii) of the Model Law in its current shape.[37] If such a recommendation was to be drafted, its operative part should include the following:

> The United Nations Commission on International Trade Law,
> [...]
> Taking into account the finality of the arbitral tribunal's decision and exclusive character of article 34 recourse
> [...]

37 Arguably, the recommendation may also cover other parts of the setting-aside provision.

1. Recommends that article 34(2)(a)(i) of the Model Law on International Commercial Arbitration be applied to any and all jurisdictional objections, including those considering the scope of the agreement to arbitrate,
2. Recommends that article 34(2)(a)(iii) of the Model Law on International Commercial Arbitration be applied only to objections that concern the tribunal's relief granted that is higher or different from the relief sought.

There is an obstacle for release of such a recommendation related to the UNCITRAL's own undertakings. The recently published UNCITRAL Secretariat Guide to the New York Convention seems to interpret the "excess of mandate" type of challenge available in the text of the Convention as referring to the challenge to the scope of the tribunal's jurisdiction and not to the issues related to the parties' *petita*.[38]

Arguably, even if the UNCITRAL will not release any interpretative recommendation for Article 34(2)(a)(iii) of the Model Law, van den Berg's proposal may still be used as a persuasive authority.[39]

3 Directions for further research

Considering an ongoing development in the field of investor – state arbitration, it might be interesting to see whether the concept of the mandate and its excess differ in the context of international commercial arbitration and investor – state arbitration.

Taking into account the number of stakeholders in investor – state arbitration, arguably, states might be eager to increase the control over the tribunal's adjudicative function, either by introducing some form of review on the merits or by improving the statutory structure of the tribunal's adjudicative mandate (which in turn would limit the parties' authority to do so). Consequently, one might further inquire if the adjudicative mandate of the arbitral tribunal in the international commercial arbitration context can be distinguished from its counterpart in investor – state arbitration.

38 See UNCITRAL, *UNCITRAL Secretariat Guide on the Convention on the Recognition and Enforcement of Foreign Arbitral Awards* (2016) p.174 ("*Consequently, where an arbitral tribunal has rendered an award which decides matters beyond the scope of the arbitration agreement, there is a ground for refusing to enforce an award under article v. (1)(c).*"), p.175 ("*[t]hough some authors have argued that article v. (1)(c) provides a second, separate ground for refusal to enforce an award rendered ultra petita, courts have rejected challenges to recognition or enforcement under article v. (1)(c) based on the fact that the arbitrators had exceeded their authority by deciding on issues or granting forms of relief beyond those pleaded by the parties.*").

39 See section 2.3.3.

4 Concluding observations

In the era of an increased judicialization and formalization of international arbitration, parties need to be prepared that the balance between their autonomy and the autonomy of arbitrators may shift for the benefit of the latter. This consequently may push the parties to apply ever more often for the "excess of mandate" type of challenge.

If this ground for recourse remains available, it will be up to the courts to decide whether the contractual or adjudicative aspect of the mandate should be prioritized. If the statutory framework changes, however, in order to make clear that only *ultra* or *extra petita* violations should be set aside, it will require the parties to shape the tribunal's mandate carefully already at the eve of the arbitral proceedings, knowing that it is their initial responsibility to do so at the outset and bearing the consequences at the later stage. It will also be clear for the tribunals that it is their *responsibility* to manage the proceedings.

Annexes

ANNEX 1

Table 1 Translations of the French setting-aside provision regarding the excess of the tribunal's mandate

Translations	Art. 1502 of the Old CCP	Art. 1518 of the Proposed CCP	Art 1520 of the CCP
	Si l'arbitre a statué sans se conformer à la mission qui lui avait été conferee	le tribunal arbitral a statué sans se conformer à la mission qui lui avait été conférée ou après l'expiration de cette mission	Le tribunal arbitral a statué sans se conformer à la mission qui lui avait été confiée
France, Decree no. 81-500 of May 12, 1981, inserting Arts. 1442-1507 into the New Code of Civil Procedure (English translation). (1982). in P. Sanders (ed.), Yearbook Commercial Arbitration Vol. VII p.281.	*If the arbitrator decided in a manner incompatible with the mission conferred upon him*	-	-
Code of Civil Procedure, Book IV, Arbitration. (1984). in J. Paulsson, & L. Bosman (eds.), ICCA International Handbook on Commercial Arbitration Supplement No. 58 p.10	*if the arbitrator has not rendered his decision in accordance with the mission conferred upon him*		
Code of Civil Procedure, Book IV, Arbitration. (2011). in J. Paulsson, & L. Bosman (eds.), ICCA International Handbook on Commercial Arbitration Supplement No. 64 (pp. 1-16). Kluwer Law International.			*the arbitral tribunal ruled without complying with the mandate conferred upon it*
http://www.parisarbitration.com/wp-content/uploads/2014/02/French-Law-on-Arbitration.pdf			*the arbitral tribunal ruled without complying with the mandate conferred upon it*
Bensaude (2015) p.1176			*the arbitral tribunal ruled without complying with the mission conferred upon it*

Translations	Art. 1502 of the Old CCP	Art. 1518 of the Proposed CCP	Art 1520 of the CCP
Rouche, Pointon, & Delvolvé (2009) p.203	*that the arbitral tribunal decided the case otherwise than in accordance with the terms of the mandate conferred on it*		
Craig, The arbitrator's mission and the application of law in international commercial arbitration (2010) p.265	*The arbitrator has decided without respecting the mission which had been given to him*		

Annex 2

Table 2 Remedies at the English court's disposal when faced with a challenge

	Challenge to substantive jurisdiction of the arbitral tribunal under Section 67(1)(a) of the Act	Challenge to substantive jurisdiction of the arbitral tribunal under Section 67(1)(b) of the Act	Challenge against serious irregularity under Section 68 of the Act	Appeal on point of law under Section 69 of the Act
Confirm the award	X	-	-	X
Vary the award	X	-	-	X
Set aside the award in whole	X	-	X	X
Set aside the award in part	X	-	X	X
Remit the award in whole	-	-	X	
Remit the award in part	-	-	X	
Remit the award to the tribunal in whole for reconsideration in the light of the court's determination				X
Remit the award to the tribunal in part for reconsideration in the light of the court's determination				X
Declare the award to be of no effect in whole	-	-	X	-
Declare the award to be of no effect in part	-	-	X	-
Declare the award on the merits to be of no effect in whole	-	X	-	
Declare the award on the merits to be of no effect in part	-	X	-	

List of cases

Arbitral Awards

ICC Case No.10625

ICC Award No.1250 (1964)

ICC Award No.2680 (1977)

ICC Case No.11264 (2002)

Himpurna California Energy Ltd v. PT (Persero) Perusahaan Listruik Negara, Final Ad Hoc Award of 4 May 1999, XXV Y.B. Comm. Arb. 13 (2000)

Canada

Bayview Irrigation District #11 v. United Mexican States, 2008 CanLII 22120 (ON SC)

Blanalko Pty Ltd v. Lysaght Building Solutions Pty Ltd [2017] VSC 97

CLOUT case No. 12 [*D. Frampton & Co. Ltd. v. Sylvio Thibeault and Navigation Harvey & Frères Inc.*, Federal Court, Trial Division, Canada, 7 April 1988]

Despetaux v. Éditions Chouette (1987) Inc., Quebec Court of Appeal, 18 April 2001, [2001] J.Q. No. 1510; JEL/2001-203

Desputeaux v. Éditions Chouette (1987) inc., [2003] 1 SCR 178, 2003 SCC 17 (CanLII)

Dunhill Personnel System Inc. v. Dunhill Temps Edmonton Ltd., 1993 CanLII 7171 (AB QB)

Louis Dreyfus, s.a.s. (SA Louis Dreyfus & Cie) c. Holding Tusculum, b.v., 2008 QCCS 5903 (CanLII)

Nearctic Nickel Mines Inc. c. Canadian Royalties Inc., 2012 QCCA 385 (CanLII)

Quintette Coal Ltd. v. Nippon Steel Corporation, 1991 CanLII 5708 (BC CA)

Smart Systems Technologies Inc. c. Domotique Secant inc., 2008 QCCA 444 (CanLII)

Telestat Canada and Juch-Tech, Inc., 2012 ONSC 2785 (CanLII)

United Mexican States v. Metalclad Corp., 2001 BCSC 664 (CanLII)

Egypt
Cairo Court of Appeal, Egypt, 8 January 2002, case No. 72/117

England
ABB AG v. Hochtief Airport GmbH and Ors [2006] 2 Lloyd's Rep. 1

Aectra Refining & Manufacturing Inc. v. Exmar NV [1994] 1 WLR 1634

Alphapoint Shipping Ltd v. Rotem Amfert Negev Ltd, The Agios Dimitrios [2005] 1 Lloyd's Rep. 23

Ameropa SA v. Lithuanian Shipping Co of Lithuania [2015] EWHC 3847 (Comm)

Ascot Commodities NV v. Olam International Ltd. [2002] C.L.C. 277

Asghar v. Legal Services Commission [2004] EWHC 1803

Athens International Airport S.A. [2006] EWHC 388 (Comm), 2006 WL 755473

Athletic Union of Constantinople v. National Basketball Association and Ors [2002] 1 Lloyd's Rep. 305, 2001 WL 825340

B v. A [2010] 2 Lloyd's Rep. 681

Bandwidth Shipping Corp v. Intaari [2008] 1 Lloyd's Rep. 7

Brockton Capital LLP v. Atlantic-Pacific Capital Inc [2014] 2 Lloyd's Rep. 275

Bromley Park Garden Estates Limited v. Gary Christopher Mallen, Bruce Maunder Taylor [2009] EWHC 609 (Ch), 2009 WL 648823

Bulfracht (Cyprus) Ltd v. Boneset Shipping Co Ltd, The MV Pamphilos [2002] 2 Lloyd's Rep. 681

Buyuk Camlica Shipping Trading and Industry Co Inc v. Progress Bulk Carriers Ltd [2010] EWHC 442 (Comm)

Checkpoint Ltd v. Strathclyde Pension Fund [2003] EWCA Civ 84

China Agribusiness Development Corporation v. Balli Trading [1998] 2 Lloyd's Rep. 76

CNH Global N.V. v. PGN Logistics Limited, Graglia SRL, Wincanton Trans European Ltd. [2009] EWHC 977 (Comm), 2009 WL 2848157

Compania Sud-Americana de Vapores S.A. v. Nippon Yusen Kaisha [2009] EWHC 1606 (Comm), 2009 WL 2392365

Demco Investments & Commercial S.A. & Others v. Se Banken Forsakring Holding Aktiebolag [2005] EWHC 1398 (Comm), 2005 WL 1534592

Double K Oil Products 1996 Limited v. Neste Oil OYJ [2010] 1 Lloyd's Rep. 141; [2009] EWHC 3380 (Comm)

Econet Satelite Services Ltd. v. Vee Networks Ltd [2006] EWHC 1664 (Comm); [2006] 2 Lloyd's Rep. 423

F Ltd v. M Ltd [2009] EWHC 275 (TCC)

Fidelity Management SA & Ors v. Myriad International Holdings BV & OR [2005] EWHC 1193 (Comm)

Fulham FC v. Richards & Anr [2008] 1 Lloyd's Rep. 616

Glencore International AG v. Beogradaska Plovidba, The Avala [1996] 2 Lloyd's Rep. 311

Gulf Azov v. Baltic Shipping [1998] C.L.C. 1240

Hussmann (Europe) Ltd v. Al Ameen Development & Trade Co & Ors. [2000] C.L.C. 1243

Hussmann (Europe) Ltd v. Pharaon (formerly trading as Al Ameen Development and Trade Establishment) [2003] 1 C.L.C. 1066

Indian Oil Corporation v. Coastal (Bermuda) Ltd. [1990] 2 Lloyd's Rep. 407

Jayaar Impex Ltd v. Toaken Group Ltd [1996] 2 Lloyd's Rep. 437

JSC Zestafoni G Nikoladze Ferroalloy Plant v. Ronly Holdings Ltd [2004] 1 C.L.C. 1146

Lesotho Highlands Development Authority v. Impregilo SpA & Ors [2005] UKHL 43

Lesser Design & Build Ltd v. University of Surrey (1991) 56 BLR 57

LG Caltex Gas Co Ltd & Anr v. China National Petroleum Corp & Anr [2001] 1 WLR 1892

Lorand Shipping Ltd v. Davof Trading (Africa) BV MV "Ocean Glory" [2014] EWHC 3521 (Comm)

K v A [2019] EWHC 1118 (Comm)

Mamidoil-Jetoil Greek Petroleum Company SA v. Okta Crude Oil Refinery AD [2001] EWCA Civ 406, 2001 WL 272881

Matthew v. Ollerton (1693) 4 Mod 226

Metal Distributors (UK) Ltd v. ZCCM Investment Holdings PLC [2005] EWHC 156 (Comm); [2005] 2 Lloyd's Rep. 37

Minmetals Germany GmbH v. Ferco Steel Ltd [1999] C.L.C. 647, [1999] 1 All E.R. (Comm) 315

Norscot Rig Management PVT Ltd v. Essar Oilfields Services Ltd [2010] EWHC 195, [2010] 2 Lloyd's Rep. 209

OAO Northern Shipping Co. v. Remol Cadores de Marin SL [2007] EWHC 1821 (Comm)

Omnibridge Consulting Ltd v. Clearsprings (Management) Ltd [2004] EWHC 2276 (Comm)

Pacol Ltd. v. Joint Stock Co Rossakhar [2000] 1 Lloyd's Rep. 109

Petrochemical Industries Co v. Dow Chemical [2012] 2 Lloyd's Rep. 691

Petroships Pte Ltd v. Petec Trading and Investment Corporation and Ors [2001] 2 Lloyd's Rep. 348

Pirtek (UK) Ltd v. Deanswood Ltd, Gordon Harris [2005] EWHC 2301 (Comm), [2005] EWHC 2301 (Comm) 2005 WL 3278910

Premium Nafta Products Ltd v. Fili Shipping Ltd [2007] UKHL 40

Primera Maritime (Hellas) Ltd & Ors v. Jiangsu Eastern Heavy Industry Co Ltd & Anor [2013] EWHC 3066 (Comm)

Primetrade AG v. Ythan Ltd. [2005] 2 C.L.C 911

Ranko Group v. Antarctic Maritime SA, The Robin [1998] ADRLN 35

Ronly Holdings Ltd v. JSC Zestafoni G Nikoladze Ferroalloy Plant [2004] EWHC 1354 (Comm)

Sanghi Polyesters Ltd v. The International Investor KCSC [2000] 1 Lloyd's Rep. 480

Schwebel v. Schwebel [2010] EWHC 3280 (TCC)

Sonatarch v. Statoil Natural Gas [2014] 2 Lloyd's Rep. 252

Telia Sonera Ab v. Hilcourt (Docklands) Limited [2003] EWHC 3540 (Ch)

Terna Bahrain Holding Co WLL v. Al Shamsi [2013] 1 Lloyd's Rep. 86

The Secretary of State for the Home Department v. Raytheon Systems Limited [2015] EWHC 311 (TCC)

The Secretary of State for the Home Department v. Raytheon Systems Ltd [2014] EWHC 4375 (TCC)

Van der Giessen-de-Noord Shipbuilding BV v. Imtech Marine & Offshore BV [2009] 1 Lloyd's Rep. 273

Warborough Investments Ltd v. S Robinson & Sons (Holding) Ltd [2003] EWCA Civ 751

Weldon Plant Ltd v. Commission for the New Towns [2000] 2 T.C.L.R. 785

Westland Helicopters Ltd v. Sheikh Salah Al-Hejailan [2004] EWHC 1625 (Comm)

Williams v. Wallis and Cox [1914] 2 KB 478

Zermalt Holdings v. Nu-Life Upholstery Repairs [1985] 2 EGLR 14

Fiona Trust & Holding Corporation & Ors v. Privalov & Ors. [2007] 1 C.L.C. 144

France

CA Paris, *Sporprom Service B.V. v. Polyfrance Immo*, Rev. Arb. 1984, p.87

CA Paris, 15 March 1984, *Soubaigne v. Limmareds Skogar*, Rev. Arb. 1985, p.285

CA Paris, 18 February 1986, *G. Aïta v. A. Ojjeh*, Rev. Arb. 1986, p.583

CA Paris, 10 March 1988, *Société Crocodile Tourist Project Company (Egypte) v. Aubert, ès qual. et autres*, Rev. Arb. 1989, p.269

CA Paris, 6 May 1988, *Société Unijet S.A. v. S.A.R.L. International Business Relations Ltd (I.B.R.)*, Rev. Arb. 1989, p.83

CA Paris, 28 June 1988, *Total Chine v. E.M.H.*, Rev. Arb. 1989, p.328

CA Paris, 14 March 1989, *Murgue Seigle v. Coflexip*, Rev. Arb. 1991, p.355

CA Paris, 28 November 1996, *Société CN France v. Société Minhal France*, Rev. Arb. 1997, p.380

CA Paris, 21 January 1997, *Société Nu Swift PLC v. Société White Knight et autres*, Rev. Arb. 1997, p.429

CA Paris, 4 November 1997, *Société Taurus Films v. SARL Les Films du jeudi*, Rev. Arb. 1998, p.699

CA Paris, 25 November 1997, *Société VRV v. Pharmachim*, Rev. Arb. 1998, p.684

CA Paris, 14 December 2000, *SA Lapeyre et autres v. Sauvage*, Rev. Arb. 2001, pp.805-810

CA Paris, 29 March 2001, *Carthago Films v. Babel Productions*, Rev. Arb. 2001, p.543

CA Paris, 27 June 2002, *SA Compagnie commerciale Comecim v. Société Theobroma NV*, Rev. Arb. 2002, p.793

CA Paris, 12 September 2002, *Société Enterprise de la Céramique Sanitaire Ouest (ECO) v. Société Eurotech SPA*, Rev. Arb. 2002, p.1044

CA Paris, 16 January 2003, *Thales Electronics v. Ingénierie des technologies nouvelles*, 2001/11782, Rev. Arb. 2003, p.249

CA Paris, 29 April 2003, *SA Impregilo v. Secrétariat aux communications et transports maritimes de la Jamahiriya arabe libyenne populaire et socialiste*, Rev. Arb. 2004, p.130

CA Paris, 22 May 2003, *SA Ess Food v. Société Caviartrade*, Rev. Arb. 2003, pp.1252-1265

CA Paris, 15 January 2004, *Société Centrale Fotovista v. Vanoverbeke et autres*, Rev. Arb. 2004, p.907

CA Paris, 6 May 2004, *Carthago Films v. Babel Productions*, Rev. Arb. 2006, p.661

CA Paris, 7 October 2004, *Société Otor Participations et autres v. Carlyle Holdings 1 et autre*, Rev. Arb. 2005, p.737

CA Paris, 18 November 2004, *SA Thalès Air Défense v. GIE Euromissile*, Rev. Arb. 2005, p.752

CA Paris, 19 May 2005, *SA Sucres et denrées v. Société Talsy Shipping Co Ltd.*, Rev. Arb. 2006, p.927

CA Paris, 23 June 2005, *Société British Motors et autre v. Société Bentley Motors Limited*, Rev. Arb. 2005, p.798

CA Paris, 16 November 2006, *Société Empresa de Telecomunicaciones de Cuba SA v. SA Telefonica Antillana et SNC Banco Nacional de Commercio Exterior*, Rev. Arb. 2008, p.109

CA Paris, 3 July 2007, *Leizer v. Bachelier*, n°RG 2006/00011, Rev. Arb. 2007, p.827

CA Paris, 27 November 2008, *Société GFI informatique SA v. Société Engineering Ingegneria Informatica SPA et autre*, Rev. Arb. 2009, p.229

CA Paris, 25 March 2010, *Société Commercial Caribean Niquel v. Société Overseas Mining Investments Ltd*, Rev. Arb. 2011, p.442

CA Paris, 29 September 2011, *M. René Scolardi et autres v. SASU Techman Head*, Rev. Arb. 2011, p.1093

CA Paris, 10 January 2012, *Société Sharikat al Ikarat Wal Abnieh (SIWA) S.A.L. v. Société Butec S.A.L.*, Rev. Arb. 2012, p.203

CA Paris, 18 September 2012, S.A. *Buildinvest et autres v. M. Guy Roy*, Rev. Arb. 2012, p.867

CA Paris, 18 June 2013, *M. Bruno Polge et autre v. M. Philippe Chaumeau et autres*, Rev. Arb. 2013, p.811

CA Paris, 20 January 2015, SA Telecel Faso v. SA Alcatel Lucent International, Rev. Arb. 2015, p.273

CA Paris, 14 April 2015, République Hellénique v. Société Bombardier Inc., Rev. Arb. 2015, p.645

CA Paris, 21 February 2017, *République du Kirghizistan v. M. Belokon*, Rev. Arb. 2017, p.336

CA Paris, 16 January 2018, Société MK Group v. SARL Onix et autre, Rev. Arb. 2018, p.295

CA Paris, 25 February 2020, *Prakash Steelage Ltd v. Uzuc SA*, n°17/18001

Cour de Cassation Civ 1ere, 25 May 1992, *Société Fougerolle v. Société Procorance*, Rev. Arb. 1993, p.91

Cour de Cassation Civ 1ère, 10 May 1988, *Wasteels v. Société Ampafrance*, Rev. Arb. 1989, p.51

Cour de Cassation Civ 1ère, 6 March 1996, *Société Farhat Trading Company v. Société Daewoo*, Rev. Arb. 1997, p.69

Cour de Cassation Civ 1ère, 20 December 2000, *Prodexport v. FMT Productions*, Rev. Arb. 2003, p.1342

Cour de Cassation Civ 1ère, 6 December 2005, *L. et B. Juliet v. X. et autres*, No. 03-13.116, Rev. Arb. 2006, p.126

Cour de Cassation Civ 1ère, 14 March 2006, *Conselho Nacional de Carregadores v. Charasse Société Groupe Antoine Tabet v. République du Congo*, Rev. Arb. 2006, p.653

Cour de Cassation Civ 1ère, 27 March 2007, *Alcatel Business Systems (ABS) v. société Amkor Technology et autres*, Rev. Arb. 2007, p.785

Cour de Cassation Civ 1ère, 4 June 2008, Société SNF SAS v. Société Cytec Industries BV, Rev. Arb. 2008, p.473

Cour de Cassation Civ 1ère, 6 October 2010, *Fondation Albert Abela Family v. Fondation Joseph Abela Family*, Rev. Arb. 2010, p.969

Cour de Cassation Civ 1ère, 1 December 2010, *Les époux X v. Société Fountaine Pajot*, No. 09-13303, Bull.civ. I, No 248

Cour de Cassation Civ 1ère, 26 January 2011, *INSERM v. Fondation Letten F. Saugstad*, No. 09-10198

Cour de Cassation Civ 1ère, 29 June 2011, Rev. Arb. 2011, p.678

Cour de Cassation Civ 1ère, 12 October 2011, *Société Groupe Antoine Tabet v. République du Congo*, Rev. Arb. 2012, p.91

Cour de Cassation Civ 1ère, 20 June 2012, *Chaudronnerie Mécanique Algéroise v. Adlor Sofal Nemoneh*, No. 10-21375

Cour de Cassation Civ 1ère, 10 October 2012, *Neoelectra Group v. Tecso*, No. 11-20299

Cour de Cassation Civ 1ère, 20 November 2013, *Giepac Bourgogne/Saica Pack v. Automation Group*, No. 12-25266

Cour de Cassation Civ 2ème, 15 February 2001, Halbout et société Matenec HG v. Epoux Hanin, Rev. Arb. 2001, p.135

Cour de Cassation Com., 9 July 2002, No. 01-01750 1ère *Southern Pacific Properties Ltd. v. Southern Pacific Properties (Middle East) Ltd., The Arab Republic of Egypt*, Cour de

Cassation [Supreme Court], Not Indicated, 6 January 1987, Y.B. Comm. Arb. 152, 154 (1988)

Sovereign Participations International S.A. v. Chadmore Developments Ltd., Cour d'Appel [Court of Appeal], 28 January 1999, XXIVa Y.B. Comm. Arb. 714 (1999)

Germany

Bank A. v. Bank B, Landesgericht [Court of First Instance], Hamburg 18 September 1997, XXV Y.B. Comm. Arb. 714 (2000)

CLOUT case No. 562 [Hanseatisches Oberlandesgericht Hamburg, Germany, 6 Sch 04/01, 8 November 2001]

Joint Stock Company A v. Joint Stock Company B, Higher Regional Court of Munich, 34 Sch 10/11, 14 November 2011, XXXVII Y.B. Comm. Arb. 231 (2012)

Oberlandesgericht Dresden, 3 Sch 3/12, 26 July 2012

Oberlandesgericht München, Germany, 34 Sch 10/05, 22 June 2005

Seller v. Buyer, Oberlandesgericht [Court of Appeal], Stuttgart, 1 Sch 12/01, 6 December 2001, XXIX Y.B. Comm. Arb. 742 (2004)

Shipowner v. Time charterer, Oberlandesgericht [Court of Appeal], Hamburg, 30 July 1998, XXV Y.B. Comm. Arb. 714(2000)

Ukrainian dealer v. German manufacturer, Oberlandesgericht, Munich, 30 July 2012 and Bundesgerichtshof, 23 April 2013, XXXIX Y.B. Comm. Arb. 394 (2014)

Hong Kong

American International Group and AIG Capital Corporation v. X Company [2016] HCCT 60/2015

Brunswick Bowling & Billiards Corp. v. Shanghai Zhonglu Indus. Co., Ltd. & Another, [2011] 1 HKLRD 707

CLOUT case no 687 [*J. J. Agro Industries (P) Ltd. v. Texuna International Ltd.*, Supreme Court of Hong Kong, High Court, 12 August 1992], [1992] 2 HKLR 402]

Luxembourg

Kersa Holding Company Luxembourg v. Infacourtage, Famajuk Investment and Isny, Cour Superieure de Justice, not indicated, 24 November 1993, XXI Y.B. Comm. Arb. 617, 625 (1996)

New Zealand

Kyburn Investments Limited v. Beca Corporate Holdings Limited [2015] NZCA 290

Parts & Services Limited v. Brooks [2005] NZHC 293

Poland

Regional Court in Katowice judgment of 23 November 2010, XIII GC 183/10 (not published)

Singapore

ABC Co. v. XYZ Ltd., High Court, Singapore, 8 May 2003], [2003] 3 SLR 546

Airtrust (Hong Kong) Ltd v. PH Hydraulics & Engineering Pte Ltd [2015] SGHC 307

AKN and another v. ALC and others and other appeals [2015] SGCA 63

Aloe Vera of America, Inc v. Asianic Food (S) Pte Ltd and Another [2006] 3 SLR 174; [2006] SGHC 78

BLB and another v. BLC and others [2013] SGHC 196

CRW Joint Operation v. PT Perusahaan Gas Negara (Persero) TBK [2011] SGCA 33, [2011] 4 SLR 305

TMM Division Maritima SA de CV v. Pacific Richfield Marine Pte Ltd [2013] SGHC 186

Spain

Jaral Decoración, S.L v. Peñasco Rodilla, SL, Madrid Court of Appeal, Spain, 2 February 2007, case No. 94/2007—7/2005

Sweden

AB Götaverken v. General National Maritime Transport Company (GMTC), Libya and others, Svea Court of Appeal (5th Dept.) Stockholm; Swedish Supreme Court, SO 1462, 13 December 1978; 13 August 1979, VI Y.B. Comm. Arb. 237 (1981)

United States of America

Abu Dhabi Inv. Auth. v. Citigroup, Inc., 557 F. App'x 66 (2d Cir.) cert. denied, 135 S. Ct. 137 L. Ed. 2d 45 (2014)

Action Industries, Inc. v. U.S. Fidelity & Guar. Co., 358 F.3d 337 (5th Cir. 2004)

AGCO Corp. v. Anglin, 216 F.3d 589 (7th Cir. 2000)

AmeriCredit Fin. Servs., Inc. v. Oxford Mgmt. Servs., 627 F. Supp. 2d 85 (E.D.N.Y. 2008)

Ancor Holdings, LLC v. Peterson, Goldman & Villani, Inc., 294 S.W.3d 818 (Tex. App. 2009)

Archer & White Sales, Inc. v. Henry Schein, Inc., 935 F.3d 274 (5th Cir. 2019), *cert. granted*, 207 L. Ed. 2d 1050 (June 15, 2020), and *cert. denied*, 207 L. Ed. 2d 1053 (June 15, 2020)

Augusta Capital, LLC v. Reich & Binstock, LLP, No. 3:09-CV-0103, 2009 WL 2065555 (M.D. Tenn. July 10, 2009)

Axia Netmedia Corp. v. Massachusetts Tech. Park Corp., 973 F.3d 133 (1st Cir. 2020)

B.L. Harbert Intern., LLC v. Hercules Steel Co., 441 F.3d 905 (11th Cir. 2006)

Bernard v. Kuhn, 65 Md. App. 557, 501 A.2d 480 (1985)

BG Grp., PLC v. Republic of Argentina, 134 S. Ct. 1198, 188 L. Ed. 2d 220 (2014)

Blanton v. Domino's Pizza Franchising LLC, 962 F.3d 842 (2020)

BNSF R. Co. v. Alstom Transp., Inc., 777 F.3d 785 (5th Cir. 2015)

Brandon, Jones, Sandall, Zeide, Kohn, Chalal & Musso, P.A. v. MedPartners, Inc., 203 F.R.D. 677, (S.D. Fla. 2001) aff'd in part, appeal dismissed in part, 312 F.3d 1349 (11th Cir. 2002)

Brijmohan v. State Farm Ins. Co., 92 N.Y.2d 821, 699 N.E.2d 414 (1998)

Brown v. Rauscher Pierce Refnes, Inc., 994 F.2d 775 (11th Cir. 1993)

Cargill Rice, Inc. v. Empresa Nicaraguense de Alimentos Basicos, 25 F.3d 223 (4th Cir. 1994)

Cat Charter, LLC v. Schurtenberger, 646 F.3d 836 (11th Cir. 2011)

Citigroup Global Markets, Inc. v. Bacon, 562 F.3d 349 (5th Cir. 2009)

Clarendon Nat'l Ins. Co. v. TIG Reinsurance Co., 990 F. Supp. 304 (S.D.N.Y. 1998)

Compania Chilena De Navegacion Interoceanica, S.A. v. Norton, Lilly & Co., 652 F. Supp. 1512 (S.D.N.Y. 1987)

Crawford Grp., Inc. v. Holekamp, No. 406-CV-1274 CAS, 2007 WL 844819 (E.D. Mo. Mar. 19, 2007)

Dean Witter Reynolds Inc. v. Byrd, 470 U.S. 213 (1985)

Ecopetrol S.A. v. Offshore Exploration & Prod. LLC, 46 F. Supp. 3d 327 (S.D.N.Y. 2014)

Emmenegger v. Bull Moose Tube Co., 324 F.3d 616 (8th Cir. 2003)

EST, LLC v. Smith, No. 5:08-CV-32, 2011 WL 2118984 (W.D.N.C. May 24, 2011)

F.A. Richard & Assocs., Inc. v. Gen. Marine Catering Co., 688 So. 2d 199 (La. Ct. App. 1997)

Faison & Gillespie v. Lorant, 187 N.C. App. 567, 654 S.E.2d 47 (2007)

Federated Dep't Stores, Inc. v. J.V.B. Indus., Inc., 894 F.2d 862 (6th Cir. 1990)

Fertilizer Corp. of India v. IDI Management, Inc., 517 F.Supp. 948 (D.C.Ohio, 1981)

Fiat S.p.A. v. Ministry of Fin. & Planning of Republic of Suriname, No. 88 CIV. 6639 (SWK), 1989 WL 122891 (S.D.N.Y. Oct. 12, 1989)

First Options of Chicago, Inc. v. Kaplan, 514 U.S. 938, 115 S. Ct. 1920, 131 L. Ed. 2d 985 (1995)

Fisher v. Gen. Steel Domestic Sales, LLC, 2011 U.S. Dist. LEXIS 125826, 2011 WL 5240372 (D. Colo. Oct. 31, 2011)

Foulger-Pratt Residential Contracting, LLC v. Madrigal Condominiums, LLC, 779 F. Supp. 2d 100 (D.D.C. 2011)

Frazier v. CitiFinancial Corp., 604 F.3d 1313 (11th Cir. 2010)

Gas Nat. Aprovisionamientos, SDG, S.A. v. Atl. LNG Co. of Trinidad & Tobago, No. 08 CIV. 1109 (DLC), 2008 WL 4344525 (S.D.N.Y. Sept. 16, 2008)

George Watts & Son, Inc. v. Tiffany & Co., 248 F.3d 577 (7th Cir. 2001)

Gonzalez v. Shearson Lehman Bros., 794 F. Supp. 53 (D.P.R. 1992)

Gordon Sel-Way, Inc. v. Spence Bros., Inc., 475 N.W.2d 704 (Mich. 1991)

GPR, Inc. v. Phoenix Petroleum Co. (1995, SDNY) 1995 US Dist LEXIS 7015

Granite Rock Co. v. Int'l Bhd. of Teamsters, 561 U.S. 287, 130 S. Ct. 2847, 177 L. Ed. 2d 567 (2010)

Grayson-Robinson Stores v. Iris Construction Co., 8 N.Y.2d 133, 168 N.E.2d 377 (1960)

Gwynn v. Clubine, 302 F. Supp. 2d 151 (W.D.N.Y. 2004)

Hall Street Assocs, LLC v. Mattel, Inc., 552 U.S. 576, 128 S. Ct. 1396, 170 L. Ed. 2d 254 (2008)

Halliburton Energy Servs., Inc. v. NL Indus., 553 F. Supp. 2d 733 (S.D. Tex. 2008)

Henry Schein, Inc. v. Archer & White Sales, Inc., 139 S. Ct. 524, 527, 202 L. Ed. 2d 480 (2019)

Howard, Weil, Labouisse, Friedrichs Inc. v. Tower Hill Trading Co Ltd, no 94 Civ 4709, 1995 WL 548846 (SDNY 1995)

Howsam v. Dean Witter Reynolds, Inc., 537 U.S. 79, 123 S. Ct. 588, 154 L. Ed. 2d 491 (2002)

Huntington Hosp. v. Huntington Hosp. Nurses' Ass'n, 302 F. Supp. 2d 34 (E.D.N.Y. 2004)

In re Arbitration Between Gen. Sec. Nat. Ins. Co. & AequiCap Program Administrators, 785 F. Supp. 2d 411 (S.D.N.Y. 2011)

In re Arbitration Between Millicom International v. N.V. and Motorola, Inc., Proempres Panama, S.A., 2002 WL 472042 (S.D.N.Y.,2002)

In re Exxon Valdez v. Exxon Corp., 484 F.3d 1098 (9th Cir. 2007)

Int'l Standard Elec. Corp. v. Bridas Sociedad Anonima Petrolera, Indus. Y Comercial, 745 F. Supp. 172 (S.D.N.Y. 1990)

J.A. Jones Const. Co. v. Flakt, Inc., 731 F. Supp. 1061 (N.D. Ga. 1990)

Jacada (Europe), Ltd. v. Int'l Mktg. Strategies, Inc., No. 1:02-CV-479, 2003 WL 24267645 (W.D. Mich. Oct. 22, 2003), aff'd, 401 F.3d 701 (6th Cir. 2005)

Jih v. Long & Foster Real Estate, Inc., 800 F. Supp. 312 (1992, DC Md)

Johnson v. Directory Assistants Inc., 797 F.3d 1294 (11th Cir. 2015)

Johnston Lemon & Co. v. Smith, 886 F. Supp. 54 (D.D.C. 1995) aff'd, 84 F.3d 1452 (D.C. Cir. 1996)

Josephthal & Co. v. Cruttenden Roth Inc., 177 F. Supp. 2d 232 (S.D.N.Y. 2001)

Kimble v. Marvel Entm't, LLC, 135 S. Ct. 2401, 192 L. Ed. 2d 463 (2015)

Kimm v. Blisset, LLC, 388 N.J. Super. 14, 25, 905 A.2d 887 (App. Div. 2006)

Liebman v. Better Way Wholesale Autos, Inc., No. 3:15CV1263 (JBA), 2017 WL 1088078 (D. Conn. Mar. 21, 2017)

Long John Silver's Restaurants, Inc. v. Cole, 514 F.3d 345 (4th Cir. 2008)

M & C Corp. v. Erwin Behr GmbH & Co., KG, 87 F.3d 844 (6th Cir. 1996)

Mastrobuono v. Sherman Lehman Hutton Inc., 514 U.S. 52, 115 S. Ct. 1212 (1995)

Matter of Carty (Nationwide Ins. Co.), 149 A.D.2d 328, 539 N.Y.S.2d 374 (1st Dep't 1989)

Med. Shoppe Int'l, Inc. v. Turner Investments, Inc., 614 F.3d 485 (8th Cir. 2010)

Mgmt. & Tech. Consultants S.A. v. Parsons-Jurden Int’l Corp., 820 F.2d 1531 (9th Cir. 1987)

Mgmt. & Tech. Consultants S.A. v. Parsons-Jurden Int'l Corp., 820 F.2d 1531 (9th Cir. 1987)

Ministry of Def. & Support for Armed Forces of Islamic Republic of Iran v. Cubic Def. Sys., Inc., 29 F. Supp. 2d 1168 (S.D. Cal. 1998), aff'd in part, vacated in part, remanded sub nom.

Ministry of Def. & Support for the Armed Forces of the Islamic Republic of Iran v. Cubic Def. Sys., Inc., 665 F.3d 1091 (9th Cir. 2011)

Mitsubishi Motors Corp. v. Soler Chrysler-Plymouth, Inc., 473 U.S. 614 (1985)

Morgan Stanley & Co., LLC v. Core Fund, 884 F. Supp. 2d 1229 (M.D. Fla. 2012)

Moses H. Cone Memorial Hospital v. Mercury Construction Corp., 460 U.S. 1, 103 S. Ct. 927 (1983)

Murtagh v. Emory Univ., 321 Ga. App. 411, 741 S.E.2d 212 (2013), reconsideration denied (Apr. 11, 2013)

Nat'l Oil Corp. v. Libyan Sun Oil Co., 733 F. Supp. 800 (D. Del. 1990)

Olympia & York Florida Equity Corp. v. Gould, 776 F.2d 42 (2d Cir. 1985)

Oxford Health Plans LLC v. Sutter, 569 U.S. 564, 133 S. Ct. 2064, 186 L. Ed. 2d 113 (2013).

Parsons & Whittemore Overseas Co., Inc. v. Societe Generale De L'Industrie Du Papier (RAKTA), 508 F.2d 969 (C.A.N.Y. 1974)

PMA Capital Ins. Co. v. Platinum Underwriters Bermuda, Ltd., 400 F. App’x 654 (3d Cir. 2010)

PNGI Charles Town Gaming, L.L.C. v. Mawing, 603 F. App’x 137 (4th Cir. 2015)

PoolRe Ins. Corp. v. Organizational Strategies, Inc., 783 F.3d 256 (5th Cir. 2015)

Porzig v. Dresdner, Kleinwort, Benson, N. Am. LLC, 497 F.3d 133 (2d Cir. 2007)

Prestige Ford v. Ford Dealer Computer Servs., Inc., 324 F.3d 391 (5th Cir. 2003)

Rain CII Carbon LLC v. ConocoPhillips Co., 2011 U.S. Dist. LEXIS 68994 (E.D. La. June 27, 2011)

Ray v. Chafetz, No. CV 16-428 (CKK), 2017 WL 663527 (D.D.C. Feb. 17, 2017)

ReliaStar Life Ins. Co. v. EMC Nat'l Life Co., 564 F.3d 81 (2d Cir. 2009)

Rent-A-Center, West, Inc. v. Jackson, 130 S. Ct. 2772, 561 U.S. 63 (U.S. 2010)

Ritterman v. Amari, 1989 U.S. Dist. LEXIS 13569 (S.D.N.Y. Nov. 14, 1989)

Schoenduve Corp. v. Lucent Technologies, Inc., 442 F.3d 727(9th Cir. 2006)

Seagate Tech., LLC v. W. Digital Corp., 854 N.W.2d 750(Minn. 2014)

Seed Holdings, Inc. v. Jiffy Int'l AS, 5 F. Supp. 3d 565 (S.D.N.Y. 2014)

Southland Corp. v. Keating, 465 U.S. 1, 104 S. Ct. 852 (1984)

Spector v. Torenberg, 852 F. Supp. 201 (S.D.N.Y. 1994)

Stolt-Nielsen S.A. v. AnimalFeeds Int'l Corp., 559 U.S. 662, 130 S. Ct. 1758, 176 L. Ed. 2d 605 (2010)

Szuts v. Dean Witter Reynolds, Inc., 931 F.2d 830 (11th Cir. 1991)

Timegate Studios, Inc. v. Southpeak Interactive, L.L.C., 713 F.3d 797 (5th Cir. 2013)

United Paperworkers Int'l Union, AFL-CIO v. Misco, Inc., 484 U.S. 29, 108 S. Ct. 364, 98 L. Ed. 2d 286 (1987)

Westminster Constr. Corp. v. PPG Indus., Inc., 376 A.2d 708 (R.I. 1977)

Wilko v. Swan, 346 U.S. 427, 74 S. Ct. 182 (1953) (overruled on other grounds by Rodriguez de Quijas v. Shearson/Am. Express, Inc., 490 U.S. 477, 109 S. Ct. 1917 (1989))

Wolf v. Sprenger + Lang, PLLC, 86 A.3d 1121 (D.C. 2013), as amended (Jan. 30, 2014).

Zephyros Mar. Agencies, Inc. v. Mexicana De Cobre, S.A., 662 F. Supp. 892 (S.D.N.Y. 1987)

Other sources

UN Documents

U.N. Doc. E/AC.42/4/Rev.1

U.N. Doc. A/CN.9/245

U.N. Doc. A/54/17

U.N. Doc. A/CN.9/216

U.N. Doc. A/CN.9/233

U.N. Doc. A/CN.9/264

U.N. Doc. A/CN.9/460

U.N. Doc. A/CN.9/SR.318

U.N. Doc. A/CN.9/WG.II/WP.41

U.N. Doc. A/CN.9/WG.II/WP.42

U.N. Doc. A/CN/23

References

Books and book chapters

Alvarez, H. C., Kaplan, N., & Rivkin, D. W. (2003). *Model Law Decisions. Cases Applying the UNCITRAL Model Law on International Commercial Arbitration (1985-2001).* Kluwer Law International.

Audit, B. (2014). Choice of the Applicable Law by the Parties. in F. Bortolotti, & P. Mayer (eds.), *The Application of Substantive Law by International Arbitrators* (pp. 10-19). ICC Publications.

Azeredo da Silveira, M., & Lévy, L. (2008). Transgression of the Arbitrators' Authority: Article V(1)(c) of the New York Convention. in E. Gaillard, & D. Di Pietro (eds.), *Enforcement of Arbitration Agreements and International Arbitral Awards. The New York Convention in Practice* (pp. 639-678). Cameron May.

Barrington, L. (2001). Law to Be Applied in International Arbitration. in D. Campbell, & S. Meek (eds.), *Arbitration Process* (pp. 77-87). Kluwer Law International.

Bensaude, D. (2015). French Code of Civil Procedure (Book IV). in L. A. Mistelis, *Concise International Arbitration* (2nd ed., pp. 1133-1188). Kluwer Law International.

Bermann, G. A. (2014). United States: Arbitration. in C. Espulgues, & S. Barona (eds.), *Global Perspectives on ADR* (pp. 485-536). Intersentia.

Bernini, G. (1983). Report: Adaptation of Contracts. in *New Trends in the Development of International Commercial Arbitration and the Role of Arbitral and Other Institutions* (pp. 193-198). Kluwer Law International.

Bernet, M., & Meier, P. (2013). Recognition and Enforcement of Arbitral Awards. in E. Geisinger, & N. Voser (eds.), *International Arbitration in Switzerland: A Handbook for Practitioners* (pp. 199-222). Kluwer Law International.

Binder, P. (2010). *International Commercial Arbitration and Conciliation in UNCITRAL Model Law Jurisdictions* (3rd ed.). Thomson Reuters.

Blackaby, N., Partasides, C., Redfern, A., & Hunter, M. J. (2015). *Redfern and Hunter on International Arbitration* (6th ed.). Oxford University Press.

Blanco White, T., & Walton, A. (1957). *Russel on the law of arbitration* (16th ed.). Stevens & Sons Limited.

Borghetti, J.-S. (2009). Punitive Damages in France. in H. Koziol, & V. Wilcox (eds.), *Punitive Damages: Common Law and Civil Law Perspectives* (pp. 55-73). SpringerWien.

Born, G. B. (2009). *International Commercial Arbitration* (1 ed.). Kluwer Law International.

Born, G. B. (2012). *International Arbitration: Law and Practice.* Kluwer Law International.

Born, G. B. (2014). *International Commercial Arbitration* (2 ed.). Kluwer Law International.

Borris, C., & Hannecke, R. (2012). Article V: Grounds for Refusal of Recognition and Enforcement of Arbitral Awards. General. in R. Wolff (ed.), *New York Convention on the Recognition and Enforcement of Foreign Arbitral Awards of 10 June 1958. Commentary* (pp. 239-267). C.H. Beck.

Borris, C., & Hannecke, R. (2012). Excess of Competence or Jurisdiction, Article V(1)(c). in R. Wolff (ed.), *New York Convention on the Recognition and Enforcement of Foreign Arbitral Awards of 10 June 1958. Commentary* (pp. 309-329). C.H. Beck.

Borris, C., & Hannecke, R. (2012). Improper Tribunal Composition and Flawed Proceedings, Article V(1)(d). in R. Wolff (ed.), *New York Convention on the Recognition and Enforcement of Foreign Arbitral Awards of 10 June 1958. Commentary* (pp. 329-355). C.H. Beck.

Briner, R., & Hamilton, V. (2008). The History and General Purpose of the Convention. The Creation of an International Standard to Ensure the Effectiveness of Arbitration Agreements and Foreign Arbitral Awards. in E. Gaillard, & D. Di Pietro (eds.), *Enforcement of Arbitration Agreements and International Arbitral Awards. The New York Convention in Practice* (pp. 3-38). Cameron May.

Broches, A. (1990). *Commentary on the UNCITRAL Model Law on International Commercial Arbitration.* Kluwer Law and Taxation Publishers.

Capper, P., Ljungström, K., & Dépinay, P. (2014). 'Proving' the Contents of the Applicable Substantive Law(s). in F. Bortolotti, & P. Mayer (eds.), *The Application of Substantive Law by International Arbitrators* (pp. 31-59). ICC Publications.

Carbonneau, T. E. (2010). *Carbonneau on Arbitration: Collected Essays.* Juris Net.

Carbonneau, T. E. (2012). *The Law and Practice of Arbitration.* Juris Net.

Carbonneau, T. E. (2014). *Toward a New Federal Law on Arbitration.* Oxford University Press.

Cave, E., & Wetton, E. (1935). *Russell on the power and duty of an arbitrator and the law of submission and awards.* Stevens & Sons Limited/Sweet & Maxwell Limited.

Chantebout, V. (2007). *Le principe de non-révision au fond des sentences arbitrales* (Vol. 2). Thèse dactyl., Paris II.

Clay, T. (2001). *L'arbitre.* Dalloz.

Clay, T. (2015). *Code de l'arbitrage commenté.* LexisNexis.

David, R. (1985). *Arbitration in International Trade.* Kluwer Law and Taxation Publishers.

de Boisséson, M. (1990). *Le droit français de l'arbitrage interne et international.* GLN-éditions.

De Ly, F. (1994). Judicial Review of the Substance of Arbitral Awards. in *Comparability and Evaluation, Essays and Comparative Law, Private International Law and International Commercial Arbitration. Liber Amicorum Mica Kokkini-Iatridou.* T.M.C. Asser Instituut.

De Ly, F. (2010). Conflicts of Law in International Arbitration - an overview. in F. Ferrari, & S. M. Kröll (eds.), *Conflict of Laws in International Arbitration* (pp. 3-16). Sellier.

De Ly, F. (2016). Paradigmatic Changes – Uniformity, Diversity, Due Process and Good Administration of Justice: The Next Thirty Years. in S. L. Brekoulakis, J. D. Lew, & L. Mistlis (eds.), *The Evolution and Future of International Arbitration* (pp. 21-33). Kluwer Law International.

Departamental Advisory Committee on Arbitration Law. (1996). *Report on the Arbitration Bill.*

Departamental Advisory Committee on Arbitration Law. (1996). *Supplementary Report on the Arbitration Act 1996.*

Derains, Y., & Kiffer, L. (2013). National Report for France. in J. Paulsson, & L. Bosman, *ICCA International Handbook on Commercial Arbitration.* Kluwer Law International.

Derains, Y., & Schwartz, E. A. (2005). *A Guide to the ICC Rules of Arbitration.* Kluwer Law International.

Di Pietro, D., & Platte, M. (2001). *Enforcement of International Arbitration Awards. The New York Convention of 1958.* Cameron May.

Dimolitsa, A. (2011). Sur l'"autorité" de l'arbitre. in L. Lévy, & Y. Derains (eds.), *Liber Amicorum en l'honneur de Serge Lazareff* (pp. 207-211). ICC Publications.

Dimolitsa, A. (2014). The Raising Ex Officio of New Issues of Law. in F. Bortolotti, & P. Mayer (eds.), *The Application of Substantive Law by International Arbitrators* (pp. 22-30). ICC Publications.

Domke, M., Wilner, G., & Edmonson, L. E. (2013). *Domke on Commercial Arbitration.* Thomson/West.

Domke, M., Wilner, G., & Edmonson, L. E. (2015). *Domke on Commercial Arbitration.* Thomson/West.

Dziurda, M., & Zielińska, A. (2015). Prohibition on Surprise Decisions on Legal Grounds by Arbitrators. in B. Gessel-Kalinowska vel Kalisz (ed.), *The Challenges and the Future of Commercial and Investment Arbitration* (pp. 315-329).

Farnsworth, E. A. (2010). *An Introduction to the Legal System of the United States* (4 ed.). Oxford University Press.

Ferrari, F., & Kröll, S. M. (eds.). (2010). *Conflict of Laws in International Commercial Arbitration.* Sellier.

Fountoulakis, C. (2011). *Set-Off Defences in International Commercial Arbitration: A comparative Analysis.* Hart Publishing.

Fortún, A. (2010). Set-offs Are Not Counterclaims in International Arbitration. in *Liber Amicorum Bernardo Cremades* (pp. 451-469). Kluwer Law International.

Frick, J. G. (2001). *Arbitration and Complex International Contracts.* Kluwer Law International.

Fullelove, G. (2016). Functus Officio? In J. C. Betancourt (ed.), *Defining Issues in International Arbitration* (pp. 257-268). Oxford University Press.

Gaillard, E. (2004). The Role of the Arbitrator in Determining the Applicable Law. in L. W. Newman, & R. D. Hill (eds.), *The Leading Arbitrators' Guide to International Arbitration* (pp. 185-216). Juris Net.

Gaillard, E. (2010). *Legal Theory of International Arbitration.* Martinus Nijhoff Publishers.

Gaillard, E., & Savage, J. (eds.). (1999). *Fouchard Gaillard Goldman on International Commercial Arbitration.* Kluwer Law International.

Gerbay, R., Richman, L., & Scherer, M. (2015). *Arbitrating under the 2014 LCIA Rules: A User's Guide.* Kluwer Law International.

Giovanni, T. (2010). International Arbitration and Jura Novit Curia. in M. Á. Fernández-Ballesteros, & D. Arias (eds.), *Liber Amicorum Bernardo Cremades* (pp. 495-509). La Ley.

Giraud, P. (2017). *Le devoir de l'arbitre de se conformer à sa mission.* Bruylant.

Grigera Naón, H. (2001). *Choice-of-Law Problems in International Commercial Arbitration.*

Haas, U. (2002). Part 3. Convention on the Recognition and Enforcement of Foreign Arbitral Awards, New York, June 10, 1958. in F.-B. Weigand (ed.), *Practitioner's Handbook on International Arbitration.* C.H. Beck.

Hanotiau, B., & Caprasse, O. (2008). Public Policy in International Commercial Arbitration. in E. Gaillard, & D. Di Pietro (eds.), *Enforcement of Arbitration Agreements and*

International Arbitral Awards. The New York Convention in Practice (pp. 787-829). Cameron May.

Harris, B., Planterose, R., & Tecks, J. (2007). *The Arbitration Act 1996.* Blackwell Publishing.

Harris, B., Planterose, R., & Tecks, J. (2014). *The Arbitration Act 1996* (5 ed.). Wiley Blackwell.

Holtzmann, H. M., & Neuhaus, J. E. (1989). *A guide to the UNCITRAL Model Law on International Commercial Arbitration: legislative history and commentary.* Kluwer Law and Taxation Publishers.

Holtzmann, H., Donovan, D. F., Tahbaz, C., & Amirfar, C. (2013). National Report for the United States of America. in J. Paulsson (ed.), *International Handbook on Commercial Arbitration* (pp. 1-109). Kluwer Law International.

Horvath, G. J. (2001). Duty of the Tribunal to Render an Enforceable Award. in D. Campbell, & S. Meek (eds.), *The Arbitration Process* (pp. 229-254). Kluwer Law International.

Hunter, M. J., & Redfern, A. (2004). *Law and Practice of International Commercial Arbitration.* Thomson Sweet & Maxwell.

ICC Commision. (2015). Report on Decisions on Costs in International Arbitration. *ICC Dispute Resolution Bulletin* (2), 1-55. ICC Publications.

ICCA's Guide to the Interpretation of the 1958 New York Convention: A Handbook for Judges. (2011). International Council for Commercial Arbitration.

International Law Association. (2002). *ILA Report on Public Policy as a Bar to Enforcement of International Arbitral Awards.*

International Law Association. (2008). *ILA Report on Ascertaining the Contents of the Applicable Law in International Commercial Arbitration.*

International Law Association. (2014). ILA Report on Inherent Powers of Arbitral Tribunal.

Jarvin, S. (2008). Irregularity in the Composition of the Arbitral Tribunal and the Procedure. in E. Gaillard, & D. Di Pietro (eds.), *Enforcement of Arbitration Agreements and*

International Arbitral Awards. The New York Convention in Practice (pp. 729-756). Cameron May.

Joseph, D. (2010). *Jurisdiction and Arbitration Agreements and their Enforcement* (2nd ed.). Sweet & Maxwell.

Kaplan, C. (2010). Brief Reflections on the Application of Norms by International Arbitrators. in *Liber Amicorum Bernardo Cremades* (pp. 671-678). La Ley.

Karali, M., & Ballantyne, J. (2009). England. in F.-B. Weigand (ed.), *Practitioner's Handbook on International Commercial Arbitration* (2nd ed., pp. 351-422). Oxford University Press.

Karrer, P. A. (2005). Must an Arbitral Tribunal Really Ensure that its Award is Enforceable? In G. Aksen, K.-H. Böckstiegel, M. J. Mustill, P. M. Patocchi, & A. M. Whitesell (eds.), *Global Reflections on International Law, Commerce and Dispute Resolution. Liber Amicorum in honour of Robert Briner* (pp. 429-436). ICC Publications.

Kaufmann-Kohler, G. (2004). "Iura Novit Arbiter" – est-ce bien raisonnable? Réflexions sur le statut du droit de fond devant l'arbitre international. in *De Lege Ferenda. Réflexions sur le droit désirable en l'honneur du professeur Alain Hirsch* (pp. 71-78). Éditions Slatkine.

Kim, K. K. (2011). Arbitrators and Choice-of-Law Decisions. in Y. Derains, & L. Lévy (ed.), *Is Arbitration Only As Good as the Arbitrator? Status, Powers and the Role of the Arbitrator* (pp. 65-67). ICC Publications.

Kolkey, D. M., Chernick, R., & Reeves Neal, B. (eds.). (2012). *Practitioner's Handbook on International Arbitration and Mediation.* Juris Net.

Konrad, S., & Hunter, R. (2013). LCIA Rules. in R. A. Schütze (ed.), *Institutional Arbitration.* C.H. Beck.

Kreindler, R., Wolff, R., & Rieder, M. S. (2016). *Commercial Arbitration in Germany.* Oxford University Press.

Kröll, S. M. (1998). *Ergänzung und Anpassung von Verträgen durch Schiedsgerichte.* Carl Heymanns Verlag.

Kröll, S. M. (2012). Arbitration. in J. M. Smits (ed.), *Elgar Encyclopedia of Comparative Law.* Edward Elgar.

Kröll, S. M., & Kraft, P. (2015). Chapter VII: Recourse against the Award, § 1059 – Application for Setting Aside. in K.-H. Böckstiegel, S. Kröll, & P. Nacimiento (eds.), *Arbitration in Germany: The Model Law in Practice* (2nd ed., pp. 383-420). Kluwer Law International.

Kronke, H. (2010). Introduction: The New York Convention Fifty Years on: Overview and Assessment. in H. Kronke, & P. Nacimiento (eds.), *Recognition and Enforcement of Foreign Arbitral Awards: A Global Commentary on the New York Convention* (pp. 1-18). Kluwer Law International.

Kurkela, M. S. (2007). *Due Process in International Commercial Arbitration.* Oceana Publications.

Kurkela, M. S., & Turunen, S. (2010). *Due Process in International Commercial Arbitration.* Oxford University Press.

Lew, J. D. (1978). *Applicable Law in International Commercial Arbitration.* Oceana Publications.

Lew, J. D. (2011). Iura Novit Curia and Due Process. in L. Lévy, & Y. Derains (eds.), *Liber Amicorum en l'honneur de Serge Lazareff* (pp. 397-417). ICC Publications.

Lew, J. D., & Holm, M. (2013). Chapter 1: Development of the Arbitral System in England. in J. Greenaway, G. Fullelove, H. Bor, & J. D. Lew (eds.), *Arbitration in England, with chapters on Scotland and Ireland* (pp. 1-18). Kluwer Law International.

Lew, J. D., Mistelis, L. A., & Kröll, S. M. (2003). *Comparative International Commercial Arbitration.* Kluwer Law International.

Lewis, D. (2016). *The Interpretation and Uniformity of the UNCITRAL Model Law on International Commercial Arbitration: Australia, Hong Kong and Singapore.* Kluwer Law International.

Liebscher, C. (2003). *Healthy Award. Challenge in International Commercial Arbitration.* Kluwer Law International.

Loquin, É. (1980). *L'amiable composition en droit comparé et international – contribution à l'étude du non-droit dans l'arbitrage international.* Librairies Techniques.

Loquin, É. (2015). *L'arbitrage du commerce international. Pratique des affaires.* Joly éditions, Lextenso éditions.

Mantilla Serrano, F. (2010). Multiple Parties and Multiple Contracts: Divergent or Comparable Issues? In B. Hanotiau, & E. A. Schwartz (eds.), *Multiparty Arbitration* (pp. 11-33). Kluwer Law International.

Maurer, A. G. (2012). *Public Policy Exception under the New York Convention: History, Interpretation and Application.* Juris Net.

Mayer, P. (2011). The Laws or Rules of Law Applicable to the Merits of a Dispute and the Freedom of the Arbitrator. in Y. Derains, & L. Lévy (eds.), *Is Arbitration Only As Good as the Arbitrator? Status, Powers and the Role of the Arbitrator* (pp. 47-63). International Chamber of Commerce.

Merkin, R., & Flannery, L. (2014). *Arbitration Act 1996* (5 ed.). Routledge.

Merkin, R., & Hjalmarsson, J. (2009). *Singapore Arbitration Legislation Annotated.* Informa.

Motulsky, H. (2010). *Écrits. Études et notes sur l'arbitrage.* Dalloz.

Mourre, A. (2011). Judicial Penalties and Specific Performance in International Arbitration. in M. E. Schneider, & J. Knoll (eds.), *ASA Special Series No. 30: Performance as a Remedy: Non-Monetary Relief in International Arbitration* (pp. 355-378). Juris Net.

Mustill, S. J., & Boyd, S. C. (1989). *The Law and Practice of Commercial Arbitration in England.* Butterworths.

Nacimiento, P. (2010). Article V(1)(a). in H. Kronke, & P. Nacimiento (eds.), *Recognition and Enforcement of Foreign Arbitral Awards: A Global Commentary on the New York Convention* (pp. 205-230). Kluwer Law International.

Oehmke, T. H., & Brovins, J. M. (2014). *Oehmke Commercial Arbitration.* Thomson Reuters.

Onyema, E. (2008). Formalities of the Enforcement Procedure. in E. Gaillard, & D. Di Pietro (eds.), *Enforcement of Arbitration Agreements and International Arbitral Awards. The New York Convention in Practice* (pp. 597-514). Cameron May.

Oppetit, B. (1998). *Théorie de l'arbitrage.* Presses Universitaires de France.

Park, W. W. (2014). The Predictability Paradox - Arbitrators and Applicable Law. in F. Bortolotti, & P. Mayer (eds.), *The Application of Substantive Law by International Arbitrators* (pp. 60-79). ICC Publications.

Patocchi, P. M. (1996). The New York Convention - The Swiss Practice. in *ASA Special Series No. 9 The New York Convention* (pp. 145-207).

Paulsson, J. (2005). Jurisdiction and Admissibility. in G. Aksen, K.-H. Böckstiegel, M. J. Mustill, P. M. Patocchi, & A. M. Whitesell (eds.), *Global Reflections on International Law, Commerce and Dispute Resolution. Liber Amicorum in honour of Robert Briner* (pp. 601-618). ICC Publications.

Paulsson, J. (2011). Thinking Simply about Public Policy. in L. Lévy, & Y. Derains (eds.), *Liber Amicorum en l'honneur de Serge Lazareff* (pp. 473-489). ICC Publications.

Paulsson, J. (2013). *The Idea of Arbitration.* Oxford University Press.

Perret, F. (1993). Les conculusions et leur cause juridique au regard de la règle ne eat judex ultra petitum partium. in C. Dominicé, R. Patry, & C. Reymond (eds.), *Études de Droit International en L'honneur de Pierre Lalive* (pp. 595-605). Helbing & Lichtenhahn.

Pichonnaz, P., & Gullifer, L. (2014). *Set-Off in Arbitration and Commercial Transactions* (1st ed.). Oxford University Press.

Piers, M. (2016). Commentary on Part VI of the Belgian Judicial Code, Chapter VI: Article 1715. in N. Bassiri, & M. Draye (eds.), *Arbitration in Belgium* (pp. 443-448). Kluwer Law International.

Port, N. C., Bowers, S. E., & Noll, B. D. (2010). Article V(1)(c). in H. Kronke, & P. Nacimiento (eds.), *Recognition and Enforcement of Foreign Arbitral Awards: A Global Commentary on the New York Convention* (pp. 257-280). Kluwer Law International.

Poudret, J.-F., & Besson, S. (2007). *Comparative Law of International Arbitration* (2nd ed.). Sweet & Maxwell.

Pryles, M., & Waincymer, J. (2009). Multiple Claims in Arbitration Between the Same Parties. in A. J. van den Berg (ed.), *50 Years of the New York Convention* (pp. 437-499). Kluwer Law International.

Pulkowski, D. (2010). Court Review of Arbitration Awards for Excès de Pouvoir. in Association for International Arbitration (ed.), *The UNCITRAL Model Law on International Commercial Arbitration: 25 years* (pp. 119-134). Maklu.

Racine, J.-B. (2016). *Droit de l'arbitrage.* Presses Universitaires de France.

Rau, A. S. (2015). "Gap Filling" by Arbitrators. in A. J. van den Berg (ed.), *Legitimacy: Myths, Realities, Challenges* (pp. 935-1005). Kluwer Law International.

Reisman, W. M., & Richardson, B. (2012). Tribunals and Courts: An Interpretation of the Architecture of International Commercial Arbitration. in A. J. van den Berg (ed.), *Arbitration - The Next Fifty Years* (pp. 17-66). Kluwer Law International.

Robert, J. (1993). *L'Arbitrage droit interne droit international privé* (6th ed.). Dalloz.

Rodner, J. O. (2011). Unilateral Setoff and the Principles of UNIDROIT. in *Liber Amicorum Serge Lazareff* (pp. 545-562). ICC Publications

Roth, M. (2009). UNCITRAL Model Law on International Commercial Arbitration. in F.-B. Weigand (ed.), *Practitioner's Handbook on International Arbitration* (pp. 953-1132). Oxford University Press.

Rouche, J., Pointon, G. H., & Delvolvé, J.-L. (2009). *French Arbitration Law and Practice: A Dynamic Civil Law Approach to International Arbitration* (2nd ed.). Kluwer Law International.

Rubino-Sammartano, M. (2001). *International Arbitration Law and Practice.* Kluwer Law International.

Russell, F. (1849). *A treatise on the power and duty of an arbitrator, and the law of submissions and awards* (1st ed.). T. & J.W. Johnson.

Rutledge, P. B., Kent, R., & Henel, C. (2009). United States. in F.-B. Weigand (ed.), *Practitioner's Handbook on International Commercial Arbitration* (2 ed.). Oxford University Press.

Sachs, K., & Lörcher, T. (2015). Chapter V: Conduct of the Arbitral Proceeding, § 1046 – Statements of Claim and Defence. in P. Nacimiento, S. Kröll, & K.-H. Böckstiegel (eds.), *Arbitration in Germany: The Model Law in Practice* (2nd ed., pp. 272-277). Kluwer Law International.

Sanders, P. (1996). Arbitration. in K. Zweigert, & U. Drobnig (eds.), *International Encyclopedia of Comparative Law* (Vol. XVI, pp. 3-171). Martinus Nijhoff, Tübingen, Mohr.

Sanders, P. (1999). The History of the New York Convention. in A. J. van den Berg (ed.), *Improving the Efficiency of Arbitration Agreements and Awards: 40 Years of Application of the New York Convention* (pp. 11-15). Kluwer Law International.

Sanders, P. (1999). The Making of the Convention. in *Enforcing Arbitration Awards under the New York Convention. Experience and Prospects* (pp. 5-9). United Nations Publication.

Schäfer, E., Verbist, H., & Imhoos, C. (2005). *ICC Arbitration in Practice.* Kluwer Law International.

Scherer, M. (2012). Violation of Due Process. in R. Wolff (ed.), *New York Convention on the Recognition and Enforcement of Foreign Arbitral Awards of 10 June 1958. Commentary* (pp. 279-311). C.H. Beck.

Scherer, M. (2015). Chapter III: The Award and the Courts, Set-Off in International Arbitration. in C. Klausegger et al. (eds.), *Austrian Yearbook on International Arbitration 2015* (pp. 451-474). Kluwer Law International.

Schmalz, B. (2015). Chapter VI: Making of the Award and Termination of the Proceedings, § 1051 – Rules Applicable to Substance of Dispute. in K.-H. Böckstiegel, S. Kröll, & P. Nacimiento (eds.). Kluwer Law International.

Schmitthoff, C. M. (1986). Finality of arbitral awards and judicial review. in J. D. Lew (ed.), *Contemporary Problems in International Arbitration* (pp. 230-237). Centre for Commercial Law Studies, Queen Mary College.

Schöldstrom, P. (1998). *The Arbitrator's Mandate.* Stockholm: Jure AB.

Schöll, M. (2006). Set-off Defences in International Arbitration. (M. Wirth, Ed.) *ASA Special Series, 26*, 97-138.

Schütze, R. A. (ed.). (2013). *Institutional Arbitration.* C.H. Beck.

Seraglini, C., & Ortscheidt, J. (2013). *Droit de l'arbitrage interne et international.* LGDJ.

Silberman, L., & Ferrari, F. (2010). Getting to the Law Applicable to the Merits in International Arbitration and the Consequences of Getting it Wrong. in F. Ferrari, & S. Kröll (eds.), *Conflict of Laws in International Commercial Arbitration* (pp. 257-324). Sellier.

Silva-Romero, E. (2004). Brief Report on Counterclaims and Cross-claims: The ICC Perspective. in *Arbitral Procedure at the Dawn of the New Millenium* (pp. 73-81). Bruylant.

Siwy, A. (2012). Mandatory Rules in International Commercial Arbitration. in C. Klausegger et al. (eds.), *Austrian Yearbook on International Arbitration 2012* (pp. 165-193). Kluwer Law International.

Southern Pacific Properties Ltd. v. Southern Pacific Properties (Middle East) Ltd., The Arab Republic of Egypt, Cour de Cassation [Supreme Court], Not Indicated, 6 January 1987. (1988). in A. J. Van den Berg (eed.), *Yearbook Commercial Arbitration 1988* (Vol. XIII, pp. 152-155). Kluwer Law International.

Stone Sweet, A., & Grisel, F. (2017). *The Evolution of International Arbitration.* Oxford University Press.

Strong, S. I. (2013). *Class, Mass, and Collective Arbitration in National and International Law.* Oxford University Press.

Suchoža, J., & Hučková Palková, R. (2012). Autonomy of Arbitrators - Decision-making on the Basis of Ex Aequo et Bono. *Czech Yearbook of Arbitration, 2*, 253-279. Juris Net.

Sutton, D. S., Gill, J., & Gearing, M. (2007). *Russell on Arbitration* (23rd ed.). Sweet & Maxwell.

Tweeddale, A., & Tweeddale, K. (2007). *Arbitration of Commercial Disputes: international and English law and practice* (Paperback ed.). Oxford University Press.

UNCITRAL 2012 Digest of Case Law on the Model Law on International Commercial Arbitration. (2012). United Nations Publication.

UNCITRAL Secretariat. (2016). *Guide on the Convention on the Recognition and Enforcement of Foreign Arbitral Awards.* United Nations Publication.

Van den Berg, A. J. (1981). *The New York Convention of 1958: Towards Uniform Judicial Interpretation.* T.M.C. Asser Institute.

Van den Berg, A. J. (1999). Striving for uniform interpretation. in *Enforcing Arbitration Awards under the New York Convention. Experience and Prospects* (pp. 41-44). United Nations Publication.

Van den Berg, A. J. (2005). Failure by Arbitrators to Apply Contract Terms from the Perspective of the New York Convention. in G. Aksen, K.-H. Böckstiegel, M. J. Mustill, P. M. Patocchi, & A. M. Whitesell (eds.), *Global Reflections on International Law, Commerce and Dispute Resolution. Liber Amicorum in honour of Robert Briner* (pp. 63-72). ICC Publications.

Van den Berg, A. J. (2008). The New York Convention of 1958: An Overview. in E. Gaillard, & D. Di Pietro (eds.), *Enforcement of Arbitration Agreements and International Arbitral Awards. The New York Convention in Practice* (pp. 39-69). Cameron May.

Van den Berg, A. J. (2009). Hypothetical Draft Convention on the International Enforcement of Arbitration Agreements and Awards. Explanatory Note. in A. J. van den Berg (ed.), *50 Years of the New York Convention* (pp. 649-667). Kluwer Law International.

Várady, T. (2011). Can Proceeding "Not in Accordance with the Agreement of the Parties" be Condoned? Remarks on Article V(1)(d) of the New York Convention. in S. M. Kröll, & L. A. Mistelis (ed.), *International Arbitration and International Commercial Law: Synergy, Convergence and Evolution* (pp. 467-487). Kluwer Law International.

Veeder, V. V. (1997). National Report for England (1997). in J. Paulsson (ed.), *International Handbook on Commercial Arbitration.* Kluwer Law International.

Veeder, V. V. (2010). Is There a Need to Revise the New York Convention. in E. Gaillard (ed.), *The Review of International Arbitration Awards* (pp. 183-194). Juris Net.

Verbist, H. (2008). Challenges on Grounds of Due Process Pursuant to Article V(1)(b) of the New York Convention. in E. Gaillard, & D. Di Pietro (eds.), *Enforcement of Arbitration Agreements and International Arbitral Awards. The New York Convention in Practice* (pp. 679-729). Cameron May.

Verbruggen, C. (2016). Commentary on Part VI of the Belgian Judicial Code, Chapter VII: Article 1717. in N. Bassiri, & M. Draye (eds.), *Arbitration in Belgium* (pp. 455-488). Kluwer Law International.

Verbruggen, C. (2016). Commentary on Part VI of the Belgian Judicial Code, Chapter VII: Article 1718. in N. Bassiri, & M. Draye (eds.), *Arbitration in Belgium* (pp. 489-494). Kluwer Law International.

Walton, A., & Vitoria, M. (1982). *Russell on the law of arbitration* (20th ed.). Stevens & Sons.

Wolfson, D., & Charlwood, S. (2013). Challenges to Arbitration Awards. in J. D. Lew, *Arbitration in England, with Chapters on Scotland and Ireland* (pp. 527-562). Kluwer Law International.

Wood, P. R. (1989). *English and International Set-Off.* Sweet & Maxwell.

ARTICLES

Aeberli, P. (1992). Abatements, Setoff and Counterclaims in Arbitration Proceedings. *Arbitration and Dispute Resolution Law Journal.*

Ancel, J.-P. (2012). L'arbitre juge. *Revue de l'Arbitrage, 2012*(4), 717-723.

Barraclough, A., & Waincymer, J. (2005). Mandatory Rules of Law in International Commercial Arbitration. *Melbourne Journal of International Law, 6*, 205-244.

Berger, K. P. (1999). Set-off in International Economic Arbitration. *Arbitration International, 15*(1), 53-83.

Berger, K. P. (2001). Power of Arbitrators to Fill Gaps and Revise Contracts to Make Sense. *Arbitration International, 17*(1), 1-17.

Bermann, G. A. (2009). Restating the U.S. Law of International Commercial Arbitration. *Journal of International Law and Politics, 42*(1), 175-199.

Bermann, G. A. (2011). 'Domesticating' the New York Convention: the Impact of the Federal Arbitration Act. *Journal of International Dispute Settlement, 2*(2), 317-332.

Bermann, G. A. (2012). The "Gateway" Problem in International Commercial Arbitration. *The Yale Journal of International Law, 37*(1), 1-50.

Bermann, G. A., Coe, J. J., Drahozal, C. R., & Rogers, C. A. (2009). Restating the U.S. Law of International Commercial Arbitration. *Penn State Law Review, 113*(4), 1333-1342.

Bernardini, P. (2004). The Role of the International Arbitrator. *Arbitration International, 20*(2), 113-122.

Bernardini, P. (2008). Stabilization and adaptation in oil and gas investments. *Journal of World Energy Law & Business, 1*(1), 98-112.

Blessing, M. (1997). Mandatory Rules of Law versus Party Autonomy in International Arbitration. *Journal of International Arbitration, 14*(4), 23-40.

Bollée, S. (2015). Les effets des sentences arbitrales a l'egard des tiers. *Revue de l'Arbitrage, 2015*(3), 695-738.

Brewer, T. J., & Mills, L. R. (2009). When Arbitrators "exceed their powers" A New Study of Vacated Arbitration Awards. *Disputer Resolution Journal, 64*(1), 46-53.

Brown, M. J. (2013). "Final" Awards Reconceptualized: A Proposal to Resolve the Hall Street Circuit Split. *Pepperdine Dispute Resolution Law Journal, 13*(2), 325-361.

Brunet, E. (2007). The Minimal Role of Federalism and State Law in Arbitration. *Nevada Law Journal, 8*, 326-340.

Burns, B. T. (2010). Freedom, Finality, and Federal Preemption: Seeking Expanded Judicial Review of Arbitration Awards Under State Law After Hall Street. *Fordham Law Review, 78*(4), 1813-1873.

Carbonneau, T. E. (1981). The Reform of the French Procedural Law on Arbitration: An Analytical Commentary on the Decree of May 14, 1980. *Hastings International and Comparative Law Review, 4*(2), 273-339.

Carbonneau, T. E. (2012). The Assault on Judicial Deference. *American Review of International Arbitration, 23*(3-4), 417-437.

Carbonneau, T. E. (2013). The Rise in Judicial Hostility to Arbitration: Revisiting Hall Street Associates. *Cardozo Journal of Conflict Resolution, 14*, 593-620.

Carducci, G. (2012). The Arbitration Reform in France: Domestic and International Arbitration Law. *Arbitration International, 28*(1), 125-157.

Carducci, G. (2013). Dealing with set-off and counterclaims in international commercial and investment arbitration. *Yearbook on International Arbitration, 3*, 173-184.

Carter, J. H. (2012). A Kiss for Arbitration Cost Allocation. *American Review of International Arbitration, 23*(3-4), 475-480.

Castagno, N. P. (2011). International Commercial Arbitration and Punitive Damages. *Resta de Arbitraje Comercial y de Inversiones, 4*(3), 729-751.

CFA. (2006) Texte proposé par le Comité Français de l'Arbitrage pour une réform du livre IV NCPC. *Revue de l'Arbitrage, 2006*(2), 499-517.

Chainais, C. (2011). Note - Société Top Bagage International v. société Wistar Entreprise Ltd, Cour de cassation (1re Ch. civ.), 23 June 2010. *Revue de l'Arbitrage, 2011*(2), 449-467.

Chen, A. (2008). The Doctrine of Manifest Disregard of the Law after Hall Street: Implications for Judicial Review of International Arbitrations in U.S. Courts. *Fordham International Law Journal, 32*(6), 1872-1910.

Cohen, S. (2008). The New York Convention at Age 50: A Primer on the International Regime for Enforcement of Foreign Arbitral Awards. *New York Dispute Resolution Lawyer, 1*(1), 47-49.

Cole, S. R. (2016). Curbing the Runaway Arbitrator in Commercial Arbitration: Making Exceeding the Powers Count. *Alabama Law Review, 68*(1), 179-224.

Colman, A. (2006). Arbitrators and judges - how much interference should we tolerate. *Arbitration, 72*(3), 217-223.

Craig, W. L. (2010). The arbitrator's mission and the application of law in international commercial arbitration. *The American Review of International Arbitration, 21*(1-4), 243-293.

Cullemark, J. (2014). Continued Hesitations Regarding "Manifest Disregard of Law" as a Basis for Setting Aside Awards. in *Young Scholars in International Arbitration* (pp. 159-182).

Dedezade, T. (2006). Are you in? Or are you out? An analysis of Section 69 of the English Arbitration Act 1996: Appeals on a question of law. *International Arbitration Law Review*(2), 56-67.

Derains, Y. (2004). Amendments to the Claims and New Claims: Where to Draw the Line? In *Arbitral Procedure at the Dawn of the New Millenium* (pp. 65-72). Bruylant.

Devolvé, J.-L. (2006). Présentation de texte proposé par le comité français de l'arbitrage pour une réforme du droit de l'arbitrage. *Revue de l'Arbitrage, 2006*(2), 491-498.

Dimolitsa, A. (2009). The equivocal power of the arbitrators to introduce ex officio new issues of law. *ASA Bulletin, 27*(3), 426-440.

Drahozal, C. R. (2002). In Defense of Southland: Reexamining the Legislative History of the Federal Arbitration Act. *Notre Dame Law Review, 78*(1), 101-170.

Drahozal, C. R. (2010). Contracting Around Hall Street. *Lewis & Clark Law Review, 14*(3), 905-927.

Drahozal, C. R. (2012). New York Convention and the American Federal System, The Symposium. *Journal of Dispute Resolution, 2012*(1), 101-117.

Eisenberg, T., & Miller, G. P. (2013). Damages versus Specific Performance: Lessons from Commercial Contracts.

Elder, T. E. (1997). The Case Against Arbitral Awards of Specific Performance in Transnational Commercial Disputes. *Arbitration International, 13*(1), 1-32.

Ellenbogen, G. (1952). English Arbitration Practice. *Law & Contemporary Problems, 17*(4), 656-678.

Ellis, R. (2009). Imperfect Minimalism: Unanswered Questions in Hall Street Associates, L.L.C. v. Mattel, Inc., 128 S. Ct. 1396 (2008). *Harvard Journal of Law & Public Policy, 32*(3), 1187-1196.

Farnsworth, E. A. (1991). Punitive Damages in Arbitration. *Arbitration International, 7*(1), 3-16.

Ferrari, F., & Silberman, L. (2010). Getting to the Law Applicable to the Merits in International Arbitration and the Consequences of Getting it Wrong. *Revista Brasileira de Arbitragem, VII*(26), 73-121.

Friedman, D. P. (2011). Set-off - avoiding the confusion. *Construction Law Journal, 27*(6), 494-505.

Gaillard, E. (2007). Extent of Court Review of Public Policy. *New York Law Journal, 237*(65).

Gaillard, E. (2011, January 24). France Adopts New Law on Arbitration. *New York Law Journal, 245*(15).

Gaillard, E. (2011). General Principles of Law in International Commercial Arbitration - Challenging the Myths. *World Arbitration & Mediation Review, 5*(2), 161-172.

Gaitis, J. M. (2006). Unraveling the Mystery of Wilko v. Swan: American Arbitration Vacatur Law and the Accidental Demise of Party Autonomy. *Pepperdine Dispute Resolution Journal, 7*(1), 1-63.

Gaitis, J. M. (2011). Clearing the Air on "Manifest Disregard" and Choice of Law in Commercial Arbitration: A Reconciliation of Wilko, Hall Street, and Stolt-Nielsen. *American Review of International Arbitration, 22*(1), 21-43.

Gee, S. (2008). Jurisdiction: the Validity and Width of Arbitration Agreements, and the House of Lords Decision in Premium Nafta Products Ltd. v. Fili Shipping Co. Ltd. *Arbitration International, 24*(3), 467-473.

Gill, L. F. (2011). Manifest Disregard After Hall Street: Back from the Dead - the Suprising Resilience of a Non-Statutory Ground for Vacatur. *Lewis & Clark Law Review, 15*(1), 265-287.

Grierson, J., & Taok, M. (2011). Dallah: Conflicting Judgments from the U.K. Supreme Court and the Paris Cour d'Appel. *Journal of International Arbitration, 28*(4), 407-422.

Gronlund, A. C. (2011). The Future of Manifest Disregard As a Valid Ground for Vacating Arbitration Awards in Light of the Supreme Court's Ruling in Hall Street Associates, L.L.C. v. Mattel, Inc. *Iowa Law Review, 96*, 1351-1376.

Gross, J. I. (2009). Hall Street Blues: The Uncertain Future of Manifest Disregard. *Securities Regulation Law Journal, 37*(3), 232-247.

Haydock, R. S., & Henderson, J. D. (2002). Arbitration and Judicial Civil Justice: An American Historical Review and a Proposal for a Private/Arbitral and Public/Judicial Partnership. *Pepperdine Dispute Resolution Law Journal, 2*(2), 141-198.

Hayford, S. L. (1995-1996). Law in Disarray: Judicial Standards for Vacatur of Commercial Arbitration Awards. *Georgia Law Review, 30*, 731-842.

Hayford, S. L. (2001). Federal Preemption and Vacatur: The Bookend Issues under the Revised Uniform Arbitration Act. *Journal of Dispute Resolution, 2001*(1), 67-88.

Horton, D. (2013). Federal Arbitration Act Preemption, Purposivism, and State Public Policy. *The Georgetown Law Journal, 101*, 1217-1273.

Hunter, M. J., & Triebel, V. (1996). Awarding Interest in International Arbitration: Some Observations Based on a Comparative Study of the Laws of England and Germany. *Journal of International Arbitration, 6*(1), 7-24.

Hwang, M., & Lai, A. (2005). Do egregious amount to a breach of public policy. *Arbitration, 71*(1), 1-24.

Jarrosson, C. (2012). L'acceptabilité de la sentence. *Revue de l'Arbitrage, 2012*(4), 793-804.

Jarvin, S. (1996). The sources and limits of the arbitrator's powers. *Arbitration International, 2*(2), 140-163.

Jones, T. L. (1996). State Law of Contract Formation in the Shadow of the Federal Arbitration Act. *Duke Law Journal, 46*, 651-678.

Karrer, P. A. (2001). Jurisdiction on set-off defences and counterclaims. *Arbitration, 67*(2), 176-178.

Kaufmann-Kohler, G. (2005). The Arbitrator and the Law: Does He/She Know It? How? And a Few More Questions. *Arbitration International, 21*(4), 631-638.

Kee, C. (2005). Set-off in International Arbitration - What Can the Asian Region Learn. *Asian International Arbitration Journal, 1*(2), 141-160.

Knuts, G. (2012). Jura Novit Curia and the Right to Be Heard - An Analysis of Recent Case Law. *Arbitration International, 28*(4), 669-688.

Kreidi, J. (2013). Infra Petita in International Arbitral Awards: The Incomplete Reforms of Two Major Operators in International Arbitration. *Versailles International Arbitration and Business Law Review*, 29-52.

Kreindler, R. (2003). Approaches to the Application of Transnational Public Policy by Arbitrators. *The Journal of World Investment, 4*(2), 239-250.

Kreindler, R. (2006). Final Rulings on Costs: Loser pays all? In M. Wirth (ed.), *ASA Special Series No.26 Best Practices in International Arbitration* (pp. 41-54).

Kröll, S. M. (1999). Contractual gap-filling by arbitration tribunals. *International Arbitration Law Review*, 9-16.

Kurkela, M. S. (2003). 'Jura Novit Curia' and the Burden of Education in International Arbitration – A Nordic Perspective. *ASA Bulletin, 21*(3), 486-500.

Lando, O. (1986). The Law Applicable to the Merits of the Dispute. *Arbitration International, 2*(2), 104-115.

Landolt, P. (2012). Arbitrators' Initiatives to Obtain Factual and Legal Evidence. *Arbitration International, 28*(2), 173-223.

Leboulanger, P. (1996). Multi-Contract Arbitration. *Journal of International Arbitration, 13*(4), 43-97.

Lécuyer, H. (2006). Exercice abusif des voies de recours contre les sentences arbitrales: de quelques manifestations de l'ire du juge judiciaire. *Revue de l'Arbitrage, 2006*(3), 573-589.

LeRoy, M. H. (2011). Are Arbitrators Above the Law? The "Manifest Disregard of the Law" Standard. *Boston College Law Review, 52*, 137-187.

Lévy, L., & Robert-Tissot, F. (2013). L'interprétation arbitrale. *Revue de l'Arbitrage, 2013*(4), 861-952.

Main, H. A. (2005). Court supervision of awards and the interpretation of the Arbitration Act 1996: Lesotho Highlands Development Authority v Impregilo SpA and Others. *Arbitration, 71*(4), 368-371.

Maniruzzaman, A. F. (1993). Conflict of Laws Issues in International Arbitration: Practice and Trends. *Arbitration International, 9*(4), 371-404.

Maniruzzaman, A. F. (1999). Choice of Law in International Contracts - Some Fundamental Conflict of Laws Issues. *Journal of International Arbitration, 16*(4), 141-172.

Maniruzzaman, A. F. (2003). The Arbitrator's Prudence in Lex Mercatoria: Amiable Composition and Ex Aecquo Et Bono in Decision Making. *Mealey's International Arbitration Report*, 1-8.

Marcantel, J. A. (2009). The Crumbled Difference Between Legal and Illegal Arbitration Awards: Hall Street Associates and the Waning Public Policy Exception. *Fordham Journal of Corporate and Financial Law, 14*(3), 597-638.

Marian, C. (2012). Proper Notice: Common Problems in Interpreting Article V(1)(b) of the New York Convention in Light of the Lernmoniiproekt Decision of the Swedish Supreme Court. *Arbitration International*, 545-566.

Mayer, P. (1986). Mandatory rules of law in international arbitration. *Arbitration International, 2*(4), 274-293.

Mayer, P. (2001). Reflections on the International Arbitrator's Duty to Apply the Law – The Freshfields Lecture 2000. *Arbitration International, 17*(3), 235-248.

Mayer, P. (2013). La liberté de l'arbitre. *Revue de l'Arbitrage, 2013*(2), 339-365.

Mills, L. R., & Brewer, T. J. (2013). 'Exceeded powers': Exploring Recent Trends in Cases Challenging Tribunal Authority. *Alternatives to the High Cost of Litigation, 31*, 113-126.

Moses, M. L. (2006). Statutory Misconstruction: How the Supreme Court Created a Federal Arbitration Law Never Enacted by Congress. *Florida State University Law Review, 34*, 99-159.

Moses, M. L. (2010). Arbitration Law: Who's in Charge? *Seton Hall Law Review, 40*(1), 147-189.

Moss, G. C. (2005). Can an arbitral tribunal disregard the choice of law made by the parties? *Stockholm International Arbitration Review*(1), 1-20.

Moss, G. C. (2006). Is the arbitral tribunal bound by the parties' factual and legal pleadings? *Stockholm International Arbitration Review*(3), 1-31.

Mourre, A. (2008). The Set-off Paradox in International Arbitration. *Arbitration International, 24*(3), 387-404.

Noussia, K. (2010). Punitive Damages in Arbitration: Panacea or Curse? *Journal of International Arbitration, 27*(3), 277-294.

O'Neal, D. L. (2001). Clarifying the Intent of Congress: Are the Federal Arbitration Act's Venue Provisions Permissive or Mandatory? Cortez Byrd Chips, Inc. v. Bill Harbert Construction Co.'. *Journal of Dispute Resolution, 2001*(1), 157-164.

Park, W. W. (2002). Amending the Federal Arbitration Act. *The American Review of International Arbitration, 13*(75), 1-66.

Park, W. W. (2005). The Nature of Arbitral Authority: A Comment on Lesotho Highlands. *Arbitration International, 21*(4), 483-491.

Park, W. W. (2010). Arbitrators and Accuracy. *Journal of International Dispute Settlement, 1*(1), 25-53.

Park, W. W. (2011). Arbitration in Autumn. *Journal of International Dispute Settlement, 2*(2), 287-315.

Parker, M. (2013). Changing Tides: The Introduction of Punitive Damages into the French Legal System. *Georgia Journal of International and Comparative Law, 41*(2), 389-432.

Paulsson, J. (1998). Enforcing arbitral awards notwithstanding a local standard annulment (LSA). *The ICC International Court of Arbitration Bulletin'*, *9*(1), 14-31.

Paulsson, J. (1998). May or Must Under the New York Convention: An Exercise in Syntax and Linguistics. *Arbitration International, 14*(2), 227-230.

Paulsson, J. (2007). Arbitration-Friendliness: Promises of Principle and Realities of Practice. *Arbitration International, 23*(3), 477-498.

Paulsson, M. R. (2012). The New York Convention: Can we finally move forward from 1958 to 1953? *European International Arbitration Review, 1*, 1-13.

Pavić, V. (2006). Counterclaim and Set-Off in International Commercial Arbitration. *Annals International Edition*, 101-116.

Petsche, M. (2013). Punitive Damages in International Commercial Arbitration: Much Ado about Nothing? *Arbitration International, 29*(1), 89-104.

Pharaon, C. (2015). The extent of arbitrators' power to order class arbitration. *Arbitration International*, 589-612.

Poznanski, B. G. (1987). The Nature and Extent of an Arbitrator's Powers in International Commercial Arbitration. *Journal of International Arbitration, 4*(3), 71-108.

Rabasca, S. C. (1989). Venue for Motions to Confirm or Vacate Arbitration Awards Under the Federal Arbitration Act. *Fordham Law Review, 57*(4), 653-663.

Radicati di Brozolo, L. (2005). L'illicéité « qui crève les yeux »: critère de contrôle des sentences au regard de l'ordre public international (à propos de l'arrêt Thalès de la Cour d'appel de Paris). *Revue de l'Arbitrage, 2005*(3), 529-560.

Radicati di Brozolo, L. (2012). Mandatory Rules and International Arbitration. *American Review of International Arbitration, 23*, 49-74.

Rau, A. S. (2006). Fear of Freedom. *American Review of International Arbitration, 17*(4), 469-511.

Rau, A. S. (2007). Federal Common Law and Arbitral Power. *Nevada Law Journal, 8*, 169-213.

Rau, A. S. (2008). Arbitral Jurisdiction and the Dimensions of "Consent". *Arbitration International, 24*(2), 199-264.

Reid, A. S. (2004). The UNCITRAL Model Law on International Commercial Arbitration and the English Arbitration Act: Are the Two Systems Poles Apart? *Journal of International Arbitration, 21*(3), 227-237.

Reisberg, S. H., & Pauley, K. M. (2013). An arbitrator's authority to award interest on an award until "date of payment": problems and limitations. *International Arbitration Law Review*, 25-30.

Reuben, R. C. (2009). Personal Autonomy and Vacatur After Hall Street. *Penn State Law Review, 113.*

Rogers, J. (2006). An English treatment of set-off in arbitration. *International Arbitration Law Review, 9*(5), 129-133.

Rowan, S. (2010). Reflections on the Introduction of Punitive Damages for Breach of Contract. *Oxford Journal of Legal Studies, 30*(3), 495-517.

Rubino-Sammartano, M. (1992). Amiable Compositeur (Joint Mandate to Settle) and Ex Bono et Aecquo (Discretional Authority to Mitigate Strict Law): Apparent Synonyms Revisited. *Journal of International Arbitration, 9*(1), 5-16.

Samuel, A. (2008). Separability and Construing Arbitration Clauses: the House of Lords' decision in Premium Nafta and the Fiona Trust. *Arbitration International, 24*(3), 489-497.

Samuel, A. (2014). Competence-Competence, Kompetenz-Kompetenz - now just an excuse for confused thinking about arbitrator jurisdiction. *Arbitration, 80*(1), 67-72.

Scherer, M. (2016). The fate of parties' agreements on judicial review of awards: a comparative and normative analysis of party-autonomy at the post-award stage. *Arbitration International, 32*(3), 437-457.

Schwartz, D. S. (2004). Correcting Federalism Mistakes in Statutory Interpretation: the Supreme Court and the Federal Arbitration Act. *Law and Contemporary Problems, 67*(1-2), 5-54.

Scodro, M. A. (2005). Deterrence and Implied Limits on Arbitral Power. *Duke Law Journal, 55*, 547-607.

Seeger, K., & Friel, S. (2004). Challenge under section 67 of the Arbitration Act 1996. *International Arbitration Law Review, 7*(3), 39-40.

Sénéchal, T. J., & Gotanda, J. Y. (2009). Interest as Damages. *Columbia Journal of Transnational Law, 47*, 491-536.

Seriki, H. (2005). Serious irregularity and the Arbitration Act 1996: Lesotho Highlands Development Authority v Impregilo SpA. *Journal of Business Law*, 745-751.

Sheppard, A. (2005). Rights of appeal under s.68 of the Arbitration Act 1996. *International Arbitration Law Review, 8*(5), N64-67.

Sims, M. K., & Bales, R. A. (2010). Much Ado About Nothing: the Future of Manifest Disregard After Hall Street. *South Carolina Law Review, 62*, 407-437.

Smit, H. (2006). Hall Street Associates v. Mattel: A Critical Comment. *American Review of International Arbitration, 17*(4), 513-523.

Smit, R. H., & Robinson, T. B. (2009). Cost Awards in International Commercial Arbitration: Proposed Guidelines for Promoting Time and Cost Efficiency. *American Review of International Arbitration, 20*(3), 267-283.

Snodgrass, E. (2007). Fiona Trust v Privalov: the Arbitration Act comes of age. *International Arbitration Law Review, 10*(2), 27-32.

Stipanowich, T. J. (2011). The Third Arbitration Trilogy: Stolt Nielsen, Rent-A-Center, Concepcion and the Future of American Arbitration. *American Review of International Arbitration, 22*(3), 323-434.

Style, C., & Knowles, M. (2008). Fiona Trust: 10 Years On, the Fresh Start Entrenched. *Arbitration International, 24*(3), 499-502.

Sweeney, P. (2014). Exceeding Their Powers: A Critique of Stolt-Nielsen and Manifest Disregard, and a Proposal for Substantive Arbitral Award Review. *Washington and Lee Law Review, 71*(2), 1571-1639.

Tan, P., & Ahmad, J. (2014). The UNCITRAL Model Law and Awards infra petita. *Journal of International Arbitration, 31*(3), 413-423.

Ulmer, N. C. (2010). The Cost Condurum. *Arbitration International, 26*(2), 221-250.

Van den Berg, A. J. (1998). Enforcement of Annuled Awards? *The ICC International Court of Arbitration Bulletin, 9*(2), 15-21.

Van den Berg, A. J. (2007). New York Convention of 1958: Refusals of Enforcement. *The ICC International Court of Arbitration Bulletin, 18*(2), 1-35.

Ware, S. J. (1997). "Opt-In" for Judicial Review of Errors of Law under the Revised Uniform Arbitration Act. *The American Review of International Arbitration, 8*(3-4), 263-272.

Waincymer, J. (2009). International Commercial Arbitration and the Application of Mandatory Rules of Law. *Asian International Arbitration Journal, 5*(1), 1-45.

West Janke, B., & Licari, F.-X. (2012). Enforcing Punitive Damage Awards in France after Fountaine Pajot. *The American Journal of Comparative Law, 60*(3), 775-804.

Wester-Ouisse, V., & Thiede, T. (2012). Punitive Damages in France: A New Deal? *Journal of European Tort Law, 3*(1), 115-122.

Weston, M. A. (2007). Preserving the Federal Arbitration Act by Reining in Judicial Expansion and Mandatory Use. *Nevada Law Journal, 8*, 385-399.

Wolff, R. (2008). Party Autonomy to Agree on Non-Final Arbitration. *ASA Bulletin, 26*(3), 626-641.

Yelnosky, M. (2012). Fully Federalizing the Federal Arbitration Act. *Oregon Law Review, 90*, 729-771.

Yu, H.-L. (2000). Amiable Composition - A Learning Curve. *Journal of International Arbitration, 17*(1), 79-98.

Lightning Source UK Ltd.
Milton Keynes UK
UKHW051558141022
410480UK00006B/173

9 789462 369917